SOLDIERS AND THE SOVIET STATE

A Research Study of the Center
for Strategic and International Studies

SOLDIERS AND THE SOVIET STATE

CIVIL-MILITARY RELATIONS FROM
BREZHNEV TO GORBACHEV

Timothy J. Colton and Thane Gustafson, Editors

PRINCETON UNIVERSITY PRESS   PRINCETON, NEW JERSEY

Library of Congress Cataloging-in-Publication Data

Soldiers and the Soviet state : civil-military relations from Brezhnev
to Gorbachev / Timothy J. Colton and Thane Gustafson, editors.
p. cm.
ISBN 0-691-07863-7 (alk. paper) — ISBN 0-691-02328-X
(pbk. alk. paper)
1. Soviet Union—Politics and government—1953–1985. 2. Soviet
Union—Politics and government—1985– . 3. Soviet Union—Military
policy. 4. Civil supremacy over the military—Soviet Union.
I. Colton, Timothy J., 1947– . II. Gustafson, Thane.
DK274.3.S63   1990
322'.5'0947—dc20   90-8104   CIP

This book has been composed in Linotron Times Roman

Princeton University Press books are printed
on acid-free paper, and meet the guidelines
for permanence and durability of the Committee
on Production Guidelines for Book Longevity
of the Council on Library Resources

Printed in the United States of America by
Princeton University Press, Princeton, New Jersey

10 9 8 7 6 5 4 3 2 1

(Pbk.)
10 9 8 7 6 5 4 3 2 1

To Lee Agree ———————————————————

WITH AFFECTION AND GRATITUDE

Contents

Tables and Figures ———————————

Acknowledgments

THE IDEA for this book came to us in 1983, well before Mikhail Gorbachev's accession, at a time when the Soviet military—at least in the eyes of most Western observers—appeared to have reached the height of their political power. Some even spoke of the possibility of a military takeover in Moscow. The finished volume now appears after five years of Gorbachev's perestroika, at a time when—again according to most Western observers—the power of the Soviet military, whether over budgets, doctrine, or policy, has fallen to an all-time low.

Are such swings in perception justified? Can the relationship between the party leadership and the military-industrial system, which has been close to the center of the Soviet polity for more than seven decades, really be so unstable and unpredictable? If the answer is yes, that would have ominous implications indeed for East-West relations, for it would mean that Soviet security policy is essentially unfathomable. As social scientists but also as citizens, we must hope for better.

What is needed, in our view, is a longer and broader perspective on civil-military relations in the Soviet system, and in particular, a more comprehensive view of what shapes the relationship. Accordingly, this book covers a twenty-five-year span, from the beginning of the Brezhnev era to the present, and it devotes separate chapters to the major factors affecting the civil-military relationship: politics, economics, technology, society, and foreign relations.

It would be bold indeed to claim that our approach yields the magic key to prediction, at a time when Soviet politics is so full of surprises. But we believe this book will show that there are significant elements of stability and continuity in civil-military relations, that different parts of the military-industrial system change in different ways, and that the resulting patterns of interest and influence are subtle and diverse—but not unfathomable or entirely unpredictable.

Along the way, this project has also had a second goal: We wanted to test whether the advent of personal computing and networking would enable us to conduct a large joint research project electronically, minimizing costly meetings and the use of that primitive analog synthesizer called the telephone. We have successfully run a large part of this project on the *Sovset* computer network, developed by us at the Soviet and East European Studies Program of the Center for Strategic and International Studies, using it to exchange news and views among ourselves and to draw in a wider circle of participants, including younger scholars and specialists from many countries. We are grateful to the many colleagues who have worked with us to develop Sovset as a practical working tool, especially Seymour Goodman and Joel Snyder, our Sovset partners at the College of Public and Business Administration of the University of Arizona.

We are indebted to many people for their kindness and support. We especially thank the F. W. Prince Charitable Trusts for their generous core support for the Soviet and East European Studies Program of the Center for Strategic and International Studies, under whose auspices our project was conducted. It was Mr. William Wood-Prince who first had the idea of an international conferencing network for Soviet studies and made possible its founding and growth.

Our project on the Soviet military was supported throughout by the Andrew W. Mellon Foundation and the Carnegie Corporation of New York, whose help is gratefully acknowledged. The editors would like to express particular appreciation to Fritz Mosher and Deana Arsenian for their personal commitment and encouragement.

By coincidence, a similar research project began at the Rand Corporation at about the same time as ours, and we have benefited from frequent and stimulating interaction (a good deal of it on Sovset) with our Rand colleagues over the last five years. In April 1988, under the auspices of the Carnegie Corporation, the two groups held a joint conference on "Civil-Military Relations in Soviet Politics" in Washington, D.C. We are grateful to the codirectors of the Rand project, Jeremy Azrael and Harry Gelman, for their friendly collaboration. We have learned from both our agreements and our disagreements, and the reader will find many references to the excellent work of the Rand group throughout this book.

Our principal findings and conclusions, together with their main policy implications, have been presented at a series of meetings at CSIS in 1988–90, to a lively and well-informed audience of journalists, policy makers, and fellow scholars. We thank the participants for their comments and criticism, most of which they will find reflected in these pages.

We have also benefited from the advice and reviews of many colleagues and friends. We would especially like to thank Condoleezza Rice, Matthew Evangelista, and Dale Herspring, who read and reread the entire manuscript. Other colleagues who gave comments and criticism are also mentioned in the individual chapters.

Finally, we would like to make special mention of the staff of the Soviet and East European Studies Program of the Center for Strategic and International Studies. We thank the program's director, Stephen Sestanovich; the program coordinators, Marina Marcoux, Kim Cox, and Alice Young; and above all Lee Agree, to whom this book is fondly dedicated.

Thane Gustafson
Project Director

Timothy J. Colton
Project Codirector

SOLDIERS AND THE SOVIET STATE

One

Perspectives on Civil-Military Relations in the Soviet Union

TIMOTHY J. COLTON

THE PURPOSE of *Soldiers and the Soviet State* is to take a fresh look at the balance between civilian and military institutions in the Soviet Union. Our immediate concern is with the shared understandings and patterns of influence prevailing under L. I. Brezhnev, the top Soviet leader from October 1964 to his death in November 1982, and under his successors, principally M. S. Gorbachev, who became general secretary of the Communist Party in March 1985. Besides scrutinizing specific events, we wish to reopen a long-standing debate over general analytical approaches to Soviet military politics. As conflict heats up over Gorbachev's attempts at reform, it is imperative that Western scholars and governments think lucidly about the bond between soldiers and the state he is trying to reinvigorate.

The Significance of Civil-Military Relations

Who rules—the statesman, whose vocation is politics, or the soldier, whose calling is war but who is capable of turning his arms on his own government? How great is military influence in politics, and how complete is the civilians' sway over defense decisions? How weighty a claim does national security exert on the community's resources and on its imagination? Answers to these and related questions tell us much about the nature of the state, even in lands such as the United States and Great Britain where they have long since been settled and passed into the realm of unexamined belief. The contract between military officers and civilian politicians is an essential clause of the operative constitution of every society save the aberrant handful that do not have armies.

In the Soviet Union, military-political issues gain import from the immense attachment the political authorities themselves have had to military might. This goes back to the regime's birth in violent revolution, its abundant experience of invasion and cold war, and its imperial ambitions, which would be unattainable without potent armed forces. In the present as in the past, the party "considers the protection of the socialist fatherland, the strengthening of the country's defense, and the maintenance of state security to be one of the most important functions of the Soviet all-people's state,'' in the words of the latest version of its program. The armed services, about five million officers and enlisted men strong, still take the biggest bite out of the national budget, digesting proportionately more resources than those of any other industrial power. Coordination of the defense effort and maintenance of ''party leadership of the armed forces,'' as party doctrine phrases it, are chronic worries for the Soviet bosses.

Granted that the civil-military connection is perennially topical, a compelling case can be made for looking closely at how it stands right now. If useful information has come out in a miscellany of specialized Western publications, no major, integrative work on civil-military relations in the USSR has been published since the 1970s.[1] What makes this omission glaring is that the Soviet system as a whole has at this very time been buffeted by unusual and at times dramatic stress.

In politics, the long Brezhnev era, which opened with such self-assurance and optimism, reached its end with a leadership enfeebled and rudderless and with pessimism spreading within the political class. The long overdue transfer of power to a new generation ignited dissension within the Soviet establishment more intense than any since the heyday of N. S. Khrushchev in the 1950s and early 1960s. The succession, moreover, was fought out against a backdrop of mounting concern about the country's ills. In economics, the gradual slide of growth rates became a drop in the latter half of the 1970s, precipitating a searching debate about resource allocation, technological innovation, and economic reform. The regime also awakened to a plethora of social problems and pathologies, new and old, ranging from the housing shortage and alcoholism to youth anomie and ethnic friction. In addition, as the souring of detente with the United States, the 1980–81 upheaval in Poland, and the miring of the Soviets in Afghanistan went to show, challenges and setbacks were plentiful in foreign relations.

Gorbachev has brought many simmering problems to a boil by encouraging candid discussion of them and proclaiming the need for *perestroika*, the ''reconstruction'' or ''rebuilding'' of inherited policies and structures. He asserts, as he put it in a landmark speech to the party Central Committee in January 1987, that ''unresolved problems began to pile up'' in Soviet society under Brezhnev. ''The country's leadership, chiefly for subjective reasons, was un-

---

[1] A number of recent Western works on civil-military relations and related questions are critically reviewed in Stephen M. Meyer, ''Soviet National Security Decisionmaking: What Do We Know and What Do We Understand?'' in *Soviet Decisionmaking for National Security*, ed. Jiri Valenta and William C. Potter (London: George Allen & Unwin, 1984), 255–297; and Dale R. Herspring, ''Soviet Military Politics,'' *Problems of Communism* 35 (March–April 1986), 93–97. A valuable compendium of information about Soviet military organization is Harriet Fast Scott and William F. Scott, *The Armed Forces of the USSR*, 3d ed. (Boulder: Westview Press, 1984).

able in good time and in full measure to see the necessity of changes and the danger of *the growth of crisis phenomena* in society, or to work out a clear line for overcoming them." Worse, it clung to "authoritarian appraisals and opinions" conceived under I. V. Stalin in the 1930s and 1940s, "when our society faced quite different problems." The Soviet Union, in Gorbachev's judgment, cannot move forward until such dogmas are confronted and revised.[2]

Suppose that Gorbachev and Western specialists are correct about the Soviet system under Brezhnev not measuring up to the political, economic, technological, social, and international problems of an advanced society. It is hard not to wonder whether these exogenous changes and the surfacing of "crisis phenomena" have affected the equilibrium between the party and the armed forces, its ultimate tool for neutralizing enemies and threats. In many other countries, armies have become politically radicalized during times of national crisis. The issue is all the more timely now that Gorbachev is attempting to reverse Soviet decline.

Now, too, after an initial phase in which Gorbachev seemed to pay little attention to military issues, his policies are impinging directly on military personnel and programs. In his January 1987 address on the malaise of the Soviet system, he reiterated the regime's commitment to the "vitally important task" of national defense and affirmed officers' "special role" in it, but he also underlined their "enormous responsibility before the people" and made a cryptic comment about them, too, "living by perestroika."[3] Only four months later, he dealt the army high command its sharpest slap since Khrushchev's sacking of the great wartime marshal, G. K. Zhukov, thirty years before. The Politburo abruptly retired Defense Minister S. L. Sokolov and replaced him with one of his lower-ranking deputies, D. T. Iazov. It accused Sokolov and the commander-in-chief of Soviet air defenses, A. I. Koldunov, of "gross derelictions" of duty for failing to prevent the deep incursion into Soviet air space of a light airplane piloted by a West German teenager, Mathias Rust.[4]

The leadership took advantage of the affair to make wider claims on the officer corps. Gorbachev linked military to civilian incompetence by observing that the Rust incident "reminds us how powerful and alive negative phenomena turn out to be in our society, even in the army."[5] Some civilian critics were less restrained.[6] General Iazov, the new minister, declared in blanket terms that Soviet officers "have still not profoundly grasped the essence of perestroika" and "have not defined their role and place in it," insisting that

---

[2] *Pravda*, 28 January 1987, 1; emphasis added.

[3] Ibid., 5.

[4] Ibid., 31 May 1987, 1.

[5] Ibid., 26 June 1987, 2.

[6] See especially the comments of B. N. Eltsin, the then first secretary of the Moscow party apparatus, in *Krasnaia zvezda*, 17 June 1987, 2.

this change forthwith.[7] Changes on a number of levels were quick to follow. Western audiences saw the most graphic sign of them in Gorbachev's address to the United Nations General Assembly in December 1988, where he committed the Soviet Union to unilateral demobilization of 500,000 troops and major revisions in its military doctrine.

Stirring though such headlines may be, it is necessary to reach behind them to underlying patterns and determinants. In planning *Soldiers and the Soviet State*, the editors have been mindful of a tendency among Western analysts to swing from one extreme to another in their evaluations of the Soviet military's role. During most of Brezhnev's reign, for example, and for several years afterward, it was standard to assert that the army's star was on the rise and, indeed, that there was a drift toward military hegemony in Soviet politics, either solo or with civilian collaborators. Today the thesis of incipient military dominance is out of fashion, and some are rushing to invert the picture, seeing discord pure and simple as the dominant feature of the civil-military relationship.

There is more to gain, in our view, from taking the long view and working toward more systematic and verifiable explanations. Without pretending to the definitive analysis that will have to await historical hindsight, we scan the Brezhnev era for clues to the present, investigate major aspects of recent military politics, and engage in some cautious forward projection. Our findings are targeted as much on the generalist reader and student of public policy as on the initiated Sovietologist.

The Comparative Context

If by theory is meant a construct that elegantly spells out all the pertinent variables and causal relationships, it has to be said that there is no such thing as an accepted global theory of civil-military relations. Perhaps for this reason, most university departments of political science pass over the subject in their curricula, subsuming it under courses on strategic studies, policy formation, and public administration. The well-known *Handbook of Political Science*, synopsizing the state of the discipline, has no chapter on it.[8]

True, the reality of military coups and governments, to say nothing of the intricacies of relations in civilian-dominated polities, has spawned a voluminous literature and a bevy of models and theorems.[9] Nonetheless, many of the

---

[7] D. T. Iazov, "Perestroika v rabote voennykh kadrov," *Voenno-istoricheskii zhurnal*, no. 7 (July 1987), 6.

[8] Fred I. Greenstein and Nelson W. Polsby, eds., *Handbook of Political Science* (Reading: Addison-Wesley, 1975).

[9] Among the most ambitious efforts to arrive at general conclusions are Samuel E. Finer, *The Man on Horseback: The Role of the Military in Politics* (London: Pall Mall Press, 1962); Eric A.

most thoughtful observers despair of arriving at all-embracing conclusions. Donald Horowitz, in a review of coup theories, finds that they often become obsolete before they are rigorously tested: "Theoretical emphasis has shifted so rapidly that there has scarcely been time to gather material that might support or refute the explanations being propounded."[10] One of the most daunting problems is that civil-military relations, rather than being a seamless whole, display such variation from country to country and situation to situation.

Conceptual Approaches to Civil-Military Relations

It is possible, nonetheless, to make at the outset of this book certain conceptual distinctions, less exacting than synoptic theory but helpful in charting the terrain and introducing the literature on Soviet military affairs. A beginning is to delineate three broad domains of civil-military relations. Each is defined by the arena within which the military wields influence. They are not mutually exclusive; traffic may and very often does occur simultaneously in more than one arena.

In the first and narrowest domain, the object is *defense policy*. The mode is problem solving, the formulation and implementation of adequate measures for protection against foreign enemies. The stakes in the second arena may be thought of as concerning *societal choice*. Military and nonmilitary elites in this instance grapple with problems and divisions within civilian society. Economic, technological, and sociocultural in nature, these issues are loosely related to military security as such, but may, if conditions are right, attract the army's attention and become bound up in its dealings with civilian officials and groups. The issue in the third domain is the most gripping: *sovereign power*. The question here can be baldly put as whether soldiers or statesmen are to be supreme in the state. Notice that in each province civil-military transactions may be broadly conflictual or cooperative and may tie civilian and military leaders in complex political tangles with one another and with third parties.

In his seminal work *The Soldier and the State*, published in 1957, Samuel Huntington outlined a framework for fitting together types much like the ones

Nordlinger, *Soldiers in Politics: Military Coups and Governments* (Englewood Cliffs, N.J.: Prentice-Hall, 1977); and Amos Perlmutter, *The Military and Politics in Modern Times* (New Haven: Yale University Press, 1977).

[10] Donald L. Horowitz, *Coup Theories and Officers' Motives: Sri Lanka in Comparative Perspective* (Princeton: Princeton University Press, 1980), 11. One survey of the literature on military rule in Africa alone finds that the analysis "is often mutually contradictory and lacking in predictive power, foundering . . . against an empirical reality resilient to easy generalization." Samuel Decalo, "Military Rule in Africa: Etiology and Morphology," in *Military Power and Politics in Black Africa*, ed. Simon Baynham (London: Croom Helm, 1986), 39.

adumbrated here, and for giving them historical referents.[11] Traditionally, Huntington said, governments in the West have been most intent on political superiority and have opted for subjective civilian control over the warrior class. This meant maximizing the power of a civilian group or groups vis-à-vis the military leadership by patronage, surveillance, class- or kinship-based recruitment, or some other intrusive device. Subjective control became politically less palatable as society industrialized, mass politics grew, and the desire of social groups to deny military support to their opponents squeezed out their wish to get it for themselves. But its greatest liability was that it was militarily inefficient and self-defeating. For Huntington, the growing scale, complexity, and destructiveness of mechanized warfare in the nineteenth and twentieth centuries virtually dictated that governments delegate management of their armies to a technically proficient, meritocratic, and cohesive corps of experts in violence.

The new settlement Huntington labeled objective civilian control, a marriage of mutual acceptance of "autonomous military professionalism" in the army's own sphere with a recognition of civilian primacy in politics at large (in the arenas I term societal choice and sovereign power). If subjective control "achieves its end by civilianizing the military, making them the mirror of the state," objective control does so "by militarizing the military, making them the tool of the state." The officer corps, now the preserve of skilled professionals rather than aristocratic amateurs, would under conditions of objective control make most routine administrative decisions within its functional area, and would advance policy demands on the basis of its corporate bias. It would not be invited or admitted into other conflicts, for purpose of which it would be rendered "politically sterile and neutral."[12]

Huntington's scheme is not without its problems and grey areas. It has been objected that military professionalism is a more elastic concept than he allowed, that it differs in content from one culture to another, and that it does not always produce optimal efficiency.[13] Nor, as Huntington recognized, does professionalism in and of itself define a watertight boundary between military and civilian concerns or a single point of equilibrium between military and civilian organizations. This is true even of the politics behind defense policy,

---

[11] Samuel P. Huntington, *The Soldier and the State: The Theory and Politics of Civil-Military Relations* (Cambridge: Harvard University Press, 1957), chaps. 1–4.

[12] Ibid., 83–84.

[13] Some of these points are made in Perlmutter, *The Military and Politics*, chap. 2. Morris Janowitz, in an influential book written mostly about the U.S. military, pointed out that the modern officer, though still in a sense a professional warrior, is acquiring engineering and communication skills found in a number of civilian professions; Morris Janowitz, *The Professional Soldier* (Glencoe, Ill.: Free Press, 1960). Some sociologists writing after Janowitz eventually began analyzing a military career as an occupation rather than a profession, and political scientists working in the same vein started looking at the officer corps "essentially as a trade union looking out for its own interests" (Horowitz, *Coup Theories*, 5).

where both military influence and civilian checks constantly have to be as- serted and affirmed through active effort.

Civilian politicians, for one thing, remain responsible for national budget- ing and financial management and normally compare the marginal utility of the expenditures recommended by their military advisers to spending on social and other programs. They also, in most modern states, retain a military per- sonnel role, reserving the right to select the most senior officers and to review appointments at lower levels. A final complication is that in many industrial societies, especially since the Second World War, important civilian organi- zations, interested in national security but not part of the uniformed military, also help mold defense programs. Examples would be weapons contractors, regional lobbies, civilian think tanks, nonmilitary intelligence services, and voluntary associations engaged with strategic affairs or arms control. For the military to deal effectively with all these forces and problems in its surround- ings, professional autonomy, as Huntington was aware but did not emphasize, is not an absolute. Objective control does not preclude soldiers acting pru- dently, within the rules of the political game, to maintain and advance the interests of the military establishment and its component parts.

If objective control is accompanied at the best of times by zones of ambi- guity, its breakdown involves their degeneration into zones of combat and confrontation. Using the categories of *The Soldier and the State*, civil-military crisis is most likely under two sets of conditions. First, military and civilian organizations may fall out if either side concludes that the other, be it due to mismanagement, denial of resources, or some other reason, is doing an unac- ceptably poor job of safeguarding national security. A bungled war, a gross discrepancy between defense budgets and security needs, heavy-handed civilian interference in internal military decision making, or creation of an anti-army militia may spark this recognition. In a second pattern, military rad- icalization follows governmental failure within the normal core of civilian jurisdiction. Military leaders here come to perceive, usually after years of grief, that the politicians and civil service are so corrupt, inept, or disorderly that the very survival of the state they are sworn to defend is in jeopardy. They will be hastened toward this conclusion if convinced that their own institution, by contrast, is operationally efficient and politically chaste.[14]

The domain of civil-military interaction most slighted in *The Soldier and the State* is that of societal choice. Subsequent events, in particular the rash of coups in the new states of the Third World in the 1960s and 1970s, showed

[14] See, for example, Horowitz, *Coup Theories*, 193–200; and John Samuel Fitch, *The Military Coup d'Etat as a Political Process: Ecuador, 1948–1966* (Baltimore: Johns Hopkins University Press, 1977). Summarizing evidence on coup motives, Nordlinger (*Soldiers in Politics*, 86) writes that general reform of the political system is rarely the main object of coup makers and that, normally, ''civilian failures strengthen the resolve to intervene when other motives—the protec- tion of the military's corporate interests in particular—are present.''

the need to take this factor into fuller account, along with immediate frictions over defense issues and, in limiting cases, sovereign power. In many countries, military officers have experienced a sweeping "role expansion" as a consequence of being deployed against striking workers, guerrilla bands, or other kinds of dissenters. Involvement in the maintenance of civil peace blurs the line between professional and political matters and may eventually find the army, as in Peru in the 1960s, "preoccupied with rural development, national planning, educational policy, and . . . foreign affairs" as much as with conventional military pursuits.[15] Other times, officers reach the same end after calculated civilian solicitation of their assistance in party, factional, or socioeconomic disputes. This pattern is illustrated by Brazil, in which politicians and interest groups "have always attempted to use the military to further their own goals," thereby ensnarling the armed forces in all manner of societal issues and inviting their intervention. Civilian pressure has been "conveyed to military officers through the medium of personal contacts, public manifestos, and newspaper editorials."[16]

The salience of the social factor in military politics in the developing nations has been evident enough for Huntington himself to concede the point. Military usurpation of civilian power in the Third World, he wrote in the late 1960s in *Political Order in Changing Societies*, is as often as not but one symptom among many of a pathology afflicting whole societies. "In every society, military men engage in politics to promote higher pay and larger military forces, even in political systems such as those of the United States and the Soviet Union, which have almost impeccable systems of civilian control. In underdeveloped societies the military are concerned not only with pay and promotion, although they are concerned with that, but also with the distribution of power and status throughout the political system."[17]

It is worth noting that, although civilian control in the Soviet Union has been, as Huntington says, almost impeccable, some other Communist countries have spottier records.[18] In China and Poland, the two most noteworthy

[15] Perlmutter, *The Military and Politics*, 197. Other examples are given in Robin Luckham, *The Nigerian Military: A Sociological Analysis of Authority and Revolt 1960–67* (Cambridge: Cambridge University Press, 1971); John Steward Ambler, *The French Army in Politics 1945–1962* (Columbus: Ohio State University Press, 1966); and Alan Rouquie, "Military Revolutions and National Independence in Latin America, 1968–1971," in *Military Rule in Latin America: Functions, Consequences, and Perspectives*, ed. Philippe C. Schmitter (Beverly Hills: Sage, 1973), 23–31.

[16] Alfred Stepan, *The Military in Politics: Changing Patterns in Brazil* (Princeton: Princeton University Press, 1971), 94–95. Army involvement in societal conflict may be greatly complicated if the society is ethnically divided and soldiers disproportionately recruited from a particular group. See Cynthia H. Enloe, *Police, Military, and Ethnicity: Foundations of State Power* (New Brunswick, N.J.: Transaction Books, 1980).

[17] Samuel P. Huntington, *Political Order in Changing Societies* (New Haven: Yale University Press, 1968), 194.

[18] Two preliminary attempts to develop a broad comparative approach to civil-military relations in Communist countries are David E. Albright, "A Comparative Conceptualization of Civil-Mil-

cases, this is mainly because external magnets have pulled officers into the resolution of questions of societal choice and sovereign power.

In China, the People's Liberation Army, having originated as a guerrilla army at the same time as the party, arguably has never been a purely professional force. It was deeply implicated in national and regional politics after 1949, and from here it amassed even more power during the Cultural Revolution. Between 1965 and 1969, writes one chronicler, "the PLA came to dominate China," with military officers constituting about half of the central party leadership and taking over most of the party's provincial committees. This was not so much an intentional power grab as a backing into it, triggered by "the collapse of nonmilitary political power" within the civilian party and ministries.[19] Many believe that the army's return to barracks, speeded up by Deng Xiaoping after 1976, has not yet been entirely achieved.

Closer to Moscow, the Polish Army, previously highly professionalized, was propelled to political center stage by the Solidarity crisis of the early 1980s. The socioeconomic failures of the civilian party quickened its loss of legitimacy and nerve and allowed the eruption of massive anti-establishment protest. It took the army and Defense Minister Wojciech Jaruzelski, elevated first to government prime minister and then to party first secretary, to quell popular resistance through martial law (administered by a Military Council of National Salvation) and, for the first time, through substantial militarization of the politics of a Soviet client state.[20] It was this hybrid regime that in 1988–89 achieved the even more startling result of partial democratization of Polish politics.

The Literature on the Soviet Case

The foregoing, while not adding up to a global theory, at least prompts important distinctions to be made in approaching the case at hand. It is most essential to clarify the following things about the Soviet Union: the military

itary Relations," *World Politics* 32 (July 1980), 553–576; and Amos Perlmutter and William M. LeoGrande, "The Party in Uniform: Toward a Theory of Civil-Military Relations in Communist Political Systems," *American Political Science Review* 76 (December 1982), 778–789. Albright attributes stability in relations in Communist systems in part to the overlap between military and civilian elites, whereas Perlmutter and LeoGrande maintain that the existence of "dual-role elites" creates the possibility of serious conflicts over military-related issues within the governing party itself.

[19] Harlan W. Jencks, *From Muskets to Missiles: Politics and Professionalism in the Chinese Army, 1945–1981* (Boulder: Westview Press, 1982), 91. See for background Ellis Joffe, *Party and Army: Professionalism and Political Control in the Chinese Officer Corps* (Cambridge: Harvard University Press, 1967); and, for special insight into the army's regional role, Harvey W. Nelsen, *The Chinese Military System: An Organizational Study of the Chinese People's Liberation Army*, 2d ed. (Boulder: Westview Press, 1981).

[20] See especially Jerzy Wiatr, *The Soldier and the Nation* (Boulder: Westview Press, 1988).

establishment's role definition, and especially whether it constitutes a professional fighting force, in the sense in which we have just defined it; the domains (defense policy, societal choice, sovereign power) within which the officer corps has exercised influence; the prevalence of either subjective or objective civilian control; the extent to which the rules of the civil-military game are stable and agreed upon; the presence or absence of the catalysts of civil-military crisis observed in other countries; and the main alignments in military politics.

How have Western specialists sized up these questions in the past? It is possible to group the existing literature into three main schools of thought. They see the civil-military relationship in the Soviet Union in different ways and discern different potentialities in it. As shorthand, I will call their conceptualizations models I, II, and III, respectively.

Model I was for some time the prevalent one in Western thinking. It is particularly associated with the work of Roman Kolkowicz, whose major study *The Soviet Military and the Communist Party*, mostly treating events under Khrushchev, was published in 1967. To Kolkowicz, the axis of Soviet military politics is conflict between civilian and military elites. Their pervasive enmity is grounded in divergent values, styles, and interests. The party, seeing in the army a potential challenger of its monopoly of power, strives to impose control by subjective means (in Huntington's classification), prime among them political indoctrination and monitoring by party and police organs; the army, for its part, tries to blunt party controls and to acquire professional autonomy, self-respect, and bigger budgets. The party's elaborate restraints "have not always succeeded in suppressing the many strains and disagreements that exist between the two institutions. At various points in Soviet history, . . . these disagreements have brought about critical tensions in their relations. . . . The relationship between the Communist Party and the Soviet military is essentially conflict-prone and thus presents a perennial threat to the political stability of the Soviet state."[21]

Model II has come together mostly in the work of William Odom, who, unfortunately, has explicated it in short essays and reviews and not yet a full-length book. Odom takes strong exception to Kolkowicz's ascription of antithetical traits to army and party: "A more accurate assessment of the institutional values of the two entities suggests congruence, not conflict." Differ-

---

[21] Quotation from Roman Kolkowicz, *The Soviet Military and the Communist Party* (Princeton: Princeton University Press, 1967), 11. A briefer statement of Kolkowicz's argument, with some differences of emphasis, can be found in Roman Kolkowicz, "The Military," in *Interest Groups in Soviet Politics*, ed. H. Gordon Skilling and Franklyn Griffiths (Princeton: Princeton University Press, 1971), 131–169. Studies that broadly share Kolkowicz's approach include Michael J. Deane, *Political Control of the Soviet Armed Forces* (New York: Crane, Russak & Co., 1977), a panoramic treatment; and Yosef Avidar, *The Party and the Army in the Soviet Union* (Jerusalem: Magnes Press, 1983), which is mostly about the 1950s.

ences of opinion do crop up from time to time, but "against a background of broad pragmatic consensus." For Odom, then, cooperation is the hallmark of the relationship. Unlike Kolkowicz, he does not concern himself much with mechanisms of civilian control, subjective or objective, defining the problem away by declaring that military professionalism in the Soviet Union (or, for that matter, in any modern country) does not generate politically significant attitudes. Soviet marshals and generals, says Odom, are better thought of as bureaucratic "executants" of the will of party bosses with whom they basically agree than as defenders of a corporate cause or would-be praetorians. As a consequence, we should worry less about how Soviet soldiers and civilians contest issues and more about how the two of them work together to use military power for their mutual benefit.[22]

Both these models have their blind spots, and in particular Model I. Its conflict-dominated approach is empirically wanting and is contradicted, for that matter, by some of the richest of Kolkowicz's own evidence.[23] Model I overgeneralizes from the fates of individuals (such as Marshal Zhukov, unseated as minister of defense by Khrushchev in 1957). It takes a simplistic view of the motives of the participants, exaggerating the mutual suspicion between the party apparatus and the military and making inadequate allowance for mixed military-civilian coalitions. It conceives of the professional expectations of the Soviet military in ways that are, by comparative standards, unrealistic—failing to heed, for example, that in other industrial countries (the United States included) civilian leaders as a matter of course hire and fire senior military officers and set both the bottom line and many of the components of military budgets.

As for Odom's Model II, its portrait of civil-military condominium, while making valid points about flaws in Model I, goes too far in the other direction. It errs by dismissing Soviet military professionalism's contribution to officer's mentality and conduct. Odom, himself a career U.S. officer, is alert to some of the ambiguities in the notion of the military ethic, but his critique is overdone. He overlooks the contribution of career specialization and professional role boundaries to limiting the lateral spread of military influence into areas of

---

[22] Quotations here are from William E. Odom, "The Party-Military Connection: A Critique" (1973), as reprinted in *Civil-Military Relations in Communist Systems*, ed. Dale R. Herspring and Ivan Volgyes (Boulder: Westview Press, 1978), 32, 36. See also Odom's "The 'Militarization' of Soviet Society," *Problems of Communism* 25 (September–October 1976), 34–51. Many of Odom's comments are directed at Kolkowicz's work. For a spirited reply, see Roman Kolkowicz, "Toward a Theory of Civil-Military Relations in Communist (Hegemonial) Systems," in *Soldiers, Peasants, and Bureaucrats: Civil-Military Relations in Communist and Modernizing Societies*, ed. Roman Kolkowicz and Andrzej Korbonski (London: George Allen & Unwin, 1982), 231–252, esp. 249–250.

[23] I am thinking especially of his analysis of the "Stalingrad group," military officers who were associated with Khrushchev during the war and were favored by him after he became head of the party. See especially Kolkowicz, *The Soviet Military and the Communist Party*, chap. 7.

societal choice and sovereign power. He also overstates the totality of the commitment to military priorities within the party and other civilian institutions.

A Model III can be inferred from my own work. A similar approach is evinced in the research of Dale Herspring, Edward Warner, and Condoleezza Rice.[24] Model III rejects unicausal explanations of the dynamics of Soviet military politics, whether based on conflict or on value congruence. It finds ingredients of both in the relationship over the years, with a certain emphasis, although not exclusively, on the latter. It stresses interaction between military and civilian elites, in which neither side attains absolute domination but the party's sovereign power is accepted. Soviet defense policies it sees as "the outcomes of extended bargaining and political maneuvering among a variety of interested institutions."[25]

For most periods of Soviet history, Model III finds military officers to have been active in this bargaining, participating in military-specific decisions—but not, as a rule, in decisions concerning societal choice and supreme power—on the basis of their professional expertise. In so doing, they often belong to webs of alliance and mutual support that crisscross institutional borders. Civilian control, which under Model I is achieved by subjective means and in Model II is not seen as problematic at all, is in Model III effected by both subjective and objective means, but with a tendency toward predominance of the objective. Military influence figures as legitimate in Model III when motivated by professional concerns and confined to defense issues, whereas Model I finds military influence to be fugitive and stability threatening, and Model II imagines it to be broad but shallow, since civilian and military leaders concur on all points of principle and bargain only over instrumentalities.

A brief excursion into Russian and Soviet military history, reviewing some of the points at issue in the models, will put us in a better position to delve into recent trends under Brezhnev and his successors.

The Historical Context

The study of civil-military relations in the latter-day Soviet Union is impeded by the dearth of research on their past. The appearance of several solid mono-

[24] See especially Timothy J. Colton, *Commissars, Commanders, and Civilian Authority: The Structure of Soviet Military Politics* (Cambridge: Harvard University Press, 1979); and, for a concise statement, "The Party-Military Connection: A Participatory Model," in *Civil-Military Relations*, ed. Herspring and Volgyes, 53–75. Compare Herspring, "Soviet Military Politics"; Edward L. Warner III, *The Military in Contemporary Soviet Politics: An Institutional Analysis* (New York: Praeger Publishers, 1977); and Condoleezza Rice, "The Party, the Military, and Decision Authority in the Soviet Union," *World Politics* 40 (October 1987), 55–81.

[25] Warner, *The Military in Contemporary Soviet Politics*, 117.

graphs on military organization before the Russian Revolution only begins to offset the neglect of decades.[26] Lacunae yawn in our knowledge of the origins and evolution of Soviet military administration, national security policy, and civil-military interplay. Even the formative period of the machinery of national defense cries out for work. Allan Wildman's two-volume study of the lower ranks in 1917 sets a stellar standard, one which, unfortunately, no scholar comes close to meeting for events after October 1917.[27] The two best summary books on the revolutionary and interwar years, by Dimitri Fedotoff-White and John Erickson, date from the 1940s and the early 1960s, before the availability of the most revealing Soviet memoirs and scholarly accounts.[28] Hard though it is to believe, no full-scale Western study exists of Soviet military decision making during the Second World War, in spite of the vast importance of the war to the development of the whole system.[29]

The gaps in historical scholarship notwithstanding, enough is knowable to hazard some summary findings and to provide yardsticks for the present.

From Tsarist Army to Red Army

Russia by the time of the 1917 revolution had possessed a regular standing army—and, most times, the largest one in Europe at that—for two centuries. Its professionalization, however, was greatly retarded by the refusal of its founder, Tsar Peter the Great, to differentiate clearly between military and civilian administration, by the persistent discrimination in officer admission and promotion in favor of the landed gentry, and by the embroilment of senior officers (members of the royal family, gentry, and commoners alike) in court intrigue and dynastic politics.

[26] John L. H. Keep, *Soldiers of the Tsar: Army and Society in Russia, 1462–1874* (Oxford: Clarendon Press, 1985); William C. Fuller, Jr., *Civil-Military Conflict in Imperial Russia, 1881–1914* (Princeton: Princeton University Press, 1985).

[27] Allan K. Wildman, *The End of the Russian Imperial Army*, 2 vols. (Princeton: Princeton University Press, 1979–1987).

[28] Dimitri Fedotoff-White, *The Growth of the Red Army* (Princeton: Princeton University Press, 1944); John Erickson, *The Soviet High Command: A Military-Political History, 1918–1941* (London: Macmillan, 1962). Mark von Hagen, Soldiers in the Proletarian Dictatorship: *The Red Army and the Soviet Socialist State, 1917–1930* (Ithaca: Cornell University Press, 1990) takes a social history approach to the army's first decade. One hopes that this sophisticated study is soon followed by others.

[29] The best source of information about military-political decisions is still Seweryn Bialer, ed., *Stalin and His Generals* (New York: Pegasus, 1969), which consists of translations from Soviet military memoirs organized and introduced by Bialer. John Erickson has published two massive volumes on the Soviet war effort, each of them thoroughly researched and engagingly written: *The Road to Stalingrad* (London: Weidenfeld and Nicolson, 1975) and *The Road to Berlin* (London: Weidenfeld and Nicolson, 1983). But this is narrative battlefield history, with little systematic attention to decision making or civil-military relations.

Imperial Russia up to the late nineteenth century can reasonably be typified as a militaristic state, in the sense of its unstinting support for the amassing of military might and its frequent recourse to armed force at home and abroad, but Russian military leaders were more general-purpose agents, ready for secondment to the civilian bureaucracy, than their counterparts in most other countries. Partly because military academies outproduced civilian schools, and partly due to the tsars' zeal for the military way of life, "much of the Imperial administration," to quote John Keep, "continued to wear a martial look right down to the Reform era" of the 1860s and 1870s.[30] Conversely, the relatively few officers who were alienated from the autocracy—notably, the instigators of the abortive rebellion of December 1825—were seized more by diffuse grievances against the regime than by military-specific ones.[31]

Stung to action by Russia's humbling in the Crimean War, D. A. Miliutin, Alexander I's war minister (1861–1881), instituted mass conscription and made strides toward bringing armaments, doctrine, logistics, and officer schooling up to contemporary European standards. Professionalization of the officer corps was accompanied by civilianization of most other branches of government, into which military men were now much more rarely slotted. To be sure, by a strict definition the Russian Army was probably not a fully pro-fessional force by the time of the First World War. The research of William Fuller demonstrates that its vocational training was too slipshod, its sense of group identity too weak, and its executives too vulnerable to political dictate for this to be so. Most telling, the tsarist government repeatedly used the army, to the detriment of its principal mission and the disgust of its commanders, to break strikes and otherwise enforce public order against rebellious groups among the populace.[32]

Nonetheless, as Fuller shows, "Military professionalism in Russia grew steadily stronger from 1881 to 1914," and War Ministry headquarters and the Imperial General Staff acquired the rudiments of a "professional culture." Unlike the radical intelligentsia in the civilian world—and unlike the Decem-brists a century before—frustrated military officers never articulated a rounded ideological exegesis of the failings of the old regime or a blueprint for a new

[30] Keep, *Soldiers of the Tsar*, 307. Keep reports (315–317) that in 1853, near the end of Nich-olas I's reign, only twelve of the forty-nine provinces of European Russia were under the control of civilian governors; of fifty-two ministers appointed under Nicholas, only ten had never served as officers.

[31] Keep does demonstrate, however (chaps. 10–11), that the poor government performance on military issues made some officers more receptive to the Decembrists' credo.

[32] Fuller, *Civil-Military Conflict*, passim. Despite their unease over the practice, most officers also continued to accept without protest the use of their troops in the nonmilitary work of produc-ing provisions and supplies, and some cooperated in the hiring out of soldiers for harvesting and other menial economic tasks outside the regiments. John Bushnell, *Mutiny amid Repression: Rus-sian Soldiers in the Revolution of 1905–1906* (Bloomington: Indiana University Press, 1985), chap. 1.

one. For all the incompleteness of their corporate evolution, they behaved in politics essentially as professionals, lobbyists who "appreciated politics less for what they meant to the country and more for the possible benefits which could accrue to Russia's military potential."[33] It is revealing that Russian governmental leaders, although entitled to do so, did not arbitrate among the several military factions supporting incompatible force postures and strategies during the leadup to general war. This civilian abdication, more complete than in any West European country, was the main reason for the calamitous double offensive against Germany and Austro-Hungary in August 1914.[34]

The tsar's army was bloodied by its wartime losses and by the mass defections and internal anarchy unloosened by the February Revolution of 1917. The Bolsheviks did away with it outright after their October Revolution. They feared it, even in its splintered condition, as a vehicle of counterrevolution. Like most European socialists, they also subscribed to the romantic notion that a part-time militia, not a standing army, would be force enough for the workers' state.

Within months of conquering power, the Bolsheviks were compelled to shelve this dream, like so many others, and to found a new army harking back in certain ways to the old, to battle both invading German divisions and their internal opposition. The Red Army was directed by an amalgam of "military specialists" from the pre-1917 officer corps (mostly junior officers, with a sprinkling of generals and colonels) and "Red commanders" signed on from the ranks, from among the NCOs, and from the civilian population. Although plagued by desertions and *partizanshchina*, the guerrilla spirit, it staggered to victory by 1921.

Reared together under revolutionary conditions, their interests overlapping but never coinciding, party and army in the early years hammered out a relationship compounded of mutual dependence and suspicion. With its fate hanging in the balance, achieving political control over its military agents was an urgent necessity for the regime. This was first sought by unabashedly subjective means (to use Huntington's classification). Prime was the assignment of pistol-packing party commissars to hover over each civil war commander, empowered to countermand politically incorrect orders and, by the early directives of L. D. Trotskii, the civilian head of the armed forces, to shoot to kill any commander attempting treason. In the majority of cases, however, even the ex-tsarist officers collaborated willingly with the new regime and its emissaries. Some of the ablest of them staffed new central staff organs that carried on the tradition of the Imperial General Staff in everything but name.[35]

[33] Fuller, *Civil-Military Conflict*, 260, 262–263.

[34] See on this point Jack Snyder, *The Ideology of the Offensive: Military Decision Making and the Disasters of 1914* (Ithaca: Cornell University Press, 1984), esp. chaps. 6–7.

[35] Matitiahu Mayzel, *An Army in Transition: The Russian High Command, October 1917–May 1918*, Slavic and Soviet Series, no. 5 (Russian and East European Research Center, Tel-Aviv

After the civil war came a chaotic demobilization of 90 percent of the troops and, briefly, a brush with party factional politics, mainly through the person of Trotskii. There were experiments, mostly for financial reasons, with a territorial militia, but the way forward was blazed by the "military reform" pushed through in 1924–25 by Trotskii's successor, M. V. Frunze. The reform regularized education, staffing, and logistics within the conscript army and gave greater identity to specialized branches (such as the new air arm), responding in the act to some of the criticisms of Russian military organization made before 1917. At most operational levels, it decreed one-man command (*edinonachalie*) and retooled most commissars as either commanders or more innocuous political assistants.[36] The initiation of secret military cooperation with Weimar Germany in 1926 helped with the resumption of Soviet armaments production and the development of training and tactics.

Stalin's Military

When Stalin at the end of the 1920s launched his "revolution from above" and ran the Soviet Union through the paces of forced-draft industrialization, he decided, after some initial hesitation, to make satisfaction of military needs an overriding priority.[37] His government scrapped the last territorial units and delivered to the cadre army, now swollen in size to several million men, vast batches of the best equipment Soviet techology could provide. The Soviet Union on the eve of the German invasion had more tanks, military aircraft, and submarines than the rest of the world put together. Military muscle and, after the defeat of Hitler, military conquests were among the self-proclaimed glories of Stalin's system. The battle cry of the Soviet soldiers who fought their way to the Elbe was *Za Rodinu, za Stalina!* (For the Motherland, for Stalin!). Stalin never looked happier in his last years than when reviewing a military parade or air show, bedecked in his immaculate white generalissimo's uniform.

Important levers of subjective civilian control persisted under Stalin. Prominent among them were independent political commissars (resurrected at most command levels between 1937 and 1942) and assignment of key posts to cronies of Stalin from the civil war—the likes of the military ignoramus and

---

University, September 1976); John Erickson, *The Russian Imperial/Soviet General Staff*, College Station Papers, no. 3 (Center for Strategic Technology, Texas A&M University, 1981), 53–83.

[36] I. B. Berkhin, *Voennaia reforma v SSSR (1924–1925 gg.)* (Moscow: Voenizdat, 1958).

[37] Stalin is said to have turned down in 1927 and 1930 suggestions by M. N. Tukhachevskii that rearmament be made the national priority, only to change his mind in 1931. Tukhachevskii, appointed armaments chief of the army in May 1931, then helped supervise its reequipment. Vitaly Rapoport and Yuri Alexeev, *High Treason: Essays on the History of the Red Army* (Durham: Duke University Press, 1985), chap. 15.

fawning Stalin supporter, K. E. Voroshilov, who was chief of the Red Army from 1925 to 1940, or the alcoholic S. E. Budennyi, the commander of the First Cavalry Army during the civil war and a believer in the decisiveness of horse-mounted troops in a future European war. Police intimidation and terror became a major factor in the Red Army in 1930, when several dozen former tsarist officers (members of a losing faction in a doctrinal dispute) were arrested. The Great Purge of 1937–38 sent three of the army's five marshals and tens of thousands of others to their deaths; numerous officers and soldiers returning from German captivity in 1945 were to be transported to labor camps and Siberian exile; and minipurges erupted at other times in different parts of the forces.[38]

Capping these harsh subjective constraints was the authority of the tyrant himself. As Marshal Zhukov, Stalin's main deputy and troubleshooter and the foremost military hero of the war, mused years later, to contradict Stalin outright "could mean at that time, to put it simply, that before leaving the building you would be invited to go for coffee with Beriia," L. P. Beriia being the sanguinary head of the political police.[39] Zhukov himself was accused of disloyalty and downgraded to command of a provincial military district in 1946, and a group of officers close to him during the war was arrested on trumped-up charges the following year. Only a timely intervention by Stalin saved Zhukov from a similar fate; in 1952 Zhukov by personal order of Stalin was returned to a command post in Moscow and reinstated in the party Central Committee.[40]

In addition to terror, Soviet generals were as captivated as civilian politicians were by the myth of Stalin's omniscience. Explaining why, as chief of the General Staff, he did not argue more assiduously for mobilization to meet the expected German attack in 1941, Zhukov recalled, "I did not feel then . . . that I was wiser and more far-seeing than Stalin, that I could appraise the situation better, or that I knew more than him. I did not have any opinion of events of my own that I could have put forward with confidence as more correct than the judgment of Stalin."[41]

[38] One unofficial Soviet history puts the number of military victims of the Great Purge at 82,000 and points out that the family members of some arrested officers were also seized and even put to death. Anton Antonov-Ovseyenko, *The Time of Stalin: Portrait of a Tyranny* (New York: Harper and Row, 1981), 183. Another (Rapoport and Alexeev, *High Treason*, 276–278) estimates total losses to be between 50,000 and 100,000, and calculates with more precision that 71 percent of all officers holding ranks equivalent to major general or higher were arrested and 65 percent of them killed.

[39] "Marshal Zhukov," *Ogonek*, nos. 48–51 (November–December 1986), pt. 4, 28. These articles consist of personal recollections of Zhukov taped by the writer Konstantin Simonov in 1971 and published only under Gorbachev.

[40] See the account, previously excised from Zhukov's memoirs, in *Pravda*, 20 January 1989, 3.

[41] "Marshal Zhukov," pt. 4, 28.

But this is only part of the story. Components of a pattern recognizable as Huntington's objective civilian control also took shape in Stalin's lifetime, so much so that he really handed his heirs a dual system, an alloy, as I would see it, of the models I and III sketched above. The key, as in the Western countries earlier, was professionalization. In one of the paradoxes in which the age abounded—analogues can be found in fields as diverse as Soviet science and technology, criminal justice, and industrial management—military professionalism congealed even as individual officers lived in fear of Stalin's wrath and of the midnight knock on the door by the secret police.

Know-nothings in the Voroshilov-Budennyi stamp never had things all their way in Stalin's Red Army, sharing control with better-schooled officers like M. N. Tukhachevskii and B. M. Shaposhnikov. Before and after the Great Purge, professionalism was inculcated via a greatly extended network of military schools and academies, the incubators of the resourceful tacticians who outwitted and overwhelmed Hitler's generals. Officers with world-class military skills, either unscathed by the purges or, in some cases, retrieved from Stalin's prisons and camps, increasingly came to the fore after the German onslaught of June 1941. In 1949 one of them, A. M. Vasilevskii, in an earlier life a junior officer in the tsarist army and eventually Stalin's chief of General Staff, was to be the first professional soldier named government minister in charge of the armed forces.[42]

Stalin was incapable of fully trusting anyone, but this did not get in the way of his making good use of his military's talent during the war. He often took unilateral decisions during the horrible first year of the conflict, but after this he depended more and more on his military subordinates. "He came," Marshal Vasilevskii recalled, "to have a different attitude toward the General Staff apparatus and front commanders, he was forced to rely constantly on the collective experience of the military. . . . Before deciding on an . . . operational question, Stalin took advice and discussed it with his deputy [Zhukov], with leading officers of the General Staff, with the main directorates of the People's Commissariat of Defense, with the commanders of fronts, and also with the executives in charge of defense production."[43] His most astute generals, Zhukov and Vasilevskii included, learned how to nudge Stalin toward a decision without talking back to him.

Professional identity was nurtured by the military's new material, social, and bureaucratic privileges, including immunity (except under extraordinary

---

[42] Marshal S. K. Timoshenko held the post from May 1940 to July 1941, but he was a self-taught veteran of the First Cavalry Army and scarcely more of a military virtuoso than Voroshilov. Vasilevskii served as minister from March 1949 to March 1953. Stalin himself was minister (people's commissar) from 1941 to 1946, and the political general N. A. Bulganin for the next three years. A professional seaman headed the navy during its two periods as a separate ministry, 1937–1946 and 1950–1953.

[43] A. M. Vasilevskii, *Delo vsei zhizni*, 2d ed. (Moscow: Politizdat, 1975), 543.

conditions) to public criticism by civilians and immurement behind a wall of secrecy that shut out even senior party leaders, short of Stalin himself, from regular contact with officers' operations. Professional consciousness was celebrated in the ranks, insignia, and other military paraphernalia reintroduced between 1935 and the early 1940s. Equally supportive was the atrophying of the function of maintenance of internal order that the tsarist military had so despised. Assignment of this task to large police and paramilitary forces left the military mostly free to concentrate on external foes, their hands unsoiled by the repression of their countrymen.[44]

There were other earmarks of movement toward objective civilian control. The hierarchy of political officers, first little more than sentries over command personnel, was substantially militarized under Stalin, channeling many of its energies into force management in concert with commanders and siding with them in political controversies. In October 1942, after several zigzags, the government eliminated commissars for the last time at most levels of the military hierarchy and substituted political deputies (*zampolity*) formally integrated into the line of command. Party admission, which after the revolution was granted selectively to political enthusiasts, became nearly universal among Soviet officers, an obligatory but easily earnable badge of the young lieutenant or captain on his way up.

In organizational terms, military professionalism and pride found a nucleus in the General Staff, which operated under different names from the civil war onward but was officially reconstituted as such in September 1935. This "brain of the army," as Shaposhnikov, a three-time chief, dubbed it, was in peacetime the authoritative forum for articulation and debate of military science and art. It overshadowed the headquarters of the lesser branches of service, and no parallel body existed within the party or elsewhere in the civilian bureaucracy.[45] In wartime the General Staff was the main collator of information and drafter of decision memoranda for Stalin's Stavka, Supreme Military Headquarters. Only after the war were it and other military agencies put in an intellectual straitjacket. Hemmed in by five epigrammatic "permanent operating principles" enunciated by Stalin in 1942, Soviet military theory was allowed to stultify. Creative thinking about strategy, force structure, and the like had to be done surreptitiously, if at all.

Although Stalin's Russia, like Peter the Great's, might be thought of as militarist in terms of its policy priorities and ethos, this was far from translating into political dominance on the part of military officers. It was the Communist Party, not the Soviet Army (as the Red Army was retitled in 1946),

---

[44] As late as the latter part of the 1940s, army troops fought anti-Soviet guerrillas in the newly annexed western border lands, but the main responsibility for this and all other internal security questions lay with the police agencies.

[45] Analysis of the early debates over the General Staff's role can be found in M. A. Gareev, *M. V. Frunze—Voennyi teoretik* (Moscow: Voenizdat, 1985), 184–191.

that took responsibility for mobilizing national resources for defense. For the purpose, the regime created new, nonmilitary institutions. The most potent were the agencies that developed and manufactured armaments. They made up a military-industrial complex that, while collaborating with military personnel, was not administratively or politically under their thumb. Aircraft and weapons design bureaus were headed by strong personalities like A. I. Mikoian and A. S. Iakovlev, who had independent lines of communication to the political leadership and many times to Stalin personally.[46]

It is fair to say that civil-military relations under Stalin, as best we understand them, had to do essentially with military policy, with issues flowing directly from the army's functional responsibilities. In deciding such questions, neither civilians nor military officers presented a united front. Alliances spanning the formal boundaries between institutions characterized military politics on issues as different as the design of weapons systems, the making of military doctrine, the direction and limits of the Great Purge in the military, preparations for the war with Germany, and the main operational decisions of the war.[47]

Stalin was adamant that the scope of military influence be duly bounded and that the army as an institution be excluded from decisions of wide societal impact. His attitude was exemplified in his angry rebuff of the commanders of the Ukrainian Military District, who joined regional party secretaries in pleading for relief for hungry peasants in the aftermath of the farm collectivization of the early 1930s: "They [military and civilians at the local level] are not to be in cooperation. The military should occupy themselves with their own business and not discuss things that do not concern them."[48]

Thus, although officers were coopted in sizable numbers to the Central Committee (where their representation was stepped up in February 1941, as war loomed), as well as to local party bodies, their role there was mostly honorific and they seem to have had little input on general questions of polit-

[46] One analyst has argued that the design philosophy for Soviet weapons under Stalin—stressing ruggedness, simplicity, and ease of production—indicates that manufacturers' interests counted at least as much as the military's. Jerry F. Hough, "The Historical Legacy in Soviet Weapons Development," in *Soviet Decisionmaking*, ed. Valenta and Potter, 87–115. This is not to say that conditions were ideal for the arms makers, any more than they were for the military. At one time or another, some of the most illustrious of them (S. P. Korolev, A. N. Tupolev, and B. L. Vannikov stand out) were arrested and forced to do their work in captivity.

[47] See, for example, ibid.; Rapoport and Alekseev, *High Treason*, chaps. 14–15; Gareev, *M. V. Frunze*; Colton, *Commissars, Commanders, and Civilian Authority*, chaps. 5–7; and Bialer, *Stalin and His Generals*.

[48] P. I. Iakir et al., *Komandarm Iakir* (Moscow: Voenizdat, 1963). Another source reports a letter on the rural crisis written by military personnel alone, after which Stalin exclaimed to Voroshilov, "Horrible! What do you have here, Kliment Efremovich, an army or a cooperative society? Why are your people sticking their noses where they don't belong?" I. Dubinskii, *Naperekor vetram* (Moscow: Voenizdat, 1964), 220.

ical power and strategy. Unlike the pre-Miliutin tsarist army, or the militaries of many Third World countries, the Soviet officer corps was rarely used to supply bureaucratic talent for nonmilitary agencies. Stalin, fond though he may have been of his generalissimo's tunic, did not coopt soldiers into his Politburo or, with rare exceptions, into the economic and other ministries of government. During the war, not a single military man was named to the State Defense Committee, which supervised war mobilization. The generals put in charge of civilian transport and communications in 1941–42, A. V. Khrulev and I. T. Peresypkin, relinquished these posts well before the war's end.[49]

The Khrushchev Interlude

When Stalin's death touched off turbulence in Soviet politics, military affairs were no exception. For the first time since the 1920s, the army became enmeshed in high party politics.

It was Zhukov and K. S. Moskalenko, commander of one of the several rival military commands in the Moscow area, who arrested Beriia on behalf of the civilian party leadership in June 1953. Named minister of defense in 1955, Zhukov threw in his lot with Khrushchev during the succession struggle. But he overplayed his hand in June 1957, at the climactic moment of Khrushchev's battle with the Stalinist "antiparty group." When the Presidium (as the Politburo was then known) voted to remove Khrushchev as first secretary, Zhukov is said to have declared, "The army is against this decision, and not a single tank will move without my order." This outburst, as the publicist Fedor Burlatskii noted in a recent article, helped Khrushchev defeat his enemies but, by suggesting the possibility of the military acting independently in high politics, "cost [Zhukov] his political career."[50] Only four months after Zhukov became the first military professional ever to sit on the Politburo, Khrushchev had him relieved of all his offices, pilloried for "Bonapartism," and retired in disgrace. According to Zhukov, Khrushchev tried after October 1957 to confiscate his government dacha, and Khrushchev supporters stooped so low as to connive to send to slaughter the cavalry horse Zhukov had ridden in the 1945 victory parade.[51]

Khrushchev's headstrong activism flared up in other episodes. In January 1960 he announced deep cuts in Soviet troop strength, on the rationale that nuclear weapons delivered by ballistic missiles should now be the nub of Soviet doctrine and weapons procurement. Many senior officers, especially the

[49] See especially I. T. Peresypkin, *A v boiu eshche vazhnei* (Moscow: Sovetskaia Rossiia, 1970); and N. A. Antipenko, *Na glavnom napravlenii* (Moscow: Nauka, 1971), 310–367.

[50] Fedor Burlatskii, "Khrushchev: Shtrikhi k politicheskomy portretu," *Literaturnaia gazeta*, no. 8 (24 February 1988), 14.

[51] "Marshal Zhukov," pt. 2, 7, and pt. 4, 27.

veterans of the great tank battles of the war, were offended. In 1962 Khrushchev made the ill-fated decision to base medium-range missiles in Cuba. During the ensuing backbiting, both the commander-in-chief of the rocket troops, Moskalenko, and the chief of the General Staff, M. V. Zakharov, were demoted.

Dramas like these should not obscure the fact that the Khrushchev leadership, although wavering and wobbling along the way, tilted the relationship with the army further toward objective civilian control pegged on military professionalism. Zhukov's ejection from the Presidium was not inconsistent with the trend, for it accentuated that the military command was first and foremost to have clout within its own bureaucratic frontyard and not on the broader plains of national politics. To the extent that Zhukov's promotion to the party Olympus represented an expansion of the military's political role, his downfall suggested a natural reflex on the part of civilian politicians to counteract any such expansion.

Zhukov's replacement as minister was a stolid but competent armored-warfare specialist, Marshal R. D. Malinovskii, who was not named to the Presidium. Officers whose wartime experience had been at the front, where Khrushchev served as a political officer, rather than in Moscow, with Stalin and Zhukov, were given precedence in promotion, but there seemed little to pick in the way of military credentials between them and the others. The party did not attack the officer corps' material perquisites, status, or administrative prerogatives. It augmented investment in military research and development, the successes of which were symbolized by the military-dominated space program.

De-Stalinization, the main plank of Khrushchev's platform, was also important for civil-military relations. It resulted in the rehabilitation of military victims of Stalin's purges and in a growing feeling of personal security among officers, as throughout the Soviet elite. This could only have been increased by Zhukov's not being physically harmed or even stripped of his marshal's stars, in spite of the lurid charges flung at him. There was no purge within the high command after his fall; executives in the Main Political Administration, the party apparatus within the military, were rotated at a higher rate after October 1957 than regular commanders were.[52] The first wave of military memoirs, appearing at the end of the 1950s, cast a sympathetic light on the epic deeds of the war, showcasing military prowess and exposing some of Stalin's strategic blunders. Slanted though most of them were against Stalin and Stavka, they allowed officers to tell their stories with a vividness not granted any other group.

De-Stalinization made room also, as Miliutin had in the 1860s, for a new latitude in public debate of questions of military doctrine and managing what was now thought of as the "revolution in military affairs" occasioned by nu-

---

[52] See Colton, *Commissars, Commanders, and Civilian Authority*, chap. 8.

clear weapons. In 1955 Stalin's "permanently operating factors," which implicitly downgraded the skill with which weapons were used, were repudiated. Henceforth, military officials and philosophers could discuss strategic concepts with a directness unallowed since the 1920s. When Khrushchev and his supporters proposed that Soviet forces be restructured around nuclear warheads and missiles, the issue was thoroughly and at times heatedly aired, with both Defense Minister Malinovskii and the military's authoritative spokesman on strategy, Marshal V. D. Sokolovskii, taking positions differing in thrust from Khrushchev's. The question was eventually settled on terms nearer to the majority military view, the "combined-arms doctrine," than to Khrushchev's opening stance.[53]

Behind closed doors, Khrushchev later wrote in his memoirs, the generals pressed their policy opinions energetically and persistently. "Soldiers will be soldiers," he said in summary. "They always want a bigger and stronger army. They always insist on having the very latest weapons and on attaining quantitative as well as qualitative superiority over the enemy."[54] When Khrushchev finally lost the support of his fellow party leaders, they toppled him from office in October 1964 without recourse to military help, as new, insider accounts of the palace coup confirm.[55] The sense on both sides of how soldiers could best "be soldiers" had as much as anything helped the relationship survive the rocky transition from Stalin.

From Brezhnev to Gorbachev

The Brezhnev Golden Age

The ouster of Khrushchev removed a thorn in the military's flesh. It marked the advent of what Jeremy Azrael, in a recent study, has called a golden age of civil-military relations in the USSR:

[53] On doctrinal debates, see especially Thomas W. Wolfe, *Soviet Strategy at the Crossroads* (Cambridge: Harvard University Press, 1964). Dale R. Herspring reassesses these and other exchanges in *The Soviet High Command, 1964–1989: Politics and Personalities* (Princeton: Princeton University Press, 1990).

[54] *Khrushchev Remembers: The Last Testament* (Boston: Little, Brown, 1974), 617. See Khrushchev's description (p. 25) of the behavior of the naval commander-in-chief, Admiral N. K. Kuznetsov, once thrown into prison by Stalin and who, before being fired by Khrushchev for impertinence in 1956, demonstrated "the same obstinacy and arrogance that had gotten him into trouble with Stalin." Kuznetsov, in Khrushchev's opinion, "felt that since Stalin was no longer alive, there was nothing to be afraid of and no one he had to respect."

[55] See especially the detailed reminiscences of Khrushchev's son Sergei, "Pensioner soiuznogo znacheniia" (Pensioner of national importance), *Ogonek*, nos. 40–43 (October 1988). It would seem from this and other accounts that Malinovskii and a few other senior officers were eventually informed of the budding anti-Khrushchev conspiracy within the civilian party leadership but took no active part in it. This contrasts with the active engagement of the KGB, the political police.

All things considered, . . . the high command had some reason to hope that Brezhnev's elevation would lead to a substantial improvement in civil-military relations. In the event, Brezhnev's favorable treatment of the military during the first decade of his rule exceeded all but the most extravagantly optimistic expectations. In virtually all respects, in fact, the last half of the 1960s and the first half of the 1970s constituted a "golden age"—in which the Soviet high command got almost everything it wanted in terms of resources, programs, status, and freedom of action in developing Soviet strategic concepts. The contrast with the "Khrushchev era" could hardly have been greater.[56]

Whether or not Azrael is entirely correct about the contrast with Khrushchev, or about the degree of favorable treatment of military interests, he is on safe ground in pointing to an unusual degree of rapport and conflict avoidance between army and party under Brezhnev's leadership, especially for the first ten or twelve years after the removal of Khrushchev. This period, in my opinion, can best be seen as a further stage in the evolution toward a Model III–type relationship hinged on military professionalism and objective civilian control.

To a considerable extent, civil-military accommodation after 1964 was a manifestation of the larger pattern of rapprochement between the party leadership and all segments of the Soviet bureaucracy. Leonid Brezhnev and his Politburo, unlike their predecessors, swore by what they termed "trust in personnel," believing that their interests were usually best served by letting established agencies get on with their jobs with a minimum of interference from without. This cautious and technocratic approach to policy making was much more to the generals' liking than anything that went before. It did not hurt their cause, one has to presume, that Brezhnev had a prior involvement with military affairs so extensive that it must have reflected a personal taste. Twice a political officer, and in the late 1950s the national party secretary supervising the armed forces and the military-industrial complex, Brezhnev had forged numerous patron-client ties to military and defense-industry figures.

Shortly after Brezhnev's inauguration, the civilian leadership restored Marshal Zakharov, fired as chief of General Staff after the Cuban fiasco, to his position.[57] With the evident assent of the party bosses, Zakharov bluntly assailed meddling in military business by "dilettantes" without "an elementary knowledge of military strategy," an obvious allusion to Khrushchev. From this juncture on, it was taken as axiomatic that military knowledge be treated

---

[56] Jeremy Azrael, *The Soviet Civilian Leadership and the Military High Command, 1976–1986*, R–3251–AF (Santa Monica: Rand Corporation, June 1987), 2.

[57] Marshal S. S. Biriuzov, who replaced Zakharov in 1963, was killed in an air crash in Yugoslavia five days after Khrushchev's removal. By coincidence, the position of chief of General Staff was thus open in October 1964—but the civilian leadership, of course, did not have to reinstate Zakharov in it.

with maximum respect. As one senior political officer stated, "The more the political leadership relies on the conclusions reached by military science, the more effective its decisions will be, the more the unity of political and military leadership will be attained."[58] To the satisfaction of party as well as military leaders, the army, and notably the General Staff, began to lay emphasis, both in its own administration and in assessment of national needs, on decision principles influenced equally by Western innovations in defense management and by cybernetic theory.[59]

Direct military access to civilian decision makers was part of the Brezhnev synthesis. Western arms-control negotiators were struck by the weight seemingly carried in Soviet delegations of the late 1960s and 1970s by representatives of the General Staff and other military bodies.[60] At the highest level, A. A. Grechko, Malinovskii's successor as defense minister and a wartime comrade of Brezhnev, was made a full member of the Politburo in April 1973. The first military officer to get this honor since Zhukov, Grechko retained the position until his death three years later. The new minister, D. F. Ustinov, was a veteran member of the party Secretariat with a lifelong involvement in weapons production. As Ustinov was already on the Politburo, the military retained a seat, albeit through a noncareer soldier, for the duration of the Brezhnev period.[61]

Equally propitious for the officer corps were Brezhnev's budgetary priorities, particularly at the start. Promptly after Brezhnev came to power, the Soviets "initiated an across-the-board modernization and buildup of both strategic and conventional forces."[62] Defense outlays climbed at an average of 5 percent a year over the next decade, the largesse being spread out over all services and major missions. It bought "strategic parity" with the United States by the early 1970s, an oblique tribute to the military, and enabled the negotiation of major arms limitation agreements with the other superpower. The military instrument was to be of growing import in Soviet foreign policy in other ways. Most noticeable were the increases in arms transfers and provision of military assistance and advisers to Third World friends and clients. The Soviets used their growing blue-water navy to project power into distant areas and sap Western strength there. In December 1979 their army for the first time since 1945 invaded a nonallied country, Afghanistan.[63]

[58] Quoted in Colton, *Commissars, Commanders, and Civilian Authority*, 202.

[59] David Holloway, *Technology, Management, and the Soviet Military Establishment*, Adelphi Papers, no. 76 (London: Institute for Strategic Studies, 1971).

[60] See especially Raymond L. Garthoff, "The Soviet Military and SALT," in *Soviet Decision-making*, ed. Valenta and Potter, 136–161.

[61] Ustinov in April 1976 had been a full member of the Politburo for only several weeks, but had previously been a candidate member for eleven years.

[62] *The Soviet Weapons Industry: An Overview* (Washington, D.C.: Central Intelligence Agency, Directorate of Intelligence, 1986), 1.

[63] The best general treatment is Michael MccGwire, *Military Objectives in Soviet Foreign Pol-*

Policy calculations aside, the party leadership also seemed to be warmly disposed toward military values and symbols. Nostalgia for the Great Patriotic War, the experience of a lifetime for many politicians of Brezhnev's generation, often shaded into an affection for all things martial, embodied in the campaigns to glorify the war effort and "military-patriotic" ideals which deluged the Soviet population in the 1960s and 1970s. A corollary of the abandonment of Khrushchev's de-Stalinization was a substantial rehabilitation of Stalin as wartime leader. With this change, which not all officers could have welcomed, came a more balanced picture of the strategic decisions of 1941–45, in which the competence of the officer corps as a whole was stressed more than under Khrushchev. Zhukov, Stalin's wartime deputy and the butt of Khrushchev's caprice, was fully exonerated in 1965 and published his best-selling memoirs to favorable reviews in the official press.

It bears underlining that Western analysts at the time widely accepted the smoothness of civil-military relations under Brezhnev. While interpreting it somewhat differently, they agreed that the tenets of Model I, built around high tension and conflict between army and party, no longer applied in Brezhnev's Russia.

Zbigniew Brzezinski, for instance, remarked in 1976 on how the military "are in a more symbiotic relationship with the ruling party" than at any prior point in Soviet political history. His view of the relationship was thus quite close to Odom's Model II.[64] Michel Tatu went even further in this direction, not only detecting an increased stature for the military but assigning it veto power over civilian decisions: "In the Soviet Union of today the supreme leader is no longer in a position to take any important decision that runs counter to the opinion of the military."[65]

Seweryn Bialer's analysis was more in the vein of Model III, as it pointed to the military's attainment of "a high degree of professional autonomy and a great voice in matters concerning military questions," this at a time when Soviet military strength was increasing.[66] It is intriguing that the consensus

---

icy (Washington, D.C.: Brookings Institution, 1987). See also Stephen S. Kaplan, *Diplomacy of Force: Soviet Armed Forces as a Political Instrument* (Washington, D.C.: Brookings, 1981); Mark N. Katz, *The Third World in Soviet Military Thought* (Baltimore: Johns Hopkins University Press, 1982); and Michael MccGwire, Ken Booth, and John McDonnell, eds., *Soviet Naval Policy: Objectives and Constraints*, (New York: Praeger, 1975).

[64] Zbigniew Brzezinski, "Soviet Politics: From the Future to the Past?" in *The Dynamics of Soviet Politics*, ed. Paul Cocks, Robert V. Daniels, and Nancy Whittier Heer (Cambridge: Harvard University Press, 1976), 351.

[65] Michel Tatu, "Decision Making in the USSR," in *Soviet Strategy in Europe*, ed. Richard Pipes (New York: Crane, Russak, 1976), 52.

[66] Seweryn Bialer, "The Political System," in *After Brezhnev: Sources of Conduct in the 1980s*, ed. Robert F. Byrnes (Bloomington: Indiana University Press, 1983), 3. Bialer said in the same passage that the military under Brezhnev "broadened its powers," but he seems to have intended this observation to apply to defense policy only.

extended to Roman Kolkowicz, whose earlier writings were classic statements of Model I. By the early 1980s, Kolkowicz was using the language of Model III to describe the Brezhnev period: "The Soviet military and the party leadership seem to have reached a workable *modus vivendi*, a political and bureaucratic accommodation. . . . The military has faithfully supported the party's policies and the party has seen to it that the military's interests are satisfied. There is a complementarity of institutional interests."[67]

Mixed Signals after Brezhnev

What would life after Brezhnev bring to the Soviet military and to civil-military relations? The preeminent point of view, put forward until well after Brezhnev's death, was that civil-military comity and the political influence of the officer corps could both be expected to increase. Western journalists writing during the Kremlin interregnums of Iu. V. Andropov and K. U. Chernenko seemed especially convinced that this was so. Typically, a magazine story several weeks before Andropov's death in 1984—under a sensational heading asking whether the military was "taking over the Kremlin"—spoke of the unprecedented "political importance and public visibility" of the armed forces. "Their growing influence shows up across the board—from the powerful role of the Defense Minister [Ustinov] in the Politburo to the impact of the military on the everyday life of Russians." Dimitri Simes of the Carnegie Endowment for International Peace was quoted as explaining in an interview that under Andropov, "the military has greater influence, higher status, and wider impact on society than ever before in Soviet history." The military, in Simes's estimation, "now comes in the front door. It is the one big winner of the Andropov era."[68]

A number of scholars were willing to go farther and to predict that the military establishment would actually move to dominate the whole Soviet system. The forecast was a reconfiguration of Odom's Model II. They posited congruence, not on the basis of a shared commitment to expansion of Soviet military power, as Odom originally saw it, but on different grounds: the shared dilemma of how to cope with a drastic decline in regime legitimacy and an exacerbation of the economic and other problems of the Soviet Union. And party-military condominium, it was thought in this new formulation, would end up with the military supplanting the party as the paramount partner, rather as proved to happen in Poland in 1981.

The words of Zbigniew Brzezinski and Roman Kolkowicz, the former a

---

[67] Kolkowicz, "Toward a Theory of Civil-Military Relations," 246, 248.

[68] Nicholas Daniloff and Robin Knight, "Is Military Taking Over the Kremlin?" *U.S. News and World Report*, 23 January 1984, 26, 30.

distinguished generalist and the latter a specialist on Soviet military affairs, may be taken as representative of the more outspoken forecasts of military ascendancy. In the 1976 essay already quoted in this chapter, Brzezinski wrote as follows:

> The military is . . . increasingly becoming the major repository of the state tradition and an alternative unifying symbol [to the party]. If political change in the Soviet Union should gradually begin to threaten the autocratic tradition, either through an evolution towards a significantly more pluralistic system, or if such change should involve a dangerous decay in the party's ability to integrate the system as a whole or to cope effectively with the social turbulence that might even by the end of this decade spread from the West to the more advanced portions of the Soviet Union, then the military would become the force most likely to respond—with new vigor—in keeping with the imperatives defined by long-enduring traditions. . . . A dictatorship fusing some of the party and some of the more politicized top military hence becomes a scenario for the future to be taken quite seriously. There is no other elite group in the Soviet Union capable either of supporting the party in the event of a major crisis, or of replacing the party in the event the crisis should get out of hand.

Brzezinski considered it not at all improbable that a Soviet marshal in full uniform might at some future party congress "mount the podium as the party's new Secretary General."[69]

Kolkowicz's prognosis, a bit more guarded but essentially similar, dates from 1982. For Kolkowicz, the most likely outcome in the near future was an incremental transfer of political power from party to army, in a prolongation of the military aggrandizement he saw as occurring under Brezhnev. "The military, in this scenario, would assume a much more active role in decision-making in the party and government, becoming a senior partner of the civilian apparat of the CPSU." If, however, the regime was beset by severe and protracted crisis, as Kolkowicz thought not unlikely, the military "would be able, and probably willing, to assume power in a transition mode." The upshot would be a "military-dominated coalition," with civilian as well as military partners, which would try to legitimize itself on the basis of patriotism, militarism, and Marxism and to deal with the backlog of national problems the party was unable to fix on its own.[70]

Even before Gorbachev's rise, a minority of Western commentators was offering quite a different analysis and prognosis. Their work, first seeing the light in the mid-1980s, but based in some cases on research begun while Brezhnev was still in power, has spotlighted what they see as a countertrend: toward less military influence and more civil-military conflict. Their recom-

---

[69] Brzezinski, "Soviet Politics," 351.

[70] Roman Kolkowicz, "Military Intervention in the Soviet Union: Scenario for Post-Hegemonial Synthesis," in *Soldiers, Peasants, and Bureaucrats*, ed. Kolkowicz and Korbonski, 111, 132.

mendation, in effect, is to resuscitate Model I, largely along the lines originally adumbrated in the 1960s by Kolkowicz.

Jeremy Azrael, in the clearest statement of this position, has maintained that
the golden age turned to brass, and civil-military discord began to rise, as early
as the mid-1970s, well before the death of Brezhnev.[71] By Azrael's account,
the appointment of the civilian Ustinov as minister of defense, upon Grechko's
death in 1976, was a serious blow to the officer corps.[72] Additional ill-will
arose, Azrael submits, from resource stringency and the party leadership's
desire to ease it at the expense of the military budget; from Brezhnev's pronouncements on military doctrine and the unwinnability of nuclear war, especially after his major speech in the city of Tula in 1977; and from the strident
public statements made by the chief of General Staff appointed in 1977, N. V.
Ogarkov, about the need for military preparedness against both conventional
and nuclear military threats from the United States.

Azrael attaches special importance to two discrete events in 1982–84. The
first was an extraordinary Kremlin audience Brezhnev held with the military
brass two weeks before his death, in which he seemed both to reassure them
that the party had economic problems in hand and to demand that officers
make better use of the resources they were getting. The second incident was
the sudden removal of Marshal Ogarkov, the USSR's most prominent professional soldier, in September 1984, midway through Chernenko's brief reign.
Azrael also argues that at the time of writing—some months before the Rust
affair of 1987—there were strong signs of "a large disparity between the ambitions and aspirations of the high command on the one hand, and Gorbachev's near-term priorities . . . on the other."[73]

It is not difficult to find developments in civil-military relations under Mikhail Gorbachev suggestive of Model I.[74] Gorbachev, unlike Brezhnev, had
no earlier career involvement with military affairs. His policy of media *glasnost* or openness is permitting more probing of military shortcomings and of
political taboos in the defense field. His declared economic priorities are consumer goods and civilian technology, not defense production. His Politburo's
arms-control initiatives—the treaty on Intermediate Nuclear Forces in Europe,
the December 1988 announcement of the demobilization of 500,000 troops,
and the assent to the broad outlines of a treaty on chemical weapons, in particular—have involved liquidation of major Soviet military assets, and they have

[71] Azrael, *The Soviet Civilian Leadership*, passim.

[72] The last nonprofessional minister of defense was Bulganin (1946–49 and 1953–55), but he
was a party generalist with a varied background (including secret police work and mayor of Moscow) and no expertise in weapons production.

[73] [73]Azrael, *The Soviet Civilian Leadership*, 40.

[74] For some brief early analysis, see Timothy J. Colton, "Gorbachev and the Soviet Military,"
in *Soviet Policy Issues*, ed. Susan Clark, Memorandum Report M-446 (Alexandria, Va.: Institute
for Defense Analyses, February 1988), 149–164; and Dale R. Herspring, "On *Perestroyka*: Gorbachev, Yazov, and the Military," *Problems of Communism* 36 (July–August 1987), 99–107.

greatly relaxed the Soviet Union's traditional hostility to on-site verification of such agreements. In addition, he has engineered the withdrawal of Soviet troops from the futile war in Afghanistan.

Gorbachev has also administered what look like a series of deliberate symbolic slights of the high command. His tone toward the army has been correct but cool, his rhetoric containing none of the laudatory phrases common in Brezhnev's. Some message must be intended in the exclusion of military officers from the pageantry of Chernenko's funeral in March 1985 and, more pointedly, in the reduction from a dozen men to four of the military contingent atop the Red Square reviewing stand at the 1986 Revolution Day parade. Both Sokolov, the minister of defense from December 1984 to May 1987, and Iazov, his replacement, have been limited to candidate members' seats on the Politburo, whereas Grechko and Ustinov before them were full members.[75] Iazov, in addition, retains the military rank of general of the army, which is second in precedence to the full marshal's rank held by all postwar defense ministers.[76]

These wisps of evidence do not, however, add up to a convincing appraisal of the condition of, or prospects for, civil-military relations. Neither the Model I analysis now gaining favor in the West nor the Model II forecast in vogue several years earlier can at this point be treated as more than a hypothesis needing proper development and testing. The same, needless to say, goes for any attempt to update Model III.

Speculation and categorical assertion are no substitute for careful empirical research. But they are exactly what have set the tone in journalists' and some academics' recent comments about political-military affairs in the USSR. The claim, for instance, that the officer corps was "the one big winner" of the Andropov era seems to have rested on little more than supposition. The Soviet decision to withdraw from Afghanistan has been widely read as a slap at the military, even though it was never clear that the military favored the original invasion—and we now have claims in the Soviet press to the effect that senior officers, Ogarkov included, opposed it and strove to limit Soviet troops' combat role in Afghanistan. Analytical statements about the rise and, lately, the fall of military influence have at times been internally contradictory and weakly, if at all, linked to concrete indicators of influence. Analysts have often not bothered to specify the exact issue area (defense policy, societal choice, sovereign power) within which they are charting influence or conflict.

[75] Foreign Minister E. A. Shevardnadze, a full member of the Politburo, outranks Iazov. The new head of the KGB, V. A. Kriuchkov, was appointed a full member in September 1989.

[76] There is also the ambiguous signal of the Soviet government's decision in June 1987 to restore the original name of a defense-industry city, Izhevsk, which had been renamed Ustinov in honor of the late minister of defense after his death in 1984. The renaming of Izhevsk had been openly criticized by several Soviet intellectuals, but it is unlikely that it would have been reversed had Gorbachev's Politburo held Ustinov in the reverence some Western commentators have believed he enjoyed.

A particular problem has been the haste to draw conclusions about interinstitutional relations from fragmentary and ambiguous information about individuals. Institutions tend to be presented as monoliths with homogeneous interests identical with those of their current leaders.

Concerning Defense Minister Sokolov's fall, for instance, Soviet sources have so far told us little of what lies behind it. It is entirely possible that the removal of the seventy-five-year-old Sokolov, handpicked for the job by the Chernenko Politburo, would have been approved by not a few military officers—those who would benefit from the promotion opportunities opened up by a new minister, those who would prefer a more vigorous boss and advocate (and one more in step with Gorbachev's thinking), those who were embarrassed by the spectacle of a foreign aircraft landing unimpeded in downtown Moscow, those who associated Sokolov with the failure in Afghanistan (Sokolov in 1979 supervised the introduction of Soviet forces there), and perhaps others. The demotion of Marshal Ogarkov in 1984 and the announced resignation in December 1988 of Marshal S. F. Akhromeev, Ogarkov's successor as chief of General Staff, also stimulated reams of commentary, most of which, sadly, remains untestable until diaries are published or the Soviets unlock archives to Western professors.[77]

High among our hopes in *Soldiers and the Soviet State*, therefore, is to clear up terms and standards of evidence, downplay personalities in favor of institutional and systemic factors, look at a common set of research questions from several vantage points, and arrive at findings that will provoke orderly debate among Western analysts.

The Perspective of This Volume

Our Broad Approach

The civil-military relationship is ultimately the expression of forces and trends that act on both sides of the boundary between military and nonmilitary organizations. What happens, we ask, if underlying variables move in such a way

[77] The Ogarkov affair might be thought symptomatic of some sort of disagreement. But who was disagreeing with whom, and about what? Some have seen Ogarkov's removal as a gesture by a party apparatus starting to reassert itself, others as evidence that the military was so strong that it was tempted to flex its muscle in ways that provoked civilian politicians. A skeptic might dismiss the incident as a not terribly consequential personnel decision. After all, Ogarkov was aged sixty-seven at demotion, had held his position for three years longer than the average for other postwar chiefs of staff, was succeeded by his ranking deputy (Akhromeev), was given another major assignment, continued to have articles published, and was reelected a full member of the party Central Committee in 1986. He was retired only in 1989.

As for Akhromeev in 1988, it was well known that he had health problems. Moreover, he was perceived by American officials with whom he had come in contact as a warm backer of Gorbachev, and he was appointed a personal adviser to Gorbachev upon his retirement from the General Staff.

as to introduce strain into the relationship? One broad possibility is mutual adaptation, in which roles, ambit of interaction, and institutional interests are adjusted with some degree of reciprocity. The other is escalation of conflict resulting from a failure of adaptation, which carries the potential of a rupture or radical revision of the core relationship; this in turn could have far-reaching consequences for the Soviet political system.

How to bring order to the inquiry? Our choice is to consider civil-military relations in the broad context of overall political, economic, technological, and social forces in the Soviet Union. Persistent and emerging realities in each of these areas constitute crucial dimensions of the action setting within which Soviet soldiers and civilians function. In each instance, our aims are to assess the strain that environmental trends have brought about in the civil-military relationship and to gauge the nature and success of the adjustment in the relationship.

Explaining and Measuring Influence

The civil-military relationship in the Soviet Union, as in any country, comprises a complex cluster of behaviors. To make our work manageable, we direct it toward the aspect of the relationship that we consider most central— the exercise of influence on issues of mutual interest by key military and civilian institutions.

Political scientists often use influence and power interchangeably. Both terms describe control exercised by some person or persons over the actions of others. Some theorists, however, draw a subtle distinction between the two concepts. We follow Robert Dahl by defining influence as the alteration of others' behavior through communication, persuasion, and inducement. Power we consider to be a special kind of influence, "when compliance is attained by creating the prospect of severe sanctions for non-compliance."[78] At least in stable societies, such sanctions, at their most severe when they entail force or coercion, are usually the monopoly of the state or those who speak in its name.

To illustrate: the Soviet military would be exercising influence if the chief of the General Staff convinced the Politburo to invest more resources in an upcoming five-year plan in tank or submarine production. It would be exercising power if the submission to the Politburo was successful because it was

---

[78] Robert A. Dahl, *Modern Political Analysis*, 4th ed. (Englewood Cliffs, N.J.: Prentice-Hall, 1984), 38–39, 41. Needless to say, different definitions of these terms abound. For instance, one well-known text considers influence to be a type of power, as "power not expressed as command"; Carl J. Friedrich, *Man and His Government: An Empirical Theory of Politics* (New York: McGraw-Hill, 1963), 200. For another stimulating analysis that treats power, not influence, as the summary variable, see Steven Lukes, *Power: A Radical View* (London: Macmillan, 1974).

accompanied by an explicit or implicit threat of what the armed forces would do if the capital were not forthcoming; the sharpest sanction, and the one most unlikely to be used in normal politics, would be the threat to use force against the civilian authorities.

It is crucial to keep in mind two methodological cautions made by political theorists. One is that any statement about political influence must specify the issue, or the range of issues, over which the influence is effective. This chapter has already made the crude division among issues of defense policy, societal choice, and sovereign power. Depending on the level of detail sought, other gradations may be advisable within those realms. Indicative of how this might be done is Condoleezza Rice's subdivision of defense policy, the main area in which the Soviet military is politically active, into a series of concentric circles. In only the innermost circle, where options for matters of organization, strategy, and force posture are developed, does she find the military normally to have the scene to itself. The further decisions move toward threat assessment, weighing of social costs, and the like, the more, Rice says, the military has found itself sharing the stage with civilian institutions that also expect to have input into decisions.[79]

Similar specificity is needed in considering issues outside the defense area. In economics, as an example, it would be one thing for military officers to seek to remedy shoddy housing construction or poor consumer goods on military bases; it would be another for them to try to shape the Soviet government's entire investment policy or dictate its attitude toward economic reform. Civilian officials, for their part, would take a different approach to determining steel or tank production than they would to interfering in the internal structure of tank divisions.

The second caveat, urged by Dahl and other scholars, is that the influence of any individual or organization must always be understood in relation to the influence of others. For the Soviet military, the others are most materially the officials in the apparatus of the Communist Party, whose power over the officer corps—civilian control, subjective or objective—is the main counterweight to military influence. But also part of the equation, and essential to any comprehensive account, are other civilian organizations, among them the defense production ministries and the KGB, the Soviet security police.

Our interest in influence inevitably alerts us to cases of observable conflict, since such behavior, like smoke to the fire, is potentially the strongest indicator of political work being done. Nonetheless, this cannot be the only such indicator, and the absence of actual and observable conflict cannot always be read as proof that power and influence are not being exercised. As has been pointed out in the Western debate on the phenomenon of power, "the most effective and insidious use of power is to prevent [actual] conflict from arising

[79] Rice, "The Party, the Military, and Decision Authority in the Soviet Union."

in the first place.''[80] Political winners in many countries and situations use their resources, not only to resolve open disagreements in their favor, but to keep potential grievances from being voiced and even to keep losers from believing themselves to be aggrieved. To compound the problem, it is a special trait of Soviet politics, nowhere more so than in the defense area, that great pains are taken to suppress information about differences of opinion and interest. Hence the analyst of civil-military relations in the Soviet Union is often faced with a depressing paucity of hard data—about who is prevailing in controversies, why this is happening, and even what the argument is really about.

Consequently, the participants in our project have had to be inventive in methods and to stretch what data they do have. Where overt conflict is not revealing as to patterns of influence, we have resorted to surrogate measures of several different kinds. Patterns of military and civilian participation in politics, through administrative involvement and expression of preferences in the official media, are of analytic importance in their own right.[81] In this volume, we use them as one important proxy for influence. Where the professional military is concerned, we are especially interested in evidence of attentiveness to issues in policy domains—industrial management, education, and justice might be cases in point—that go beyond the defense realm proper. Where civilian leaders are concerned, we will especially want to know if they are taking a stronger interest in issues over which military personnel have habitually had the main say.

Apparent policy outcomes will be another surrogate for direct measures of influence. They may help the analyst to make inferences about power and influence relations even when Soviet censorship or other interference precludes full reconstruction of the way in which those results were generated. Policy outcomes may take forms such as budgetary allocations, revised administrative procedures or operating theories, or breaks in the continuity of personnel. Alternatively, they may be expressed as altered institutional arrangements. Examples from the past would be the abolition of commissars in Soviet divisions and regiments in 1942 or the 1959 establishment of a new branch of service, the Strategic Rocket Forces. An institutional change will be of special interest to us if it affects military and civilian organizations simultaneously—as would, to take a hypothetical example, creation of a Soviet analogue to the National Security Council in the United States.[82]

A final surrogate measure is the political authority of the military and civil-

---

[80] Lukes, *Power: A Radical View*, 23.

[81] See the argument in Colton, *Commissars, Commanders, and Civilian Authority*, chaps. 10–12.

[82] The Defense Council, chaired by the head of the party, advises the Soviet party leadership on national security issues, but it has no bureaucracy of its own and depends on the military's General Staff for staffing.

ian agencies involved. Authority is influence vested with legitimacy, conveying the belief that its exercise is proper or morally good.[83] It is thus a resource that may, when called upon, add to the influence or power of the individual or organization possessing it. It is valuable to know if the apparent decision authority of any of the major players in Soviet military politics is changing, even if, again, invocation of that authority in the making of concrete decisions cannot be conclusively demonstrated. Indicators of authority are essentially status indicators, and evidence as plain as a seat on the Politburo or as abstruse as the number of generals atop Lenin's tomb may, if judiciously used, be of assistance in gauging status.

Environmental Challenges and the Structure of the Book

Each author has been asked to take as an independent variable a specific facet of the environment of civil-military relations. Strictly speaking, it has been impossible to define variables that are completely independent of the civil-military connection. Somewhat arbitrarily, we have defined important aspects of the environment that are more or less exogenous to the relationship, and we have asked authors to take stock of significant trends in it. This is an important task in its own right, since such trends have been incompletely and inconsistently analyzed in previous Western studies.

From here, the authors proceed to military and civilian response to environmental challenges, and then on to possible change in our principal dependent variable, influence of civilian and military actors. The responses to environmental change, although varying from case to case, would hypothetically include changes in the nature of the issues and stakes of civil-military relations, in perceptions of the issues and stakes, in the roles and alignments of the institutional players, and in the political assets they are able to bring to bear. From these intermediate variables we hope to be able to proceed to explain changes, if any, in the civil-military balance.

I shall preview the substantive chapters briefly by summarizing the environmental tendencies, and the puzzles arising from them, that we thought in advance to be of greatest importance.

CHALLENGE NUMBER ONE: CHANGES IN LEADERSHIP POLITICS

The first environmental disturbance that could feasibly have been affecting civil-military relations has been on the plane of political leadership. It is taken up in chapter 2 by Bruce Parrott.

The Brezhnev Politburo's inability to renew itself or to refurbish its policies

[83] Dahl, *Modern Political Analysis*, 53–54.

was integral to Soviet national politics from the mid-1970s on. The Andropov-Chernenko interregnum of 1982–85 only underscored the image of an oligarchy out of touch with society and unwilling to make the hard choices needed to address its problems. The accession of Gorbachev, and with it the political breakthrough of a younger generation of leaders, has broken the logjam within the leadership. It has also occasioned a flurry of policy innovations and a debate over deeper, structural reforms. Divisions over Gorbachev's program are deeper, and the stakes higher, than any within the Soviet political elite since Khrushchev.

Conceivably, inertia, weakness, and division within the civilian leadership, in a party in which the rules governing replacement of the top leader are informal only, have afforded the military the opportunity and motivation for extending its influence in high politics. Michel Tatu, Roman Kolkowicz, and others have listed the uncertainty over succession as one of the most important factors favorable to an increase in military politicization and influence.[84] The same was intimated in the many reports of a greater military presence during Andropov's and Chernenko's interlude in power.[85]

A variety of specific questions thus present themselves. Have conditions in leadership politics actually been conducive to a more expansive military role? Has the feeling of brooding crisis in the Soviet Union, finally brought into the open by Gorbachev, worked to the advantage or disadvantage of the military? Has the party's internal malaise approached that which drew the Chinese and Polish militaries into elite politics in those countries? Is there any reliable evidence that Soviet military figures acted as kingmaker in the recent chain of mini-successions? Have the generals actively participated in the main policy disagreements within the civilian leadership, or have they taken advantage of succession circumstances to raise grievances of their own? Have they been faring better or worse with the Gorbachev generation of civilian bosses? Changes in public policy bearing on military sensitivities should help with answers. So should trends in the treatment of senior military personnel, in military representation on party executive bodies, and in cross-posting of officers to civilian agencies.

The issue of possible civilian allies for a politically assertive military must also be taken up. Of unusual interest is the tie with the KGB, the Soviet Union's political police. The KGB shares certain organizational traits with the

[84] See especially Michel Tatu, *Eux et nous* (Paris: Fayard, 1985), 24–30, and Kolkowicz, "Military Intervention," 122–126. In a later account (*Gorbatchev: L'U.R.S.S. va-t-elle changer?* [Paris: Le Centurion, 1987], chap. 9), Tatu argues that the majority of military officers oppose Gorbachev and his reforms, and that they are important members of an anti-Gorbachev coalition that has a serious chance of defeating Gorbachev's policies or even removing him from office.

[85] The 1984 *U.S. News and World Report* article already cited (Daniloff and Knight, "Is Military Taking Over the Kremlin?" 26) reported "growing signs that the Soviet military may be moving to fill a power vacuum in the Kremlin."

army: a specialization in the application of violence, a strict internal hierarchy, a growing professionalization. Various of its operations also interlock with the military's. Besides helping keep watch on military commanders, military installations, and nuclear weapons through its "special departments" within the armed forces, the KGB patrols frontier areas and mounts a variety of intelligence and subversive operations abroad. The KGB seemed to gain new political prominence in the Soviet Union with the appointment of Andropov, its chief for fifteen years, as head of the party in 1982.

The KGB has often been bracketed with the army in Western discussions of an augmentation of military power, but with little evidence being adduced. Is the KGB apt to act as political friend or foe of the military establishment? And how do KGB-military relations, good or bad, affect civil-military relations?[86] Amy Knight, the author of a new book on the KGB, addresses these and related questions in chapter 3.[87]

CHALLENGE NUMBER TWO: ECONOMIC STRINGENCY

The secular decline in Soviet economic performance, which accelerated after 1975 and continued into the 1980s, constitutes another potential wellspring of change in civil-military relations. Falling growth rates; tighter supply of labor, raw materials, energy, and investment capital; and a climate of austerity and gloom about future growth spelled bad news for the military leadership as much as they did for Soviet civilians. Resource allocation and the other economic dilemmas of the 1970s continue to confront the new party leadership, which under Gorbachev is committed to reforming the economy but so far has been temporizing over how to do so.

Exactly what real tradeoffs have Soviet planners faced between military and civilian programs? How has the military been affected by economic hard times and the intensifying competition for resource shares? Has it been at all inclined to blame economic decline on civilian mismanagement or press reform prescriptions of its own? Has the army's standing as a Soviet success story been translated into any special authority to speak out, or to be courted as a bureaucratic ally, on management and reform issues? Or, alternatively, has the military sector been seen as a source of resources available for recommitment by civilian economic reformers?[88]

---

[86] One who emphasizes the contradictions between military and KGB interests, not their commonalities, is Roman Kolkowicz. See Kolkowicz, "Toward a Theory of Civil-Military Relations," 246–247.

[87] See Amy W. Knight, *The KGB: Police and Politics in the Soviet Union* (Boston: George Allen & Unwin, 1988).

[88] Western observers have sometimes drawn a direct link between economic decline and the Soviet military's prestige. One specialist on international economics, Paul Craig Roberts of Georgetown University, is quoted as saying during the Andropov interlude: "No one should be

These complicated issues are dealt with in chapter 4, by Robert Campbell. Whereas most analysts have accepted the finding of the U.S. Central Intelligence Agency that the annual rate of decline of Soviet defense spending declined from 4 to 5 percent to roughly 2 percent around 1976, one of Campbell's conclusions is that the sag occurred about a half-decade later, and that problems of definition and measurement continue to vex Western and, indeed, Soviet efforts to understanding trends in Soviet military outlays. We have also thought it essential to commission a separate essay on the Soviet armaments industry, asking how various environmental changes have affected its operations and what part it has been playing in the overall interaction between civilian and military institutions. Chapter 5, by Julian Cooper, complements not only Campbell's chapter but Thane Gustafson's on military technology.

CHALLENGE NUMBER THREE: TECHNOLOGICAL DYNAMISM

The point of departure for Gustafson in chapter 6 is another environmental stimulus, the swift pace of modern technology. To stay in the arms race with the United States, and even to be well-placed to control it through negotiation, the Soviets must cope with new generations of weapons systems, incorporating breakthroughs in communication and guidance systems, materials, optics, propulsion, and more. These extraordinary changes affect conventional as well as nuclear arms; indeed, some military thinkers believe that they are shrinking the gap in destructiveness between the two families of weapons. Awareness has mounted in the Soviet Union of the magnitude of the technological gap between East and West and of its consequences for national security. Moscow's alarm at the announcement of the United States's Strategic Defense Initiative in 1983 is the most eloquent demonstration of this, but far from the only one.

Stephen Meyer has reasoned that technological change has already built up the Soviet military's leverage over defense policy, because of "the military's virtual monopoly on the analytic tools of military science." Further, he says, "military decision influence could spill over into areas of general economic-industrial policy" due to the need in future to mobilize wider sectors of the economy for defense purposes.[89] Jerry Hough believes that the younger gen-

surprised at the military's prominence. It is the bodyguard of the Communist system and its road to ultimate triumph. It is also the only successful institution in the system at a time when the pressure of economic failure is intensifying." Daniloff and Knight, "Is Military Taking Over the Kremlin?" 26.

Some preliminary discussion of the reform issue can be found in George C. Weickhardt, "The Soviet Military-Industrial Complex and Economic Reform," *Soviet Economy* 2 (July–September 1986), 193–220, and in the comments by Julian Cooper and me at 221–232.

[89] Stephen M. Meyer, "Civilian and Military Influence in Managing the Arms Race in the USSR," in *Reorganizing America's Defense: Leadership in War and Peace*, ed. Robert J. Art, Vincent Davis, and Samuel P. Huntington (Washington, D.C.: Pergamon-Brassey's, 1985), 53.

eration of military officers is becoming so disenchanted with the level of Soviet technology that it will be urging and even threatening the party apparatus to undertake radical economic reforms to right the situation: "Their anger at a defense industry that cannot keep up with the West will grow, and a military that becomes convinced that the civilians are destroying the nation's capacity to defend itself becomes more than a mere interest-group claimant in the budgetary process."[90]

How much is there to these suggestions? How is technological advance affecting the military's operations and its needs for hardware and other civilian inputs? What is it doing to military and party doctrines of the battlefield and of the political consequences of warfare? In what ways is it working in the military's political favor? Does technology, or the ways it is channeled into the military sector, have any contrary effects? Are Soviet officers ahead of civilians in their recognition of the need for institutional changes to improve technological innovation? What does Soviet experience with previous revolutions in military technology, such as the nuclear revolution of the 1950s and 1960s, suggest about the capacity of established institutions to adapt?

CHALLENGE NUMBER FOUR: SOCIAL MATURATION AND MALAISE

Consciousness has also jelled in the Soviet Union of changes in the country's social system and of the emergence of problems previously seen as of secondary importance by the regime. Some of these social ills are ripening only in the long term; others seem to be of shorter duration. Some are common to most mature industrial nations and, in fact, are indicative up to a point of the Soviets' success at modernization—declining birth rates and urban congestion being good examples. Others are peculiar at least in their severity to the USSR and reflect more poorly on the capacity of Soviet institutions. Cases in point are deterioration of health standards, alcohol abuse, increases in crime and bureaucratic corruption, and the signs of alienation from authority among today's better-educated younger generation. Tension among the Soviet Union's dozens of ethnic groups, which may in the long haul be its most combustible social issue, has also become more prominent in recent years.

Taken together, these various social and sociocultural factors constitute a fourth setting within which civil-military relations take place. For the officer corps, the external social environment is graphically brought home inside their own units in the person of the conscript soldiers who make up the bulk of Soviet military manpower.

What difference, Ellen Jones asks in chapter 7, have social trends, especially negative ones, made for the performance of the military's administrative

[90] Jerry F. Hough, "Soviet Decision-Making on Defense," *Bulletin of the Atomic Scientists* 41 (August 1985), 88.

role?[91] Can we say that officers are becoming more alarmed than before about the deterioration of the country's social fabric? Are they more critical of state policy in the social area? Have they been leading or following civilians in diagnosing problems and defining solutions? What conclusions have civilian leaders drawn about the relative priority of military needs?

CHALLENGE NUMBER FIVE: FOREIGN INVOLVEMENT

We considered and rejected the option of defining the international environment as a separate source of strain in civil-military relations. Given the Soviet Union's superpower standing, some of the most salient characteristics of international politics in recent decades—the East-West detente of the early 1970s, the new cold war of the early 1980s, and the easing of tensions since then—have to a considerable degree been the product of Soviet actions. We also preferred to eschew detailed discussion of military doctrine, the main medium through which the Soviets formalize their understanding of the proper uses of force beyond their borders. This subject would have demanded more thorough and technical treatment than we could have provided in our volume.

While especially conspicuous in Bruce Parrott's contribution on political change, the international and foreign-policy factor aptly figures in all the chapters of the book. Chapter 8, by Bruce Porter, singles out for consideration one specific piece of the problem, namely, the increased foreign commitments of the Soviet military establishment.

A major achievement of military policy under Brezhnev was the improved capacity for projecting force outside the Soviets' familiar European theater of operations and the heightened willingness to use military means to further Soviet interests. The enlargement of the blue-water fleet, multiplication of arms sales and military assistance agreements, provision of combat-ancillary crews and, on occasion, combat personnel all greatly expanded the numbers of So-

---

[91] Western sources are inconsistent on the extent of problems such as alcohol abuse in the Soviet military. A semipopular study, based in part on random interviews with former Soviet citizens, portrays drunkenness as rampant (Andrew Cockburn, *The Threat: Inside the Soviet Military Machine* [New York: Random House, 1983]) and asserts with confidence (p. 40) that American servicemen "drink less than their Soviet counterparts." But a comparison of U.S. and Soviet military combat effectiveness, relying on a survey of 134 Russian émigrés and on surveys done in the American military, finds the opposite: "Although both Soviet and American soldiers appear to drink heavily, far fewer of the Soviet soldiers admitted to being drunk on duty than did American soldiers." Richard A. Gabriel, *The Antagonists: A Comparative Combat Assessment of the Soviet and American Soldier* (Westport, Conn.: Greenwood Press, 1984), 119. The most thorough study of social relations in the Soviet military describes the problem, but concludes that, in the military as well as the civilian world, "Available data do not permit a direct comparison between current levels of alcohol abuse or alcoholism in the USSR as compared to other industrial societies." Ellen Jones, *Red Army and Society: A Sociology of the Soviet Military* (Boston: George Allen & Unwin, 1985), 138.

viet military personnel outside Soviet borders and thereby the openness of the military establishment to foreign experience. The two major involvements at the beginning and end of the 1970s—in the "war of attrition" along the Suez Canal and in Afghanistan—were the boldest steps. With the introduction of more than 100,000 troops into Afghanistan, Soviet forces for the first time since the Second World War were fighting a major and protracted shooting war—and a war that ended for the Soviets with the 1988–89 withdrawal of those troops without assuring the stabilization of the pro-Soviet regime in Kabul.

There have been many occasions in history when military involvement abroad has had an effect on the military's political behavior and power at home. Of the USSR, Kolkowicz writes that "The military's institutional and political influence has been further strengthened by the growing external commitments of the Soviet state."[92] Is this in actuality the case, and, if so, just what has the connection been? Do Soviet officers look at the world or their own country differently than before as a result of service in Afghanistan or elsewhere in the Third World? Have they been spurred to make new demands of civilian politicians? Are they now afforded greater deference because of their wider experience? These are some of the questions put by Porter, who concentrates, mainly because of the availability of data, on the consequences of the Afghanistan intervention.

In chapter 9, finally, the project director and my co-editor, Thane Gustafson, returns to the propositions raised at the outset of the joint study, knits our findings together, and sketches some implications for our understanding of civil-military relations and political development in the Soviet Union.

[92] Kolkowicz, "Toward a Theory of Civil-Military Relations," 246.

Two

Political Change and Civil-Military Relations

BRUCE PARROTT

A FEW YEARS ago scholars who glanced back over recent Soviet history saw terrain that was reassuringly familiar, but today we confront a landscape nearly transformed by massive earthquakes. Many of our working assumptions about the Soviet system—including our assumptions about civil-military relations—have been called into doubt. In the Brezhnev era Soviet marshals served long terms in senior defense posts, but under Gorbachev the minister of defense and other senior officers have been harshly criticized and summarily removed from office. Accolades to military efficiency and integrity have been superseded by blistering public criticisms of the military hierarchy for inefficiency and corruption. The long row of senior officers standing with party leaders on reviewing platforms has been drastically shortened, and civilian advocates of the ''new political thinking'' have begun to espouse strategic concepts that most military professionals until recently would have rejected out of hand. These dramatic developments demand that we reexamine our views about the nature and evolution of the civil-military relationship.

Taking as a point of departure the analytical approach outlined in Timothy Colton's introductory chapter, this chapter analyzes the effect of Soviet politics and political change on the balance between civilian and military leaders since the fall of Khrushchev. The chapter first examines the decade-long ''golden age'' of civil-military accommodation that followed L. I. Brezhnev's selection as party first secretary in 1964. Did this accommodation reflect the full congruence of civilian and military outlooks posited by Model II? In searching for the causes of the accommodation, the analysis considers both the Brezhnev leadership's inbred attachment to military power and the USSR's fluctuating fortunes in the international military competition with rival states. The investigation examines how the new leaders' technocratic style of leadership—so different from Khrushchev's risky political improvisations and organizational shakeups—affected the military's policy-making role and authority as a specialized caste with a monopoly of military expertise. It also

I wish to thank Stephen Foye, Andrew Kuchins, and Barry Ehrlich for their assistance in preparing this chapter.

explores how the competition for power within the party's collective leadership impinged on the civil-military balance.

Next the chapter scrutinizes the perturbations and adjustments in civil-military ties that occurred as Brezhnev consolidated his personal power and gradually modified Soviet security policy during the 1970s. To what extent did the members of the civilian and military elites reappraise the "lessons of the past," particularly lessons about the importance of military power, and how did such changes affect the relationship between them? The analysis also inquires whether the civil-military frictions sparked by the slowdown of the growth of weapons procurement intensified continuously from the mid-1970s. Were such tensions easily absorbed by the system of "objective" control—the commonly accepted division of labor between civilian politicians and autonomous military professionals—or did Brezhnev and his allies resort to "subjective" mechanisms (i.e., direct political intervention) to manage them? How successful were these efforts to dampen civil-military tensions, and why?

Against this backdrop the chapter traces the sharp rise in civil-military conflict at the close of the 1970s. Around the end of the decade the regime was shaken by the collapse of detente with the United States, the Polish crisis, and a precipitous decline in the rate of Soviet economic growth. The party leadership, increasingly infirm and divided by the onset of a protracted succession struggle, barely responded to these shocks, whereas senior officers became deeply alarmed by what they regarded as adverse trends favoring hostile states. How well did the system of civilian control cope with these pressures? In view of the civilian leadership's weakness and internal rivalries, one might have expected military men to try to shape the outcome of the succession struggle, and civilian politicians to solicit support from the officer corps. The analysis explores whether this sort of military entanglement in politics actually occurred. Weighing policy outcomes, it also inquires whether heightened frictions with the party leadership reflected professional officers' growing influence over policy or their inability to affect policy.

Finally, the chapter surveys the civil-military consequences of the dramatic political changes unleashed after M. S. Gorbachev became party general secretary in 1985. It examines how the elevation of a new generation of leaders who came of age after World War II has shaped civilian attitudes toward military power and the role of the military in the Soviet system. In addition, it considers the effects of the civilian reformers' abandonment of technocratic methods of decision making. How, for instance, has civilian specialists' growing involvement in developing the "new thinking" about security affected professional soldiers' claim to novel expertise on military issues, and how have senior officers reacted to Gorbachev's innovations in security policy? The chapter also evaluates military attitudes toward perestroika, Gorbachev's ambitious program to revitalize the domestic economic and political order, and the implications of this program for the military establishment's position in the Soviet system.

The Age of Accommodation, 1965–1974

In security policy as well as domestic affairs, the men who removed Khrushchev reacted against the practices of his final years in power. Their values and priorities were substantially different from Khrushchev's, and they embraced a cautious style of leadership that contrasted sharply with Khrushchev's flamboyant improvisations. The new leaders' attitudes and style of governance made them naturally more receptive to military requests and military participation in security policy making. In addition, the jockeying for power within the collective leadership made most of the party chiefs reluctant to challenge military interests for fear of giving their civilian rivals an opportunity to use defense issues for partisan advantage. The result was a striking improvement in civil-military relations—although some tensions persisted— and an expansion of the officer corps' influence over defense policy.

Civilian Values and Priorities

One cause of the improvement of civil-military ties was the new leaders' emphatic recommitment to the expansion of Soviet military power. After the appearance of the alleged "missile gap" in the late 1950s, Khrushchev tried to capitalize on Western fears by substituting inflated military claims and bluff for the real expansion of Soviet strategic power.[1] At the same time, in an effort to justify proposed defense cuts to a domestic audience, he also argued that changes in the military balance in favor of the United States would not encourage more aggressive American behavior.[2] By contrast, the men who ousted Khrushchev believed that a major expansion of the military establishment was crucial to deter foreign attack and establish the USSR as America's geopolitical equal.

This belief derived from a combination of historical experiences and recent events. Brezhnev and his cohorts had lived through the devastation of World War II as adults and seen the near-destruction of the Soviet system by a foreign invader. Although not all civilian leaders had been equally marked, the first-hand experience of the cataclysmic war with Nazi Germany gave most of them an instinctive sympathy for military programs. Briefly eclipsed in the second

---

[1] Arnold Horelick and Myron Rush, *Strategic Power and Soviet Foreign Policy* (Chicago: University of Chicago Press, 1966).
[2] *Pravda*, 15 January 1960, 1–5.

half of Khrushchev's reign, this attitude was again brought to the fore by the U.S. strategic buildup under President John Kennedy, the ensuing Soviet humiliation during the Cuban missile crisis, and the U.S. military intervention in Vietnam.[3] In 1965 the new party leader, Brezhnev, betraying obvious concern about U.S. claims of strategic superiority over the USSR, called for a stepped-up Soviet military effort. Past experience, he remarked, taught that "the stronger our army and our vigilance, the stronger [will be] the peace on our borders and on our earth."[4]

The premium that Khrushchev's successors put on military power was reinforced by their career involvements in military affairs. In 1966, 32 percent of the Politburo members had spent at least seven years of their earlier career in military or military-related occupations.[5] This percentage was lower than during the 1950s, when a larger proportion of the members had served in military-related jobs connected with the war, but in 1966 several senior Politburo members had prior work experience that gave them close ties to top military men. For instance, Brezhnev's personal ties with Minister of Defense R. D. Malinovskii, First Deputy Minister A. A. Grechko, and quite likely S. G. Gorshkov, the commander-in-chief of the navy, dated back to his wartime service as a political officer in the military. During the 1950s he had also served in a series of party posts involving the supervision of the military and military industry.[6] Among the other leading members of the Politburo, A. P. Kirilenko, M. A. Suslov, and P. E. Shelest had enjoyed sustained contacts with military officers earlier in their careers. Perhaps just as important, no Politburo member had worked for a long period in foreign affairs or nonmilitary intelligence.[7] In other words, all the Politburo members who had extensive specialized experience in security affairs had worked in posts that provided an incentive to view security issues primarily in military terms.

Such career experience evidently had a major impact on civilian attitudes toward military questions, since it distinguished most of the senior Politburo members who championed greater military expenditures from the few who did not. Almost all the senior figures who advocated a rapid arms buildup in the mid-1960s—Brezhnev, Kirilenko, Suslov, A. N. Shelepin, and Shelest—had

[3] Bruce Parrott, *Politics and Technology in the Soviet Union* (Cambridge: MIT Press, 1983), 182–185.

[4] L. I. Brezhnev, *Leninskim kursom* (Moscow: Politizdat, 1973–1982), 1:160–162.

[5] Stephen M. Meyer, "Civilian and Military Influence in Managing the Arms Race in the U.S.S.R.," in *Reorganizing America's Defense: Leadership in War and Peace*, ed. Robert Art and Samuel Huntington (Elmsford, N.Y.: Pergamon Press, 1985), 50.

[6] Jerry F. Hough, *Soviet Leadership in Transition* (Washington, D.C.: Brookings, 1980), 97–98.

[7] Meyer, "Civilian and Military Influence," 59. One member, Aleksandr Shelepin, had served for three years as head of the KGB in the late 1950s and early 1960s. By Meyer's criteria, this period was too short to qualify.

extensive prior experience in military-related work.[8] By contrast, the two who argued against a rapid buildup—A. N. Kosygin and N. V. Podgornyi—lacked such experience.[9] Taken as a group, career experience predisposed the party leaders to spend heavily on military programs, and the growth of international tensions after 1965 made them especially determined to eliminate the USSR's inferiority to the United States in strategic forces. The resulting Soviet buildup, which won high praise from Malinovksii and his successor as minister, Marshal Grechko, obviously played a major role in improving the party leadership's relations with the officer corps.[10]

The party leaders' belief in the centrality of military power was accompanied by a disposition to promote conservative political and social values. While they stopped short of rehabilitating Stalin, they strove to block intellectual challenges to the party's legitimacy and repressed dissenters who tried to raise such questions. More than Khrushchev, the new leaders solicited policy-oriented analysis and advice, but they sought analysis of narrowly compartmentalized issues, not broad evaluations that impinged on the regime's basic structure and policies. Laying new weight on inculcating patriotic sentiments and combating "pacifist" ideas, they also engaged in a massive, long-term public campaign to extol Soviet feats in World War II.[11] This campaign reflected a desire to communicate the meaning of the wartime upheaval to younger generations who had not witnessed it; it also reflected the powerful hold that the experience exercised on the political imagination of those who had lived through it.

This conservative shift in political values suited most professional officers. Soon after Khrushchev's fall a group of military officers publicly criticized the liberal journal *Novyi mir* for questioning traditional accounts of Bolshevik military heroics during the revolution; reportedly officials of the Central Committee backed them by quashing a rebuttal prepared by the journal.[12] In the same spirit Malinovskii and especially Grechko pressed for more positive treatment of "the heroic past" and more effective military-patriotic education, particularly for youth.[13] Although military spokesmen continued to express

---

[8] Parrott, *Politics and Technology*, 182–185, and A. P. Kirilenko, *Izbrannye rechi i stati* (Moscow: Politizdat, 1976), 34–35. Shelepin was the exception.

[9] Parrott, *Politics and Technology*, 182–185.

[10] See Malinovskii's remarks in *XXIII sezd Kommunisticheskoi partii Sovetskogo Soiuza* (Moscow: Politizdat, 1966), 1:413, and *Pravda*, 2 May 1966. Cf. *Pravda*, 9 May 1966. See Grechko's comments in *Pravda*, 23 February 1968, 2–3; 9 May 1969, 2; and 9 May 1970, 2–3.

[11] Timothy J. Colton, *The Dilemma of Reform in the Soviet Union*, rev. ed. (New York: Council on Foreign Relations, 1986), 14–15.

[12] Lilita Dzirkals, Thane Gustafson, and A. Ross Johnson, *The Media and Intra-Elite Communication in the USSR*, R-2869 (Santa Monica: Rand Corporation, September 1982), 68. See also Harry Gelman, *The Brezhnev Politburo and the Decline of Detente* (Ithaca: Cornell University Press, 1984), 242n.

[13] See Malinovskii's comments in *XXIII sezd*, 1:416, and Grechko's much sharper attack on

concern about this matter for the whole of the Brezhnev period, senior military men apparently felt that the party leadership—if not some lesser social groups—was more committed to the inculcation of patriotic values than it had been in Khrushchev's time. Grechko, for example, seemed quite pleased with the effects of the system of preinduction training and patriotic education introduced in 1967.[14]

Civilian Decision-Making Style

The effect of this shared belief in military power and conservative values was reinforced by the new party leadership's style of decision making, which differed sharply from Khrushchev's. Khrushchev's reservations about the utility of military power sharpened his native inclination to make snap decisions about security policy and to force these choices on his subordinates. He tried, for instance, to compel many skeptical officers to accept his belief that several major types of conventional weapons had become outmoded and should be supplanted by nuclear missiles. Put differently, he adopted basic security assumptions that contradicted the assumptions of most military professionals, and in doing so he threatened the efficacy of their technical expertise as a source of influence in security policy making.

By contrast, Brezhnev and his civilian colleagues embraced a technocratic style of decision making based on deference to specialized agencies and the resolution of disagreements through bureaucratic compromise. By renewing the traditional commitment to the doctrine of "combined arms," the new leaders avoided many of the Khrushchev era's clashes over basic security assumptions and offered senior officers more latitude to work out military policy among themselves. One reflection of the technocratic style was the expanding effort of the General Staff to use sophisticated new mathematical techniques to choose among military policy options and develop the Soviet forces along optimal lines.[15] In principle the party's simultaneous decision to bolster the network of civilian foreign-affairs think-tanks—for example, by setting up the Institute of the USA and Canada within the USSR Academy of Sciences— might have created a source of countervailing information and advice on trends in the East-West military balance. But while the civilian institutes

---

the "blackening" of the "heroic past" by some writers, playwrights, and filmmakers (*Izvestiia*, 18 June 1966, 6).

[14] Timothy R. Colton, *Commissars and Commanders: The Structure of Soviet Military Politics* (Cambridge: Harvard University Press, 1979), 208–210, 213; Roman Kolkowicz, *The Soviet Military and the Communist Party* (Princeton: Princeton University Press, 1967), 319; *Pravda*, 13 October 1967, 5–6, and 23 February 1971, 2.

[15] Brezhnev, *Leninskim kursom*, 1:162; Condoleezza Rice, "The Party, the Military and Decision Authority in the Soviet Union," *World Politics* 60, 1 (October 1987), 61–62.

played a significant role in promoting the move toward political detente and arms negotiations with the West near the end of the 1960s, they appear to have been largely excluded from discussions of the size of the Soviet military effort and the specifics of military policy.[16] In the years immediately after Khrushchev's ouster, uniformed officers probably came closer to enjoying a monopoly of expertise on military-technical matters than ever before, and the party decision makers' reflexive belief in military power enabled officers to override any civilian specialists who might question their recommendations on defense. Leading officers plainly found the Brezhnev leadership's "scientific approach" to military matters a welcome change from Khrushchev's forceful intrusion into the specifics of military policy.[17]

Conflict and Co-optation

Although Khrushchev's successors developed a more symbiotic relationship with the officer corps, the relationship was not trouble-free. When Malinovskii died in the spring of 1967, tensions arose over whether his successor as defense minister should be a professional officer or a civilian. After Malinovskii died, there was a twelve-day delay in naming his successor; since he had been terminally ill, the delay must have been due to indecision rather than to the unexpectedness of his death.[18] According to rumors circulating at the time, some party leaders favored appointing D. F. Ustinov, a civilian official with a long career in managing defense production.[19] The fact that the Politburo apparently considered installing a civilian minister indicates that the professional military's influence on military policy was not entirely beyond challenge.

Any attempt to reconstruct this episode must be speculative. If Ustinov was in fact put forward for the post, he probably appealed to Brezhnev because the two men had a long personal relationship that would have strengthened Brezhnev's influence in this crucial ministry. During 1967 Brezhnev was striving to install his supporters and remove his rivals' clients in other important agencies, such as the Ministry of Interior and the KGB. At the same time, the idea of appointing a civilian minister may have appealed to members of the Politburo minority, led by Kosygin, which wished to restrain the growth of military

---

[16] Parrott, *Politics and Technology*, 192–201.

[17] See in particular the remarks of Marshal M. V. Zakharov, chief of the General Staff, in *Krasnaia zvezda*, 4 February 1965, 2–3, and of Malinovskii in ibid., 24 September 1965, 2. Both men indirectly censured some officers who had advocated Khrushchev's unorthodox military ideas.

[18] By comparison, in 1976 it took three days to name a new minister of defense after the incumbent's unexpected death.

[19] Michael J. Deane, *Political Control of the Soviet Armed Forces* (New York: Crane, Russak, 1977), 171.

spending and was eager to respond to the recent U.S. invitation to begin strategic arms negotiations.[20] To judge by the fact that he delivered the funeral eulogy for Malinovskii, Kosygin was closely involved in arranging the ministerial changeover.

Whichever leaders tried to appoint a civilian minister, the diffusion of power within the Politburo apparently prevented them from doing so. A group of senior Politburo members met with the assembled high command, and the stalemate was resolved in favor of the officer corps.[21] The final choice of Marshal Grechko buttressed the influence of military men and the party's technocratic style of governance. Grechko was a professional soldier who had served as Malinovskii's first deputy for ten years. His selection exemplified the party leadership's emerging practice of choosing the new head of an agency from within the agency itself, rather than installing an outsider who might be unresponsive to its interests and policy preferences. Grechko's selection guaranteed that the officer corps would continue to play a central role in formulating security policy, and perhaps in other realms as well. The episode suggests that civilian politicians vying for power found it difficult to circumscribe the military's influence over defense policy.

By the same token, the incident foreshadowed Brezhnev's problems in seeking to establish himself as the acknowledged leader of the Politburo. In the mid-1960s Brezhnev had increased his personal power by advocating a package of policies that included the rapid expansion of the armed forces. Apart from addressing a perceived Western threat to Soviet security, this stance strengthened his position vis-à-vis less promilitary Politburo competitors, such as Kosygin and Podgornyi. But Brezhnev was not the only leader to accentuate military growth—Shelest and especially Shelepin staked out similar positions—and he had not yet consolidated his power over foreign relations or even domestic economic policy.[22] If he antagonized the officer corps, he risked giving political ammunition to national-security conservatives within the collective leadership. The stance adopted by senior military officers was thus of considerable personal importance to Brezhnev, and his efforts to maintain the support of the minister of defense contributed to an expansion of military influence.

One key issue on which Grechko and other officers held strong views was arms control. During the period when the United States privately began urging

---

[20] Parrott, *Politics and Technology*, 192–193.

[21] Jeremy R. Azrael, *The Soviet Civilian Leadership and The Military High Command: 1976–1986*, R 3501-AF (Santa Monica: Rand Corporation, 1987), 25n.

[22] Until 1970, Kosygin continued to take the lead in negotiations with Western and Third World governments. Jerry Hough, "Gorbachev Consolidating Power," *Problems of Communism* 36, 4 (August–September 1987), 23–24. Domestically, Brezhnev quickly established his primacy in agricultural policy making, but Kosygin continued to play the leading role in industrial reform and overall economic planning.

the new leaders to enter strategic arms negotiations, Marshal Grechko made a general statement that dismissed U.S. interest in cooperation and was probably meant as a signal that strategic arms talks should be avoided.[23] Other indications of military resistance came from the military press, which excised statements about arms talks from the speeches given by Soviet supporters of the idea.[24] The rationale for this resistance was spelled out by two military theoreticians who discounted political efforts to slow the arms race and contended that arms-control agreements could not reduce the danger of war. A number of officers plainly feared that strategic-arms negotiations would hinder the military buildup and harm Soviet security interests.[25]

Through careful bureaucratic logrolling with Grechko, Brezhnev managed to expand his personal power without precipitating a political coalition between the military leadership and his Politburo rivals. At the December 1969 plenum of the Central Committee, Brezhnev launched a major effort to expand his authority over domestic policy and foreign relations. Several Politburo members reportedly opposed this move, and sharp leadership tensions quickly emerged.[26] According to an unofficial account, in the midst of this struggle Brezhnev traveled to Belorussia, where major military maneuvers were under way, and asked Grechko for a pledge of support, which he obtained.[27] Circumstantial evidence suggests that such an understanding probably included Brezhnev's commitment to support the continued rapid growth of military spending in exchange for Grechko's promise not to challenge the advisability of the strategic arms talks that had begun six months earlier with Brezhnev's cautious approval. During his visit to Belorussia, Brezhnev made a strong speech justifying high levels of military spending and reminding civilian as well as military scientists of the necessity for rapid weapons innovation.[28] Two months later, Grechko gave the first public signal that he might support a strategic arms control agreement and other accords with the West.[29]

[23] "Under cover of conversations about peace and cooperation, the ruling circles of the United States of America are strengthening military preparations against the USSR and other socialist countries and are creating dangerous hotbeds of war in various regions of the world," said Grechko (*Pravda*, 13 October 1967). This broad statement may conceivably have referred to other questions, such as the U.S. position on negotiations to end the war in Indochina.

[24] Thomas Wolfe in United States Senate Committee on Armed Services, Subcommittee on Strategic Arms Limitation Talks, *The Limitation of Strategic Arms*, part 2 (Washington, D.C., 1970), 63.

[25] Colonel E. Rybkin in *Kommunist Vooruzhennykh Sil* (hereafter cited as *KVS*), no. 18 (1968), 89–90, and Colonel V. Bondarenko in *KVS*, no. 24 (1968), 24; Garthoff, "The Military and SALT," 140; Parrott, *Politics and Technology*, 192–200.

[26] Parrott, *Politics and Technology*, 239–244.

[27] Roy Medvedev, 1976 interview with Edward L. Warner III, as cited in Edward L. Warner III, *The Military in Contemporary Soviet Politics* (New York: Praeger, 1977), 53. The report does not indicate whether Grechko took any action other than promising to support Brezhnev.

[28] *"Dvina": voiskovye manevry, provedennye na territorii Belorussii v marte 1970 goda* (Moscow: Voenizdat, 1970), 6–7.

[29] "Following the principles of peaceful coexistence," said Grechko, "the socialist countries

Further signs of political collaboration between the party leader and the military chief appeared in 1972. During the spring, tension grew within the civilian leadership as the date approached for President Richard Nixon to visit Moscow to complete the negotiation of the SALT I and other accords. A month before Nixon's scheduled arrival, Brezhnev, accompanied by Grechko, addressed a meeting of the high command and offered a justification for his security policy.[30] Shortly afterward, Grechko, who delivered the concluding speech at the meeting, acclaimed Brezhnev's address as a "remarkable event" in the life of Soviet soldiers.[31] Most likely Grechko participated in the meeting in order to help calm persisting apprehensions within the officer corps about the wisdom of concluding strategic arms-control agreements with the United States.[32]

Just before the summit, when an intense Politburo conflict flared up over whether to cancel Nixon's visit because of stepped-up U.S. military action against North Vietnam, Brezhnev's hand must have been strengthened by his mutual understanding with Grechko and by Grechko's support for the SALT I package.[33] In the end Brezhnev overcame the Politburo opposition, which centered on the hard-line Shelest, the summit proceeded, and the treaties were completed. When they were presented to the Supreme Soviet for ratification, Grechko and the new chief of the General Staff, V. G. Kulikov, firmly endorsed them.[34] Although Grechko and Kulikov implicitly conditioned their support for the treaties on continued strengthening of the armed forces, they manifestly believed that a combination of military growth and arms control would enhance the Soviet strategic position.

The note of amity in civil-military relations was confirmed by events in the spring of 1973. In March a national conference of military party secretaries met. Brezhnev's message to the meeting noted that the international situation had recently improved, but reiterated the party's "sacred obligation" to ensure the "comprehensive strengthening . . . of the armed forces."[35] Grechko, for his part, warned against imperialism's military plans, yet praised the "enormous work . . . done in developing and perfecting [our] weaponry" and remarked that the forces currently possessed "everything necessary." The Politburo, said Grechko, always kept defense questions at the center of its

---

do not call into doubt the efficacy of these or those concrete agreements with the capitalist world or the possibility and necessity of regulating unsolved problems by diplomatic means" (*Pravda*, 9 May 1970, 3).

[30] Ibid., 26 April 1972, 1.

[31] Ibid., 9 May 1972, 2.

[32] For evidence of such apprehensions, see Raymond L. Garthoff, "BMD and East-West Relations," in *Ballistic Missile Defense*, ed. Ashton B. Carter and David N. Schwartz (Washington, D.C.: Brookings, 1984), 311.

[33] On Grechko's support, see Garthoff, "The Military and SALT," 140, 155–156.

[34] Kulikov replaced Zakharov as chief of the General Staff in 1971.

[35] *KVS*, no. 8 (1973), 11

attention, and every significant question of military construction was handled "directly by the Politburo headed by comrade L. I. Brezhnev."[36] Grechko thus signalled his approval of Brezhnev's defense policy. Just as important, by describing Brezhnev as head of the Politburo he endorsed Brezhnev's political supremacy over other members of the civilian leadership at a moment of serious controversy within the party.

The next month two of Brezhnev's civilian rivals, including Shelest, were expelled from the Politburo, and Grechko was made a full member. The only precedent for the election of a professional officer to the ruling party body was Marshal Zhukov's brief membership during 1956–57. By comparison with Zhukov's meteoric rise and fall, Grechko's election reflected a firmer decision to give Politburo representation to professional soldiers. Although most major military issues were probably decided in the Defense Council, the thorniest questions were presumably passed up for resolution by the Politburo.[37] Grechko's election thus gave the officer corps greater access to the making of security policy, as well as to the broader societal choices decided by the Politburo. As of 1973, there seemed little doubt that the influence of the military establishment was greater than it had been in many years.

Agitation and Adjustment, 1974–1979

Civilian Values and Priorities

Although Brezhnev's alliance with Grechko was based on agreement about the overriding importance of military power, Brezhnev's stance on this matter started to shift around 1974. Putting a new accent on the stability of East-West detente, he began to hint that further increases in Soviet military power would not guarantee peace. For centuries, he remarked, mankind "has been guided by the formula: If you want peace, be ready for war. In our nuclear age this formula conceals particular danger. Man dies only once. However, in recent years a quantity of weapons has already been amassed sufficient to destroy everything living on earth several times."[38] Early in 1976 Brezhnev told the Twenty-fifth Party Congress that recent Soviet successes in the struggle for a decisive turn from cold war to peaceful coexistence had "truly enduring sig-

[36] Ibid., 14–15. An editorial note indicates that Grechko's address was printed "in abbreviated form."

[37] For example, during the Moscow summit that hammered out the final terms of the SALT I agreements, the Politburo met at least four times in five days to discuss the content of the treaties. Raymond Garthoff, "The Military and SALT," in Soviet Decision-making for National Security, ed. Jiri Valenta and William Potter (Boston: George Allen & Unwin, 1984), 145.

[38] Pravda, 22 July 1974, 3, as quoted in Thomas N. Bjorkman and Thomas J. Zamostny, "Soviet Politics and Strategy toward the West: Three Cases," World Politics (January 1984), 202.

nificance.'' Soviet diplomacy and agreements with the West had laid a "solid political and legal foundation" for peaceful cooperation between the superpowers, and the danger of nuclear war had receded.[39]

Brezhnev approached the formulation of the Tenth Five-Year Plan (1976–1980) in the same spirit. Telling the congress that further arms agreements would allow both superpowers to save "significant sums" on arms expenditures, he pledged that the party would seek to replace the "steady growth" of the defense budgets of "many states" with a "systematic reduction" of expenditures. He also chastised unidentified individuals for underestimating the political importance of Soviet consumer goods and services and urged that higher growth targets be established for these sectors.[40] Brezhnev appeared to believe that since the USSR had closed the strategic gap with the United States, it could reduce the rate of its military buildup and increase its reliance on diplomacy and negotiation to protect and advance Soviet interests.

In striking this new note, Brezhnev drew on the ideas of civilian foreign-affairs analysts who emphasized the prospects for East-West accommodation and favored slowing the pace of Soviet military growth. These ideas, for example, had been vigorously advocated by N. N. Inozemtsev, director of the Academy of Science's Institute of the World Economy and International Relations (IMEMO).[41] Brezhnev, in keeping with his instinct for charting a middle course between divergent views and interests, treated the advice of these analysts cautiously. He never endorsed their occasional hints that further Soviet military growth would actually worsen the country's security by provoking a powerful counterbuildup in the West.[42] Nor did he encourage civilian foreign-policy intellectuals to play a more active role in the making of military-technical decisions. At the level of basic working assumptions about military power, however, the ideas of civilian specialists were beginning to exert some influence on receptive civilian leaders and to play a role in deliberations over military choices.[43]

Brezhnev's shift of emphasis was facilitated by the consolidation of his personal power and by changes in the composition of the Politburo. Having finally established his primacy in all policy arenas, foreign as well as domestic, Brezhnev succeeded in expelling several rivals from the Politburo. In 1973 Shelest, who had favored heavy military spending and opposed Brezhnev's detente policy, was removed from the top ruling body, and in 1975 Shelepin,

[39] *XXV sezd Kommunisticheskoi partii Sovetskogo Soiuza: stenograficheskii otchet* (Moscow: Politizdat, 1976), 1:26–27, 43.

[40] Ibid., 1:47–49, 78–79; Parrott, *Politics and Technology*, 261–262.

[41] N. N. Inozemtsev, *Sovremennyi kapitalizm: novye iavleniia i protivorechiia* (Moscow: Mysl, 1972), esp. 116–117; Parrott, *Politics and Technology*, 194–199, 245–248, 251.

[42] See, for instance, the comment by the director of the USA Institute, G. A. Arbatov, in *Pravda*, 22 July 1973, 4–5, as quoted by Bjorkman and Zamostny, "Soviet Politics," 200.

[43] Samuel Payne, *The Soviet Union and SALT* (Cambridge: MIT Press, 1980), 7 and passim.

another hard-liner, suffered a similar fate. Together with the 1973 removal of a third Brezhnev critic, G. I. Voronov, this show of political muscle must have won him greater deference from the leaders who remained.

On balance, the Politburo promotions announced during 1973 also strengthened Brezhnev's hand in defense matters. Grechko's election to full membership, of course, added a staunch defender of military interests, and G. V. Romanov, a new candidate member, may have felt an instinctive sympathy for the military's point of view.[44] These promotions, however, were more than counterbalanced by the appointment of Foreign Minister A. A. Gromyko and the chief of the KGB, Iu. V. Andropov, as full members of the ruling body. Gromyko and Andropov had long worked in posts that dealt with national security from nonmilitary perspectives, and their administrative responsibilities entailed participation in arms-control negotiations and in monitoring Western military activities and plans.[45] Positioned bureaucratically to justify alternative views on security questions, both men adopted an attitude toward detente that was more optimistic than Grechko's and that highlighted the economic benefits of arms control for the USSR.[46] According to one unconfirmed account, Brezhnev sought to use Gromyko and Andropov to reduce Grechko's influence by including all three men in a new Politburo committee on arms control that he organized and chaired.[47]

Military Disagreement

In response to Brezhnev's shift of emphasis and the preliminary drafting of the new five-year plan, senior military men began to issue veiled warnings about the danger of miscalculations in Soviet defense policy. In a book published in 1974 Grechko, warning that American military policy had recently become "even more aggressive," reasserted the goal of Soviet strategic superiority by appealing to the authority of Lenin.[48] Because Western governments "depend on force and take account only of force," he said, they could

[44] In theory Romanov's extensive military-related career experience should have caused him to side with Grechko. On the other hand, he clearly owed his promotion to Brezhnev, and he was probably reluctant to challenge his patron.

[45] On the role of the KGB, see Amy Knight's chapter in this volume.

[46] For Andropov's views, see Amy Knight's chapter and Sidney Ploss, "Signs of Struggle," *Problems of Communism* (September–October 1982), 47. For Gromyko's attitudes, see *Pravda*, 28 June 1968, 3, and 1 April 1977, 2; A. A. Gromyko, *Leninskim kursom mira: izbrannye rechi i stati* (Moscow: Politizdat, 1984), 5–27; Arkady N. Shevchenko, *Breaking with Moscow* (New York: Knopf, 1985), 151, 162–163.

[47] Dusko Doder, *Shadows and Whispers* (New York: Random House, 1986), 221, cited in Azrael, *The Soviet Civilian Leadership*, 4.

[48] A. A. Grechko, *Vooruzhennye Sily Sovetskogo gosudarstva* (Moscow: Voenizdat, 1974), 290, 318.

gain advantage from "the smallest weakening" of Soviet defenses. Failure to prepare to counter an adversary's military programs could allow the enemy to seize the initiative, which would be "extremely difficult" to regain.[49] Grechko sharpened these warnings in a revised edition of his book published a year later. In a new section on the prospects for developing novel weaponry, he cautioned that the USSR must not let its defense efforts lag behind contemporary requirements and hinted at fears that slapdash planning might hamper the emergence of new armaments. Careful long-term military planning, he urged, was vital because "there is nothing more difficult than to make up for what has been neglected, if that is possible to do at all."[50]

Grechko took pains to counter the view that the growth of Soviet military power could be slowed without undermining East-West detente. He acknowledged that the USSR's overall economic and political policies were components of defense capacity, but in the second edition of his book he added pointedly that the further strengthening of the armed forces constituted the main component of national defense.[51] According to Grechko, Lenin had stipulated that a shift to cooperation with the imperialist countries must be based on an intensive Soviet military effort and the avoidance of disarmament.[52] Plainly he doubted that military power was becoming a less important part of the international correlation of forces, as some civilians implied, and he was wary of depending heavily on arms control to protect Soviet security.

In early 1976, when Brezhnev's report to the party congress suggested that favorable international trends permitted a slackening of the Soviet military buildup, military objections became especially pronounced. Kulikov, chief of the General Staff, cautioned against underestimating the danger of war, and the Ministry of Defense published a book spelling out the dangers in detail.[53] In contrast to Brezhnev's upbeat picture of international trends, the author, Colonel V. M. Bondarenko, warned that influential "reactionary" circles in the West were still tempted by the idea of launching a nuclear strike against the USSR, and he asserted repeatedly that detente had not become an irreversible process.[54] Elsewhere in the book Bondarenko forcefully appealed for the acceleration of Soviet military research programs, particularly anti-ballistic missile programs, and rebutted unnamed Soviet writers who contended that the large military share of the national research-and-development budget was

[49] Ibid., 82–83, 101.

[50] A. A. Grechko, *Vooruzhennye Sily Sovetskogo gosudarstva*, 2d ed. (Moscow: Voenizdat, 1975), 192–193, 198. See also Raymond L. Garthoff, *Detente and Confrontation: American-Soviet Relations from Nixon to Reagan* (Washington, D.C.: Brookings, 1985), 467.

[51] Grechko, *Vooruzhennye Sily Sovetskogo gosudarstva*, 1st ed., 31; 2d ed., 31, 114, 198.

[52] Ibid., 2d ed., 31, 49.

[53] Army General Kulikov in *Izvestiia*, 8 May 1976, 2, and Colonel V. M. Bondarenko, *Sovremennaia nauka i razvitie voennogo dela* (Moscow: Voenizdat, 1976).

[54] Bondarenko, *Sovremennaia nauka*, 32, 130–131, 184.

hampering the country's economic development.[55] The book also contained a hint of controversy between the military establishment and civilian agencies, possibly including the Ministry of Foreign Affairs, about who was entitled to decide on the development and deployment of new weapons.[56]

Viewed in isolation, such remarks might be discounted as a sign of heightened civil-military tensions. Professional officers are supposed to prepare for war, and in worrying aloud about this contingency they may merely be fulfilling the responsibility assigned by their civilian superiors or engaging in routine maneuvers to obtain larger defense budgets. These explanations, however, fail to account for the increased sharpness of military statements during 1974–1976 by comparison with the preceding decade. Never since becoming minister had Grechko hinted that the USSR might fall behind the West militarily, or that basic errors might be made in defense policy. Nor had the preparation of the preceding five-year plan been accompanied by disputatious statements like Bondarenko's.[57] Only the approach of superpower arms talks had provoked a flurry of overt military protest. In other words, during the mid-1970s, outspoken officers were not engaging in business as usual but were objecting to trends in civilian thinking that they regarded as mistaken.

Brezhnev Consolidates His Hold on the Ministry of Defense

Faced with these objections from Grechko and like-minded officers, Brezhnev consolidated his hold on the military establishment through a combination of political maneuver and luck. Around 1974 a campaign was launched under the auspices of the Main Political Administration, the principal agency overseeing the political training of military cadres, to propagate Brezhnev's views within the armed forces. One of the first steps in the campaign was to shake up the personnel of the MPA itself, which had shown a recurrent tendency to identify with professional military views and had harbored some of the most outspoken proponents of Soviet military superiority in the late 1960s.[58] The campaign's

---

[55] Ibid., 32, 41, 46–49, 62, 64, 131, 184; Parrott, *Politics and Technology*, 2725. Bruce Parrott, *The Soviet Union and Ballistic Missile Defense* (Boulder: Westview Press, 1987), 33–35.

[56] Bondarenko, *Sovremennaia nauka*, 41; Parrott, *The Soviet Union*, 33–34. Bondarenko's book was sent to the printer about the time that Soviet arms-control negotiators gave their American counterparts definitive assurances that the USSR construed the 1972 ABM Treaty as prohibiting the development of extensive ABM defenses based on exotic technologies. Another important Soviet weapons decision that may have been under consideration at the time was the deployment of SS-20 missiles, which got under way near the end of 1977.

[57] Compare, for example, Bondarenko's book with his earlier articles in *KVS*, no. 17 (1966), 8–14, and no. 18 (1974), 22–30.

[58] Colonel General G. Sredin, the first deputy chief of the MPA who spearheaded the campaign, referred to the need to take "definite organizational steps" in selecting and training military ideological workers. *KVS*, no. 21 (1974), 10.

main purpose was to counter "scholastic" thinking among officers, help them grasp "the major positive changes" resulting from East-West detente, and show that new party policies were an "organic" part of Marxism-Leninism.[59] As part of this campaign the first deputy chief of the MPA criticized "theoretical errors" in the writings of Soviet military specialists on military theory and party policy and called for them to work more closely with specialists in the social sciences.[60] The campaign culminated in a national conference of military ideological workers in 1975. In contrast to similar gatherings held in earlier years, Grechko was forced to share the rostrum at this conference with a prominent civilian politician, Politburo candidate member B. N. Ponomarev, who offered a much more up-beat reading of recent international trends and progress in arms control.[61]

Brezhnev also made other efforts to reduce Grechko's influence. Departing from the precedent established at the previous three party congresses, he denied Grechko the opportunity to address the Twenty-fifth Congress, where the triumph of detente was proclaimed and the guidelines for the new five-year plan were approved.[62] Ill health can be ruled out as an explanation of Grechko's failure to speak, since he attended the congress and made a number of subsequent public appearances before dying unexpectedly at the end of April.[63] A more plausible explanation is that Brezhnev prevented Grechko from addressing the congress because he and his views were in disfavor. Immediately afterward, D. F. Ustinov, the party secretary charged with supervising military and police activities, was promoted from candidate to full membership in the Politburo. Ustinov had already adopted a public stance toward detente manifestly softer than Grechko's, and his promotion was probably meant as a further check on the minister of defense.[64]

Grechko's death the following month allowed Brezhnev to appoint Ustinov in his place. The appointment was crucial. Although Ustinov had spent much of his career as an administrator and party overseer of the military industries, he was a longtime ally of Brezhnev and the first civilian to be minister of defense since 1955. Ustinov began his tenure by issuing an order on Victory Day that was the first since 1964 to omit any mention of strengthening the

[59] Sredin in *KVS*, no. 2 (1974), 17, 19, 23–24.

[60] Sredin in *KVS*, no. 1 (1975), 9–13, 18. See also Colonel V. Merkulov in *KVS*, no. 2 (1975), 9–16.

[61] At the national conferences of military party officials and Komsomol officials in 1973 and 1974, MPA chief Epishev had spoken, but no high-level civilian speaker had addressed the meeting. For the 1975 conference, see *Pravda*, 29 January 1975, 2, and *KVS*, no. 4 (1975), 3–5.

[62] The minister of defense addressed the Twentieth, Twenty-second, Twenty-third, and Twenty-fourth party congresses, but not the Twenty-fifth. Warner, *The Military in Contemporary Soviet Politics*, 37–38.

[63] *The New York Times*, 27 April 1976, 1.

[64] For Ustinov's position on detente, see Dmitri Ustinov, *Izbrannye rechi i stati* (Moscow: Politizdat, 1979), 253, 270–271.

armed forces. Instead he emphasized that current Soviet weaponry was sufficient and that improved combat readiness depended on military personnel themselves.[65] Presumably Ustinov also played an important role in Brezhnev's efforts to don the symbols of military authority as part of his budding personality cult. In mid-1976 Brezhnev was awarded the military rank of marshal, and the military press began to extol his qualities as a military leader by publishing exaggerated accounts of his past military accomplishments.[66] The next year it was revealed for the first time that Brezhnev was chairman of the Defense Council.

In addition, Brezhnev strengthened his position by replacing some of his military critics with officers more sympathetic to his views. In January 1977 Kulikov was transferred from his post as chief of the General Staff and made commander-in-chief of the Warsaw Pact forces. He was replaced with N. V. Ogarkov. Previously first deputy chief of the General Staff, Ogarkov had served as one of two senior military representatives at the SALT I talks, where he is reported to have endorsed some negotiating positions that Grechko and other officers opposed.[67] In the mid-1970s Ogarkov's attitude toward Brezhnev's security policy was considerably more positive than Grechko's or Kulikov's. Although he asserted the need for further improvements in Soviet defenses, he did not echo Grechko's hints that the party leadership was in danger of adopting mistaken military policies. Instead he treated the notion that detente might become "irreversible" as a serious possibility, and shortly after the Twenty-fifth Party Congress he declared that the relaxation of international tensions "has become dominant in international life." Crediting this shift largely to Brezhnev's personal efforts, Ogarkov voiced servicemen's "deep gratitude" for Brezhnev's warm attitude toward them, and in 1976 he acclaimed the general secretary as head of the Politburo.[68] No doubt these views, which were at odds with the prevailing military sentiments represented by Grechko and Kulikov, help account for the political leadership's selection of Ogarkov to lead the General Staff.

The consolidation of Brezhnev's authority vis-à-vis the officer corps allowed him to allay the controversy over military policy and push through an important change in military doctrine. In January 1977—the same month in which Ogarkov replaced Kulikov—Brezhnev took the dramatic step of formally disavowing strategic superiority as a Soviet goal.[69] Some military officials plainly disliked the change, and signs of foot-dragging showed that the

[65] Azrael, *The Soviet Civilian Leadership*, 6; Ustinov, *Izbrannye rechi i stati*, 285.

[66] Peter Kruzhin, "The Contribution of the Military Journals to the Brezhnev Cult," *Radio Liberty Research Bulletin*, no. 38, 16 February 1977.

[67] Shevchenko, *Breaking with Moscow*, 202–204.

[68] N. V. Ogarkov in *Sovetskaia Litva*, 23 February 1974, 2; *Sovetskaia Rossiia*, 8 May 1975, 2; *Uchitelskaia gazeta*, 2 February 1975, 2; and *Pravda vostoka*, 9 May 1976, 1, 3.

[69] Brezhnev, *Leninskim kursom*, 6:293–294.

new declaratory policy was not merely an exercise in international propaganda. Months after Brezhnev enunciated the doctrine a few articles in military journals were still making positive references to the goal of Soviet strategic superiority.[70] Nonetheless, no civil-military rift ensued. Most military commentators gradually fell in behind the new position with a minimum of argument. For instance, Colonel E. Rybkin, previously a hard-line champion of pursuing superiority, did a sudden about-face and accepted the idea that the further growth of nuclear arsenals would not improve Soviet security. Marshal Kulikov likewise adopted a more favorable attitude toward Brezhnev's defense policies.[71]

Although this relatively compliant adjustment to Brezhnev's doctrinal innovations stemmed partly from Brezhnev's success in installing less militant individuals at the helm of the Ministry of Defense, it was also due to favorable trends in the international situation. During the mid-1970s the United States seemingly accepted the USSR as a geopolitical and military equal, and progress was being made toward the conclusion of a SALT II treaty that would impose permanent restraints on the U.S. nuclear arsenal. In Europe the Soviet Union had finally obtained a long-desired settlement of such unresolved postwar issues as the legitimacy of the German Democratic Republic, and in the Third World Soviet diplomacy was scoring dramatic gains at the expense of the United States.[72] Viewed from a Soviet standpoint, these achievements were impressive. By 1977 Brezhnev and his allies could make a persuasive case that the USSR's defense capacity "has never before been so strong and reliable,"[73] and such military skeptics as Kulikov found themselves reluctantly agreeing, despite their narrow interest in the continued rapid growth of military procurement and expenditures.[74]

These favorable international trends must have helped assuage military discontent over the slower pace of military expansion and Brezhnev's interventionist role in the formulation of military doctrine during the second half of the 1970s. Although the growth rate of inputs into military production during the second half of the decade may have remained quite high, the curve representing the growth of weapons procurement flattened out.[75] Even if economic bot-

---

[70] Col. K. Paiusov in *Vestnik protivovozdushnoi oborony*, no. 6, (1977), 77–80, and A. Aleksandrov in *KVS*, no. 20 (1977).

[71] Bjorkman and Zamostny, "Soviet Politics," 203–204; for Kulikov's position, see *KVS*, no. 3 (1978), 22–23, 26–27. See also the article by Marshal Ogarkov in *Kommunist*, no. 7 (1978).

[72] Several of these arguments were set forth in the MPA's guidelines for political study by Soviet officers. See *KVS*, no. 20 (1974), 68–75.

[73] Leonid Brezhnev, *Na strazhe mira i sotsializma* (Moscow, 1979), 534. This statement was made in November 1977.

[74] In 1978 Kulikov quoted this statement and credited Brezhnev personally with reducing— although not eliminating—the danger of war. *KVS*, no. 3 (1978), 22, 28.

[75] For an analysis of inputs into military programs, see Robert Campbell's chapter in this vol-

tlenecks help explain the initial procurement slowdown, Brezhnev and his civilian supporters plainly favored the trend. The new pattern of procurement
was consistent with Brezhnev's doctrinal innovations, and once the trend became clear, he and his civilian supporters made no visible attempt to boost the
growth rate of procurement back to its former level. Although they might have
mounted a crash campaign along the lines of the massive energy program that
they launched at the end of 1977, they eschewed such a step. By the same
token, senior officers cannot have taken much comfort from figures indicating
high inputs into defense production, since they were primarily interested in
obtaining progressively greater quantities of finished weapons. That professional soldiers eventually acquiesced in the flattening of procurement is a tribute both to Brezhnev's political maneuvering and to the international events
that seemed to have made the USSR, at long last, a full-fledged superpower.

Years of Conflict, 1980–1984

Around the end of the 1970s the relatively high level of consensus over security policy began to disintegrate. One major cause was that Brezhnev and his
cohorts had become wedded to a set of foreign and domestic policies that they
were unwilling to change. Increasingly wary of policy innovation and of potential political challengers, the aging oligarchs were reluctant to groom and
promote able young leaders. For the most part they filled the occasional open-
ings in their ranks with members of their own generation. K. U. Chernenko's
promotion to full Politburo membership in 1978 was typical; M. S. Gorbachev's promotion in 1980 was the exception that proves the rule. These efforts
to stabilize the party leadership did not prevent the growth of rivalries among
the aspirants for power, but they did obstruct major policy change. Under the
declining Brezhnev, and then under his ailing successors, Andropov and Chernenko, political infighting and uncertainty about the future became pervasive.

Civilian Priorities and the Security Debate

This political uncertainty coincided with the advent of severe foreign and domestic troubles. After the Soviet invasion of Afghanistan, growing American
skepticism about arms control led the United States to shelve the unratified
SALT II treaty, and the Reagan administration came to power with the avowed
intention of reestablishing U.S. military superiority. Meanwhile NATO confirmed a plan to deploy new U.S. intermediate-range nuclear forces (INF) in

---

ume. For discussion of the data on Soviet procurement trends, see Richard Kaufman, "Causes of
the Slowdown in Soviet Defense," *Soviet Economy* 1, 1 (1985), 9–41.

Europe if the Soviets refused to dismantle their SS-20s. No less important, the Polish crisis threatened Soviet dominance of Eastern Europe and raised doubts about the stability of USSR's own domestic political order. All these clouds appeared on the horizon at a time when a sudden and worrying drop in economic growth was exacerbating the tensions among the various claimants on the national budget.[76]

In the early 1980s the civilian leadership had great difficulty deciding how to cope with these security and resource-allocation choices. Bruising budgetary conflicts broke out over military policy, investment in heavy industry, and investment in agriculture and consumer-goods production.[77] These conflicts, in turn, gave rise to an intense theoretical dispute over the relative importance of the various components of the USSR's international power. The most striking feature of this dispute was the willingness of some of the participants to argue that current military spending was less important than economic growth or even domestic consumption in safeguarding the regime's security.[78]

On a practical level, the debate over military policy centered on whether the existing mix of diplomacy and military programs was adequate to cope with the West's more assertive behavior, or whether greater emphasis must be put on the unilateral accumulation of military power. An influential but heterogeneous Politburo coalition, which included Brezhnev, Chernenko, Gromyko, and a few others, contended that the mix was correct. Their defensive efforts to justify this viewpoint, however, revealed that some of their Politburo colleagues disagreed.[79] Precisely who these skeptics were remains uncertain, although they probably included Romanov, V. V. Shcherbitskii, and V. V. Grishin.[80] The essential point is that the civilian leadership was divided over security policy.

When added to Politburo succession rivalries, this division of opinion invited military intrusion into the party's policy decisions and possibly even its choice of future leadership. Starting in 1980 members of the officer corps,

---

[76] The main fall-off in economic growth occurred in 1979 and 1980. See Herbert Levine, "Possible Causes of the Deterioration of Soviet Productivity Growth in the Period 1976–1980," in U.S. Congress, Joint Economic Committee, *Soviet Economy in the 1980s: Problems and Prospects*, part 1 (Washington, D.C.: GPO, 1982), 154.

[77] V. Medvedev in *Kommunist*, no. 4 (1980), 22–23; the editorial in *Kommunist*, no. 11 (1982), 7; and G. Sorokin in *Planovoe khoziastvo*, no. 5 (1982), 65–67.

[78] Compare V. Kornienko in *KVS*, no. 2 (1980), 22–26 and S. Bartenev in *KVS*, no. 14 (1980), 66, 70–71, with Iu. Vlasevich in *KVS*, no. 4 (1980), 18–19, 22, 25.

[79] See, for example, Gromyko's article in *Kommunist*, no. 11 (1980), 9, 11, 23; and the article by Aleksandr Bovin in *Kommunist*, no. 10 (1980), 73–75, 77–80. See also Brezhnev's defense of detente at the Twenty-sixth Party Congress against the charge that it was "a groundless utopia." *XXVI sezd KPSS*, 1:43.

[80] For Romanov's and Shcherbitskii's hard-line attitudes, see George B. Weickhardt, "Foreign Policy Disputes in the Gorbachev Succession," forthcoming in *Soviet Union*, and the following section. For indirect evidence that Grishin may have criticized Brezhnev's policy toward the West, see *Moskovskaia pravda*, 16 June 1982, 1.

alarmed by international trends, became increasingly restive. In a dramatic change of stance, Marshal Ogarkov began to speak out forcefully on behalf of the apprehensive military professionals. Ironically, Ogarkov, who had previously helped Brezhnev establish his authority over the officer corps, now became the harshest public critic of his security policies. Ogarkov's change of attitude probably reflected a belief that Western trends had vindicated fellow officers' skepticism toward detente, and it may have been compounded by resentment that Brezhnev's ill-informed decision to invade Afghanistan had unwittingly undercut the detente line that Ogarkov had previously championed.[81] In any case, the fact that Ogarkov had previously backed Brezhnev's policies made his criticism all the more telling.

Brezhnev, his health and vitality obviously declining, sought to vindicate his past policies rather than find more effective alternatives. Persistent Soviet diplomacy and political splits within the West, he argued, would gradually bring the United States back to an acceptable pattern of conduct.[82] The past decade of detente had gained the USSR many benefits, particularly because the party had showed "self-control" and not allowed itself to be deflected from its established international strategy.[83] Brezhnev acknowledged that the United States and its allies had become more aggressive, but he voiced the hope that the Reagan administration would "ultimately succeed in looking at things more realistically." Denouncing any attempt to win the arms race as "dangerous madness," Brezhnev contended that existing Soviet defense spending was sufficient, and he emphatically reiterated his commitment to arms control as a task of "special meaning and urgency."[84] The economic burden of the military budget was obviously one motive for this commitment.[85]

For Brezhnev, coping with domestic needs was a higher priority than addressing potential new military dangers. He called for a shuffling of the R&D system and recommended that defense-oriented research establishments devote more effort to civilian needs, not to the faster creation of weapons.[86] Taking note of recent disruptions in the population's food supply, Brezhnev

[81] Recent testimony suggests that Ogarkov and other General Staff officers initially opposed the idea of invading Afghanistan. The invasion reinforced the hardening of American attitudes toward the USSR and strengthened Sino-American military cooperation, about which Ogarkov subsequently expressed deep concern. (Interview with Deputy Minister of Defense V. I. Varennikov, "Afganistan: podvodia itogi," *Ogonek*, 18 March 1989, 6); Bruce Parrott, "The Soviet System, Military Power, and Diplomacy," in *The Dynamics of Soviet Defense Policy*, ed. Bruce Parrott (Washington, D.C.: The Wilson Center Press, 1990).

[82] Brezhnev, *Leninskim kursom*, 8:249–250, 285, 419.

[83] Ibid., 364, 419.

[84] *XXVI sezd Kommunisticheskoi partii Sovetskogo Soiuza: stenograficheskii otchet* (Moscow: Politizdat, 1981), 1:21, 40–45, 84.

[85] According to Brezhnev, the arms race had created "no small burden" at home, and "quite a number of difficulties" had recently emerged, "both in the economic development of the country and in the international situation." Ibid., 21, 26.

[86] Ibid., 60, 62; Brezhnev, *Leninskim kursom*, 8:472–473.

pushed to overcome political resistance to his proposed "Food Program" and additional heavy investment in agriculture.[87] He also called for faster development of the consumer industries. These tasks, he emphasized, were vitally important not simply from an economic but from a political standpoint.[88]

It fell to Chernenko, Brezhnev's closest political ally, to spell out the significance of welfare spending for the stability of the domestic political system. Obviously frightened by the massive worker protests in Poland, Chernenko remarked that the experience of other socialist countries showed that a party's ties with the masses "cannot be established once and for all." The party must win the trust of the masses "again and again," and the people would judge the party not by "words and promises" but by "tangible results." Neglect of any class's interests, Chernenko added pointedly, was "fraught with the danger of social tension and of political and socioeconomic crisis."[89] Consistent with this concern, Chernenko indicated repeatedly that the government would not curb its social and welfare plans for the sake of greater military spending.[90]

In 1981, prompted partly by the struggle over the targets to be included in the Eleventh Five-Year Plan, Marshal Ogarkov published a hard-hitting article challenging Brezhnev's security policies and demanding a larger defense effort.[91] Ogarkov, who had already shown a marked skepticism about the capacity of diplomacy and arms control to protect Soviet security,[92] discounted Brezhnev's expressions of hope that the Reagan administration would become more moderate. Instead he maintained that the new administration's military-political strategy had "already been revealed sufficiently clearly," and that the United States had taken a "still more dangerous, reactionary course" since the presidential elections.[93] Members of the two most recent Soviet generations, warned Ogarkov, were inclined to underestimate the danger of war, and this mistaken view could have "serious consequences." Given the worsening world situation, not only the political organs of the armed forces, but all party and soviet organizations had to make citizens more aware of the present military danger.[94] This comment amounted to more than the customary military complaint about inadequate patriotic indoctrination. It was a rebuke of both

---

[87] Brezhnev, *Leninskim kursom*, 7:469; *XXVI sezd KPSS*, 1:63.

[88] *Kommunist*, no. 13 (1981), 3–8; Brezhnev, *Leninskim kursom*, 8:206–7, 415, 469.

[89] *Kommunist*, no. 13 (1981), 11, 14.

[90] *Pravda*, 7 February 1982, 4.

[91] Although Ogarkov had already been signalling his dissatisfaction for at least a year, those signals were mild compared to the 1981 article. See, e.g., *KVS*, no. 14 (1980), 24–30. Cf. *Partiinaia zhizn*, no. 3 (1979), 27.

[92] Whereas some civilian foreign-policy analysts emphasized the possibility of using "inter-imperialist contradictions" to curb the "aggressiveness" of the United States, Ogarkov claimed to discern an emerging Sino-American-Japanese military alliance reminiscent of the Rome-Berlin-Tokyo axis of the 1930s. *KVS*, no. 14 (1980), 24–30.

[93] *Kommunist*, no. 10 (1981), 81–82. Before the party congress Ogarkov asserted that the West was seeking "overwhelming military superiority" over the Soviet bloc, and that this policy was "in all probability calculated for the long run" *KVS*, no. 14 (1980), 24–30.

[94] *Kommunist*, no. 10 (1981), 90–91.

the MPA and civilian party propagandists. With rare directness, Ogarkov was urging that the party change its working assumptions about the strategic situation and the likelihood of war.

Ogarkov was unwilling to postpone increased military expenditures on the grounds that domestic economic development had become the party's dominant task, as some other commentators claimed. Immediately after alluding to the new economic tasks facing the country, he observed that military art "has no right" to lag behind military possibilities in circumstances where basic weapons systems were changing at great speed. In these conditions, he warned, the belated revision of views and "stagnation in the development and especially in the practical assimilation" of new means of war "are fraught with serious consequences." Ogarkov also called for measures to create adequate economic reserves for war and heighten the self-sufficiency of defense industrial enterprises in energy, equipment, and other supplies.[95] Plainly he was demanding large increases in a wide range of military expenditures, including the defense production needed for "the practical assimilation" of new weapons. Given the strains on the state budget many officers, probably including Ogarkov, were opposed to Brezhnev's schemes for heavy new spending on agriculture.[96] The publication of Ogarkov's article in *Kommunist*, the party's main theoretical journal, suggests that his alarmist views enjoyed significant support within the upper echelons of the party.[97]

Faced with military demands for a jump in defense spending, Brezhnev and his supporters launched a campaign to persuade or discipline their military critics. An editorial in *Voenno-istoricheskii zhurnal* (Journal of military history) reiterated that economic might, including sectors such as agriculture, is the foundation of the state's defense capacity. Citing Lenin for authority, the editorial called for the "qualitative solution" of the tasks of national defense with "the allocated or even fewer resources."[98] Another article underlined the military's responsibility to defend the country and pointedly quoted Brezhnev: "We have everything necessary . . . for ensuring the Soviet Armed Forces' high and reliable battle preparedness. Therefore the further raising of the level of battle readiness of the army and navy depends . . . on the practical activity of military cadres, on their skill, will, energy and persistence."[99]

Brezhnev and his supporters buttressed the argument for military belt-tight-

---

[95] Ibid., 89.

[96] *Krasnaia zvezda*, 29 May 1982, 1; *Pravda*, 1 July 1982, 2.

[97] It is true, of course, that senior military men frequently publish articles in the main party journals. But the decision to publish an article so clearly at odds with the general secretary's preferences would require special political support. For evidence of intraparty controversy over the wisdom of Brezhnev's foreign policy, see the editorial in *Kommunist*, no. 8 (1982), 10–20.

[98] *Voenno-istoricheskii zhurnal* (hereafter cited as *VIZh*), no. 10 (1981), 3–4, 6–9. See also *KVS*, no. 17 (1981), 10–20.

[99] Rear Admiral V. Gulin and Captain I. Kondyrev in *KVS*, no. 24 (1981), 20, 27. The authors gave no published source for the Brezhnev quotation.

ening by calling the MPA and other political mechanisms into play. Starting in 1980 the annual rate of turnover among the military's establishment's senior political officers, which had recently been rather low, rose sharply to almost 30 percent per year for three years running. As with the sharp rise in turnover among political officers in 1975, this jump suggests that Brezhnev and his backers were again seeking to strengthen the MPA as a means of indoctrinating regular military commanders with party-approved views. Brezhnev's backers also convened a national conference of secretaries of the military's primary party organizations to shore up the general secretary's support within the officer corps.[100] About the time the date of the conference was announced, a deputy head of the MPA complained that "not all party organizations" had ensured the "deepened study" of the Twenty-sixth Party Congress's defense decisions. Some military men had approached the links of theory to practical affairs "extremely primitively" and should be able to draw "practical conclusions" from the decisions of the party and the government.[101] When the national conference met in mid-1982, it gave a blanket endorsement to Brezhnev's policies, particularly his stance on the military budget.[102]

Brezhnev and his supporters also threatened political retribution against officers who failed to toe the line. Shortly after the conclusion of the national conference the first deputy chief of the Defense Ministry's Main Cadres Administration called for tighter screening and control of commanders. Regular attestation of officers, he said, could serve as a "powerful stimulus" to the fulfillment of party and service obligations, and officers should understand that attestation was not a formality but a procedure "determining for years" the position in which an individual would serve. Officers were needed who could establish friendly working relations within large collectives and could do so without "turmoil and noise." "*Only*" such people should be promoted, said the cadres official. Although an officer's or general's sense of responsibility usually increased with his rank, occasionally an immature officer began to consider himself "infallible." Sometimes it was necessary to consider removing leaders who depended too little on the military party organization and could not create a sense of solidarity within their military units.[103]

Security and the Question of Expertise

A key aspect of this struggle over security policy was the claim of Ogarkov and his military backers to special expertise. In arguing for higher defense

---

[100] See the announcement of the meeting in *KVS*, no. 21 (1981), 8. This was the first such conference to be convened in almost ten years.

[101] Colonel General M. Sobolev in *KVS*, no. 1 (1982), 58, 62.

[102] *KVS*, no. 11 (1982), 32.

[103] Colonel General V. Goncharov in *VIZh*, no. 6 (1982), 4–7, 9. Emphasis in original.

spending, Ogarkov heavily underscored the importance of assessing international threats objectively, "without any elements of one-sidedness and subjectivism."[104] The reaction of Ogarkov's opponents shows that such appeals to "objectivity" were a potent weapon. Editorials polemicizing in favor of Brezhnev's policies made special efforts to justify the scientific accuracy of the party's assessment of the international scene, and one MPA proponent of capping military growth even argued that "selectivity" in explaining the country's military policy to military men "does not at all contradict truthfulness and objectivity" but helps officers to evaluate political phenomena correctly.[105] Another article asserted that the party's role "in deciding fundamental military-theoretical problems—in particular, research on the possibility of preventing war and maintaining the military balance—is growing." The Central Committee "orients military cadres toward a deep mastery of the military art and an effective application of battle technology and weaponry."[106] In other words, the party reserved the right to assess the danger of war and whether the strategic balance was moving against the USSR. The duty of military men was to master and apply the resources given to them.

Civilian foreign-affairs specialists also played a role in this struggle over the relationship between political authority and military expertise. Previously kept at a distance from defense decision making, some civilian specialists were eager to gain a hearing for their views on military policy. One important step toward this goal was the creation in 1979 of a Scientific Research Council on Problems of Peace and Disarmament to coordinate research on arms control and military detente.[107] Although set up partly to influence Western public opinion, the council sought to shape the outlook of Soviet policy makers as well.[108] It was chaired by Inozemtsev, the director of IMEMO and a longtime proponent of East-West detente. Its section heads included G. A. Arbatov, director of the Institute on the USA and Canada (IUSAC), M. A. Markov, academic secretary of the Academy of Sciences' Division of Nuclear Physics, and D. M. Gvishiani, the first deputy chairman of the State Committee for Science and Technology.

As debate over security and military spending intensified, influential council members advocated views at odds with the ideas articulated by Ogarkov. Arbatov, for instance, was a leading proponent of the view that diplomacy and patience could bring the United States back to the bargaining table, and he and

[104] N. V. Ogarkov, *Vsegda v gotovnosti k zashchite Otechestva* (Moscow, 1982), 26–27.

[105] *Kommunist*, no. 8 (1982), 18–20; B. Utkin in *VIZh*, no. 8 (1983), 7–8. Utkin was a deputy head of the MPA.

[106] Colonel V. Zotov in *KVS*, no. 23 (1982), 51.

[107] The organizing agencies were the Academy of Sciences, the State Committee for Science and Technology, and the Soviet Peace Committee.

[108] *Mirovaia ekonomika i mezhdunarodnye otnosheniia* (hereafter cited as *MEMO*), no. 7 (1979), 106–111.

some of his colleagues intimated that the USSR should avoid falling into the American trap of an arms race designed to bankrupt the Soviet economy. Early in 1982 the Academy of Sciences convoked a large symposium to discuss the nature of American military-political strategy. A number of the civilian participants at this meeting were far more sanguine about the security situation and more wary of an accelerated arms race than was the representative from the General Staff.[109] Later that year, after Ogarkov had twice called for fuller party recognition of the danger of war and civil-military tensions had sharply increased, a deputy director of IUSAC published an article that warned against overestimating the danger of war.[110] In other words, some leading foreign-affairs specialists put their expertise at the disposal of the Brezhnev coalition against the national-security conservatives personified by Ogarkov.

Thanks to its emphasis on uniting the work of social and natural scientists, the Scientific Research Council laid the basis for teamwork between civilian foreign-affairs specialists and scientific researchers in behalf of arms control.[111] This marriage of civilian political and technical expertise, which had not previously existed in the USSR, was first brought to bear on matters of military doctrine in a study coauthored by space scientists and members of IUSAC. The study dealt with a military subject—space-based ballistic missile defenses—that was peripheral to the Soviet military's current force structure and plans for deployment.[112] But it foreshadowed a coming shift in the roles of civilian specialists and military professionals in resolving pivotal questions of force structure and military doctrine. Fragmentary evidence suggests that specialists associated with the Scientific Research Council, taking a cue from Brezhnev, may also have attempted to promote research plans that heightened the accent on civilian technology at the expense of military R&D.[113]

The Military and Succession Politics

The tensions between party leaders and restive officers reached a crescendo in October 1982, when Brezhnev and a few other Politburo members met with a large contingent of the high command.[114] Assuring the gathering that his de-

---

[109] SShA, nos. 5 and 6 (1982).

[110] Richard Bogdanov in Sovetskaia Rossiia, 24 October 1982, 5, trans. in FBIS, Daily Report: Soviet Union (hereafter cited as FBIS), 1 November 1982, AA1–AA3.

[111] MEMO, no. 7 (1979), 106–108.

[112] Komitet sovetskikh uchenykh v zashchitu mira, protiv iadernoi ugrozy, Strategicheskie i mezhdunarodno-politicheskie posledstviia sozdaniia kosmicheskoi protivoraketnoi sistemy s ispolzovaniem oruzhiia napravlennoi peredachi energii (Moscow: Institut kosmicheskikh issledovanii AN SSSR, 1984).

[113] G. Marchuk in Kommunist, no. 4 (1983), 68.

[114] The other Politburo members in attendance were Andropov, Gromyko, Tikhonov, Ustinov,

tente policy would enable the USSR to keep the geopolitical initiative, Brezhnev remarked that "we are equipping the armed forces with the most advanced weapons" and taking steps "in order that you need nothing [more]." His comment that "the armed forces should always be worthy of this concern" contained a hint of reproach, and his reference to bottlenecks in the fuel and metal industries was probably meant to underscore the limits on the number of new weapons that could be produced. Brezhnev also emphasized the security benefits of his agricultural policies and the "exceptional importance" of the Food Program. At the same time, he conceded that a lag in the intensifying international competition in weapons technology was impermissible, and he voiced the expectation that all researchers and engineers would do "everything possible" for military programs. Although reluctant to speed up the production of new weapons, he appeared to be promising to accelerate the pace of weapons development.[115]

Brezhnev's death shortly afterward provided a test case of an aroused officer corps' ability to influence succession politics. Some observers have suggested that Ustinov, as minister of defense, shaped the party succession on behalf of the high command. At the time of Brezhnev's death, the dwindling Politburo inner circle included Ustinov, Grishin, Gromyko, Andropov, and Chernenko.[116] Andropov and Chernenko, the two leading candidates to succeed Brezhnev, both had an organizational base in the party secretariat, but their political profiles were quite distinct.[117] Having served for almost fifteen years as chief of the KGB, Andropov had acquired extensive foreign-policy experience and had demonstrated a political firmness that probably appealed to officials worried about coping with the USSR's mounting problems. By contrast, Chernenko lacked leadership experience and had shown little concern about the needs of the military establishment or the worsening international situation. Around the time of Brezhnev's death, the comments of Ustinov and Andropov on military questions were noticeably firmer than those of Chernenko, who seemed extraordinarily sanguine about the ultimate victory of "reason" in relations with the United States.[118] Under these conditions it seems likely that Ustinov backed Andropov as Brezhnev's successor, and that his support was an important ingredient in Andropov's victory.

---

and Chernenko. According to the press account, Ustinov delivered a speech. *Pravda*, 28 October 1982, 1; see also *Krasnaia zvezda*, 21 October 1982, 1.

[115] *Pravda*, 28 October 1982, 1–2.

[116] During the past five years, several previous members of the Politburo core group had dropped out. Podgornyi had been ousted, Kosygin and Suslov had died, and Kirilenko had fallen into disgrace.

[117] In May 1982, following Suslov's death, Andropov had moved from his post as KGB head and become a member of the Secretariat—no doubt to strengthen his hand in the succession struggle that was already under way.

[118] *Pravda*, 30 October 1982, 2; 8 November 1982, 2; and 13 November 1982, 1–2; *Kommunist*, no. 16 (1982), 29; and *Pravda*, 30 October 1982, 2, in *FBIS*, 3 November 1982, R15–R17.

Ustinov did not, however, represent the interests of the military establishment within the Politburo. To say that he represented the views of the Politburo within the Ministry of Defense would be much closer to the truth. In Brezhnev's final years, Ustinov worked hard to sell the officer corps on the general secretary's expensive nonmilitary programs. It was Ustinov, for example, who called on Soviet soldiers not to stand apart from the Food Program.[119] Ustinov also urged repeatedly that the growth of the armed forces be kept in balance with the development of the other political and economic components of national defense capacity, and he claimed that the "decisive front" in the East-West competition lay "precisely in the sphere of the economy."[120] In 1982, when senior officers became acutely dissatisfied with Brezhnev's agricultural and foreign policies, Ustinov extolled Brezhnev's "truly titanic" contribution to defense at the national conference of military party secretaries organized to shore up the party chief's authority.[121] Moreover, Ustinov denied the suggestive parallels that Ogarkov repeatedly drew between the late 1930s and the current period, and he differed openly with Ogarkov over the pace of weapons innovation and deployment.[122]

Thus, while professional soldiers must have found Andropov more appealing than Chernenko, he was not installed at their behest. Nor did he proceed to carry out the wishes of the most assertive officers. Although Andropov made an occasional bow to the importance of the military and pledged to restore tight labor discipline, his warnings against underestimating the danger of "serious collisions" within society seemed to reflect a deep concern about domestic political stability not unlike that of Brezhnev and Chernenko.[123] Moreover, he refrained from endorsing a large increase in defense expenditures, as continued expressions of military dissatisfaction over the budget attest.[124] Instead, taking a leaf from liberal foreign-affairs specialists, he espoused Lenin's dictum that the USSR exerts its main influence on the world revolutionary process through its economic policies—and not, by implication, through military power.[125] He also declared his belief in the historic possibility of restoring East-West detente.[126]

As part of his attempt to achieve this goal, Andropov took steps to

---

[119] *Krasnaia zvezda*, 29 May 1982, 1; *Pravda*, 1 July 1982, 2.

[120] B. F. Ustinov, *Sluzhim Rodine, delu kommunizma* (Moscow, 1982), 23, 30.

[121] *KVS*, no. 11 (1982), 7; see also Ustinov, *Sluzhim Rodine*, 36–38.

[122] Whereas Ogarkov emphasized the importance of rapidly deploying a new generation of sophisticated weapons, Ustinov said pointedly that the capabilities of the weapons currently in service should not be underestimated. Ustinov, *Sluzhim Rodine*, 86–87.

[123] *Kommunist*, no. 3 (1983), 21. Andropov seemed especially worried about tensions among ethnic groups; see *Kommunist*, no. 1 (1983), 8.

[124] See, for example, Col. A. Dmitriev in *KVS*, no. 3 (1983), 17.

[125] Iu. V. Andropov, *Izbrannye rechi i stati*, 2d ed. (Moscow: Politizdat, 1983), 215. Aleksandr Bovin presented the same argument in an article published in *Kommunist* in 1980.

[126] *Izbrannye rechi i stati*, 2d ed., 216; see also *Pravda*, 18 February 1980, 2.

strengthen his position vis-à-vis the officer corps. Thanks to Ustinov's efforts, he soon acquired a fabricated military reputation.[127] Shortly after Andropov took office, the MPA and its military sympathizers sharply underscored the party's primacy over the military establishment and the impermissibility of "partisan warfare" over military policy within the Ministry of Defense.[128] Just as important, Andropov—or perhaps Ustinov acting with his tacit approval—moved to curb Ogarkov's influence. In the spring of 1983 a deputy chief of the General Staff, S. F. Akhromeev, was awarded the rank of marshal and promoted from candidate to full membership in the party Central Committee. In view of Akhromeev's military post, his promotion to marshal was unprecedented, and it marked him as someone enjoying high-level political patronage.[129] The promotion, which may have been intended as a step toward replacing Ogarkov or as a signal that he should stop criticizing established security policy in public, was followed by a momentary softening of Ogarkov's public statements. But Ogarkov, as Andropov's health worsened, again renewed his criticism, and some military commentators pointedly observed that an army's failure to prepare to master all the weapons its enemy might obtain would be "foolish or even criminal."[130] When Andropov died in early 1984, the officer corps was no less restive than during Brezhnev's final year.

This dissatisfaction, however, had no impact on the selection of Andropov's successor. Although Ustinov warmly endorsed Chernenko's selection as general secretary and praised him for his contribution to Soviet defense, the military press treated the news coldly, and Chernenko's attempts to transmute his brief service as a border guard into military experience must have rubbed salt in the wound.[131] Of all the contenders for power, Chernenko was the least concerned about the military danger emanating from the West and the most optimistic that the security situation could be improved through patience, diplomatic negotiation, and the resumption of the arms-control talks that the USSR had broken off in 1983 in retaliation for the start of the new American INF deployments in Europe. If Ogarkov and the rest of the officer corps had

---

[127] Timothy J. Colton, *The Dilemma of Reform in the Soviet Union* (New York: Council on Foreign Relations, 1984), 52.

[128] *KVS*, no. 23 (1982), 30–31, 51, and especially *VIZh*, no. 1 (1983), 11–12.

[129] This was the first time since the creation of the General Staff in 1935 that a deputy chief had held the rank of marshal. Peter Kruzhin, "The New Marshals—A Sign of Change in the Soviet Ministry of Defense?" *Radio Liberty Research Bulletin*, no. 148, 11 April 1983.

[130] Compare *Krasnaia zvezda*, 23 February 1983, 1–2, with *Izvestiia*, 23 September 1983, 4–5, in *FBIS*, 23 September 1983, AA1–AA6. See also the article by Marshal V. Petrov, commander-in-chief of the ground forces, in *Kommunist*, no. 3 (1984), 84–85.

[131] The coverage of Chernenko's election in *Krasnaia zvezda* was quite different from the coverage in *Pravda* and *Izvestiia*. See David R. Jones, "The Soviet Military Year in Review," in *Soviet Armed Forces Review Annual*, ed. David R. Jones (Gulf Breeze, Fla.: Academic International Press, 1985), 8:6–7. Chernenko had served as a member of the border guard troops in Kazakhstan from 1930 to 1933; see his comments in *Kommunist*, no. 9 (1984), 3.

had a say in selecting the top leader, they undoubtedly would have picked someone like Romanov or Grishin. Fragmentary evidence suggests that during the Andropov period Romanov, or else his sympathizers within the military establishment, did try obliquely to advertise his credentials as a defender of Soviet security. It is a reasonable surmise that the step was intended to strengthen Romanov's standing as a competitor for the general secretaryship, but it failed to achieve this effect.[132]

Soon after Chernenko assumed the general secretaryship the running civil-military controversy broke into the open with new force. Issuing a clarion call for greater attention to military needs, Ogarkov warned that American imperialism was becoming far more aggressive and drew a parallel between alleged neo-fascist trends in Western Europe and developments in Germany on the eve of World War II. Citing Chernenko's promise the previous month to strengthen Soviet defenses, Ogarkov remarked that "this demand must be fulfilled undeviatingly"—wording which implied that the promise was not at present being fulfilled. The emergence of revolutionary new weapons in countries such as the United States was "a reality of the immediate future," Ogarkov said, and "not to take account of this now would be a serious error." Failure to respond promptly to these trends, the marshal added darkly, could not fail to alter existing conceptions of "the military might of the state."[133] In a scarcely veiled way, Ogarkov was warning that current policy was endangering the country's military security.

Chernenko was unswayed. Two weeks prior to the appearance of Ogarkov's article he had explicitly rejected a proposal for a special public campaign to support a larger military effort and had dwelt instead on the needs of agriculture and consumer welfare. Shortly after Ogarkov's blast, Chernenko, although decrying the deterioration of superpower relations, refrained from mentioning any need to strengthen the armed forces. Instead he told a national meeting of military Komsomol (youth league) officials that the regime was doing "everything" required to ensure peaceful relations with the West.[134]

Within two months party overseers moved to tighten political discipline inside the military establishment. In an article probably directed at Ogarkov and his military supporters, the first deputy head of the MPA condemned irresponsible behavior by staff officers and noted that some military men wrongly tried to concentrate exclusively on weaponry and purely specialized questions. A leader was always on view, the MPA official wrote, and the higher the leader's post, the more people looked to him as an example of someone who took an "active political position" and put the interests of the party above all else. But

---

[132] Shortly after Brezhnev's death, a military journal ran an article that was apparently an Aesopian attempt to single out Romanov as a champion of the military's interests. See V. Ershov in *VIZh*, no. 1 (1983), 69–74.

[133] *Krasnaia zvezda*, 9 May 1984, 2–3.

[134] *Kommunist*, no. 7 (1984), 15–17; no. 9 (1984), 4.

subordinates also noticed the "arrogance" and "tactlessness" of a leader. The party organizations within the military must strictly apply the Central Committee's firm line against those who rejected criticism; there could be no indulgences for persons who forgot their duties as Communists. The MPA spokesman concluded that "conceit" and "excessive ambitions" should be quickly blocked to ensure that every military leader adopted a Leninist leadership style.[135]

Two months later, in a move triggered partly by Ustinov's deteriorating health, Ogarkov was demoted as chief of the General Staff and replaced with Akhromeev. In the absence of this step, Ogarkov's prominence would have given him a serious chance of becoming the new defense minister, and recent precedents would have made it difficult to deny him a seat on the Politburo. Both Chernenko and Ustinov undoubtedly wanted to block this eventuality, and Gromyko most likely concurred.[136] Gorbachev, whose power within the leadership was rapidly growing, probably also supported the demotion.[137] On the other hand, such hard-liners as Romanov and Shcherbitskii had policy reasons to oppose it. Romanov apparently helped cushion Ogarkov's fall, although not before the marshal was compelled to recant many of his previous views.[138] Apart from being linked with Ustinov's impending death, the timing of the demotion indicates that it was also connected with simmering controversies over the military budget and over easing the Soviet position on the American INF deployments in order to resume arms negotiations.[139]

When Ustinov died in December, the Politburo chose S. L. Sokolov, a first deputy minister of defense, as his replacement. In one sense this choice was a positive gesture to the officer corps, because it meant that the ministry would once again be run by a professional officer. Many party politicians probably welcomed Sokolov as an officer who was less forceful and outspoken than Ogarkov, and they may also have felt that he would be less likely to become entangled in the next phase of the succession, which was obviously approach-

---

[135] Admiral A. Sorokin in *KVS*, no. 14 (1984), 9, 11.

[136] Gromyko had vigorously championed diplomatic means of ensuring Soviet security and played down military ones. For a comparison of his views with those of Ogarkov and other military commentators during 1983, see Bruce Parrott, "Soviet Policy Toward the United States: A Fork in the Road?" *SAIS Review* 5, 1 (Winter–Spring 1985), 115–116.

[137] Like Andropov and Gromyko, Gorbachev strongly emphasized the utility of diplomatic means to resolve East-West differences. He stressed the stability of the strategic balance and minimized the need for growth of the military establishment. He also backed Chernenko in the debate with hard-liners over policy toward the United States. *Pravda*, 23 April 1983, 2–3; 19 May 1983, 4; Parrott, *The Soviet Union*, 56.

[138] *KVS*, no. 21 (1984), 22–25; Parrott, *The Soviet Union*, 56. It was Romanov who finally revealed that Ogarkov would be assigned to an important military command and not, as previously rumored, to a military academy.

[139] See the editorial in *Pravda*, 5 September 1984, 1; Marc Zlotnik, "Chernenko Succeeds," *Problems of Communism* (March–April 1984), 27; and Parrott, *The Soviet Union*, 55–56.

ing due to Chernenko's precarious health. The prospect of military neutrality may have displeased some Politburo competitors who wished to obtain political support from the officer corps.[140] Nonetheless, when Chernenko died in February 1985, the military, lacking either a civilian or a professional military representative on the Politburo, was ill-equipped to exert a significant influence on the party's choice.

The Consolidation of Civilian Dominance, 1985–1988

The New Leadership and Its Priorities

After being selected general secretary, Gorbachev quickly inaugurated an ambitious effort to revitalize the Soviet system and improve its international situation. As a relative newcomer to the Politburo, Gorbachev had little personal stake in defending the political legacy of his immediate predecessors, and he was far more willing to use the powers of the general secretaryship to force political change. Breaking decisively with Brezhnev's legacy in domestic affairs, he claimed that the policies of the past two decades had led the Soviet system to a state of near-crisis that must be scrutinized in the harsh light of glasnost. Brezhnev had enshrined a consensual leadership style that papered over conflicting assumptions, focused on a narrow range of policy options, and tended to compartmentalize the channels for receiving specialized advice.[141] Rejecting this technocratic pattern of leadership, Gorbachev actively encouraged competing views and public debate over the basic tenets of party theory and policy. By allowing intellectuals to range across political subjects with unprecedented freedom, his approach undermined the monopolies of expertise that many groups of specialists, such as the officer corps, had sought to preserve during the Brezhnev era. Moreover, Gorbachev showed a new willingness to adopt unorthodox ideas as the basis for action. Less than a year after his accession to power, the cascade of policy innovation, first felt in domestic affairs, spread to security policy as well.

The leadership turnover initiated under Gorbachev marked a further weakening of the career linkages between the civilian and military elites. In mid-1987, although a number of Politburo civilians had done short prior stints in military-related occupations, only 15 percent of the members had extensive

---

[140] About the time of Ustinov's death, *Kommunist Vooruzhennykh Sil* ran an editorial that inveighed against Trotskii's attempts in 1922 and 1923 to use illegitimate tactics, including "splitting" activity within military party organizations, to become Lenin's successor. See *KVS*, no. 24 (1984), 19–23. The timing of the editorial suggests that it may have been an esoteric communication intended to counter the lobbying of the officer corps by some of the competitors for Chernenko's mantle.

[141] See Fedor Burlatskii's discussion of Brezhnev's leadership style in *Literaturnaia gazeta*, no. 37 (1988), 14.

military-related work experience, compared with about 25 percent in 1978 and 32 percent in 1966.[142] Equally significant, 20 percent of the 1987 members had worked for an extended period in the Foreign Ministry or intelligence, thus earning some professional claim to speak on security issues from a non-military perspective.[143] Gorbachev himself came to office without significant career ties to the officer corps, and he made no effort to identify himself with professional officers. Unlike Brezhnev, Andropov, and Chernenko, he did not contrive a reputation to give himself an aura of special military experience or authority.[144] Apparently Gorbachev's lack of experience in security matters raised doubts within the party elite, since at the time of his selection Gromyko made an unusual effort to reassure the Central Committee that he was well-versed in defense and foreign-policy matters.[145]

If some of the doubters were senior military men, Gorbachev made no attempt to placate them by giving the officer corps a strong voice in the Politburo. After coming to power he promoted Minister of Defense Sokolov only to candidate rather than to full Politburo membership. Meanwhile two of Gorbachev's political allies—N. I. Ryzhkov and E. K. Ligachev—were promoted to full membership without passing through the candidate stage, and another backer, KGB Chairman V. M. Chebrikov, advanced from candidate to full membership. The result was to give the other principal state organizations concerned with external relations—the Foreign Ministry and the KGB—a stronger voice in top-level deliberations than the military establishment enjoyed. The KGB's growing influence also overshadowed the military's ability to affect policy making in regional party bodies (see table 2.1). On a symbolic level, the officer corps' diminished political standing was reflected in a sharp drop in the number of senior military men on the reviewing stand at the annual parades celebrating May Day and the anniversary of the revolution.[146]

These bureaucratic slights were compounded by Gorbachev's pronouncements on security policy. Gorbachev promised not to let the United States

---

[142] The 1978 percentage is based on Meyer's classification of full and candidate Politburo members for that year; the 1987 calculation is based on my classification of all Politburo members using Meyer's seven-year criterion of extensive work experience. The individuals who met this standard were Chebrikov, Vorotnikov, and Iazov.

[143] The group included Gromyko, Aliev, and Iakovlev, who had served for more than a decade as Soviet ambassador to Canada and later headed up the Academy of Sciences' Institute of the World Economy and International Relations. It also included Chebrikov, who had done lengthy assignments in both military-related and intelligence work. The formal list did not include Shevardnadze, who became foreign minister in 1985 and therefore did not satisfy Meyer's seven-year criterion for extensive work experience.

[144] He did, on the other hand, assume the chairmanship of the Defense Council, which had great importance for the formulation of Soviet defense policy.

[145] Archie Brown, "Gorbachev," *Problems of Communism* (May–June 1985), 15–16; *Kommunist*, no. 5 (1985), 6–7.

[146] *The Radio Free Europe/Radio Liberty Daily Report*, 7 May 1987.

TABLE 2.1

Number of Republican Party Bureaus Containing a Military or KGB Representative, 1966–1986

	1966	1971	1976	1981	1986
Total Bureaus	14	14	14	14	14
Number Containing:					
Military Full Member	6	6	7	7	7
Military Candidate	1	1	1	0	0
Total Military	7	7	8	7	7
KGB Full Member	1	2	5	6	12/13[a]
KGB Candidate	3	5	7	8	2/13[a]
Total KGB	4	7	12	14	14/13[a]

Sources: Derived from Grey Hodnett and Val Ogareff, *Leaders of the Soviet Republics* (Canberra: Department of Political Science, Research School of Social Sciences, Australian National University, 1973), and biographical directories.

[a] The affiliations of the members of one bureau could not be fully established. Another bureau contained two KGB officials.

obtain strategic superiority, but he showed no inclination to underwrite increased defense spending. Instead, claiming that the future of the Soviet system and world socialism hinged on accelerated economic development, he suggested that added increments of military power should not be equated with an increase in the state's security.[147] "Reasonable sufficiency" should be the standard for scaling down the superpowers' military arsenals, he said, and the USSR and its allies should reshape their defense establishments to give them "an exclusively defensive character."[148] Although Gorbachev made revitalizing the high-technology industries the top economic priority, his extremely ambitious investment plans intensified short-term demands on resources and strengthened the temptation to siphon off inputs previously earmarked for military use.[149] During July 1985 he met in Minsk with the high command and, according to informal accounts of his unpublished speech, told military plan-

[147] *Pravda*, 24 April 1985, 1; Parrott, *The Soviet Union*, chap. 5.

[148] *XXVII sezd KPSS*, 1:89, 98; Mikhail Gorbachev, *Perestroika: New Thinking for Our Country and the World* (New York: Harper & Row, 1987), quoted in Robert Legvold, "Gorbachev's New Approach to Conventional Arms Control," *The Harriman Institute Forum* 1, 1 (January 1988), 6.

[149] Jan Vanous and Bryan Roberts, "Time to Choose Between Tanks and Tractors: Why Gorbachev Must Come to the Negotiating Table or Face a Collapse of His Ambitious Modernization Program," *PlanEcon Report: Developments in the Economies of the Soviet Union and Eastern Europe* 2, nos. 25–26, 1–16.

ners that stringent limits would be imposed on the growth of military expenditures.[150]

Gorbachev viewed these strategic issues through a historical lens quite different from the one used by most previous party leaders. Personal memories of the epic strife and suffering of World War II had shaped the imaginations of all past leaders and had provided a compelling argument in favor of contemporary military requirements. Gorbachev, however, was too young to have experienced the war as an adult, and he gave an early signal that he rejected the promilitary lessons ordinarily drawn from that cataclysmic struggle. Subtly initiating a portentous new evaluation of the war's causes, he drew the lesson that farsighted diplomacy, not an all-out effort to build up the armed forces, was the key to protecting Soviet security. This view set him at odds with some leaders from the older generation, such as Shcherbitskii, who continued to justify their calls for military expansion with analogies to the prewar period.[151] As shown below, later polemics about the history of Soviet foreign relations revealed that Gorbachev and his supporters held a deeply critical attitude toward the past use of Soviet military power and its effectiveness in protecting the country's security.

Although some thoughtful officers agreed with Gorbachev that the armed forces must accept short-term sacrifices as the price of maintaining military effectiveness over the long term, Marshal Sokolov did not concur. In his view, the "severe lessons" of World War II showed the vital importance of strengthening the contemporary armed forces.[152] Plainly at odds with the new general secretary, Sokolov made common cause with the civilian Politburo members who were trying to brake the momentum of Gorbachev's campaign for economic revitalization, and for nearly six months he ostentatiously refrained from mentioning Gorbachev's name in print.[153]

Signs of military dissatisfaction over the defense budget also surfaced in the publication of a new pamphlet by the resilient Marshal Ogarkov. Although slightly milder than most of Ogarkov's pronouncements in the 1980s, the new pamphlet rescinded the recantation that had been extracted from him in the fall of 1984. Once more underscoring the parallel between current circumstances and the international situation on the eve of World War II, Ogarkov called the further strengthening of Soviet defenses "an objectively vital necessity." New American weapons, he warned, were a "special threat," and "extremely weighty errors" could result from misinterpreting present military-technolog-

---

[150] Dale Herspring, "The Soviet Military in the Aftermath of the 27th Party Congress," *Orbis* 30, 2 (Summer 1986), 311.

[151] Mikhail Gorbachev, *Izbrannye rechi i stati* (Moscow: Politizdat, 1987–1988), 2:136, 180; *Kommunist*, no. 8 (1985), 13–14; *Pravda Ukrainy*, 8 May 1985, 2; Bruce Parrott, "Soviet National Security under Gorbachev," *Problems of Communism* (November–December 1988), 4–5.

[152] *Kommunist*, no. 6 (1985), 67.

[153] Parrott, "Soviet National Security," 7; *Krasnaia zvezda*, 25 May 1985, 2.

ical trends.[154] Ogarkov was not speaking for the whole military establishment; Marshal Akhromeev, for one, took a less anxious view.[155] But many senior commanders, including Sokolov, probably sympathized with Ogarkov's position on defense spending. Ogarkov's restatement of his alarmist views was also backed by such civilian politicians as Romanov, a key Gorbachev rival, and Shcherbitskii.[156]

After July 1985, when Gorbachev expelled Romanov from the Politburo and called for military belt-tightening, military spokesmen became more cautious. As part of the leadership shakeup Gorbachev engineered the promotion of E. A. Shevardnadze, a close ally, to full Politburo membership and persuaded Gromyko to vacate the Foreign Ministry in Shevardnadze's favor.[157] In response to this political shift Sokolov trimmed his sails and affirmed that the armed forces had all they needed to defend the country.[158] But new tensions arose as the drafting of the Twelfth Five-year Plan (1986–1990) neared completion. Patchy evidence suggests that some members of the General Staff were uneasy with the line taken by Gorbachev in his Minsk speech.[159] Moreover, during the preparation of the new draft party program, past military champions of bigger defense budgets urged that the draft program's rather equivocal formulas about equipping and manning the armed forces be strengthened.[160] Basically rejecting these appeals, Gorbachev went out of his way to assure "many of our people" that the USSR was not falling behind the United States militarily, and L. N. Zaikov, a Politburo ally, called for the defense industry to give more assistance to consumer-goods production.[161] Undaunted, Sokolov reacted by reinterpreting the new party program to fit his budgetary claims. Asserting that the West was seeking "decisive" military superiority over the USSR, Sokolov claimed—inaccurately—that the party program called for "the balanced, dynamic development of all the elements of the combat potential of the Soviet Armed Forces." In fact, the new program's commitment to the military establishment was considerably more cautious.[162]

Tensions also arose over the efforts of Gorbachev's political coalition to recast military doctrine and enhance the influence of civilian analysts on defense questions. As Gorbachev consolidated his political position, he shifted

[154] N. Ogarkov, *Istoriia uchit bditelnosti* (Moscow, 1985), 24, 43–47, 80–81, 93.

[155] *Izvestiia*, 7 May 1985.

[156] Parrott, "Soviet National Security," 5–6.

[157] Gromyko, in turn, was appointed chairman of the Presidium of the Supreme Soviet.

[158] *Pravda*, 8 November 1985, 1–2; 23 February 1986, 2; Parrott, "Soviet National Security," 14.

[159] *Krasnaia zvezda*, 31 December 1985.

[160] See especially *KVS*, no. 2 (1986), 28–30, and *Krasnaia zvezda*, 27 June 1986, 2–3.

[161] Parrott, *The Soviet Union*, 49; *Pravda*, 29 June 1986, 2.

[162] *Pravda*, 9 May 1986, 2; *XXVII sezd KPSS*, 1:453, 595–96; Parrott, "Soviet National Security," 14.

toward a radical stance on several doctrinal issues ranging from nuclear deterrence to policy on conventional arms. Even if the USSR maintained strategic parity with the United States, he said, in the future nuclear deterrence might not prevent a general war.[163] Because the doctrine of deterrence was spawning ever larger numbers of complex weapons susceptible to catastrophic technical or human error, it actually raised rather than decreased the likelihood of military conflicts. World war had not been avoided because of nuclear weapons, but in spite of them, Gorbachev claimed.[164] He also indicated that the yardstick of ''reasonable sufficiency'' should be applied to conventional as well as nuclear arms, and he acknowledged that the East possessed some military ''surpluses'' that it would trade for reductions of weapons in which the West enjoyed an advantage.[165] These formulas carried major implications for military policy and for the military establishment's role in defense policy making.

A principal actor in Gorbachev's early attempts to revamp security policy and expand the influence of civilian experts was A. F. Dobrynin, who became the party secretary overseeing foreign policy in the spring of 1986. In a key article, Dobrynin argued that the USSR had succeeded in avoiding general war during the last forty years not because of its military power, but because of its diplomacy and the existence of moderate political groups in the West.[166] Observing that many contemporary military problems still required scholarly analysis, Dobrynin listed a series of topics without mentioning any of the military academies and institutes that had already given those topics years of professional study. Instead he singled out the Scientific Research Council on Peace and Disarmament and the institutes of the Academy of Sciences as the locus of promising research on these subjects.[167] Dobrynin's pointed omission of professional officers and their specialized knowledge signaled an attempt to downgrade military expertise in favor of the authority of civilian defense specialists. This effort received vigorous backing from Foreign Minister Shevardnadzde and from A. N. Iakovlev, a former director of IMEMO who joined the Politburo in early 1987, as they assumed increasing responsibility for managing foreign relations.[168]

This effort to expand civilian influence over security policy was reflected in organizational changes. Dobrynin organized a military affairs section within

[163] *XXVII sezd KPSS*, 1:7–8. This was a major change of position from 1985, when Gorbachev had described strategic parity as an effective source of deterrence. (See, e.g., *Pravda*, 24 April 1985, 1–2.)

[164] *Pravda*, 17 February 1987, 2; 17 September 1987, 2.

[165] Ibid., 11 April 1987, 2; 8 July 1986, 5.

[166] Anatolii Dobrynin in *Kommunist*, no. 9 (1986), 20.

[167] Ibid., 19, 26–28.

[168] *FBIS*, 16 March 1987, G12; A. Iakovlev in *Kommunist*, no. 8 (1987), 18. Toward the end of 1988 Dobrynin was edged out of his post as party secretary and head of the International Department, but Shevardnadze and Iakovlev continued to push hard for more civilian input into military policy.

the Central Committee's International Department, Iakovlev established a small arms-control section under the Propaganda Department, and Shevardnadze began to mobilize civilian specialists for research work on disarmament through a special coordinating center in his ministry.[169] Some of the staff members of the new units were retired officers or military men seconded from regular military assignments; General Viktor Starodubov, who joined the new section in the International Department, was a case in point. As a rule, however, the views of these officers tended to fall outside the mainstream of conventional military thought, and they functioned as allies of the civilian officials and experts working to recast security policy.

With encouragement from the party apex, civilian commentators and officials soon staked out a series of controversial positions on security matters. In the spring of 1987, Aleksandr Bovin, a journalist who had long favored a more conciliatory policy toward the West, hinted strongly that the original Soviet decision to deploy SS-20 missiles in the European theater had been a mistake.[170] Acting, no doubt, with the approval of Shevardnadze, Deputy Foreign Minister A. A. Bessmertnykh openly condemned the SS-20 decision and hinted that the Ministry of Foreign Affairs should have a say in future choices about developing and deploying new weapons.[171] Meanwhile two other foreign-affairs analysts—one an academic, the other a retired officer—argued that Soviet doctrine on conventional operations should be made genuinely defensive by altering force structures and deployments.[172] Perhaps most dramatically, several civilian writers began to describe the troop cuts of the Khrushchev era favorably and to contend that current Soviet forces should be reduced unilaterally, without waiting for the West to commit itself to corresponding reductions.[173]

These civilian forays into military doctrine and policy sparked military resistance, although there were significant variations in the responses of senior officers. Sokolov showed an obvious aversion to downgrading the significance assigned to Soviet military power as a deterrent of Western attack. Asserting that the armed forces "are a real factor deterring the aggressive strivings of imperialist reaction," Sokolov defended the notion of deterrence by arguing

[169] *Krasnaia zvezda*, 24 March 1988, 3, trans. in *FBIS*, 24 March 1988, 2.

[170] *Moscow News*, no. 10 (1987), as cited in *Radio Liberty Daily Report*, 20 March 1987.

[171] Aleksandr Bessmertnykh in *New Times*, no. 46 (1987), quoted in Harry Gelman, *The Soviet Military Leadership and the Question of Soviet Deployment Retreats*, R-3664-AF (Santa Monica: Rand Corporation, 1988). Shevardnadze had already taken a line broadly compatible with this demand, and he later personally endorsed it.

[172] A. Kokoshin and V. Larionov, "Kurskaia bitva v svete oboronitelnoi doktriny," *Mezhdunarodnaia ekonomika i mezhdunarodnye otnosheniia*, no. 8 (1987), 13–15, quoted in Legvold, "Gorbachev's New Approach," 4.

[173] Vitalii Zhurkin, Sergei Karaganov, and Andrei Kortunov in *Novoe vremia*, no. 40 (1987), quoted in Gelman, *The Soviet Military Leadership*; A. G. Arbatov in *MEMO*, no. 5 (1988), 152.

that the avoidance of general war in the recent past had been due above all to Soviet might and the unavoidability of retaliation against an attacker.[174]

On more specific points, Major General Iu. V. Lebedev, a General Staff officer, rebuffed civilian criticism of the SS-20 deployments by contending that the decision to deploy the missiles had been the correct response to Western military programs.[175] A number of senior officers were plainly unhappy with the drift of civilian thinking on the themes of unilateral cuts and "defensive" doctrine. Deputy Defense Minister I. M. Tretiak, for example, bitterly criticized the lingering effects of Khrushchev's troop cuts in terms leaving no doubt that he opposed such steps.[176] Even the relatively flexible Akhromeev seemed to harbor doubts about some of the new ideas. Describing Warsaw Pact doctrine as already defensive in every sense, he especially cautioned against interpreting the notion of sufficiency "one-sidedly" and engaging in a "unilateral reduction of our defense forces." Such apprehensions became more pronounced as the civilian leadership moved to accept a highly asymmetrical cut in the stock of SS-20s in order to obtain a U.S.-Soviet treaty on intermediate-range nuclear forces.[177]

Civil-Military Relations and Domestic Liberalization

Partly because of this resistance, civil-military relations gradually became intertwined with Gorbachev's quest for internal reform. Initially Gorbachev's campaign for national revitalization stressed greater discipline and order, together with accelerated economic development, or *uskorenie*. These goals proved elusive, however, and Gorbachev's campaign gradually assumed a far more radical coloration under the rubric of perestroika. Perestroika entailed increasingly blunt criticism of many bureaucratic hierarchies and vigorous public pressures for them to "restructure" themselves in order to respond to societal needs. By 1987 Gorbachev and his civilian Politburo allies had concluded that bureaucratic efficiency and responsiveness could be achieved only by instituting a far-reaching liberalization of the whole political order.

This conclusion, which Gorbachev set forth in a controversial speech at the January 1987 Central Committee plenum, had implications for the military establishment. At the plenum Gorbachev, highlighting the existence of "crisis

---

[174] *Pravda*, 23 February 1986, 2; *XXVII sezd KPSS*, 1:454. Marshal Kulikov, one of Sokolov's three top deputies, adopted a similar position. See *Trud*, 22 February 1987, 1–2.

[175] *Moscow News*, no. 11 (1987). Lebedev served as military adviser at the unsuccessful U.S.-Soviet INF negotiations in the early 1980s.

[176] *Moscow News*, no. 8 (1988), quoted in Gelman, *The Soviet Military Leadership*, 14.

[177] The Akhromeev statement is from *Problemy mira i sotsializma*, no. 12 (1987), 24, as quoted in Legvold, "Gorbachev's New Approach," 5. For the internal politics of the treaty, signed in December 1987, see also Parrott, "Soviet National Security," 19–23.

phenomena'' within the Soviet system, proposed the introduction of multiple candidacies in elections to the soviets and to party organs at all levels except the all-union one. He also advocated a further expansion of glasnost and faster personnel turnover to avoid the "absurd" results of the past "artificial stability" of cadres.[178] When he touched on security issues, Gorbachev played down the need for additional military spending in favor of domestic concerns and remarked that the armed forces "also live by perestroika." Stressing that Soviet society was doing "everything" to strengthen the military and had a right to assume that no aggression could catch the USSR unawares, Gorbachev remarked that officers bore "an enormous responsibility before the people" and voiced the expectation that they would act "with the greatest responsibility." The veiled note of impatience in these remarks was reminiscent of Brezhnev's suggestion in 1982 that the military already had the resources it needed and should attend to the business of defending the country.[179]

Gorbachev's effort to reshape security policy was complicated by the Central Committee's obvious reluctance to endorse his diagnosis of the domestic and international situations. The final Central Committee resolution made no reference to domestic "crisis phenomena." Moreover, its comments on the armed forces dropped Gorbachev's undertone of criticism while putting heavier stress on the alleged Western military threat and the need to expand Soviet defense capacity.[180] Once again Sokolov joined conservative civilians seeking to limit Gorbachev's reform drive by invoking more conservative party policies from earlier years, and the military press, most likely with Sokolov's encouragement, initially omitted references to the notion of a domestic crisis from its accounts of Gorbachev's speech.[181]

Evidently a substantial portion of the officer corps shared Sokolov's reservations about the desirability of internal military reform. During the preceding two years most commanders, with the exception of MPA officials, had responded sluggishly to Gorbachev's calls for "criticism and self-criticism" and the introduction of "fresh forces" into positions of leadership.[182] After the January plenum Marshal Akhromeev treated internal military reform, including the rejuvenation of the high command, as a serious matter. Marshals Sokolov and Kulikov, on the other hand, paid only lip service to the idea and expatiated instead on the "high evaluation" the armed forces had received in

[178] *Pravda*, 28 January 1987, 1–3.

[179] Ibid., 5. Gorbachev's comments about the KGB, for example, were far more positive. He noted the tempered ideology and high professional qualities of KGB cadres and said nothing about *perestroika* of the KGB.

[180] Ibid., 29 January 1987, 2.

[181] Ibid., 23 February 1987, 2; Parrott, "Soviet National Security," 17–18.

[182] Herspring, "On *Perestroika*: Gorbachev, Yazov, and the Military," *Problems of Communism* (July–August 1987), 101.

the January plenum's final resolution.[183] Although middle-level military Communists endorsed changes in cadres policy, including a downgrading of seniority and service records in making military appointments, Sokolov did not.[184] Instead he underscored the need for a large measure of stability among military cadres to ensure the maximum use of the experience of older officers.[185] No doubt many officers at the top of the military hierarchy agreed with him.

Two weeks later the party activists (*aktiv*) of the Ministry of Defense convened under the watchful eye of Central Committee overseers to analyze the military implications of the January plenum.[186] Sokolov's endorsement of perestroika was again perfunctory, but the endorsements of other participants seemingly carried more conviction. Calling for the MPA's political departments in the General Staff and in the ministry's central administrations to play a much more active role, speakers complained that military ethics and standards would not have declined if the ministry's personnel administration had taken corrective steps and introduced "fresh forces" into military commands.[187] This stress on personnel change was linked to demands for a sharp improvement in the ministry's planning of future military strategy and force structure.[188] Evidently Gorbachev, faced with military foot-dragging, was reinforcing his campaign for doctrinal change with pressures for stepped-up turnover inside the high command.

In view of the tugging and hauling between Gorbachev's coalition and many senior commanders, the Rust affair in May 1987 was a stroke of luck for Gorbachev. Better than any rhetoric about perestroika, the ability of a young West German pilot to traverse Soviet airspace and land his small private plane near the Kremlin illustrated the need for military reform. The incident provided a perfect justification for sacking Sokolov, as well as the chief of the air defense forces, and publicly chastising the high command in a fashion not seen for decades. At the June 1987 Central Committee plenum Gorbachev remarked critically that the "unprecedented" event demonstrated the existence of "powerful" negative phenomena in the military, and he proclaimed that there must be no doubt either within the party or among the people about the armed forces' ability to defend the country.[189] Similar military lapses during the

---

[183] In particular, Akhromeev acknowledged the need for better cadres policy (*Sovetskaia Rossiia*, 21 February 1987, 1). Compare Sokolov in *Pravda*, 23 February 1987, 2, and Kulikov in *Trud*, 22 February 1987, 3.

[184] See, for example, the report from a meeting of the party aktiv of the Group of Soviet Forces in Germany in *Krasnaia zvezda*, 7 March 1987, 2.

[185] *Pravda*, 23 February 1987, 2.

[186] Colonel B. Pokholenchuk in *Krasnaia zvezda*, 18 March 1987, 2.

[187] Ibid. The source does not indicate who advocated this view. MPA officials, deputy ministers, and Central Committee overseers participated in the meeting.

[188] Ibid.

[189] *Pravda*, 26 June 1987, 2.

Brezhnev years might have provoked the quiet punishment of lower-ranking officers, but not the public humiliation of the minister of defense.

In selecting Sokolov's replacement, Gorbachev avoided the affront of installing a civilian minister, but he bypassed all the obvious candidates at the top of the military hierarchy. Instead he reached down to select Army General D. T. Iazov. Iazov had demonstrated a concern for eliminating military inefficiency and corruption before these issues had become fashionable.[190] Moreover, he had been installed as head of the Defense Ministry's Cadres Administration just three months earlier, around the time that the ministry's personnel policy had been harshly criticized at the meeting of the party aktiv. After becoming minister Iazov pushed hard to improve personal and professional standards inside the officer corps. His appointment clearly strengthened Gorbachev's hold over the military establishment and gave Gorbachev more room for maneuver on military policy.

Together with the drive to redefine security policy, Gorbachev's increasingly radical drive for political liberalization unleashed new forces that challenged the military establishment's social standing and institutional role. Perhaps the most vivid example was B. N. Eltsin's lacerating public attack on the military at a meeting of the Moscow Air Defense District's party aktiv held in the wake of the Rust incident. In the name of the workers of Moscow, Eltsin demanded that military men explain how such an incident could occur. During the past year, he complained, "nothing had changed": there had been virtually no restructuring of the air defense unit's work. Eltsin flayed commanders for deceptive reporting, "anachronistic" leadership of soldiers by "authoritarian dictate," and "elitism." In making military promotions, he said, the decisions of party organizations had frequently been ignored. Moreover, there had not been "any sort of glasnost, as if you are unaffected by the decisions of the [Twenty-seventh Party] Congress and the plenums of the Central Committee." Eltsin noted that some persons—who doubtless included many professional officers—had expressed the belief that public discussion of military deficiencies might be harmful. He answered that "the lesson of truth" must be administered, even if it came two years too late.[191]

Although Eltsin's diatribe was far harsher than anything Gorbachev had said publicly, the expression of such views by a candidate member of the Politburo must have reinforced the inclination of liberal intellectuals to voice antimilitary sentiments. In one striking incident, A. M. Adamovich, a prominent Belorussian writer, argued that even if the West launched a massive first strike, Soviet nuclear retaliation would still be unjustified. Adamovich also praised the superior courage of military men who "give their military exper-

[190] Herspring, "On *Perestroika.*"
[191] *Krasnaia zvezda*, 17 June 1987, 2.

tise to the antiwar movement.''[192] Leading MPA and General Staff officers replied with angry denunciations of such ''pacificism.''[193] Nonetheless, these liberal intellectuals reasserted their position unequivocally, arguing that ''the truth of the new thinking is obligatory even for military thought,'' and some objected to the traditional practice of interrupting the education of promising young specialists by drafting them for military service.[194] One writer went so far as to argue that the military establishment had a vested interest in opposing peace and was willfully misinterpreting Gorbachev's pronouncements on security.[195]

These controversies signified a widening struggle between the advocates of traditional promilitary values and the exponents of a new liberalism distrustful of the military establishment. In place of the previous Marxist-Leninist emphasis on the aggressive character of imperialism, exponents of this liberal attitude now argued with extraordinary bluntness that bourgeois democracies were essentially peaceful, and that the Western powers would never launch a premeditated attack on the Eastern bloc.[196] Liberal analysts likewise invaded the field of Soviet military history, previously the exclusive preserve of officers and historians connected with the Ministry of Defense, and advocated changes in Soviet force structure and deployments very different from the traditional ''lessons of history'' favored by the bulk of the officer corps.[197] Perhaps most dramatically, civilian specialists published articles suggesting that the Soviet Union bore a large part of the responsibility for the outbreak of World War II and the rise of the Cold War, primarily because of its confrontational diplomatic posture and excessive reliance on military force.[198] Taken together, these developments constituted a wide-ranging cultural offensive against the values that had long undergirded the militarization of Soviet foreign policy and the preferential standing of the armed forces within the Soviet system.

Many military men and political conservatives were deeply alarmed by this

[192] *Moskovskie novosti*, 8 March 1987, as quoted in Stephen Foye, ''Intellectuals Attack the Military,'' *Sovset News* 3, 9 (30 July 1987).

[193] *Literaturnaia gazeta*, 8 May 1987, as quoted in Foye, ''Intellectuals Attack the Military.''

[194] Some civilian scientists questioned whether the military's need for highly qualified students is more important than society's need for ''physicists, biologists, engineers, and social scientists.'' *Literaturnaia gazeta*, 22 May 1987 and 8 June 1987, as quoted in Foye, ''Intellectuals Attack the Military.''

[195] A. Nuikin in *Vek XX i mir*, as cited by A. Pavlov and V. Liashenko in *KVS*, no. 21 (1988), 24.

[196] V. Zhurkin, S. Karaganov, and A. Kortunov in *Kommunist*, no. 1 (1988), 43–46, 49. Zhurkin was a deputy director of IUSAC.

[197] See, for example, Kokoshin and Larionov, ''Kurskaia bitva''; see also the editorial in *VIZh*, no. 5 (1986), 9, and P. A. Zhilin in *VIZh*, no. 7 (1986), 10.

[198] See especially the article by Viacheslav Dashichev in *Literaturnaia gazeta*, 18 May 1988, and *Komsomol'skaia pravda*, 19 June 1988, 3.

trend. For example, Defense Minister Iazov, who adopted a cautious attitude toward the liberalization of the political system, seemed especially upset by the sort of slashing attack on the military that Eltsin had delivered.[199] Military theorists vigorously criticized the liberal view of the West and reiterated that imperialism was inherently aggressive.[200] In an effort to shore up the military's crumbling monopoly over the extraction of policy lessons from past military events, Iazov also cautioned against a loss of objectivity in the writing of military history.[201] Although he and some other officers made considerable concessions in the realm of military doctrine and accepted the goal of negotiating reductions in the size of the Soviet arsenal, they firmly rejected civilian arguments that unilateral reductions were either inherently desirable or a useful means of spurring progress in East-West arms negotiations.

Nonetheless, Gorbachev and his Politburo allies gradually espoused more and more of the ideas advocated by liberal civilian analysts. The benign view of Western political intentions was implicit in their espousal of the idea that "common human values," rather than class conflict, had assumed overriding importance in the dealings between East and West.[202] Gorbachev, Iakovlev, and Shevardnadze all took pains to emphasize the basic differences between the current era and the military conflicts of the 1930s and 1940s. Shevardnadze, in particular, embraced the liberal indictment of Stalin's foreign policy, arguing that it had been militarized and counterproductive, and called for the reinterpretation of the traditional lessons of World War II on the basis of "new experience" showing that national economic dynamism, not military forces in being, was the key to security.[203] The espousal of this revisionist view of the purge and war years was a major development. It marked the emergence of a new generation of leaders young enough not to have been stamped indelibly by the Nazi onslaught and less inclined to believe instinctively that national security required the continuous expansion of the armed forces.

On the institutional level, the party reformers pressed to give the Ministry of Foreign Affairs a decisive voice in security policy and to link this change with legislative reform. Taking his cue from Gorbachev's report to the Nineteenth Party Conference in the summer of 1988, Shevardnadze publicly assailed the policy makers of the Brezhnev era for such mistakes as deploying the SS-20s and dragging out the MBFR negotiations over conventional arms

---

[199] *Krasnaia zvezda*, 18 July 1987, 2; 29 July 1987, 1; and 13 September 1987, 1. Criticism, Iazov remarked, is a sharp weapon, and in using it sensationalism and a disrespectful attitude toward military cadres should be avoided. See *Krasnaia zvezda*, 13 August 1987, 2. For attacks on the military's liberal critics by Iazov and associated conservative intellectuals, see particularly *FBIS*, 22 January 1988, 68–69.

[200] S. Tiushkevich in *KVS*, no. 8 (1988), 85–86; A. Pavlov and V. Liashenko in *KVS*, no. 21 (1988), 24, 26.

[201] *FBIS*, 26 February 1988, 68; *Pravda*, 9 May 1988, 2.

[202] Parrott, "Soviet National Security," 30–31.

[203] *Vestnik Ministerstva inostrannykh del SSSR*, no. 15 (1988), 32–33, 35.

in Europe. The context of these remarks left no doubt that he regarded senior military men as some of the chief culprits. Shevardnadze bluntly demanded that the Ministry of Foreign Affairs receive full information and the right to vet prospective weapons programs to ensure that they matched the USSR's diplomatic line and treaty obligations. Elaborating on Gorbachev's summons to give the revamped Supreme Soviet real power and to publish a meaningful defense budget, Shevardnadze advocated holding open legislative hearings to scrutinize the defense budget and weigh possible decisions to use military force abroad.[204]

If fully implemented, these steps will sharply reduce the armed forces' influence on military decision making. By removing the secrecy that has traditionally shrouded the cost of the national military effort to society, they will make military programs vulnerable to the public criticism and mounting consumer dissatisfaction already welling up through the reformed legislative structure. This, in turn, will provide a new source of political support for Gorbachev and other leaders eager to cut military spending.[205]

Gorbachev's United Nations speech in December 1988 marked a watershed in the internal debate over security policy. By announcing plans for a unilateral reduction of 500,000 soldiers over the next two years, Gorbachev reversed recent assurances to the officer corps and swung publicly toward the liberal civilian argument that unilateral Soviet cuts could provide a rapid solution to mounting internal economic hardships and serve as a political stimulus to Western arms reductions.[206] Gorbachev's pledge to withdraw some five thousand tanks and bridging equipment from Eastern Europe was also an important step toward making Soviet military doctrine defensive in an operational rather than only a rhetorical sense. Apparently these dramatic policy changes generated civil-military tensions and contributed to the retirement of Marshal Akhromeev as chief of the General Staff. Although Akhromeev allegedly retired strictly on grounds of health, he had consistently resisted unilateral cuts, and the fact that his retirement became known on the day of Gorbachev's speech suggests that it may have been precipitated by disagreement

[204] Ibid., 29, 36–37. In August 1987 Gorbachev promised that as the regime carried out internal economic reforms it would publish a defense budget comparable to Western budgets. *Pravda*, 27 August 1987, 4.

[205] In June 1989 Gorbachev told the newly created Congress of People's Deputies that Soviet defense expenditures would be reduced by 14 percent during the next two years. A subsequent public opinion poll in six major Soviet cities showed that large majorities of the respondents— ranging from 62 percent in Leningrad to 82 percent in Tallinn—favored the 14 percent cut or even greater reductions. Fewer than 10 percent of those polled in any city opposed the cut, and the rest of the responses were "don't knows." *Izvestiia*, 4 June 1989, 1, cited in Archie Brown, "Political Change in the Soviet Union," *World Policy Review* (Summer 1989), 496–497.

[206] Only two months before, Gorbachev had strongly implied that the USSR would cut its forces only through negotiations with other governments. See *Pravda*, 1 November 1988, 2, as quoted by Stephen Foye in *Radio Liberty Research Bulletin*, RL 504/88.

with the general secretary.[207] Akhromeev's successor, General M. A. Moiseev, was elevated from the command of a military district and had not previously held any assignments at the General Staff. Like other Gorbachev appointments involving rapid promotions or lateral transfers, Moiseev's
selection was apparently designed to create a military policy maker who is
heavily dependent on the general secretary and prepared to attack the prevailing security views entrenched in the organization he will lead.

Conclusions

Which model of civil-military relations corresponds most fully to the political
interplay between the civilian and military elites since Khrushchev's fall? To
be useful analytically, a model must encompass the swings in civil-military
relations since 1964, and it must offer a multicausal perspective that helps
explain the shifts from one phase to another. Models I and II fall short in both
respects. Model I, grounded on the assumption that the party and the military
are necessarily divided by contradictory institutional imperatives, cannot explain the accommodation that occurred after Khrushchev's fall. On the other
hand, Model II, based on the assumption that the civilian and military elites
have nearly identical values and interests, cannot explain the sharp conflicts
that later appeared, especially during the early 1980s. Neither model, in other
words, sheds much light on the process of evolution that has characterized
civil-military ties since Khrushchev. Because Model III posits numerous
sources of both cooperation and conflict in civil-military dealings, it provides
a sounder basis for explaining the process of historical change.

The choice might not seem so clear-cut if the only period under discussion
were the first decade following Brezhnev's accession to power. That era did
indeed come closer than any other to being a golden age of civil-military relations. The large measure of party-military consensus on the strategic importance of enhanced military power, the party leaders' technocratic willingness
to give military professionals a central role in security policy making, and the
rapid buildup of the armed forces all gave superficial grounds for concluding
that Model II captured the essence of the civil-military relationship. The ad-
mixture of controversy, however, showed that reality was closer to Model III.
The conflicts over the identity of Malinovskii's successor and over the wisdom
of opening strategic arms talks with the United States demonstrated that significant disagreements could arise between civilian and military leaders even

[207] See Milan Hauner and Alexander Rahr, "New Chief of Soviet General Staff Appointed,"
Radio Liberty Research Bulletin, RL546/88, 16 December 1988. The two men's disagreements,
however, were obviously not as sharp as the disputes between Ogarkov and Brezhnev. Akhromeev was soon made a special military adviser to Gorbachev in the latter's new capacity as head
of the Supreme Soviet.

in the golden age. The large measure of civil-military cooperation that did exist derived partly from ingrained characteristics of the military and political elites, such as the common frame of reference established by the shared experiences of World War II. But the high level of cooperation also resulted from other conditions—such as the USSR's strategic inferiority in the early 1960s and the vagaries of the post-Khrushchev succession struggle—which could change more quickly.

In the early 1970s, as the USSR approached strategic parity with the United States and Brezhnev consolidated his position in the Politburo, Brezhnev cautiously began to modify the compact with the officer corps. He expelled two of his rivals and added two new full members, Gromyko and Andropov, whose responsibilities for foreign relations and intelligence led them to favor a national security policy that gave less weight to military power. Drawing selectively on the thinking of civilian foreign-affairs specialists, Brezhnev qualified his earlier commitment to the growth of weapons production, introduced corresponding changes in military doctrine, and advocated greater emphasis on arms control and domestic socioeconomic needs. Although senior military spokesmen protested these alterations, Brezhnev was able to still the protests by installing the civilian Ustinov as minister of defense and appointing Ogarkov, whose views initially fell outside the military mainstream, as chief of the General Staff. Perhaps equally important, in the mid-1970s the USSR's impressive geopolitical gains, which contrasted markedly with the setbacks of the early 1960s, bolstered Brezhnev's authority and helped him allay apprehensions within the officer corps.

Starting about 1980, this adjusted civil-military compact was buffeted by the collapse of East-West detente, the Polish upheaval, a precipitous drop in economic growth, and the onset of the succession struggle. Under these pressures, civil-military frictions, previously easily manageable, became acute. For three years Ogarkov openly disputed the validity of the party's established security policy, and the party leadership, weak and internally divided, failed to silence him. This episode, which may have constituted the longest and most open military challenge to party policy in Soviet history, showed that the compact between civilian politicians and the officer corps was under serious strain.

This strain, however, was not a harbinger of the military dominance or military takeover forecast by some Western observers. Despite the civilian leadership's internal divisions and a widening fear of social instability, there was little of the military "role expansion" that might have preceded a genuinely dangerous civil-military clash. Although wisps of evidence suggest some oblique military efforts to affect the terms of the succession competition, military men had little or no influence on the selection of the three general secretaries who followed Brezhnev. Ogarkov and his military sympathizers made few critical comments about economic and social policy, save for expressions of concern about growing pacificist sentiment in the country. Even in the realm of security policy, where their claim to expertise was strongest, their repeated statements of alarm failed to persuade a Politburo majority to accept their point of view. Instead, faced with an unusually assertive effort to expand the military's influence over policy, the civilian leadership finally responded by demoting Ogarkov. Though fraught with tension, the early 1980s demonstrated the underlying strength of the mechanisms of civilian control and marked an important step in the gradual reduction of military influence within the political system.

That process has accelerated under Gorbachev. His accession marks the arrival of a new generation of leaders whose experiences and leadership style differ sharply from those of their predecessors. Drawing on heterodox ideas once discussed primarily in civilian think-tanks, the new leaders have launched a critical reevaluation of the amalgam of ideological precepts and historical experiences that made military growth and international conflict dominant elements in the outlook of previous leaders. Gorbachev and his allies have gradually strengthened the subordination of the military establishment to the party leadership and have increasingly demanded that the military focus its energies on internal reform as a key element of a reliable defense. After first drawing civilian experts into deliberations over military policy, they have begun to adopt recommendations that diverge sharply from the policies customarily favored by most officers. Perhaps most important, the reformers have unleashed a broader process of domestic political change that calls into question the promilitary social values that have traditionally undergirded the standing of the Soviet military establishment. If these trends continue, they will drastically reduce the influence of the officer corps in the Soviet political order.

Whether these trends will provoke open military opposition and acute civil-military conflict is uncertain. Gorbachev's skepticism toward military power and his conciliatory unilateral gestures toward the West clearly trouble many officers. Professional soldiers are also troubled by tumultuous domestic developments that challenge their cherished institutional traditions and even their honor. To date, however, Gorbachev and his supporters have overcome military resistance through a combination of political pressure and vigorous argumentation, and the rate of policy change suggests that they have kept the initiative firmly in their hands.

Whether they continue to prevail will depend partly on Gorbachev's ability to protect his personal power within the political leadership and thereby block possible cooperation between his military and civilian critics. Although bureaucratic manipulation and ingenious political tactics will play an important part in preventing the emergence of such an alliance, so will the substantive effectiveness of Gorbachev's policies. Further successes in dealing with the outside world will strengthen his hand, but major setbacks will give political ammunition to critics who subscribe to the view that his policies threaten the country's security. Equally important, Gorbachev and his backers must reduce the potential for a conservative civil-military backlash by demonstrating that they can introduce liberal domestic reforms without triggering an internal collapse of the Soviet state.

Finally, the tenor of future civil-military ties will depend on the results of reform within the military establishment itself. Under the intellectual impact of glasnost, the process of military reform may establish a new generation of less parochial senior officers genuinely enthusiastic about Gorbachev's new approach to security, or it may produce a new generation of commanders still wedded to traditional views of military power and eager to reassert their corporate interests at the first favorable opportunity. In any event, the political relationship between the civilian and military elites has reached a watershed, and if the reformers have their way the relationship, like the Soviet system as a whole, will be changed virtually beyond recognition.

Three

The KGB and Civil-Military Relations

AMY KNIGHT

WESTERN analysts often lump the KGB, or Committee on State Security, together with the military establishment and assume that their interests are essentially the same, particularly in terms of how they relate to the party. At first sight, relations between the party apparatus and the KGB do have much in common with party-military relations. In both cases the party leadership faces the problem of controlling a "coercive elite," a prestigious and secretive body of career officers with strong traditions and esprit de corps. Both the military and the KGB enjoy special legal and administrative status in the government structure. The KGB, like the military, controls armed units and key security resources that could make it, in extreme circumstances, a threat to the political leadership itself. Indeed the KGB and its predecessors have been active players in power politics on several occasions; as recently as 1964, the KGB played a central role in the overthrow of Khrushchev.[1] Consequently, relations between the party apparatus and the KGB raise many of the same fundamental issues as party-military relations.

But the KGB and the military are also very different services: their missions, though partially overlapping, are mostly distinct; and so are their histories, their skills, and their resources. One should expect, therefore, that the trends of the last twenty-five years have affected the two services in different ways, and therefore that the evolution of party-KGB relations over this period has not necessarily mirrored that of party-military relations.

This chapter, then, has two purposes. The first is to compare party-KGB with party-military relations, and in particular to look at the problem of "professionalism" as it applies to the secret police. Have the trends that have led to an increasingly professionalized military and a stable civil-military relationship (at least until the death of Brezhnev) had the same effect on the party leadership's relations with the secret police? Is there any counterpart to the specialized division of labor that has evolved between the political and the

[1] A detailed account of the role of the KGB in Khrushchev's overthrow appears in the excerpted memoirs of Khrushchev's son Sergei, "Pensioner soiuznogo znacheniia," *Ogonek*, nos. 40–43 (October 1988). The essentials of Sergei Khrushchev's account are confirmed in an interview with V. P. Semichastnyi, then chairman of the KGB, in "Kak smeshchali N.S. Khrushcheva," *Argumenty i fakty*, no. 20 (1989), 5.

military leaderships, that is, the phenomenon of "loose coupling"? Have there been parallel changes in the political influence and resources of the two coercive elites? Finally, has the impact of Gorbachev's reforms on the party's relations with the secret police been similar to the impact on the military?

The second purpose of this chapter is to assess the importance of the KGB as a factor in the civil-military relationship. Here the central question is the extent to which the KGB and the military are allies or competitors, and indeed, whether the party leadership deliberately encourages rivalry between the two institutions, using each as a tool to control the other. How has the balance of cooperation and competition changed under Gorbachev? To address these issues, this chapter will compare the KGB and the military establishments in terms of both long-standing institutional arrangements and the ways in which the two groups have responded to the changing Soviet scene in recent years. Of particular interest is how the KGB's responses to environmental changes have affected its relationship with the Soviet military, and what impact these responses have had on the military's position within the Soviet regime. To what extent does increased KGB influence diminish or offset that of the military, and to what extent, conversely, are the KGB and the military both on the same side of the power equation?

The KGB and the Military: Commonalities and Competition

In a closed, quasi-militarized society like the Soviet Union, where the goals of political and military defense are placed far above those of individual rights or consumer well-being, the armed forces and the security police occupy important places in the political system. Because both serve as coercive forces designed to protect the Soviet state from its enemies, the KGB and the military have much in common as institutions, and it is not without significance that KGB officials have military ranks and are often seen in uniform. Even the Soviets themselves, in discussing their country's defense, have referred to the armed forces and the organs of state security in the same vein, as they did in the Party program adopted at the Twenty-seventh Party Congress.[2]

The KGB and the military share a common institutional status within the Soviet regime, in the sense that, although both are formally under the authority of the USSR Council of Ministers, they operate with more autonomy than other ministerial bodies. The KGB and the Ministry of Defense function on the basis of statutes (*polozheniia*), which set forth their respective rights and duties in legal terms. Although the majority of statutes governing ministerial agencies are published, this is not so with the KGB and the Defense Ministry, presumably because of the sensitive nature of their tasks and the fact that the

[2] The text of the program appeared in *Pravda*, 7 March 1986, 3–8. See note 38 below.

party controls these two institutions directly rather than through some intermediate government body.[3]

The State-Legal Department (formerly the Administrative Organs Department) of the party Central Committee exercises general oversight over the
police and the military and apparently vets personnel appointments.[4] The head
of this department from 1968 to 1988 was N. I. Savinkin, a low-profile bu-
reaucrat with a military-political background. In late 1988, A. S. Pavlov, a
legal expert and a sector chief in the department, replaced Savinkin. As part
of the reorganization of the party apparatus that occurred in the autumn of
1988, the Central Committee established a Legal Affairs Commission, headed
by former KGB Chairman V. M. Chebrikov, to oversee the State-Legal Department and issue general guidelines on legislative policy for this area.[5]

Like the military, the KGB has armed security and border troops at its disposal, which perform such highly sensitive tasks as guarding the Kremlin, the
party leadership, and nuclear installations, suppressing public unrest, and protecting the USSR's state borders.[6] Although border troops are under the sole
legal authority of the KGB, they were until recently conscripted as part of the
bi-annual call-up of the Ministry of Defense, and their induction was regulated
by the 1967 USSR Law on Universal Military Service.[7] During World War II
both the security and border troops of the then NKVD (People's Commissariat
of Internal Affairs, the equivalent to the KGB) performed military functions,
including armed combat, and NKVD units were frequently integrated into the
regular army. Such NKVD generals as I. I. Maslennikov and P. A. Artemev

[3] See Dietrich A. Loeber, "Statutes of Agencies with Ministerial Status in the USSR: List of
Sources as of 1 July 1982," *Review of Socialist Law* 8, 4 (1982), 359–367; and Iu. M. Kozlov,
Sovetskoe administrativnoe pravo: posobie dlia slushatelei (Moscow: Znanie, 1984), 80–84. Before July 1978, the KGB, which stands for Komitet gosudarstvennoi bezopasnosti, was a state
committee attached to the USSR Council of Ministers. Since July 1978 it has been a state committee of the USSR. A new law on state security is scheduled to be issued in 1990, but this
apparently will not include specific regulations on the KGB.

[4] On the history and evolution of this department, see Amy Knight, *The KGB: Police and
Politics in the Soviet Union* (London and Boston: Unwin/Hyman, 1988), 125–143.

[5] Judging from its activities thus far, this commission has broad powers and responsibilities,
including not only security, defense, and legal issues, but also interethnic relations. See a report
on one of its sessions published in *Pravda*, 14 March 1989, 4.

[6] According to the International Institute for Strategic Studies in London, there are about
40,000 KGB security troops and about 230,000 border troops. See *The Military Balance, 1988–
89* (London: International Institute for Strategic Studies, 1988), 45. The MVD's internal troops
assist the KGB security troops in some of these functions. See William Fuller Jr., "The Internal
Troops of the MVD SSSR," College Station Papers, no. 6 (College Station, Texas, 1983).

[7] In March 1989 the USSR Supreme Soviet issued a decree removing the border, internal, and
railway troops from the Soviet Armed Forces, so presumably their induction and call-up will
henceforth be regulated separately. See *Vedomosti verkhovnogo soveta SSSR*, no. 12 (22 March
1989), 136. The legal status, duties, and rights of the border troops are set forth in the 1982 Law
on the USSR State Border, reprinted in *Izvestiia*, 26 November 1982.

even took up front commands.[8] Presumably, similar coordination between police and military would take place in the event of a future war.

The KGB and the military are both highly professional, closed bureaucracies with strong institutional interests to protect. Like their military counterparts, KGB officials exhibit a sense of loyalty to their organization and an esprit de corps that is lacking in many other Soviet institutions. The natural attraction to hierarchy and command of police and military professionals and the fact that they operate under conditions of extreme secrecy (even in the era of glasnost) strengthen the service ethos that characterizes each organization.

Although these commonalities may lead the KGB and the military to agree on many issues, significant differences between the two institutions belie the assumption that they constitute essentially a single interest group. First, the Soviet military has, since the late 1940s, exercised its coercive function primarily beyond Soviet borders. With some recent exceptions, the military has not combatted civilian disobedience or antigovernment dissent.[9] The KGB, while given the task of protecting the regime from foreign spies and enemy agents, has a crucial domestic security function as well—that of ensuring the political conformity of Soviet citizens and warding off threats to the stability of the regime. To put it simply, the KGB's coercive role is a political rather than a military one.

Because of the disavowal of terror by the post-Stalin leadership, the KGB has not resorted to the widespread physical violence used by its predecessors to ensure political compliance. Unlike the military, its coercion is based mainly on psychological techniques and encompasses all-pervasive information-gathering functions. As the eyes and ears of the regime, the KGB acts on behalf of the government to protect it from society, while the military's job has been to protect both the government and the population as a whole from outside incursions.

Institutional arrangements—in particular, the KGB's numerous military-related functions—create opportunities not only for coordination but also for competition between the KGB and the military. The Soviet Union, for example, is one of the few modern states where military counterintelligence (the prevention of espionage against the military) is the responsibility of the security police rather than the armed forces. The KGB's Directorate of Special

[8] Artemev was an NKVD troop commander, who later served as chief of the Moscow Military District. In 1953, at the time of police chief L. P. Beriia's ouster, he was transferred to another district because of his ties with Beriia. See *Voennyi entsiklopedicheskii slovar* (Moscow: Voenizdat, 1983), 48, and note 17 below. On Maslennikov, see ibid., 430, and John Erickson, *The Soviet High Command: A Military-Political History, 1918–1941* (London: Macmillan, 1962), 651.

[9] Regular Soviet troops have been called in to assist special police troops in restoring order in areas such as Armenia, Azerbaidzhan, Georgia, and Uzbekistan, where ethnic strife has grown to serious proportions. This trend could continue if ethnic disruptions persist.

Departments, or Third Chief Directorate, which carries out this function, has broad powers of political surveillance and criminal investigation within the armed forces.[10] This enables the party leadership to protect itself from the possibility that the military would exercise its enormous potential for organized, forceful opposition. Although the party leadership has long maintained a system of party controls within the armed forces—the Main Political Administration (MPA)—the KGB provides the ultimate defense against subversion within the military.[11]

The KGB's political surveillance no doubt causes resentment on the part of military officers, particularly in view of historical experience. In 1937–38, the Special Departments, at the time headed by M. P. Frinovskii, played a key role in the massive purges of the armed forces.[12] This experience had a profound and lasting impact on military-police relations, serving as a reminder, even today, of the punitive powers of the security police against the military. The military's resentment may be compounded by the fact that, with the exception of the border troops, which have a network of political organs similar to, but entirely separate from the MPA, the regular KGB apparatus does not have a system of party monitoring within its ranks.[13]

There is also the question of antagonism between the KGB and the GRU (Glavnoe razvedyvatelnoe upravlenie or Main Intelligence Administration) of the Ministry of Defense. Although the GRU is responsible for gathering military intelligence, its functions sometimes overlap with those of the security police. (For a brief period after World War II, in fact, these organizations were merged.)[14] Both the KGB and the GRU are tasked with acquiring technological secrets from the West. Both are also involved with the collection of intelligence for strategic warning. The GRU concentrates on the so-called hard indicators, monitoring Western military communications and other electronic emissions, while the KGB focuses on soft strategic indicators, such as human intelligence and social and political developments. The KGB and the GRU, as Stephen Meyer notes, carry out their assessments independently. Although the

[10] On the history and current operations of the Special Departments, see A. Knight, ''The KGB's Special Departments in the Soviet Armed Forces,'' *Orbis* 28, 2 (Summer 1984), 257–280; and Knight, *The KGB*, chap. 8.

[11] The Directorate of Special Departments commemorated its seventieth anniversary on 19 December 1988. According to an interview with its current chief, V. S. Sergeev, KGB investigators have exposed a number of spies within the armed forces in recent years. See *Krasnaia zvezda*, 16 December 1988, 2.

[12] For a recent account of the purges of the Red Army in the thirties, see Vitaly Rapoport and Yuri Alexeev, *High Treason: Essays on the History of the Red Army* (Durham: Duke University Press, 1985), 219–390.

[13] Like all Soviet institutions, the KGB has party units within its organization at all levels, but they perform administrative and propaganda functions, rather than control.

[14] See Simon Wolin and Robert M. Slusser, *The Soviet Secret Police* (New York: Praeger, 1957), 25–26.

military bears the main responsibility for providing strategic warning, Soviet leaders are probably open to independent KGB assessments.[15] Overlapping functions have created a long-standing antagonism between the GRU and the security police, which dates back to the early Stalin period.[16]

Another likely source of rivalry between the KGB and the military is KGB involvement in the nuclear weapons program. In the early postwar years the security police had overall authority over the atomic energy industry. Following the introduction of nuclear weapons into the Soviet arsenal, the KGB was given custody and transport responsibilities for nuclear charges, which were separated from missiles and aircraft until the late 1960s. At this time the KGB relinquished its physical control over nuclear warheads.[17] But KGB troops still guard weapons installations, and the KGB's responsibility for protecting nuclear secrets gives it access to military plans regarding the use of nuclear weapons.

With these common functions and jurisdictional rivalries in mind, it is useful to compare the responses of the security police with those of the military in terms of the challenges they have faced since the early Brezhnev era. Those same environmental changes that have affected the Soviet military establishment and the full range of civilian institutions have had an impact on the power and influence of the political police. How have these changes affected the KGB's institutional outlook, its participation in policy making, and its prestige as an organization?

The political changes that have taken place since the early 1980s have posed a significant challenge for the KGB. Like the military, the KGB enjoyed increased influence in the Kremlin under Brezhnev, particularly from the late 1960s onward. The political police and the party leadership achieved a modus vivendi whereby the latter's interests were well-served by the former, and there was little evidence of institutional conflict. The struggle for the Brezhnev succession, however, produced disruptions in this peaceful coexistence between party and police. The KGB played a significant role in the intense Kremlin infighting that surrounded the accession of former KGB chief Iu. V. Andropov to the post of general secretary of the party in November 1982, as well as in the political turmoil wrought by the two subsequent succession crises. Gorbachev's accession to power in March 1985 initially signalled both a

[15] Stephen M. Meyer, "Soviet Nuclear Operations," in *Managing Nuclear Operations*, ed. Aston B. Carter, John D. Steinbruner and Charles A. Zracket (Washington, D.C.: Brookings, 1987), 500.

[16] See Oleg Penkovskiy, *The Penkovskiy Papers*, trans. Peter Deriabin (New York: Doubleday, 1965), 53, 267; and a book by a former member of the Soviet diplomatic corps, Nicolas Polianski, *M.I.D. 12 ans dans les services diplomatiques du Kremlin* (Paris: Pierre Belfond, 1984), 211–212.

[17] Wolin and Slusser, *The Soviet Secret Police*, 25; and Meyer, "Soviet Nuclear Operations," 487.

strong KGB influence and a cordial relationship between the KGB and the party leadership. But the reforms he promoted with growing forcefulness raised the specter of institutionalized limitations on its domestic powers and created strong tensions between the KGB and Gorbachev's coalition.

The increasingly severe economic troubles faced by the Soviet regime from the mid-1970s onward, the new challenges posed by technological changes, and growing social and cultural problems, such as economic crime, alcoholism, and changes in the ethnic balance, have had a further impact on the KGB and its institutional role in Soviet society. The KGB has also been very much affected by the expansion in the USSR's military and political involvement abroad.

It should be emphasized at the outset that the KGB, like any other Soviet institution, probably does not present a united front on all important issues. In particular, officials responsible for domestic security and those who work in foreign operations may well have different views on policy questions. The First Directorate, for example, which concerns itself with KGB operations abroad, may have welcomed Brezhnev's efforts at detente initiated in 1972, because they offered greater opportunities for KGB agents to infiltrate into Western countries under legal cover. On the other hand, detente made the job of those in charge of internal security more difficult, since it meant an increase in contacts between Soviet citizens and foreigners, a relaxation of restraints on communications, and curbs on the KGB's campaign against political dissent. Thus, when one considers the KGB's probable stance on certain issues and its response to challenges, one must look at both the domestic and foreign policy implications and assume that the chairman of the KGB as a whole participates in the policy process as a coordinator of both the KGB's internal and foreign operations, integrating the views of the various KGB directorates.

Political Change: The Greatest Challenge

The KGB's Political Evolution under Brezhnev

Brezhnev's policies toward the KGB are best understood when seen in contrast to those of his predecessor, Khrushchev, whose reforms had reduced the power and influence of this institution. After defeating L. P. Beriia in July 1953, Khrushchev and his colleagues dismantled Beriia's vast police apparatus and strengthened party control over the political police. Such reforms were no doubt favored by the Soviet military, whose leaders, Marshals Zhukov and Moskalenko in particular, played decisive roles in overcoming Beriia.[18] Not

---

[18] On Beriia's arrest and the role of the Soviet military, see a recently published account based on the recollections of Major General I. Zub, in *Krasnaia zvezda*, 18–20 March 1988. Also see "Marshal Zhukov: krutye stupeni i sudby," *Sovetskii voin* 17 (1988), 13–15.

only was terror disavowed as a method, legal reforms were introduced to protect Soviet citizens from arbitrary police persecution. These legal and institutional changes, together with amnesties for political prisoners, cultural liberalization, and public denunciations of Stalin, marked a period of decline for the political police, which lasted until the early 1960s. Although information on budgetary allocations to the KGB is unavailable, numerous sources have reported that its size was trimmed and that the Administrative Organs Department of the Central Committee, responsible for supervising personnel appointments to the KGB, the regular legal organs, and the military, was strengthened.

Khrushchev's stress on popular participation in government and his reforms and innovations offended the KGB's institutional interests as understood by its leaders. This is no doubt one reason why A. N. Shelepin, who had served as KGB chairman from 1958 to 1961, took a leading part in the ouster of Khrushchev in October 1964, enlisting his protégé, KGB chairman V. P. Semichastnyi, to help carry out the plot.[19] Although many elements of the military also resented Khrushchev, their role in his ouster was minimal, particularly in comparison with 1953.[20] With the political police on their side, Khrushchev's opponents did not have to rely on the military's support.

Thus, unlike the case of party-military relations, the twenty-five-year period covered by this book opens with a crisis of civilian control over the political police. In October 1964 the KGB leadership had actively conspired with a faction of the Politburo, tailed the deposed leader's family and tapped their telephones, and moved armed units about to support a coup. The new administration now faced a KGB leader and a former (but still de facto) KGB leader who expected as their reward a major role—perhaps even the leading role—in the new administration. The party leadership could not tolerate such a situation without risking a return to the violent politics of Beriia's day. In short, while in party-military relations Brezhnev's accession reinforced trends that had been under way for more than a decade, in party-KGB relations the partial depoliticization achieved with such difficulty after Stalin's death was once more in question.

Brezhnev managed to defeat this threat by gradually undermining Shelepin's authority in the Central Committee Secretariat and by achieving the dis-

[19] See note 1 and Fedor Burlatskii, "Brezhnev i krushenie ottepeli," *Literaturnaia gazeta* 37 (14 September 1988), 13–14. Burlatskii claims that Shelepin, rather than Brezhnev, was the instigator of the coup. Both Shelepin and Semichastnyi were rewarded for their efforts by promotions in November 1964. Semichastnyi was promoted to full Central Committee membership and Shelepin was made a full member of the Politburo.

[20] Also in contrast to 1957, when the military led by Zhukov saved Khrushchev from an attempted coup. On the military's subsequent dissatisfaction with Khrushchev over cuts in the defense budget, see part 2 of the memoirs of Sergei Khrushchev in *Ogonek*, no. 41 (8–15 October 1988), 26–29.

missal of Semichastnyi in May 1967. He then installed several of his own supporters in key KGB posts. He was not in a position to name a protégé to replace Semichastnyi as KGB chief in 1967, but the recipient of that post, Andropov, appeared to be politically neutral, and Brezhnev's allies served directly below him. These included S. K. Tsvigun, appointed first deputy chairman in late 1967; V. M. Chebrikov, a party apparatchik from Dnepropetrovsk, who became a deputy chairman in 1968; and G. K. Tsinev, former chief of the KGB's Third Directorate and a deputy chairman since 1970. With some leverage over the KGB through this patronage, Brezhnev proceeded with a program to strengthen the organization and raise its professional stature.

Brezhnev's policies toward the KGB were similar to those he developed toward the military. As George Breslauer and others have pointed out, Brezhnev's approach to politics was one of seeking elite consensus.[21] Unlike Khrushchev, who trampled on established interests and offended key groups such as the military and the KGB, Brezhnev avoided confrontation and sought instead to build his political support on a coalition of the various political groups. He satisfied the demands of both the KGB and the military by giving them generous material support and high public prestige, while fostering the development of professionalism in their ranks.

Numerous sources have referred to the high salaries and perquisites enjoyed by the KGB under Brezhnev.[22] Also, CPSU cadres policy toward the KGB stressed the recruitment of well-educated, highly-qualified personnel and the development of experience and expertise through security of tenure. The party transferred many apparatchiks into the KGB immediately after Stalin's death, but these were not temporary assignments. The majority of these men remained in the KGB permanently, gaining, to all appearances, a strong sense of identity with this organization. Party outsiders were not brought into the KGB on a regular basis, and there was a low rate of turnover in KGB posts relative to other careers. Thus, under Brezhnev the KGB evolved into a closed, specialized bureaucracy, whose employees had homogeneous backgrounds and career experiences. Aside from cleavages between foreign and domestic cadres, which represent essentially separate bureaucracies with little interchange of personnel, KGB officials developed a strong sense of solidarity. Judging from numerous memoirs and articles on the KGB, this spirit was especially strong among older officers, who joined the security police before

---

[21] See George Breslauer, *Khrushchev and Brezhnev as Leaders: Building Authority in Soviet Politics* (London: Allen & Unwin, 1982).

[22] According to Soviet defector and former diplomat Arkady Shevchenko, "Only the KGB pays its people well enough for them to afford the best in Western clothing." Arkady Shevchenko, *Breaking With Moscow* (New York: Ballantine Books, 1985), 322. Also see Aleksei Myagkov, *Inside the KGB* (Surrey: Foreign Affairs Publishing, 1976), 90–91; and Polianski, *M.I.D.* According to Polianski, p. 308, KGB officers receive salaries that are one and a half to two times higher than those for corresponding ranks in other organizations.

or during the war, but it was also carried over to the younger generation of KGB professionals.[23]

The Brezhnev leadership went out of its way to promote a favorable public image of the KGB and to ensure its elite status, just as it did with the military. In the mid-1960s the regime launched a publicity campaign to glorify the KGB and its predecessors. The campaign continued unabated throughout the Brezhnev era. Alongside the multitude of publications honoring the Soviet armed forces, thousands of memoirs, biographies, histories, and adventure stories were published on the security police.[24] The literature portrayed the typical Chekist, as employees of the KGB are still referred to (after the Cheka of the original years), as a dedicated Communist, with high moral standards and lofty ideals, who rigorously defended Soviet society from the evil designs of foreign spies and wayward Soviet citizens. A cult of the security police was developed, with the intention of inspiring reverence and awe among the population.

Like the military, the KGB broadened its powers and gained a greater voice in policy making. The regime extended the KGB's legal prerogatives in December 1965, when it authorized the KGB to investigate cases of misappropriation of state property. After the notorious trial of writers Andrei Siniavsky and Iulii Daniel in 1966, the Brezhnev regime gave it wide latitude in repressing political dissent. The leadership enlisted the KGB to carry out a vigorous campaign against dissidents and allowed it to flout Soviet laws with impunity.

To be sure, the Kremlin had considerations beyond those of dissent, and there were times, particularly from 1973 to 1979, when it placed limits on the KGB's persecution of dissidents because of efforts to improve relations with the West.[25] In general, however, the Brezhnev leadership adhered to the maxim that domestic political concerns took precedence over the observance of legality. Without being privy to Kremlin conclaves, one cannot determine the KGB's precise role in domestic decision making under Brezhnev. But the fact that domestic policy was geared to the demands of internal security suggests that the KGB, as the main purveyor of information on dissent and the political mood of Soviet citizens, must have made its influence felt.

The steady increase in KGB representation on key party bodies offered further evidence of its growing political influence. At the republic level, where

[23] For a detailed discussion of cadres policy in the KGB, see Knight, *The KGB*, chap. 5.

[24] By 1977, according to one estimate, over two thousand books extolling the deeds of the security police had been published in the Soviet Union. See *Soviet Analyst* 6, 19 (28 September 1977), 5.

[25] For a discussion of the factors motivating Kremlin policy toward dissent during these years, see Peter Reddaway, "Policy Towards Dissent Since Khrushchev," in *Authority, Power and Policy in the USSR: Essays Dedicated to Leonard Schapiro*, ed. T. H. Rigby, Archie Brown and Peter Reddaway, 2d ed. (New York: St. Martin's Press, 1980), 158–192; and Peter Reddaway, "Dissent in the Soviet Union," *Problems of Communism* (November–December 1983), 1–15.

none of the fourteen KGB chairmen enjoyed full membership and only one
had candidate membership on the party bureaus in 1961, seven KGB chairmen
were full members and seven were candidate members by 1981. In the party
Central Committee the KGB was represented in 1961 only by Semichastnyi,
who was a candidate member. By 1981, at the Twenty-sixth Party Congress,
four KGB officials were elected full members of the Central Committee. This
representation was still slight in comparison with the military, which had
twenty-three senior officers elected as full members at the 1981 congress.[26]
But the KGB is a much smaller organization and, by virtue of its functions,
has always maintained a more discreet presence than the armed forces at political gatherings. However much the regime tried to dispel the image of the
KGB as a "secret police," large numbers of KGB officials could not have
been elected to the Central Committee without causing alarm among both the
elite and the public as a whole.

   An important gauge of political influence for a Soviet institution is representation on the Politburo. There, along with the ministries of Defense and
Foreign Affairs, the KGB gained representation in April 1973, when Andropov was made a full member of this body (he had been a candidate member
since 1967). The KGB was now a part of the elite decision-making process,
where its views could have a direct impact, and Andropov was recognized as
a key Kremlin official. It is important to stress that, while Brezhnev's policies
favored the growing effectiveness and professionalism of the KGB, Andropov's own skillful leadership of this organization also deserved much credit.
He was evidently keenly aware of the KGB's public image, encouraging his
employees to take a sophisticated approach to their tasks and to avoid the
strong-armed tactics of their predecessors. Instead of overt coercion, the stress
was increasingly on prevention of crimes and molding public attitudes through
KGB propaganda.[27]

   The term "golden age," which has been used to characterize the relationship between the party and the Soviet armed forces during Brezhnev's middle
years, could be applied just as aptly to the relationship between the KGB and
the party.[28] Brezhnev's cordial relations with the military and the police no

---

[26] On military representation in the Central Committee, see Dale R. Herspring, "The Soviet
Military in the Aftermath of the 27th Party Congress," *Orbis* 30, 2 (Summer 1986), 297–316. It
might be added that the KGB's influence was furthered by the "export" of selected personnel to
other agencies, in particular to the MVD and the party apparatus. One such example was Geidar
Aliev, tranferred in 1967 from the post of Azerbaidzhan KGB chairman to party chief in that
republic.

[27] For details on Andropov and his tenure in the KGB, see A. Knight, "Andropov: Myths and
Realities," *Survey* 28, 1 (120) (Spring 1984), 22–44. For an example of how Andropov involved
himself with the struggle against dissent and his clever use of the "carrot and stick" approach,
see an account of his prison visit to dissident Viktor Krasin in Krasin's book, *Sud* (New York:
Chalidze Publications, 1983).

[28] Andropov's elevation to the rank of army general (unprecedented for a security chief since

doubt contributed to the stability of his leadership. As far as the KGB's relations with the military were concerned, Brezhnev's policies may have soothed antagonisms caused by built-in institutional arrangements and differences in outlook. Because the Brezhnev leadership accommodated the interests of both organizations, there was less cause for discord than had previously been the case. Also, perhaps, Brezhnev's own position was secure enough that he did not need to play off the KGB and the military against each other.

The KGB and the Struggle for Succession

Despite the overall resemblance of party-KGB relations to party-military relations during the Brezhnev years, the kind of "objective control" referred to in chapter 1—a depoliticized relationship between the political leadership and the security police, based on a stable division of labor between "political" and "technical" tasks and between policy formation and execution—did not develop. The problem is that, at least where the KGB's domestic duties are concerned, even its technical tasks have inherently political implications. Gathering domestic intelligence about corruption in the Brezhnev era, for example, led straight to the political elite, indeed, to Brezhnev's own family. Even in ordinary times, the KGB's watchdog mission pits it against every other institution in the political system, and the KGB's routine monitoring of communications yields a constant flow of sensitive information about the views and movements of all political players.

The KGB's responsibility for ensuring the personal safety of the political leadership puts it in an even more sensitive political position. Consequently, it is hard to speak of a sphere of nonpolitical, "routine technical implementation" in the KGB's domestic missions. The limits to the KGB's depoliticization became especially clear during the succession crises that ensued after Brezhnev's death.

While analysts began to see signs of a breakdown in the "marriage of mutual convenience" between the party and the military as early as 1976, there were no such signs with the party and the KGB until the early 1980s, when the struggle over Brezhnev's succession began in earnest and Andropov and Chernenko began vying for the post of general secretary. It was at this time that the KGB was brought into the succession struggle as a weapon in the anticorruption campaign initiated by Andropov to attack those close to Brezhnev.

The KGB had been empowered by law since 1965 to investigate cases of large-scale corruption, but these powers had hitherto been employed only on

Beriia's days) in September 1976 and the subsequent promotion of three deputy KGB chiefs to that rank in December 1978 reinforced this picture of amity and cohesion between the KGB and the Kremlin leadership.

a limited scale. Now they were unleashed against the official corruption that was rampant among the Brezhnevites. Key targets were top-level officials of the Ministry of Internal Affairs (MVD), or regular police, several of whom were cronies of Brezhnev.[29] After becoming general secretary in November 1982, Andropov transferred KGB chairman V. V. Fedorchuk, who had held this job only since May, to the post of MVD chief with the apparent purpose of further purging this organization, as well as other elements of the party and state apparatus. Fedorchuk was replaced in the KGB by Chebrikov, at the time a first deputy chairman. The extent of Andropov's reliance on the KGB as a base of support to gain the general secretaryship is difficult to gauge, but it may be assumed that his success in reaching the top party post can be at least partly attributed to the considerable political clout this institution had acquired under his chairmanship.

Some experts have depicted an alliance between the KGB and the military in the drive for the Brezhnev succession.[30] While it is possible that Defense Minister Ustinov threw in his lot with the Andropov faction, there is little evidence that the military's role in the Brezhnev succession was anything more than marginal.[31] This was equally the case when Chernenko succeeded Andropov. If the military had been a strong force behind Chernenko, it is unlikely that its interests would have been so neglected during his brief tenure as party leader. Not only was Marshal Ogarkov demoted from the General Staff under his leadership; the military lost its representation on the Politburo in the wake of Ustinov's death in December 1984.

The KGB's political interests, by contrast, did not suffer, even after August 1983, when Andropov became incapacitated and Chernenko was apparently second in command. Letters poured into the press praising the security police; Chebrikov was promoted to the rank of army general in November 1983 and the following month was made a candidate member of the Politburo (a promotion that was overdue). In January 1984 changes in the law on state crimes gave the KGB increased latitude in struggling against political nonconformity; and in February 1984, after Chernenko's accession as general secretary, the number of KGB officials elected to the USSR Supreme Soviet rose to an unprecedented eighteen.[32]

[29] Andropov probably encountered opposition to his anticorruption drive among those KGB officials with personal ties to Brezhnev, such as Brezhnev's brother-in law, First Deputy Chairman Tsvigun, who died suddenly (reportedly a suicide) in January 1982. Tsvigun's death may have helped to clear the way for Andropov to pursue his program. For details see Amy Knight, "Soviet Politics and the KGB-MVD Relationship," *Soviet Union* 11, pt. 2 (1984), 157–181.

[30] See, for example, Zhores Medvedev, *Andropov* (New York: W. W. Norton, 1983); and Jeremy Azrael, *The Soviet Civilian Leadership and the High Command: 1976–1986* (Santa Monica: Rand Corporation, 1986).

[31] On this point, in addition to Bruce Parrott's chapter in this volume see Jerry Hough, "Andropov's First Year," *Problems of Communism* (November–December, 1983), 49–64.

[32] By comparison, in 1958 only six delegates were elected to the USSR Supreme Soviet from the KGB, and in 1979 fifteen KGB delegates were elected.

It may be that Chernenko was not strong enough politically to risk an attempt at curbing the KGB's influence. It is also possible that he had ties with those remaining elements of the KGB leadership who had been cultivated by Brezhnev. It is not easy to determine Chebrikov's loyalties, for example, despite the fact that he was named to the top KGB post when Andropov became party leader. Given the fact that he hailed from Brezhnev's old bailiwick of Dnepropetrovsk (he had worked closely with Shcherbitskii in the party apparatus there), he may not have opposed a Chernenko interregnum, particularly if, as Jerry Hough has suggested, Gorbachev had already been designated the long-term successor.[33]

As far as Gorbachev was concerned, the April 1985 promotions to full Politburo membership of Chebrikov, E. K. Ligachev, and N. I. Ryzhkov revealed the coalition he had forged to reach the top party post in March 1985. Three years later, in a speech to the Nineteenth Party Conference, Ligachev confirmed that Chebrikov had been among Gorbachev's backers.[34]

The fact that, like Andropov, Gorbachev used the anticorruption campaign as one means of purging entrenched Brezhnevites was a sign that the KGB helped Gorbachev to consolidate his power. As one of the criminal investigatory agencies, the KGB is authorized to uncover cases of official corruption; it is difficult to imagine that Gorbachev and his associates could have conducted this campaign without the close cooperation of the KGB. During Gorbachev's first eighteen months in power, he seemed to be cultivating good relations with the KGB by maintaining its high prestige and political status. Chebrikov himself was featured prominently in the Soviet media, and, while the regular law enforcement agencies were under continuous fire in the press for their failures to curtail economic crime and corruption, the KGB remained unscathed.

Significantly, Ligachev's party conference speech made no mention of where Sokolov, who had been minister of defense at the time, stood in relation to Gorbachev's appointment as general secretary. And indeed there was little indication that Gorbachev was beholden to the military for support. The position of the military contrasted sharply with that of the KGB after Gorbachev assumed power. Contrary to what might have been expected, Marshal Sokolov was not promoted to full Politburo membership. Nor did Marshal Ogarkov make a comeback, as some had predicted.

Moreover, G. V. Romanov, a civilian politician often believed to have been sympathetic to the military who served from June 1983 onward as party sec-

---

[33] See Jerry Hough, *Russia and the West: Gorbachev and the Politics of Reform* (New York: Simon & Schuster, 1988), 154–155.

[34] The speech was reprinted in *Pravda*, 2 July 1988. Ligachev also listed Gromyko and Solomentsev as backing Gorbachev at the time. His apparent purpose was to warn Gorbachev and his allies that the views of those responsible for the selection of Gorbachev should be heeded, but shortly thereafter Gromyko and Solomentsev were dropped from the leadership.

retary responsible for administrative organs and the defense industry, was dropped from the Politburo in July 1985 and his responsibilities for the police and military assumed by Ligachev (and, subsequently, by L. N. Zaikov in early 1986).[35] In Romanov, the military to all appearances lost a vigorous advocate within the party leadership.[36] While the KGB was able to continue its harsh treatment of political dissent, the military leadership, as Parrott points out, was engaged in a struggle with the party over arms control issues, and its expertise appeared to be downgraded in favor of civilian specialists.

The Twenty-seventh Party Congress in February–March 1986, at which the number of KGB officials elected to the Central Committee reached four full members and one candidate member, offered further evidence that the KGB was faring better than the military under Gorbachev. Chebrikov delivered a speech at the congress (the first time since 1961 that the KGB chairman was accorded this honor) in which he gave an extremely aggressive and broad interpretation of the functions of the security police, offering none of the usual assurances that his organization would observe socialist legality.[37] In addition, the new party program, approved in draft before the congress, included references to the importance of state security in the section on defense, implying that political security is equal in importance to military might.[38]

Gorbachev's Reforms and the KGB

The honeymoon between the KGB and the Gorbachev leadership was not destined to last, however. By the autumn of 1986, Gorbachev's policies of reform began to take hold, causing disquiet at KGB headquarters. The campaign for openness in the press, the liberalization of cultural policies, and the movement toward greater public participation in the political system are not policies that lend themselves to strong controls by the security police. Discussions by legal experts of judicial and legal reforms, voiced with increasing frequency from

[35] The first indication that Ligachev was supervising the Department of Administrative Organs was his attendance at a conference of subordinate officials in December 1984 (*Izvestiia*, 21 December 1984, 2). He continued to attend departmental functions until Zaikov stepped in. Zaikov's signature on the obituary of the chief military procurator, A. G. Gornyi, was the first sign of this change (*Krasnaia zvezda*, 9 January 1986, 4).

[36] On Romanov and the military, see Hough, "Andropov's First Year," 53; and Azrael, *The Soviet Civilian Leadership*, 39.

[37] *Pravda*, 7 March 1986, 5–6.

[38] In the section on defense, the new program reads: "The CPSU regards the defense of the socialist homeland, the strengthening of the country's defense, *and the safeguarding of state security* as one of the most important functions of the Soviet state of the whole people" (emphasis added). In the earlier program "safeguarding of state security" had not been mentioned. The next paragraph contains a reference to the importance of "reinforcing the USSR's defensive might and *strengthening its security*." The italicized words did not appear in the 1961 program.

the autumn of 1986 forward, along with calls for "restructuring" of Soviet law enforcement agencies probably alarmed KGB officials even more.

A turning point was reached in KGB-party relations when the policy of glasnost was extended to the KGB in January 1987, and the role of the KGB in the so-called Berkhin affair was exposed by the press. (Berkhin was a journalist who was unlawfully arrested by KGB investigators because he had attempted to expose corruption in the Ukraine.) Chebrikov himself issued a front-page announcement in *Pravda* to the effect that several KGB officials in the Ukraine had been disciplined for violations of the law. He was also compelled to state that the KGB was taking further measures to assure compliance with legal norms on the part of its staff.[39]

The significance of this case cannot easily be exaggerated. The KGB had in the past been allowed to flout legal norms in its work, and KGB interference in investigations by the regular law enforcement organs, though explicitly illegal since the reforms of the 1950s, had been an accepted practice. By publicly exposing such illegalities, the Gorbachev leadership dealt a heavy blow to the KGB's prestige and authority. This move may have been intended as an attack on Chebrikov personally (and perhaps also, as some evidence suggests, on the Ukrainian party leader, Shcherbitskii). But it had distinct ramifications for the KGB as an institution.

Further scandals since that time have impugned the reputation of KGB employees. In late 1987, the Soviet press exposed a case in Odessa where KGB investigators had fabricated bribery charges against an innocent MVD official. One investigator was accused of having appropriated money in an earlier case and beaten witnesses to extract false confessions.[40] Reports of KGB improprieties and criticism of its activities became increasingly frequent in 1988–89. It is no exaggeration to say that some of these revelations touched on the very legitimacy of the KGB.[41]

The KGB also had its operations against domestic dissent sharply curtailed. By the end of 1988 more than three hundred political prisoners had been released from prisons and camps, and arrests for political crimes had all but ceased. Proposed reforms of the legal system raised the specter of permanent, institutionalized restrictions on KGB activities. Calls for a relaxation in the secrecy laws and for stricter criteria in determining what information should be classified as secret posed a further threat, since a principal justification for the security police is the need to protect state and military secrets.[42]

---

[39] See *Pravda*, 8 January 1987.

[40] See *Literaturnaia gazeta*, 2 December 1987; 3 February 1988; and 24 August 1988.

[41] For details, see Amy Knight, "The KGB and Soviet Reform," *Problems of Communism* (September–October 1988), 61–70. The KGB came under especially heavy criticism at the Congress of People's Deputies in May 1989, in a speech by a deputy from Moscow, Iu. P. Vlasov. See the report in *FBIS*, 1 June 1989, 31–34.

[42] See, for example, a piece by S. Pestov in *Argumenty i fakty* 33 (13–19 August 1988); and

Thus, just as Gorbachev offended the interests of the military by permitting harsh public criticism of its officers and questioning the need for military solutions to international problems, he also initiated some policies that appeared unfavorable to the KGB. (In the case of relaxing secrecy rules, the military establishment is equally threatened, since it zealously protects information about its operations.)

The negative impact of Gorbachev's reform program, insofar as it relates to the KGB, has been mitigated by several circumstances. First of all, Gorbachev has been careful not go too far in challenging the vested interests of the KGB. His pressure on the domestic operations of the KGB has been measured: the media have been allowed limited criticism of local KGB officials, but not a witch-hunt. The meetings of the People's Congress and the Supreme Soviet in May and June 1989 witnessed spectacular public criticism of the KGB and renewed demands for public control over its operations. But the relevant committee of the new Supreme Soviet that is charged with oversight for the KGB is staffed (for the time being at least) with trusted officials, and it is not clear that the powers of this committee will be sufficient to restrict effectively KGB (or military) activities.[43] Official rules concerning secrecy have been eased slightly, but the KGB's archives are still off-limits, and much of the official rethinking of policy on secrecy has been entrusted to KGB officials. Gorbachev himself mixes mild criticism of the KGB with emphatic praise, and his treatment of top KGB officials, beginning with Viktor Chebrikov, has been a model of caution.

Furthermore, KGB officials have been able to use glasnost to their own advantage by engaging in public relations on the KGB's behalf. In the spring of 1988, the KGB mounted an unprecedented propaganda campaign, featuring a spate of speeches by and interviews with KGB officials. Although portraying themselves as champions of glasnost and perestroika, they stressed that the USSR is now more vulnerable than ever to the subversive designs of Western intelligence services and warned of the dangers of perestroika going too far.[44] The high point of this campaign was an unprecedented *Pravda* interview with KGB Chairman Chebrikov in September 1988. It gave Chebrikov the oppor-

---

V. A. Rubanov, ''From the Cult of Secrecy to an Information Culture,'' *Kommunist* 13 (September 1988), 24–36. Rubanov, who was scathingly critical of the existing security regulations, was identified as a section head in the KGB's scientific research institute. Since his views run counter to those expressed by other KGB officials he may well have been enlisted by more radical proponents of perestroika to write the article.

[43] The composition of the new Committee for Defense and State Security was revealed in *Izvestiia*, 13 July 1989. It includes a significant number of deputies from the military-industrial sector as well as three KGB officials among its members. For an idea of how the committee views its tasks, see an interview with its chairman, V. L. Lapygin, in *Krasnaia zvezda*, 22 June 1989, 1–2. KGB Chairman Kriuchkov has said that he welcomes the creation of this committee, because it will give the KGB an opportunity to get more public support.

[44] See Knight, ''The KGB and Soviet Reform.''

tunity to convey a positive image of the KGB, while making a case for vigilance and strong security measures.

A month after this interview Chebrikov was transferred to the Secretariat of the party, where he continued to supervise police (and possibly military) affairs as chairman of the newly created Legal Affairs Commission of the Central Committee.[45] His replacement as KGB chairman is V. A. Kriuchkov, a KGB official for over twenty years. Kriuchkov had been a deputy chairman and chief of the First Chief Directorate of the KGB, which is responsible for foreign operations. His background is thus different from that of Chebrikov, who had concentrated more on domestic affairs. Although he may not have been Chebrikov's first choice to take over the chairmanship, the two have worked closely together for several years, so the change should not be too disruptive. Perhaps the most significant aspect of Kriuchkov's appointment is that the KGB has one of its own at the helm and has not had its professionalism challenged by having an outsider brought in to assume the KGB leadership.

Despite Gorbachev's seemingly cautious approach to the KGB, his relationship with the latter is still far from that of the ''golden age'' that characterized party-KGB relations under Brezhnev. While KGB officials acknowledge the need for restructuring within the KGB and have paid tribute to the ''positive changes'' in the Soviet Union, they have continually warned that the West is using Soviet democratization for subversive purposes, and their concept of perestroika seems to be much more limited than that of Gorbachev. As far as Kriuchkov himself is concerned, he has made every effort, in numerous television and newspaper interviews, to portray himself as a reasonable and moderate administrator who eschews the methods of his predecessors and is much more interested in ''legitimate'' security and intelligence operations than in pursuing dissent. But, having served many years directly under Andropov, beginning in Hungary during the 1956 Soviet invasion, Kriuchkov is probably not willing to see the reforms get too far out of hand.

It is thus possible that Gorbachev's reform program could become increasingly intolerable to KGB officials, particularly if ethnic and/or labor unrest seriously threatens domestic political stability. Could this lead the KGB and the military to find common cause in their grievances with the leadership? Before considering this possibility and the future of the KGB-military relationship, let us look at the impact of the other environmental changes on the KGB. What has been the KGB's stance on the issues that began causing tensions between the party and the military in the Brezhnev era and have continued to present themselves with increasing urgency?

[45] Previously a Gorbachev ally, A. I. Lukianov, had been supervising this area. It was not surprising, and not a departure from the usual procedure, that it took a year for Kriuchkov to be appointed to the Politburo. In September 1989, after this chapter was completed, Chebrikov was retired.

The Impact of Other Environmental Changes

Economic Problems

The KGB has had good reason to worry about the USSR's growing economic problems, but budgetary constraints on its own operations have not, until recently at least, been the primary concern. Of course, the growing technological sophistication of intelligence-gathering methods has put strains on the KGB's budget, as has the increase in active measures and other illegal activities by the KGB abroad, which call for more and better manpower. In their public statements, KGB officials have reminded their audiences and readers that Western governments spare nothing in providing their intelligence services with manpower, up-to-date equipment, and other resources. As the chairman of the Latvian KGB, S. V. Zukul, observed in 1988, "they are appropriated substantial sums of money."[46]

Such statements indicate a lobbying effort to keep resources flowing into KGB coffers. But the evidence suggests that the regime has satisfied most KGB requirements. I have already mentioned the high salaries and material rewards enjoyed by KGB employees, and it is known from Western sources that the number of KGB agents engaged in intelligence gathering and other covert actions has expanded steadily since the early 1970s.[47] With regard to the KGB's domestic apparatus, there have been no reports of a cut in personnel since the Khrushchev era, when operations were pared down.[48] As a relatively small agency, the KGB has budgetary requirements that can be no more than a tiny fraction of the military's. Open-source estimates of the total number of KGB employees are in the range of seven hundred thousand, which is small in comparison with the more than five million members of the armed forces.[49]

Nevertheless, there have been public calls for a curtailment of KGB personnel and operations. Boris Eltsin, for example, at the Supreme Soviet hearings

[46] *Sovetskaia Latviia*, 26 October 1988, 3. In an earlier interview USSR Deputy KGB Chairman G. E. Ageev noted pointedly: "According to certain data, the U.S. CIA now employs more than twenty thousand persons, and its budgetary appropriations have reached six billion dollars per annum. In the U.S. intelligence community as a whole an important role is assigned to the National Security Agency, whose annual budget amounts to ten to fifteen billion dollars" (*Trud*, 19 April 1987, 4).

[47] According to Shevchenko, Andropov increased the number of Soviet foreign agents two- to threefold. Shevchenko, *Breaking With Moscow*, 315.

[48] Personnel cuts were discussed by Shelepin, for example, in his speech to the Twenty-first Party Congress. See *Vneocherednoi XXI Sezd KPSS: Stenograficheskii otchet* (Moscow: Gosizdat, 1959), 2:251–252.

[49] See John Barron, *KGB Today: The Hidden Hand* (New York: Readers Digest Press, 1983), 41; Richard F. Staar, *USSR Foreign Policies after Detente*, rev. ed. (Stanford: Hoover Institution Press, 1987), 107 n. 5; and International Institute for Strategic Studies, *The Military Balance, 1988–1989*, 33.

on Kriuchkov's reappointment as KGB chairman, voiced alarm at the growth of the KGB and proposed a drastic reduction in its domestic operations.[50] Others have called for cuts in KGB foreign activities and personnel.[51] Kriuchkov, at his confirmation hearings, claimed that at least one KGB subdepartment for dealing with internal dissent had already been abolished, but he made no reference to personnel or budget cuts. Judging from his strong efforts to demonstrate, in his speech to the Supreme Soviet, how essential the KGB is to the Soviet state, it is doubtful that he will easily give in to further demands to streamline his organization.[52]

Although the KGB probably does not compete directly for resources with the military, its officials have not been indifferent to the debates over the economy and defense spending, which became especially sharp by the early 1980s. In a speech to honor the 110th anniversary of the birth of F. E. Dzerzhinskii, the chief of the first Soviet security police, the Cheka, Chebrikov, who was still KGB chairman at the time, spoke at length on Dzerzhinskii's role in alleviating the economic problems faced by Lenin's regime.[53] Dzerzhinskii was appointed chief of the Supreme Council of the National Economy (VSNKh), the state organization responsible for industry, in 1924, while retaining his police post. Chebrikov implied that the economy was still a legitimate realm of concern for the security police.

Those involved in both domestic and foreign KGB operations may well favor curbing budgetary allocations to the military. High defense spending has drained resources away from the already weak consumer sector as well as from investment programs. KGB officials may especially worry that food shortages and other failures to meet consumer needs create the potential for the kind of political unrest seen in Poland in the early 1980s. Although there was little to indicate that Polish dissent threatened to spill over into the Soviet Union, KGB officials voiced specific concerns about Poland at the time.[54] More recently, KGB worries about economic discontent have doubtless grown as a result of

---

[50] See the report from Moscow Television as published in *FBIS*, 17 July 1989, 47–48.

[51] See, for example, a piece by Mikhail Liubimov in *Moscow News*, no. 9 (5–12 March 1989).

[52] For excerpts from his speech see *FBIS*, 17 July 1989, 51–54. Gorbachev has thus far said nothing about budget cuts for the KGB, although he did agree with a deputy at the Kriuchkov hearings who said that the KGB should not be moving into the best and largest buildings.

[53] *Pravda*, 11 September 1987, 3.

[54] V. V. Fedorchuk, at that time KGB chairman in the Ukraine, noted in 1981: "Today the enemies of peace and socialism are linking their insidious designs with growing political and economic pressure on the socialist community; this can be seen clearly from the example of Poland." Quoted in Roman Solchanyk, "Ukrainian KGB Chief Warns of Ideological Sabotage," *Radio Liberty Research Bulletin*, RL 422/81, 22 October 1981. Also see an article by Chebrikov on the subversion of Soviet youth in *Molodoi kommunist*, no. 4 (1981); and Sidney I. Ploss, *Moscow and the Polish Crisis: An Interpretation of Soviet Policies and Intentions* (Boulder: Westview Press, 1986), 94–95. Ploss concludes from the evidence of KGB concern that its officials favored military intervention, but this claim is debatable. See the discussion of the Polish crisis later in this chapter.

the strikes that broke out in July 1989, which presented the Kremlin leadership with a grave crisis. If for no other reason than the possibility that economic discontent could cause political instability, the KGB has a vested interest in the success of some type of economic reform. Such success is predicated, according to the Gorbachev leadership's present thinking, on reductions in defense spending.

It might be added that the Soviet Union's economic problems have had some beneficial consequences for the KGB. Gross deficiencies in the centrally planned economy have resulted in an upsurge of black-marketeering and white-collar, organized crime. As more and more members of the political elite have been implicated in corruption, there have been calls for the KGB to take a more active role in the investigation of organized crime.[55] Authority over these investigations gives the KGB a potentially powerful political weapon. Second, in seeking to offset domestic economic weaknesses by expanding trade with the West, the regime has had to call on the KGB to prevent corrupt practices in foreign trade and also to protect commercial secrets.[56]

Technological Change

While KGB officials may be among those who seek to curb military spending, they have supported the military's efforts to narrow the technological gap by acquiring militarily significant Western technology. According to a U.S. government study, the KGB has been a key participant in an active program executed by the Military Industrial Commission (VPK) of the Council of Ministers since at least the mid-1970s to gain access to Western products and technological secrets. This report asserts that the KGB conducts its collection operations for the VPK by means of some three hundred foreign agents, who work for Directorate T of the KGB's First Chief Directorate.[57] This, then, is an area where the KGB and the military act in concert, and where they both would advocate increased budgetary resources.

The KGB itself benefits directly from the technology it acquires for the military, particularly in the areas of computers, radar, and telecommunications. The rapid development of technology has indeed had a significant im-

---

[55] See Julia Wishnevsky, ''KGB to Take Over Investigation of Organized Crime,'' *Radio Liberty Report on the USSR* 1, 27 (7 July 1989). Kriuchkov himself has advocated more active KGB involvement in this area. See a letter by him in *Nedelia*, no. 22 (29 May–4 June 1989), 10.

[56] Kriuchkov made this point at his confirmation hearings before the Supreme Soviet: ''The fact is that thousands and thousands of our enterprises have embarked upon direct trade and economic ties with other countries. But we are still very bad businessmen. Unless we guard commercial secrecy, the losses for our state could run into thousands of millions.'' *FBIS*, 17 July 1989, p. 52.

[57] *Soviet Acquisition of Militarily Significant Western Technology: An Update*, September 1985.

pact on the KGB's operations in recent years. To the extent that the KGB has been able to keep pace with technological change, this trend has been highly beneficial to its operations. For an agency whose main tasks involve gathering and processing information, the computer age has come as a great boon. While the use of computers by the KGB specifically is not mentioned by the Soviet press, general discussions of cybernetics in the field of law enforcement do appear from time to time.[58] It can be inferred from these discussions that KGB employees have been availing themselves of computers for several years. As one Western study noted, "It is not hard to imagine applications that would be within their interests and capabilities. To mention a few: mainframes for large centralized databases, micro-electronic-based surveillance systems and personal computer use by KGB case officers."[59] The KGB also uses satellite communications for worldwide intelligence collection.[60] Although some satellite intelligence may be strictly for military purposes and therefore under the purview of the GRU, much of it is probably used by the KGB.

Of course, the telecommunications and computer revolution has also had serious drawbacks for the KGB, since its job (prior to the era of glasnost at least) has been to prevent challenges to the regime's control of information and to filter communications from the West. The use of personal computers and word processors—although by no means widespread as of yet—offers Soviet citizens a means of communicating and transmitting information that is beyond KGB control.[61] The same might be said of audio and videocassettes, which are steadily making their way into the USSR. Speaking as KGB chairman at the Twenty-seventh Congress, Chebrikov referred to videotechnology as a problem for the KGB: "While this technology is by itself a progressive phenomenon, it is sometimes used for the propagation of alien ideas, of the cult of greed, violence, and amorality."[62] Later, in September 1987, Chebri-

[58] See, for example, G. A. Tumanov and A. P. Gerasimov, "Metodologicheskie vozmozhnosti kibernetiki v gosudarstvenno-pravovoi sfere," *Sovetskoe gosudarstvo i pravo* 9 (1982), 29–37.

[59] S. E. Goodman and W. K. McHenry, "Computing in the USSR: Recent Progress and Policies," *Soviet Economy* 2 (1986), 339–340.

[60] Robert W. Campbell, "Satellite Communications in the USSR," *Soviet Economy* 1, 4 (October–December 1985), 330.

[61] Although the Soviets have ambitious plans for computerization of Soviet society, they still lag far behind the West. See, for example, Bren West, "Soviet Computing Comes Under Review," *Radio Liberty Research Bulletin*, RL 385/88, 23 August 1988. Also see Walter R. Roberts and Harold E. Engle, "The Global Information Revolution and the Communist World," *The Washington Quarterly* 9, 2 (Spring 1986), 141–156; and Loren R. Graham, "Science and Computers in Soviet Society," in *The Soviet Union in the 1980's*, ed. Eric Hoffmann (New York: Academy of Political Science, 1984), 124–134.

[62] See *Pravda*, 1 March 1986, 5–6. On the spread of video networks in the Soviet Union, see *Soviet Analyst* 16, 7 (8 April 1987), 6–7; and Viktor Yasmann, "How Many Video Cassette Recorders Are There in the USSR?," *Radio Liberty Research Bulletin*, RL 211/99, 17 May 1988. According to Yasmann, Soviet citizens owned between 500,000 and 950,000 VCRs in 1988.

kov observed that "imperialism's special services are trying to find new loop-holes through which to penetrate our society and are exerting targeted, differ-entiated influence on various population groups in the USSR."[63] Thus, the global information revolution presents both opportunities and formidable chal-lenges to the KGB.

One can only speculate about the effect of these changes on the KGB itself, but they must be considerable. The expanding scale and scope of Soviet for-eign-intelligence and technology-transfer operations have brought heightened requirements for new technologies and new skills, which the KGB has had to meet. It is plausible that modernization of the KGB's foreign-intelligence op-erations will shift the balance of influence inside the KGB as a whole, as re-sources flow toward foreign intelligence at the expense of the domestic side of the house, and as a new generation of foreign-intelligence professionals rises to high rank. Such a scenario would fit in with Kriuchkov's efforts to down-play the KGB's role in combatting internal dissent while stressing the impor-tance of its intelligence-gathering functions. But Kriuchkov and his colleagues will doubtless not lose sight of the continuing possibilities for applying tech-nological innovation to the KGB's domestic tasks as well.

Societal Disruptions

In contrast with technological challenges, the growing social and cultural problems that have beset the Soviet Union over the past decade have probably had a more direct impact on the KGB than on the Soviet military. The de-mands placed on the KGB by social changes have strongly affected its role as an institution and its relationship with the party.

To be sure, the KGB, as an isolated, elite organization, is not closely linked to the civilian population in the way that the military is. As Jones points out, the military draws on all elements of society for its manpower, and therefore the characteristics of its conscripts mirror those of society as a whole. Changes in the ethnic balance, educational levels, and cultural values of Soviet society are all reflected in the military's manpower, as are such problems as alcohol-ism, drug abuse, political disaffection, and declining morale. The KGB, by contrast, chooses its recruits selectively, seeking out well-educated, politically reliable young men, often from the Komsomol. The fact that the KGB can offer recruits high salaries and numerous other perquisites that are not avail-able to those entering the armed forces helps the KGB to filter out undesirable applicants and to create a more homogeneous group of cadres. As far as ethnic questions are concerned, the KGB is dominated by Russians and other Slavs.

---

[63] *Pravda*, 11 September 1987, 3.

Non-Russian natives are sometimes appointed to KGB posts in the republics (for language and public relations reasons), yet there is little evidence that the KGB makes an effort in its hiring practices to reflect the changing ethnic composition of the USSR.[64] Equal opportunity for ethnic groups probably conflicts with the KGB's goals of effectiveness, just as it does in the Soviet armed forces.

While the KGB's own personnel may be relatively invulnerable to social problems, the tasks they perform are directly affected. Alcohol and drug abuse, rejection of official ideology, decline in worker discipline, growth in crime and ethnic tensions all pose a potential threat to the USSR's internal security and therefore are a concern for the KGB. KGB officials have stressed in their public statements and writings that these social problems make their job more difficult because of their political implications. The standard KGB line has long been that social and ethnic problems are the direct result of the machinations of evil foreign organizations aimed at subverting the USSR. Thus Chebrikov wrote in the June 1981 edition of *Molodoi kommunist*, a Komsomol journal: "Extolling the 'drug culture,' for example, the radio saboteurs are throwing out to morally unstable young people the appeal: 'tune in, turn on, drop out.' The purpose, of course, is clear—turning young people aside from the path of an active, conscious life."[65]

Similarly, the KGB has often blamed ethnic unrest on foreign efforts to arouse unhealthy nationalist sentiments by means of radio broadcasts and subversive publications. At a meeting of the Armenian KGB in November 1988, the republic's KGB chairman, V. G. Badamiants, spoke of the "hostile plans and intentions of the imperialist states' special services, anti-Soviet organizations abroad, and ideological subversion centers, which are seeking to use the complex processes occurring in the republic in their own interests."[66] The KGB chairman in Kirghizia was more explicit, citing examples of how foreign agents from the West incited ethnic disturbances in his country.[67] Kriuchkov himself has been somewhat hesitant in blaming ethnic problems directly on Western subversion. When asked at his confirmation hearings about the causes of ethnic strife, he said only that "what is happening in our country is of interest and very great interest to the special services of Western countries."[68]

Unrest in the Caucasian and Baltic republics, as well as in Uzbekistan and elsewhere, which reached alarming and often violent proportions in 1988–89,

---

[64] See Knight, *The KGB: Police and Politics*, chap. 5.

[65] Chebrikov in *Molodoi kommunist*, 38–39.

[66] *Kommunist*, 18 November 1988, 4.

[67] *Sovetik Kyrgyzstan*, 30 December 1988, 2–3, as cited in *JPRS: Soviet Union Political Report*, 19 May 1989, 79.

[68] *FBIS*, 17 July 1985, 54.

has posed especially serious problems for the KGB and other law enforcement organs. KGB officials have frequently claimed that, in addition to foreign subversion, the unrest can be attributed to extremist elements among the advocates of perestroika, and they have stressed the dangers of perestroika being carried too far. At the Nineteenth Party Conference in June 1988, the KGB's spokesman called for stronger measures against "arbitrary interpretations of socialist pluralism."[69]

While ordinary crime is primarily the responsibility of the MVD and the Procuracy, the KGB has good reason to worry about any increase in the crime rate, since it has a potentially destabilizing effect on society. In addition, the KGB itself is legally empowered to investigate cases of large-scale economic crime, currency speculation, and certain other offenses. So it has been taking an active role in the anticorruption campaign conducted with varying degrees of intensity since the early 1980s. As the discussion below suggests, the KGB's involvement in fighting corruption has resulted in a significant expansion of its influence upon Kremlin politics.

Another area where social problems have modified and expanded the KGB's mission is that of political indoctrination. As Ellen Jones points out, the apparent decline in patriotism and in readiness to serve in the armed forces has been of considerable concern to the military, causing it to put increased pressure on civilian socialization agencies to promote "military-patriotic" values. While political indoctrination and propaganda have traditionally been considered a task of the party and the mass media, their efforts have not been deemed particularly successful in recent years, and Soviet authorities have sought to devise new approaches to the problem.[70]

One solution has been to enlist the KGB to help by conveying the regime's message in speeches and reports on political vigilance and ideological questions. KGB officials at all levels have been contributing more to the political indoctrination process in recent years. According to Chebrikov: "KGB members actively participate in work conducted by party organs to raise the political vigilance of Soviet people, systematically deliver lectures at enterprises and institutions, hold talks in collectives, and make extensive use of the potential of the press, radio, and television for this purpose."[71] The specific goal of the KGB is to raise the awareness of Soviet citizenry of the dangers of subversive ideas spread by "bourgeois propagandists," but its political indoc-

---

[69] See Knight, "The KGB and Soviet Reform," 64. KGB troops have been called in, along with MVD Internal Troops, to break up riots and demonstrations.

[70] See Stephen White, "Propagating Communist Values in the USSR," *Problems of Communism* (November–December 1985), 1–17.

[71] V. M. Chebrikov, "Sverias s Leninym, rukovodstvuias trebovaniem partii," *Kommunist* 9 (June 1985), 51–52.

trination efforts benefit the party and the military as well. Thus, this is an area where the KGB, the military, and the party act in concert toward a common aim.

International Developments and Foreign Involvement

While the KGB attempts to promote feelings of patriotism among the Soviet population, it has not necessarily favored the growth of military involvement abroad from the late 1970s onward. I have already mentioned KGB concerns about strains on the economy caused by an expansion of the military's material demands. There is another reason why the KGB prefers nonmilitary solutions to foreign policy problems. In situations where there are opportunities to exploit social and political factors to the benefit of the Soviet Union, nonmilitary approaches offer the KGB a greater role in global affairs. It is difficult for the KGB to influence public opinion through propaganda and disinformation when the Soviet Union has the image of an aggressor. The Soviet invasion of Afghanistan, for example, created obstacles for the KGB in its efforts to halt NATO's INF deployment by means of arousing antinuclear sentiments among West Europeans because these efforts entailed convincing people of the benevolent intentions of the USSR. Andropov's subsequent remarks indicated that he had not favored the Soviet decision to invade Afghanistan and was most unhappy about the outcome.[72]

The KGB may have taken a similar stance, with greater success, on the Polish crisis of 1980–1981. While its officials undoubtedly had concerns about a possible spillover of political unrest into the USSR, military intervention would have done serious damage to the USSR's international image at the height of the KGB's campaign against INF. Furthermore, a Soviet invasion of Poland could have been expected to enhance the influence of the Soviet military over foreign policy, a trend that the KGB does not welcome. Andropov himself did not comment publicly on the Polish situation, but as an expert on Eastern Europe, the chief of the agency responsible for providing information on Poland, and a full member of the Politburo, he no doubt had a role in the decision to refrain from military intervention in Poland, a decision that may not have been favored by all elements of the military.[73]

---

[72] Andropov was the only Politburo member to express pessimism over the world situation after the invasion. See his speech for the RSFSR Supreme Soviet elections, reprinted in *Pravda*, 12 February 1980.

[73] On the efforts of the Soviet high command to push for military intervention, see Richard D. Anderson Jr., "Soviet Decision-making and Poland," *Problems of Communism* (March–April 1982), 22–36. This is not to say that no elements of the KGB leadership favored military intervention in Poland. As mentioned above, Fedorchuk may have been concerned about Poland because of the possibility of unrest in the Ukraine. Tsvigun too expressed strong disquiet about

It might be added that Andropov was among the most outspoken critics of open-ended Soviet military and economic assistance to Third World states, even before he became head of the party. According to Francis Fukuyama, Andropov was the first senior political leader to renew the idea stressed earlier by both Lenin and Khrushchev that the Soviet Union can better exert its influence over the world revolutionary movement by means of its example as a socialist society than through direct economic assistance.[74] Presumably, Andropov worried about the deleterious effects of such involvement on East-West relations, as well as about the economic burden.

One cannot assume from these cases, however, that the KGB and the military are always at odds on questions of foreign policy and military intervention. There is considerable evidence, for example, that the KGB was strongly behind those who favored the 1968 invasion of Czechoslovakia.[75] Soviet foreign policy over the past two decades has successfully integrated military and political strategies, so that the "battle of ideas" has often taken place simultaneously with the use of military means. Increasingly since the early 1970s, KGB covert actions and active measures (disinformation, forgeries, propaganda campaigns) have been employed alongside the provision of military advisers and supplies in support of Soviet objectives in the Third World. Also, of course, the KGB's intelligence functions have served as an essential underpinning to Soviet force projection abroad.[76] But the lessons of Afghanistan and the clear risks of using military force in a nuclear age have created a situation where the Kremlin is increasingly likely to employ nonmilitary means to achieve its objectives, which points to an even greater role for the KGB in foreign policy.

On the question of arms control and East-West relations, the KGB's responses have been mixed. Andropov presented himself as an advocate of detente during the 1970s. In a speech delivered in late 1973 he noted enthusiastically: "Never before has the foreign policy of the Soviet Union been so effective within so short a time. . . . The entire foreign policy of our party has led to the fact that the international situation is now being shaped to a great extent under the influence of the peace initiative of the Soviet Union."[77] With

---

Poland, blaming disturbances there on "a slanderous propaganda campaign recently launched against Poland in order to destabilize the country and its position in the international arena. Opponents of socialism even go so far as to directly interfere in Poland's internal affairs." See S. K. Tsvigun, "O proiskakh imperialisticheskikh razvedok," *Kommunist* 14 (September 1981), 88.

[74] Francis Fukuyama, "Gorbachev and the Third World," *Foreign Affairs* (Spring 1986), 719.

[75] See Jiri Valenta, *Soviet Intervention in Czechoslovakia, 1968: Anatomy of a Decision* (Baltimore: Johns Hopkins University Press, 1979), 23, 107.

[76] The KGB's role in providing intelligence during crises like the Yom Kippur War has been highly important. See Jacques Derogy and Hesi Carmel, *The Untold History of Israel* (New York: Grove Press, 1979), 294–297.

[77] From an Estonian Radio Broadcast on 27 December 1973, translated in *FBIS*, vol. 3, 2 January 1974, R6. It should be noted that Andropov's views were not shared by all of his col-

his strong expertise in foreign policy, Andropov was able to see the value of detente. At the same time he never failed to remind his audiences that the West was engaged in a dangerous game of "ideological sabotage" against the Soviet Union.

Chebrikov did not appear as favorably disposed toward efforts to improve relations with the West. Having worked mainly in the domestic sphere before becoming head of the KGB, he had a more skeptical attitude. While he initially showed some enthusiasm for the peace process, he grew increasingly negative in 1986–87. He was virulent in his criticism of the United States in his speech to the Twenty-seventh Party Congress in early 1986.[78] In his September 1987 Dzerzhinskii speech, he went out of his way to stress the evil motives of the West. He cited Dzerzhinskii's opposition to the 1918 Brest-Litovsk peace treaty, and later in the speech he remarked how relevant Dzerzhinskii's concerns were to the present day. This may be a hint that Chebrikov opposed the missile treaty about to be signed in December by Gorbachev and Ronald Reagan in Washington. The KGB's handling of Nicolas Daniloff, the American journalist arrested for spying in 1986, and its treatment of the West German pilot, Mathias Rust, who landed his plane in Red Square in May 1987, further indicated its disinclination to be flexible in the interests of smoother East-West relations at the time.[79]

Chebrikov may have supported the arms control process as a means of curtailing military spending, but he was uneasy about the thorny problem of verification of arms control agreements. In late 1984 he accused the Americans of placing too much emphasis on verification as a means of dragging out negotiations.[80] Since the KGB is responsible for protecting all military secrets, Chebrikov was concerned about allowing Western representatives access to Soviet defense installations. Also, he probably viewed Gorbachev's arms-control initiatives as part of his drive to democratize and liberalize Soviet society, to be suspect for that reason.

Judging from his remarks thus far, the new KGB chairman, Kriuchkov, is more pragmatic than Chebrikov in his approach to the West. Having served as head of the KGB's First Chief Directorate since the mid-1970s, he has strong expertise in foreign affairs. In a speech delivered at a July 1988 Ministry of Foreign Affairs Conference, shortly before his promotion to KGB chairman

---

leagues. First Deputy Chairman Tsvigun, who apparently oversaw the KGB's domestic operations, had nothing positive to say about detente. In 1977 he even observed that detente was providing the imperialists with new opportunities for subversion against the USSR.

[78] *Pravda*, 1 March 1986.

[79] Both these cases were under the investigatory purview of the KGB. There was some indication in the Rust case that certain elements within the Kremlin leadership would have preferred treat him more leniently.

[80] See a speech delivered in honor of the fortieth anniversary of the "liberation" of Estoni reprinted in *Sovetskaia Estoniia*, 23 September 1984.

Kriuchkov endorsed Gorbachev's "new thinking" in foreign policy and welcomed the progress achieved in disarmament.[81] He noted that a change in the West's traditional view of the Soviet Union as a totalitarian enemy has had a positive influence on external politics. Calling for a reassessment of Soviet views of the West by discarding old stereotypes, he stressed the importance of cultivating, by means of propaganda, those segments of the Western public that favor disarmament.

Although he advocated a more flexible approach toward the West in his speech, it would be a mistake to place Kriuchkov firmly in the reformist camp. He reverted back to the standard KGB line when he discussed the provocative activities of Western intelligence services, which he said were devoted to subverting the process of perestroika in the Soviet Union. In speaking of disarmament, he pointed out that "we must not forget the efforts of NATO countries to compensate for the liquidation of short- and medium-range missiles and the significant reductions in strategic missiles. We must call world attention to these plans and not allow the West to evade us." Although Kriuchkov's tone was much less alarmist than that of his predecessor, he did stress that the West was continuing its subversive efforts and urged Soviet citizens and officials, especially those going abroad, to be more vigilant.

Kriuchkov noted the need for improvement in the KGB's foreign operations and mentioned a "fundamental restructuring" in the KGB's foreign services, but he would have been treading on thin ice if he went too far in criticizing past Soviet policy, since he has been a leading member of the foreign policy establishment for a decade and a half. The main thrust of Kriuchkov's speech was that perestroika and the changing international environment call for a greater foreign involvement on the part of the KGB, as well as a different approach. He appears to be an "Andropovite" in the sense that he favors diplomatic over military solutions and supports Gorbachev's arms-control efforts—a stance that may not go down well with Gorbachev's generals—but the substance of his message has not radically departed from the standard KGB line.

The KGB-Military-Party Triad: Future Prospects

The broad trends of the last generation have affected the military and the KGB in different ways and have evoked different responses. In the political sphere, party-KGB and party-military relations actually began by moving in opposite directions, as Brezhnev started his reign with a successful bid to reassert the

---

[81] The speech was reprinted in *Mezhdunarodnaia zhizn* 10 (October 1988), 34–37. Kriuchkov was part of the team that accompanied Gorbachev on his trip to the United States in December 1987, so presumably he was already an important actor in Gorbachev's foreign-policy process.

party's supremacy over the KGB and to remove it once again from leadership politics, whereas in party-military relations Brezhnev was sufficiently confident of the military's neutral professionalism that he gave its leaders an expanded voice in debates over security policy. In both cases, however, the net result was the same: sympathizing with the values and sharing the objectives of both coercive elites, the party leadership systematically raised their prestige and privileges. For much of the Brezhnev era, both the KGB and the military enjoyed essentially the same golden age.

Similarly, for both institutions the golden age drew to an end toward the end of the 1970s, and in both cases the main underlying reason was the deterioration of the regime's performance and Brezhnev's personal decline. But here the military and KGB cases diverge, because the tensions that arose in the party's relations with its two coercive elites at the end of the 1970s took two different forms. The military leadership, alarmed by the growing military strength of the West and angered by what it perceived to be the attempts of the Brezhnev administration to cut back its resource share, lobbied actively to defend its interests. But its objectives remained confined to policy issues.

In contrast, the KGB's behavior (or at least that of its leadership) appears to have been driven by an explicitly political perception and an explicitly political ambition—namely, that the party apparatus had failed in its duties, and that the man required to implement the needed overhaul was Andropov. In short, while the military leadership remained largely apolitical, the KGB leadership returned overtly to politics, taking a key role in the series of succession crises that ensued after Brezhnev's death and actively exerting its influence on Gorbachev's reform policies.

Gorbachev's reforms have unleashed an extraordinary wave of popular resentment against all three of the traditionally dominant institutions of the country—the party apparatus, the military-industrial system, and the KGB. As seen throughout this book, the military is growing resentful in return, and this chapter has shown that the same is increasingly true of the KGB. Gorbachev has no doubt become acutely aware of the potential for disaffection on the part of the coercive elites, and he seems to be adjusting his strategy accordingly. Rather than pursue a policy of confrontation, he has followed a strategy that mixes pressure with co-optation and conciliation, in an attempt to reshape the missions of the coercive elites and to promote those who are willing to cooperate with him, while sidelining those who resist. He appears to have a long-range goal of depoliticizing party-KGB relations and achieving what previous leaders have failed to do, namely, to develop something approximating a system of "objective control." But the KGB's functions and resources are inherently more political than those of the military, and whether they can be brought under nonpartisan control, either by the party or by the Supreme Soviet, depends a great deal on how indispensable those functions turn out to be in coming years.

Thus far the KGB has fared better than the military in terms of political authority under the Gorbachev leadership. While the KGB no longer has unrestrained coercive powers, it still has other highly effective means of exerting its influence. First, the KGB is the main source of information on corruption and other scandals involving party and state officials. This information can serve as a powerful political weapon, as the anticorruption campaign has demonstrated. Second, insofar as the KGB has moved from coercion to manipulation, and from punishment to prevention in dealing with real or perceived dissent, it has gained a better public image. To be sure, the KGB is precluded by the nature of its functions from gaining the kind of moral authority that the Soviet armed forces have, but, despite the recent press criticism, it has been successful in at least diluting the unsavory reputation of its predecessors.

Kriuchkov's seat on the Politburo gives the KGB a spokesman there, which the military does not have. Also, while the KGB has been subjected to turnover of leading personnel, this has not been of the sweeping nature of the turnover that the military has undergone. (Ten KGB republic chairmen have been replaced in Gorbachev's first fours years in power, along with First Deputy Chairman Tsinev and the chiefs of the Moscow and Leningrad KGB apparatuses.)[82] From what evidence there is on newly appointed KGB officials, most are career security policemen, like Kriuchkov, rather than party men, which implies that Gorbachev is not attempting to undermine the KGB's institutional cohesiveness and professionalism.[83]

The extent to which the Soviet regime still relies on a strong political police should not be underestimated. The leadership is not in a position to tolerate open criticism of the political system unless it is prepared to relinquish the party's monopoly of power. Indeed, it is possible that the KGB's services will be needed more than ever as glasnost gains a momentum of its own and gives rise to dangerous expressions of political discontent.

In evaluating KGB influence in terms of policy outcomes, the picture is mixed. Gorbachev's efforts to restrict military spending and raise economic efficiency may be welcomed by the political police. On the foreign side, the Kremlin continues to show a preference for diplomacy and "active measures" rather than military interventionism to further Soviet objectives abroad, and Gorbachev's foreign policy has revealed significantly more pragmatism and flexibility than that of earlier leaders. His forward-looking national security

[82] KGB chairmen have been replaced in all the non-Russian republics except Belorussia, Estonia, Latvia, and Tadzhikistan. A similar rate of turnover occurred after 1966, when Brezhnev was building up patronage in the KGB. Unlike the Brezhnev case, however, there are no evident career connections between the new KGB appointees and Gorbachev or, for that matter, Kriuchkov.

[83] See Knight, "The KGB and Soviet Reform"; and Amy Knight, "Personnel Changes in KGB as Public Relations Campaign Continues," *Radio Liberty Report on the Soviet Union* 1, 10 (10 March 1989), 7–9.

team places strong emphasis on public relations and dynamic approaches to international problems. With their reputation for expertise and political sophistication, KGB foreign intelligence cadres should be valuable assets for implementing Soviet foreign policy. The fact that the current KGB chairman has established his credentials as a foreign-policy expert and occupies a place on the newly created International Affairs Commission of the Central Committee suggests that the KGB will have a strong voice in this area, possibly infringing on the military's traditional domain.

On the negative side, Gorbachev's internal policies have subjected the KGB to unprecedented criticism, undercut its monopoly of information, and constrained the KGB in combatting dissent. The proposed reforms in the legal code and the Law on State Security, due to appear in 1990, could institutionalize these constraints and significantly reduce the KGB's scope for arbitrariness. The much-discussed liberalization of secrecy regulations could force the KGB (and the military) to reveal much more about its operations and could throw into question one of the KGB's main functions—to protect state and military secrets. If democratization were carried to its logical extremes, it could pose a significant challenge to the KGB's legitimacy as a domestic institution.

A crucial variable for Gorbachev in his efforts to reform the Soviet system while at the same time keeping his coercive elites in line is the relationship between the KGB and the military and how this relationship is likely to evolve if Gorbachev continues to dominate the political scene. Despite the factors that point to a competitive and antagonistic relationship between the KGB and the military, which in some ways serves the party leadership well, there is no evidence of overt conflict between military and KGB leaders during the period of political upheaval that has beset the Kremlin since Brezhnev's death, and their common grievances with the reform-minded leadership could draw them together. If Khrushchev's ouster is taken as a precedent, the military and the KGB need not be on the best of terms to form a temporary alliance for the purpose of opposing the policies of a leader that they view with disfavor.[84]

Whatever Gorbachev's popular appeal, the Soviet Union is still a one-party, authoritarian state that relies on force as its ultimate bulwark. Although democracy may be gradually developing, the institutions of coercion rather than the public continue to play the key role in supporting or opposing leaders. The party depends on the KGB to help ensure the military's loyalty and has created specific institutional arrangements that counterpose the KGB to the armed forces. As a general rule, these arrangements work. But the KGB shares with

[84] These two institutions were probably not congenial toward the end of the Khrushchev era. The KGB's exposure of the Penkovskii affair had left scars within the armed forces. Further resentment toward the security police was probably aroused by Khrushchev's appointment in 1962 of A. A. Epishev, a former deputy chief of the security police, as head of the MPA and USSR KGB Deputy Chairman Petr Ivashutin to head the GRU.

the military a vested interest in promoting a hard line against spontaneous political expression and stressing the security threat from the West—a central justification for both a strong military and a strong security police in the Soviet Union. Thus a leader who goes too far in accommodating the West and who questions the need for strict internal political controls could give the police and the military a common cause. Although they would probably not attempt to oust Gorbachev on their own, they could act together with conservatives in the party in pressuring him to stem the tide of reform.

Four

Resource Stringency and Civil-Military Resource Allocation

ROBERT CAMPBELL

THE TASK of this chapter is to consider how the long-term decline of economic growth and changing views on national security have influenced each other and affected the civil-military competition for resources and the nature of civil-military relations. As in the other chapters of this book, the period examined here runs from the mid-1960s to the present.

The main background circumstances are by now familiar: growth in GNP declined from a little over 5 percent per year in the 1960s to about 2 percent per year by the second half of the 1970s. But the causes of this slowdown and the interplay of various forces in it are not yet fully understood. Nor is there any general agreement on the impact of the economic slowdown on military spending or the impact of military expenditures on growth. The timing of defense-civilian interactions in resource allocation in the 1970s remains especially puzzling.

In view of these unresolved questions, the issue of the military's influence over economic allocations has been especially controversial for Western analysts. Some believe that the military establishment had so much power, and traditional national security goals had so strong a hold on the thinking of the leaders, that economic slowdown could not have had any significant impact on the allocation of resources to defense. Others maintain that increasing economic stringency must inevitably have constrained growth in the resources flowing to military uses.

The same argument continues today, but with the added element of the new economic strategy introduced under Gorbachev. This strategy heightens the conflict between military expenditure and other uses to which the economy's output could be allocated, namely, consumption and investment. Gorbachev's speeches tell us that he has faced up to the disastrous economic conditions passed on by the previous leadership, and that he understands that the USSR must focus on restoring the vitality of the economy and cannot afford to continue an arms competition with the United States. But many observers believe that for all of Gorbachev's emphasis on restructuring the economy, solving the agricultural problem, and providing for the social needs of the population, the leadership remains committed to maintaining its position as a military superpower vis-à-vis the West and is prepared to spend whatever it needs to do so. The latest Soviet statements claim that they began cutting defense spending in 1985, but U.S. intelligence sources do not have convincing evidence of that. Until there is firmer information about how resources are actually being allocated, one cannot be sure of what Gorbachev really intends, or whether his intentions are being carried out.

A second background circumstance is the growing technological interdependence between civilian and military production, which leads in turn to increased interdependence both within the military-industrial sector and between military and civilian production. In the West today, as Thane Gustafson observes in chapter 6 of this volume, much of the recent progress in military technology has come from innovations first developed for civilian uses. The same is true for the Soviet economy. A senior scientist asserts, for example, that, "Contrary to a widely held view, the military sphere borrows a great deal more from the civilian sphere than vice versa."[1] This issue is discussed in detail in Julian Cooper's chapter in this volume, but it is important to observe here that continuing to favor military claims on resources for research and development (R&D) over civilian needs will in the long run damage military capabilities.

This chapter will first try to unravel what happened over roughly the two decades between 1965 and 1985 and to discern what Gorbachev's options and intentions are today. There is not much disagreement among Western observers over the first decade: from the mid-1960s to the mid-1970s, military spending grew rapidly, expanding its share of a national product that was still increasing vigorously. The problems arise in interpreting the period since 1975. The general line of argument to be developed in what follows can be summarized in a few broad conclusions:

1. The evidence suggests that in terms of opportunity cost to the civilian economy, resource allocation to the military sector became increasingly burdensome during the Tenth and Eleventh Five-Year Plan (FYP) periods (1976–1980 and 1981–1985, respectively). It was an important contributor to the slowdown in economic growth, primarily through its deleterious impact on the civilian machinery industry and on investment.

2. In the argument over whether there was a policy decision in the mid-1970s (roughly at the time the Tenth FYP was put together) to slow procurement and to ease the burden defense posed for other objectives, my conclusion is that the leaders sensed the burden and made an effort to do something about it, but that this effort was not big enough to alter allocations. The effort became more serious in the Eleventh FYP than it had been in the Tenth.[2]

How do I reconcile this picture with the CIA's well-known report of a slow-

[1] L. P. Feoktistov, "Gonka vooruzhenii, voina i nauchno-tekhnicheskii progress nesovmestimy," *Kommunist*, no. 15 (1986), 104.

[2] U.S. Congress, Joint Economic Committee, *Allocation of Resources in the Soviet Union and China—1984* (Washington, D.C.: GPO, 1984), 23.

down in the amount of hardware procured beginning in 1976? I believe that the slowdown in procurement was caused mainly by technical challenges that stymied productivity growth in defense production, not by a cut in the growth of resources allocated. Indeed, the inertia of the informal priority system continued to let a growing volume of resources flow to military production. The latter was facilitated by a statistical system that masked what was really happening.

3. Gorbachev is taking a much harder run at the problem. He is determined to try to reallocate resources toward civilian needs. Moreover, he is focusing on the correct leverage points in trying to break down the wall that separates weapons production from the rest of the economy, particularly from the civilian part of the machinery sector, and in trying to redirect investment to civilian machinery production. One of the short-run compensations he is offering the military while the civilian basis of the economy is being renovated is more R&D. But Gorbachev's effort to turn the attention of the defense-industrial sector to civilian tasks now comes up against the familiar informal priority system favoring the military. The flow of actual resources—particularly machinery—to the military in the Twelfth FYP (1986–1990) seems not to have been seriously restricted, but a significant reallocation will probably be a major issue in formulating the Thirteenth FYP (1991–1995).

These are my arguments in broad outline. In what follows I will show the evidence for them.

Resource Allocation Before Gorbachev

A brief narrative of what happened in the allocation of resources between military and other uses over the last couple of decades will provide crucial background for analysis of the degree and substance of civil-military conflict and of shifts in relative influence.

The economist's instinct is to turn to the statistical record to trace the shifts in resource-allocation policy. That turns out to be difficult inasmuch as the statistics on economic aggregates are unreliable and ill-suited to this purpose. But these data must be analyzed as well as possible to see what interpretations they can support. Firmer conclusions may emerge, first, if the question is considered not only at the level of the major end-use aggregates (military expenditure versus investment and consumption), but also in terms of particular components of military expenditure (hardware, R&D resources, and manpower). Second, money quantities are frequently misleading; a more accurate picture may be obtained by focusing on the flow of physical and human resources.

Macro Stringency

Growth has decelerated steadily, according to both Western estimates of gross national product (GNP) and the official Soviet series on net material product (NMP).[3] In 1966–1970, GNP grew at 5.3 percent per year, in the Ninth FYP (1971–1975) at 3.8, but dropped to 2.7 in the Tenth FYP (1976–1980), with an especially notable fall-off in 1978–1980. GNP growth continued to be low during the Eleventh FYP (1980–1985) at 2.4 percent per year, and also during 1986–1988 at 2.3 percent.[4] Official data for growth of NMP show a drop from 5.7 percent per year in the Ninth FYP to 4.4 percent per year in the Tenth, and 3.6 percent in the Eleventh.

MILITARY EXPENDITURES

Such a deceleration must inevitably have raised the issue of the opportunity cost of military claims in terms of other objectives sacrificed. Did the leaders choose to reevaluate their priorities and put part of the burden of slowing growth on the military? The CIA reports that beginning in the mid-1970s the growth of resources allocated to the military establishment did slow. Resource allocation had grown at about 4 percent per year between 1965 and 1975, but according to the CIA, growth "since 1976 has been slower . . . about 2 percent per year. . . . Procurement of military hardware . . . was almost flat in 1976–81."[5] Later estimates showed this pattern continuing through the mid–1980s. "The CIA believes that defense procurement was essentially flat during [the 1982–1984] period."[6] Moreover, "since 1976, the main driver of defense spending has been the rapid growth of RDT&E [research, development, testing, and evaluation]."[7] In its latest estimates, the CIA shows mili-

---

[3] Western analysts make their own independent estimates of Soviet GNP, since the Soviet NMP series is a less than comprehensive measure of economic activity and, moreover, is biased upward.

[4] Average GNP growth from 1986–1988 in the USSR was 2.3 percent. See U.S. Congress, Joint Economic Committee, *The Soviet Economy in 1988: Gorbachev Changes Course*, 14 April 1989, 41, table B–4.

[5] U.S. Congress, Joint Economic Committee, *Allocation of Resources*, 23. In the CIA's concept, "resources allocated to the military" are measured where the armed forces interface with the rest of the economy and are aggregated using prices of a given year. This leaves open a complicated set of issues as to whether cost overruns and production problems could make allocations of resources to defense production grow at a rate different from procurement.

[6] "The Soviet Economy under a New Leader," 19 March 1986, paper prepared jointly by the Central Intelligence Agency and the Defense Intelligence Agency for submission to the Subcommittee on Economic Resources, Competitiveness, and Security Economics of the Joint Economic Committee, Congress of the United States, 8.

[7] U.S. Congress, Joint Economic Committee, *Allocation of Resources*, 55.

tary expenditure in the mid-1980s growing once again, led by hardware procurement, which has been increasing at about 3 percent per year.[8]

How are these findings to be explained? One possibility is that beginning in the mid-1970s the leaders deliberately decided to damp the growth of military spending to permit more attention to other end uses. To check that idea, one should consider how the main competing uses fared. If there was a slowdown in military spending, are there indications that either consumption or investment benefited?

INVESTMENT AND CONSUMPTION IN THE TENTH FYP

Unfortunately, the CIA's estimates of military expenditures are developed independently of its measures of general economic growth (in which allocations to the military are mixed in with other categories), making it difficult to reconstruct how the leaders may have balanced the military allocation against consumption and investment. The question must be approached in an eclectic way. At the beginning of the Tenth FYP (1976–1980) the leaders declared they wanted to cut the growth rate of investment, and at least one Western observer interpreted this as a policy decision to sacrifice investment to permit military expenditures to continue to grow at the old rates.[9] The evidence is ambiguous, however, on whether this is what actually happened. Most investment measures in the CIA national income accounts (table 4.1) continued, as in the Ninth FYP, to rise faster than total output. The CIA data for consumption show it rising in the Tenth FYP at the same rate as GNP, 2.7 percent per year. It is not possible for investment to have grown at over 4 percent per year and consumption at 2.7 percent if military expenditures grew at 2 percent, but since the CIA's military expenditure series and its GNP accounts are estimated separately, they are not well enough reconciled to prove the point one way or the other.[10]

Official Soviet statistics, on the other hand, do clearly show a sacrifice of investment, suggesting that the growth of investment was checked differentially so that something else could grow more rapidly. Net material product (NMP) statistics suggest a big differential in favor of consumption, but, given that Soviet NMP statistics make no reference to military expenditure, they are hard to take seriously.

In short, neither the Soviet NMP data nor the CIA GNP data help to tell

[8] U.S. Congress, Joint Economic Committee, *The Soviet Economy in 1988*, 15.

[9] Myron Rush, "The Soviet Policy Favoring Arms over Investment since 1975," in U.S. Congress, Joint Economic Committee, *Soviet Economy in the 1980's: Problems and Prospects*, part 1 (Washington, D.C.: GPO, 1982), 319–330.

[10] *USSR: Measures of Economic Development and Growth, 1950–80*, studies prepared for the use of the Joint Economic Committee, Congress of the United States (Washington, D.C.: GPO, 1982), 121.

Table 4.1

Comparison of Soviet and CIA Measures of Soviet National Income Accounts

	(1) Ninth FYP	(2) Tenth FYP	(3) (2)/(1)
CIA Measures			
GNP	3.8	2.7	.71
All Investment	5.38	4.27	.79
Fixed Investment	4.78	3.81	.78
Investment in Machinery and Equipment	8.78	6.53	.74
Consumption	2.6	2.7	1.04
Soviet Measures			
NMP	4.4	3.6	.818
Net Fixed Investment[a]	4.96	1.27	.256
Net Fixed Investment, Plus Inventories	5.5	2.6	.42

Sources: Goskomstat SSSR, *Narodnoe khoziaistvo SSSR*, various years; U.S. Congress, Joint Economic Committee, *USSR: Measures of Economic Growth and Development, 1950–1980* (Washington, D.C.: GPO, 1982).

[a] Since NMP includes only net investment, official investment figures have been adjusted for depreciation.

whether investment or consumption were sacrificed to maintain the growth of military spending in the Tenth FYP, or the opposite.

INVESTMENT AND CONSUMPTION IN THE ELEVENTH FYP

For the Eleventh FYP, the initial priorities guiding the plan seem clearer. In developing and approving the plan, the leaders called more explicitly than they had in the Tenth for a drastic curtailment of investment growth. A provisional investment plan, already low, was cut further in the final stages.[11] In the official targets finally accepted, investment was to stay almost flat at the 1980 level. One hypothesis is that the leaders may have hoped by this decision to be able to keep military expenditure rising.

But as the Eleventh FYP went along, investment growth was not curtailed, as shown by the rates of growth for various Soviet and CIA measures, given

[11] Rush, "The Soviet Policy Favoring Arms," 327–328. The plan adopted cut the five-year figure of the original guidelines by 30 billion rubles, or 4.5 percent. See also N. K. Baibakov in *Planovoe khoziaistvo*, no. 1 (1982), 11.

in table 4.2.[12] Investment growth ended up well above the planned rate, even though there was no recovery or overfulfillment of the overall growth plan to provide a resource windfall. Why did such a reversal in favor of investment occur? It seems likely that an original promise to continue defense expenditure growth by sacrificing investment was reversed soon after the Eleventh FYP was under way.

In short, the economic evidence for a policy decision to curb the rate of growth of resources to the military in the Tenth FYP, or even in working up the Eleventh FYP, is not very convincing. It is easily conceivable that an effort to divert resources from defense to investment began in the late 1970s, but that it was only in the early 1980s, after the Eleventh FYP was under way, that the leaders moved decisively to effect such a shift in the annual plans. In the thinking for the Eleventh FYP, there had been a heavy emphasis on reequipping the economy and renovating the capital stock,[13] and Brezhnev was calling as early as 1980 on the Academy of Sciences and defense R&D institutions to help improve the level of civilian machine building.[14] But the first acknowledgment

TABLE 4.2
Soviet and CIA Measures of Soviet Investment Growth

| | Tenth FYP | Eleventh FYP | |
	Actual	Plan	Actual
Measures			
NMP	4.4	3.4	3.5
All Investment	3.3	2.0	3.5
State Investment	3.5	1.05	3.5
CIA Measures			
Fixed Investment	3.8	na	3.5
GNP	2.7	na	1.9

Sources: Goskomstat SSSR, *Narodnoe khoziaistvo SSSR*, various years; U.S. Congress, Joint Economic Committee, *USSR: Measures of Economic Growth and Development*.

[12] Plan figures from speech by N. K. Baibakov, *Ekonomicheskaia gazeta*, no. 48 (1981), 9–15.

[13] Ibid.

[14] In his speech to the Central Committee of 21 October 1980, Brezhnev said: "The tasks of renovating fixed assets and technically reequipping the various branches of the national economy will become increasingly acute. . . . We must instruct the Council of Ministers to determine with the aid of specialists exactly what scientific and design collectives of the defense industry could assist various branches of civilian machine building" (*Pravda*, 22 October 1980, 1–2).

that investment was being raised above the FYP targets came later, when the plan for 1983 was announced in the fall of 1982.[15]

Neither does it appear that consumption benefited much in the five-year plan ratified at the Twenty-sixth Congress, although Brezhnev had been extremely eloquent about the importance of consumption in his speech to the congress in 1981.[16] The Eleventh FYP envisaged a rise in the share of consumption in national income from 75.3 percent to 77.3 percent, but in fact it fell to 73.5 percent.[17] According to the CIA figures, annual consumption growth dropped from 2.63 percent in the Tenth FYP to 2.17 in the Eleventh, whereas the GNP growth rate stayed almost unchanged.

My conclusion is that, although the data provide little support for the idea of a policy decision to reduce the growth of military spending as early as 1975–76, there was indeed a decision early in the Eleventh FYP to accelerate investment spending and to put the brakes on the growth of military expenditure.

There is some corroboration of this interpretation in some of the key events in the early 1980s. General Secretary Chernenko stated in 1984 that "in the last five-year plan [1976–1980] the complexities of international life forced us to divert significant resources to needs connected with strengthening the security of the country."[18] Another item that fits with the above interpretation is a report of a confrontation between Brezhnev and the top military commanders in October 1982.[19] If a decision was taken sometime in 1981–82 to renege on military expectations in order to restore investment expenditures, this had to be explained to the military. Similarly interesting is an analysis by F. Klotsvog (who ought to have a good idea of structural changes in output, since he is a principal Gosplan research specialist on input-output). He wrote that in the years of the Tenth FYP, "nonproductive consumption" rose, and the share of capital investment fell. This language suggests that he was blaming excessive

---

[15] N. K. Baibakov, *O gosudarstvennom plane ekonomicheskogo i sotsialnogo razvitiia SSSR na 1983 god i khode vypolneniia plana v 1981 godu* (Moscow, 1982).

[16] He put it as follows: "As you know, comrades, the draft of the guidelines for the next five years embodies a certain acceleration of the rate of growth of Group B, to exceed the rate of growth of Group A. That is good. The problem is to create a really modern sector producing consumer goods and services for the population, which meets their demands. In concluding this point, I would like to consider it as more than a purely economic problem, and pose the question in broader terms. The things we are speaking of—food, consumer goods, service—are issues in the daily life of millions and millions of people. The store, the cafeteria, the laundry, the dry cleaners are places people visit every day. What can they buy? How are they treated? How are they spoken to? How much time do they spend on all kinds of daily cares? The people will judge our work in large measure by how these questions are solved. They will judge strictly, exactingly. And that, comrades, we must remember" (*Ekonomicheskaia gazeta*, no. 9 [1981], 10–11).

[17] G. Kuranov, "Strukturnye izmeneniia v narodnom khoziaistve," *Planovoe khoziaistvo*, no. 5 (1986), 77.

[18] *Ekonomicheskaia gazeta*, no. 11 (1984), 2.

[19] The report of this meeting appears in *Pravda*, 28 October 1982, 1.

military spending for the economic slowdown, and he went on to say that what was needed was a change in the structure of final use to facilitate a faster solution of "socio-economic" (i.e., nonmilitary) tasks.[20]

That this reversion to investment growth and the easing of the investment bottleneck did little to improve economic growth is not surprising, and can be explained by gestation lags. But there is a more subtle and ironic possibility: the leaders may have *thought* they were expanding production capacity by accelerating investment, but in reality no change took place, because the informal priority system continued to drain off real resources into military production even faster than before.[21] In that case, why did the leaders not realize what was happening? Because the statistics misled them into thinking that the ordered shift was in fact taking place. To see how this could have happened, a more detailed examination of subaggregates and nonmoney allocations is necessary.

Competition Between Hardware Procurement and Equipment for Investment

Within the general competition for resources between defense expenditure and investment, there is a more direct competition between subcomponents of each, that is, between military hardware procurement (accounting for almost half of total defense expenditure) and expenditures on capital equipment (accounting for about 38 percent of investment). (The other major component of investment is construction.) Both come from a relatively specialized sector of the economy with significant capacity inelasticity—the machinery-producing sector. There is strong internal specialization in this sector between civilian and military output in the sense that it is difficult to produce textile machinery in missile plants and vice-versa. There is also an institutional wall running through the administrative structure dividing the machinery sector into a civilian wing and a defense-industry wing. The first has consisted in recent years of eleven ministries producing primarily civilian machinery (the number was reduced to nine in the summer of 1987, to eight in 1988, and to six in 1989). The second includes the ministries serving primarily military needs, overseen and coordinated by a deputy prime minister and by the Military Industrial Commission (Komissiia po Voenno-Promyshlennym Voprosam, usually known by the initials VPK) under the Council of Ministers, which is chaired

---

[20] *Planovoe khoziaistvo*, no. 11 (1983), 31–39.

[21] One explanation that has been offered to reconcile the low growth of procurement with the failure of other end uses to spurt upward is that resources were still being poured into the military sector, but because of problems with technology they were not emerging as finished military hardware. This is suggested in the CIA testimony in U.S. Congress, Joint Economic Committee, *Allocation of Resources*, 56.

by that deputy prime minister. The institutional separation of this defense-industry sector is expressed in the top levels of the party hierarchy in the form of a Central Committee department in charge of defense industrial production, and a party secretary whose responsibility is primarily for defense industry. At the top level of the planning hierarchy it is expressed in the form of a separate military department in Gosplan, the State Planning Committee.

Until recently, Western observers usually maintained that these institutional walls separated the machinery sector into two distinct worlds, one civilian and the other military. But now there is agreement that the flow of resources between the two halves of the machinery sector is fairly large, because the defense industry ministries produce a great deal of civilian machinery (as Julian Cooper shows in chapter 5).[22] In addition, the military machinery sector produces general-purpose intermediate goods and capital equipment for its own needs.

Despite these qualifications, if there had been a change in relative investment-military priorities beginning in the second half of the 1970s or in the early 1980s, it should have been detected through changes in the allocation of machinery output to investment. In the CIA picture of a check to defense expenditure beginning in the mid-1970s, the major factor was that the procurement of military hardware stopped growing. But careful consideration of the evidence on what happened to machinery output and investment in equipment does not, in my view, support the interpretation that the civilian sector gained priority in the allocation of machinery. Since examination of the evidence on this point is arcane and tedious, it has been removed to an appendix, but the conclusions to be drawn from it may be summarized as follows.

It turns out to be impossible to draw any certain conclusions about the civil-military equipment split using either CIA or Soviet data on output of machinery. All these series are rubber yardsticks, not reliable enough to elucidate the point at issue, and arguments that depend on them should be treated with skepticism. Given the fallibility of the ostensibly relevant numbers, one must resort to a more qualitative and intuitive assessment. After all, our interest is less in what was really happening than in how policy makers saw the situation, and what they thought they were doing as they balanced the desire of the military establishment for more weapons against the general desire to stimulate growth. An interpretation along the following lines seems plausible:

- The growth of finished products from the machinery sector has been considerably slower than statistics show, although perhaps a bit faster than shown by the CIA's series for growth of machinery output.

[22] For an estimate by the same author of the relative shares of output involved, see Julian M. Cooper, "The Scales of Output of Civilian Products by Enterprises of the Soviet Defense Industry," *Discussion Papers of the Centre for Russian and East European Studies*, Soviet Industry and Technology Series no. 3, University of Birmingham, August 1988.

- This discrepancy distorts the associated figures for investment and capital stock that both U.S. analysts and Soviet leaders look at to monitor what is happening to capacity. Both investment and growth of capital stock throughout the Soviet economy are exaggerated, and this applies to the machinery sector as well as to any other. This helps explain the pinch on growth of real machinery output, especially its civilian component, compared to the official figures.
- Military procurement has retained a hold on resource allocations via the informal priority mechanism. Real resources flowing to military production were not stemmed after the mid-1970s despite leadership intentions, and the leaders were unsuccessful in achieving the expansion of real investment in the civilian economy that they sought. (Incidentally, this helps to explain the phenomenon of inflation in the civilian machine building and investment series. The lack of a hard budget constraint permits weapons procurement and civilian equipment demand together to exceed supply, and the gap is filled by machinery producers' continually raising the allegedly "constant prices." This may well be easier to do for civilian than for military goods.)

In short, it is possible that the leaders were simply unable to exercise control over the allocation of real machinery output between military procurement and growth-enhancing capital investment. They thought they were accelerating investment and adding to the economy's production capacities, but that was an illusion, and resources continued to flow into military production. It may be that the investment and machinery statistics are so out of touch with reality that planners have had a hard time understanding what is happening. One Soviet economist asserts precisely this, namely, that misleading investment and capital stock figures have prompted wrong allocations.[23] This interpretation gains additional credibility from the revelations by Gorbachev and other authorities that they feel there is something peculiar about how weapons procurements are priced and financed, and from their decision to appoint a special commission to look into the issue.[24]

R&D Expenditures

A second component in the estimates of defense expenditures produced by the CIA is research and development expenditures for new weapons systems, which represent large commitments of resources—nearly one-quarter of all

[23] G. Khanin, "Sochtem fondy," *Sotsialisticheskaia industriia*, 29 August 1986, 2.

[24] Very little is known about this, but there is an interesting hint that prices of military goods might be understated in the statement of Deputy Foreign Minister V. F. Petrovskii at the UN conference on disarmament and development that there are "differences in principle in the structure of prices for weapons and in the mechanism of price formation" *Izvestiia*, 27 August 1987, 4.

military expenditures.[25] The CIA says that from 1976 through the mid-1980s most of the growth in its series for military expenditures is accounted for by R&D, but at the same time it says that its figure for R&D expenditures is the least solid element in its overall estimate. If military R&D was growing at anything like the 6 percent or so required to raise total military expenditure at 2 percent yearly when procurement and other components were essentially flat, it had to be crowding out civilian R&D, since total expenditures on R&D grew very slowly during both the 1976–1980 and 1981–1985 quinquennia. The slowdown in the growth of overall R&D activity has been more striking than that of the economy as a whole, as the figures in table 4.3 indicate.

For GNP the average annual rate of growth was about halved between 1966–1970 and 1980–1985, but the growth rate for scientific workers fell over the same period to one-fifth of the earlier tempo, and for all employees in the science and science service sector from a rate close to GNP growth to virtually nothing. The index for expenditures on science fell less sharply. Price increases and increasing material intensity of R&D keep its growth rate above the labor input series, but even so its growth from 1980 to 1985 dropped to two-fifths of its rate for 1965 to 1970.

It is frequently asserted that the demands of military R&D have indeed en-

TABLE 4.3
Slowdown in the Growth of Soviet R&D Activity (1965 = 100)

Year	GNP (CIA)	Scientific Workers	Employees in Science and Science Service	Expenditures on Science (Undeflated)
1965	100	100	100	100
1970	129 (5.2)	140 (6.9)	125 (4.5)	170 (11.1)
1975	155 (3.7)	184 (5.7)	158 (4.8)	252 (8.3)
1980	177 (2.7)	207 (2.3)	182 (2.9)	323 (5.1)
1985	199 (2.4)	226 (1.8)	190 (.008)	399 (4.3)
1986	202 (4.2)	226 (1.2)	191 (.004)	409 (2.5)
1987	203 (0.5)	228 (0.6)	na	na
1990 Plan	na	na	na	545 (8.2)

Source: Except for GNP, these data are based on Robert Campbell, *R&D Statistics*, a report prepared for the National Science Foundation, June 1984, updated with current statistical handbooks, budget speeches, and plan speeches.
Note: Figures in parentheses refer to average annual rates since the preceding year shown.

[25] CIA, National Foreign Assessment Center, *Estimated Soviet Defense Spending: Trends and Prospects*, June 1978, 3.

croached more and more on civilian uses. The work of the Academy of Sciences is alleged to have become increasingly militarized.[26] On the other hand, a long series of statements by the leadership during this period directed the military R&D establishment to help with civilian problems. At the Twenty-sixth Party Congress in 1981, Brezhnev called for some "realignment" of the network of R&D establishments, and for R&D organizations in the defense industry to help raise the level of technology in civilian activities.[27]

The disparity between virtually stagnant total R&D and military R&D growing at the alleged 6 percent provides obvious grounds for a conflict over the allocation of R&D capabilities between civilian and military uses. There are enough statements about the issue to suggest that there has been such a conflict. To repeat, there is little solid evidence to enable us to judge what may have happened to the growth of military R&D in the Tenth or the Eleventh FYPs. Western commentators tend to make strong statements on the basis of flimsy evidence, and even the best work is full of heroic assumptions.[28] But one can find some instructive hints.

The R&D establishment has four main components: the branch system, the academy system, the higher education (VUZ) system, and the so-called factory sector. R&D for military purposes is performed in all of the R&D subsystems, but primarily in the scientific research institutes (NIIs) and design bureaus (KBs) of the branch system. One estimate is that 90 percent of it is located there, which is an important point to keep in mind in dealing with assertions that the Academy of Sciences and the VUZy perform a great deal of R&D work for the military. The share of these two systems in employment

[26] John R. Thomas, "Militarization of the Soviet Academy of Sciences," *Survey* 29, 1 (Spring 1985). On the basis of conversations with Soviet scientists, Robert Kaiser reports a growing militarization of scientific research. For example, Defense Minister Ustinov is said to have "brought an increasing number of the country's scientific research institutes under military control by requiring that any institute that does research for the military must be subject to military discipline" *Washington Post*, 24 September, 1984, A14.

[27] His speech is available in *Ekonomicheskaia gazeta*, no. 9 (1981). Actually, Brezhnev had expressed this desideratum earlier, at the Twenty-fourth Party Congress in 1971: "Taking into account the high scientific-technical level of the defense industry, the transmission of its experience, inventions and discoveries to all spheres of our economy acquires the highest importance." Cited in David Holloway, *The Soviet Union and the Arms Race* (New Haven: Yale University Press, 1983), 171.

[28] Nancy Nimitz, *The Structure of Soviet R and D Outlays*, WN 7463-PR (Santa Monica: Rand Corporation, August 1971); and *The Structure of Soviet Outlays on R and D in 1960 and 1968*, R-1207-DDRE (Santa Monica: Rand Corporation, June 1974). A recent survey in a chapter in Mary Acland-Hood, *Military R and D: Resource Use and Arms Control*, is a careful review of previous work but is unable to do more than squeeze earlier assumptions and data bases a bit harder for conjectures regarding the current situation. An example of an inflated claim on flimsy evidence is William Lee's estimate that military R&D was 19 BR in 1980 in 1970 prices (taking the midpoint of his range), when the Soviet figure in current prices for all R&D is 22 BR. See William T. Lee and Richard Staar, *Soviet Military Policy since World War II* (Stanford: Hoover Institution Press, 1986), 112.

(in the narrower concept of scientific workers) and in expenditures is small, and no matter how carefully one analyzes the evidence relating to the academy and the VUZy, it does not tell much about expenditure on military R&D.

Rather, the place to investigate the civilian-military split in R&D is in the NIIs, KBs, and factory-sector institutions of the machinery sector. Having sorted over the numerous scraps of evidence available on the matter, I offer the tabulation in table 4.4 as the most likely to provide some insight as to how the total is split between military and nonmilitary ministries. The measure used for R&D activity is R&D manpower, conceptualized as the number of "diploma-level personnel" working in the specialized R&D organizations.[29]

The figures through 1980 are reasonably solid, as are those for the whole

TABLE 4.4
Diploma Holders Employed in Science Sector Institutions (in thousands)

Year	All Economy (1)	Nonindustrial Mins. and Depts. (2)	Industrial Mins. and Depts. (3)	Machinery Ministries (4)	Civilian Machinery Ministries (5)
1965	588	300	288 (49%)	169 (59%)	na
1970	873	481	392 (45%)	236 (60%)	na
1975	1,311	766	545 (42%)	336 (61%)	na
1977	1,417	811	606 (43%)	374 (62%)	na
1980	1,614	913	701 (43%)	na	na
1985	1,800	900	900 (50%)	700 (77%)	400 (57%)

Sources: Column (1) is from Campbell, *R&D Statistics*, June 1984. Columns (3) and (4) for 1965–1977 represent my interpretation of Plekhov, which differs from that of Julian Cooper but is fairly close to Nancy Nimitz's interpretation. Column (2) is by subtraction. Figures in parentheses show the share of the relevant figure in the next larger category. Industrial ministries and departments for 1980 are based on Nauchno-issledovatelskii ekonomicheskii institut Gosplana UkrSSR, *Planovoe upravlenie razvitiem nauki i tekhniki v soiuznoi respubliki* (Kiev, 1981), 42. Some further support for the industrial-nonindustrial split comes from the fact that a similar split (47.5 percent in industry) was found in the Moscow economy. T. V. Riabushkin, ed., *Sotsialnye i ekonomicheskie problemy povysheniia effektivnosti nauki* (Moscow, 1985), 198.

[29] All the Soviet statements I consider most important can be construed as referring to diploma-level personnel, especially those of Lebedev and Plekhov. The Soviet sources speak of *uchenye i inzhenery*, or sometimes they speak of developing their data using TsSU information on *spetsy* with higher education (diploma holders in my terminology) by specialty, which would make it possible to take out diploma holders not in the science or engineering fields. My hypothesis is that this TsSU data can be assigned by industrial branch only on a ministerial basis, so that what the numbers show is that the *spetsy* in science-sector organizations are subordinated to the various ministries.

economy for 1985. The figure for machine building in 1985 is solid in the sense that it is given explicitly by an authoritative source. Premier N. I. Ryzhkov said at the Supreme Soviet meeting approving the Twelfth FYP that the machine-building industry employs "700,000 scientific workers, designers, and technologists,"[30] a formulation interpreted here as conceptually consistent with the rest of the tabulation. The split between industrial ministries and departments and other ministries and departments for 1985, however, is largely a hypothesis.

What portion of those working in the machinery industry would be in the civilian ministries versus those in the VPK ministries? The best indication is an article by B. M. Martynov, chief of a Gosplan department that, according to other evidence, is concerned with the civilian machinery branches. Martynov asserts that the machine-building sector has a large R&D establishment consisting of 700 "large NII and PK organizations," employing 400,000 persons.[31] There is always a danger that Martynov is using a concept with different coverage than that in table 4.4, but, given his concern with civilian machine building, it seems likely that he is referring to R&D personnel in the civilian machinery ministries, whereas Ryzhkov was referring to those in the whole sector.

There is little information regarding employment growth in civilian machine building, but a useful recent source contains systematic information on R&D expenditures of the six civilian machine-building ministries. Most of the data are in percentages, but it is claimed that these ministries account for about 7 percent of all R&D expenditures in the economy, and that the ratio has stayed remarkably stable. This yields an absolute expenditure figure for the six together in 1975, which can be distributed among the six and extended to other years on the basis of other tables in the source. Data on the outlay structure permit calculation of the wage component, and division by the annual wage in the R&D sector gives the employment estimates in table 4.5.

These are imprecise calculations, and comparison with scattered information on individual ministries suggests that they may be somewhat small. Of the omitted ministries, Mintiazhmash and Minenergomash are likely to have establishments like those of Minkhimmash or Minpribor, but Minzhivmash and Minstroidormash must have very small numbers. Correction for their omission suggests a number a little less than 350,000, somewhat smaller than the 400,000 cited by Martynov for civilian machine building. But Martynov's formulation suggests that he probably includes people in organizations other than NIIs and KBs. The numbers here refer to employment in NII and KB, a concept that is more comprehensive than "scientists, engineers, and technol-

[30] *Izvestiia*, 19 June 1986, 2.

[31] B. M. Martynov, "Razvitie mashinostroitelnogo kompleksa strany," *Planovoe khoziaistvo*, no. 9 (1986), 16.

TABLE 4.5
R&D Employment of Soviet Civilian Machine Building Ministries (in thousands)

	1965	1970	1975	1980	1985
Minelektrotekhprom	45	65	72	82	84
Minpribor	32	39	68	68	73
Minkhimmash	22	30	35	33	33
Minstankoprom	23	25	26	24	25
Minlegpishchemash	13	17	19	19	21
Minavtoprom	13	15	17	17	17
Total	148	191	237	243	253

Source: V. M. Logachev et al., *Finansy i khozraschet v NII i KB* (Moscow, 1987).

Note: The ministries referred to in the table are as follows: Minelektrotekhprom: Ministry of the Electrical Equipment Industry; Minpribor: Ministry of Instrument Making, Automation Equipment, and Control Systems; Minkhimmash: Ministry of Chemical and Petroleum Machine Building; Minstankoprom: Ministry of the Machine Tool Industry; Minlegpishchemash: Ministry of Machine Building for Light and Food Industry and Household Appliances; Minavtoprom: Ministry of the Automotive Industry.

ogists engaged in R&D,'' but perhaps narrower in that it does not include employment in such activities as experimental plants and some kinds of design organizations, as I suspect the figures cited by Ryzhkov and Martynov do.

But these coverage problems do not affect the dynamics. Comparison of these data with the estimate for all machine building implies a strong differential unfavorable for civilian machine building. The figures calculated above fall from over 80 percent of the number estimated for all machinery ministries in 1970 to only 37 percent by the mid-1980s. For the years 1970–1984, they represent an annual growth rate for these six ministries of 2 percent versus 8 percent for all machinery ministries together. In sum, the VPK ministries were absorbing the lion's share of the resource increment in R&D in the decade preceding 1985, starving the civilian R&D function.

This conclusion is also suggested by a study indicating that the number of new models of machinery in civilian areas has slowed compared to the number in military-related areas.[32] Statistical handbooks report the number of prototypes of new machines and instruments created, both in total and for some subcategories of machinery. It is possible to relate the explicitly indicated subcategories to groups of civilian machinery, leaving a residual that can be interpreted as prototypes of military equipment. Since the mid-1960s, this resid-

[32] Vladimir Kontorovich, ''R and D in Soviet Military and Civilian Machine Building,'' 1987, ms.

ual indicates, the number of civilian prototypes has been declining, and that of military types increasing.

Division of Investment Between Civilian and Military Machine Building

A final indicator of resource conflict between the civilian and military wings of the machinery sector is the division of investment.

Gorbachev appears to have seen neglect of civilian machinery production as a crucial factor causing the deterioration of the general performance of the economy. He raised the issue in one of his first important announcements as general secretary, at the June 1985 conference on scientific-technical progress, stating that in the Eleventh FYP (1981–1985) civilian machine building had received only 5 percent of productive capital investment in the economy.[33] Despite the approximate figures and ambiguous definitions being used, if his figure is taken at face value and compared with what the Central Statistical Administration reports as total investment in machine building, a split of roughly 40 percent can be arrived at for the civilian machine building ministries, and 60 percent for the VPK ministries.

Information as to how this division has moved over time is spotty, but one source provides some investment figures for the early 1970s indicating that the investment share of the civilian ministries was then significantly higher—over half of the total.[34] Thus, during the 1970s and 1980s, the VPK ministries were winning out over the civilian ministries in the struggle for investment resources. Another Soviet source notes that in the first three years of the Eleventh FYP the eleven civilian machinery ministries utilized only 90 percent of the capital investment budget line allocated to them,[35] meaning that the ministries in question were unable to obtain the physical resources corresponding to their budget allocation. Since investment plans were generally overfulfilled in the Eleventh FYP, this, too, suggests that the civilian wing was losing out to the VPK ministries through the informal priority system.

These movements in investment ultimately had an impact on the growth of capacity and output in civilian machine building. A number of economists have offered this, in a veiled sort of way, as the diagnosis of what was wrong in the machinery sector. The economist K. K. Valtukh, for example, focuses

[33] "Korennoi vopros ekonomicheskoi politiki partii," in M. S. Gorbachev, *Izbrannye rechi i stati* (Moscow: Izdatelstvo Politicheskoi Literatury, 1985), 118. Gorbachev's statement would most likely refer to ministerial data. Evidence of Gorbachev's concern over civilian machinery can be found as early as 1983.

[34] P. N. Zhevtiak and V. I. Kolesnikov, *Pribyl v sotsialisticheskom rasshyrennom vosproizvodstve* (Moscow: Izdatelstvo Finansy, 1976), 157.

[35] *Planovoe khoziaistvo*, no. 7 (1985), 14.

on "productive" machine building as the bottleneck, and the term seems to be a clear euphemism for civilian as opposed to military hardware production.[36]

Conclusions Regarding the Pre-Gorbachev Period

This survey of the civil-military competition in three crucial areas strongly suggests that the resource requirements of the military program had a serious dampening effect on the performance of the economy as a whole between 1975 and 1985, especially toward the end of the 1970s. Excessive support of the military claim was killing the goose that laid the golden eggs. This was an insidious process, starting with shifts at the R&D and investment stages that took a while to show up in output and quality.

How to interpret the behavior of the political leadership and its relations with the military establishment as this process unfolded remains a puzzle. Room should probably be allowed in the explanation for the possibility that the leaders did not fully understand what was happening, but I believe that between 1975 and 1985 they became increasingly aware that military commitments were imposing a heavy opportunity cost in the form of poor performance in the civilian economy. If so, they may have lacked the will to confront the military. But the explanation suggested here is that they also lacked the ability to control the informal priority mechanisms so as to reorient decisively the real flow of resources.

Developments in the Twelfth Five-Year Plan

Under Gorbachev the political leadership has moved with determination to try to reallocate resources between civilian and military goals. To get the economy growing again, Gorbachev has adopted a strategy that sharpens the competition between military and civilian uses at all the levels discussed above.

The centerpiece of the Gorbachev strategy for accelerating growth is renovation of the economy's capital stock. In the process, the structure of investment is being shifted away from construction of new plant toward modernization of existing plant, chiefly in the form of new equipment. This strategy means: (1) a higher overall priority for investment; (2) a disproportionate rise in equipment requirements; with (3) an especially sharp emphasis on high-

[36] K. K. Valtukh and B. L. Lavrovskii, "Proizvodstvennyi apparat strany: ispolzovanie i rekonstruktsiia," *Ekonomika i organizatsiia promyshlennogo proizvodstva (EKO)*, no. 2 (1986), 28.

technology machinery. As a corollary of point 2, the competition with military procurement inevitably intensifies; as a corollary of point 3, the demand for the services of competent R&D institutions and personnel to improve the technical level of civilian machinery output also accelerates. The Gorbachev strategy requires reallocation of resources at all these levels.

Investment-Consumption-Defense

The Twelfth FYP (1986–1990) envisages an acceleration of investment well above past rates, and above the rate of growth for net material product. One source for increasing investment is to squeeze consumption, and clearly there was pressure on consumption in the Twelfth FYP as first approved and as carried out during the first two or three years. According to Premier Ryzhkov in June 1986, the share of consumption would fall from 74.1 percent in 1985 to 72.4 percent in 1990.[37]

But this acceleration of investment also required a diversion of resources from military end-uses. The Twelfth FYP envisaged an investment program that was front-loaded, but investment shot far ahead of the FYP pace in 1986, and its growth has not slackened as much in subsequent years as was originally intended.[38]

Once again, however, money quantities are not the best guide to what is really going on. The real question is, what are Gorbachev and the reformers doing to challenge the informal allocation system in machinery and R&D resources?

Division of Investment Within Machine Building

The leaders have targeted a reallocation of investment within the machine-building sector to expand the capacity of the civilian machine-building ministries. Gorbachev raised this issue early, and it seems probable that this was one of the changes he insisted on as successive drafts of the Twelfth FYP were sent back to Gosplan for reworking. At the 1986 Supreme Soviet meeting that approved the plan, Ryzhkov said, "We need to remind ourselves once again that in the years of the last five-year plans attention to development of the

---

[37] Speech by N. I. Ryzhkov presenting the Twelfth FYP to the Supreme Soviet, *Pravda*, 19 June 1986, 1.

[38] The five-year plan projected an increase of 23.6 percent in central capital investment, but after just three years the increase already stood at 19.9 percent. *Narodnoe khoziaistvo SSSR za 1987 g.*, 295, and *Izvestiia*, 21 January 1989.

machine-building branch [in its capacity of providing equipment for invest-
ment] flagged."[39]

The data on investment in the Twelfth FYP are incomplete and contradictory. My reconstruction suggests that, in contrast to the experience of the past,
the civilian machinery ministries are indeed enjoying higher growth rates of
investment than the VPK ministries, and that they will increase their share of
the total somewhat. The differential is less than might have been expected,
but, as will be explained below, the VPK ministries are being assigned more
civilian tasks, and the investment allocated to them may not necessarily be for
military production. (See also chapter 5.)

Civilian Machinery versus Military Hardware

In the Twelfth FYP, capital equipment for investment is targeted to grow much
faster than machinery output. The share of all investment to be used for reconstruction and reequipping is to rise from 37 percent in 1985 to 50 percent by
1990 (1.35 times), and state productive investment is to increase by 1.26
times, so that the reconstruction and reequipment category should grow by 1.7
times by 1990. Although not all investment in reconstruction and reequipment
is for machinery, the latter dominates, and this kind of structural change has
to put pressure on machine-building output, which is forecast to grow by only
43 percent by 1990.

The evidence as the Twelfth FYP period unfolds is that investment probably
is cutting into procurement. In 1986, while machinery output (probably civilian only) rose by 7.7 percent and net imports of machinery dropped by 400
million rubles, investment in reconstruction and reequipment rose by 17 percent. In 1987 net imports dropped again, machinery output rose at only 4.6
percent, but investment in reconstruction and reequipment rose by 7 percent.

During the Gorbachev period, there has been increasing pressure on the
VPK ministries to serve civilian needs. In the plan, the defense industries were
explicitly instructed to help retool the consumer goods industries. The latter
demand was greatly intensified in 1988 when the leaders decided that a quick
fix of the obsolete food and consumer goods industries was the most urgent
task.

This pressure also applies to consumer goods. The plan guidelines called on
the defense industries "to raise significantly their contribution to supplying
consumer durables to the population." *Pravda* carried an attack on 3 June
1986 on the Radio Industry, General Machine Building, and Electronics Industry ministries for poor performance in improving the quality of television
sets, and the ministers were warned they would be held personally responsible

[39] *Izvestiia*, 19 June 1986.

for this task. A similar attack in *Pravda* one week later involved videocassette recorders. The Ministry of the Aviation Industry has also been criticized for its unsatisfactory contribution to improving the supply of building materials to households.[40] Such admonitions continued unabated through 1988.

Research and Development

The planners apparently expected to ease the civil-military competition for scarce R&D resources by expanding capacity after the stagnation of recent years. Expenditures on science, including capital investment, are to grow from 27.5 billion rubles in 1985 to 38.6 billion rubles in 1990.[41] Current expenditures will grow by a third (from 24.8 billion rubles to 33 billion rubles), while investment in R&D facilities will grow by 1.7 times.

But such skilled manpower cannot be educated overnight. Given that constraint, will it really be possible to expand current expenditures so fast? Assuming that the expenditure figure is in constant prices and that the growth ratio of expenditures and manpower does not change from that in the Eleventh FYP (see table 4.4), scientific workers would have to increase from 1,491,000 to 1,753,000 over the five-year period. That will be difficult to do, especially since a parallel effort has been launched to weed out incompetent R&D personnel. If this purge is extensive, large manpower additions will be needed to achieve the growth envisaged in the plan.

In any case, Gorbachev will likely have to engage the help of the R&D establishment as it already exists in the VPK if the modern equipment needed for the renovation program is to be developed. G. B. Stroganov, a deputy chairman of Gosplan whose portfolio apparently includes machine building, says that in planning the development of machine building in the Twelfth FYP, "we give special attention to diffusing the experience of the most advanced collectives of our country."[42] This "most advanced collectives" formulation is what Brezhnev used when he called for the military R&D establishment to assist in solving civilian problems.

The Academy of Sciences is apparently to have an enhanced role in improving the technological level of machinery, a change that is probably intended to aid military as well as civilian production. In his 1986 speech at the academy's annual meeting, the then president of the academy, A. P. Aleksandrov, mentioned its close ties with the ministries of the Electronics and Communi-

---

[40] Ibid., 18 July 1987.

[41] *Ekonomicheskaia gazeta*, no. 11 (1986). Expenditure has traditionally been reported inclusive of capital investment. In his speech to the congress, Ryzhkov gave figures for current expenditure alone, which makes it possible to deduce capital investment in 1985, i.e., 2.7 BR. Ryzhkov also gave the planned growth index for capital investment for the Twelfth FYP.

[42] *Kommunist*, no. 10 (1986), 74.

cations Equipment Industries and said that ties with the Ministry of the Radio Industry were less good but improving.[43]

The annual meeting of the academy in March 1986 authorized the creation of a new Division of Problems of Machine Building, Mechanics, and Control Processes (Otdelenie problem mashinostroeniia, mekhaniki i protsessov upravleniia).[44] Academician K. V. Frolov, the academy vice-president responsible for this division, has implied that it will contribute to both the military and civilian tasks of the machinery sector. The newspaper report on the 1986 annual meeting indicated that the division would include some newly created institutes and noted that new branches of one of its institutes (Institut mashinovedeniia) are to be organized in Gorky, Sverdlovsk, Leningrad, and Saratov. These measures to provide more help to machine building should "in no way crowd out the fundamental research already being done. What is necessary is a sensible combination and interaction of different fields of knowledge in the solution of urgent problems of science and practice."[45] That combination of cities, all of them centers of military-industrial production, suggests that what is envisaged is an increase in work for the military.

One wonders how such a role will sit with the scientists. Any shift of basic science resources to military work is likely to cause some opposition, although so far there has been little indication of actual changes. But an article by L. P. Feoktistov, deputy director of the Kurchatov Institute of Atomic Power (the director of which is academy vice-president E. P. Velikhov), makes one wonder if heated disputes may not be going on in the science establishment. "Scientific-technical progress . . . ," he writes, "is stimulated by the needs of the civilian, not the military sector. . . . It is progress in the civilian sector that plays a decisive role in raising productivity and economic growth. . . . Thus far, military technology has provided few results which have had decisive direct significance for scientific-technical progress in the civilian sector. Only 20 percent of the results of military R&D (NIOKR) are used in any way for civilian purposes."[46] Feoktistov's own research specialty is nuclear fusion, and he seems to be an expert on laser-powered implosion approaches to fusion for electric power.[47] One can well imagine that he fears that Star Wars–type research will interfere with civilian objectives.

---

[43] *Vestnik Akademii Nauk SSSR*, no. 5 (1986), 6. E. K. Pervyshin, minister of Minpromsviazi, adds that this cooperation is based on a plan of joint work developed in 1978. Ibid., 16.

[44] *Kommunist*, no. 6 (1986), 37. This was previously the Otdelenie mekhaniki i protsessov upravleniia. It worked on reliability, especially for aircraft, so it has close ties to Minaviaprom and military R&D. The change in its name and function is not mentioned in the *Vestnik AN SSSR* issue reporting the annual meeting (no. 5, 1986), or thus far in any later issue.

[45] *Izvestiia*, 20 March 1986.

[46] L. P. Feoktistov, "Gonka vooruzhenii," 101–102.

[47] L. P. Feoktistov, "Gorizonty LTS," *Budushchee nauki, 1985* (Moscow: Znanie, 1985), 168–182.

Organizational Changes

Support for the proposition that the reform program seeks to divert resources from military uses is found in the organizational shifts made under Gorbachev. In the summer of 1985 the Politburo apparently decided to shake up the machinery sector. A report of a Politburo session in late July or early August 1985 stated that it had approved a decree on the machinery sector.[48] The content of that decree is elusive,[49] probably because it involves some attenuation of the independence of the VPK branches within the machinery sector and allocation shifts that Gorbachev would just as soon not reveal fully to either outsiders or insiders.

My interpretation is that this "program" involves diffusing VPK ministry experience to the civilian ministries, using VPK resources—experience, production capacity, R&D institutes, and so forth—for civilian production tasks, and attempting to break down the wall that has separated the two wings of the machinery sector. One of the measures in this program was the creation of the Bureau for Machine Building (Biuro po mashinostroeniiu) of the Council of Ministers. The way this bureau was created suggests that the idea was controversial.

The bureau was first mentioned in a Politburo summary, but the decree establishing it has never been published. For a while its name was sometimes spelled with a lower-case B. The first reference to I. S. Silaev as its head was not through an appointment announcement but in a television program in which he appeared.[50]

[48] Report of the Politburo meeting (date not given) in *Pravda*, 2 August 1985, 1.

[49] The decree was never published, and no title or date is ever cited for it. At a conference on the tasks of the machinery sector held at the Central Committee on 8 August 1986, L. N. Zaikov asserted that the government did pass such a decree in 1985. *Izvestiia*, 9 August 1986, 1. Abel Aganbegian spoke of it as a detailed and comprehensive decree (*razvernutoe postanovlenie*) on the further development of machine building *EKO*, no. 6 (1986), 13. It is frequently referred to as a "complex of measures" constituting a "national program" for the machinery sector. (See, for example, a review of the machine building sector in *Ekonomicheskaia gazeta*, no. 35 [1985], 1. G. Stroganov, deputy chairman of Gosplan, spoke of a set of measures constituting an "all-state program for the development of the machine-building sector" *Ekonomicheskaia gazeta*, no. 38 [1986], 2, 4. The "all-state" qualifier is another clue that this "complex of measures" covers the nine VPK ministries as well as the eleven civilian ones.) It is treated as if it contains provisions that are not to be spoken of openly. In his speech to the Supreme Soviet on 18 June, 1986, Ryzhkov said that the investment plans for the machinery sector were fully in accord with the "well-known decree" of the Politburo on machine building. *Ekonomicheskaia gazeta*, no. 26 (1986), 13. At the first big meeting on the tasks of the machinery sector held at the Central Committee on 21 May 1986, Gorbachev gave "a long speech," in which he spoke of the "all-state program for the development of machine building." The meeting is reported in *Ekonomicheskaia gazeta*, no. 22 (1986), 3, but the story gives no information on the content of the speech, and the speech has so far not been released.

[50] Reported in FBIS, vol. 3, 3 December 1985, U1.

The important point is that the leadership did not succeed in getting a unified administration of the two wings of the machinery industry.[51] The bureau has jurisdiction over the civilian machinery ministries only.[52] There is still a deputy premier with primary responsibility for the VPK ministries (I. S. Belousov since early 1988), and no doubt still a VPK. The new bureau was probably intended as a body parallel to the VPK, expected to emulate the kind of practices that have been employed in the VPK ministries to achieve technological progress and quality goals, and, the reformers hoped, with enough bureaucratic weight to compete with the VPK for resources and influence. Silaev, as a former minister of the aviation industry, certainly brings a great deal more clout to the civilian machinery sector than it had previously. Silaev and Belousov (and Iu. D. Masliukov before him) seem in certain respects to operate as a team jointly responsible for machine building, as at the Central Committee conference on machine building on 8 August 1986, but each controls independent assets.[53]

Another important measure evidently intended to apply the experience of the defense industries to the civilian sector is the decree on quality control adopted in the summer of 1986.[54] An important departure in this decree is the institution of an independent quality-control establishment under the State Committee of Standards rather than under enterprise management. It also contains provisions giving a designer of final products the right to demand that design subcontractors meet his specifications for components, and that material suppliers also meet his specifications. Both of these sound like ideas from the military sector. The parallel is drawn explicitly by academician V. A. Trapeznikov in an article in *Pravda*, 2 October 1985. He says that "the technology and quality of output in our defense industry are much higher than in the civilian fields," and that it is necessary to "use the experience of the defense production people, particularly in instituting a strong influence on quality from the side of the user."

It is tempting to interpret the formation of interbranch scientific and technical complexes (MNTKs) for the major directions of scientific technical progress as a similiar borrowing. The MNTKs are intended to bring together sci-

---

[51] It is possible that no effort was actually made to get a single body to oversee the whole machinery sector. In even the most "centralizing" of earlier proposals for new administrative structures to unify machinery production, administration of defense production was to be kept separate from the rest of machine building. See B. P. Kurashvili, "Sudby otraslevogo upravleniia," *EKO*, no. 10 (1983), 44–45.

[52] I. S. Silaev in *Izvestiia*, 11 April 1986.

[53] *Izvestiia*, 9 August 1986, 2.

[54] This is a decree "On Measures for the Radical Improvement of the Quality of Production," adopted by the Central Committee and the Council of Ministers. There is a commentary in *Izvestiia*, 2 July 1986, and a discussion by G. D. Kolmogorov, chairman of the State Committee on Standards, in *Ekonomicheskaia gazeta*, no. 30 (1986), 5, specifically on the plans for "outside acceptance."

entific research institutes, design bureaus, and experimental production facilities of different branches to force progress in specific areas. But of the twenty-three that have so far been identified as in operation, only the Rotor MNTK is subordinated to one of the VPK ministries; descriptions of the others offer only occasional hints that they are to draw on the resources of defense-industrial R&D organs.

Another change that might be expected if there is to be some unification of R&D effort seems not yet to have occurred. When the new method of financing the whole cycle of R&D and innovation through the Unified Fund for Development of Science and Technology (EFRNT) was established some years ago, the VPK ministries were specifically excluded. In 1986 the transfer of all the civilian machine-building ministries to the EFRNT system was completed, but to my knowledge no mention has been made of introducing this change in the defense-industry ministries.

Another area where the reformers may be trying to breach civil-military barriers is technical information. One of the measures mentioned at the May 1986 conference on machine building was the need "to improve the whole system of scientific-technical information." The patent and technical information system has long been divided into secret and nonsecret systems.[55] The system has envisaged civilian application of innovations developed for military purposes, but it seems likely that there has been a highly impermeable barrier here. Serious efforts to enlist the aid of military industry in upgrading civilian machinery technology should certainly address that issue.

As the neglected civilian claimants have acquired a more vigorous voice under glasnost, there is more and more evidence that the defense-industrial branches have given short shrift over the years to serving the civilian needs that were part of their assignment. There are numerous examples in areas such as consumer electronics, telecommunications equipment, and printing equipment. The most interesting aspect of this is the difficulty Gorbachev has had in altering that informal system. Two examples are especially instructive.

One of the most urgent but so far fecklessly handled tasks in improving the telephone network is to create fiber-optic technology. The Svetovod MNTK was established under the aegis of the USSR Academy of Sciences to try to make some progress on this difficult interbranch task. But this was a failure, and in early 1988 Svetovod was abolished or reorganized. It had discovered that earlier, "when everyone was solving the fiber-optic technology problem on their own," a design bureau in the Ministry of the Electronics Industry, a VPK ministry, had developed the equipment to produce fiber-optic cable. But Svetovod was unable to enlist the efforts of that design bureau, even though

---

[55] There is an elaborate system of registering the results of R&D work, but with secret and open discoveries kept secret. Some information on the handling of classified technical information is given in *Zakonodatelnye akty po voprosam narodnogo khoziaistva SSSR* (Moscow, 1961), 1:646–651.

its staff showed "a readiness to deal with this task on a statewide scale," because "in that departmental fence there is no gate." [56]

The second example is what happened to Minlegpishcheprom, the ministry producing equipment for the light and food industries. Despite clear directions in the Twelfth FYP, the defense industrial ministries had failed to assist it. In a desperation move in 1988, Minlegpishcheprom was liquidated and most of its plants transferred to the defense industrial branches. In addition, a special unit was established within the VPK with direct responsibility for the transferred plants, headed by the former minister of Minlegpishcheprom. This is a revealing illustration of Gorbachev's determination and tactical flexibility—if the aid of the VPK ministries can be enlisted, he seems to be reasoning, give them the whole task! But this tactic has not been particularly successful, and Belousov, the deputy prime minister in charge of the VPK, has been publicly reprimanded by Prime Minister Ryzhkov for failing to follow through.

The effort to enlist the help of the defense industry in dealing with civilian tasks to further economic recovery shifted in early 1989 to a full-scale campaign for conversion of military industry to civilian production. In his speech to the United Nations in December 1988, Gorbachev proposed a conversion "from an economy of armament to an economy of disarmament" on a global scale. Apparently a decision for a more aggressive program of conversion in the USSR was taken at the party plenum in April 1989. In his closing remarks to the plenum, Gorbachev said that the defense industries would have to help, and he called on VPK Chairman Belousov to devote more attention to the needs of the civilian economy.[57] The now modish conversion theme covers a heterogeneous set of shifts. One form is converting equipment scrapped as a result of arms-cut agreements to civilian purposes—using tanks as bulldozers, converting missile transporters to cranes, using military aircraft for civilian transport, and so on.[58] But the most significant form of conversion is of existing plants in the defense-industrial complex from military to civilian production. There apparently now exists an elaborate plan that calls for the defense-industrial ministries to expand production of consumer durables and of equipment for reequipping the light and food industries, extending to the year 1995. Prime Minister Ryzhkov has said that the share of civilian output in the total output of the defense industrial sector is to go from 40 percent at present to 60 percent by 1995. Belousov has since provided some additional details,[59] stressing the great variety of food-processing equipment the defense industries are to produce. Some 209 R&D organs in the defense-industrial ministries are

---

[56] *Pravda*, 26 February 1988, 2.

[57] Gorbachev speech reported in *Ekonomicheskaia gazeta*, no 18 (1989).

[58] On a civilian transport role for military aircraft, see "Mirnye reisy boevykh samoletov," *Pravitelstvennyi vestnik*, no. 8 (1989).

[59] I. S. Belousov, "Adresovano agropromu," *Pravitelstvennyi vestnik*, no. 4 (1989), 2. He has a similar article in *Sovetskaia Rossiia*, 10 February 1989.

being assigned to design the new civilian equipment. Other ministers of the defense-industrial ministries have added numerous statements about their plans for conversion.[60] Some showcase plants have been selected for conversion, including a MIG-29 plant in Moscow. There was a great deal of talk about conversion at the Congress of People's Deputies in May–June 1989, and in his speech after being named prime minister, Ryzhkov gave this theme an important place. The idea of conversion is also being applied to the space program, which is dominated by military missions.[61]

But in all this flurry of discussion about conversion, there are numerous confirmations of how difficult it has been even to begin to reorient the defense-industrial ministries away from military to civilian production. V. A. Shamshin, minister of communications, has complained about the unresponsiveness of the Ministry of the Communications Equipment Industry to its needs and has revealed that only 5–6 percent of the output of the latter is civilian equipment.[62] The latest organizational shakeup, however, may put communications equipment under his direct command.

The most interesting hint of difficulty is a statement by Ryzhkov in his speech to the Congress of People's Deputies in May 1989 that in the Twelfth FYP "we were compelled to envision a growth of defense expenditures at a pace exceeding the growth of the national income."[63] An interesting conjecture, as one looks back over the various elements in Gorbachev's moves to reduce the influence of the military establishment and its drain on the economy, is that he seems to have found the military-industrial establishment more difficult to deal with than the uniformed military themselves.

In retrospect, the limited success that even Gorbachev has had in trying to alter behavior in the defense-industrial sector strengthens the view that, to the extent the leaders tried in the Tenth and Eleventh FYPs to reallocate resources, they continued to be frustrated by the informal priority system favoring military procurement.

Manpower Policy

From an economist's perspective, military manpower policy serves national goals badly, especially in the light of a tight labor market, increasingly so-

---

[60] For examples, see P. Finogenov, minister of the defense industry, in *Pravda*, 15 March 1989, and L. D. Riabev, then minister of medium machine building, in *Pravitelstvennyi vestnik*, no. 4 (1989).

[61] See "Kosmos—narodnomu khoziaistvu," *Pravda*, 2 February 1989, reporting on a visit by O. D. Baklanov, party secretary in charge of military-industrial affairs, and V. Kh. Doguzhiev, then minister of general machine building, to the plant producing the Energiia-Buran space shuttle.

[62] *Pravitelstvennyi vestnik*, no. 9 (1989).

[63] *Sotsialisticheskaia industriia*, 8 June 1989.

phisticated military technology, and a changing ethnic mix in the draft pool. Forces consisting of short-service, poorly motivated conscripts, with a rising share of non-Slavic minorities, would seem to fit poorly with advanced weaponry. A pay scale far below the opportunity cost of manpower encourages wasteful use of a crucially short national resource. Draftees are paid only a few rubles a month, as against an average wage in the economy of over two hundred rubles a month. Although military manpower policy answers to many considerations other than economic rationality, and although there are benefits as well as opportunity costs to the present system,[64] military manpower would seem to be an area where a changing economic environment ought to be a powerful stimulus to a rethinking of past policies.

The draft pool is decreasing in size and changing in composition. The 18-year-old cohort, having fallen from 1.639 million persons in 1979 to 1.382 million in 1985, is expected to be a mere 1.362 million in 1990 and to rise slightly thereafter.[65] It is necessary to call up a large fraction of this pool each year to maintain the armed forces at the estimated current level of 5.3 million men.[66] The share of those taken must have risen as the pool shrank, though there are enough puzzles in reconciling the estimated size of the draft-age cohort with the commonly accepted estimates of manpower in the armed forces to call the latter into question.

Within the group taken, the share of non-Russian nationalities must also be rising. Young men from the Muslim areas of the USSR represent a growing share of the total. It has been estimated that in the 1980 cohort, 23.5 percent of the 18-year-old males were Muslim-Turkic by ethnic origin, but by 1990 it will be 26.5 percent, and by 2000, 28 percent.[67] These groups generally have lower educational attainment, and many of them do not speak Russian, the language of command in the armed forces. Moreover, the preinduction training they receive through paramilitary programs and in the schools in their national areas is said to be weak compared to the national average.[68]

The traditional way to meet military manpower needs out of this cohort is by selection according to a services pecking order. Many of those considered unsuitable for the main kinds of service are placed in construction battalions and railroad troops. But it will be increasingly difficult to continue to use this

[64] Soviet manpower policy and its rationale are described in Ellen Jones, *Red Army and Society* (Boston: Allen and Unwin, 1985), chaps. 2 and 3; and Harriet Fast Scott and William F. Scott, *The Armed Forces of the USSR*, 2d ed. (Boulder: Westview Press, 1981), chap. 10.

[65] Edmund Brunner, Jr., *Soviet Demographic Trends and the Ethnic Composition of Draft Age Males, 1980–1995*, N-1654-NA (Santa Monica: Rand Corporation, February 1981).

[66] International Institute of Strategic Studies, *The Military Balance, 1985/86.*

[67] Brunner, *Soviet Demographic Trends.*

[68] Dennis J. Bowden, "Islam in the Soviet Military: Implications and Prospects," M.A. thesis, Indiana University, 1985, 23–24.

approach. One would think there would be dissatisfaction on the part of military leaders with the changing nature of the draft pool.

Soviet military sources recognize the point that quality of manpower must rise to handle more sophisticated weapons. According to a recent book, "At the present time the role of engineering and technical cadres and technical specialists is rising. . . . If technicians (*tekhnicheskie spetsy*) in 1945 constituted only 15 percent of the personnel of the armed forces, in 1983 they constituted 40.1 percent. . . . Today use of weapons of heightened destructiveness makes manpower skills ever more important and makes the outcome dependent on practically every soldier, not just officers." The importance of mental and educational qualities is increasing, requiring from each person "a high level of educational attainment, profound professional military knowledge, abilities and habits, heightened responsibility and self-discipline, initiative, and creativity."[69]

But this source seems not to consider conscript qualifications a problem. As of 1 January 1983, 92.3 percent of the enlisted men and noncommissioned officers had education not below middle school, compared to 33.1 percent in 1965.[70] A favorable environmental change is the spread of secondary education since World War II. By the mid-1970s, incomplete secondary education had become almost universal in the USSR, and it is claimed that by 1978, 96 percent of young people were obtaining some form of complete secondary education.[71] This trend has greatly improved the overall quality of the pool, and the impact of Muslimization has yet to dilute these gains.

One interesting clue to current leadership preoccupations is the fact that preinduction training was essentially ignored in the educational reform that began in the fall of 1985.[72] It was mentioned in an insignificant way in the reform document, and scarcely addressed in the extensive public discussion of the reform. Harley Balzer notes that much of the work on the reform was done while Gorbachev was party secretary for ideology, which suggests that he was not greatly interested in the state of military manpower. This oversight may have been recognized belatedly. In mid-1986 the Politburo adopted a decree intended to improve preinduction preparation for military service, especially mentioning the health and physical conditioning of potential draftees, along with indoctrination in military-patriotic values. Although the decree

---

[69] A. I. Sorokin, ed., *Sovetskie vooruzhennye sily v usloviiakh razvitogo sotsializma* (Moscow: Nauka, 1985), 163.

[70] Ibid., 168.

[71] Robert Campbell et al., *Soviet Science and Technology Education* (Washington, D.C.: Foreign Applied Sciences Assessment Center, 1985).

[72] Harley Balzer, *Effects of Soviet Education Reform on the Military* (Washington, D.C.: Foreign Applied Sciences Assessment Center, 1985).

seems not to have been published, the Politburo summary did not mention language as a problem.[73]

Occasionally one can find a statement expressing worry about the quality of these conscripts, including inadequate Russian. Marshal Ogarkov, for example, noted that "the high level of technical equipment of the army and navy presents serious demands regarding the quality of the draft pool. Today it is hard to find a place for an uneducated person in a military unit or on a ship." He adds that the military must obtain people of adequate general education and technical preparation, and, "remembering the multinational composition of the armed forces, knowing Russian well."[74] In general, comments on the language problem of non-Russian conscripts are becoming more common.

There are many indicators that the leaders have concluded that treatment of military manpower is counterproductive, as in a 1986 Politburo call for measures to improve the living conditions of soldiers,[75] and approval of improved benefits for the dependents and widows of short-term servers.[76] As perestroika and glasnost have spread to the armed forces, there has been an explosion of criticism of living conditions, mostly referring to conscripts, but also to officers. Murray Feshbach reports extensive discussion in the specialized press of health care deficiencies in the military.[77] Politburo discussions have become more and more critical of the conditions under which conscripts serve.[78]

Civilian critics have complained of the deleterious effects of interrupting education for military duty, and although this is disputed by military spokesmen, who fear a decline in the size of forces, apparently educational deferments have once again been expanded.[79]

In the first several years of the Gorbachev period, one could search in vain for evidence that any consideration was being given to a new manpower policy that would pay servicemen a real wage, drastically reduce the numbers in service, enhance the attractiveness of extended service for the enlisted ranks, and generally professionalize those ranks. But that issue seems gradually to be moving onto the agenda. Criticism of the draft and suggestions of a volunteer army began to appear in letters and articles in the press in late 1988, suggesting that the matter is about to be considered seriously by policy makers.[80]

[73] *Ekonomicheskaia gazeta*, no. 24 (1986), 3.

[74] "Na strazhe mirnogo truda," *Kommunist*, no. 10 (1981), 90.

[75] Politburo summary in *Ekonomicheskaia gazeta*, no. 49 (1985), 3.

[76] Politburo summary in ibid., no. 3 (1986), 3.

[77] Murray Feshbach, "Medical Problems in the Soviet Military," *Kennan Institute Meeting Report*, 1986.

[78] Summary of the Politburo session of 13 October 1988, in *Ekonomicheskaia gazeta*, no. 42 (1988), 7.

[79] According to *Literaturnaia gazeta*, no. 52 (1987), 1, "A decision has been taken to restore deferments for students of a number of the most important vuzy."

[80] A reader's letter in *Izvestiia*, 6 October 1988, suggested the possible desirability of a volun-

Implications for Civil-Military Relations

To assess the import of these changes for the broader issue of civil-military relations, it will be useful to expand on the general description of civil-military relations laid out in chapter 1.

The "civil" aspect of the relationship, in my view, should be understood in terms of a means-ends hierarchy of social goals in which the use of military force, and the institutionalized responsibility for creating and using it, are understood as an instrument of higher-level societal goals, such as continued party control, economic growth, fulfillment of ideological aspirations, and satisfying the population. To ensure that the military remains in its instrumental role, modern states resort to the professionalization of the military, defining their responsibility as an instrument and limiting soldiers' authority to discharge that responsibility, but not define it. Socialist states differ from pluralist ones, of course, in that responsibility and authority for pursuing "civil" purposes are largely in the hands of the Communist Party and its instruments.

"Military" refers in the first instance to the armed forces and the Ministry of Defense. Yet, to fulfill their responsibility in the modern world, the military professionals need a huge volume of resources beyond manpower alone, and the institutions responsible for producing weapons take on a military character. They are secret, they operate outside the norms characteristic for civilian producers, and they are closely directed by the military proper. In short, the definition of the "military" should properly include defense industry.

In fulfilling its responsibility, the military establishment has several kinds of claims against the civil component. First, it needs a great many resources. Second, its technique of using force to attain national security and international relations goals competes with other methods of pursuing the same ends, such as diplomatic means, or arms control. Third, it is sensitive about professional independence; it does not want civilians telling it how to run its business in such areas as creating a fighting spirit or setting criteria of effective performance and promotion. Fourth, this latter sensitivity sometimes spills over into pretensions regarding proper public values in the larger society—military-patriotic ideals, appreciation and support of the military mission, willingness to sacrifice, and the like. Fifth, its capability for the use of force creates the possibility that it could defy and subvert the civil authority it is intended to serve, so that potentially it could claim sovereign power.

"Relations" refers to the various institutions and processes through which the military interacts with the civil society in exercising these claims. Examples of formalized institutions are the Defense Council and the law on univer-

---

teer army; at about the same time, *Moscow News* carried an article by a military officer along the same lines.

sal military service. "Processes" refers to the less constitutionalized features of how those institutions work. In each of these claim areas and forums, the civilian side is organized to handle its end in negotiating these claims. The party is represented in the Defense Council; there is a structure relating Gosplan in general to its own military department; the new Bureau for Machine Building is a counterweight to the VPK; the MPA has a defined status in relation to the Central Committee apparatus; and so on. Outcomes in these interactions are governed by access, rules for participation, knowledge, and other kinds of resources brought to bear by each side.

To repeat, the interface in civil-military relations is not necessarily between the "uniformed" forces and the rest of society. Under the draft system, conscripts bring civilian values and goals to their interaction with the cadre forces. The defense industry complex is closely enough allied with the military establishment that a crucial civil-military interface—one might say *the* crucial interface—is within the VPK or between the VPK and civilian industry, rather than between industry and the armed forces. Once the science establishment becomes highly involved in creating the means of force, a portion of that establishment gets co-opted into military activities, and the civil-military dividing line runs through the science establishment itself. The arena in which the "military" claim is fought over is partly within the Academy of Sciences, rather than in a setting pitting "the military" against some civilian body.

These interactions inevitably involve differences in points of view, namely, civil-military conflict, but for the most part the interaction proceeds productively within a kind of equilibrium. That equilibrium has a constitutional aspect, in which there is a routine set of understandings about settings, access, roles, and procedures, and another aspect that is more a state variable characterizing the balance of military claims against the civil side of society, such as the share of GNP going to defense, the degree of symbolic honoring of military values, or the governing doctrine and allocation of responsibilities for dealing with international relations. The distinction between constitutional status and process outcomes is slippery, and one should think in terms of a spectrum of relationships.

It is easy to apply these ideas about changes in civil-military relations to this chapter. If the wall between defense industry and civil machine building were to be torn down, that would be institutional change weakening the claim of the military for preferential treatment in resource allocation. If particular plants were to produce telecommunications equipment for the Ministry of Communications rather than for the military, that would be an operational outcome reflecting diminution of military strength in this relationship. If the draft law were to be changed so that conscription were more selective and servicemen were paid a wage more nearly comparable to civilian occupations, that would inject a new criterion, efficiency, into the military's deliberations about the manpower input they want. This would diminish the military's ability to press their claim, since it sets up a test they did not previously have to pass.

Another relevant dimension of civil-military relations is how one understands "politics," which has to do mainly with the "civil" part of this relationship. Gorbachev arguably is trying to create a "civil society," separable from the state, of the Western kind. He is groping toward a variable-sum concept of politics, which views politics not as a process that divides up a fixed sum of "power" but as a process that both generates and allocates power. It uses participation, trust, and other such novel tactics to elicit commitments, energies, and initiative, enhancing the capability of the society to achieve the goals that are at the top of the means-ends hierarchy mentioned earlier.

This enrichment and complexification of the "civil" side of the relationship itself changes civil-military relations, although what the effect might be in the USSR is only beginning to be seen. A hypothetical example might be the American phenomenon of university scientists trying to organize a boycott against participation in SDI research. Such an action would have been impossible in the USSR in the past; a shift toward a civilian society there will enhance that possibility. This claim would in the traditional system be adjudicated at the top of the hierarchy, but, with modernization, lower-level players and institutions will become involved in it. The quest of the Baltic states for more autonomy has included a demand that central ministries build additional plants in the area only with the agreement of the local authorities. This will undercut the ability of the defense industries to gain access to the superior resources of the Baltic area for their high-technology projects.

The emergence of "civil society" phenomena might seem to decrease military power in civil-military relations, but whether it does, and by how much, depends on the response of the military. One could imagine the military deciding to go outside its own professional sphere to develop a public relations capability and to strengthen its role in the interaction with new political players. This would be analogous to the polished way it responded to the Pentagon publication *Military Power* by producing a Soviet clone. The more complex interaction that resulted might not necessarily represent a net shift toward civil *or* military influence. It seems clear that, thus far, there has been very little response to the new situation on the military side.

Economic stringency has clearly generated civil-military conflict and led to some renegotiation of the contract governing relations between the civilian and military leaderships. No outsider knows exactly how that contract was thought of by the two parties, but the military leaders probably thought of it as a kind of guaranteed priority growth of resources available to them to carry out their responsibility for national security. Ultimately, the economic slowdown raised the issue of the ability of the civilian leadership to assert the primacy of a more general goal structure over the military desire for more resources.

The leadership's control over the civil-military resource split was hindered by a supersecret decision-making process, and a walled-off defense-industrial sector. This was an extension of the professionalization tactic beyond the military establishment proper to the sector serving its weapons needs, which has made it difficult to implement a change in priorities. The weapons-producing establishment had too much autonomy; the mechanism that assured it priority treatment took on a life of its own. When Gorbachev came to reassert the authority of the civilian side, he seems to have been able to co-opt the leaders of the defense production establishment as individuals to help improve management in the rest of the economy. But it has been difficult to deal with the more institutionalized bodies in that complex to get weapons producers to reorient their activities.

This extension of the professionalization formula to the weapons producers exemplifies a more general problem. The growing complexity of military technology raises the dependence of both the military professionals and the weapons producers on still another societal institution, the science establishment. The growing literature on the relationship of the military to science suggests that, on the personal level, scientists are ambivalent about military R&D. The relatively better material and professional working conditions of military R&D are an important attraction to researchers. But such work also has unattractive features—isolation, few publications, obstacles to association with the international scientific community, and so on. On the institutional level, however, the leaders of the society seem to have been able to recruit whatever amount of science they want for military purposes.

If this is a useful way to think about the problem, it might inspire a broader generalization: the general tactic of delimiting the role of the military by professionalizing it gets more complicated as time goes on. The increasing importance of weapons acquisition, and then of science, brings in more groups with an interest in the outcome. And although the efforts to create a civil society are still tentative and fragile, such an evolution will further complicate the task faced by the civilian political leadership in managing the process.

Such an extensive reconstellation of the civil-military relationship is less a present reality than a possible future evolution. In the economic area, although the party leadership seems not to be finding the professional military establishment an unconquerable obstacle, it has had much more difficulty with the defense industry. It is surely premature, however, to conclude that a stable new equilibrium with significantly diminished power for the military has been reached.

Appendix A: The Split Between Capital Equipment and Weapons Procurement

The use of data on machinery output and investment to evaluate the flow of machinery to procurement has been discussed too carelessly in much of the argument about military expenditures. Looking for evidence of shifts between procurement and investment in the allocation of machinery output is more complicated than it seems at first, since other sources and uses for machinery output complicate the picture.

A basic consideration is the importance of *finished products*—weapons or equipment for investment. Unfortunately, most of the available information about machinery output refers to "gross output," which includes sales of components and intermediate goods to other firms as well as finished products for delivery to final uses. The share of such intermediate sales in gross output can change. Since information on what the trend has been is sparse, reconciliation of the two concepts is uncertain. A further complication is that domestic production is decreased and augmented by exports and imports of both intermediates and finished products. Furthermore, the resulting net domestic supply of finished machinery items includes consumer durables, as well as equipment for investment and military hardware.

Numerous attempts have been made to use these relationships in a so-called residual method that corrects for net machinery trade and subtracts equipment investment and consumer durables from final output of machinery to estimate the amount of hardware available for the military. In general, such attempts lack precision, since each step in the procedure suffers from conceptual fuzziness, uncertainties of data interpretation, and differences in price base.[81] Having tried my own hand at this, I find it so fraught with difficulties that I have given it up as not worth the effort. My goal here is less ambitious, namely, to see if trends in these end-uses seem consistent with the hypothesized changes in allocation priorities, and their timing.

A tabulation of average annual rates of growth of machinery output and related series generally shows no significant interperiod anomalies over the four FYPs between 1965 and 1985 that would suggest a differential check to

---

[81] Daniel L. Bond and Herbert S. Levine, "The Soviet Machinery Balance and Military Durables in SOVMOD," in U.S. Congress, Joint Economic Committee, *Soviet Economy in the 1980's: Problems and Prospects*, part 1 (Washington, D.C.: GPO, 1982), 296–318; Bonnie Matosich, "Estimating Soviet Military Hardware Purchases: The 'Residual Approach,' " in U.S. Congress Joint Economic Committee, *Gorbachev's Economic Plans* (Washington, D.C.: USGPO, 1987), 1:431–461; *Planecon Report*, vol. 2, nos. 25–26; William T. Lee, *The Estimation of Soviet Defense Expenditures, 1955–75: An Unconventional Approach* (New York: Praeger, 1977).

Average Annual Rates of Growth of Soviet Machinery Output

	1970/1965	1975/1970	1980/1975	1985/1980
Machinery Output (TsSU, gross)	12.1	12.1	8.6	6.2
Machinery Output (CIA, value added)	7.3	7.7	4.0	2.7
Net Machinery imports (CIA)	31.6	51.6	18.7	36.7
Investment in Equipment (TsSU)	7.6	8.8	6.5	4.5
Consumer Durables Output (CIA)	11.3	11.7	13.9	na

Sources: GNP and machinery output from handbooks and CIA, *Handbook of Economic Statistics*, 1985 edition, and for later years from speeches and plans. Net machinery imports and consumer durables are from Bonnie K. Matosich, ''Estimating Military Hardware Purchases: The 'Residual' Approach,'' in Joint Economic Committee, *Gorbachev's Economic Plans* (Washington, D.C., 1987), 1:431, 461.

growth of hardware procurement in 1976–1980 or 1980–1985. Investment in equipment slowed more or less *pari passu* with total machinery output; the only hint of a reduction in supply for procurement is the diminished augmentation of supply through trade in the Tenth, compared to the Ninth FYP.

These figures do more to raise questions than to settle them. It is implausible that growth of machinery output could consistently exceed growth of investment in equipment to the degree the two TsSU (Central Statistical Administration) series imply. With net imports growing faster than machinery output, and with consumer durables too small in the total for their faster growth to make any appreciable difference, the implication is that final output grows considerably slower than gross, or military procurement faster than total machinery output. The available evidence suggests that final output grows only slightly slower than gross output.[82] The rate of growth of military procurement required to reconcile the difference is too large to be plausible. The index of machinery output, though said to be in constant prices, is seriously biased upward through price inflation and a secular increase in double counting. It is generally accepted that this is so, even by economists.[83]

[82] The share of gross value of output of machine building used as intermediate consumption as shown in Soviet input-output tables was 42 percent in 1966, 45 percent in 1972, and 48 percent in 1977. See Bond-Levine, *The Soviet Machinery Balance*, and CIR staff paper, *Construction of a 1977 Input-Output Table*, January 1984.

[83] As one among many instances, see K. K. Val'tukh and B. L. Lavrovskii, ''Proizvodstvennyi apparat strany; ispol'zovanie i rekonstruktsiia,'' *EKO*, no. 2 (1986), 17–32, who say on page 28, regarding machine building, ''It is impossible to assess the growth of this branch by its gross output index; here an especially important role is played by pure price inflation caused by changes in the *nomenklatura* of output. The development of ineffective specialization also plays a certain role [i.e. an increase in double counting]. Finally, one must remember that gross output encom-

Comparison of the supply and use of machinery for investment is complicated by the fact that it is generally thought that the investment series is also inflated. A number of economists have made a convincing case.[84] But the degree of inflation in the equipment component of investment may be less than that in the output of machinery. One possibility for differential inflation is that machinery output is inflated by increases in the degree of double counting, while investment in machinery is not. Another is that all the inflation in machinery prices may not be carried over into the supposedly constant-price estimate prices in which investment is reported. The "estimate costs," on the basis of which investment is financed and in which investment is tracked, do not keep up with the rise in machinery prices. They are adjusted upward from time to time, but with lags.[85]

The problem is different if one begins with the CIA index for machinery output. Because the machinery output series is thought to be seriously inflated, the CIA produces its own index of machinery output, conceptualized as an index of value added.[86] It grows only about half as fast as the index, and even slower than the "equipment-for-investment" index. Note that the gap between the CIA's machinery output growth rate and the higher investment-in-equipment growth rate has tended to increase. This would be consistent with

---

passes all output of machine building, while analyzing the growth of production capacity requires looking at the final output of machine building that goes for productive use.''

[84] V. K. Faltsman, "Mashinostroenie: puti peremen," *EKO*, no. 12 (1985), 3–20; G. Khanin, "Sochtem fondy," *Sotsialisticheskaia industriia*, 29 August 1986, 2.

[85] Faltsman and Kornev speak of "cost increases [*udorozhanie*] arising in the review of estimates in the process of construction." I imagine a process like the following: the price for a piece of equipment shown in the *smeta* could be higher than for a nearly identical piece of equipment in an earlier project. That is how inflation enters the equipment part of the investment series. But even after a price is fixed, one might still have to pay more for the machine (substitution, price rise) than shown in the smeta. This would be financed by going to the Stroibank, with the original smeta still used for reporting investment volume. These authors say the Stroibank has done many studies showing the prevalence of financing above the smeta. See V. K. Faltsman and A. Kornev, "Rezervy snizheniia kapitaloemkosti moshchnostei promyshlennosti," *Voprosy ekonomiki*, no. 6 (1984), 36–45. One source says that a fifth of the rise in investment costs is caused by price increases on equipment over the prices used in the original design. L. Braginskii, in *Izvestiia*, 23 January 1986, 2.

There is a big argument about the relative plausibility of the machinery output index and the index of investment in machinery, the unsettled state of which is on public display in Abram Bergson, Philip Hanson, and Alec Nove, "On Soviet Real Investment Growth," *Soviet Studies* (July 1987), 406–433.

[86] For descriptions of how the index is constructed, see F. Douglas Whitehouse and Ray Converse, "Soviet Industry: Recent Performance and Future Prospects," U.S. Congress, Joint Economic Committee, *Soviet Economy in a Time of Change* (Washington, D.C.: GPO, 1979), 1:402–422; and Ray Converse, "An Index of Industrial Production in the USSR," in *USSR: Measures of Economic Development and Growth, 1950–80*, Studies prepared for the use of the Joint Economic Committee, Congress of the United States (Washington, D.C.: GPO, 1982), 169–244.

the hypothesis that machinery output has indeed been diverted from procurement to investment, as the reported slowdown in procurement would imply. But two other plausible causes are that the CIA machinery output index is increasingly understating real growth, or the machinery output indexes and equipment for investment indexes are increasingly inflated. It is likely that all three are happening.[87]

[87] It seems suspicious that in the earlier years the CIA's growth rate for machine building was 60 percent of the Soviet rate, but since 1975 less than half. The CIA procedure includes one feature that biases its index upward—i.e., it uses Soviet constant price indexes for some components—and one that biases it downward—i.e., use of a fixed sample of outputs in physical terms covering today a very small share of total output, mostly only stagnant kinds of output. My view is that these two factors do not cancel each other out—rather, the latter prevails, to give an overall downward bias. An increase in the degree of inflation in the investment-in-equipment index could be caused by the role of imported equipment. The Soviet economist V. K. Faltsman says that a third of all equipment going into investment is imported. See V. K. Faltsman, "Mashinostroenie: puti peremen," *EKO*, no. 12 (1985), 5. It is likely that prices of imported equipment, which have risen rapidly in recent years, go into the reported investment figures without deflation. A rising share of imported equipment in total investment would make the investment series increasingly inflated.

Five

The Defense Industry and Civil-Military Relations

THE AIM of this chapter is to explore the implications for Soviet civil-military relations of the changing position in the economy of the defense industry in the period from Brezhnev to Gorbachev. This period has seen significant changes in the defense industry and the environment within which it works, including changes not only in the political sphere, but also in the general state of the economy, technology, and the international context. Given the crucial role for the military of the weapons industry, and also its importance for the economy and the research and development system, it would be surprising if it played no part in the state of civil-military relations. The available evidence is far from adequate, but it does permit the drawing of some tentative conclusions.

The Military-Industrial Sector

The Soviet military-industrial sector can be seen as a set of institutions for the development and production of weapons and for the planning, management, and political oversight of these processes. Most end-product weapons production and manufacture of major components is undertaken by enterprises subordinate to nine industrial ministries generally considered as constituting the Soviet defense industry.[1] The number of enterprises and the size of the labor force employed in these ministries have not been revealed and are impossible to determine with any accuracy from Soviet published sources. According to U.S. intelligence estimates, more than 150 major plants produce weapons, with a further 150 supplying combat support equipment.[2] In addition, some

---

[1] In the reorganization of the government that took place in June 1989, the number of defense-industrial ministries was reduced from nine to seven. The Ministry of Machine Building and the Ministry of the Communications Equipment Industry were folded into other ministries; the Ministry of Medium Machine Building took over the civilian nuclear power industry and was renamed the Ministry of Atomic Energy and Industry. See the list of new ministries published in *Pravda*, 6 July 1989, and the account of Prime Minister Ryzhkov's remarks on the new nuclear ministry in *Pravda*, 5 July 1989.

[2] U.S. Department of Defense, *Soviet Military Power*, 5th ed. (Washington, D.C.: GPO, 1986), 115.

military-related products and also materials, components, and production equipment are supplied by enterprises of nominally civilian industrial ministries.

Most research and development for new weapons systems is undertaken by institutes and design bureaus under the seven defense-sector ministries. Again according to U.S. intelligence sources, there are at least 450 R&D organizations concerned with weaponry, including some 50 major design organizations responsible for major systems.[3] This industrial R&D base is supported by weapons-related research carried out by institutes of the USSR and republican academies of sciences, the higher education system, and the customer, the Ministry of Defense. It is generally accepted that up to half the country's total R&D expenditure is for military purposes.

The activities of the defense-industry ministries are coordinated by the VPK, the Military-Industrial Commission of the USSR Council of Ministers. It is likely that there is close cooperation between the VPK and the defense-sector departments of Gosplan, one of the first deputy chairmen of which leads its military economic planning activities. This set of government agencies is supplemented by the party's own policy and oversight bodies. In the Central Committee Secretariat there is a Defense Industry Department,[4] but overall responsibility usually rests with one of the senior secretaries of the committee, almost invariably a member of the Politburo; the latter body has ultimate authority to resolve policy issues concerning the defense sector and its resource allocations.

The interface with the Ministry of Defense and the service arms is best seen in the context of the weapons-procurement process. On the military side, the principal actors are the deputy minister of defense for armaments, who leads the work of the Ministry of Defense's administrations concerned with weapons R&D and technical policy, and the deputy commanders-in-chief responsible for procurement and leadership of technical administrations within each of the services. These administrations play a central role in the procurement process as they define requirements for new systems, monitor the fulfillment of R&D contracts, organize acceptance trials before new weapons are approved for serial production, and, through their representatives at industrial enterprises (the *voenpredy*), check that the forces receive systems fully corresponding to the agreed technical specifications and quality standards.[5]

[3] U.S. Central Intelligence Agency, *The Soviet Weapons Industry: An Overview* (Washington, D.C.: CIA, 1986), 1.

[4] In the reorganization of September 1988, the Defense Industry Department was renamed the Defense Department, although its chief, O.S. Beliakov, remained unchanged. See *Izvestiia TSK KPSS*, no. 1 [1989], 86. In a note to the Politburo in August 1988, Gorbachev indicated that this department was a temporary concession to the "transitional stage" of economic reform and would eventually be abolished (ibid., 85).

[5] David Holloway, "Innovation in the Defense Sector," *Industrial Innovation in the Soviet Union*, ed. Ronald Amann and Julian Cooper (London: Yale University Press, 1982), 321–331.

In discussion of Soviet military affairs, the uniformed military and the defense industry are at times discussed as if they constituted a single "military" interest. In my view, such conflation is incorrect. The defense industry and the armed forces have their own distinct organizational structures and concerns. In Soviet understanding the former is part of the "national economy" and as such must share many of the interests and concerns of other sectors of the economy. The armed forces, notwithstanding the fact that they embrace a range of economic activities and depend on the economy for their supplies, are above all concerned with military matters.

If one examines the career structures of members of the forces and of leading administrators and technical personnel of the weapons industry, one finds that they are strikingly distinct, with few examples of individuals who have switched from one to the other. In fact, recent years have seen only two notable exceptions, both at a senior level: D. F. Ustinov's appointment as minister of defense in 1976, and V. M. Shabanov's crossover from the radio industry, where he was a deputy minister, to become deputy defense minister for armaments in 1978.[6] Contacts between the two organizational hierarchies appear to be structured by the stages and procedures of the procurement process, with the technical administrations fulfilling a mediating function. Major issues of policy concerning both parties, or serious conflicts between them, will be referred to the Defense Council, the party Secretariat, or the Politburo.

The Brezhnev Years: A Golden Age?

The new general secretary who succeeded Khrushchev was no stranger to the defense industry. During the late 1950s, as Central Committee secretary responsible for the oversight of heavy industry, the defense sector, and the space program, Leonid Brezhnev became familiar with many of its leading figures. In the words of a participant in the missile program, "During those years the office of the secretary of the CC [Central Committee] was a kind of staff headquarters where the most important problems of missile technology were resolved, and meetings held with the participation of the most eminent scientists, designers, and specialists in various fields of science, technology and production. L. I. Brezhnev was often seen in the factories where missile technology was being created."[7] Indeed, it may well have been this experience and the contacts forged during it that were crucial in securing his rise to supreme power in October 1964.

---

[6] Shabanov, however, could be said to have returned to his original career track as he initially served in the air force as an acceptance tester of new radar systems. See M. M. Lobanov, *Razvitie sovetskoi radiolokatsionnoi tekhniki* (Moscow: Voenizdat, 1982), 170 and 231.

[7] V. Tolubko, *Nedelin: pervyi glavkom strategicheskikh* (Moscow: Molodaia Gvardiia, 1979), 183.

A striking feature of the Brezhnev period was the stability and cohesiveness of the defense industry's administrative elite.[8] The defense industry had been less affected by Khrushchev's reforms than the rest of the economy: whereas civilian industries suffered considerable organizational fragmentation during the time of the *sovnarkhozy*, the territorial system of industrial administration introduced in 1957, the defense sector maintained a more centralized command structure. This probably helped to strengthen the cohesiveness of an already well-established group with ties dating back to the war and even earlier, and it also may have enhanced its position vis-à-vis the leadership of civilian ministries.

The key figures of this period had long had close working relations with one another and with Brezhnev. The center of this network was Ustinov. Commissar for armaments during the war and minister during the postwar years, Ustinov was almost certainly chairman of the VPK during the time Brezhnev was overseeing the defense industry. An important element in Ustinov's rise may have been his ministry's responsibility for the rapidly expanding missile industry. Association with this industry, again during Brezhnev's period of oversight, carried L. V. Smirnov to leadership of the VPK in 1963. I. D. Serbin became head of the Central Committee's Defense Industry Department in 1958 and was to retain this important post for more than twenty-two years. From 1965 his first deputy was I. F. Dmitriev, a close associate of Ustinov from his student days in Leningrad. Dmitriev succeeded Serbin as head of the department, following the latter's death in 1981. A deputy under Ustinov during the war, V. M. Riabikov led Gosplan's defense-sector planning from 1965 until his death in 1974.

Other associates from Ustinov's past in the armaments industry included S. A. Afanasev, responsible for the missile industry from 1965 until the end of the Brezhnev period; S. A. Zverev, minister of the defense industry until his death in 1979; V. V. Bakhirev, leader of the new munitions-producing Ministry of Machine Building created in 1968; and V. N. Novikov, a deputy chairman of the Council of Ministers with responsibility for the engineering industry. According to Khrushchev's son Sergei, at the time of his father's downfall a specialist of the missile design bureau headed by V. N. Chelomei, the forceful Ustinov had no difficulty in getting his way with the pliable Brezhnev.[9]

The stability of personnel characteristic of the Brezhnev years led to an inevitable aging of the defense sector's leadership. Taking the industrial ministers and the chairman of the VKP as a group, their average age in 1965 was approximately fifty-five; by 1975 it had risen to sixty-one; and by the end of the period, 1982, it had reached sixty-five years. Following the restoration of

---

[8] See also Julian Cooper, ''The Elite of the Defense Industry Complex,'' in *Elites and Political Power*, ed. David Lane (Aldershot: Edward Elgar, 1988).

[9] Sergei Khrushchev, ''Pensioner soiuznogo znacheniia,'' *Ogonëk*, no. 41 (1988), 26.

the defense-industry ministries in March 1965 (a few months before the civilian ministries were reorganized), there were no institutional changes apart from the creation of the above-mentioned Ministry of Machine Building in 1968, and in 1974 the separating out from the radio industry of a Ministry of the Communications Equipment Industry. This stability of institutions and personnel was matched by an almost unchanging pattern of political representation of the industry.

As a proportion of full members of the Central Committee, the defense industry group (defined as party and government officials, industrial ministers, and designers and scientists associated with the defense sector) showed a modest tendency to decline, from 6.7 percent in 1966 to 5.6 percent in 1976 and 5.0 percent in 1981; as a proportion of both full and candidate members, the percentage shares were 4.2, 4.5, and 3.8 percent, respectively.[10] Throughout the period the chairman of the VKP and the Gosplan first deputy responsible for defense-sector planning were both full members, as were almost all the ministers, but the head of the Defense Industry Department of the Central Committee remained a candidate member. The only real change in the pattern of representation was the elevation to full membership from 1976 of a group of "general designers" associated with the missile industry (V. P. Glushko, P. D. Grushin, and V. F. Utkin).

Representation on the USSR Supreme Soviet showed an even more marked stability. The defense-industry group (as before, but with the addition of directors of enterprises of the defense-sector ministries) accounted for an unchanged 2.4 percent of the total number of delegates in 1966, 1970, and 1979, with only a modest dip to 2.2 percent in 1974.[11] Again, the scientists and designers were predominantly those associated with the missile industry, but the aviation industry was also strongly represented, especially if account is also taken of enterprise directors. One surprise is that, notwithstanding the expansion of the navy and the associated building program, representation of the ship-building industry remained extremely modest. The well-entrenched aerospace interest may have blocked the advancement of the shipbuilders, but the latter may also have been disadvantaged by their peripheral location: the missile and aviation industries have powerful design, research, and production facilities in or near Moscow; shipbuilding is based in Leningrad, Nikolaev, and other locations far from the capital.

At various times during the Brezhnev period, there were attempts to engage the defense industry to a greater extent in the civilian economy. The Soviet weapons industry has always had a large civilian side to its activities, but the intensity of leadership effort to increase this contribution has fluctuated over

---

[10] Calculated from lists of Central Committee members elected at the congresses of the respective years. Note that the 1981 shares are lower in part because at the time there does not appear to have been a Central Committee secretary with direct responsibility for the defense industry.

[11] Calculated from *Deputaty Verkhovnogo Soveta SSSR* for the relevant years.

time.[12] Many enterprises of the defense sector produce consumer goods, sometimes on a substantial scale. The aviation industry, for example, increased its production of consumer goods from 142 million rubles in 1965 to more than 900 million rubles in 1980.[13] During the 1960s, party and government decrees set out tasks for the defense-sector ministries in such fields as the development and production of medical equipment, the improvement of consumer services, and the extension of land reclamation, but it was only during the early 1970s that the military may have had some grounds for concern that the armaments industry was to be diverted from its basic task.

In 1970 Brezhnev attempted, with some success, to increase the sector's contribution to the supply of agricultural equipment. This was an interesting episode, reflecting the relations between the leadership and the defense industry. There were no direct orders from above; instead, Brezhnev appealed to the political understanding and good will of the ministers concerned. It was made clear that these additional obligations, voluntarily entered into, would be fulfilled without detriment to the ministries' basic activities.[14] In the following year, at the Twenty-fourth Party Congress, Brezhnev went out of his way to emphasize that the defense sector was contributing to the civilian economy and called for more transfers of experience and technology.

There is evidence that this pressure had some impact, at least during the first half of the 1970s. The ship-building industry began producing its large, mobile "Fregat" irrigators, now a quite common sight in the Soviet countryside; output increased from 100 units in 1970 to 1,850 in 1981.[15] Deliveries to the agricultural sector of the heavy-duty "Kirovets" tractor of the Ministry of the Defense Industry increased from 7,400 units in 1970 to 14,500 in 1975, but the rate of growth then slowed, reaching 16,800 units in 1982.[16] In 1966 the vast Izhmash works of the same ministry began building its own version of the "Moskvich" car: output increased from 36,000 vehicles in 1970 to 114,800 in 1975 and 144,000 in 1981.[17]

Until almost the end of the Brezhnev period, however, there were no further public appeals for a greater civilian role for the defense industry. For much of the Brezhnev era there was thus an apparent harmony in the relationship between the military-industrial sector and the political leadership. One dimension of this harmonious relationship was the manner in which the activities of

---

[12] See Julian Cooper, "The Civilian Production of the Soviet Defense Industry," in *Technical Progress and Soviet Economic Development*, ed. Ronald Amann and Julian Cooper (Oxford: Blackwell, 1986), 31–50.

[13] *Trud*, 18 December 1979; *Izvestiia*, 16 February 1980. By 1986 the volume of civilian production had risen to 1,600 million rubles (*Sovetskaia torgovlia*, 11 September 1986).

[14] *Ekonomicheskaia gazeta*, no. 28 (1970), 7–9.

[15] Ibid., no. 26 (1982), 2.

[16] *Narodnoe khoziaistvo SSSR v 1982g.* (Moscow: Finansy i statistika, 1983), 206.

[17] *Narodnoe khoziaistvo Udmurtskoi ASSR za 60 let* (Izhevsk: Udmurtiia, 1980), 34; *Narodnoe khoziaistvo SSSR v 1982 g.*, 180; *Avtomobilnaia promyshlennost*, no. 3 (1982), 1.

the military sector were shrouded in secrecy and protected from public criticism. The only exceptions to this rule were occasional complaints of inadequate quality of consumer goods produced by enterprises of the defense-industry ministries. It is possible, of course, that this shield of secrecy concealed real differences and conflicts, some of which may yet be exposed in the new era of glasnost. Nonetheless, compared with both the preceding and following years, the first decade at least of the Brezhnev period is likely to emerge in relative terms as a golden age.

Pressures for Change

It is not difficult to imagine that by the mid-1970s there was complacency in the top levels of leadership of both the military-industrial sector and its political masters. Thanks to the efforts of the former, the goal of nuclear strategic parity had been achieved; and while Soviet conventional weapons lacked the technological sophistication of their Western counterparts, it was probably accepted that the defense industry's ability to produce in quantity provided adequate compensation. But a plausible case can be argued that there were also mounting pressures for change. By this time, however, both parties were poorly equipped to respond to new challenges.

The Accumulation of Problems

The principal force for change was the rapid development of technology, in particular the growing importance of microelectronics and new materials. This technological challenge and the defense industry's response are discussed more fully in chapter 6.

One aspect of the new developments was the threat to well-established relations within the defense industry: the electronics-related branches were likely to gain at the expense of more traditional, but firmly entrenched, activities. The creation in 1974 of the new Ministry of the Communications Equipment Industry was an early manifestation of this new trend.

Another important source of pressure for change was the state of the economy, in particular the declining rate of growth. The trend of development of the economy and the appearance of disproportions and strains must have caused concern to the leadership of the military-industrial sector. It is unlikely that the sector's privileged position guaranteed immunity from short-term dislocations during what are now termed the "years of stagnation," and there must have been anxiety about the long-term implications of the current trends for the capability to produce the quantity and quality of weapons required by the country's armed forces.

The remarkable stability of the defense industries' leading personnel and the nature of the relationship with the top party hierarchy must have limited the ability to perceive the seriousness of the situation and to devise appropriate policy responses. As noted above, by 1982 the average age of the administrative elite of the defense industry had reached sixty-five years. At eighty-four, E. P. Slavskii, responsible for the production of nuclear weapons, was the country's oldest industrial minister. Smirnov, chairman of the VPK, had been in his post for almost twenty years. The conservatism and fear of change of the leadership are exemplified by the appointment of Ustinov's long-time colleague I. F. Dmitriev as head of the Central Committee's Defense Industry Department in 1981 at an age of over seventy-two years.

The replacement of many elderly directors of enterprises of the military sector in the post-Brezhnev period and criticisms of their work suggest that, as in other spheres of Soviet life, complacency and a general lowering of expectations for effort and discipline became widespread. While the defense industry probably remained the most highly disciplined sector of the economy, it had the advantage that poor performance could be more easily concealed through secrecy and the long-standing protective relations of its leading personnel.

The appointment of Ustinov as minister of defense in 1976 may have had some bearing on the above insofar as it probably led to some weakening of party supervision over the activities of the defense industry. Initially, the relatively inexperienced Ia. P. Riabov was Central Committee secretary responsible for oversight of the military-industrial sector. This was Riabov's first appointment in the central party apparatus; all his previous experience had been in Sverdlovsk. In practice, it is likely that the real power rested with the committee's Defense Industry Department under Serbin, who had occupied the post since 1958, assisted by his first deputy, Dmitriev. When Riabov was moved to Gosplan early in 1979, he was not replaced, and it is generally assumed that Ustinov combined the role of party overlord of the armaments industry with his brief as defense minister. Again, it is likely that the department exercised effective control. This provides further evidence that party-defense industry relations were not perceived as problematic.

As economic problems accumulated, the political leadership began to look to the military sector for solutions. In 1981, at the Twenty-sixth Party Congress, Brezhnev renewed his call for greater defense-industry involvement in research and development for consumer-related activities.[18] The planning and management practices of the military sector began to be seen as means of improving the innovative performance of the civilian economy.[19]

[18] *Materialy XXVI sezd KPSS* (Moscow: Politizdat, 1981), 43–44.
[19] Ronald Amann and Julian Cooper, eds., *Industrial Innovation in the Soviet Union* (London: Yale University Press, 1982), 507–511.

The years 1980–81 saw the beginning of transfers of leading administrators from the defense industry to civilian economic institutions. The first case was the transfer of I. S. Silaev from the aviation industry to the post of minister of the machine tool industry. This proved short-lived as the early death of the aviation industry's minister led to Silaev's return as his replacement, but the new leader of the machine tool industry, B. V. Balmont, was also a transferee, this time from the missile-producing Ministry of General Machine Building. While the defense sector meets some of its own requirements for machine tools, it is still to a large extent dependent on the civilian machine tool industry. Thus, this transfer could be interpreted as an attempt to use the skills and experience of the military sector to improve the work of a branch of industry vital to both sectors of the economy. Until the death of Brezhnev, however, this transfer remained an isolated case.

In sum, at the time of Brezhnev's death in 1982, the country had a defense-industry administrative elite that, like the political leadership, had become elderly, conservative, and complacent, ill-equipped to tackle the problems of economic stagnation and rapid technological change. The lack of personnel renewal and the consolidation over many years of close relations between the two elites must have created substantial inertia: even if the party had decided on the necessity of a reorientation of the military sector, it is questionable whether this could have been achieved.

First Attempts at Renewal and Reorientation

Since the death of Brezhnev, there have been many changes both within the military industrial sector and in its relations with the top political leadership. There were some developments under both Andropov and Chernenko, but the pace of change, as in so many aspects of Soviet life, accelerated markedly following Gorbachev's accession.

Given the policy emphasis on restoring order and discipline which characterized Andropov's brief rule, it is not surprising that the defense sector was seen as a source of personnel, ideas, and experience. The switch of ministerial briefs of S. A. Afanasev from the missile industry to heavy and transport machine building in April 1983 could be so interpreted, as could the prominent role granted to Gosplan's first deputy chief, L. A. Voronin, in leading work for the experimental introduction of new planning and management methods in industry. Voronin, who later became head of the state supply agency, Gossnab, was previously responsible for military-sector planning in Gosplan.

Andropov's experiment in industrial management placed considerable emphasis on contract discipline and may well have been influenced by defense-industry experience.[20] In August 1983, a package of measures for improving innovative performance also showed evidence of borrowing from the military sector. Another development of note was the appointment of G. V. Romanov as Central Committee secretary responsible for oversight of the military production, which could be interpreted as evidence of a desire to strengthen party control. There is no evidence, however, that Romanov used his post to appoint clients within the military-industrial complex.

During the Chernenko interlude of 1984–85, there was one development of large potential significance, namely, the death in December 1984 of Ustinov. With his demise, the defense sector lost its powerful patron, and it was probably this, plus the removal of Romanov a few months later, that created favorable conditions for the sweeping personnel changes and reorientation that were soon to follow under Gorbachev.

Gorbachev and the Military-Industrial Sector

Unlike Brezhnev, Gorbachev has had no association with the military-industrial sector at any stage of his career. This may well provide him with greater freedom of action insofar as he is not indebted to it for his rise to power. Leaving aside the exceptional case of L. N. Zaikov, a Central Committee secretary and for a time first secretary of the Moscow party committee, some other members of the Politburo have had more contact, but often for only a few years early in their careers.[21]

Examples include Zaikov's fellow secretary, E. K. Ligachev, who graduated from the Moscow Aviation Institute in 1943 and then worked for a period at the Novosibirsk aviation works, and V. I. Vorotnikov, who has served mostly as head of government of the Russian republic and who graduated from the Kuibyshev Aviation Institute in 1954 and then worked for several years at the local aircraft factory. An important figure with somewhat more direct experience is N. I. Ryzhkov, the new head of the Soviet government, who worked for many years at the Uralmash heavy engineering works in Sverdlovsk. The wide product range of this vast production association is reported to include artillery systems,[22] but Uralmash is under the civilian heavy-ma-

---

[20] According to a 1978 work on the economics of the aviation industry, one of the main indicators for evaluating enterprise performance was the volume of sales with account of the fulfillment of delivery contract obligations, that is, the same principal as for the Andropov industrial experiment. See V. I. Tikhomirov, *Organizatsiia, planirovanie i upravlenie proizvodstvom letatelnykh apparatov* (Moscow: Mashinostroenie, 1978), 17. Also D. E. Starik, *Ekonomika aviatsionnoi promyshlennosti* (Moscow: Vysshaia Shkola, 1980), 211, which puts even greater emphasis on the link between bonuses and the fulfillment of contractual obligations.

[21] The biographical information that follows is based on *Deputaty Verkhovnogo Soveta SSSR*, Moscow, various years.

[22] See CIA, *The Soviet Weapons Industry*, 14.

chine building ministry and Ryzhkov's later work in Gosplan was not directly concerned with the armaments industry.

In general, by their backgrounds and experience, the top political leaders under Gorbachev are unusually remote from the military sector. Of rising figures not yet in the Politburo, the two with the most experience are O. D. Baklanov, discussed below, and the head of the People's Control Committee, G. V. Kolbin, who began his career at an enterprise in Nizhnii Tagil in the Urals. The enterprise has not been identified but was probably the giant Uralvagonzavod tank and rail freight car works. Kolbin subsequently occupied leading party posts in industrial centers with important defense sector enterprises: Nizhnii Tagil itself, Sverdlovsk, and Ulianovsk.

Changes in personnel gathered pace following the appointment in July 1985 of Zaikov as Romanov's replacement as Central Committee secretary for oversight of the military-industrial sector. This was an interesting appointment. After extensive experience of management in the Leningrad radio-electronics industry, rising to the directorship of a major science-production association, Zaikov served as leader of the Leningrad municipal government and, from 1983, as party first secretary of the Leningrad region. In this latter post, he led work on the local program "Intensification-90," providing for the modernization of Leningrad industry on the basis of the latest technologies and involving cooperation between military and civilian R&D and production organizations. This initiative gained the backing of the Central Committee and was soon taken up by many other industrial centers, in particular those known for their military production role.[23] Zaikov was thus well-qualified to lead a reorientation of the military-industrial sector. After his election as leader of the Moscow city party organization in 1987, Zaikov appears to have retained overall responsibility for oversight of the military-industrial sector, with day-to-day oversight being exercised by O. D. Baklanov, appointed a Central Committee Secretary in early 1988 after serving for five years as minister of general machine building. By the end of 1988, however, it began to appear increasingly likely that Baklanov had taken over full responsibility, although since Zaikov's removal as leader of the Moscow party organization in late 1989, the situation is once more unclear.

One of Zaikov's first changes was the replacement of the seventy-five-year-old Dmitriev as head of the Defense Industry Department by O. S. Beliakov, more than twenty years his junior.[24] Like Zaikov, Beliakov appears to be a

[23] See the author's "Technology Transfer Between Military and Civilian Ministries," in U.S. Congress, Joint Economic Committee, *Gorbachev's Economic Plans* (Washington, D.C.: GPO, 1987), 1:396.

[24] Possibly the earliest evidence of Beliakov's promotion can be found in *Sotsialisticheskaia industriia*, 24 August 1985 (obituary of I. F. Belorodov). Born in 1933, Beliakov worked in the Central Committee apparatus from 1972. Between 1983 and 1985 he served as an assistant to one

radio-electronics specialist.[25] It should be noted that these appointments help to shift the balance away from the artillery-rocket bias of the Ustinov appointees in favor of the new information technologies. This trend has been reinforced by Baklanov's appointment: for twenty-five years he worked at an electronics-related plant of the missile industry. Other leading figures with similar backgrounds include Shabanov, deputy minister of defense for armaments (until 1978 in the radio industry and possibly well-acquainted with Zaikov), and the new Gosplan first deputy for general affairs, A. A. Reut, yet another radio-industry transferee. V. I. Smyslov, the new Gosplan first deputy for military-sector planning, has a shipbuilding background, but this does not rule out the possibility that he also has experience of the electronics-related technologies.

It may well have been Zaikov's influence that accounted for both this trend and the striking bias toward Leningrad as a source of leading personnel. Besides Zaikov himself, those with Leningrad associations now include Beliakov and his first deputy, N. M. Luzhin (at one time chief engineer of the Admiralty shipyard),[26] I. S. Belousov (chairman of the VPK), Iu. D. Masliukov (chairman of Gosplan and a member of the Politburo), Smyslov, and I. V. Koksanov (minister of the shipbuilding industry).

Another significant change was the replacement of Smirnov as chairman of the VPK. His immediate successor, Masliukov, was previously the Gosplan first deputy for the defense sector, and prior to that a deputy minister of the defense industry. Born in 1937, Masliukov is one of the youngest of all the Gorbachev appointees to a senior government post. In February 1988 he was appointed chairman of Gosplan and his successor as VPK chairman became Belousov, previously shipbuilding minister.

Of the nine defense-industry ministries overseen by the VPK, by the end of 1988 only two, the Ministry of the Defense Industry (P. V. Finogenov, appointed in 1979) and the Ministry of the Communications Equipment Industry (E. K. Pervyshin, appointed in 1974) still had ministers appointed in the Brezhnev period. Both were removed in the government reorganization of July 1989. While it is the case that the majority of the new ministers have been internal promotions from first deputy or deputy minister positions, the new leaders are much younger and more highly educated than their predecessors. In three cases they have had experience of work in the party Central Commit-

---

of the Central Committee secretaries (probably Romanov). See *Sovetskii entsiklopedicheskii slovar* (Moscow: Sovetskaia Entsiklopediia, 1986), 127.

[25] In 1982 as deputy head of the department he attended a meeting of the trade union for workers of the radio-electronics industry. *Trud*, 18 February 1982.

[26] Luzhin was identified as first deputy head of an unidentified Central Committee department in May 1988 (*Leningradskaia pravda*, 12 May 1988) but is known to have served previously as a deputy head of the Defense Industry Department. For his Admiralty shipyard post in the early 1970s, see G. V. Romanov, *Izbrannye rechi i stati*, 2d ed. (Moscow: Politizdat, 1983), 25.

tee: V. I. Shimko (born 1938), the minister of the radio industry (until October 1988 and again from July 1989), transferred directly from the Central Committee Defense Industry Department;[27] Slavskii's replacement as minister of medium machine building, L. D. Riabev (born 1933), worked in the Central Committee apparatus for six years before briefly serving as deputy minister (he has since been named deputy prime minister with authority over the energy sector);[28] and the shipbuilding minister, I. V. Koksanov, worked as a sector head in the Central Committee for almost twelve years before becoming first deputy minister of shipbuilding in 1985.[29]

The rejuvenation has been impressive. By the beginning of 1988, the average age of the nine ministers plus the VPK chairman had fallen to fifty-seven, compared with sixty-five just five years earlier. Those who had previously dominated the military-industrial sector rose to positions of power during the war, under Stalin; many of the new generation were only children during the war and embarked on their careers during the Khrushchev and Brezhnev years. The long-standing dominance of the Ustinov group has finally come to an end.

The break-up of the formerly cohesive military-industrial elite and the existence of a new party leadership with limited connections with the military sector is likely to have diminished the political influence of the defense industry. Perhaps as partial compensation for this loss of effective power, the representation of the military-industrial sector on the party Central Committee elected at the Twenty-seventh Congress in 1986 showed a modest increase. For the first time, the head of the Secretariat's Defense Industry Department gained full membership on the committee, raising the share of full members to 5.9 percent compared with 5.0 percent in 1981. Overall, the sector's share of full and candidate members rose to 4.8 percent, a higher level than at any time during the Brezhnev years.[30] The new appointments after the congress, however, left the sector less favorably represented. By the time of the Nineteenth Party Conference in June 1988, five of the nine industrial ministers (B. M. Belousov, V. Kh. Doguzhiev, Koksanov, Riabev, and Shimko) were not members. In the elections for the Supreme Soviet in 1984, the sector's representation increased from 2.4 percent in 1979 to 2.9 percent: again, a higher level than at any time during the Brezhnev period. In this case, the designers achieved the largest gain in representation.[31]

[27] *Izvestiia*, 8 June 1987 and 16 November 1987.

[28] Ibid., 23 November 1986. For a period prior to 1978 Riabev appears to have served as director of a major research institute of the Ministry of Medium Machine Building in the Gorkii region.

[29] Ibid., 22 February 1988.

[30] One reason for the higher share was the election as candidate member of the first deputy minister of the nuclear weapons building Ministry of Medium Machine Building, A. G. Meshkov. This was evidently done on the expectation that he would relieve the elderly Slavskii as minister, but soon after the congress Meshkov was sacked following the Chernobyl accident.

[31] It is interesting to note that during the twenty-year period 1966–1986, scientists and designers experienced the largest increase in representation of all the groups concerned with the military-

Transfers and Cooperation

The hypothesis advanced here is that the diminished political influence of the military-industrial sector is associated with the desire of the party leadership to achieve some reorientation of the work of the defense industry. One aspect of such a reorientation is evident from recent developments: a commitment to harnessing the skills and experience of the military sector to the task of modernizing the civilian economy. But it is possible that there is also a perception that the defense industry needs to be reoriented to meet more fully the requirements of the armed forces, in particular the needs for more rapid and effective technological innovation and for a strengthening of the capability in vital new technology fields, in particular microelectronics, computing, and advanced materials.

There is little doubt that the Gorbachev leadership is seeking a greater contribution to the civilian economy from the military-industrial sector. Gorbachev has shown himself to be well aware of the differential technological capabilities of the two sectors: "Our rockets can find Halley's comet and fly to Venus with amazing accuracy, but side by side with these scientific triumphs is an obvious lack of efficiency in using scientific achievements for economic needs, and many Soviet household appliances are of poor quality."[32] But the achievements of the military sector may also be a source of confidence for the leadership that the Soviet socialist economy *can* produce to the highest world standards: the problem is one of diffusing this positive experience more widely to the general benefit of the economy, or at least, in the first instance, its most important civilian sectors.

One method of diffusing experience is the transfer of personnel, already started on a tentative basis before Gorbachev's election. Under Gorbachev, transfers of personnel have become so extensive that one must conclude that they have been the outcome of a deliberate policy. There must be a perception that military-sector administrators possess skills and other qualities appropriate to the current needs of the economy, and possibly also an expectation that their transfer will improve intersectoral relations and cooperation.

This transfer process is illustrated strikingly by Gosplan. As noted above, its chairman, Masliukov, previously headed the VPK. Reut, his top deputy until July 1989, had a background in the radio industry and served for a time as director of the Minsk computer works. The deputy chairman responsible for the civilian engineering industry, G. B. Stroganov, was previously a dep-

---

industrial sector on both the Central Committee and the Supreme Soviet. This could be interpreted as a deliberate attempt by the party to strengthen the influence of those concerned with innovation as opposed to current production.

[32] Mikhail Gorbachev, *Perestroika: New Thinking for Our Country and the World* (London: Collins, 1987), 21.

uty minister of the aviation industry, while another deputy chairman, Iu. P. Khomenko, was transferred from the communications equipment industry. The former head of the latter ministry's scientific and technical administration, V. V. Simakov, is head of Gosplan's department of science and technology. Besides Gosplan, during Gorbachev's first four years, three other central economic agencies had chairmen with military-sector backgrounds: the State Committee for Material and Technical Supply (Voronin); the State Committee for Standards (G. D. Kolmogorov, again from the communications equipment ministry); and the State Committee for Science and Technology (B. L. Tolstykh, from the electronics industry, where he served for several years as general director of the Voronezh Elektronika Association, one of the leading plants in the field of microelectronics).

The civilian engineering industry has also been a recipient of defense-sector transferees. The two early cases, Afanasev and Balmont, have both been retired, indicating that not all such administrators are suited to the demands of perestroika. Afanasev was older, a representative of the Ustinov group, and therefore his retirement is less surprising. But prior to the reorganization of mid-1989, at least three of the seven ministers of the "machine-building complex," as it is now known, had association with enterprises producing at least in part for the military: V. M. Velichko, of the Ministry of Heavy, Transport, and Power Engineering; N. A. Pugin, of the Ministry of the Automobile and Agricultural Machine Building Industry; and E. A. Varnachev, of the Ministry of Construction and Road Machine Building.[33] With the creation in late 1985 of the Bureau of Machine Building of the Council of Ministers, a supraministerial agency for coordinating the activities of the civilian engineering industry, apparently modeled on the VPK, the influence of defense-sector transferees was further enhanced. The bureau chairman, Silaev, was previously minister of the aviation industry, and one of his deputies, Iu. V. Konyshev, was previously a deputy minister. In this case the aspect of military-sector experience of greatest value to the civilian economy is probably the aviation industry's ability to produce to consistently high standards of quality. Significantly, Silaev's appointment also involved oversight of the work of the State Committee for Standards.[34]

This transfer policy was maintained and even strengthened in the major government reorganization of the summer of 1989. As a result of the changes, at least 30 percent of those appointed to the fifty-eight ministerial posts have defense-industry backgrounds, including six of the thirteen first deputy and deputy chairmen of the Council of Ministers. This led the deputy editor of the

[33] Velichko was director of the Leningrad Bolshevik works, a major military sector enterprise; Pugin of the Gorkii GAZ association, the products of which include military trucks and tracked vehicles; and Varnachev of the Sverdlovsk Uralmash works, the products of which include artillery systems.

[34] See *Ogonëk*, no. 48 (1987), 4 (interview with Silaev).

paper *Moskovskaia pravda* to observe that "the head of government obviously has confidence in people from the defense industry—over a third of the new government comes from there. By the way, this was noticed at once, but then dismissed with a joke—we're in a period of conversion."[35]

It could be argued that the military sector itself must resent this loss of administrative talent to the civilian economy, but looked at from another point of view, there may be reassurance that the sector's interests will be understood and respected during a time of uncertainty and change through the occupation of key posts by its former members. Furthermore, if as seems likely the military sector now appreciates the necessity of a modernization of the civilian economy, it may be more confident of success having its "own people" in commanding positions.

Under Gorbachev the attempt to transfer organizational arrangements and management practices from the military sector to the civilian economy has been stepped up.[36] As noted above, the new bureaus of the Council of Ministers, providing high-level coordination of groups, or "complexes" (in the Soviet terminology) of related ministries, appear to be modeled on the VPK. But probably the most significant recent borrowing has been in the field of quality management and control: the introduction of the state quality acceptance system, *gospriemka*, modeled on the military sector's *voenpred* system. In the words of Gorbachev: "Many things are done well in the country. Take defense. Here we are not lagging behind in anything. This means that we know how to work. But here, I have to say, the inspectors work in such a way that they make it hot for everyone—workers, designers, engineers, and managers alike. This is how gospriemka should work. Then we will have the technology and goods we want."[37]

Like the *voenpredy*, the state quality inspectors work alongside enterprise quality controllers and are responsible for the acceptance of final production. They are highly paid and subordinate to an independent body, in this case the State Committee for Standards. Wisely, no attempt has been made to diffuse this practice throughout the whole of industry; instead, it has been restricted to enterprises producing what are considered to be important products. The gospriemka system has generated many problems and has the weakness that the State Standards Committee does not directly represent the interests of the

[35] See BBC, *Summary of World Broadcasts*, SU/0341 B/16, 22 December 1988, for explicit reference to the retention of the defense industry department in the Georgian party Central Committee. It can be deduced that similar departments have been retained in the Leningrad obkom and Moscow gorkom (*Leningradksaia pravda*, 29 November 1988; *Vecherniaia Moskva*, 9 December 1988).

[36] For more detailed discussion see Paul Cocks, "Soviet Science and Technology Strategy: Borrowing from the Defense Sector," in U.S. Congress, Joint Economic Committee, *Gorbachev's Economic Plans*, 2:145–160.

[37] *Ekonomicheskaia gazeta*, no. 41 (1987), 3.

customers concerned, but nevertheless it is probably a worthwhile measure for inducing greater order and discipline in important branches of the civilian economy.[38] Transfers of organizational arrangements and management practices from the defense sector should probably be seen not as components of a radical economic reform (indeed, as some Soviet economists have pointed out, gospriemka represents a traditional "administrative" method), but as transitional means of creating a more ordered environment favorable to the success of such a reform. As economic reform takes hold, the military sector will probably have more to learn about management practices from the civilian economy than vice versa.

A third type of transfer could be the most important in the long run, namely, transfers of technology and improved cooperation between the military and civilian economies. There is no doubt about the policy commitment: it was made clear by Gorbachev from the outset. Speaking in June 1985, he declared that "the experience of the defense branches must be used in full measure. We have begun this work. It has to be continued actively."[39]

As under Brezhnev, there has been particular reference to assistance from the military sector in modernizing consumer-related activities, but the evidence now points to the desire for a much broader contribution to the general modernization process. And, whereas under Brezhnev the leadership requested assistance from the defense industry, now it appears ready to resort to measures obliging the latter to contribute. Thus, as early as June 1986 Zaikov made explicit reference to a decision to engage the military sector in the technical reequipment of the light and food industries, public catering, and the retail trade system, and at about the same time this was confirmed by the then minister of the shipbuilding industry, I. S. Belousov, who revealed that the Central Committee had obliged his ministry to assist in the provision of new equipment for light industry.[40]

As the reform process has gathered pace, efforts to engage the military sector in civilian tasks have intensified. This became especially apparent from the second half of 1987; by this time the difficulties of modernizing the civilian engineering industry had become evident. In October, at a meeting in the Central Committee on the development of the food-processing industry, Ryzhkov noted that "the powerful production and scientific-technical potential of the defense branches of industry" had to be engaged in the modernization drive. Both Ryzhkov and Gorbachev left no doubt as to the leadership's dissatisfac-

---

[38] The committee has now been renamed the State Committee for the Management of the Auditing of Production and Standards, and, significantly, its new head, V. V. Sychev, was formerly deputy chairman of the VPK. See *Trud*, 14 June 1989, and *Pravda*, 12 July 1989.

[39] *BBC Summary of World Broadcasts*, SU/7976/C/8, 13 June 1975.

[40] *Pravda*, 29 June 1986; *Piataia sessiia Verkhovnogo Soveta SSSR (odinnadtsatyi sozyv), 18–19 iiunia 1986g., stenograficheskii otchet* (fifth session of the USSR Supreme Soviet, 18–19 June 1986, verbatim report) (Moscow, 1986), 268.

tion with the work of the relevant specialized civilian agency, the Ministry of Machine Building for the Light and Food Industries (Minlegpishchemash). Speakers at the meeting included Baklanov, then minister of general machine building.[41] There is evidence that by this time there was already increasing involvement of defense-sector ministries in the development and production of equipment for consumer industries, with examples of joint projects with Minlegpishchemash organizations. Thus the aviation and missile industries had been engaged in the manufacture of presses and extractors for the production of vegetable oils; the shipbuilding and electronics branches in the creation and production of equipment for the textile industry; and new products of enterprises of the Ministry of the Defense Industry included potato-packaging machines and rotary lines for the making of ice cream.[42]

In the spring of 1988, as Robert Campbell also notes in chapter 4, a more radical solution was adopted. Minlegpishchemash was disbanded outright, and many of its 260 enterprises transferred to the defense-sector ministries.[43] The former minister, L. B. Vasilev, was appointed deputy chairman of "one of the commissions of the Council of Ministers," namely, the VPK, to head a department with a staff of twenty or more officials charged with overall coordination of the activities of the enterprises concerned. Each ministry was to appoint an additional deputy minister.[44] The defense sector now has a major new responsibility: it must secure a rapid growth of the output of equipment for consumer-related industries, and it has been made clear that the equipment must be competitive by world standards.

At the time of writing, details of the new responsibilities are incomplete, but it has become apparent that some of the ministers concerned are having to adapt to unaccustomed roles. Riabev, minister for nuclear weapons until his recent promotion to deputy prime minister, had responsibility for the development and production of equipment for the dairy industry and in this capacity had meetings with representatives of Western firms and discussed his ministry's new civilian work in the pages of *Izvestiia*. Not only is the Ministry of Medium Machine Building making dairy equipment, it is also planning to expand sharply its output of consumer goods: new products will include Polaroid cameras (a U.S.-Soviet joint venture), video equipment, computers, and, possibly, refrigerators. From Riabev's account it is clear that resource transfers from military to civilian purposes are becoming a reality. Some military pro-

---

[41] *Pravda*, 19 October 1987.

[42] *Leningradskaia pravda*, 15 May 1987; *Piataia sessiia*, 268; *Tekstilnaia promyshlennost*, no. 1 (1987), 9–11; *Leningradskaia pravda*, 13 March 1987; *Izvestiia*, 23 November 1986.

[43] See *Izvestiia*, 2 March 1988; *Ekonomicheskaia gazeta*, no. 14 (1988), 4; *Pravda*, 2 March 1988. The defense-sector ministries concerned exclude those for the radio, communications, and electronics industries; some enterprises were transferred to two civilian ministries, those for automobiles and electrical equipment.

[44] *Izvestiia*, 2 March 1988.

grams have been halted, two enterprises of the ministry are being reprofiled to civilian work, and the reconstruction of enterprises to make dairy equipment involves the redirection of the ministry's own internal resources.[45] The evidence suggests that similar developments are taking place in other defense-sector ministries. In the radio industry, for instance, work is under way for increasing rapidly the production of refrigeration units for the agroindustrial complex, and this new activity is beginning to engage not only thirteen newly transferred enterprises, but also the well-established facilities of the ministry.[46]

In switching consumer-related activities to the military sector, there must be a danger that the culture of secrecy will frustrate cooperation with customers and inhibit public criticism of shortcomings. At first, in apparent confirmation of these fears, there was little information about the former Minleg-pishchemash enterprises, but by the autumn of 1988 this situation began to change. In October, at a session of the Council of Ministers, the first ever to be shown on television, Belousov, Riabev, A. S. Systsov (of the aviation industry), and others had to answer criticism of work for the development and production of equipment for the food industry. Two main points emerged: first, discontent with the pace of development; second, concern that the ministries were charging inflated prices for civilian items. Concluding the session, Ryzhkov declared, "We are deeply convinced that what has been done with regard to transferring enterprises, institutes, and design bureaus from the former Minlegpishchemash to the defense industries has been done correctly, and we do have confidence that in a year or two we will begin to get the equipment."[47]

Following the Council of Ministers meeting, political pressure on the military sector for improved work for the food industry intensified, accompanied by a further deepening of glasnost. Developments included visits by Ligachev and Baklanov to a number of defense-sector ministries to discuss their work for the food industry, and a visit by Gorbachev and other leaders to an exhibition of new food-processing equipment. The report of the latter revealed that by late 1988, 355 defense-industry enterprises were involved in supplying the food industry.[48] Meanwhile, the energetic Baklanov, in a series of publicized visits to leading establishments of the defense industry, consistently stressed

[45] Ibid., 10 November 1988. Note that some of these new civilian activities (for example, the Polaroid deal) are being handled through the civil arm of the Ministry of Medium Machine Building, namely, the State Committee for the Utilization of Atomic Energy. See *NTR: Nauchno-tekhnicheskaia revoliutsiia*, no. 11 (1988) (74), 2.

[46] *Ekonomicheskaia gazeta*, no. 48 (1988), 4.

[47] BBC, *Summary of World Broadcasts*, SU/0292 C/9, 26 October 1988; *Pravda*, 20 October 1988.

[48] *Pravda*, 19 and 26 November 1988; BBC, *Summary of World Broadcasts*, SU/0320 C/1, 28 November 1988.

the importance of civilian work, in particular the provision of consumer-related equipment.[49]

The case of Minlegpishchemash is not the only example of efforts to increase the involvement of the defense sector in civilian activities. In the early months of 1988, leading representatives of the sector, in particular Baklanov, Belousov, and Beliakov, found themselves involved in discussion of the provision of equipment for such diverse fields as the printing industry, sport and tourism, the animal feed industry, and the education system.[50] Baklanov's responsibilities appear to involve general oversight of the chemical industry: in May 1988 he opened a meeting in the Central Committee on the development of the industry and just before visited one of its leading science-production associations.[51] This interest may arise at least in part from an evident concern to accelerate the development and production of new composite materials, the use of which until recently was restricted almost exclusively to the military sector, in particular the aerospace industry. Given Baklanov's background in the missile industry, he would appear to be in a good position to promote this important technology, which has made little progress outside the military sector.[52]

The issue of composites provides a good illustration of a general point: both civil and military sectors stand to gain from improved cooperation. In this case, the initiative has come from the latter, with the aviation industry taking the lead in a vigorous campaign for a rapid expansion of the use of composites in the economy.[53] The motivation is clear: an increased scale of production and use of composites will lower costs, and an enhanced priority will be associated with a strengthening of the research effort in this important field.

Elsewhere the author has discussed examples of intersectoral transfers and cooperation in the development of such technologies as machine tools, flexible manufacturing systems, industrial robots, and rotary production lines.[54] Over the years the military sector has created a strong research and manufacturing

[49] Examples in the latter half of 1988 include the Leningrad Kirov works, an NPO near Moscow concerned with space technology, the Moscow Skorost works of the aviation industry, and the factory of the Sukhoi design bureau. *Pravda*, 3 September, 19 October, 2 and 17 December 1988.

[50] See ibid., 11 March 1988, 13 May 1988, 23 March 1988, and 21 February 1988.

[51] Ibid., 22 and 17 May 1988.

[52] The interest of the missile industry in composite materials is shown by the prominence in the technology of the late V. P. Makeev, the general designer of sea-launched systems, and V. D. Protasov, who now appears also to be a missile general designer. See, for example, *Zhurnal vsesoiuznogo khimicheskogo obshchestva im D. I. Mendeleeva*, no. 3 (1978), 245–248 and 289. That the use of advanced composites has been restricted to the Soviet aerospace sector has been confirmed by leading representatives of the aviation industry. *Izvestiia*, 2 February 1988.

[53] See *Izvestiia*, 1 September 1986, 12 August 1987 and 2 February 1988, *Pravda*, 8 July 1987; *Sotsialisticheskaia industriia*, 27 October 1987. The principal protagonists have been R. Shalin and I. Fridliander of the All-Union Institute of Aviation Materials and A. Bratukhin, a deputy minister of the aviation industry.

[54] See U. S. Congress, Joint Economic Committee, *Gorbachev's Economic Plans*, 1:388–404.

capability in these and other production technologies, and this offers possibilities for fruitful, mutually beneficial, cooperation with the civilian engineering industry. In recent years such cooperation has been developed at a local level within the framework of city and regional scientific and technical programs of the kind pioneered under Zaikov in Leningrad. It is interesting that since Zaikov's appointment as Moscow party chief, work has started on the elaboration of a comprehensive city economic development plan, ''Progress-95,'' similar in concept to the Leningrad program ''Intensification-90,'' and the evidence indicates that this will also involve organizations of both the civilian and military sectors. Moscow already has a less elaborate modernization program during the current, Twelfth FYP, and, significantly, its scientific leader is P. N. Belianin, director of the aviation industry's central technology institute.[55]

The reorientation of the defense sector is not restricted to the above-mentioned transfers. One of the principal thrusts of current economic policy is the drive to accelerate the development of strategic new technologies, in particular, microelectronics, computing, and other information technologies. But research, development, and production in many of these fields takes place to a large extent within the military sector. The modernization of the civilian engineering industry, a central goal of the current five-year plan, must inevitably involve the ministries of the defense industry, above all the electronics, radio, and communications equipment ministries. Because of their role in supplying computers and other electronic equipment to the civilian economy, it is likely that within the defense industry these ministries are currently receiving preferential resource allocations and undergoing more dynamic development than more traditional activities. Significant in this respect was the Politburo approval in April 1988 of a comprehensive set of measures to accelerate the development of the electronics industry.[56]

It is therefore likely that enthusiasm for the Gorbachev reforms may be unevenly distributed within the military-industrial sector, and the above-mentioned personnel changes in favor of the radio-electronics interest may well reflect a real shift of power now taking place to the disadvantage of some of the traditional weapons-producing ministries. But to the extent that the armed forces now require weapons incorporating advanced electronics, and also modern command, control, and communications systems, such a shift may not be displeasing to the military.

Until the autumn of 1988, the scale of transfer activity and cooperation does not appear to have been very substantial and is unlikely to have contributed much to the rate of growth of the economy. Experience was gained, however, and it is likely that this served to strengthen the leadership's conviction that this is a worthwhile policy to pursue in the interests of rapid industrial mod-

[55] *Izvestiia*, 4 February 1985.
[56] *Pravda*, 29 April 1988.

ernization. As noted above, by the end of 1988, evidence was beginning to mount that resource reallocation was underway.

The INF agreement, for example, created possibilities for expanding the civilian activities of the enterprises previously engaged in the production of intermediate-range missiles and their transport-launch vehicles. Even before the agreement, the Votkinsk machine-building works, responsible for final assembly of the SS-20, was manufacturing NC machine tools, robots, components for the "Izh" cars and pick-ups, and a range of consumer goods, including baby carriages and washing machines.[57] It has been reported that the works will now substantially increase its civilian output: the machine tool building capacity is being increased, and new products will include equipment for underwater drilling rigs and milk processing units for the dairy industry.[58] According to Foreign Minister Shevardnadze, the SS-20 design bureau will now work on a new meteorological rocket, which in future may be offered for export.[59] Claimed savings to the economy from the INF treaty in 1989 alone amount to 300 million rubles.[60]

The INF treaty put conversion from military to civilian production on the policy agenda, but it was Gorbachev's speech at the United Nations in December 1988, with its dramatic announcement of unilateral force reductions, that gave the green light to a national conversion program. Over two years, the production of armaments and other military equipment would be cut by almost 20 percent. In March the following year, Ryzhkov revealed a substantial shift in the structure of output of the defense-industry ministries: from current shares of 60 percent military and 40 percent civilian, by 1991 the ratio would be 50:50, reaching 40:60 in 1995.[61] Work started on a national plan for conversion, and defense-sector enterprises began to report reduced military orders and efforts to switch to new civilian work. Whereas it had been argued in earlier Soviet publications that social ownership of the means of production coupled with central planning would permit trouble-free conversion, it began to be acknowledged that difficulties would be encountered in adapting specialized facilities and skills to new civil purposes.[62] For the defense sector there was an additional complication: the turn to partial conversion coincided with the transition to economic reform.

---

[57] *Izvestiia*, 4 January 1983; *Pravda*, 14 June 1982. The Votkinsk works is also one of three enterprises now attempting to organize the first Soviet production of dishwashing machines. See *Kommercheskii vestnik*, no. 22 (1986), 43. In 1988 the works was planning to make more than 400,000 of the popular Feia small washing machine (*Pravda*, 7 May 1988).

[58] *Sovetskaia Rossiia*, 15 December 1988; *Pravda*, 13 March 1988.

[59] *Pravda*, 29 May 1988.

[60] BBC, *Summary of World Broadcasts*, SU/0338 a1/2, 19 December 1988 (statement by Deputy Foreign Minister Viktor Karpov).

[61] *Sotsialisticheskaia industriia*, 7 October 1989.

[62] See, for example, *International Affairs*, no. 5 (1988), 82–88; *Novoe Vremia*, no. 29 (1987), 8–11; no. 1 (1988), 24–27; no. 27, 20–21; no. 30. 21–22.

The Military-Industrial Sector, Economic Reform, and Glasnost

There has been much speculation about the attitude of the military to the economic reforms proposed by the Gorbachev leadership.[63] It has been argued that there is acceptance of the necessity of modernizing the civilian economy and of some measures of reform, provided that the latter do not involve the widespread use of market relations potentially threatening to the privileged position of the military-industrial sector.

The package of reform measures adopted in the summer of 1987 is not likely to give the defense industry serious grounds for anxiety. While it may experience greater pressure to operate within more strictly enforced financial constraints, the familiar methods of planning and management employed within the military sector are unlikely to change to any appreciable extent. Instead of the existing system of directive output plans, the military sector, together with priority civilian activities, will work to "state orders" with corresponding privileged conditions of work. In particular, the defense industry will retain the traditional system of funded supply for material and equipment inputs.[64]

Thus, the market (or, more accurately, quasi-market) aspects of the reform, such as wholesale trade in inputs and freedom to set output plans and prices in consultation with customers, are likely to impinge only on some of the civilian activities of the military sector. To the extent, however, that the reform puts some important civilian activities on a state-order basis and provides them with relatively favored conditions, it could be argued that the priority line has been redrawn with some potential loss of privilege for the defense sector. But if these civilian activities are necessary to the effective operation of the military sector itself, it is unlikely that this redefinition of priority will be opposed.

One aspect of the reform that could prove unsettling to the military sector is the transition from January 1989 to self-financing, with the expectation that enterprises will operate on a profitable basis. Much will depend on the impact of the forthcoming price reform and also the willingness of the authorities to subsidize unprofitable activities. The self-financing provision could provide an incentive for greater engagement in civilian production insofar as it may facilitate the fulfillment of financial plans. The complaints of excessive prices of items of food-industry equipment manufactured by defense-sector enterprises suggest that the possibilities offered for financial betterment were already being exploited in advance of the new reform measure.

There have been indications that the system of payment for military supplies

---

[63] See, in particular, G. C. Weickhardt, "The Soviet Military-Industrial Complex and Economic Reform," *Soviet Economy* 2, 3 (1986); 193–220.

[64] See *Ekonomicheskaia gazeta*, no. 32 (1987); 6, for explicit acknowledgment that the defense industry will retain funded supply.

may also be changed as organizations of the armed forces go over in 1989 to full economic accounting, with a reduction of budget financing.[65] One author has argued that the "appetite" of the forces will be restrained by the new provisions, forcing military-industry enterprises to seek more orders for civilian work.[66]

What could be opposed is any attempt to introduce even more radical measures within the military sector of the economy. According to the well-known, reform-minded, economist Gavriil Popov, "Many technicians, especially workers in the defense industry, are among those who oppose *perestroika*. I think the defense industry personnel is still deeply confident that everything is in order in their branch and that no changes are needed in defense-related spheres of the economy. Hence the illusions among its staff that command-and-administer methods of management are effective."[67] In the early months of 1989, however, there were signs that some in the defense sector were willing to entertain more radical solutions, including the adoption of leasing arrangements and the creation of cooperatives. Indeed, Popov himself modified his earlier assessment, including representatives of the military sector and the armed forces among the supporters of genuine perestroika. In reality, there is probably a broad spectrum of opinion, but if attempts to radicalize the economic reform as it applies to the military sector were to meet resistance, it would probably be to Gorbachev's advantage to have a politically weakened defense industry.

The transfers of personnel, practices, and technologies, and the terms of the economic reform, all suggest a trend toward a convergence of arrangements and a greater integration between the military-industrial sector and at least the priority sectors of the civilian economy, to the potential mutual benefit of both sides. There is another dimension of convergence that in some respects will be less welcome to the defense industry: its activities are gradually becoming more exposed to public view. Institutions previously concealed are being openly acknowledged (for example, the Zelenograd research center of the electronics industry, and organizations concerned with missile production and the space program); leading personnel previously in the shadows are beginning to emerge as personalities; military-sector products are being displayed and openly discussed (both the latter exemplified by the unprecedented publicity granted to the Buran-Energiia space shuttle and launcher); and poor work is being exposed to criticism in the press. Those employed in the military sector are likely to approve of the greater openness in relation to personnel and institutions but may be concerned at the trend toward public criticism, espe-

---

[65] See N. Karasev, "Novoe kachestvo khozrascheta," *Kommunist vooruzhennykh sil*, no. 22 (1988), 39–43.

[66] *Sotsialisticheskaia industriia*, 13 November 1988. (The author, Iu. S. Valkov, a former chief designer of a military enterprise, welcomes these new developments.)

[67] *Moscow News* (English edition), no. 15 (1988), 13.

cially when it is accompanied by demands for a review of the practices of strict secrecy, which have hitherto shielded the activities of the Soviet defense industry.

Since Gorbachev became general secretary, no ministry of the military sector has escaped public criticism. Some of the revelations of poor work have been damaging to the sector's reputation. Well-known enterprise directors of the Brezhnev period, often held up as models in the press, have been removed from office for their shortcomings, the most striking case being P. Derunov, director of the Andropov (Rybinsk) aeroengine works, who appears to have personified the ''command-and-administer'' methods of management now in disfavor.[68] Others have been removed for abuse of office. One of the most striking cases, requiring the intervention of the party Control Committee, was that of Iu. Pugin, the director of the Moscow Saliut aeroengine works, whose offenses included a lavish, alcoholic fiftieth birthday celebration financed from enterprise funds.[69]

Criticism has also extended to poor plan fulfillment, inadequate innovation, civilian goods of inferior quality (in particular, television sets), and neglect of social obligations, including housing and welfare facilities and worker training.[70] Critics of poor-quality civilian goods manufactured at defense-industry enterprises now openly express their frustration at the way in which secrecy is used to obstruct the investigation and exposure of shortcomings. One author, discussing the fire hazard presented by low-quality televisions, notes that some of the producers ''have hidden themselves in zones literally closed to criticism. State 'secrets' are invoked. Even people's control [inspection officials] has difficulty breaking through into the 'boxes' (*iashchiki*).''[71]

Another author, in a remarkably outspoken article entitled ''On 'Boxes,' Open Secrets, and Departmental Interests,'' berates the aviation industry for its use of secrecy to protect its own interests and shows the absurdity of some of the security measures adopted.[72] Articles of this kind would have been un-

[68] See *Sovetskaia Rossiia*, 15 June 1986.

[69] *Pravda*, 3 April 1988.

[70] Examples include criticism of the aviation industry for serious shortcomings in the supply of aeroengine drive units to gas pipeline compressor stations, and failure to meet the engine requirements of Aeroflot (*Gazovaia promyshlennost*, no. 11 [1987], 28, and *Sotsialisticheskaia industriia*, 23 April 1988); a rebuke for the nuclear weapons industry for delays in producing modern equipment for the food industry (*Pravda*, 26 May 1987); a surprisingly negative assessment of the new K-701M heavy tractor of the Ministry of the Defense Industry (*Trud*, 12 April 1988); and criticism of the aviation, missile, and communications equipment industries for neglect of social provision in Moscow (*Moskovskaia pravda*, 21 October 1987; 10 March 1988).

[71] *Pravda*, 9 May 1988. The ''boxes'' are the postal box numbers used to identify what are considered to be militarily sensitive enterprises. All Soviet television sets are made by enterprises of four defense-sector ministries—in order of importance, the communications equipment industry, the radio industry, the missile-producing Ministry of General Machine Building, and the electronics industry.

[72] *Moskovskaia pravda*, 21 April 1988.

thinkable under Brezhnev. In the new political circumstances, the defense industry is no longer a "zone closed to criticism," and this fact reflects the
emerging new relationship between it and the country's party and state leadership.

The Military-Industrial Sector and Civil-Military Relations

It has been argued that during the Brezhnev period the military-industrial sector represented a strong, cohesive interest enjoying close relations with the top
political leadership. Its administrative elite was remarkable for its stability and
longevity, and in Ustinov it had a powerful patron. The defense industry could
claim solid achievements: it provided the weaponry enabling the Soviet Union
to achieve strategic parity with the United States, secured the volume production of conventional arms of an acceptable, if not ideal, level of modernity,
and built the systems for prestige-winning successes in space.

In the course of time new challenges accumulated. Response to the relent-
less advance of technology became increasingly difficult as economic growth
faltered and stability of cadres reached the point of sclerosis. Since the death
of Brezhnev, and especially under Gorbachev, a policy of renewal and reorientation has been pursued by the leadership, now more independent vis-à-
vis a politically weakened, less cohesive, military-industrial sector. The
reorientation, it has been argued, has a dual nature: an attempt to harness defense-industry expertise and experience to the general task of economic modernization and, within the sector, a strengthening of the capability in vital new
technology fields, shifting the balance of power away from more traditional
activities privileged during the Brezhnev golden age.

· The question remains: what are the implications of the above for the general
state of civil-military relations? Here we need to bring in the military establishment as such. While the Brezhnev years may have been a golden age for
the military-industrial sector, there are grounds for doubting whether the
armed forces perceived their relations with the weapons suppliers in quite the
same way. The powerfully entrenched defense industry with its high-level political support was not necessarily responsive to customer demands. It is not
difficult to imagine that there was frustration and occasional conflict during
the 1970s as the forces posed demands for weapons of greater technological
complexity, although not perhaps the degree of conflict suggested by Jerry
Hough.[73]

From this perspective, the armed forces may not be unhappy about some
weakening of the power of the military-industrial elite and the transition to a

---

[73] Jerry F. Hough, "Soviet Decision-Making on Defense," *Bulletin of the Atomic Scientists*
(August 1985), 84–88.

more distanced relationship between it and the political leadership. The newly emerging balance of power could provide the services with a more responsive and compliant supplier, especially if the reorientation of the military-industrial sector leads to a genuine enhancement of the capability in vital new technology fields.

What of the military's reaction to the other dimension of reorientation, pressure for an expanded civilian role of the defense industry? This will surely depend on how far the process is taken. Any substantial loss of capacity and skills to the civilian economy is likely to be perceived as threatening to the interests of the armed forces, unless at the same time the armed forces themselves are being restructured in such a manner that their demand for weaponry is also being cut back. Force reductions could well be associated with a reduced scale of annual output of many weapons systems. In these circumstances, the ability of the defense industry to supply modern, high-technology systems could become much more important than its ability to produce in volume. To date any adjustment has been marginal, but the indications are that much more dramatic change may be in prospect. It is likely that resource shifts from the military to civil purposes will go in parallel with an on-going reconsideration of issues of military doctrine and force structures, with the possibility of a major reorganization leading to the formation of smaller professional armed forces, or a combined professional-militia system.

What would be the reaction of the defense industry to a substantial switch from military to civil work? Could such a switch lead to conflict with the political leadership? This is a difficult question to answer. It is unlikely that there is any single, unchanging set of attitudes characteristic of the elite of the military sector. Some ministries have traditionally been more involved in civilian work than others, while the direction of change is likely to enhance further the civilian role of the electronics-related branches in particular.

Attitudes could well be undergoing substantial change when compared with the Brezhnev golden age. If the general prestige and traditional, unquestioned priority granted to the military are perceived to be under challenge, will the nuclear weapons minister and his colleagues necessarily resist greater involvement in such manifestly peaceful activities as the manufacture of milking machines and video equipment? In the author's view, those responsible for the Soviet defense industry are above all senior economic administrators and not military personnel devoted single-mindedly to the development and manufacture of armaments. Support for this judgment is provided by the pattern of transfers of personnel in recent years: defense-industry ministers, and their deputies, can expect to rise to the highest government and party posts. From the narrow perspective of career interests alone, it seems unlikely that this elite group would go out on a limb and challenge a fundamental issue of party and state policy.

None of the above provides grounds for perceiving any serious civil-military disharmony. By its very nature, the triangular relationship among the party apparatus, defense industry, and professional military must inevitably involve conflicts of interest and clashes on particular issues. But it could be argued that fundamental conflict would be more likely if a bipolar relationship prevailed: political leadership versus the armed forces *plus* the military-industrial sector. In my view, one of the reasons for the basic stability of civil-military relations in the USSR is precisely the fact that such a bipolarity does not characterize the relationship. For this reason, analyses which take as their starting point an assumed singular "military-industrial complex" cannot but fail to illuminate Soviet civil-military relations.

From this perspective it could be argued that conflict might arise if for some reason the industrial and military points of the triangle found truly serious common cause vis-à-vis the political leadership. This could occur, for example, if Gorbachev simultaneously attempted to weaken seriously the influence of both parties. Whether conflict occurred and the form it took would then also depend on the extent to which each could present a coherent, united position. While Gorbachev probably has weakened the influence of both the armed forces and the military-industrial sector compared with the Brezhnev period, the degree of weakening has not been such as to generate serious conflict.

The processes set in motion, however, must have the potential for disharmony of a kind not seen during the golden age. To avoid the risk of damaging conflict, Gorbachev has to continue to manage the complex dialectic of political, economic, and military change. The future may be uncertain, but for many this will be a price of change preferable to the certainties of stagnation.

Six

The Response to Technological Challenge

THANE GUSTAFSON

SOVIET military technology has been a remarkable success story. Two decades after the triple cataclysm of world war, revolution, and civil war, the fledgling Soviet defense industries were able to match the best that Germany could produce. Only two decades after that they could hold their own against the technological might of the United States. All this was done with an industrial and technological base smaller and less advanced than that of its competitors.

But since the mid-1960s the latest wave of technological innovation from the West has posed a formidable new challenge for a Soviet industrial and technological base that remains, as before, smaller and weaker than that of the competition.[1] Around 1970 Soviet industry reached its maximum relative strength compared to the United States and then fell back.[2] In other words, over the last twenty years the Soviet military-industrial system has come under new competitive pressure even as its relative position has been deteriorating.

In this chapter, I raise two principal questions: How have the Soviets perceived and responded to the latest challenge of military technology since the mid-1960s? And how has this altered civil-military relations in the Soviet po-

For their advice and criticism the author is indebted to Arthur Alexander, Peter Almquist, Harley Balzer, Lewis Branscomb, Harvey Brooks, Rose Gottemoeller, Loren Graham, Cynthia Roberts, Thomas Nichols, Merritt Roe Smith, George Steeg, and Leon Trilling, as well as the other contributing authors of this volume. Finally, without Stephen Meyer this chapter would not have been written.

[1] In sheer numbers of scientists and engineers, the Soviet Union leads the world. But many of these are actually closer to technicians in their training and tasks. The number of those who actually work in their specialties and at levels corresponding to their training and rank is smaller than in the United States. For useful background see S. A. Kugel, "Kvalifikatsiia i realnaia deiatelnost inzhenera," *Sotsiologicheskie issledovaniia*, no. 1 (1983), 91–98; and Louvan R. Nolting and Murray Feshbach, "R&D Employment in the USSR," *Science*, vol. 207 (1 February 1980), 493–503.

[2] Mikhail Gorbachev in his speeches states that Soviet industrial output reached a maximum of about 75 percent of the U.S. level in 1970 and then receded throughout the decade and into the early 1980s. See especially Gorbachev's speech to the June 1986 plenary session of the Central Committee of the Communist Party of the Soviet Union, as reprinted in his collected speeches, in M. S. Gorbachev, *Izbrannye rechi i stati* (Moscow: Izdatelstvo politicheskoi literatury, 1987), 3:428.

litical system; specifically, the balance of influence, authority, and power among the participants?

As a general matter, how might one expect technological challenge to affect civil-military relations? First, technological change, by creating new threats and new opportunities, and thus altering the balance among missions and services, creates pressures for changes in military doctrine. In the Soviet system, where the formation of military doctrine is one of the main arenas of civil-military interaction, such technological influences have always raised highly political issues.[3] Technological change also brings new knowledge and skills to the fore, fostering new professions and specialties while depreciating older ones, thus creating new organizations, new roles, and assets that profit some players more than others. Finally, depending on whether the responses of the players to technological challenges are perceived as successful or not (from the standpoint not only of military effectiveness but also of cost), their relative prestige and authority rises or falls, and tensions and grievances among them may mount or abate. In sum, as a result of technological pressures, the tone, the terms, and the topics of civil-military interaction may all be altered, and these are the ingredients of influence, power, and authority.

Three Western scholars who have written recently on this subject have reached strikingly different conclusions. Stephen Meyer argues that there is a long-term trend toward enhanced military influence in Soviet national security decision making, mainly because of the growing complexity, specialization, and expense of military technology.[4] Indeed, although Meyer stresses that he means decision influence, and not decision authority (and, presumably, still less power), by the end of his essay he broadens his argument considerably: "Technology seems to have accomplished what sixty-five years of Soviet party-military relations have attempted to prevent, the movement of the professional military into the heart of the defense decision-making structure."[5]

There are four trends, in Meyer's view, that tend to shift the balance of decision-making influence in favor of the "professional military": (1) the increasing technological content of defense and arms-control policy; (2) the continuing monopoly on military analytic capabilities held by the Soviet professional military elite; (3) the lack of relevant politico-military experience among the new generation of Soviet political leaders; and (4) the increasing

[3] For an excellent analysis of the politics of Soviet military doctrine in historical perspective, see Thomas M. Nichols, "The Politics of Doctrine: Khrushchev, Gorbachev, and the Soviet Military," Ph.D. dissertation, Georgetown University, 1988.

[4] Stephen M. Meyer, "Civilian and Military Influence in Managing the Arms Race in the USSR," in *Reorganizing America's Defense*, ed. Robert M. Art and Samuel P. Huntington (Lexington, Mass.: Lexington Books, 1985), 37–61.

[5] Ibid., 53. It is not entirely clear, incidentally, just whom Meyer meant by the "professional military," but he seemed to have in mind mainly the uniformed officers, rather than the military-industrial sector as a whole.

divergence in structure and orientation between the Soviet civilian and military economies.[6] These add up, in particular, to a "facts gap" between military and civilian leaders, affecting not only "microtechnical data," but equally data about systems, costs, and force balances.[7]

Meyer's analysis is predicated on the assumption that the military's response to technological challenge has been largely successful. Jerry Hough, in contrast, starts from the opposite proposition: by the late 1970s, he argues, there was a crisis in Soviet weapons development, primarily as a result of technological conservatism in Soviet military industry. The uniformed military were growing alarmed and impatient, and the most visible symbol of their mounting anger was Marshal Nikolai Ogarkov, then chief of the General Staff, whose criticisms of Soviet military readiness Hough interprets as a direct attack on Defense Minister Dmitrii Ustinov's management of the defense industry. Hough goes on to predict that the defense industry's incompetence, combined with the mounting indignation of the uniformed military, could eventually lead to dramatic consequences in civil-military relations:

> Their [the military's] anger at a defense industry that cannot keep up with the West will grow, and a military that becomes convinced that the civilians are destroying the nation's capacity to defend itself becomes more than a mere interest-group claimant in the budgetary process.

> If the Soviet Union does not begin to solve the problem of technological lag, it faces the prospect of real political instability. The threat will come from the military, if from nowhere else.[8]

Behind this warning is Hough's judgment that the tension between the military and defense industrialists is of long standing. In his view, the Soviet defense industry has long been the dominant partner, and the uniformed military are powerless to obtain the greater innovativeness they require to match the Western challenge.

Still a third view is that the Soviet response to technological challenge has had very little impact on civil-military relations at all. Condoleezza Rice describes the Soviet decision-making system in military matters as one of "loose coupling" between two main zones. In the first, the political leadership sets the broad outlines of policy; in the second, military-industrial professionals formulate options and implement policy.[9] Overall, this arrangement gives the political leadership clear supremacy, and in Rice's view, the substantial changes that have taken place in military technology and the ways the Soviets

---

[6] Ibid., 40.

[7] Ibid., 42.

[8] Jerry Hough, "Soviet Decision-making on Defense," *Bulletin of the Atomic Scientists* (August 1985), 85–88.

[9] Condoleezza Rice, "The Party, the Military, and Decision Authority in the Soviet Union," *World Politics* 40, 1 (October 1987), 55–81.

have responded have not disrupted this essential hierarchy of authority. Loose coupling, she concludes, has "worked pretty well" and remains an accurate description of the way the system works today.

These three views will serve as hypotheses for this chapter, and at the conclusion I shall return to an evaluation of them. In the meantime, this chapter proceeds as follows: Part 1 describes the traditional system of weapons acquisition and the ways the Soviets coped with technological challenge in the past. Part 2 discusses what makes today's challenge different. Part 3 examines the main lines of Soviet perception and response. Part 4 explores the consequences for military-industrial issues, roles, assets, and thus, at last, the powers of the players and the impact on civil-military relations.

In dealing with so large a subject in a small space, we must draw some boundaries. Technological change affects every aspect of the military enterprise; and no treatment of the consequences for civil-military relations could be complete without a detailed examination of doctrine, force dispositions, military organization, and weapons development and procurement. But that is far beyond the scope of one chapter. I have chosen to focus on one aspect of the military-industrial system that lies at the intersection of all of the above, namely, the process of Soviet weapons design and development, or, as it is commonly known in the literature, weapons acquisition.

Weapons acquisition is the stage at which military and political requirements must be reconciled with technological opportunities and constraints. Design and development unavoidably represent a process of choice and compromise, not only among competing technical parameters (such as performance versus cost, power and speed versus weight and firepower, and innovation versus reliability), but also among competing agencies and people, each with different objectives and views. Consequently the bargaining and reconciliation that take place in weapons design and development are not only constant and inescapable, but they are also inherently political, and hence they constitute an important measure of the impact of technological change on civil-military relations.

The Traditional System of Soviet Weapons Acquisition

Before appraising the Soviet responses to the latest technological challenges, we need a bench mark against which to measure them. Accordingly, I turn first to the setting in which Soviet weapons design and acquisition grew up from the 1930s to the 1960s and examine the characteristics of Soviet weapons design as they developed during this period. Three main questions arise: first, what caused this system to take the shape it did? Second, what were the resulting relations of power and influence among the actors in this system? And third, how effective was this system in coping with technological challenges?

A substantial collection of Soviet memoirs and biographies has been devoted to the major weapons designers and builders, providing one of the most useful sources of information about decision making in Soviet weapons procurement. It has been extensively mined by a handful of Western scholars, who have combined it with data from Western sources to build a composite picture of the weapons design-and-development process through the early 1970s.[10] So far, Gorbachev's glasnost has not added much new material to this collection, particularly for the 1970s and 1980s, although there are signs that more is on the way.[11] A recent flow of émigré accounts gives glimpses, sometimes quite valuable ones, of more recent developments, stretching in some cases to the beginning of the 1980s.[12] Consequently, against the background

[10] The two most valuable syntheses are Arthur J. Alexander, "Decision-Making in Soviet Weapons Procurement," *Adelphi Papers*, nos. 147/148 (London: International Institute for Strategic Studies, 1978); and David Holloway, "Innovation in the Defense Sector," in *Industrial Innovation in the Soviet Union*, ed. Ronald Amann and Julian Cooper (New Haven: Yale University Press, 1982), 276–414. Both of these studies build on several previous works by both scholars. See especially Alexander, *R&D in Soviet Aviation*, R-589-PR (Santa Monica: Rand Corporation, 1970); Alexander, *Armor Development in the Soviet Union and the United States*, R-1860-NA (Santa Monica: Rand Corporation, 1976); David Holloway, "Military Technology," in *The Technological Level of Soviet Industry*, ed. R. Amann, J. M. Cooper, and R. W. Davies (New Haven: Yale University Press, 1977), 407–489.

In addition, on the subject of aviation, one should mention the excellent work of Richard D. Ward, in particular, *Soviet Military Aircraft Design and Procurement: A Historical Perspective*, 2d ed. (Fort Worth: General Dynamics Corporation, 1983).

The military industrialists and designers have received much more attention in the Soviet literature than have the military commanders in charge of armaments, especially for the postwar period. In addition, aviation and space have received more attention than land warfare, and especially the navy. Consequently, we are handicapped from the beginning in understanding the relations between the players and the differences from service to service.

[11] The most important recent memoirs to date are those of Dmitri Ustinov, *Vo imia pobedy: zapiski narkoma vooruzheniia* (Moscow: Voennoe izdatelstvo, 1988), which unfortunately cover only World War II, and V. N. Novikov, *Nakanune i v dni ispytanii: vospominaniia* (Moscow: Politizdat, 1988).

Among other works, one should mention especially the memoirs of Air Marshal E. Ia. Savitskii, former deputy commander of the air defense forces, *Polveka s nebom* (Moscow: Voennoe izdatelstvo, 1988); and a biography of Marshal N. I. Krylov, commander of the Strategic Rocket Forces from 1963 to 1972, by I. G. Dragan, *Marshal N. I. Krylov* (Moscow: Voennoe izdatelstvo, 1987).

Gradually the veil may be lifting from the lives and work of the military naval designers, especially those of nuclear submarines. In October 1988 *Krasnaia zvezda* carried a biographical sketch of the chief designer of the first Soviet nuclear submarine, V. N. Peregudov. Iu. Stvolinskii, "Konstruktor podvodnogo atomokhoda," *Krasnaia zvezda*, 15 October 1988. Stvolinskii is a submarine commander turned naval writer who has recently published a book on pre–World War II surface ship designers, *Konstruktory nadvodnykh korablei* (Leningrad: Lenizdat, 1987). In 1989, such material began appearing frequently in the Soviet press, especially in *Krasnaia zvezda*.

[12] Delphic Associates, of Falls Church, Virginia, has published several dozen autobiographical accounts by former Soviet technical specialists, of which a dozen or so of military interest have been used for this chapter.

of a knowledge of the traditional procurement process, one can get inklings of the more recent responses to technological challenge.

The Soviet system for weapons design and development grew up in the 1920s and 1930s and, like the command economy as a whole, had taken essentially its modern form by the time of the German invasion in 1941.[13] It was shaped by three principal influences: industrial and technological backwardness (albeit eased by the existence of a talented scientific and engineering elite and a vigorous technical culture);[14] a continuous and pervading sense of threat from the West, combined with the challenge (but also, at intervals, the powerful assistance) of Western technological example; and finally, a domestic political atmosphere of fear and compulsion, which, though gradually tempered after Stalin's death, continued in the form of a tradition of administrative pressure.

The groups conveying these influences into the design and development process were also essentially three: the uniformed military as customers; the military-industrial ministries as contractors; and the political leadership, most prominently Stalin himself, as overseers and expediters.[15]

The Uniformed Military and the Defense Industries

The uniformed military and the defense industrialists have always formed two quite distinct groups. As Julian Cooper shows in chapter 5, there have been few cases in which individuals have crossed over from the uniformed services to industry and vice-versa. This, added to differences of outlook and behavior stemming from the two groups' contrasting roles, might have been expected to breed an antagonistic relationship. But in most cases the roles and objectives of the uniformed military and the defense industrialists were shifting and complex, and consequently the relationship was far from clear-cut. Thus, the uniformed military, day-to-day the originators of most weapons requirements, wanted the most advanced performance and were typically a force for innovation; but they also wanted systems that would be easy and safe to use and

---

[13] A useful study of the early days of the Soviet weapons procurement system, in addition to the sources already mentioned, is Mikhail Tsypkin, "The Origins of the Soviet Military Research and Development System," Ph.D. dissertation, Harvard University, 1985.

[14] Kendall E. Bailes, *Technology and Society under Lenin and Stalin* (Princeton: Princeton University Press, 1978).

[15] For detailed descriptions of the decision-making structure for weapons R&D and procurement, see Holloway, "Innovations in the Defense Sector," and Alexander, "Decision-Making." See also Jerry F. Hough, "The Historical Legacy in Soviet Weapons Development," in *Soviet Decisionmaking for National Security*, ed. Jiri Valenta and William Potter (London: Allen and Unwin, 1984), 87–115; and Peter Almquist, *Red Forge: Soviet Military Industry since 1965* (New York: Columbia University Press, 1990).

maintain, and they wanted them in large numbers.[16] Moreover, the military were not necessarily united: service rivalries, personal enmities, competing doctrines, or simply different professional roles not infrequently colored their views on requirements.[17]

Most important, the military, backed by the political leadership, wanted fast results. All Soviet memoirists and biographers stress the constant, unremitting pressure for speed that drove designers and their teams day and night. New military requirements frequently arose suddenly, as political leaders reacted to military challenges arising abroad. It was only in the mid-1950s, A. I. Mikoian's biographer tells us, that the pressure for breakneck speed abated somewhat.[18]

The defense industry, contending with taut plan targets and tight production constraints, might have been expected to act as a conservative force, resisting the military's demands for innovation, higher quality, and more exacting standards. The actual situation, however, as with the uniformed military, was more complex.[19] For example, the network of research institutes attached to the aviation industry (for aerodynamics, materials, engines, and so on) played a mixed role: though responsible for standard setting and thus inclined toward conservative uniformity, they also conducted research on new designs, materials, and production techniques and can frequently be glimpsed in Soviet sources on the side of the innovators.[20]

[16] One example of such mixed motives concerns the Sukhoi-9 (Fishpot-B), Sukhoi's first delta-wing interceptor. Highly praised by test pilots and air-defense (PVO) commanders, the plane was unpopular with air-defense pilots as being too difficult to fly safely. This led to noisy confrontations, in which some industry officials aligned themselves with the pilots, while the PVO air commander, Air Marshal Ie. Ia. Savitskii, remained a staunch defender of the designer. L. Kuzmina, *Generalnyi konstruktor Pavel Sukhoi* (Moscow: Molodaia gvardiia, 1983), 188–189.

Resistance to innovation by pilots was especially great when the Soviet air forces made the transition to jet aircraft. Pilots and instructors did not trust jet engines, and this "user resistance" was one reason why Iakovlev designed the Yak-15 to handle like a Yak-3, so as to put pilots in as familiar a setting as possible. The PVO pilots were particularly hostile to jet aircraft. Savitskii, *Polveka s nebom*, 301 passim.

[17] Thus the adaptation of the Red Army to tank warfare in the 1930s was delayed by deep divisions over doctrine among top commanders—on one side, the cavalry veterans of the civil war; on the other, the followers of Marshal M. N. Tukhachevskii, advocates of mechanized warfare. See the remarkably frank reminiscences of G. Iserson, "Razvitie teorii sovetskogo operativnogo iskusstva v 30-e gody," *Voenno-istoricheskii zhurnal*, nos. 1 and 3 (1965), 36–46 and 48–61.

[18] Mikhail Arlazorov, *Artem Mikoian* (Moscow: Molodaia gvardiia, 1978), 231. Writing about the circumstances under which the MiG-21 was designed, Arlazorov comments, "The stabilization of the international situation freed the designers from the extraordinarily nerve-racking, exhausting tempo in which previous fighters had been created." One suspects that the change was connected above all to Stalin's death; the first MiG-21 prototype was built in 1955, two years after Stalin's death.

[19] See Almquist, *Red Forge*, for many valuable illustrations of the mixed roles of the defense industrialists.

[20] Thus, for example, throughout its history the All-Union Institute for Aviation Materials

As with the uniformed military, military industry was divided by competing criteria and objectives. A frequent theme in Soviet sources is technological conservatism at lower levels, offset by more far-sighted executives higher up. Thus, one learns that in the early days of Soviet jet aviation, lower-ranking officials of the Ministry of Aviation Industry were inclined to copy the German IUMO jet engine; it was the direct intervention of then first deputy minister P. V. Dementev that swung the balance in favor of a home-grown model developed by A. M. Liulka, whose jet engines subsequently powered Sukhoi's airplanes.[21] Some of the most determined conservatism came from the producer enterprises, which bore the brunt of integrating higher performance standards, new techniques, and materials with demanding production schedules.[22]

Moreover, the defense industry as a whole was far from a united conservative front. The Ministry of the Aviation Industry, for example, faced with requirements for higher performance, consistently played the innovator in dealing with manufacturers of engines and electronic systems. Throughout the major designers' memoirs and biographies, one finds frequent complaints of lag among avionics suppliers.[23] In the mid-1950s the Ministry of the Aviation Industry, frustrated by the slow response of the radio industry to new advances in electronics, even sought to establish its own microelectronics empire.[24]

In sum, it is difficult to show that the military have dominated the defense industrialists or vice-versa, that relations between them have been consistently contentious, or that one has been the innovative force while the other has been the conservative. Rather, the relations and roles of the two appear to depend

---

(VIAM) has played the important role of developing and testing new alloys for the aviation industry; and more recently a counterpart institute has been created to deal with synthetics and composites. For a history of materials development, see A. T. Tumanov et al., "Aviatsionnoe materialovedenie," in *Razvitie aviatsionnoi nauki i tekhniki v SSSR* (Moscow Nauka, 1980), 318–351). But VIAM also plays a conservative, rule-setting role, by specifying which materials may be used for what purposes.

[21] L. Kuzmina, *Ognennoe serdtse* (Moscow: Moskovskii rabochii, 1983), 82–84.

[22] For an example concerning mass production of Sukhoi's first delta-wing design, see Kuzmina, *Sukhoi*, 180. For another illustration from the life of tank builder V. A. Malyshev on the eve of World War II, see V. A. Chalmaev, *Malyshev* (Moscow: Molodaia gvardiia, 1978), 115–116.

[23] The designer A. S. Iakovlev tells how around 1956 he denounced the shortcomings of the radio industry in a report to the CPSU Central Committee, which led to an acrimonious confrontation with officials of the Ministry of the Radio Industry (Minradioprom) in front of a high-level commission chaired by then secretary Brezhnev. Radio industry officials accused Iakovlev, an aviation man, of meddling in matters he knew nothing about and of trying to disrupt relations. A. S. Iakovlev, *Zapiski konstruktora* (Moscow: Politizdat, 1979), 285.

[24] The former first deputy minister of the aviation industry, P. V. Dementev, traveled to Prague in the mid-1950s to recruit the American defector Philip Staros, who became one of the founders of the Soviet microelectronics industry, initially under aviation industry auspices. The story of Staros is told in Henry Eric Firdman, *Decision-Making in The Soviet Microelectronics Industry: the Leningrad Design Bureau, a Case Study* (Falls Church, Va.: Delphic Associates, 1985).

very much on the period, the nature of the technology, the competitive pressure from the West, and the personalities involved. Finally, one major factor, not yet discussed, is the crucial role of the political leadership.

The Impact of the Political Leaders

Perhaps the most distinctive feature of the Soviet military design and development system was the detailed personal involvement of the top political leaders, beginning with the party general secretary himself. This was especially true of Stalin, who according to the Soviet memoir literature appears to have been personally involved in most, if not all, of the major design and procurement decisions of the 1930s and 1940s, particularly for manned aircraft, artillery, and tanks, but even on occasion for small arms as well.[25]

It is less clear how Stalin's close involvement affected the net direction and effectiveness of Soviet military design and development. Stalin brought the same management style to military procurement as he did to everything else, shifting course as new favorites caught his ear, shuffling the same small cast of top lieutenants from one post to another, always seeming to prefer administrative fluidity and amorphousness to order. Frequently indecisive and always unpredictable, Stalin was never particularly receptive to new ideas and grew less so as he aged, tending to react (and overreact) to developments abroad rather than to ideas generated at home.[26] Stalin's doctrinal notions, political phobias, and personal aversions played havoc with military planning.

[25] Stalin's role in weapons design and procurement is discussed in Holloway, "Innovations in the Defense Sector," 301–303; and especially in Tsypkin, "The Origins of Soviet Military Research," 165–179. See also Vernon V. Aspaturian, "The Stalinist Legacy in Soviet National Security Decisionmaking," in *Soviet Decisionmaking*, ed. Valenta and Potter, 23–73. According to Khrushchev, "Defense was [Stalin's] exclusive concern, and he guarded it fiercely. If someone else expressed the slightest interest or curiosity about this or that new weapon, Stalin immediately became jealous or suspicious." N. S. Khrushchev, *Khrushchev Remembers: the Last Testament* (Boston: Little, Brown, 1974), 11.

[26] Thus, Stalin did not assign consistently top priority to the atom-bomb project until after Truman informed him at Potsdam of the first U.S. nuclear test in August 1945. Holloway, "Innovations in the Defense Sector," 389.

Similarly, according to an émigré account, Stalin showed no particular interest in helicopters until the American landing at Inchon in September 1950, in which helicopters played a key role. Then, under Beriia's personal supervision, M. L. Mil built the first Soviet transport helicopter, the Mi-4, in less than a year. Lev Chaiko, *Helicopter Construction in the USSR* (Falls Church, Va.: Delphic Associates, 1986), 3–5.

As for missiles, Soviet memoirs give special credit to Ustinov for the development of Soviet rocketry after World War II. Thus space-capsule designer Konstantin Feoktistov records that "Stalin didn't have much faith in missiles right down to the first flights of the R-1." Konstantin Feoktistov and Igor Bubnov, *O kosmoletakh* (Moscow: Molodaia gvardiia, 1982), 46–47. Missile designer S. P. Korolev, in an interview given in 1963 but published only in 1988, criticized Stalin's lack of enthusiasm for missiles, adding, "Only after 1953 were the essential conditions

Both the style of Stalin's participation and its effects on military procurement changed somewhat after the war, as they did throughout the system. The acute upheavals and terrors of the 1930s settled into the more institutionalized dictatorship of the late 1940s and early 1950s, and the dictator himself became more willing to delegate stable authority to the military-industrial chieftains who had played key roles in organizing military industry during the war. Though conservative on most points (and notably on doctrine), he gave enough strong backing to people like B. L. Vannikov, D. F. Ustinov, and L. P. Beriia to lay the basis for the development of missiles, nuclear weapons, and jet aircraft.

Nevertheless, several essential features of Stalinist decision making dominated Soviet weapons design and development for a quarter century and were slow to dissipate thereafter: priority access to scarce resources, an atmosphere of constant urgency, acute competition among designers and agencies, high rewards but also extreme threats and chilling fear of failure, and a highly personalized, administratively fluid system of policy making.

The evidence concerning Khrushchev's personal role is less clear because there is no equivalent for the 1950s and 1960s of the mass of war time Soviet memoirs, but the fragments available (especially from Khrushchev's own recollections in retirement)[27] suggest that he took less of a direct part in design questions and was less involved in day-to-day decision making on procurement and defense construction than Stalin.[28] But the effects of Khrushchev's strong views on doctrine and strategy could be nearly as sweeping.[29] Thus, at the beginning of the 1960s Khrushchev's enthusiasm for rockets and his bias against manned aircraft had repercussions among all the major plane designers.[30] Similarly, Khrushchev's admiration for submarines and his mistrust of

---

created for really intensive work.'' A. Romanov, ''Raskhody na kosmos okupiatsia vo sto krat,'' *Pravda*, 6 January 1989.

[27] N. S. Khrushchev, *Khrushchev Remembers* (Boston: Little, Brown, 1970), and especially the second volume, *Khrushchev Remembers*, particularly chaps. 1–4.

[28] The difference, to be sure, was a matter of degree. Khrushchev's memoirs and other sources make clear that he was frequently involved in detailed decisions concerning procurement. But the point is that Khrushchev's interest was not as detailed, sustained, or, for that matter, necessarily as decisive as Stalin's. For a recent example, see the memoirs of Khrushchev's son Sergei concerning Khrushchev's role in choosing between two competing ICBM designs on the eve of his fall in 1964. Sergei Khrushchev argues that Dmitri Ustinov's view, rather than Khrushchev's or Brezhnev's, was decisive. Sergei Kkhrushchev, ''Pensioner soiuznogo znacheniia,'' *Ogonëk*, no. 40 (1988), 26–29.

[29] See Raymond Garthoff, *Soviet Strategy in the Nuclear Age* (New York: Praeger, 1962); Thomas Wolfe, *Soviet Strategy at the Crossroads* (Cambridge: Harvard University Press, 1964). For a recent analysis that incorporates the latest available Soviet memoir literature, see Nichols, ''The Politics of Doctrine.''

[30] The bomber designer V. M. Miasishchev was dismissed and his design bureau converted to missile work. D. Gai, *Nebesnoe pritiazhenie* (Moscow: Moskovskii rabochii, 1984). Sukhoi was prevented from working on fighters for several years and was obliged instead to switch to rockets

surface vessels led to major cuts in the latter. Khrushchev's endorsements could be as sudden and sweeping as his vetoes; for example, infuriated by American overflights of Soviet territory in the mid-1950s, he reacted with emergency orders for new missiles and interceptors.[31]

As for day-to-day management, the Central Committee apparatus under Khrushchev remained closely involved in overseeing weapons programs, but the style was more relaxed, more supportive, and less disruptive than under Stalin. Leonid Brezhnev was Khrushchev's secretary for military industry for about half of the latter's reign,[32] and brought to military procurement even then something of the style that later became his trademark as general secretary: "trust in cadres," a respect for military-industrial expertise, and a preference for long personal associations.

In sum, from the 1930s to the 1960s the personal participation of the general secretary grew less detailed and intrusive, and the previous atmosphere of fear and pressure slowly abated. In other words, one of the most important forces shaping the traditional procurement system had already changed significantly even before the mid-1960s, opening the way for greater institutionalization and regularized procedures.

The Roles of the General Designer

The unique pressures and constraints bearing on Soviet weapons design and procurement in the 1930s and 1940s combined to create a unique figure, that of the "hero-designer." Managing the trade-offs inherent in weapons design is an essential task in any country's military-industrial system,[33] but nowhere has the figure of the general designer been so important as in the Soviet Union from the 1930s to the present day.

The Soviet general designer's role was twofold. He was, first of all, the

---

(Kuzmina, *Sukhoi*, 195–196, 201, 211); Mikoian came under the same pressure, although he apparently was able to stand firm (thanks perhaps to support from his high-placed brother). See Mikhail Arlazorov, *Vint i krylo: neskolko stranits istorii aviatsii* (Moscow: Znanie, 1980), 148. Iakovlev likewise reports coldness from Khrushchev and from Central Committee staff at about the same time. A. Iakovlev, *Zapiski konstruktora* (Moscow: Izdatelstvo politicheskoi literatury, 1979), 286–287.

[31] Kuzmina, *Sukhoi*, 182.

[32] Leonid Brezhnev was Central Committee secretary from 1956 to 1960 and again from 1963 through Khrushchev's fall, with primary responsibility for military industry. He had previously held the same position in Stalin's last years (from 1952 to 1953); and he remained involved in military-industrial affairs at other times as well. Thus his memoirs suggest that he played some part in overseeing the construction of Baikonur while first secretary of Kazakhstan in 1954–56. L. I. Brezhnev, "Glavy iz knigi 'Vospominaniia,' " *Novyi mir*, no. 1 (1983), 28. They also indicate that he retained some responsibility for oversight of the manned space program even after 1960, when he was no longer secretary (p. 36).

[33] For suggestive comparisons, see Arthur J. Alexander, *Weapons Procurement in the Soviet Union, United States, and France*, P-4989 (Santa Monica: Rand Corporation, March 1973).

broker between the military's requirements and the industry's capabilities. Second, he was the embodiment of the political leaders' will; in the amorphous and shifting environment of Stalinist administration, the general designer acted as an expediter and coordinator, transmitting the political leaders' pressure for fast results. In both roles the general designer served as a gatekeeper for technological innovation, striking the balance between performance and risk, and ultimately also as a "risk buffer," absorbing the consequences personally in the event of failure.[34]

A *generalnyi* had to know how to use his fists in dealing with fellow designers, managers of producer plants, military test personnel, and quality-control representatives.[35] The designers' doughtiness can be seen, for example, in the way Sukhoi at the end of the 1960s lectured a pair of air force generals who accused him of exceeding their requirements and threatened to transfer a project to another design bureau: "A good tailor's shop [Sukhoi told them] educates his customer's taste. If a 22-cm trouser cuff is the fashion now, we will not make you a suit with a 30-cm one, even if you want it badly. If you want bell-bottoms you're going to have to go across the street."[36]

Air Marshal E. Ia. Savitskii, formerly commander of the air defense forces, remembers traveling to Iakovlev's dacha to convince him to change the disposition of the instruments inside the cockpit of the early Iak-15. Although in this case he was successful, he comments, "People like Iakovlev, Lavochkin, Tupolev, Iliushin, Mikoian, Sukhoi had colossal, at times unchallengeable prestige (*avtoritet*). And it was not at all easy at times to change their minds."[37]

The designers' power was not absolute; the military still held the ultimate weapon of being able to turn down a design or a prototype. Thus, after lengthy and acrimonious bargaining failed to induce Mikoian to include suitable air brakes on the first MiG-15s, the military simply scrapped the prototypes and ordered Mikoian to start over.[38]

The general designers were not themselves the direct innovators; rather, their roles consisted of making the key decisions whether or not to incorporate innovations made by others and duly approved by the standards-setting insti-

---

[34] It is striking that many of the leading military designers and executives were arrested in the late 1930s and served lengthy prison terms, frequently working in special laboratories under NKVD jurisdiction. The famous names include Vannikov, Peregudov, Korolev, and Tupolev.

[35] Thus, Marshal Tolubko's biography of Nedelin shows Korolev fighting hard to get rid of a military engineer whom Korolev accused of finding fault with trifling problems in Korolev's missiles. V. Tolubko, *Nedelin: pervyi glavkom strategicheskikh* (Moscow: Molodaia gvardiia, 1979), 180. Iakovlev likewise tried to get rid of pesky military test pilots who criticized his creations (Iakovlev, "Zapiski konstruktora," 285–286). Sukhoi struggled with enterprise directors who surreptitiously added weight. The examples in this literature are legion.

[36] Kuzmina, *Sukhoi*, 228–229.

[37] Savitskii, *Polveka s nebom*, 267. Savitskii was not yet air defense commander at the time, but chief of fighter training.

[38] Savitskii, *Polveka s nebom*, 268.

tutes.[39] A similar class of "creative brokerage" problems involved integrating the airplane platform with subsystems (rockets, cannon, avionics) developed in other organizations. This brokerage function was frequently active rather than passive: thus, airframe and engine designers are described as having taken the initiative in stimulating applications of titanium fabrication and use of plastics, sometimes moving ahead of official approval from the industry research institutes and bucking considerable opposition in the bargain.

Such choices involved gauging risk, and despite striking differences in personality from one designer to another, their behavior fit the description that test pilot M. L. Gallai once gave of A. N. Tupolev: "He always strove to use in his new designs a maximum of tested [design concepts] that had proven their worth on planes that were already in the air. It's a little bit like what chess players call 'safe moves.' "[40]

In sum, the importance of the Soviet general designers derived from their function as technological brokers. This had two separate dimensions: first, a horizontal one, in which the *generalnye* managed the complex relations between customers and suppliers within the military-industrial sector; second, a vertical dimension, in which they acted as conduits between the political leadership and the military. It was this second role, which cast them as advisers, entrepreneurs, expediters, and occasional scapegoats, that gave the "classic" general designers their power and visibility.

The Resulting Characteristics of Traditional Soviet Design

Starting with Arthur Alexander's pioneering work in the late 1960s and early 1970s, Western studies of Soviet weapons design have identified a characteristic Soviet style in design across a broad range of weapons systems from the 1930s through the beginning of the 1970s.[41] Soviet designers traditionally stressed simplicity, commonality, heredity, and economy. Wherever possible,

---

[39] Thus one sees Mikoian hesitating between a swept wing and a delta wing for the MiG-21, but the innovation was not his: both had already been extensively studied and approved by the Central Aerodynamics Institute (TsAGI) (Arlazorov, *Vint i krylo*, 219, 221–222).

[40] Ibid., 221, 225.

[41] Thus Alexander followed his earlier work on aviation with a study of Soviet armor, previously cited; and David Holloway wrote valuable case studies of Soviet armor and missile development, also previously cited. Western studies of Soviet naval design are less detailed, but they point in the same direction; see J. W. Kehoe and K. S. Brower, "U.S. and Soviet Weapon System Design Practices," *International Defense Review*, no. 6 (1982), 705–712, which sums up a decade of previous works by both men and generalizes to other systems. A Western work on Soviet helicopters makes many of the same findings about Soviet design style: John Everett-Heath, *Soviet Helicopters: Design, Development and Tactics* (London: Jane's, 1983).

Soviet authors agree, although for obvious reasons they are inclined to dwell on the innovative, risk-taking traits of their heroes. See, for example, I. Tsygankov, "Sovetskaia voennaia tekhnika: razvitie konstruktorskoi mysli," *Tekhnika i vooruzhenie*, no. 2 (1978), 6–9.

Soviet designers borrowed proven subsystems from earlier designs rather than designing each successive system anew. As a result, designs evolved incrementally, in clear lines of descent sometimes spanning decades, with many small improvements in between major models,[42] and numerous adaptations to new environments in response to user feedback.

Commonality of basic systems and techniques was reinforced by the strong standards-setting controls of the military-industrial research institutes, which scrutinized new materials and design types before incorporating them in official handbooks.[43] Thus all first-generation Soviet jets used lateral "fences" along wing surfaces, and T-tails, which were the standard designs tested and approved by TsAGI (the Central Aerodynamics Institute, in Moscow).

Uniformity in design solutions was combined with innovation through competition among designers, who were pitted against one another by the political leadership. This orchestrated rivalry was especially vigorous in aviation, where competing models were actually built and flown until well into the 1950s.[44]

The simplicity of older Soviet designs, compared to equivalent American ones, was sometimes astonishing. The engine that Tumanskii designed for the MiG-21, for example, contains about one-tenth as many parts as the one used in its U.S. counterpart of the day, the F-4 Phantom.[45] Another famous example was the Kalashnikov assault rifle, which contains fewer than one hundred parts.[46] As the designer of the Katiusha rocket, V. P. Barmin, was fond of saying, "The most reliable part is the one that isn't there."[47]

[42] There are many examples, but perhaps the most famous case is that of the innumerable modifications of the Sukhoi-7 (Fitter) from the mid-1950s down to the beginning of the 1980s. In the mid-1950s Sukhoi designed a delta-wing modification (Sukhoi-9, or Fishpot), using the same basic engine (Liulka AL-7F), airframe, control systems, cockpit and ejection system, and landing gear. Kuzmina, *Sukhoi*, 169. A few years later the Sukhoi-7 interceptor was modified as a fighter-bomber (Sukhoi-9), and in the mid-1960s it served as the basis for a series of variable-geometry models, which were improved throughout the 1970s.

Revealingly enough, all of the modifications of the basic Sukhoi-7 design over a quarter century were overseen by the same man, N. G. Zyrin, who was deputy general designer from 1955 to 1980. Kuzmina, *Sukhoi*, 223–224.

[43] This helps to explain why innovations tended to be adopted by several designers simultaneously. Thus the wing shapes (swept-wing and delta) used by Soviet aircraft designers in the 1950s reflected TsAGI-approved standards. In the 1960s, when TsAGI authorized the use of variable-sweep designs, they spread quickly across all manufacturers. (Ward, *Soviet Military Aircraft Design*, 9–11.)

[44] Ward, *Soviet Military Aircraft Design*, 26–28.

[45] Central Intelligence Agency, Directorate of Intelligence, *The Soviet Weapons Industry: An Overview*, DI 86-10016 (Washington, D.C.: CIA, September 1986), 25. The Soviet engine is the R-11 300, which uses only 2,500 parts compared to the Pratt and Whitney J-79's 22,500.

[46] "Sekret nadezhnosti," *Krasnaia zvezda*, 14 December 1985.

[47] A. Vasilev and G. Nazarov 1985, "Vdokhnovlenie starta," *Sotsialisticheskaia industriia*, 25 September 1985. Strictly speaking, Barmin did not design the rocket itself but the support vehicles for it. He went on to become the Soviets' leading designer of rocket launch facilities. See M. Rebrov, "Delo na zavtra," *Krasnaia zvezda*, 22 October 1988.

As a result, traditional Soviet designs were cheap and highly producible, and thus well adapted to long production runs. This trait was reinforced by the use of manufacturing techniques that were labor-intensive but required a minimum of advanced skills or technologies.[48] In the field, Soviet soldiers and fliers found such simple weapons rugged, reliable, and easy to operate.

Since design involves trade-offs, the military customer paid a price, in the form of reduced service life, diminished versatility, and more modest performance. Soviet tanks and airplanes were not easy to maintain and repair in the field; that had to be done in rear depots or back at the factory. But such drawbacks were not necessarily disastrous in the military's eyes; long service life and versatility could be wasted assets in the short, intense war they believed the most likely, and as for lesser performance, they may have agreed that under such circumstances sheer quantity could well be more valuable than sophisticated quality.

When designing major new types of weapons, such as the first missiles or nuclear bombs, the Soviets were obviously obliged to depart from their incremental style and make long leaps in innovation. As a result, Western literature tends to represent the design and development process for "new-in-principle" weapons as sharply different from run-of-the-mill weapons acquisition, stressing the importance of direct oversight by the highest political authorities, top-priority access to materials and manpower, a greater willingness to take risks in the face of technological unknowns, and the role of special-purpose organizations dedicated solely to the new weapons technologies. In short, the literature indicates that there may be two different worlds of design and development, with two different philosophies and two very different sorts of products.

In fact, the difference is not as extreme as is sometimes portrayed; it would be more accurate to view it as a matter of degree. For example, the high political priority of "new-in-principle" weaponry projects did not spare them from problems of supply and coordination; and the designers of rockets and nuclear weapons had to show the same ingenuity as their colleagues in conventional weaponry.[49] The early space program had to reckon with the relative backwardness of the Soviet electronics industry, and consequently it used desk calculators and slide rules to design the first reentry vehicles; used off-the-shelf instruments (despite their greater weight); and borrowed whole subsys-

---

[48] Thus Soviet manufacturers frequently use spot-welding instead of rivets, and castings and forgings instead of built-up or wholly machined parts. Standard production techniques in the aircraft industry, for example, are prescribed in specialized handbooks, such as books of standard extrusions listing the shapes designers are allowed to use. See Richard D. Ward, *1985 Paris Air Show: Report*, MR-D-781 (Fort Worth: General Dynamics Corp., October 1985), 65.

[49] Thus, one of S. P. Korolev's closest associates, P. V. Flerov, was considered especially valuable because of his unparalleled connections with all the aviation organizations and designers who could possibly be useful to Korolev—in effect, a high-level *tolkach* (expediter). See Konstantin Feoktistov and Igor' Bubnov, *O kosmoletakh* (Moscow: Molodiaia gvardiia, 1982), 30.

tems from other programs.[50] As a consequence, the space program's design philosophy could have come straight from a saying attributed to Soviet helicopter designer M. L. Mil: "Make it simple, make it reliable, make it rugged, and make it work."[51]

Even more important, one should not underestimate the extent to which even "incremental" designers have been competing in a fast race to innovate, in which new materials and techniques have been incorporated at a breathtaking rate. Thus, in the aviation industry the use of materials over the decades has been anything but incremental: from wood to steel and aluminum, then to titanium and high-performance alloys—each step has required a whole new industry behind it and a whole generation of engineering research to exploit new possibilities, but also to deal with new constraints.

In sum, the secret to the Soviets' success has been remarkably the same for all weapons: concentration of priority, intense development of science and engineering, exploitation of the follower's advantage, ingenuity in offsetting the weaknesses of an inferior economy, and determined military and political leadership.

The material in this section suggests that there were two causes of the traditional Soviet design style. The first was "historic-political": much of the traditional system was a reflection of the stressful and disorderly, but administratively fluid and professionally mobile, environment produced by Stalin's dictatorship, combined with the upheavals of the first five-year plans, World War II, and the Cold War, and unremitting technological competition from the West. The second was "technical-functional": in this view, the behavior of the traditional system can be explained primarily as a result of the mixture of the technical constraints bearing on weapons design and development—uneven and frequently inferior technology, constraints in production capabilities, limited access (partly self-imposed) to imported equipment and materials, and, finally, unskilled users.

These are not alternative explanations; from the 1930s through the 1960s they acted together to produce the characteristic Soviet style. But do they still, and is the result still the same? In particular, what has happened to the nature of the technological challenge from the West?

The New Technological Challenge

Just What Is New about New Weapons Technologies?

In the history of war and weaponry nothing is so constant as technological change, yet the period from the 1930s to the 1960s, which witnessed the ad-

---

[50] Ibid., 53, 25, and 48. Thus the air-purification systems used in the *Vostok* capsule were taken from submarines.

[51] Everett-Heath, *Soviet Helicopters*, 119.

vent of nuclear weapons, guided missiles, jet engines, and electronics, was especially tumultuous. The Soviets responded to it successfully, and they look back on this period with pride. But the last twenty years have opened a qualitatively new phase of competition in military technology. One might argue that if the Soviets met the last challenge they can surely meet any new one. But the latest stage poses special problems for the Soviet system. The differences can be summed up in five points:

1. *Broader and closer dependence on new science.* In earlier decades most technological innovations, both military and civilian, were based not directly on new scientific discoveries, but on known principles, the accumulated, "packed-down" science taught in engineering textbooks.[52] But it is now increasingly the case that new weapons systems draw simultaneously on a broad range of advances in basic knowledge. In contrast to the dramatic breakthroughs of the previous generation, such as the atom bomb, the major development of recent years is the multiplication of more subtle advances arising at many different points along the development cycle. Thus, composite materials depend directly on theoretical knowledge of interfaces, semiconductors and lasers on understanding of thin films, and control systems on the mathematics of pattern recognition.[53] As these examples suggest, the change is not so much in the newer weapons' core concepts as in the design and production processes that underlie them, and in the components and subsystems they contain. Engineering and science have become virtually indistinguishable.[54]

---

[52] In the 1960s a Pentagon-sponsored study, Project Hindsight, argued that the most significant advances in military technology of the previous twenty-five years, though ultimately traceable to basic science, owed their immediate origin to innovations in design and applied science. This provoked vigorous dissent and a debate that continues to this day. Unfortunately, to my knowledge there have been no further investigations of this important question. For reviews of the principal studies and controversies surrounding them, see C. W. Sherwin and R. S. Isensen, "Project Hindsight," *Science* 156 (1967), 1571–1577; and Karl Kreilkramp, "Hindsight and the Real World of Science Policy," *Science Studies*, no. 1 (1971), 43–66.

The main weakness of the "Hindsight" approach is that it assumed a straight line between basic discovery and application. But much more frequently basic research is the basis for solving problems that arise in the course of development after the original technical invention is made. See Stephen J. Kline and Nathan Rosenberg, "An Overview of Innovation," in *The Positive Sum Strategy: Harnessing Technology for Economic Growth*, ed. Stephen J. Kline and Nathan Rosenberg (Washington, D.C.: National Academy Press, 1986).

[53] For illustrative examples, see National Academy of Sciences, Committee on Science, Engineering, and Public Policy, "Report of the Research Briefing Panel on Science of Interfaces and Thin Films," *Research Briefings 1986* (Washington, D.C.: National Academy Press, 1986), 1–16, and "Report of the Research Briefing Panel on Computer Research and Pattern Recognition," *Research Briefings 1985* (Washington, D.C.: National Academy Press, 1985), 87–100. See also National Research Council, Physics Survey Committee, *Physics Through the 1990s: Scientific Interfaces and Technological Applications* (Washington D.C.: National Academy Press, 1986), 217–224.

[54] An important aspect of this is the direct contribution to engineering of laboratory techniques and equipment first developed for basic research in physics. The newest generation of submicron-

The growing "science content" of today's weapons systems poses two special problems for Soviet military industry. The greatest strengths of Soviet science and technology, on the whole, are in basic science; and the closer to the theoretical, "blackboard" end of the spectrum, the stronger the Soviets tend to be.[55] But the Soviets are weaker in branches of science that require a multitude of smaller, sophisticated instruments, computers, or ultra-pure, custom-designed materials and reagents, such as chemistry, electronics, or the biological sciences. Their special weakness, in short, is a high wall between science and engineering. The crumbling of that wall in the West (where it was always lower to begin with) puts the Soviets at a special disadvantage.

The second Soviet disadvantage is that much of the contribution of science to military industry in the West comes at the initiative of scientific and industrial entrepreneurs, whose stake in obtaining grants and contracts, combined with a tradition of weak central supervision and control, produces a strong "science-push" bias to the weapons acquisition system, especially in the United States.[56] In the Soviet Union, though the phenomenon of scientific entrepreneurship is by no means uncommon, the scientists' and industrialists' incentives for promoting engineering applications and new weapons concepts are typically weaker, and bureaucratic obstacles to home-grown ideas are greater. Thus, it is not unusual for discoveries made by Soviet scientists to be applied first in Japan or the United States;[57] and in weapons acquisition it is generally (though not exclusively) the case that the Soviets respond to developments begun elsewhere. The traditional Soviet process, in short, is "government-pull" rather than "science-push."[58]

2. *Increasing dominance of civilian innovations and applications.* In earlier decades military applications typically came ahead of civilian ones; indeed,

---

resolution chips, for example, requires X-rays generated from synchrotron radiation sources that originated in high-energy physics research. Herman Winick, "Synchtrotron Radiation," *Scientific American* 257, 5, (November 1987), 88–101. I am grateful to Professor Harvey Brooks of Harvard University for many valuable ideas for this section.

[55] For a discussion of the "blackboard" pattern of excellence in Soviet science, see Thane Gustafson, "Why Doesn't Soviet Science Do Better than It Does?" in *The Social Context of Soviet Science,* ed. Linda L. Lubrano and Susan Gross Solomon (Boulder: Westview Press, 1980), 31–68.

[56] See Franklin A. Long and Judith Reppy, eds., *The Genesis of New Weapons: Decision Making for Military R&D* (New York: Pergamon Press, 1980).

[57] A spectacular recent example with many potential military applications is the technique of depositing thin diamond films from methane or alcohol vapor, co-discovered by B. V. Deriagin in the Soviet Union but first exploited in Japan. Walter A. Yarborough and Russell Messier, "Current Issues and Problems in the Chemical Vapor Deposition of Diamond," *Science* 247, 4943 (February 9 1990), 688–696. Malcolm W. Browne, "New Diamond Coatings Find Broad Application," *The New York Times,* October 25 1988, A1.

[58] See Matthew Evangelista, *Innovation and the Arms Race: How the United States and the Soviet Union Develop New Military Technologies* (Ithaca: Cornell University Press, 1988), 69–70 and passim.

military support played a crucial role in the early development (if not the actual invention) of such major technologies as semiconductors, xerography, polaroid photography, numerically controlled machine tools, and of course nuclear power and jet engines. This is still broadly the case in many specialized areas today, such as compound semiconductors (for example, gallium arsenide) or nonferrous magnetic materials.[59]

But in a growing array of technologies, such as semiconductors and computers, fiber optics, ceramics, new magnetic alloys, new battery materials, and laser applications to manufacturing, civilian applications preceded military ones and continue to lead. This is due partly to growing lead-times for military development and the restrictions imposed by conservative military specifications, but partly also to a more fundamental trend: the companies making new technologies today increasingly serve civilian markets primarily and are less and less influenced by military contracting. In the future, as the needs of the military shift from volume production of weapons to information products, many of their requirements will resemble those of large civilian consumers, and their dependence on civilian innovation will grow further.

Many of these innovations arise in large multinational corporations. As a result, the Western military increasingly depend on civilian materials and equipment imported from other Western countries, especially Japan.[60] This may create problems in times of war, but it is a fact that military competition in peacetime requires collaboration across international boundaries.

This second feature of the new technological challenge finds the Soviets at

[59] In the 1940s and 1950s, a major role in sponsoring basic research in promising directions was played by the Office of Naval Research. See Sanford L. Weiner, "Resource Allocation in Basic Research and Organizational Design," *Public Policy* 20, 2 (Spring 1972), 231–238; Harvey Brooks, "Basic Science and Agency Missions," in *Research in the Service of National Purpose*, ed. F. J. Weyl (Washington, D.C.: Office of Naval Research, 1966).

Though the transistor was first invented at Bell Labs as part of a search for a replacement for mechanical telephone relays, the Army Signal Corps played a crucial role in the transition phase between invention and commercial marketing. See Thomas J. Misa, "Military Needs, Commercial Realities, and the Development of the Transistor, 1948–1958," in *Military Enterprise and Technological Change: Perspectives on the American Experience*, ed. Merritt Roe Smith (Cambridge: MIT Press, 1985), 253–288.

On numerically controlled machine tools, see David F. Noble, *Forces of Production* (New York: Alfred A. Knopf, 1984). For nuclear power, Richard Hewlett and Francis Duncan, *The Nuclear Navy* (Chicago: University of Chicago Press, 1974). Useful background on the development of jet engines will be found in Edward Constant, *The Turbojet Revolution* (Baltimore: Johns Hopkins University Press, 1980).

[60] The growing direct role of Japan's industry in U.S. military procurement is described in Kent E. Calder, "The Rise of Japan's Military-Industrial Base," *Asia Pacific Community* (Summer 1982), 26–41. For an evaluation of U.S. dependence on foreign suppliers in militarily relevant branches of electronics, see National Research Council, Board on Army Science and Technology, *Foreign Production of Electronic Components and Army Systems Vulnerabilities* (Washington, D.C.: National Academy Press, 1985).

a special disadvantage, too, because of the historic weaknesses of most of its civilian sectors compared to the military ones. In the Soviet system, it has been almost exclusively the military-industrial sector that has contributed innovation and entrepreneurship to the civilian sector, not the reverse.[61] Moreover, because of Western trade restrictions and their own aversion to technological dependence, the Soviets are unable to draw efficiently on civilian innovations outside their own bloc, and when they do, it is through the least efficient transfer mechanisms.[62]

3. *New weapons systems really are systems.* No modern weapon stands alone. But the latest weapons are highly elaborate systems at every stage of their existence, from manufacture to use. First, because their requirements for precision, quality, and reliability are greater than ever before, each new system draws on a broader range of a nation's total technical skills than its predecessors and puts a greater premium on coordination and communication. In particular, the new materials and components require new production processes: new alloying and fabricating techniques for titanium alloys, composites, and laminated materials; forging and extrusion presses; new welding techniques and precision machining. This fact in turn requires more elaborate industrial management and planning. Such heightened requirements for integration and the management of complexity and risk pose a special problem for Soviet industry, which is vertically organized and finds horizontal coordination and exchange of information difficult.

On the other hand, the Soviets' tradition of centralization may be a source of strength in dealing with the other half of this trend, namely, the requirements of new weapons in use. New weapons need elaborate supporting systems to filter and process information and to coordinate operations. The Soviets' long-standing emphasis on combined arms, their preference for close ground control of flight operations, and the priority they have long given to centralized military communications may serve them well, provided they are able to deploy the necessary technologies for command and control. In this area too, however, the Soviets have long-standing weaknesses.

4. *The growing importance of software.* At every step of the development of new weapons systems, from design and production to deployment and use,

---

[61] Julian Cooper, "The Civilian Production of the Soviet Defense Industry," in *Technical Progress and Soviet Economic Development*, ed. Ronald Amann and Julian Cooper (Oxford: Basil Blackwell, 1986), 31–50.

[62] The most elaborate study of these questions, industry by industry, is the pair of volumes written by a team of British researchers at the Center for Russian and East European Studies of the University of Birmingham. See R. Amann, J. M. Cooper, and R. W. Davies, *The Technological Level of Soviet Industry* (New Haven: Yale University Press, 1977), and R. Amann and J. M. Cooper, *Industrial Innovation in the Soviet Union* (New Haven: Yale University Press, 1982). See also Philip Hanson, *Trade and Technology in Soviet-Western Relations* (New York: Columbia University Press, 1981).

the most critical factor is now the quality and modernity of software and human skills. Computer-assisted design and manufacturing are limited by the available programs, not by hardware. The sophistication of technical means available on the battlefield surpasses the algorithms and skills available to exploit and control them effectively.

These requirements hit the Soviets at an especially vulnerable point. Computing is a crucial example: if Soviet computer hardware is still weak compared to that of the West,[63] Soviet software is far weaker, and the necessary human skills are weaker still.[64] A massive program to teach computing in secondary schools, adopted by the Soviet Politburo in 1985, has been delayed by the lack of the necessary microcomputers and peripherals in the schools, but a more serious constraint has been a lack of suitably trained teachers.[65] One of the most chronic complaints in the Soviet military press is the low level of computing skills in military ranks, the lack of enthusiasm for computerization among line officers, the shortage of instructors and equipment, and the consequences for training.

5. *New opportunities for reliability, ruggedness, flexibility, custom design, and flexibility.* The gains in firepower, mobility, precision, and miniaturization available from new weapons technologies are well known and require little comment here. But what may be equally revolutionary is the new technologies' potential for producing systems that are more reliable, rugged, flexible, redundant, and custom-designed for precise situations—and therefore ultimately (despite initial trends to the contrary) cheaper. In the thirty years from 1950 to 1980, for example, the thrust-to-weight ratio of jet engines has tripled, fuel efficiencies have more than doubled, and the time between overhauls has increased from 100 to 10,000 hours.[66] Much of this is due to advances in materials science.[67]

---

[63] As in everything else concerning Soviet technology, there is substantial variation in Soviet capabilities even within a single specialty. For an overview, see S. E. Goodman and W. K. McHenry, ''Computing in the USSR: Recent Progress and Policies,'' *Soviet Economy* 2, 4 (October–December 1986), 327–354. On the other hand, Soviet development of high-speed, advanced-architecture computers is a zone of relative strength. Peter Wolcott and S. E. Goodman, ''High-Speed Computers of the Soviet Union,'' *Computer* (September 1988), 32–41.

[64] See S. E. Goodman, ''The Information Technologies and Soviet Society: Problems and Prospects,'' *IEEE Transactions on Systems, Man, and Cybernetics* SMC-17, 4 (July–August 1987), 529–552.

[65] Soviet efforts to develop mass computing skills are covered regularly by Viktor Yasmann of the Radio Liberty research staff, in *Radio Liberty Research Bulletin* and in *Soviet Analyst*.

[66] V. H. Kear and E. H. Thompson, ''Aircraft Gas Turbine Materials and Processes,'' *Science*, vol. 208 (23 May 1980), 847–855. See also R. V. Jones, *Future Conflict and New Technology*, The Washington Papers, vol. 9, no. 88 (Beverly Hills, Calif.: Sage Publications, 1981).

[67] Nickel- and cobalt-based superalloys to withstand high temperatures (advances of the 1950s), new processes such as directional and single-crystal solidification in the fabrication of turbine vanes (advances of the 1960s), and the advent of composites such as boron/aluminum for fan

One more quality of the new technologies is increased versatility, leading to greater flexibility in responding to opponents' countermeasures. Thus, cyclotron resonance masers (CRM) offer the potential of being tuned by the operator to produce radiation of any desired wavelength across a broad band, a powerful asset in defense against stealth weapons.[68] Versatility of another sort comes from computer-assisted design and manufacturing, which, together with new materials such as compound semiconductors, create the possibility of responding quickly to new military requirements with customized adaptations that do not require lengthy retooling.

These qualities reinforce one another: miniaturization, for example, creates new possibilities for redundancy and thus for increased reliability. It is now possible to machine miniature sensors from a single crystal of silicon, which take up so little space that they can be used in replaceable modules or multiple, parallel systems.[69] The consequences for the architecture of new weapons are frequently dramatic, but also potentially disruptive for all established weapons systems.

Design has traditionally been a strong point in Soviet weapons development, but its aims were typically to circumvent technological constraints rather than exploit technological opportunities, to contain rather than take risks. The new technologies challenge Soviet designers to trade proven strategies for new ones and to take more risks. The positive opportunities created by the new technologies may require not only a physical retooling but a mental one as well.

These five features, taken together, add to up to a qualitative difference in military technology—and the key point is that they all strike the Soviet system at a traditional weak point. The weak connections between basic science and technological applications, the lag in civilian technologies, the long-standing isolation from the world economy and persistence of autarkic attitudes, the vertical organization of Soviet industry and its incapacity for horizontal coordination, the underdeveloped software and human skills, the traditional conservatism of military design—these are chronic weaknesses that the Soviet traditional military-industrial system has managed to offset in the past. But the five trends just described pose an unprecedented new challenge to the Soviet military and the military-industrial system.

---

blades (advances of the 1970s and 1980s)—all these have vastly improved the efficiency and service life of turbine parts. Better understanding of fiber-matrix interfaces produces composites that resist sheer, yielding weapons that are both lightweight and rugged. See Kear and Thompson, "Aircraft Gas Turbine Materials and Processes."

[68] *Physics Through the 1990s*, 219.

[69] James B. Angell, Stephen C. Terry, and Phillip W. Barth, "Silicon Micromechanical Devices," *Scientific American* 248, 4 (April 1983), 44–55.

But What Is the Threat?

It is clear enough that the changes sketched above produce new capabilities and raise new challenges. But the key question is how the new technologies affect the art of war. They do not change war's essential tasks (training and organizing, gathering information, commanding, striking, protecting, moving) or its fundamental principles (surprise, concentration, economy/simplicity, adaptability), but they clearly alter the way these are carried out.[70] Just how this will happen is still ambiguous. Will the defense benefit more than the offense? The conventional more than the nuclear? What are the implications for the use of war as an instrument of politics? In short, are the changes of the last twenty years revolutionary or not?

The consequences of technological change for nuclear weapons are the most clearly understood. Delivery vehicles have become versatile and precise, warheads small and quickly retargetable, and basing systems both harder to protect and easier to conceal. At first sight these developments seemed to make nuclear weapons easier to use, but after a decade of debate over the future of the land-based strategic deterrent and over the right way to shore up the strategic triad, it appears that the net effect of technological advance has been to bolster, not to weaken, the robustness of both sides' strategic forces. In short, no new technological revolution has occurred on the nuclear side.

What is far less clear is the effect of new technologies on conventional warfare. It is certain that conventional forces are increasingly lethal over longer distances; indeed, for some purposes they approach the destructive power of nuclear weapons, and this has led some analysts to speculate that new conventional weapons could replace nuclear devices for all major strategic purposes.[71] This greater lethality, combined with greater speed and precision over longer ranges, creates unprecedented possibilities for concentrating fire quickly at a defender's weakest points or disrupting his rear. But the defense, too, gains the capability of blunting massed offensive forces or destroying follow-on forces before they can be brought into action. As a result, for commanders of both sides the management of the battlefield and the integration of each side's forces loom as more vital than ever before. The positional defender is doomed, but the mobile, high-tech defender may actually enjoy an edge over the attacker.[72]

Some are still skeptical about the effects of the new weapons in actual war-

---

[70] See Steven L. Canby, "New Conventional Force Technology and the NATO-Warsaw Pact Balance: Part I," in New Technology and Western Security Policy, ed. Robert O'Neill (London: Macmillan, 1985), 66ff.

[71] See, for example, Carl H. Builder, Strategic Conflict Without Nuclear Weapons, R-2980-FF/RC (Santa Monica: Rand Corporation, April 1983).

[72] Donald R. Cotter, "New Conventional Force Technology and the NATO-Warsaw Pact Balance: Part II," in New Technology, ed. O'Neill, 84–97.

fare. The new technologies are easily countered or counterattacked, say the critics; indeed, while the new "smart" munitions are extraordinarily expensive, countermeasures such as smoke, chaff, and reflectors are cheap. In the "semi-organized melee of many on many," in unfavorable weather and over bad terrain, the advantages of sophistication are lost, and automated systems prove to be inflexible, vulnerable to deception or unexpected tactical reactions by the enemy. The small warheads of precision-guided munitions can be protected against through fairly simple adaptations in design, materials, and disposition.

In short, the critics contend, under battlefield conditions the traditional virtues of simplicity and adaptability remain essential. Neither defense nor offense is favored; in this respect, technology is neutral, and the day will belong, as always in the past, to the side that is better organized, better trained, and more numerous.[73] A corollary proposition is that high-tech forces in being and the facilities needed to produce them will be rapidly neutralized in the preliminary stages of a major war, leaving the advantage to the side that retains a large industrial capacity for producing less vulnerable and demanding weapons.

What makes the effects of new military technologies still more ambiguous is a growing gap between anticipation and actuality. Most of the systems hailed as revolutionary in the press over the last two decades are still being developed or field-tested; very few have reached the battlefield, and fewer still have seen wide action. This complicates further the task of defining the threat posed by new technologies and integrating it into actual military planning.

Three times in the last century, major scientific or technological advances have revolutionized military doctrine and practice—the development of automatic weapons in the late nineteenth century, the advent of mechanized land and air war in the 1920s, and the invention of missile-launched nuclear weapons in the 1940s and 50s. What makes the present changes different from the preceding ones is that planners are under pressure to respond before it is even clear what the threat consists of. In the first three cases the weapons came first, and the task of doctrine was to work out the implications of a new threat that already existed and had already been used in a major war. What is ambiguous about the "fourth revolution" is precisely whether it is a revolution at all, and if so, when it will come and what form it will take.

There is, indeed, another way of looking at recent trends, and that is to emphasize their essential continuity. Since the beginning of this century, advances in electronics have been a continuous force in military design, first in radio, then in radar, and more recently in computers and microelectronics. Looked at in this light, the sources of challenge do not change, and the process of adapting to them is continuous.

[73] Canby, "New Conventional Force Technology, Part I."

Soviet Perceptions and Opinions

How have the Soviets themselves viewed the technological challenge? The central question here is whether Soviet observers themselves agree that the five traits just described spell a qualitative new stage in military technology and in the character of war, and whether this perception has led them to alter their traditional approach to weapons development.

First, a comment on timing. The perception that military technology was taking a major new turn did not become widespread even in the West until the mid-1970s. During the first half of the period covered by this study, from the mid-1960s to the mid-1970s, the Soviets were absorbed in achieving strategic parity with the United States and broadening their conventional forces, developing the technological possibilities opened up by the developments of the 1940s and 1950s. It would be too much to say that during this period the Soviets were serenely confident about their own technological capabilities; indeed, the mid- to late 1960s mark the onset of nagging anxieties about the innovative capabilities of the civilian economy and the first efforts to reform civilian R&D.[74] But the Soviets appeared satisfied that their military-industrial sector was doing a good job and viewed it as a model for the rest of the economy to emulate.[75] The principal concern expressed by Soviet military authors was that they were not assimilating new weapons as fast as they should, but they appeared to take for granted the ability of their military industry to produce them.[76]

In the second half of the 1970s and the first half of the 1980s, this self-confident tone was replaced by one of growing anxiety, but it is difficult to tell whether the change was caused by worries about technology per se or about politics and doctrine, since one would naturally expect the two to overlap. There is little doubt that the Soviet military showed rising alarm as U.S.-Soviet relations worsened, as U.S. military spending began growing rapidly under Carter and then under Reagan, and as Washington adopted doctrinal innovations such as counterforce strategy and conventional attack-in-depth, followed by the Strategic Defense Initiative. But the key question is, did the Soviets also perceive a qualitative change in the nature of the technological challenge itself?

I shall begin with the best-known "alarmist," Marshal Ogarkov, chief of

---

[74] Bruce Parrott, *Politics and Technology in the Soviet Union* (Cambridge: MIT Press, 1983), chap. 6. See also Paul M. Cocks, *Science Policy in the Soviet Union*, vol. 2 of U.S. Government, National Science Foundation, *Science Policy: USA/USSR* (Washington, D.C.: GPO, 1980), chap. 11. See also Amann and Cooper, *Industrial Innovation*.

[75] See M. Cherednichenko, "Nauchno-tekhnicheskii progress i nekotorye problemy voennoi nauki," *Kommunist vooruzhennykh sil*, no. 3 (1976), 8–15.

[76] John Erickson, "Trends in the Soviet Combined Arms Concept," *Strategic Review* (Winter 1977), 39, cited in Nichols, "The Politics of Doctrine," 276.

the Soviet General Staff from 1977 to 1984. The evolution of Ogarkov's expressed views over those years mirrored that of the Soviet military as a whole, as he moved from a tone of confident, if watchful, caution to one of clear worry.[77] From the beginning, Ogarkov acknowledged the increased role of science in weapons development.[78] He saw an unprecedented acceleration in the rate of technological change, because of which, Ogarkov wrote, "basic weapons systems in practice turn over every ten to twelve years."[79]

Ogarkov had no doubts about the impact of this revolution on strategic weapons, but in the late 1970s he still appeared to hesitate over whether the consequences were equally sweeping for conventional ones. In particular, he was cautious about the implications of advances in antitank weaponry.[80] It was not until the early 1980s that he sounded convinced that the changes in conventional warfare were indeed "qualitative" and "revolutionary."[81] His language about antitank weapons grew more pointed; now the new trends, he wrote, would be "dangerous to ignore."[82] By the spring of 1984, Ogarkov had reached a conclusion with weighty doctrinal implications: Since conventional weapons now had a global reach and their destructive potential "had increased by an order of magnitude," their strategic effects approached those of nuclear weapons themselves.[83]

Not all Soviet military writers, however, were prepared to concede that the actual impact of technological change on conventional warfare was quite as revolutionary as Ogarkov claimed, at least for the near term. An interesting example is a book published in 1982 by M. M. Kirian, who followed Ogarkov in recognizing the enormous changes under way in conventional weapons but

[77] As late as 1979 Ogarkov could still write, "The Soviet Armed Forces have today the most advanced (*samoi sovershennoi*) military technology and armament." N. Ogarkov, "Na strazhe interesov sovetskoi rodiny," *Partiinaia zhizn*, no. 4 (1979), 29.

[78] Thus his famous phrase about "weapons based on fundamentally (*printsipialno*) new physical principles." N. Ogarkov, "Voennaia nauka i zashchita sotsialisticheskogo obshchestva," *Kommunist*, no. 7 (1978), 116. The same phrase recurs in most of Ogarkov's later writings.

[79] N. Ogarkov, "Na strazhe mirnogo truda," *Kommunist*, no. 10 (1981), 86. Most of the themes and phrases of the 1978 and 1981 *Kommunist* articles reappear, frequently in amplified form, in Ogarkov's 1982 pamphlet, *Vsegda v gotovnosti k zashchite otechestva* (Moscow: Voenizdat, 1982).

[80] See "Voennaia nauka," 115 and 120. Calling for "attentive study," Ogarkov added, "Of course, while being bold in improving and modernizing what exists, one should not rush ahead, and one should embark on innovations only when the new is ripe for application."

[81] *Vsegda v gotovnostoi*, 31 and 39. Whereas earlier Ogarkov had limited the use of the word "qualitative" (*kachestvenno*) to innovations in the weapons themselves, now he applied it to the resulting "new forms of military operations."

[82] Ibid., 43.

[83] N. Ogarkov, "Zashchita sotsializma, opyt istorii i sovremmenost," *Krasnaia zvezda*, 9 May 1984. These conclusions have received enormous attention from Western analysts. For a thorough discussion of Ogarkov's writings, see Mary Fitzgerald, "Marshal Ogarkov on the Modern Theater Operation," *Naval War College Review* 39, 4 (Autumn 1986), 6–25.

stopped short of accepting Ogarkov's claims for the consequences.[84] Many of the latest developments could be effectively counteracted; tanks, in particular, could be designed with greater firing ranges, higher speeds, and above all, new kinds of armor (such as cheap and effective reactive armors), and there was no sign that Kirian considered them obsolete. To be sure, new conventional weaponry would require new tactics, but here Kirian evidently believed psychological qualities, even more than new technical skills, would remain paramount.[85] Kirian was not alone; elsewhere in the Soviet literature, even as political-doctrinal alarm mounted to a fever pitch in the first half of the 1980s, one could find articles that still took a relatively relaxed attitude toward the technological threat and stressed the importance of training and tactics as the most effective near-term responses.[86]

As political and doctrinal anxiety rose, calls for more military spending, and even veiled criticism of the political leadership, rose too. But one finds little criticism of military industry or calls for reforms in military R&D and weapons acquisition, even in Ogarkov's writings.[87] His most pointed barbs were aimed at his fellow officers and at top policy makers.[88] This cannot be

---

[84] M. M. Kirian, ed., *Voenno-tekhnicheskii progress i vooruzhennye sily SSSR* (Moscow: Voennoe Izdatel'stvo, 1982), chap. 7. Kirian is a professor at the Institute of Military History of the Ministry of Defense. He and his associates apparently play a role as ghost-writers for senior Ministry of Defense officials, at least to judge from the fact that a paragraph of one of Deputy Minister V. Shabanov's articles ("Shchit rodiny," *Ekonomicheskaia gazeta*, no. 8 [1988], 18) was lifted verbatim from Kirian's 1982 edited book, page 326. That does not necessarily mean that Kirian serves as an adviser to Shabanov, but it suggests at least that he is close to Shabanov's views (or vice-versa).

[85] Ibid., 276–77, 318–325.

[86] A particularly interesting item in this genre is an article by an officer of the East German Volksarmee, V. Wuensche ("Chelovek i tekhnika v sovremennoi voine," *Voennyi Vestnik*, no. 2 [1984], 89–93). Wuensche, while also acknowledging the importance of technological developments in conventional weaponry, is openly skeptical of the claims of the weapons manufacturers that they have come up with "miracle weapons" (pp. 92–93).

For references to similar literature bylined by leading Soviet commanders, see Gottemoeller, "Conflict and Consensus in the Soviet Armed Forces," in *The Dynamics of Soviet Defense Policy*, ed. Bruce Parrott (Washington, D.C.: Wilson Center Press, 1990).

[87] Until 1984 Ogarkov assured his readers, on the contrary, that Soviet technology and the economy were fully up to their tasks. "The Soviet Union," he wrote in 1982, "has a sufficient material base to defend its interests" (*Vsegda v gotovnosti*, 44). The present level of development of the economy "enables it to solve successfully the most technologically complex tasks and to create in a short time any type of weapon" (ibid., 57). Even in the famous 1984 interview, Ogarkov did not criticize military industry or R&D but hinted instead at a broader economic weakness, by quoting Engels to the effect that "nothing depends so much on economic conditions as the army and the fleet" ("Zashchita sotsializma").

[88] Thus, the basic problem seemed to be the unwillingness of top policy makers to give the key go-ahead to develop the newer weapons. In the 1984 interview Ogarkov said, "Work on these kinds of weapons is already under way in a number of countries, for example the United States. Their creation is a reality of the very near future, and not to take that into account right away would be a serious mistake." The previous year Ogarkov had written, "We must have daring

dismissed simply as the result of censorship, unless one is willing to assume that Soviet editors were censoring his remarks about scientists and industrialists even as they were printing his criticisms of the political and military leadership.[89]

The pattern of Soviet reactions to the Strategic Defense Initiative in 1984 and since shows a similar split between political-doctrinal and technological anxiety. In the Soviets' eyes, SDI was an immediate threat because it signaled that the Americans were about to reject the doctrine of mutual deterrence. This endangered the political basis of the strategic balance, which was the Soviets' central diplomatic achievement of the last two decades, and called into question the carefully built doctrinal assumptions underlying every arms-control accord since ABM. But, for the near term at least, the Soviets' reaction to the strictly technological threat posed by SDI was much milder, which suggested that their own active antimissile and antisatellite programs made them fully aware of the technological obstacles to SDI and of the easily available countermeasures.[90]

It would be foolish to claim to know the perceptions of the Soviet military from a limited sampling of published sources, but the foregoing analysis suggests that Ogarkov did not speak for the service chiefs, for the Ustinov protégés in charge of military industry, or for the top political leadership. These groups' views may well have been more like those expressed by Kirian. After all, they had worked hard for a generation to achieve parity with the United States. Having succeeded in matching the United States in the "third revolution," they may have had little stomach for the thought that they were already behind in a fourth one.

This does not exclude the possibility, of course, that under the top very different perceptions were spreading, and that Ogarkov's views were widespread among more junior officers, particularly within the General Staff. Indeed, this was the pattern of the Brezhnev era in nearly every sphere of policy,

---

experiments and solutions, not stopping before the logic of outdated traditions, views, and positions'' (''Miru—nadezhnuiu zashchitu,'' *Krasnaia zvezda*, 23 September 1983). The following year he grew more pointed still: ''Military cadres must accept justifiable risks, if necessary. It is better to test out new methods in peacetime than to look for them in the middle of a war'' (''Zashchitu sotsializma'').

Jerry Hough is undoubtedly right to construe Ogarkov's remarks as an attack on Ustinov, but it is equally clear that they were an attack on the service chiefs as well.

[89] This is not to argue, of course, that censorship and self-censorship are not factors to reckon with. To see their impact on Ogarkov's writings, one need only glance at the much tamer version of his views published after his 1984 demotion, *Istoriia uchit bditelnosti* (Moscow: Voenizdat, 1985). Nevertheless, what is striking about Ogarkov's earlier writings (especially the two *Kommunist* articles) is precisely their critical boldness (by preglasnost standards, of course).

[90] On this point see the analysis of Benjamin Lambeth and Kevin Lewis, in *The Strategic Defense Initiative in Soviet Planning and Policy*, Report R-3550-AF (Santa Monica: Rand Corporation, January 1988), esp. 27–31.

a process that one might call "perestroika before perestroika." But what matters for the purposes of this study is the perceptions of those who had the power to make decisions, including that of removing a chief of the General Staff. If such people did not perceive a technological crisis in the military-industrial system, one would predict that the pattern of their responses to technological challenge would be largely incremental from the mid-1960s to the mid-1980s, consisting essentially of a modernization of the traditional approach described earlier. I turn now to an examination of those responses to see whether this prediction is borne out.

Patterns of Response to Technological Challenge, 1965–1985

From the mid-1960s to the mid-1980s substantial changes took place in five areas affecting weapons acquisition: a growing institutionalization and centralization of the decision-making structure for weapons development; changes in the design process; closer working relations with Soviet basic science; modernization of the design process and of production technologies in military industry; and more active mobilization and use of proven Western design concepts and technology.

Evolution of the Decision-Making System

As in the rest of the Soviet system, the Brezhnev era in the military-industrial sector was the era of the technocrat, of technocratic bureaucracy, and of technocratic rhetoric. This was the culmination of trends that had begun even before Stalin's death; and indeed, the style of the Brezhnev era was itself an extension to the Soviet system as a whole of the personnel, management methods, and models of thinking of the military-industrial complex that had evolved since World War II. The symbol of the technocrat triumphant was Dmitrii Ustinov, who long before he became minister of defense had been the dominant voice in military procurement. The Ustinov years witnessed major changes in the organization of the defense-industrial system, marking further steps toward regularization of procedures and centralization of decision making.

On the side of the uniformed military, the most striking development was the growth in size and functions of the General Staff. Under Stalin the General Staff did not play a major role in weapons development and procurement (except for the relatively brief period when Marshal M. N. Tukhachevskii was at its head). But the advent of nuclear weapons and ballistic missiles, modern combined-arms operations, and more recently of rapidly growing requirements for global command and control systems, has brought the General Staff into the center of force planning and development,[91] and both of the last two chiefs of the General Staff have stated that its roles have expanded.[92] From at least the late 1950s, the General Staff began to play a more systematic role in weapons development and procurement policy, and its apparatus includes a Scientific-Technical Committee.[93]

A similar trend toward centralization and systematization appears to have occurred on the side of the defense industries, particularly with the creation (or more exactly, re-creation) in about 1957 of a Military-Industrial Commission (VPK) under the USSR Council of Ministers.[94] The VPK coordinates weapons development and procurement, oversees the acquisition and application of foreign technology, and has at least some control of allocation of resources. On the party side, a similar institutionalizion took place, with the creation of a Central Committee Department for Defense Industry in 1958.

The rhetoric of the Brezhnev era favored "scientific" decision making, and especially in the 1960s and early 1970s there was much enthusiasm for operations research, systems analysis, and computerized planning. Most of these techniques were tried out first in the military sector. The Soviet military showed considerable interest in the decision-making techniques Robert McNamara instituted in the Pentagon, and some Soviet officers, including very high-ranking ones, became strong advocates of them.[95] These may have reinforced the trends to centralization: just as PPBS and its sister techniques put more power in the hands of the office of the U.S. secretary of defense, so

[91] See Rice, "The Party, the Military, and Decision Authority," and Kenneth Currie, "The Soviet General Staff's New Role," *Problems of Communism* 33, 2 (March–April 1984), 32–40.

[92] N. Ogarkov, *Pravda*, 2 October 1981; Sergei Akhromeev, *FBIS*, 9 December 1988.

[93] Western observers have little concrete information on this body, and not all agree it still exists. It is believed that the General Staff had an Armaments Directorate until 1978, which was then transferred to the Ministry of Defense. No new head of a General Staff committee has been identified. See Kenneth M. Currie, "The Soviet General Staff: Its Impact on Military Professionalism and National Security Decisionmaking," Ph.D. dissertation, George Washington University, 1987, 134.

Nevertheless, the impression persists that the General Staff remains involved in policy making for weapons procurement. According to one émigré account, for example, the General Staff since the late 1950s has maintained an office on helicopters that formulates missions and requirements for new helicopters, bargains with the designers over quality specifications, and even goes into fair detail over specific components and equipment during the design process. Lev Chaiko, *Helicopter Construction in the USSR* (Falls Church, Va.: Delphic Associates, 1986), 15–20.

[94] An earlier version of the VPK was created in 1938, but during World War II and the late Stalin period more informal arrangements were the rule. Under Khrushchev the oversight of defense industry became more institutionalized. See Holloway, "Innovation in the Defense Sector," 310–311.

[95] For an excellent early survey, see David Holloway, "Technology, Management, and the Soviet Military Establishment," *Adelphi Papers*, no. 76 (London: Institute for Strategic Studies, 1971). There can be no doubt that many high-placed officers were involved in these techniques. See Jacob W. Kipp, "The Role of Staff Culture in the Development of Soviet Military Theory," *Signal* (December 1985), 87–92.

in Moscow they may have served as a vehicle for the growing influence of the General Staff.

Having noted these trends, one should express some reservations about their significance as responses to the latest technological challenges. Most of them began in the 1950s and should thus probably be seen as part of a general process of formalization of decision making that came after Stalin's death. Indeed, most of the bodies just described have antecedents going back to the 1930s, and thus one may question how new they really were.

It is difficult to say whether these organizational changes altered the balance of influence among the armed services or between the uniformed military and the defense industrialists, or affected the control of the party apparatus over either. The main result may have been to drive the bargaining between the military customer and the industrial contractor to a higher level, turning it into more a contest among technocratic staffs at the top than among "plenipotentiary brokers" representing the political leadership at middle and upper-middle levels.

Adaptations in the Design Process

A second set of changes took place at the level of weapons design and production. One way of offsetting mounting costs was to reduce duplication and competition among designers, and to aim for more standardization and commonality of subsystems. The aircraft designer A. S. Iakovlev observes that one of Brezhnev's frequent themes in conversation was the need to reduce the number of different models of aircraft, so as to simplify development, maintenance and repair, and the supply of spare parts.[96] After 1960, for example, the number of military aviation design bureaus, whose rivalries had been so prominent a feature of the traditional system, was reduced, and the ones that remained became more specialized.[97]

Increasing technical sophistication required specialization; but the need to control costs called for more standardization and commonality. To combine these two requirements, the aviation industry increasingly developed special-purpose design offices for subsystems and encouraged (indeed, sometimes compelled) the major designers to use them. Thus, whereas a designer such as Sukhoi previously developed his own ejection seats, by the late 1960s Sukhoi

[96] A. S. Iakovlev, *Zapiski konstruktora* (Moscow: Politizdat, 1979), 286, 288.

[97] Miasishchev's bomber design group was switched to missile work in 1961; Lavochkin's fighter group was switched to drones and missiles. A. S. Iakovlev, *Sovetskie samolety* (Moscow: "Nauka," 1982), 283. Iakovlev's bureau, though it remained active in civilian aviation, likewise left the fighter business, except for a VSTOL project that resulted in the Yak-36. See also Richard D. Ward, *Soviet Military Aircraft Design and Procurement*, MR-D-809 (Fort Worth: General Dynamics Corporation, 12 September 1986), 31.

was looking over an early standard model at an interministerial exhibit designed to promote commonality; by the early 1970s, such standard ejection-seat systems had become general practice.[98]

These developments were bound to affect the roles and status of the general designer, because from the late 1950s on it was evident that he could no longer handle personally the design of an entire airplane, and responsibility was increasingly divided among separate organizations.[99] To a degree, this was simply the latest stage in a long-standing trend; airframe and engine design, for example, had become administratively separate specialties early in the 1930s, to which the traditional Soviet response was the stable duo of airframe man and engine man.[100] But as the trend toward specialization continued into the 1960s and 1970s, the problems of coordination mounted correspondingly.

Partly as a result, during the 1970s and 1980s the role of the chief designer tended to shift to one of overall coordinator. This was accompanied by some decline in prestige and visibility, which was to be expected in any case, because the generation of the giants of the Stalin era began to disappear, and by the mid-1980s nearly all were retired or dead.[101] Their successors were usually long-time deputies of the famous names, who in most cases remained far less visible as public figures even after the succession.[102] But this may only reflect a decline in the importance of the general designers' role as political brokers and entrepreneurs in a more institutionalized system, while their importance as managers and coordinators may be just as great as before.[103]

[98] L. Kuzmina, *Generalnyi konstruktor Pavel Sukhoi* (Minsk: Belarus, 1985), 219–222. As Kuzmina tells the story, a campaign for standardization and commonality was launched in the late 1960s, presumably at a high level, since it affected all the defense ministries. This fits with what Iakovlev states about Brezhnev's views.

[99] This is a prominent theme in the Soviet biographies of the major designers. See, for example, that of the engine designer A. M. Liulka. L. Kuzmina, *Ognennoe serdtse* (Moscow: Moskovskii rabochii, 1983), 167.

[100] Thus we have the pair of Sukhoi and Liulka, Mikoian and Tumanskii, Antonov and Ivchenko/Lotarev, whose partnerships in the early decades of Soviet jet development have become part of the official hagiography. In addition to the biography of Liul'ka, already mentioned, other works devoted to engine designers include L. L. Lazarev, *Vzlet* (Moscow: Profizdat, 1978), which is devoted to A. A. Mikulin; and M. Arlazorov, *Doroga na kosmodrom* (Moscow: Politizdat, 1984), on the life of A. M. Isaev, designer of liquid-fueled rocket engines.

[101] The decline of the aircraft designers has been more noticeable than that of the missile and space designers, partly because the golden age of the latter came later, so that a number of the original heroes are still alive.

[102] Only A. N. Tupolev's son (A. A. Tupolev), S. V. Iliushin's successor (G. V. Novozhilov), and to a lesser extent M. K. Yangel's successor (V. F. Utkin) are comparable in public prestige. The current director of the Sukhoi KB, for example, is M. P. Simonov, who was one of a group of new deputy general designers appointed in the early 1970s. After E. A. Ivanov, Sukhoi's long-time right-hand man, served as *generalnyi* from 1975 to 1981 (possibly 1982), Simonov succeeded him. (Kuzmina, *Sukhoi*, 224–225).

[103] The veteran designer Iakovlev tells an anecdote from the mid-1960s that suggests how much the initiation of new weapons systems had already come to depend on the ministries, rather than

Closer Ties with Basic Science

A third response to technological challenge from the mid-1960s to the mid-1980s has been a reinforcement of military-industrial ties with basic science. The Soviet military-industrial sector has long had close associations with basic science, partly through its own network of ministerial R&D institutes, but mainly through the Academy of Sciences.[104] Before World War II, the academy's role in military R&D was mainly advisory, but during and after the war it became directly and continuously involved in military work, most notably in "new-in-principle" systems such as nuclear weapons, nuclear propulsion, and radar.[105] Much of the academy's work in applied science and technological development was clustered in its Department of Engineering Sciences, which included such well-known bodies as the Kurchatov Institute of Atomic Energy and the Institute of Radio Engineering and Electronics, but also lesser-known ones such as the Institute of Precision Mechanics and Computing Technology, an early leader in computer research. But in 1961–63 the academy was extensively reorganized to strengthen the quality of its work in basic science; the Department of Engineering Sciences was abolished, and its engineering institutes were redistributed among the industrial ministries.[106]

It appeared at first as though the academy's involvement in applied research generally, and military R&D in particular, might have declined after the reorganization of 1961–63, but as Western observers have continued to follow the evolution of the academy's leadership and structure since the early 1960s,

---

on informal lobbying of political leaders by entrepreneurs (Iakovlev, *Zapiski konstruktora*, 289–290).

[104] The research system of the Academy of Sciences includes the USSR Academy and a galaxy of republic-level academies. In the following discussion the term "academy" will be used as a shorthand for the USSR Academy, which is the leading center for basic research. Most of the republic-level academies are much more heavily involved in applied research; the Ukrainian Academy, in particular, will be mentioned separately below.

[105] Thus, for example, the physicist A. P. Aleksandrov, who subsequently became president of the academy under Brezhnev, was the principal scientific adviser in the development of the first Soviet nuclear submarine in the late 1950s, while the noted nuclear engineer N. A. Dollezhal was the principal designer of the reactor. (Stvolinskii, "Konstruktor podvodnogo atomokhoda.")

Academic talent was brought to bear on traditional military specialties as well, but perhaps through consulting relationships involving individual scientists rather than whole institutes. Thus, among many examples in Soviet sources, the mathematician A. N. Kolmogorov is mentioned in an artillery text as one of the leading theoreticians of artillery fire (G. E. Peredelskii, ed., *Otechestvennaia artilleriia—600 let* [Moscow: Voenizdat, 1986], 343); the aerodynamicists G. I. Petrov and S. A. Khristianovich collaborated with Liulka in jet engine development (Kuzmina, *Ognennoe serdtse*, 81); and Sukhoi drew on the services of academicians N. N. Moiseev on early CAD systems and K. A. Andrianov on plastics and other nonmetallic materials (Kuzmina, *Pavel Sukhoi*, 212).

[106] Loren R. Graham, "The Reorganization of the USSR Academy of Sciences," in *Soviet Policy-Making*, ed. Peter Juviler and Henry Morton (New York: Praeger, 1967), 133–162.

they have concluded that, if anything, the academy's military work has probably grown instead. The evidence is circumstantial but consistent.

All three of the USSR Academy's presidents since the reorganization, M. V. Keldysh, A. P. Aleksandrov, and G. I. Marchuk, have had extensive backgrounds in applied science, primarily military for the former two and partly so for the latter.[107] All three have steadily stressed the importance of applied science,[108] sometimes over vigorous objections from other members of the academy, who have complained that the weight of applied research has grown too much in the academy since the early 1960s.[109] That the military have been an important part of this increase is suggested by the fact that the fastest-growing branch of the academy since the early 1960s has been the Department of Mechanics and Control Processes, which has taken over some of the functions of the old Department of Engineering Sciences, and which includes among its members a number of defense scientists (notably, in recent years, P. D. Grushin and V. P. Makeev).[110] Finally, the Presidium of the academy contains a Section of Applied Problems, which appears to have coordinated the academy's defense work since the 1961–63 reorganization.[111]

Another possible sign of a growing military role in the work of the Academy of Sciences was the growing use of research contracts, which emerged as a major source of financing for the academy network in the 1970s, especially in the Ukrainian Academy and the Siberian Division of the USSR Academy.[112] Since contracts are project-oriented, they give the customer influence and flexibility, in contrast to the inflexible institutional budget by which most academy

[107] For brief biographical sketches of all three men, see Stephen Fortescue, *The Academy Reorganized: The R&D Role of the Soviet Academy of Sciences since 1961*, Occasional Paper no. 17, Department of Political Science, Research School of Social Science (Canberra: Australian National University, 1983), 16–17, 47–49, and 54 respectively.

[108] Keldysh, in particular, opposed the disbanding of the academy's Department of Engineering Sciences in 1961–63, and Aleksandrov's views at about the same time suggest that he may have, too. Marchuk was the protégé and successor of M. A. Lavrentev, the founder of the Siberian Department of the academy, which has always insisted on the importance of applied research and has long pioneered innovative techniques for strengthening the ties between basic and applied. From 1980 to 1986, moreover, Marchuk headed the State Committee on Science and Technology, and since his election as president of the academy he has continued to stress applied research.

[109] Fortescue, *The Academy Reorganized*, 28–30.

[110] Ibid., 56–57. This department has since been renamed the Department of Problems of Machine Building, Mechanics, and Control Processes.

[111] Since its creation in 1964, the Presidium's Section on Applied Problems has been headed by experts in control systems and operations research with ties to military and space programs. From 1964 to 1971, its chairman was E. P. Popov (who is identified in the 1986 *Sovetskii entsiklopedicheskii slovar* as a major general); from 1971 to 1973, G. S. Pospelov; and after 1974, Iu. V. Chuev. I am indebted to Julian Cooper and Peter Almquist for this information.

[112] On the growing importance of research contracts generally, see Fortescue, *The Academy Reorganized*, 71ff. Specific data on the Ukrainian Academy and the Siberian Division will be found in Thane Gustafson, *Selling the Russians the Rope? Soviet Technology Policy and U.S. Export Controls*, R-2649-ARPA (Santa Monica: Rand Corporation, 1981), 61, 65.

institutes are traditionally supported. In addition, as in the past, individual academy researchers served industrial customers as consultants.[113]

In evaluating the significance of these military ties to fundamental science as a response to the growing "science content" of military technology, one important issue is whether the military customer (or the political leadership, for that matter) took responsibility for strengthening basic science to help it play its expanded role, or whether it simply "harvested" it, taking its strengths and weaknesses as it found them. It is worth noting that by the mid-1980s there was a strong perception in the Soviet Union that basic science had weakened over the previous twenty years. After decades of rapid expansion, the growth rate of funding for Soviet R&D slowed markedly during the 1970s and fell well behind that of the OECD, as did the growth rate of scientific personnel.[114] Basic science was especially hard hit.[115] The average age of the research personnel of the academy rose steadily, while the salaries paid to junior researchers made entry into science relatively less attractive.[116] Long-standing imbalances in the quality of the academy's work, making it stronger on the theoretical side but weaker on the applied side,[117] apparently continued largely unchanged into the 1980s, presumably lessening the academy's value to military customers.[118] It appears that the military's use of science increased,

[113] An interesting picture of such contracting and consulting in action comes from a specialist on protective coating formerly employed in Korolev's rocket design bureau. Victor Yevsikov, *Reentry Technology and the Soviet Space Program (Some Personal Observations)* (Falls Church, Va.: Delphic Associates, 1982), 19–30. According to Yevsikov, the dealings of Korolev's bureau with the Academy of Sciences took a variety of forms. Yevsikov records that the High Temperatures Institute carried out a series of tests for no payment. The Ioffe Institute solicited a contract but did not obtain it because its proposed topic overlapped with work under way at VIAM. Academician I. V. Tananaev, a prominent chemist with the Kurnakov Institute, worked for the bureau as a consultant, while the Ukrainian Academy's Physico-Technical Institute held a standing contract.

[114] Philip Hanson, "Gorbachev's Economic Policies: Technology and Innovation," in *The Comparative Economics of Research, Development, and Innovation in East and West: A Survey*, ed. P. Hanson and K. Pavitt (Harwood Academic Publisher, 1988).

[115] See Gorbachev's opening speech to the Nineteenth Party Conference, *Pravda*, 29 June 1988.

[116] See Loren R. Graham, "Science and Technology Trends in the Soviet Union," in *Framework for Interaction: Technical Structure in Selected Countries Outside the European Community*, ed. Herbert J. Fusfeld (Troy, N.Y.: Center for Science and Technology Policy, Rensselaer Polytechnic Institute, 1987), II-D-1-44.

[117] For a comparative analysis, see Thane Gustafson, "Why Doesn't Soviet Science Do Better than It Does?" in *The Social Context of Soviet Science*, ed. Linda Lubrano and Susan Gross Solomon (Boulder: Westview Press, 1980), 31–67.

[118] One increasingly important aspect of this is the academy's relative weakness in computers and information technologies. Only in 1983 did the academy take major steps to remedy the gap, by creating a new Department of Informatics, Computer Technology, and Automation. See Simon Kassel, *A New Force in the Soviet Computer Industry: the Reorganization of the USSR Academy of Sciences in the Computer Field*, N-2486-ARPA (Santa Monica: Rand Corporation, August 1986).

but the military's relationship with the scientists remained essentially unchanged.

Modernization of Industrial Support

Technological challenge requires not only closer ties to basic science, but also improved engineering and manufacturing techniques. In this area the Soviet response has been strong and apparently effective, particularly in developing new materials and techniques for fabricating them. Westerners who inspected the Antonov-124 (Ruslan) super-transport in the mid-1980s, for example, were surprised by the extensive use of composites and advanced alloys, as well as sophisticated casting, forging, and extrusion techniques associated with them.[119] Behind these advances lies a long history of Soviet strength in metallurgy and materials, much of which has been developed within the Ministry of the Aviation Industry itself.

The military-industrial sector has made determined efforts for the last two decades to overcome its lag in electronics, and there has been striking progress since the Ministry of the Electronics Industry was created in 1961. Soviet industry still trails the West in most areas of advanced microelectronics, but it has become strong enough to build rapidly on Western examples and to innovate on its own, supplying Soviet space and defense programs with serviceable if not state-of-the-art systems, so that designers are not so tightly constrained by technological weakness as they once were.[120]

Industrial support for the design process has improved as well. The Ministry of the Aviation Industry has invested heavily in aerodynamics research and up-to-date facilities, including one of the world's largest wind tunnels.[121] The successful flight of the Soviet space shuttle, "Buran," testifies to the growth of the testing and simulation capabilities of the ministry's research institutes such as TsAGI.[122]

The main thing to note about this industrial modernization, however, is that it took place along traditional lines, that is, it was largely concentrated within the military-industrial system. Despite growing recognition in Soviet writings of the threat posed by the chronic weaknesses of civilian industry, modernization efforts continued to neglect the civilian sector.

---

[119] Ward, *1985 Paris Air Show*, 61–76.

[120] For two contrasting views that differ mainly in emphasis, see Cooper, "Western Technology and the Soviet Defense Industry," 194–196; and U.S. Department of Defense, *Soviet Military Power: An Assessment of the Threat, 1988* (Washington, D.C.: GPO, 1988), 144–149.

[121] U.S. Department of Defense, *Soviet Military Power*, 143.

[122] G. Zaganov and I. Ageev, "Tsentr aviatsionnoi nauki," *Krasnaia zvezda*, 1 December 1988.

Increasing Resort to Technology Transfer from the West

Since the 1920s technological advances in new Soviet weapons have come from a mixture of domestic innovation and foreign borrowing. The blend of the two is not random; for each new type of weapon it has taken the form of a cycle. As Julian Cooper describes it, each cycle begins with a burst of borrowing abroad, as the Soviets seek to accelerate development and diminish design risks in a new area. Even during this phase Soviet reliance on foreign example is never total or passive. But the key feature is that once a new weapons technology has been successfully absorbed, Soviet use of outside contributions drops off sharply.[123] Throughout, the Soviets have always developed their own distinctive designs in the style described at the beginning of this chapter. Overall, the foreign borrowing phase was especially prominent in the 1930s and 1940s, when the Soviets were assimilating the principal weapons types of mechanized and nuclear warfare, whereas the "domestic elaboration" phase dominated the 1950s and 1960s.

In the 1970s new signs appeared that could be interpreted as the beginning of a new cycle of borrowing, or possibly as the beginning of a chronic dependence.[124] The main direct evidence for this is that the "special" information system (in Russian, *spetsinformatsiia*), by which Western technology is collected outside normal trade channels and supplied to Soviet military R&D, grew in size and importance, especially toward the end of the decade.

The principal covert system for gathering information on Western technology is managed by the VPK,[125] which in 1973 created an Interdepartmental Commission to act as a clearing-house for spetsinformatsiia. Acting through an agency called VIMI (Vsesoiuznyi institut mezhvedomstvennoi informatsii, or All-Union Institute for Interagency Information),[126] the commission pro-

[123] Julian Cooper, "Western Technology and the Soviet Defense Industry," in *Trade, Technology, and Soviet-American Relations*, ed. Bruce Parrott (Bloomington: Indiana University Press, 1985), 169–202, esp. 190–193.

[124] See U.S. Government, Technology Transfer Assessment Center, *Soviet Acquisition of Militarily Significant Technology: An Update* (Washington, D.C.: GPO, September 1985). The U.S. government report appears to have been based in part on Soviet documents that came into French hands in 1981–1982. These purport to be reports by the Military-Industrial Commission and the KGB on the activities of the *spetsinformatsiia* gathering system in 1976–1980. In 1985 several Western scholars, including the present author, were allowed to study copies of the Soviet texts in Paris. A description and analysis are contained in Philip Hanson, *Soviet Industrial Espionage: Some New Information* (London: Royal Institute of International Affairs, 1987). In this chapter, material based on my own notes is referenced as "VPK Reports."

[125] According to the U.S. government report cited above, there is also a separate network for illicit trade operations, operated by the Ministry of Foreign Trade. That network is not discussed here.

[126] Although apparently subordinated to the VPK, VIMI's role is not confined to processing classified information. VIMI also provides a mechanism for the transfer of technologies from the defense sector to the civilian economy.

cesses requests originating from the military-industrial ministries, assigns collection tasks to the gatherers (principally the KGB and the GRU), receives the results, and evaluates the use made of them by the originating ministry.

The year 1973 was surely not the beginning of the spetsinformatsiia system, but the early 1970s may have witnessed an initial expansion and formalization of it, particularly in the area of microelectronics. Then, toward the end of the 1970s, the spetsinformatsiia collection system became more centralized and institutionalized. In 1979 the Interdepartmental Commission was renamed and expanded; ministry-level counterparts were established;[127] and for the first time the acquisitions program was funded through the hard-currency funds of the "client" ministries, again suggesting a systematization of procedure.[128]

The key question is whether this evidence signals the beginning of a vast new cycle of borrowing or a marginal expansion of previous practices. Several features suggest the latter: Funding for the VPK spetsinformatsiia program appears to be only a small fraction of total Soviet military R&D or even of Soviet imports of machinery and equipment, and the number of projects in which spetsinformatsiia is claimed to be used is also modest. As one might expect from a technology-transfer mechanism that goes through several intermediaries, much of the information provided by the VPK system consists of low-grade ore. It contains little classified material or embargoed equipment. Years may go by between the request and its fulfillment. Thus, there are glaring inefficiencies in the ways information is ordered, processed, and used. Despite a handful of important exceptions, much of the significance of the VPK-generated flow appears to be that it enables Soviet designers and technologists to monitor Western design concepts and learn from them without actually depending on them.

Western defense analysts argue that recent Soviet weapons systems hew more closely than in the past to proven Western design concepts and configurations. This would be logical: it is plausible, on the face of it, that as the pace of innovation increases, as the costs and risks of developing new systems rise and evolutionary precedents become fewer, and as decision making grows more bureaucratized and therefore perhaps more cautious, there is more of a tendency to draw on foreign example. In some areas of technology for which more public knowledge is available, the growing force of Western design example is manifest.[129]

But for the moment, the limited public evidence available does not support

---

[127] In the Ministry of Machine Building a Tsentralnaia otraslevaia spetsialnaia tekhnicheskaia sluzhba (Special Technical Service) was created in 1979, in the ministry's Glavnoe upravlenie nauchnykh issledovaii i razrabotok (Main Directorate for R&D). (Author's notes, VPK Reports.)

[128] Author's notes, VPK Reports.

[129] The classic case is that of computers. See National Research Council, *Global Trends in Computer Technology and Their Impact on Export Control* (Washington, D.C.: National Academy Press, 1988), chap. 6.

the case that the 1970s and 1980s witnessed the beginning of a massive new cycle of foreign borrowing, let alone an era of dependence. The most one can say is that there appears to have been some increase in the volume of borrowing, and some effort to systematize the connections between borrowers and users. This is not to belittle the security implications of the transfers that have taken place, especially the handful of clearly grave cases.[130] But considered as a response to technological challenge, these changes, while suggesting some strain on the Soviet side, do not amount to a crisis reaction, a wholesale revamping of past practices, or any weakening in the Soviets' determination to provide for themselves.

Evaluating the Soviet Responses

The five responses just reviewed form a definite pattern: in weapons acquisition, from the mid-1960s to the mid-1980s, the Soviets responded to technological challenge with incremental adaptation and evolutionary modernization rather than wholesale change. Decision making became more centralized and rationalized; political leaders grew less and less involved with the minutiae of weapons design and procurement; and the two major players—the defense industry and the uniformed military—concentrated growing authority in the Military-Industrial Commission and the General Staff, as well as the upper reaches of the Ministry of Defense. The design process became less personalized and more institutionalized; the general designers acted less as political brokers, and the semimythical figure of the "hero-designer" faded from the scene. Traditional Soviet engineering strengths were further developed and manufacturing technology improved, while the basis for a modern microelectronics industry was laid. Ties with basic science were strengthened and made more flexible; and new mechanisms were developed to increase the flow of technological information from the West and its absorption into the design process.

But one should also point out what did not change: the basic organization of both the military and the defense industries was not altered; the structure of the design bureaus and military research institutes remained largely the same, and the roles of the general designers as horizontal coordinators became, if anything, more important than before. Little was done to shake up the basic science establishment or to overcome the obstacles to innovation; and the pattern of use of Western technology remained a familiar one. These responses continued the trends of the 1940s and 1950s instead of breaking with them.

---

[130] A clear recent case of an illicit transfer that is both militarily significant and indicative of a purposeful and well-coordinated effort on the Soviet side is the sale of computerized milling equipment used in the manufacture of submarine propeller blades. See David Sanger, "A Bizarre Deal Diverts Vital Tools to Russians," *The New York Times*, 12 June 1987.

The same evolutionary pattern could be seen in the products of the system. A steady modernization has taken place; the newer Soviet weapons were designed to meet much more ambitious standards of performance; and in some respects, the Soviet pattern of design trade-offs became more "American"— for example, Soviet designers made their ships and planes more habitable, easier to repair in the field, and, above all, capable of performing multiple missions. But the traditional features of Soviet design practice could still be traced in the new systems, implying many of the same basic trade-offs, objectives, and priorities as in the past.[131] The basic Soviet "style" of weapons design did not fundamentally change, any more than the organizations and decision-making system that created such weapons.

The same general pattern of response could also be seen outside the area of weapons acquisition, in the organization and force deployments of the Soviet military. In particular, Marshal Ogarkov's prescriptions for radical change in Soviet conventional forces were rejected in favor of a more evolutionary approach, which retained armored ground forces, based on the tank, as the centerpiece of Soviet conventional strength.[132]

It is important to stress again that evolutionary response is not the same thing as nonresponse: Soviet military innovation in the two decades up to 1985 was energetic and impressive. What is argued here, however, is that this was, on the whole, an extension of the response to the "third revolution," not to the new, "fourth revolution" described earlier in this chapter.

But did the Soviets themselves consider this pattern of response adequate? Western analysts believe that, starting from the mid-1970s, there were increasing signs of strain in Soviet weapons development and procurement. This can be seen in the volume of output of Soviet weaponry from the mid-1960s to the 1980s, as well as in the Western reconstructions of Soviet unit costs.

According to CIA data, from the mid-1960s to the mid-80s output has fallen in almost every category of weapons, in some cases from the early 1970s and in all cases from the end of the decade. In the category of tactical aircraft, output may have declined by as much as half in the first half of the 1980s alone, from about 1,300 new aircraft per year to about 650 in 1985.[133] DIA data, with some exceptions show a broadly similar trend (table 6.1).

During the same period, unit costs of major weapons systems rose dramatically: the T-80 tank, for example, is estimated by the CIA to cost three times as much as the T-55 of two decades before;[134] the MiG-29 Fulcrum, nearly

[131] This is the essential conclusion of the CIA, Kehoe and Brower, and Richard Ward. In addition to other works by Ward previously cited, see *MiG-2000: The Next Soviet Challenge*, MR-D-781 (Fort Worth: General Dynamics Corporation, 11 September 1985).

[132] See the excellent discussion by Rose E. Gottemoeller, "Conflict and Consensus."

[133] David M. North, "Soviet Advances Spurring Western Aircraft Upgrades," *Aviation Week and Space Technology*, 21 July 1986.

[134] Central Intelligence Agency, *The Soviet Weapons System Industry: An Overview*, DI 86-10016 (Washington, D.C.: CIA, December 1986), 27.

TABLE 6.1
Soviet Military Material Production, 1960–1985

General equipment type	1960	1965	1970	1975	1980	1985
ICBMs	25	300	275	250	250	100
LRINF[a]	500	0	0	25	100	125
SRBMs	200	200	400	1,200	500	450
SLCMs	300	300	400	500	550	700
SLBMs	100	25	250	200	150	100
Bombers	75	130	55	20	30	50
Fighters/Fighter Bombers	600	900	800	1,300	1,300	650
ASW Aircraft	0	10	35	5	10	5
Towed Field Artillery	3,300	2,325	1,950	2,000	1,800	2,000
Self-propelled Field Artillery	0	0	0	250	900	950
Submarines	25	15	16	10	13	8
Major Surface Ship Combatants	5	11	12	13	11	8
Minor Surface Ship Combatants	170	115	85	60	65	50

Source: Defense Intelligence Agency (U-45,542/DB-4).
[a] Longer-Range Intermediate-Range Nuclear Force.

three times as much as the Mig-21 Fishbed C/E; and the SS-18 MOD-4, almost four times as much as the SS-7.[135]

The combination of rising cost and declining output does not necessarily add up to a crisis in weapons acquisition, however. To make that case, one would need evidence that the top political leadership was dissatisfied with the performance of military R&D and weapons acquisition. The few available signs suggest otherwise.

Gorbachev's own treatment of the defense industries is revealing: whereas he has downgraded the status of the military commanders in several symbolic ways, there has been no similar treatment of the defense industrialists. On the contrary, Gorbachev, even more than his predecessors, has held up the military-industrial system as a model for the rest of Soviet industry to follow. As Julian Cooper recounts in his chapter in this book, more military-industrial executives have been promoted to high positions since Brezhnev's death than at any time in the past; and the VPK ministries have been mobilized to con-

[135] Ibid., 5.

tribute to the modernization of the civilian economy. Gorbachev has praised the high quality of the space program.[136] The traditional system of quality control used in military industry (through the use of "military representatives," or *voenpredy*)[137] has been invoked by Gorbachev as the model for the "state acceptance" (*gospriemka*) quality-control system implemented at the beginning of 1987.[138] Finally, there is the testimony of the president of the USSR Academy of Sciences in 1986 that, unlike some parts of Soviet industry, the military-industrial sector had not increased its dependence on Western technology.[139] One similarly fails to find criticism of military R&D or the weapons acquisition system from high-ranking uniformed officers.[140] In short, one is led to the conclusion that, at least as late as the mid-1980s and perhaps up to the present, most of the principal players considered Soviet technological performance in the military area to be adequate.

The issue of cost is more difficult to judge. It is now clear that the new leadership considers the burden of military spending excessive and means to lighten it. But there are only passing hints to suggest that Gorbachev blames military industry for the rising unit costs of weaponry.

[136] Thus, his words at Baikonur in 1987: "Everything here at the space center, from the most complex launch structures, test facilities, and laboratories, to the powerful boosters, space capsules, and life-support systems for them, equipped with up-to-date computer technology and highly sensitive instruments—everything is Soviet-made, of the highest quality and at the most up-to-date technological level. That raises in my mind a simple but very important question: why do we try to acquire from abroad sometimes even simple things, if even now we are capable of resolving such enormous, large-scale, and complex tasks?" "Byt patriotom svoei rodiny, zhit i rabotat po sovesti," *Pravda*, 14 May 1987.

[137] The *voenpred* system has been in use in the military-industrial sector since the 1930s. (Artem Mikoian, for example, got his start as a voenpred in an aviation plant before being appointed deputy designer in a design bureau.) For background see David Holloway, "Soviet Military R&D: Managing the Research-Production Cycle," in *Soviet Science and Technology: Domestic and Foreign Perspectives*, ed. John Thomas and Ursula M. Kruse-Vaucienne (Washington, D.C.: National Science Foundation, 1977), 205.

Jerry Hough discusses their powers and roles in "The Historical Legacy of Soviet Weapons Development," 94–95. According to one émigré who worked in S. P. Korolev's TsKBEM near Kaliningrad, there were voenpredy performing quality-control functions even in space projects there. Yevsikov, *Reentry Technology*, 41.

[138] As Gorbachev told an audience in Murmansk in the fall of 1987, "Take defense: here we are not behind in any way. So we are capable of doing good work. But in that sector, I must tell you, the quality-control officers make it hot for everybody: the workers, the designers, the engineers, and the managers. That is how *gospriemka* must work." ("Nemerknushchii podvig geroev Zapolaria," *Pravda*, 2 October 1987)

[139] Speech by A. P. Aleksandrov at the Twenty-seventh Party Congress: "It has become a habit to buy technology and products abroad. In many cases this has led to stagnation in several branches of science and technology, and to dependence on deliveries from foreign countries. . . . Fortunately, this import plague has not affected, or has only weakly affected, the industries (*otrasli*) that determine the security of our country." *XXVII Sezd Kommunisticheskoi Partii Sovetskogo Soiuza: stenograficheskii otchet* (Moscow: Politizdat, 1986), 1:171.

[140] Gottemoeller, "Conflict and Consensus."

Why did the Soviets' response to the new challenges of military technology amount to a continuation of previous trends? The last two sections suggest some answers: first, the record of the previous twenty years had been a considerable success; second, the implications of the new, "fourth" revolution for war were ambiguous; and third, the military were reluctant to tamper with the established priorities and missions of the services. But there was probably one more reason: responding to the "fourth revolution" would have required the high command and the defense industrialists to step outside their bounded professional roles and speak out on fundamental social and economic issues that were the preserve of the political leadership. Ogarkov's fate reminded them where the boundaries of approved participation lay. As will be seen below, those broader questions have now been addressed head-on—but by the civilian leadership, with the military as reluctant followers.

Implications for Civil-Military Relations

This chapter has divided the recent technological challenge into two periods. During the first, roughly through the mid-1970s, the Soviet military-industrial sector was mainly preoccupied with adapting to the continuing consequences of what I have called, following Soviet parlance, the "third revolution," that is, the explosive evolution of the major new weapons that appeared during and just after World War II. During the second period, since the mid-1970s, the writings and behavior of the Soviet military-industrial leadership suggest that they recognized a qualitative change in weapons technology but viewed the threat as long range and limited their response in weapons acquisitions to essentially evolutionary adjustments.

In short, the central finding of this chapter is the contrast between a qualitative change in the technological challenge and the absence of a perceived near-term crisis in military technology or a correspondingly radical Soviet response.

What were the consequences for civil-military relations and for the relative strength and influence of the players? Returning to the list set out at the beginning of this chapter, we are looking for changes in issues, assets, and roles arising as the result of strains in military doctrine, the advent of (or need for) new knowledge and skills, or perceptions about performance.

In the area of doctrine, the mid-1960s began with a reaction against Khrushchev's enthusiasm for strategic missiles and his attempts to reshape the military-industrial system to fit his views. The political leadership during the Brezhnev years showed an unprecedented willingness to let the military debate and shape strategy and doctrine.[141] But one cannot show that the uniformed

---

[141] Nichols, "The Politics of Doctrine."

military or the defense industrialists gained from this a lasting expansion of participation or permanent additional political assets. The temporarily increased role of the military in security policy caused a counterreaction from the party leadership, perhaps as early as 1977 but certainly by 1984 and 1985, when Ogarkov was dismissed, Ustinov died, and the military lost their voting membership in the Politburo.

Throughout this twenty-year period Soviet military strategists placed steadily growing emphasis on conventional war and weaponry.[142] But this did not lead to a downgrading of the prestige or resources of strategic services, taken as a group, or to a lasting increase in the standing of the surface navy. On the other hand, neither did the warnings of technologists that the tank would soon be obsolete produce a decline in the position of the ground forces; as has been seen, moves in that direction were defeated. In short, adjustments in doctrine in response to technological changes did not produce long-term changes in the relative resources or standing of the players.

Similarly, although the advent of new technologies generated adjustments in training, organization, and ways of mobilizing knowledge, it did not bring discernible changes in the previous balance of influence or power. Two successive waves of technocrats reached leading positions, displacing the tank commanders of World War II: a generation of missile specialists associated with Ustinov, and, more recently, a generation of electronics experts. Their rise was accompanied by a degree of centralization in both the military and the defense industries, most noticeably in the General Staff and the VPK. But Western analysts remain uncertain how much real centralization of decision making has been achieved. One of the lessons of Ogarkov's tenure as chief of the General Staff is that the service chiefs retain considerable power to resist change, and the manifest weakness of the VPK-like bodies recently installed in the Council of Ministers suggests that the same may be true of the military-industrial ministries. In any case, the political consequences of centralization are ambiguous: a centralized organization is more easily controlled than a decentralized one, since one need only control its leadership.

This brings us back to the hypotheses of Meyer and Hough. Turning first to Meyer's prediction that the influence of the military is growing, it should be noted that the political effects of technological trends are many-sided. Since it is not only the technology content but especially the science content of new weapons that is growing, the essential information that political leaders need about proposed new systems and processes is above all whether they are scientifically feasible; and as military-industrial ties to basic science increase, so also does the number of scientists who are informed about new military technologies and are in a position to give their views.

---

[142] Michael MccGwire, *Military Objectives in Soviet Foreign Policy* (Washington, D.C.: Brookings, 1987).

The consequences of ''increasing technological content'' are many-sided, too. An aura of expertise in the management of large integrated systems undoubtedly adds to the military's authority, but authority tied to expertise can collapse if the expertise fails or even appears to fail, as shown by the Korean Air Lines affair of 1983 and the Rust scandal of 1987.

The lack of military experience by the new generation of political leaders is ambiguous as well. Such leaders may focus less on technical issues as the military define them, and more on the broad political implications of defense decisions. Moreover, civilian politicians are presumably experts at their own business of politics—which includes the arts of co-optation and patronage. Nothing is easier than recruiting military expertise through judicious appointments and transfers.

Finally, one may question whether there really have been an increasing divergence between the Soviet military and civilian economies and a growing dominance of the former over the latter. There has always been more overlap between the two than is commonly portrayed, and while the dominance of military industry has been quite clear, that dominance is neither new nor increasing.

The Hough hypothesis likewise finds little support from the evidence in this chapter. The defense industry has not been nearly so conservative and monolithic, nor the uniformed military so innovative, as Hough suggests. Neither has the defense industry necessarily been the dominant partner. It is true that alumni of the defense industry have always been found throughout the government elite, but this may be primarily because the defense industrialists are perceived to have transferable managerial skills and the uniformed military have not.

To argue that the military have an inferior position is to underestimate the importance of the requirements laid down by the military, the tight control over quality exercised by the ubiquitous voenpredy, and the demands of the military users for design changes following testing and even field experience—all consistently backed by the political leadership. This is not to say that the uniformed commanders are the dominant partner either; rather, the point is that the relationship between the two is more fluid and more complex than one of simple dominance and hostility, shifting between partnership and antagonism in response to circumstances, with neither side dominant overall.[143]

---

[143] Indeed, these are Hough's own conclusions in *Soviet Decisionmaking*, ed. Valenta and Potter, 101–103. ''One should, of course, not exaggerate the degree of conservatism among the defense industry administrators'' (p. 101). ''One should also not exaggerate the certainty of conflict between the military and the defense industry administrators'' (p. 101). ''If we turn to the question of the relative influence of the military and the defense industry on weapons development, here too we find variability, but probably in the framework of some equality'' (p. 102).

Finally, it is not clear that the military commanders blamed the defense industry for poor performance in keeping up with technological advances. The evidence of concern and criticism reviewed here suggests that it was aimed primarily at the Brezhnev/Chernenko political leadership and at broad economic and defense policy, rather than at the defense industries in particular.

The overall conclusion of this chapter is that during the period from the mid-1960s to the mid-1980s, technological challenge and the Soviet responses to it in the area of weapons acquisition brought little change in civil-military relations. The roles and assets of the players hardly changed. New issues arose, but they were either kept off the agenda or blunted through compromise. No net changes occurred in the players' relative influence or apparent authority as a result of their successes or failures in technology. In short, in the area of weapons acquisition during this twenty-year period, there was a further growth of "professionalism" and "objective control," described by Colton in the opening chapter, and of "loose coupling," as used by Rice.

What caused what? When subjected to a sharp outside perturbation, the system failed to develop radical new responses, but instead resorted to established routines, a classic case of what organizational theorists call "cybernetic response." Logically, there are two possible explanations in such a case: either the perturbation was not large enough or immediate enough, or its effects were deliberately damped by the controlling players in the system to avoid disrupting settled procedures, roles, and rankings. Evidence of both has been seen in this chapter. There is also a classic sequel: if external perturbation continues to grow, the damping effort fails, and the search for a new response strategy begins. At that point, relations among the players are disrupted and must be renegotiated.

That is precisely what appears to be happening under Gorbachev. For Gorbachev the challenge of the emerging technologies is so extreme that it calls into question not only the traditional system of military organization and weapons acquisition but the very role of the military factor in Soviet national security. In the long run, the latest technological challenge is to the viability of the socialist system as a whole.

Gorbachev's prescriptions are correspondingly radical: Since civilian technologies increasingly provide the basis for national strength, it is Soviet civilian industry that must be attended to first and foremost, and military industry must help. Since the new technologies are international, the barriers to technology transfer must be broken down, and Soviet industry must be exposed to international competition and communication. If software and user skills are paramount in today's emerging technologies, then the educational system must be transformed; and if science is what drives engineering today, Soviet

---

"The normal influence of the defense industry and the military likely varied with the type of question" (p. 102).

science must be improved and its ties to engineering overhauled. The parallel to the traits listed earlier in this chapter is striking. It is clear that Gorbachev and his government are no longer responding to the "third revolution," but to the fourth.

The very least one can say about this agenda is that it implies a historic change in the traditional Soviet style for dealing with military-technological challenge. Created to cope with industrial backwardness and constant external change, the existing system has succeeded by concentrating priority and limiting technological risk—precisely the behavior it is now supposed to abandon. The military-industrial system of weapons acquisition was Stalin's proudest creation, and it expressed the very essence of the Stalinist strategy of development—but it is now being asked to lead the way in a dismantling of the Stalinist order.

It follows that the Gorbachev program will bring with it a wholesale disruption in the traditional issues, roles, assets, and procedures in civil-military relations. Already being seen is a massive civilian intrusion into the formation of doctrine, which will lead to an assault on the military's monopoly of data on strategy and force deployment. R&D resources will need to be reallocated to civilian industries. Internal barriers to the flow of information and data will have to be taken down, and the traditional system of illicit technology transfer replaced by more open, more efficient, less disruptive mechanisms. Simply to name these requirements is to see what havoc they will cause—indeed, are already causing—in civil-military relations.

One should not necessarily jump to the conclusion that all officers and defense industrialists will resist tooth and nail. In the long run the Gorbachev approach is the only way to create the basis for Soviet national strength in the next century. But what is perhaps most fateful for the future of professionalism in civil-military relations is that the questions of societal choice that were previously off-limits to soldiers and weapons builders are now wide open, and the military are being invited, even prodded and scolded, into expanding their roles and addressing new issues.

One is reminded here of two thought-provoking themes from the history of civil-military relations in other societies: first, military commanders grow most discontent when they perceive that they are prevented from carrying out their military duty as they see it. Second, military influence and power grow most surely, not when the military venture on their own initiative into the realms of societal choice and political sovereignty, but when they are invited to do so by political leaders.

Seven

Social Change and Civil-Military Relations

ELLEN JONES

WHEN the typical Soviet conscript reports to his military commissariat to fulfill his draft obligation, he bids farewell to family and friends as one sentenced to two years of forced segregation from familiar faces and places. Typically, he spends his two years of military service in an environment largely insulated from civilian life. There is no off-base housing for conscripts, who live in open-bay barracks. Most of their strictly regimented day is spent with their unit, beginning with reveille in the morning and continuing through drill, work detail, and training sessions. There are no automatic home leaves or weekend pass privileges. Free time is limited, and much of it is spent in organized and closely monitored outings with other soldiers from the unit. In short, military life for the Soviet draftee is physically rigorous, sometimes boring, often unpleasant and lonely, and largely divorced from civilian society.

While military life for the individual soldier may be lonely and isolated, the Soviet military as an institution is closely linked to the larger social setting. To some degree, after all, this is true of all military organizations. Armies must draw on the civilian world for manpower and so are inevitably affected by the nature of civilian life: the life-styles, value systems, behavior, and educational and technical qualifications of potential soldiers. Conscript armies, like the USSR Armed Forces, have especially close links with civilian society. In volunteer armies, recruits are self-selected. Individuals with attributes that are incompatible with military life can be filtered out. Draft armies, by contrast, must cope with a much wider spectrum of civilian life-styles.[1]

This is particularly true of the Soviet Union, where military service is seen as an obligation of citizenship, and deferments and exemptions are limited. Because a high percentage of draft-age males are drafted, the conscript contingent mirrors the social characteristics of the cohort from which it is drawn: 18-to-21-year-old males.[2] Virtually all social, regional, ethnic, and cultural

---

[1] Robert K. Griffith, Jr., "About Face? The U.S. Army and the Draft," *Armed Forces and Society* (Fall 1985); and V. Martin Anderson, ed., *The Military Draft: Selected Readings on Conscription* (Stanford: Hoover Institution Press, 1983), passim.

[2] On the link between citizenship and military service see Article 63 of the 1977 Soviet Constitution: "Konstitutsiia (osnovnoi zakon) soiuza sovetskikh sotsialisticheskikh respublik," *Svod zakonov* (Moscow: Iuridizdat, 1980), 1:14–42. See also part 4 of the most recent edition of the

groups are represented in the intake of new conscripts. The military, particularly components such as the ground forces where the conscript-to-career ratio is highest, is dominated numerically by citizens in uniform who bring with them the strengths and weaknesses of the civilian world. Changes in the social environment—the military's manpower base—are inevitably felt in the armed forces.

This chapter examines those changes and what they mean for civil-military relations. I begin by summarizing Soviet social trends, then move on to an exploration of how the environmental challenges associated with changes in the social setting have affected the military: impact on manpower quality and quantity, developments in military discipline and training, the treatment of minority soldiers, and changes affecting the career force. In the final section, I turn to the variable with which the overall volume is ultimately concerned: changes in the civil-military relationship. There I assess the extent to which social changes have affected the military as a political institution, examining how social change has led to either a more conflictual or more congenial relationship between civil and military elites. For example, one consequence of social change might be a change in the expectations the military elite has of the civilian system. Alternatively, social change might result in a modification of the missions that the civilian political leadership assigns to the military. Either development could affect civil-military relations by changing the way the military participates in the policy process and affecting the interplay between military and civilian interests.

Change and Continuity in Soviet Society

Social Modernization and Progress

Many of the most significant changes affecting the military's human capital are long-term shifts associated with socioeconomic modernization: urbanization, education, structural modernization, and changes in living standards, lifestyles, and values. These developments have been accompanied by demographic changes that have resulted in a major change in the ethnic, regional and language makeup of the draft-age cohort, as well as changes in the overall availability of manpower resources. The nature of the modernization process is profoundly affected by the political system in which it occurs. In the Soviet case, the main engine propelling modernization was an authoritarian political elite committed to rapid industrialization. The transition from a largely agrarian society to a largely urban one was purchased at immense human cost and

---

CPSU program in *Pravda*, 7 March 1986, 3–8. Relevant passages from the Universal Military Service law (as amended) are found in articles 1–3: *Zakon SSSR o vseobshchei voinskoi obiazanosti* (Moscow: Voyenizdat, 1986).

Figure 7.1. Urbanization in the USSR.

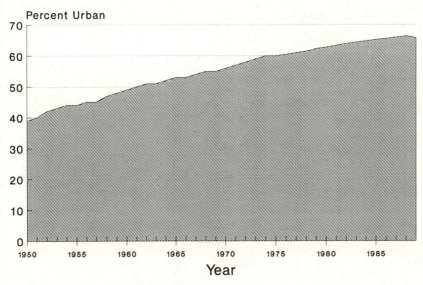

Source: Soviet statistical handbooks.

achieved through a top-heavy planning system that sacrificed economic efficiency for political control. It is important to remember, however, that many
of the social changes affecting the armed forces are not unique to the Soviet
Union, but reflect similar developments in other patriarchal societies undergoing modernization.

The major social change affecting the military's human resources has been
the shift from a rural, largely uneducated peasant society to an urban, relatively well-educated industrial society. While both rates of urbanization and
the shift from agricultural to industrial occupations have leveled off in the past
decade, the trend has had major consequences for Soviet life-styles and for the
social makeup of the military's manpower base. It means that most Soviets
live and work in urban settings, and that most will grow up to take industrial
or white-collar jobs, rather than agricultural ones. The structural changes that
accompany modernization also created a high level of occupational mobility
as the expansion of white-collar specialist and managerial positions and skilled
blue-collar jobs provided avenues for advancement for peasants and unskilled
workers.[3] These changes in the way people live have been accompanied by a
major expansion of the educational system and increase in access to education
(table 7.1).

[3] Richard B. Dobson, "Socialism and Social Stratification," in *Contemporary Soviet Society:
Sociological Perspectives*, ed. Jerry G. Pankhurst and Michael Paul Sacks (New York: Praeger
Publishers, 1980), 88–114.

FIGURE 7.2. Changes in Labor Force Composition.

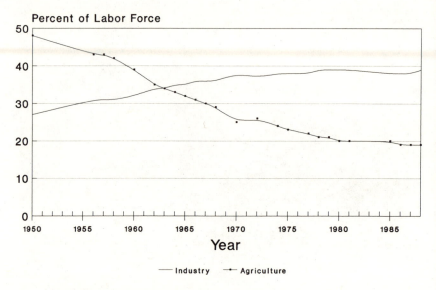

Percent of Labor Force

- Industry   -•- Agriculture

Source: Soviet statistical handbooks.

The modernization process also modified values, especially those affecting the role of the family and community. The gradual weakening of patriarchal values, particularly those affecting approved roles for women, has resulted in major demographic changes, including a long-term decline in fertility. This trend had major significance for military issues by its impact on the military manpower supply. Moreover, because these developments took place at different times for different regions and ethno-linguistic groups, the share of the population (and hence the military manpower pool) from late-modernizing southern tier regions (dominated by Islamic minorities) has been growing at the expense of the more urbanized European regions and the Slavic ethno-linguistic groups. In the urbanized European regions, the decline of the extended family, increasing geographical mobility, and the increase in the one-child family have resulted in a gradual weakening of parental and community controls.[4]

There have also been major enhancements in living standards. There were substantial improvements in the quantity and quality of housing, food, consumer durables, clothing, services, and health care.[5] Housing is one example.

---

[4] Ellen Jones and Fred W. Grupp, *Modernization, Value Change and Fertility in the Soviet Union* (Cambridge: Cambridge University Press, 1987), passim.

[5] Gertrude E. Schroeder, "Soviet Living Standards: Achievements and Prospects," *Soviet Economy in the Eighties: Problems and Prospects*, part 2, Selected Papers Submitted to the Joint Economic Committee, Congress of the United States, 31 December 1982 (Washington, D.C.:

TABLE 7.1

Educational Levels of Soviet Conscripts (percent)

Level of Education	1939	1959	1962	1964	1976	1983
Higher and Secondary	12	24.5	27	31.1	72	92.3
Incomplete Secondary	28	47.4	52.8	49.5	27	7–8
Elementary and Below	60	28.1	20.2	19.4	.8	–

Sources: Data for 1939 refer to short-term servicemen on the eve of World War II. I. I. Sorokin, ed., *Sovetksie vooruzhennye sily v usloviiakh razvitogo sotsializma* (Moscow: Nauka, 1985), 142. Another source cites identical data, noting that it applies to "draftees" for 1939. See V. I. Drugov, *voenno-patrioticheskoe vospitanie na uroven trebovanii partii* (Moscow: Izdtel'stvo DOSAAF SSSR, 1984), 11. Data for 1959, 1962, and 1964 refer to "draftees," M. M. Lisenkov, *Kulturnaia revolutsiia v SSSR i armiia* (Moscow: Voenizdat, 1977), 110. For 1976, the data are for "draftees." B. Sapunov, "Our Spiritual Wealth," *Kommunist vooruzhennykh sil*, no. 12 (1978), 18–27.

Note: For 1983, it is not completely clear whether the category "higher and secondary education" refers to completed secondary and above; however, the comparisons cited in the text suggest that this is the case. Sorokin, ed., *Sovetksie*, pp. 142, 168.

Average housing space per capita for urbanites nearly doubled in thirty years, from 7.4 square meters to 14.3 square meters in 1986. Qualitative indices, too, rose dramatically. In 1960, only 40 percent of urbanites lived in separate apartments, with the rest in communal arrangements. In 1986, about 85 percent were housed in separate apartments.[6] The proportion of urban housing units provided with such basic amenities as running water, central heating, and baths rose significantly. In 1959, less than a third of the urban housing had a bath; now 84 percent does. As late as 1970, only a third of the urban housing stock was supplied with hot water; the analogous proportion in 1986 was 72 percent.[7] These data are given here to provide a sense of the extremely low living standards inherited from Stalin, and the extent to which conditions have improved since the 1950s.

The pronounced enhancement in living standards in the postwar period,

---

GPO, 1983), 367–387. More recent data on consumer welfare can be obtained in *Statisticheskii ezhegodnik stran-chlenov soveta vzaimopomoshchi* (Moscow: Finansy i Statistika, 1985). Per capita consumption of selected food items is provided on pages 66–67; data on consumer durables is provided on page 68. Recent data on consumer durables, standardized by family, are provided in *SSSR v tsifrakh v 1985 godu*, 220.

[6] Average housing space per capita for 1955 is from Willard S. Smith, "Housing in the Soviet Union—Big Plans, Little Action," *Soviet Economic Prospects in the Seventies*, 27 June 1973, 404–406. The 1986 figures for housing space and separate vs. communal apartments are from *Narodnoe khoziaistvo SSSR za 70 let. Iubileinyi statisticheskii ezhegodnik* (Moscow: Finansy i Statistika, 1987), 517.

[7] Smith, "Housing in the Soviet Union," 417; *Narodnoe khoziaistvo SSSR za 70 let*, 521.

FIGURE 7.3. Educational Trends in the USSR.

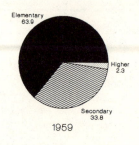

1959

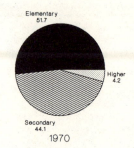

1970

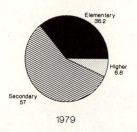

1979

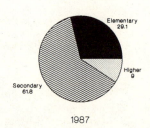

1987

Source: Narodnoe khoziaistvo SSSR V 1987 g., p. 476.

coupled with high occupational mobility, produced a widespread optimism and increased public confidence in the political leadership. It also produced an upsurge in consumer expectations.[8] The regime's ability to carry out its promise of continued consumer improvements became an important component of its political legitimacy.

The Growth of Social Stress

Economic performance, however, did not live up to heightened consumer expectations. As economic growth slowed in the 1970s and early 1980s (national income growth slowed from 7.2 percent between 1966 and 1970 to 3.8 percent between 1976 and 1980, and 3.1 percent between 1981 and 1985), so too did improvements in consumer welfare. Annual rates of growth in consumption per capita, which averaged 5.1 percent in the late 1960s, plummeted to 2.4

[8] Gail Warshofsky Lapidus, "Social Trends," in *After Brezhnev: Sources of Soviet Conduct in the 1980s*, ed. Robert F. Byrnes (Bloomington: Indiana University Press, 1983), 186–249.

percent in the late 1970s and declined even further, to 1.9 percent, in 1981.[9] Although there were substantial improvements in diet and access to consumer items, in many cases, growth rates leveled out in the late 1970s and early 1980s.

These trends produced an increase in consumer dissatisfaction. A generation of young Soviets who saw their parents get televisions and refrigerators now clamored for cars and more fashionable clothing. Increasing awareness of Western life-styles (a by-product of detente and the upsurge of emigration in the 1970s) served to fuel consumer demands by establishing new, higher standards against which to judge Soviet goods. When expectations failed to materialize, the earlier optimism was replaced by a growth in public pessimism.[10]

This development is reflected in Soviet studies on popular perceptions of living standards. One such study was conducted in 1981. Researchers sampled individuals employed in "leading sectors of the economy" in four large cities: Alma Ata, Baku, Kiev, and Moscow. In addition, they administered the survey to a broader cross-section of Leningraders (which included teachers, trade workers, and hotel-restaurant personnel, as well as those employed in industry) and to residents of twenty-seven large Soviet cities.[11] Satisfaction with quality of life varied from city to city and from indicator to indicator. Respondents gave the most positive evaluation to opportunities to educate their children. They were less satisfied with trade and transport services. Respondents evaluated medical services more positively than public catering, food more positively than clothing. Perhaps because of the inclusion of trade and food-service workers (two poorly paid groups), the Leningrad sample consistently reported the lowest levels of satisfaction. A third of the Leningraders felt their medical, everyday service, and transport situation had worsened over the previous five years. Only a quarter reported that their food situation was improving, while nearly a fifth complained that their housing was getting worse instead of better. These data, while hardly conclusive, suggest that the social price of the slowdown in consumer welfare improvements was a growth in pessimism and a decline in morale among those portions of the population most affected by the slowdown.

At the same time, the 1960s and 1970s saw a steady decline in wage differentials—a development that the current Soviet leadership terms "wage leveling." Variations in worker productivity were not reflected in differentials in pay.[12] Wage leveling was particularly demoralizing for highly-trained engi-

[9] Schroeder, "Soviet Living Standards," 370.

[10] Lapidus, "Social Trends."

[11] O. B. Bozhkov and V. B. Golofast, "Popular Evaluation of the Conditions of Life in Large Cities," *Sotsiologicheskie issledovaniia*, no. 3 (1985), 95–101.

[12] M. S. Gorbachev, "On Reorganization and the Party's Personnel Policy," *Pravda*, 28 January 1987.

neering and technical employees who saw a gradual diminution of the economic advantage they had previously enjoyed over blue-collar labor.

These negative economic trends coincided with a period of increasingly immobile political leadership. "Stability of cadres"—the political contract between Brezhnev and the bureaucratic elite—gradually took the form of a lifetime guarantee of job tenure, even for officials who were grossly inept or blatantly corrupt. Public faith in officials at all levels was shaken by growth in corruption and a decline in the ethic of public service.[13]

These trends undermined popular confidence in the Soviet system and in the regime's ability to meet consumer expectations. Cynicism toward official values increased, as did such symptoms of social malaise as crime and alcoholism. The population also became increasingly skeptical of Soviet foreign policy.

The decline in confidence in Soviet economic performance reinforced a growing alienation from officially approved values. The growing disconnection between worker performance and remuneration undermined the work ethic. Consumers unable to satisfy their material desires through the official distribution system turned to moonlighting and black market activities. Consumerism increased: "The stratum of people, some of them young people, whose ultimate goal in life was material well-being and gain by any means, grew wider."[14]

Another indicator of declining civic morale was an increase in symptoms of social pathology: the spread of drug abuse and a rise in crime.[15] Encouraged by the example of a political elite preoccupied with creating and enhancing a preserve of special privileges, Soviets at all levels turned increasingly to corruption.

Alcohol abuse increased as well. The problem is not new, of course. Heavy drinking is a cultural tradition in the USSR, one that predates the Bolshevik revolution. There is, however, a persuasive body of evidence indicating that the problem worsened in the 1970s. Vladimir Treml's estimates of alcohol consumption in the USSR show a steady rise in per capita alcohol consumption.[16] Soviet data indicate that consumption of alcoholic beverages grew an annual average of 3.2 percent from 1970 to 1979. Soviet authorities link these increases to the effects of urbanization. They also concede that cultural tradition plays a role: alcohol consumption and alcoholic illnesses are substantially higher in the RSFSR than in Central Asia and the Caucasus (regions that lack a long-term tradition of excessive alcohol use).[17]

[13] Ibid.
[14] Ibid.
[15] Ibid.
[16] Vladimir G. Treml, *Alcohol in the USSR: A Statistical Study* (Durham: Duke University Press, 1982), 68.
[17] G. G. Zaigrayev, *Borba s alkogolizmom: problemy, puti, reshenie* (Moscow: Mysl, 1986), 8, 14, 25–26.

Most worrisome to Soviet authorities about alcohol consumption was its rapid increase among young people in the 1970s. A 1965 study of several cities in the RSFSR, which was repeated in 1980, revealed that episodic use of alcohol increased from 49 percent to 75 percent for girls and from 68 percent to 90 percent for boys.[18] These data suggest that, by the mid-1980s, a long-term social problem had reached new and more alarming proportions.

In addition, the Soviet public became increasingly skeptical about certain aspects of Soviet foreign policy, in particular, the USSR's military involvement in Afghanistan. Despite the relatively limited numbers of troops involved, the Soviet role in the war had domestic significance because it was a dramatic reminder of the Kremlin's foreign commitments—ones that cost Soviet lives and diverted resources from domestic needs at a time when living standards were stagnating.

Public skepticism concerning the war was partly the result of the way the regime handled it from a public relations standpoint. The initial invasion in December 1979 was not acknowledged in the Soviet media. The first public mention of the troops there depicted Soviet forces in nonmilitary, humanitarian assistance roles. Despite this effort to minimize publicity, the Soviet public learned of the war through Western radio and through word of mouth from family and friends serving in Afghanistan. Public reaction was predictably negative. Anxiety and resentment were particularly strong among those whose lives were personally threatened: families of draft-age youth. Moreover, the media silence precluded public recognition of the sacrifice and heroism of Afghanistan veterans. Recognizing that continued secrecy about the war was counterproductive, Soviet authorities gradually began to expand media reporting on Afghanistan, including coverage of combat. Reporting on the problems "internationalist servicemen" encountered upon return to civilian life was also expanded.

The expansion of media coverage did not, however, prevent a growth in public disapproval of the war. This conclusion is tentative because we lack access to time-series opinion polls. What we do have are impressions gathered by Western visitors and the results of surveys of Soviet travelers, conducted under the auspices of Radio Liberty's Soviet Area Audience and Opinion Research.[19] What these surveys tell us is that the Soviet public, at least in urban

[18] Ibid, 110. See also G. G. Zaigraev, "The Alcoholic Situation: An Object of Preventative Measures," *Sotsiologicheskie issledovaniia*, no. 4 (1985), 47–54.

[19] The main problem with this material is that travel in the West is a privilege granted to those deemed politically reliable. Urban residents, males, the well-educated, and party members are overrepresented among Soviet tourists. Many Soviets, moreover, are understandably leery about sharing their opinions on politically sensitive topics with Western interviewers (a factor that accounts for the high level of ambivalent or "no opinion" responses). Some Soviet travelers may express opinions that they feel to be officially approved, while others express those that they feel would please the interviewer. Conclusions based on the Radio Liberty material, then, must remain tentative. Radio Free Europe–Radio Liberty, Soviet Area Audience and Opinion Research, "The

areas, became more skeptical of regime policies in Afghanistan during the first half of the decade. Surveys conducted in 1980, soon after the invasion, reveal an approval:disapproval ratio of roughly two to one. By 1984, public disapproval of the Soviet Union's Afghanistan policy had grown. By 1985–86, both approval and disapproval rates had grown, with the proportion holding no clear opinion on the war dropping from half to a third. One-third expressed approval and the remaining one-third expressed disapproval, with highly educated people more likely to express disapproval.

These data, while by no means conclusive, suggest that the military involvement in Afghanistan resulted in an increasing skepticism about the war, particularly among the well-educated urban elite and among those with greater access to Western information on the war. The war in Afghanistan, then, appears to have accentuated the decline in civic morale of the late 1970s and early 1980s.

Gorbachev and the Attempt at Social Reinvigoration

The appearance of a new generation of political leaders, by contrast, reversed this trend. Gorbachev advertised his economic modernization program as a boon to the Soviet consumer, with policies that would reverse wage leveling and enhance work-force incentives. He also promoted a crackdown on official corruption, unearned income, alcohol and drug abuse, and other manifestations of what he calls the "social corrosion" he inherited from his predecessors.

In response to increasing popular mistrust of the domestic media, Gorbachev adopted a policy of glasnost: fuller media reporting of negative domestic news and foreign-policy issues previously suppressed by Soviet censors. There has also been significant loosening of the strictures on cultural expression, with a much wider range of themes, including some that are politically sensitive, tolerated in literature and art.[20]

In the first two years of his tenure, Gorbachev could claim a degree of success in reversing the decline in civic morale. Loss of working time declined during 1986 for the first time since the 1960s. Labor discipline improved. Reported incidents of crime decreased. Soviet authorities also claimed some key victories in the war on alcohol. In 1986, they note, the consumption of alcohol fell by almost half compared with 1984. The number of alcohol-related crimes declined by 26 percent. Other indicators of alcohol abuse, such

Soviet Public and the War in Afghanistan: Perceptions, Prognosis, Information Sources," AR 4-85, June 1985; "The Soviet Public and the War in Afghanistan: A Trend Toward Polarization," AR 1-87.

[20] Ellen Jones and Benjamin L. Woodbury, II, "Chernobyl and *Glasnost*," *Problems of Communism* (November–December 1986), 28–39.

FIGURE 7.4. Crime in the USSR.

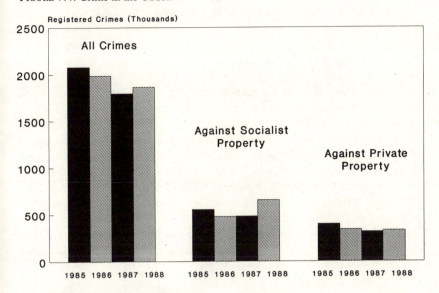

Source: *SSSR v tsifrakh v 1988, p. 136.*

as industrial, domestic, and highway accidents, also declined.[21] Gorbachev also claimed that the public mood improved appreciably. While some of these claims may be attributed to judicious self-promotion by a political leadership discovering the benefits of positive public relations, there was almost certainly an upsurge in civic energy and enthusiasm during this period.

Gorbachev's early success in reversing the "social corrosion" of the Brezhnev era proved to be temporary. By 1988, Soviet poll results were showing growing citizen skepticism of selected aspects of Gorbachev's domestic programs.[22] This development is due in part to the contrast between the benefits promised by perestroika and the actual results, which to date have been quite modest. The initial successes of the alcohol campaign were not sustained. Crime increased in 1988 and continued its upward trend in the first six months of 1989.[23] Gorbachev's initial attempts to loosen social controls resulted in an escalation of social unrest, strikes, and violence inspired by nationality, labor, and ecological issues—a development that led, in Gorbachev's words, to charges that "restructuring leads to chaos" and to nostalgic calls for the "firm hand" of the "good old days." Moreover, over four years of perestroika have

---

[21] Gorbachev, "On Reorganization"; Gorbachev's interview with Italian CP paper, *Pravda*, 20 May 1987; Moscow Domestic Service 0800 GMT, 1 June 1987; Moscow Television 21700.

[22] On public opinion regarding the reforms, see Zh. Toshchenko, "In the Mirror of Opinion," *Sotsialisticheskaia industriia*, 9 February 1988, 2.

[23] *Pravda*, 19 July 1989.

produced few tangible benefits to the Soviet consumer. Many Soviet citizens, it seems, now see living standards worsening, rather than improving.[24]

Social Change and the Military

The social trends discussed above affected the Soviet military directly, by modifying the nature of the manpower pool from which the military draws its human resources, and indirectly, by modifying the kinds of missions assigned to the armed forces by the political leadership. In this portion of the chapter, I will focus on the direct impact of social change on the military environment: the ways in which social change has affected the manpower pool from which the military draws its human resources. There are two main types of military personnel: draftees (who are conscripted for two- to three-year tours under the provisions of the 1967 military service law) and the military career force (commissioned officers, warrant officers, long-term reenlistees, and women). Because social trends have had a different impact on each of the two major groups, they will be discussed separately.

Social Change and the Conscript

The most significant impacts of social change on the military environment come by way of the conscript contingent. The most immediate, and easily documented, impact is on the supply of manpower. There has been a wide variation in supply of eighteen-year-old males over the last three decades. These trends are a delayed reflection of significant shifts in fertility. In the 1980s, there was a sharp turn-down in the supply of eighteen-year-olds. This decline bottomed out in the mid-1980s, and the number of eighteen-year-olds is now on the rise again.

It is important to note that any sudden change in the size of the eighteen-year-old pool—up or down—represents a problem for Soviet military authorities. Active duty service is the main source of reservist training, and discharged draftees (who are enrolled automatically in the reserves) are a crucial

[24] These complaints are summarized in Gorbachev's 6 January 1989 meeting with scientists and cultural figures. On public fears that Gorbachev's reforms have led to "discord and confusion," see Iu. Orlik, "Democracy Without Anarchy," *Izvestiia*, 7 January 1989. According to Orlik, one irate letter writer complained bitterly that "the heroes of today are strikers, informals, homosexuals, and Riga Market bingo players." On problems with the anti-alcohol campaign, see the Central Committee resolution, "On Progress in Fulfilling CPSU CC Resolutions on Questions of Intensifying the Campaign Against Drunkenness and Alcoholism," *Pravda*, 26 October 1988, 9. On the 1988 crime rate, see the interview with Minister of Internal Affairs V. V. Bakatin, "The Law's Duty Is to Protect," *Pravda*, 19 January 1989, 3; and A. Illesh, "*Glasnost* on Crime," *Izvestiia*, 9 February 1989, 6.

FIGURE 7.5. Trends in the Soviet Draft Pool.

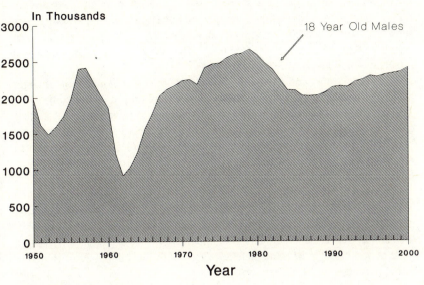

Source: Bureau of the Census.

component of the reserve base. Moreover, the two-year military experience is an important component of political socialization for young men. For these reasons, there is considerable incentive to achieve a "real universality of military service" by maximizing the proportion of young males inducted.[25]

Increases in the conscript pool place serious pressures on the complex system of identifying, screening, assigning, and training draftees. A decline in the supply of eighteen-year-olds presents its own set of problems, because it poses the issue of whether to retain the high force levels achieved during a period of manpower glut. For instance, Soviet leaders responded to the declining supply of eighteen-year-olds during the 1980s by changing the rules governing educational deferments. In December 1980, they introduced a provision limiting deferments granted for higher education. This change, which was implemented in 1982, was an attempt to maximize the proportion of the draft pool actually called to service by cutting back deferments.[26]

The impact of social change on the quality of the manpower supply is more difficult to measure. The military benefited from some trends and was disadvantaged by others. Of clearest immediate benefit was the increase in educational qualifications. The increased complexity of military equipment in-

[25] Iu. M. Kozlov et al., eds., *Upravlenie v oblasti administrativno-politicheskoi deiatelnosti* (Moscow: Iuridicheskaia literatura, 1979), 58–59.
[26] *Vedomosti Verkhovnogo soveta*, no. 52, 24 December 1980, 1142.

creased the importance of educational qualifications, both for conscripts and for the career force. It also enhanced the importance of technical qualifications.[27] The gradual transition from a basic eight-year package of obligatory schooling (introduced in 1959) to a ten-year package (the implementation of which was largely completed in the late 1970s) was reflected in an increase in the educational levels of Soviet conscripts.[28]

The military also derived some indirect benefits from more recent changes affecting the school system, in particular the school reform instituted in 1984. The reform increased the basic educational package to eleven years by starting children at age six instead of age seven, a change that has greatest potential benefit for Russian-language training in non-Russian areas.[29] The military also benefited, at least in a marginal way, from the expansion of mandatory vocational training in general educational schools and the expanding access to secondary vocational-technical schools and specialized secondary schools.[30] These trends probably increased general technical qualifications of incoming draftees. The increased priority on computer literacy among school-age children might also enhance the technical qualifications of the eighteen-year-old male pool, although the immediate relevance of this development is limited to future members of the officer corps.[31]

Probably the most important effect of increasing educational levels was the consequence of this development for predraft military training. The predraft training system involves two programs: the mandatory beginning military training (*nachalnaia voennaia podgotovka*, or NVP) and specialist training courses. Soviet authorities began implementing the NVP program in 1968 in a move intended partly to offset the decrease in service terms from three years to two years. Those young men who remained in school after finishing grade eight took the program in their last two years of secondary school. Youths who entered the labor force after completing grade eight were required to take the course at civilian training points. Extending the program to this latter group proved extremely difficult, and the transition to universal complete secondary schooling was a boon to the NVP program, because it meant that most youths attend the program within the school system. As a result of this development, plus ongoing efforts to improve curriculum, staff, and training facilities, the quality of NVP courses undoubtedly improved during the 1970s.[32]

[27] A. I. Sorokin, ed., *Sovetskie vooruzhennie sily v usloviiakh razvitogo sotsializma* (Moscow: Nauka, 1985), 163.

[28] On Soviet educational policy, see "Vseobshchee obuchenie," *Sovetskii entsiklopedicheskii slovar*, 256.

[29] *Pravda*, 14 April 1984, 3–4; 29 April 1984, 1, 3.

[30] Ellen Jones, *Red Army and Society: A Sociology of the Soviet Military* (London: George Allen & Unwin, 1985), 61–63.

[31] *Izvestiia*, 22 April 1986, 3. See also Harley D. Balzer, *Effects of Soviet Education Reform on the Military* (Foreign Applied Sciences Assessment Center, November 1985), VI-5–V-6.

[32] Jones, *Red Army and Society*, 63–70.

Less clear are trends affecting the other part of the predraft training program—specialist training. Specialist training courses are given to a selected group of predraft youths. Although Soviet authorities routinely claim that every third draftee enters the military with a military specialty earned at a DOSAAF (paramilitary) training organization, they provide no data that would allow us to track developments over time.[33]

The impact of increasing access to education on the Soviet conscript pool may be summarized as follows. The increase in the basic educational package from eight to ten years greatly simplified efforts to implement the NVP program. The improved educational qualifications of the conscript pool, coupled with more modest improvements in technical qualifications, were of unambiguous benefit in facilitating military training during active-duty service. Improvements in educational qualifications also eased the military's growing language problem, because they kept young non-Russians in the school system (where they take mandatory Russian classes) for longer periods of time. At least one facet of the socioeconomic modernization process, then, proved of benefit to the armed forces.

The same modernization process that produced increasing educational levels also involved a shift from an agrarian to an industrialized society. This development is reflected in the changing class composition of the conscript contingent. In the late 1950s and 1960s, about half of the conscripts came from the blue-collar working class, with the other half from the peasantry. By the mid-1980s, the share of workers among conscripts had increased to 67.6 percent, while that of peasants had decreased to 13.3 percent.[34]

This trend, coupled with increases in living standards and decreases in the strong social controls characteristic of traditional peasant communities and families, resulted in a major change in the Soviet conscript. The draftee of the past was likely to be a relatively uneducated peasant. The low living standards and harshness of rural life facilitated adjustment to the physical rigors and poor living conditions of the army. The stronger parental and community controls in the countryside eased adjustment to the rigid military discipline.

Today's conscripts, while better educated, are far less tolerant of the sacrifices and demands of military service.[35] According to the Soviet military media, conscripts reared in small families, particularly draftees who are only children, tend to be more spoiled, less disciplined, and less used to hard work than those from the large, rural families of the past. Their parents, complain mili-

---

[33] The "one in three" figure has been cited for over a decade. See for example N. A. Koshelev, *Komsomol v stroie armeiskom* (Moscow: Izdatelstvo DOSAAF SSSR, 1985), 3.

[34] Sorokin, "Sovetskie Vooruzhennie Sily," 167.

[35] O. Belkov, "Defense of the Socialized Fatherland—A Matter of the Entire People," *Sovetskii patriot*, 3 August 1986; "Military-Patriotic Indoctrination under Conditions of Intensification of the Ideological Struggle," *Slovo lektora*, no. 9 (1984), 1; and "Political Culture of Soviet Servicemen," *Krasnaia zvezda*, 16 February 1984, 2–3.

tary officials,[36] are overly protective and excessively permissive, creating a home environment that is not conducive to easy acceptance of the deprivations and unquestioning obedience demanded of conscripts:

> Young people joining the army and navy ranks in our days are in many respects different from those who entered military service twenty to thirty years ago. They have not a few positive qualities, and this fact is most obviously confirmed by the fitting performance of the military and the contingent of Soviet troops in Afghanistan. There are, however, other aspects, such as the lack of experience of life, of physical and labor tempering, and of other habits of military life.[37]

> Unfortunately, far from all young people come into the army with the same degree of tempering and indoctrination to reach immediately the level of the demands that military service places on them. Among the inductees, there are politically naive individuals who at times do not have elementary labor skills. Spoiled by family, many can neither sew on a button nor mop the floor.[38]

Military officials complain that many draftees from such pampered environments arrive at their units in such poor condition that they have trouble with the physical demands of military training.[39] Inadequate physical fitness, it seems, is a particular concern for military authorities.[40] Other draftees bring with them alcohol problems—a reflection of the increasing alcohol abuse in civilian society—and drug addiction.[41] Others display evidence of the increase in Western-style consumerism that has Soviet socializers particularly worried. Soviet authorities see interest in Western rock music, jeans, tee-shirts and other symbols of Western culture as harmful because it is supposedly detrimental to the development of Soviet patriotism.[42]

These developments are linked to pacifism, "political naïveté," and a decline in civic responsibility among Soviet youth.[43] Soviet young people, claim their elders, have been spoiled by a generation of peace and prosperity. They have not known the hardships of previous generations, and, most important,

[36] *Krasnaia zvezda*, 5 October 1983, 2.

[37] Ibid., 6 June 1986, 2, 3.

[38] A. Lizichev, "On Guard for the Victories of Socialism," *Agitator*, no. 2 (1986), 25–29.

[39] A. Boiko, "A Writer's Reflections: Become Strong, Sons," *Sovetskaia Rossia*, 24 March 1985, 1; and Iu. Sapozhnikov, "Time for Maturation," *Pravda*, 2 August 1986, 2.

[40] *Krasnaia zvezda*, 19 March 1987, 2; *Kazakhstanskaia pravda*, 24 December 1986, 3; *Sovetskii patriot*, 2 November 1986, 2.

[41] *Krasnaia zvezda*, 5 March 1987, 1.

[42] V. I. Mironenko, "The Sons Are Falling into Line," *Pravda Ukrainy*, 24 November 1983, 2; N. Mashovets, "Our Own Pride," *Pravda*, 31 October 7; *Komsomolskaia pravda*, 7 August 1984, 2; and *Komunisti*, 26 January 1985, 4.

[43] M. Popkov, "Implement the June CPSU CC Plenum Resolutions: Indoctrinate Patriots of the Motherland," *Znamenosets*, no. 11 (1983); A. Sorokin, "A School for the Ideological Tempering and Indoctrination of the Motherland's Defenders," *Politicheskoe samoobrazovanie*, no. 2 (1984), 28–35.

have not lived through World War II.[44] They tend to underestimate the threat;[45] and they lack, complain their elders, an emotional sense of the terrible "price we had to pay" for peace:[46] "During the postwar years, new generations have grown up which have not experienced war. In their view, peace is the normal state of society. This can, involuntarily, lead to complacency, to underestimation of the real threat of war."[47]

A Komsomol sociologist reported that Soviet youth in the past were more willing to bear personal sacrifices for defense.[48] Over two-thirds responded positively to a question that asked whether they were prepared for a cutback in the growth of their personal well-being, if the interests of strengthening defense required it. Only 6 percent said no. It would be hard to say, the sociologist concluded, how today's youth would respond to the same question, implying that he had strong doubts that the current generation would be so unselfish.

Soviet military authorities are concerned about these trends because they are related to a decline in the acceptance of the military service obligation among draft-age youth. One published report on attitudes toward military service in the 1970s surveyed draftees and draft eligibles in Moscow, Moscow oblast, Moscow State University, and the Baltic Military District. This survey indicated that most youths at the time accepted the draft as an inescapable fact of life (a conclusion echoed, incidentally, by reports from former Soviet citizens). By the late 1980s, however, First Deputy Defense Minister Lushev was complaining that "In recent years, a certain proportion of young people have shown a marked lessening of interest in military service, while pacifist sentiments have appeared in certain young men."[49]

Another senior military officer, commenting that "anti-army sentiments are also flourishing among young people," cited the results of a survey of draft-age males that indicated that only 47.2 percent said they would enter the army willingly. Nearly half (47.4 percent) said that army service was merely one's

[44] D. Volkogonov, "Defense of Socialism and Military-Patriotic Socialization," *Pravda*, 15 August 1986, 2, 3; and Iu. Ozhegov, "Political Naïveté," *Sovetskaia Rossiia*, 30 September 1983, 6.

[45] V. G. Kulikov, "Mighty Guardian of Peace," *Trud*, 22 February 1987, 3. See also Iu. Deriugin, "We Swear Allegiance to the Fatherland," *Sovetskaia Rossiia*, 30 September 1984, 1.

[46] "Fulfilling a Noble Mission: At the 8th Congress of USSR Writers," *Krasnaia zvezda*, 27 June 1986, 1, 3.

[47] I. M. Ilinskii, "Our Contemporary Youth," *Sotsiologicheskie issledovaniia*, no. 2 (1987), 16–22.

[48] N. N. Efimov and Iu. I Deriugin, "Ways to Increase the Effectiveness of Military-Patriotic Socialization of Youth," *Sotsiologicheskie issledovaniia*, no. 1, 60–66. Soviet sources give no statistical data on this issue, referring only to "individual instances" of unwillingness to serve. A. I. Sorokin, "The Armed Forces of Developed Socialism," *Voprosy filosofii*, no. 2 (1983), 3–17.

[49] G. Lushev, "No Holiday is Brighter," *Komsomolskaia pravda*, 9 May 1988, 1.

civic duty and must be carried out. Only half said that they were prepared to undergo the hardships of military service.[50]

The increase in media reporting on draft evasion also suggests that the Soviet public is becoming less supportive of the draft. One episode of the television program "I Serve the Soviet Union" admitted the existence of both opposition to the draft and draft dodging.[51] MPA chief Lizichev noted in a *Literaturnaia gazeta* interview: "We raise complacent snivellers who think it is not compulsory to prepare for army service, and if you have to serve, it would be nice to install yourself wherever things are easiest and most peaceful."[52]

Although Lizichev's comments, and other manifestations of public attention to the issue, are surely part of a greater willingness to report negative trends, they also reflect an increase in draft dodging itself. Indeed, one officer—noting that cases of "irresponsible attitudes" toward the draft are becoming "increasingly frequent"—cites a military commissariat official from Moscow oblast who complains of "an increase in the number of young people trying to dodge army service." The official goes on to say that draft dodging is most prevalent among higher-status families.[53] There were also sporadic protests among the civil populace (primarily parents) against posting of sons and relatives to Afghanistan,[54] as well as indications that the strong public disapproval of draft evasion has been replaced by indifference. One father who lost two sons in Afghanistan reported that he became the object of scorn for begrudging the one or two thousand rubles it would have taken to secure a safe assignment for his sons.[55]

This evidence, while by no means conclusive, suggests that the increased media attention to a declining acceptance of the draft is something more than just an increased willingness to publicize an existing problem. In part, the increase in draft evasion was a natural reaction to the cutback in legal deferments. Families whose sons could previously avoid conscript service legally

[50] The poll on attitudes toward the draft was reported in E. Savitskii, "Our Service Is Not for Parades," ibid., 22 June 1988, 2.

[51] Moscow Television Service, 10 October 1987. For other examples, see *Kommunisti*, 15 September 1982, 2, translated in JPRS 82270; *Turkmenskaia iskra*, 8 July 1983, 4; *Krasnaia zvezda*, 5 December 1985, 2; 11 August 1985, 2; 28 June 1985, 2; 20 March 1987, 4; 31 March 1987, 2.

[52] "A Place in the Formation," *Literaturnaia gazeta*, 25 February 1987, 10.

[53] A. Khorev, "Echo of Malicious Talk," *Krasnaia zvezda*, 12 December 1987, 4. A similar link between social status and draft avoidance was found in the Soviet Interview Project. See William Zimmerman and Michael L. Berbaum, "Soviet Military Manpower Policy: Regime Goals, Social Origins, and Working the System," unpublished paper.

[54] See, for example, an AFP report on a reported protest by two hundred Armenians, protesting their sons' being sent to Afghanistan. Paris AFP 1707 GMT 14 June 1985, in FBIS, USSR National Affairs, 18 June 1985, R1. See also "I Serve the Soviet Union," Moscow Television Service, 9 January 1988.

[55] V. Evseev and P. Studenkin, "Man's Work—Service in the Armed Forces," *Pravda*, 18 March 1987, 4.

through attending a higher educational institution attempted to avoid military duty illegally, for instance, by purchasing a medical exemption.

The Military's Reaction to Social Change

The military's reaction to these developments has been fairly limited. Increasing consumerism in the civilian populace has led military authorities to undertake marginal improvements in troop living standards.[56] In 1977 and again in 1985, the Defense Ministry held an All-Army Conference on Improving Troop Living Standards. While the focus of both conferences was on the welfare of military professionals, some attention was given as well to the need to upgrade conscript conditions—barracks, mess halls, and recreational facilities.[57]

Another Defense Ministry response to the social changes in the draft pool is a shift in emphasis away from physical coercion and toward persuasion. In theory, there are three approved ways of dealing with disciplinary and behavioral problems within military units: public censure, disciplinary punishment, and criminal prosecution. Physical punishment is not authorized by military regulations. Nonetheless, it has traditionally been a common means of controlling conscripts.[58] The increasing educational levels and changing attitudes of Soviet conscripts have resulted in efforts within the Defense Ministry to curtail use of physical coercion as a control mechanism. The ministry, prodded by increasingly outspoken media and outraged public, has also taken steps to curtail another unauthorized but widespread method of controlling young soldiers: the hazing of young draftees by older ones.[59]

These developments have not significantly altered military life-styles. In this sense, the response of the Soviet Defense Ministry to social changes within the manpower base has been very different from that of some Western militaries. During the 1960s and 1970s, there were major countercultural challenges in the United States and several West European countries. Several of these countries responded by modifying military regulations, for example,

---

[56] S. Kurkotkin, "Indispensable Condition of Combat Capability of the Troops," *Tyl i snabzhenie*, no. 11 (1977), 12–19.

[57] The 1977 conference was held 19–20 December. "All-Army Conference for Improving Troop Living Standards," ibid., no. 1 (1978), 3–34. The 1985 conference was held 28–29 November. "All-Army Conference for Improving Troop Living Conditions," ibid., no. 1 (1986), 3–26.

[58] "Ditsiplinarnyi ustav vooruzhennykh sil SSSR," *Svod zakonov* (Moscow: Izvestiia, 1982), 463–494; S. Ilin, "Methods of Educating Soviet Soldiers," *Voennaia mysl*, no. 5 (1968); and P. Slepukhin, "The Role of Interrelationships in the System of Military Indoctrination," *Voennaia mysl*, no. 10.

[59] See, for instance, the report on the 13 October 1988 Politburo session in *Pravda*, 14 October 1988, 1.

easing restrictions on off-base housing and strengthening the rights of individual soldiers vis-à-vis the command structure.[60]

In the Soviet case, the social changes were less radical and the Defense Ministry's response was far more limited. Despite the marginal improvements in conscript life-styles, the typical conscript still experiences a clear-cut decrease in living standards when he enters the military. Despite efforts by the military socialization establishment to minimize unauthorized physical punishments, career enlisted men and warrant officers in the Soviet military are still prone to a quick blow when more approved measures of modifying behavior fail. Despite attempts to curtail the practice, hazing of young draftees continues. More important, there is no evidence that Soviet military authorities are trying to accommodate a new, less tractable generation of conscripts by easing the regimentation of conscript life. In short, Soviet military authorities have thus far avoided the sorts of disciplinary concessions adopted in Western Europe and the United States.

Ethnic Change and the Conscripts

The evidence reviewed thus far suggests that the Defense Ministry has made only limited internal adjustments to the social changes taking place in the conscript pool. Similar comments apply to the military's reaction to another change in the social environment affecting the conscript pool: the increasing percentage of non-Slavic conscripts from the Soviet southern tier. This development is a reflection of the late entry of the USSR's Islamic minorities into what demographers call the fertility transition. While European nationalities, including Slavic groups, were already well into the transition to small families, Islamic minorities were still experiencing extremely high fertility.[61] As a result, the ethnic composition of the conscript pool shifted in favor of the late-modernizing regions and minorities. Of major importance were the decline in the Slavic share of the draft pool and the increase in the percentage of the pool made up of Islamic nationalities.

This development affected military manpower in several ways. The modest infusion of glasnost in the military press has permitted a somewhat franker treatment of the problem by Soviet authorities, giving us better insight into how they view it. Minority reliability does not seem to be a major problem. Nor do non-Slavic draftees suffer in an educational sense.[62] Interpersonal

---

[60] Catherine McArdle Kelleher, "Mass Armies in the 1970s: The Debate in Western Europe," *Armed Forces and Society* 5, 1 (Fall 1978), 3–30.

[61] Jones and Grupp, *Modernization, Value Change, and Fertility*, passim.

[62] V. Bezrodnyi and A. Goncharov, "The Multinational Military Collective—A Dialogue Between a Military Sociologist and a Deputy Regimental Commander for Political Affairs, " *Krasnaia zvezda*, 12 March 1987, 2, 3.

FIGURE 7.6. Ethnic Composition of the Soviet Draft Pool.

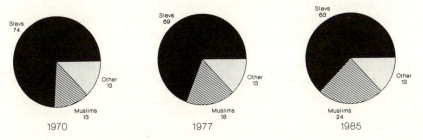

1970   1977   1985

Source: Compiled from age-specific data from the 1970 Soviet Census.

problems do not appear to be a major problem in most units. There are some manifestations of traditional ethnic animosities, ranging from ethnic name calling to fist fights, but these problems are fairly manageable and pale in significance compared to more serious cohesion issues, such as the problem of hazing. It is interesting to note that, during the Afghanistan war, ethnic-based interpersonal problems were apparently worse in the internal military districts; in Afghanistan, it seems, the dangers of combat produced a cohesion that counteracted potential ethnic tensions.[63] The most common consequence of ethnic diversity for interpersonal relations is the development of ethnic-based friendship patterns. This is viewed as a potential danger because it creates the possibility for ethnic friction.[64]

The most serious consequence of the change in the ethnic composition of the draft pool on military capabilities, from the standpoint of Soviet military authorities, is the language problem.[65] Census data indicate that nearly 90 percent of the 1970 draft pool was fluent in Russian. In subsequent years, there were improvements in Russian language training in the school system (which probably increased fluency levels among school-age non-Russians), but, at the same time, the overall proportion of non-Russians in the pool increased. The net result is that the military lost ground in terms of Russian fluency.[66] By 1985, perhaps 80 percent of the eighteen-year-old pool was fluent, with the remainder speaking and understanding Russian with difficulty. The decreasing supply of Russian-fluent conscripts, coupled with the increasing demand for Russian fluency associated with the increased technical complexity of weapons, means that military authorities face increasing problems in assigning

[63] V. Filatov, "National Color," ibid., 28 March 1987, 3.

[64] Bezrodnyi and Goncharov, "The Multinational Military Collective."

[65] Ibid. See also the comments of MPA chief Lizichev, "October and the Leninist Teaching on the Defense of the Revolution," *Kommunist*, no. 3 (1987), 85–96.

[66] Jones, "Red Army and Society," 188–195.

draftees who are less than fluent in the command language, in particular Islamic minorities, who have relatively low fluency levels.

The military's growing problem with Russian fluency is politically sensitive because it brings military needs into sharper conflict with the goals of party nationality policy in the sense that military needs dictate one pattern of assignment, while nationality policy dictates another. An assignment pattern based on military needs is one in which conscripts are assigned to slots based on their language and specialist qualifications, regardless of the impact on the ethnic composition of military units. An assignment pattern based on party nationality policy produces a different pattern of ethnic assignments, since a key component of this policy is a series of programs to reduce differences between minority groups and regions.[67] The Soviet ideological commitment to ethnic equality means that every group should have equal access to obligations and rewards. There are clearly circumstances, however, when commitment to quality conflicts with the need for efficiency. The balance between these two conflicting goals has shifted back and forth as the leadership has tried to facilitate minority social mobility.

In many ways, this changing balance between ideological commitment to ethnic equality and the pragmatic need for efficiency has been mirrored in the treatment of minorities in the military. The goal of ethnic equalization requires that all citizens, regardless of ethnic origin, serve in the armed forces on the same basis. The legal equality of all nationalities in terms of military obligation is underlined in the 1967 Universal Military Service Law. Article 3 states: "All male citizens of the USSR, regardless of origin, social and property status, ethnic and national affiliation, education, language, attitude toward religion, type and nature of employment and place of residence, must undergo active military service in the USSR Armed Forces."[68] The goal of equalizing socioeconomic status requires that minority soldiers be assigned to military posts on the same basis as ethnic Russians. In practice, this goal has frequently come into conflict with the competing goal of military efficiency. As the Soviet historical experience makes clear, the balance between equality and efficiency in the armed forces has always favored efficiency. There is no evidence of past willingness to sacrifice combat capability to achieve the goals of party nationality policy.

The same may be said of current patterns of minority participation within the conscript contingent. The ideal military unit, from the standpoint of nationality policy, is one that reflects the USSR's ethnic diversity.[69] In actuality,

[67] On Soviet nationality policy, see article 36 of the Soviet constitution and chapter 3 of the new version of the party program. "Konstitutsiia (osnovnoi zakon) soiuza sovetskikh sotsialisticheskikh respublik," *Svod zakonov* (Moscow: Izvestiia, 1980), 1:13–42; and *Pravda*, 7 March 1986, 3–8.

[68] Universal Military Service Law, article 3.

[69] Bezrodnyi and Goncharov, "The Multinational Military Collective."

draftees tend to be assigned to units and positions based on their individual aptitudes and qualifications.[70] As a consequence, units with a higher proportion of conscript slots requiring high levels of Russian fluency (for example, units in the Strategic Rocket Forces) tend to have a lower proportion of non-Russian draftees than those (for example, construction troops or the motorized rifles forces) where technical requirements and fluency needs are lower. In other words, language, specialist, educational, and security requirements based on military needs result in underrepresentation of some ethnic groups in certain types of units and overrepresentation in others. The Soviet military leadership, it seems, feels no compulsion to ensure proportional ethnic representation in every unit. Military needs, clearly, come first.

Nor is there any evidence that the Defense Ministry is enthusiastic about the prospect of expending military training time to remedy conscript language problems. Although some military units have responded with programs to identify soldiers in need of language instruction and assign them to remedial Russian programs, there is little enthusiasm for this approach within the ministry.[71] Military authorities point out that the primary responsibility for ensuring that incoming draftees have the necessary Russian skills falls to the school system and other civilian agencies charged with preparing young men for military service.[72]

Russian-language preparation within the school system has, in fact, improved significantly over the last several decades. The 1984 school reform included a provision increasing Russian-language requirements in non-Russian schools; this was only the latest in a lengthy series of measures to beef up Russian instruction in the school system. The motivation goes far beyond immediate military needs, but the Defense Ministry shared the benefits. There are also special programs tailored to military needs. Several republics have set up programs (required courses, Russian-language camps, and study groups) for draft-age males with language problems.[73] Remedial Russian, with special emphasis on military vocabulary, is also provided through local military commissariats and DOSAAF organizations.[74]

Despite these efforts, there have been numerous signals from military officials that the Defense Ministry is dissatisfied with the language qualifications of incoming draftees. Although they claim that there has been a "perceptible

[70] Jones, "Red Army and Society," 194–195.

[71] A. Overchuk, "Our Brotherhood is Indivisible," *Krasnaia zvezda*, 15 August 1979, 2; and "The Language of Friendship and Fraternity," ibid., 20 January 1973, 1.

[72] N. V. Ogarkov, *Vsegda v gotovnosti k zashchite otechestva* (Moscow: Voenizdat, 1982), 64; and A. A. Epishev, *Sviashchennyi dolg, pochetnaia obiazannost* (Moscow: DOSAAF, 1983), 75–76.

[73] T. Usabaliev, "Our Common Concern," *Krasnaia zvezda*, 16 December 1983, 2–3.

[74] V. Samoilenko, "Blossoming and Mutually Enriching Cultures of the Brotherly Peoples," *Kommunist vooruzhennykh sil*, no. 21 (1972), 28–33.

decline'' in the number of draftees with low levels of Russian capability, they argue that the increased complexity of conscript training (due to the increasing technical complexity of current weapons systems) has increased language requirements.[75]

This survey of minority conscripts provides additional evidence of the limited nature of the military establishment's accommodation to social change. Ethnic change has had significant consequences for the cultural and linguistic makeup of the conscript pool. The Defense Ministry has absorbed minority soldiers by assigning those with limited Russian to positions where fluency is not an important qualification. This became less easy as the share of conscripts with language problems has increased. The military responded to this development by pressuring civilian agencies to do their job better. Officers apparently argued, with some success, that civilian agencies must take steps to cushion the negative side-effects of ethnic trends on the conscript pool.

Social Change and the Career Force

The effect of social changes on the military career force has been far more limited than on the conscript contingent. There have been three consequences of social change: (1) the Defense Ministry (and to a lesser extent the socialization agencies) have taken measures to enhance the attractiveness of military careers; (2) both civilian and military agencies have made modest efforts to increase the proportion of non-Russians in the career force, in particular, the officer corps; and (3) the pressures of a larger influx of better-educated draftees have contributed to the development of a nonprofessional career force. As with the response to social changes in the conscript pool, the extent of Defense Ministry accommodation to social change affecting the career force has been relatively modest.

Most significant of the changes resulting from social trends has been the impact on recruitment of the military's career force. There are two basic types of nonprofessional careerists: long-term servicemen (*voennosluzhashchie sverkhsrochnoi sluzhby*) and warrant officers (*praporshchiki i michmany*). Long-term servicemen are conscripts who reenlist beyond their two-year obligation; they perform limited roles and constitute an extremely small portion of the career force. Warrant officers are the mainstay of the nonprofessional career force; they fill a variety of roles and constitute a small but growing portion of the career force. Largest in numerical strength and importance are the commissioned officers (*ofitserskii sostav*), comprising perhaps 80 percent of the career cadre. Because they are the most important component of the

---

[75] O. A. Belkov, ''The Military-Patriotic Importance of the Soviet Peoples' International Unity,'' *Nauchnyi kommunizm*, no. 1 (1983), 3–10.

military career force, this discussion focuses on how changes in the social environment affect officer recruitment and military roles.

The supply of potential officers has been affected by the same demographic trends that affect the conscript pool. The impact on officer recruitment is less direct, because it is mediated by access to secondary schooling. Most officers are recruited from among secondary school graduates, so it is the trend in this variable, not in overall eighteen-year-olds, that is of most significance in assessing potential supplies of recruits for the officer corps.[76] As with the supply of eighteen-year-olds, the supply of both secondary school graduates and those from day divisions peaked in the late 1970s and then declined (fig. 6). As a result, officer commissioning schools must compete with civilian educational establishments.

Numbers, of course, are only one aspect of the problem of officer recruitment. There is also the issue of the attractiveness of an officer career. The downturn in supply of secondary school graduates coincided with several other developments affecting the social status of the officer corps. During the Brezhnev era, a career as a military officer enjoyed fairly high prestige in the USSR. Most of the published studies on Soviet youth attitudes toward such a career date from the late 1960s and early 1970s. One study of fifteen professions found that military careers ranked between second and fourth.[77] Another study, this time of forty occupations, found that an officer's career ranked in sixth to eighth place.[78] Other surveys found that respondents prized careers in the officer corps because they were seen as challenging and interesting.[79]

The prestige of the officer corps declined substantially in the 1980s. One study published in 1986 noted that, while officer careers are still attractive to young people, the prestige of other careers has been rising.[80] As a result, the relative prestige of military careers declined. The author referenced a study showing that in a number of oblasts in Russia, officer careers ranked tenth after such professions as doctor, teacher, and engineer. In some areas of the country, the prestige of an officer's career was even lower, particularly in some districts of Moscow, Leningrad, and other major cities, and in the Central Asian, Transcaucasus, and Baltic republics. The author urged more attention to promoting officer careers so that ''the tendency of denigrating the military profession and officer service such as occurred in the late 1950s and early

---

[76] "Rules for Acceptance in Higher Military Educational Institutions," *Komsomolskaia Pravda*, 26 March 1986, 4. See also *Krasnaia zvezda*, 3 February 1985, 4.

[77] A. F. Tarasov et al., "Professional Orientation of Rural School-age Youth," *Opyt sotsialno-professionalnoi orientatsii selskoi molodezhi* (Rostov-Na-Donu: Gosudarstvenni Pedagogicheskii Institut, 1974), 25–81.

[78] V. F. Chernovolenko et al., *Prestizh professii i problemy sotsialno-professionalnoi orientatsii molodezhi: opyt sotsiologicheskogo issledovaniia* (Kiev: Naukova Dumka, 1979), 203–204.

[79] O. I. Shkaratan and V. O. Rukavishnikov, "Social Strata in the Class Structure of Socialist Society," *Sotsiologicheskie issledovaniia*, no. 2 (1977), 62–73.

[80] V. Kovalevskii, "A Profession that Society Needs," *Slovo lektora*, no. 8 (1986), 18–22.

1960s''—a development, he claimed, that was noticeably reflected in the quality of officer corps recruits—does not recur. There are also indications that the declining prestige of an officer's career is resulting in recruitment difficulties. The chief of Soviet air defenses, I. M. Tretiak, in an interview in *Moscow News*, publicly lamented that ''it is much easier to join a military school than a university . . . because of the shortage of personnel.''[81]

There are several explanations for the decline in the prestige of military careers in the early 1980s. One is the long-term increase in the civilian standard of living, a development that surely must have affected public perceptions of the economic benefits of a military career. The other development affecting officer recruitment was Soviet military involvement in Afghanistan. Although some potential recruits to the military career force may have viewed the war as an opportunity for career advancement, the possibility of being posted to Afghanistan probably lowered the attractiveness of a military career for many others.

Defense officials responded to these developments in several ways. First, they have made an effort to increase the attractiveness of military careers by improving officers' living standards. One 1984 sociological survey of the families of one thousand young officers revealed strong dissatisfaction with the quantity and quality of housing, child care, and recreational facilities on military posts.[82] Military authorities claim that they have taken some steps to improve living conditions, particularly the availability and quality of housing for the career military. Housing conditions apparently vary substantially from garrison to garrison. Amenities for the overall military housing stock are comparable to those for the urban civilian housing stock, but military authorities admit that some military families continue to live in substandard housing, despite modest gains since 1977.[83] The military also claims some improvement in quality of military health care: general morbidity, for example, declined by 12 percent between 1977 and 1985.[84]

Second, the military has turned to the civilian socialization agencies (media, schools, and youth groups) to step up efforts to popularize military careers.[85] In the early Brezhnev era, the military received favorable publicity across all organs of Soviet mass communication, especially television. A 1970 study of levels of media coverage of fifty-four professions indicated that ''line

[81] I. Tretiak, ''Reliable Defense First and Foremost,'' *Moscow News*, no. 8, 21 February 1988, 12.

[82] *Krasnaia zvezda*, 14 January 1984, 2.

[83] N. V. Gryaznov, ''The Path to Increasing the Amenities of Military Towns,'' *Tyl i snabzhenie*, no. 1 (1986), 18–19.

[84] S. K. Kurkotkin, ''To Resolve Questions of Everyday Life,'' ibid., no. 1 (1986), 4–9; and F. I. Komarov, ''In Answer to Troop Health,'' ibid., no. 1 (1986), 6–17.

[85] V. Gurin, ''Preparation to be in Service,'' *Krasnaia zvezda*, 10 August 1986, 4.

officer'' ranked tenth. For national-level television, it ranked second.[86] The military fared less well under Gorbachev's glasnost policy. Military officials are pointedly calling on the civilian socialization agencies to work harder to ''enhance the prestige of the military profession.''[87]

The second social development affecting the military career force is the evolution in the ethnic composition of the population and the conscript force. During the interwar period, when minority soldiers were organized into nationality-specific units, Soviet military authorities were anxious to recruit minority military professionals to lead minority soldiers.[88] Use of nationality units during this period accelerated the development of the minority officer corps because it increased pressure to recruit minority command cadres, fluent in both Russian and the native language. Non-Russians were trained in special native-language command schools and were not forced to compete with the better-educated ethnic Russians. While less modernized nationalities may have been somewhat underrepresented in the officer corps, they were better represented than would have been predicted given the educational and linguistic disadvantages they suffered in comparison with the dominant Slavs. The minority units were disbanded on the eve of the war, briefly reconstituted during the war, then later disbanded again. While extensive data are not available, it appears that minorities were substantially less well represented in the officer corps during the war than in the armed forces as a whole.

Minorities continue to be underrepresented in the contemporary officer corps, particularly at the highest levels. This is partly because of language and partly because until fairly recently there were substantial educational disparities affecting the late-modernizing minorities. Even now, when the program to achieve universal secondary education has largely counteracted educational disparities, the language barrier continues to limit minority access to officer careers. Examinations for admittance to officer candidate schools are given in Russian and include materials on Russian language and, in some cases, Russian literature. Clearly, even the best-educated Uzbek will be at a disadvantage competing with a native Russian speaker.

Soviet authorities are demonstrating growing concern that all minority groups be ''adequately represented'' in the officer corps.[89] One solution is Soviet-style affirmative action: setting aside a number of places in each school

[86] A. V. Korbut, "The Treatment of Professionals in Mass Communications," in *Sotsiologicheskie problemy obshchestvennogo mneniia sredstv massovoi informatsii* (Moscow: Institute for Sociological Research, 1975), 138–47, 201.

[87] See, for example, Lizichev's address to artists and writers. *Krasnaia zvezda*, 6 June 1986, 2.

[88] Jones, "Red Army and Society," 198–200.

[89] B. Utkin, "The Soviet Army—An Army of Friendship of the Peoples," *Voenno-istoricheskii zhurnal*, no. 2 (1983), 3–11; E. Nikitin, "The Triumph of Leninist Nationality Policy," *Agitator armii i flota*, no. 3 (1982), 10–14; and O. Belkov, "An Army of Friendship and Fraternity of Peoples," *Kommunist vooruzhennykh sil*, no. 12 (1981), 9–16.

for minority applicants, regardless of their performance on the entrance exam. This appears to have been done in a very limited way.[90] The other solution, and the one that has generated most support within the Defense Ministry, is to enhance minority ability to compete effectively with Russians by establishing special remedial programs to prepare minority youth who have expressed a desire for a military career. Several republics have set such programs up, and they appear to enjoy strong support from the military establishment, probably because it expands minority access to officer careers without sacrificing effectiveness. There are also efforts, particularly within southern-tier republics that lack a strong military tradition, to popularize military careers among high-school boys.[91]

A third, more indirect, impact of social trends on the officer corps is a shift in the officer's role in the command hierarchy associated with the development of the warrant officer program. Until the early 1970s, the Soviet Armed Forces had very few career enlisted personnel. Conscript sergeants served in the lowest command posts, such as that of squad leader. Most of the remaining command posts (including many that in other armies are normally filled by career enlisted personnel) were assigned to officers. This system was a major burden on both junior officers (who often found themselves assigned to duties for which they were overqualified) and conscript sergeants (who were often given responsibilities for which they were underqualified).

In response, the Soviets in 1971 established a warrant officer program. Ten years later, they introduced the rank of senior warrant officer to provide more opportunities for career advancement. Both warrants and senior warrants occupy posts similar to those previously occupied by junior officers. As such, they fill a gap between the conscripts and the increasingly well-educated commissioned officers. This development probably helped enhance the officer corps' professional identity because it freed them from a number of posts for which they were overqualified in terms of education and military credentials.

To sum up the foregoing discussion: the direct impact of social change on the military establishment was both positive and negative. It produced significant, sometimes rapid, increases and decreases in the supply of draft-age males—a development that challenged the military's ability to adjust its induction, training, and socialization program. It also produced a better-educated, more sophisticated pool of draftees and potential officer recruits, but one that conversely is less willing to accept obligatory military service or to make the necessary adjustments to the demands of military life. In addition, it

[90] *Kommunisti*, 19 July 1984, 4; excerpted in JPRS-UPS-84-106, 25.
[91] A. Melkumyan, "To Raise Defenders of the Motherland," *Kommunist* (Frevan), 17 February, 2. On efforts in minority areas to popularize officer careers, see "Candidates Shall Be Worthy," *Esh leninchi*, 24 May 1984, 3; V. Govorov, "Criteria of Quality," *Krasnaia zvezda*, 17 July 1986, 2, 3.

resulted in a manpower pool less Slavic and less fluent in the command language.

Impact on Civil-Military Relations

These social developments affected the military environment to some degree, but the negative impact—until recently—was buffered by a political leadership that placed a high priority on military power and was willing to pay a heavy price to shelter the armed forces from adverse economic and demographic trends. To anticipate an argument presented in more detail below, Gorbachev's predecessors valued military power as the very cornerstone of the USSR's claim to great-power status. As a consequence, the military—that "holy of holies" (in the words of then Politburo member Andrei Gromyko)— was largely buffered against social change.[92] During the Brezhnev years and the post-Brezhnev interregnum, the primary response of the Defense Ministry to changes in the social environment was to increase its demands on the civilian agencies involved in supplying the military with its primary human input, manpower. Social and demographic trends produced an increasing conflict between military and civilian needs, but the political leadership resolved this conflict largely in favor of the military. As a result, social change did not result in a significant shift in civil-military relations.

This congenial state of affairs (from the military's standpoint) changed under Gorbachev, though not immediately. Gorbachev's original version of perestroika was an attempt to reform the faltering economy without sacrificing military power. By 1987, however, there were increasing signs of sharpening competition between military and civilian needs, as well as signals that the military's traditional high priority was coming under increasingly critical scrutiny at the same time that the role of military power in peacetime foreign policy and in ensuring security was being seriously questioned. On 7 December 1988, Gorbachev announced a major reduction in manpower and equipment.[93] On 6 January 1989 he revealed that a "preliminary study" had shown that defense outlays could be trimmed without sacrificing military capability.[94] In effect, Gorbachev is disavowing the priority system that ensured that the military would be buffered against the effects of economic and demographic change. At the same time, he has initiated a political reform program that represents an even more troubling threat to military interests because it enfranchises constituencies that are, in some cases, actively hostile to the military.

---

[92] See Gromyko's nominating speech for Gorbachev on the occasion of Gorbachev's election to general secretary, *Izvestiia*, 12 March 1985, 1. Gromyko's nominating speech was included in a brochure on the plenum released on 14 March.

[93] *Pravda*, 8 December 1988, 1, 2.

[94] Gorbachev's 6 January 1989 speech.

Military Power and Social Change before Gorbachev

Gorbachev's predecessors placed a high priority on military power. The USSR's claim to great-power status rested squarely on the shoulders of its soldiers. Economic growth may have faltered, and Soviet living standards may have fallen further behind the Western industrialized powers. But the Soviet army was feared and respected. It bought Soviet leaders an important place on the international stage. Soviet national security was based on overwhelming military strength, and military muscle was a key component of peacetime foreign policy. The military performed, in addition, several secondary, but still useful, socioeconomic roles: providing assistance to the civilian economy, helping to socialize young men, and assisting in control of internal unrest.

On balance, the social trends outlined above did not have a significant net impact on the military's ability to fulfill its primary mission: to ensure security and serve as the basis of the USSR's superpower status. The consequences of social change were both positive and negative. The increase in educational levels, coupled with an increasing stress on technical competency within the school system and an improved predraft training system, benefitted the military. On the other hand, the increase in the share of non-Slavs in the draft pool had a negative impact. On balance, the negative impact of social change cancelled out the positive.

Social change did, however, affect the military's political socialization role, both by increasing its importance and by increasing the complexity of the mission. The nature of the military's socialization role, of course, changed in the postwar period. In the 1920s, the military was used in the nationwide literacy campaign. By the Brezhnev era, the military's two major socialization missions were to promote socialist values (particularly among what the military viewed as increasingly spoiled, self-centered, and materialistic young soldiers) and to enhance integration and increase Russian fluency among non-Slavic soldiers. This development had an impact on those agencies within the military whose primary role is socialization, in particular, the Main Political Administration (MPA). These increasing demands on the MPA came at a time when it was already under increasing pressure to use its resources for more narrowly military purposes. This development may serve to increase potential for conflict between the military commander and the political officer.

These changes did not, however, affect the armed forces' primary missions during the Brezhnev era, the post-Brezhnev interregnum, and the early Gorbachev years. The political leadership continued to see the military as the main guarantor of security in an uncertain, still hostile world, and the primary insurance that the USSR would be taken seriously on the international stage.

Because the military performed such vital missions, Soviet leaders were willing to pay a high price for military power. As social and economic trends became less favorable, the military burden increased, but Soviet leaders accepted the growing burden. As a result, they were willing to shelter the military from the most damaging consequences of social and demographic trends.

This "buffering" of the military took place in several ways. First, the armed forces made only modest efforts to modify military life in response to social changes in the civilian world. Disciplinary standards were not significantly reduced. Despite the increasing proportion of non-Russians in the draft pool and in the pool of potential officers, the military continued to assign non-Russians to mixed ethnic units where Russian is the command language and servicemen are expected to make the necessary adjustments.

Second, the sharpening of competition between military manpower needs and nonmilitary demands for manpower was resolved in favor of the military. In the early 1980s, deferments and exemptions were tightened and an increasing proportion of draft-eligible males were conscripted. Of particular importance to the military was the cutback of the higher-education deferment, because this provision had provided a legal method of draft avoidance for higher-status youth and had thus contributed to a public perception that the service obligation was unfairly applied. The tightening of deferments in the early 1980s served both to cushion the impact of the declining supply of eligible males and to underline the leadership's commitment to real universality of service.

Accommodation and Conflict under Gorbachev

The military's privileged niche in the Soviet system was not immediately threatened by the advent of Gorbachev. The original Gorbachev leadership coalition was clearly alarmed by the problems besetting the Soviet system, in particular, the stagnating economy. However, the original remedy—the earliest version of perestroika—was a fairly conservative cure that invoked traditional levers (such as the anti-alcohol campaign and the reorientation of investment resources toward civil machinebuilding) while promising that no major claimant on resources (the consumer, the military, and long-term investment) would be harmed. The high command had a great deal to gain from the benefits Gorbachev promised in terms of a robust economy capable of supporting the technologically advanced weaponry the military would need for the battlefield of the future. In the early months of his tenure, Gorbachev went out of his way to assure the military publicly that Soviet security would not be sacrificed for economic reform.[95]

[95] See, for example, Gorbachev's report at the 11 June 1985 conference on scientific and technical policy in *Kommunist*, no. 9 (1985), 13–33. See also Gorbachev's speech at a meeting with the Dnepropetrovsk Foundry collective in *Aktivno deistvovat, ne teriat vremeni* (Moscow, 1985).

The military leadership was fairly successful in achieving a formal recognition of the validity of its continuing claims on one increasingly scarce resource: manpower. The 1986 revision of the Communist Party Program incorporated a ritual reference to the link between citizenship and military service. The new program echoed both the 1961 version and the 1977 USSR Constitution in its insistence that military service was an obligation of citizenship. While this formula was the traditional one, its incorporation in the revised program reaffirmed the political leadership's commitment to a military manning policy based on universal military service. The military's interests were also endorsed by the incorporation of a statement on the importance of military-patriotic socialization: "An important task of the party's ideological education work remains military-patriotic socialization, the formation of readiness to defend the socialist fatherland and to give it all one's efforts and if necessary one's life too."[96] Military manpower issues were also recognized by the incorporation of a formulation linking physical fitness with the preparation of youth for military service.

The single military issue that emerged as a point of contention during the public discussion of the program, the disagreement over the relative importance of party loyalty and military expertise, was resolved in favor of the latter—a development that must surely have pleased professional military men. The disagreement arose over the precise wording of a section on combat potential. (There was no directly analogous section in the 1961 program.) The relevant section of the draft program read as follows:

> The CPSU will continue to show invariable concern for ensuring that the Soviet Armed Forces' combat potential constitutes a strong fusion of military skill, ideological staunchness, organization and discipline on the part of personnel, their loyalty to their patriotic and international duty, and a high level of technical equipment.[97]

This formulation placed human factors first, with greater stress on the military skills of armed forces personnel (i.e., the degree of mastery of combat hardware and weaponry). Level of technical equipment appeared at the end of the list.

In the discussion that ensued, several Defense Ministry officials applauded the emphasis on the human factor but urged adoption of a formulation that would elevate the importance of "ideological staunchness"—codewords for party loyalty—and downgrade "military mastery."[98] This appears to have been part of a larger conflict over the relative balance of political and techni-

---

[96] *Pravda*, 7 March 1986, 3–8.

[97] Ibid., 26 October 1985, 1–7.

[98] I. Sidelnikov, "Socialism's Historic Vocation: Problems of War, Peace, and the Protection of Socialism in a New Edition of the CPSU Program," *Krasnaia zvezda*, 25 December 1985, 2–3; and V. Samoylenko, "Let Us Provide a Reliable Defense for Communist Creation," *Kommunist*, no. 17 (1985), 7.

cal/managerial qualifications in Soviet cadre policy. In the military case, the advocates of greater stress on party loyalty lost out. In the final version of the program, "military skill" retained its top billing on the list of factors constituting combat potential. Moreover, "high technical equipment" moved up to second place on the list, suggesting a bow to the technocrats within the Defense Ministry.

In short, the 1986 version of the program was fairly supportive of military interests, in terms of human factors at least. There was no evidence of major discord between military and civilian authorities over those portions of the program relevant to military manpower. The only conflict that surfaced in the press, on party versus professional qualifications, was one that cut across institutional lines.

Another indicator of the political leadership's recognition of the validity of the military's manpower needs was the June 1986 joint resolution by the Central Committee and the Council of Ministers on the need to improve preparation for military service.[99] The decree itself covered virtually all aspects of predraft military preparation: elementary military training, specialist training, physical fitness, health classes, and military-patriotic socialization. Many of the provisions of the resolution echoed the traditional, long-standing complaints of military educators about the poor facilities and incompetent instructors of the predraft training system.[100] In short, the decree touched upon nearly every aspect of concern to military authorities, except, interestingly enough, Russian language problems.[101]

The treatment of the Afghanistan war likewise suggested that the political leadership was clearly sensitive to military concerns (see also the discussion by Bruce Porter in chapter 8). Here the primary military concern, in terms of social issues, was the impact of the war on public opinion about the military as an institution and about military service. During the war, these concerns were partly addressed by stepping up the public relations campaign that predated the Gorbachev era. Fuller coverage of the war was partly the result of leadership awareness of the political sensitivity of Soviet involvement. The development also benefitted the military because it presented a flattering picture of Soviet military activities in Afghanistan. In addition, Soviet socializers were able to use Afghanistan veterans in programs designed to promote popular acceptance of the draft.[102] The more open media treatment of the war thus

---

[99] "In the CC CPSU Politburo," *Pravda*, 6 June 1986, 1. See also "Preparation for Service," *Krasnaia zvezda*, 25 June 1986, 1. Like many other planks in Gorbachev's platform, rhetoric has not been matched by reality. See the report on the January 1988 Defense Ministry Collegium session in "Raising Patriots," *Pravda*, 24 January 1988, 6.

[100] G. Egorov, "Prepare Youth for Military Service," *Kommunist vooruzhennykh sil*, no. 18 (1986), 31–37.

[101] *Sovetskii patriot*, 6 July 1986, 3; 20 July 1986, 3.

[102] "Raising Patriots," *Pravda*, 24 January 1988, 6.

allowed the Soviet leadership to acknowledge and express appreciation publicly for the actions of Soviet servicemen in the combat. Expressions of leadership support, such as Gorbachev's words of praise at the April 1987 congress of the Komsomol, were important in building a positive public image of
Afghan war veterans.[103]

The Gorbachev leadership took care to handle the Afghanistan withdrawal
in a way that would avoid any implication of a military failure and, just as
important, to pay appropriate homage to (as Gorbachev put it) "our boys in
Afghanistan."[104] This latter issue is of continuing concern to military authorities in light of the growing public skepticism about the wisdom of the original
invasion.

The leadership also made some attempts to respond to the social and economic problems of Afghan war veterans. A rehabilitation center for disabled
veterans was opened in the Crimea in the early 1980s. In February 1988, the
Central Committee issued a resolution on veterans.[105] Although the resolution
included provisions relating to the vets' reintegration into civilian life, the
focus was on measures to harness the energies of Afghan vets to the promotion
of promilitary attitudes on the part of Soviet teenagers. This represents a bow
to military concerns, since military authorities see the veterans as important
allies in their efforts to counter youth pacifism.[106]

In sum, Gorbachev initially adopted the traditional high priority his predecessors assigned to military power and, in the early months of his tenure,
acceded to policies that minimized the impact of social change on the armed
forces. Most important, he did not force the military to make adjustments that
would surely be repugnant to it, such as extending the draft to women, under-
taking major manpower reductions, or abandoning conscription.

This is not to argue that the military was unaffected by social change. As
seen above, social trends did have some negative consequences on the supply
of manpower. The military responded to these consequences by placing in-

[103] M. S. Gorbachev, "The Creative Strength of Revolutionary Renewal," ibid., 17 April
1987, 1, 2.

[104] Ibid., 9 February 1988, 1.

[105] *Sovetskaia Rossiia*, 23 February 1988, 3. See also *Moskovskaia pravda*, 22 December 1987,
4; A. Titarenko, "I Did Not Send You to Afghanistan," *Pravda*, 20 August 1987, 2; A. Simurov
and P. Studenkin, "Your Heart Feels No Gratitude," ibid., 25 November 1987, 6; and P. Studenkin, "I Did Not Send You to Afghanistan," ibid., 5 August 1987, 3. It is interesting to note that
a poll conducted jointly by the Soviet Sociological Research Institute and the French polling
agency IPSOS found that while most respondents expressed support for the leadership position
on a negotiated withdrawal, a large minority (27 percent) was opposed to a troop pull-out under
any circumstances. Christopher Walker, "Poll Reveals Most Russians Want Afghanistan Pull-
out," *The Times* (London), 2 November 1987, 9.

[106] Viktor Turshatov, "Afghanistan Veterans: Society Owes Them," *Moscow News*, no. 50,
13 December 1987, 13; and P. Tkachenko, "Staying a Soldier," *Krasnaia zvezda*, 11 December
1987, 4. See also the resolution adopted at the all-union rally of reserve servicemen in Ashkhabad
on 20 November 1987, *Komsomolskaia pravda*, 22 November 1987, 1.

creased pressures on civilian socializing agencies (the school system, media, and youth organizations) to promote military goals and values. To be sure, the Defense Ministry did make some limited adjustments to social change—the effort to achieve a representative ethnic mix in small units, the ministry's in-house Russian language program, and the increasing stress on persuasion rather than coercion in handling conscripts. The Defense Ministry's primary response, however, was to escalate its demands on civilian agencies (1) to meet the need for a more literate draft pool in order to facilitate absorption of technical training, and (2) to counter the deleterious side-effects of socioeconomic modernization in terms of attitudes toward military service and willingness to adjust to the deprivations of military life.

The Defense Ministry's reaction to social change was hardly surprising in light of its traditional response to other agencies that service its needs. The military had long enjoyed a preferential position as a customer organization vis-à-vis defense-product ministries; it demanded and received top-quality weapons and equipment. The Defense Ministry clearly viewed the socialization agencies as "suppliers" of another needed product—military manpower. In increasing its requirement on the civilian institutions, the military was operating in its traditional mode as a preferred customer that traditionally demanded and received high priority treatment.

One consequence of the increase in military demands was a heightened level of conflict in the early Gorbachev years between military and civilian organizations. Initially, this conflict was played out in the media between Soviet military authorities and the civilian bodies that bear the major responsibility for the moral and physical fitness of incoming conscripts: schools, media, youth groups, and the various social organizations devoted to security issues—DOSAAF and the veterans association.[107]

The decline in public acceptance of the draft became a major issue of contention—a development that both military authorities and more conservative journalists blamed squarely on the major youth socialization agencies. Military officials were particularly critical of the media. They criticized the film "Is It Easy to Be Young?" for "cast[ing] doubt on the need for young people to fulfill their military service."[108] At a June 1986 meeting with leading literary and art figures at the Ministry of Defense, MPA chief Lizichev charged that "individual works" on World War II contained "notes of pacifism." He went on to complain that writers and artists should do more to prepare youth for the "real difficulties" of adjusting to the demands of military service. Several weeks later, at the congress of the Union of Writers, Lizichev took up the call again, complaining that contemporary military activities—the sacri-

---

[107] Iu. S. Vasiutin, *Voenno-patrioticheskoe vospitanie: teoriia, opyt* (Moscow: Mysl', 1984), 30, 45–56.

[108] *Krasnaia zvezda*, 16 September 1987.

fices of military personnel in Afghanistan and in the clean-up of the Chernobyl nuclear power plant disaster—"deserved more attention and greater interest from the country's best literary forces."[109]

Some military officials went further, arguing that the media, instead of doing everything possible to "debunk pacifism," were instead actively contributing to it.[110] Military officials, for instance, took umbrage at the media's suggestions that the production of toy guns be curtailed.[111] They also questioned
the wisdom of the media's increasing tolerance for youth interest in Western
music.[112]

Military officials also charged the Komsomol with shirking its responsibilities in preparing youth for military service. In April 1987, a heated polemic
erupted at the Komsomol congress.[113] According to the report in *Krasnaia
zvezda*, the Ministry of Defense's newspaper, Defense Minister Sokolov criticized the Komsomol for shortcomings in military-patriotic socialization. Sokolov was in turn taken to task by Ia. P. Gundogdyev, first secretary of the
Komsomol of Turkmenia (and, incidentally a Gorbachev-era appointee). Gundogdyev censured Sokolov for not proposing any concrete measures to improve the premilitary program. He then outlined a three-part program that he
argued the military itself should undertake to help improve premilitary training
of draft-eligibles.

The debate was joined by a young soldier who jumped to Sokolov's defense, arguing vehemently that the Komsomol official was placing the entire
responsibility for premilitary preparation on the army. The soldier objected to
this, nothing pointedly that "the main concern of the army is to train [soldiers]
to fight." Not surprisingly, *Krasnaia zvezda* took the military point of view,
insisting that "commanders and political workers have the right to expect"
the Komsomol to play a more effective role in preparing draft-age males for
service.

Another controversy erupted around the same time over draft deferments.
In May 1987, several scientists participating in a round-table discussion took
strong exception to the curtailment of higher-education deferments, insisting
that military service should not interfere with study. Young people who entered their studies after military service were less creative, they claimed, than
those who continued straight from high school. The long-term impact on fundamental science would be "dangerous," and this would be "for defense
also." One of the round-table participants drew a parallel with the interwar
years, when Germany exempted its intelligentsia and students from military
obligations and was able to achieve scientific superiority over England and

[109] Ibid., 27 June 1986, 1,3.
[110] Ibid., 11 December 1987, 4.
[111] Ibid., 16 September 1987.
[112] *Der Spiegel*, 15 January 1988, 138–161.
[113] N. Belan, "Preparation for Service," *Krasnaia zvezda*, 25 April 1987, 3.

France. "For this reason," he concluded, "I am absolutely agreed that it is stupid and short-sighted to draft students." A rebuttal from the military was not long in coming. Colonel General D. A. Volkogonov, a ranking MPA officer, chastised the scientists in *Krasnaia zvezda* for their "mistaken" views, reminding them that military service serves a social role as well.[114]

As this exchange illustrated, many scientists and intellectuals strongly opposed the party leadership's decision in the early 1980s to curtail the higher education deferment. The intellectuals favored a return to the previous policy allowing college students, particularly those in high-prestige scientific disciplines, to postpone or avoid service. Military officers, by contrast, opposed a selective reinstatement of the deferment for high-prestige fields, even though only a small number of conscripts would be affected, because reinstating the deferment represented a dilution of the principle of universal service.

The public controversy over draft deferments was partly a disagreement about competing military-civilian manpower priorities and partly a reflection of the larger controversy over the application of glasnost to military issues. Military officials and some of the more conservative media figures are extremely uncomfortable with the notion that the army's problems should be held up to public scrutiny. Their concern crystallized during a disagreement over the hazing problem ("nonregulation relations," as it has euphemistically been referred to).

In 1987, the writer Iurii Poliakov, over strong military objections, succeeded in publishing a novella exposing the negative effects of hazing and indirectly criticizing the officer corps for ignoring the problem. The novella was positively reviewed in *Literaturnaia gazeta*, the Union of Writers' newspaper.[115] It was panned viciously in the military press.[116] Defense Ministry officials argued angrily that uninformed outsiders were exaggerating the scope of the problem and ignoring the steps the military was taking to control it.[117] General Tretiak, commander of the air defense forces, took the counteroffensive, arguing that "if such things happen, it is not the army that is guilty, it is rather a reflection of the education the young men are getting in the pre-army environment."[118]

Controversy over the implications of glasnost for the military escalated at a 15 December 1987 meeting between Defense Minister Iazov and a group of writers. Iazov bitterly attacked the scientists who advocated reinstating the

[114] D. Volkogonov, "Imperatives of the Nuclear Age," ibid., 22 May 1987, 2, 3. The roundtable is in *Literaturnaia gazeta*, 13 May 1987, 12.

[115] V. Kondratev, "An Urgent Matter," *Literaturnaia gazeta*, 10 February 1988, 4.

[116] A. Khorev, "Is the Artillery Firing on Its Own Men?" *Krasnaia zvezda*, 29 August 1987, 3.

[117] A. Khorev, "Echo of Malicious Talk," ibid., 12 December 1987, 4.

[118] I. Tretiak, "Reliable Defense First and Foremost," *Moscow News*, no. 8, 21 February 1988, 12.

draft deferment for scientific students and raised the broader issue of the potential dangers of applying glasnost to military issues. He argued, in effect, that media efforts to unmask problems in the armed forces were misguided because they damaged the military's image and undermined patriotic values. Another participant at the December 1987 meeting, Aleksandr Prokhanov, a conservative journalist, also took issue with writers who try to "run down" the army, noting pointedly that the military was one of the few institutions that worked efficiently during the Brezhnev years of stagnation:

> It is strange business, but we are going through a period when our culture in the shape of some writers is trying somehow to "run down" the army and impute nonexistent sins to it. And that despite the fact that the army in the period of so-called stagnation was thriving, worked conscientiously, and achieved strategic parity. A pacifist, abstract peace-making mentality, after all, would not have allowed us to talk with the United States as equals or achieve the signing of a treaty on medium-range and shorter-range missiles.[119]

As the forgoing discussion makes clear, the military's typical response to changes in the social environment was to demand that civilian agencies step up their efforts to cushion the negative impact of adverse social trends. After Gorbachev's accession to power, however, civilian organizations became less cooperative, setting the stage for an increasingly acrid public conflict between civilian and military officials at lower levels. While military leaders were fairly successful in winning formal recognition of the validity of their claims on civilian socialization agencies, they were less successful in extracting from the political leadership the sustained, top-level attention required to force civilian agencies to respond as fully as the Defense Ministry desired.

In short, in the early years of his tenure, Gorbachev retained the priority system he inherited from his predecessors and continued to accord the military its traditional preference. There were disquieting signs, however, most notably in the newly critical tone of military organizations in the Soviet media. These developments were ominous because they signaled the beginning of a change in the very basis of the political contract between soldiers and the Soviet state: the military's place in the system of policy priorities. This shift in priorities was to alter the rules of civil-military relations in ways that might ultimately change the game radically.

Military Power and the Gorbachev Revolution

The major factor changing civil-military relations was a major change in perestroika itself. The original, noncontroversial version of perestroika was fairly

---

[119] "I Serve the Soviet Union," Moscow Television Service, 16 January 1988.

successful from a political standpoint: civic morale increased at home and Soviet prestige increased abroad. The economy, however, despite a temporary upturn in 1986, showed no signs of long-term improvement; and the leadership's revised strategy of systemic reform, unveiled at the June 1987 plenum, had become hopelessly bogged down in a morass of bureaucratic and popular resistance. By 1988, Gorbachev had shifted gears once again. In the international arena, he was pressing forward with a host of arms-control initiatives to implement what he called his "new political thinking" in foreign policy—a process culminating in his dramatic announcement of unilateral military reductions in December 1988. The reduction fit in well with his moves to placate the increasingly disgruntled Soviet consumer by shifting resources from defense to the consumer sector. Gorbachev also initiated a series of political reforms designed to transfer power from the party machine, which was blocking his economic reforms, to a newly revamped legislative hierarchy. This process of political reform is enfranchising consitutencies that are far less congenial to military interests than the party apparatchiky who monopolized defense decision making under Brezhnev. At the same time, the loosening of political controls has unleashed social unrest in the form of increased crime, sporadic strikes, continuing ethnic flare-ups, and communal violence—developments that are alarming to many within the Soviet elite, including the military high command.

The most immediate threat to the military's interests stems from Gorbachev's conceptual revision of foreign policy through "new political thinking." This approach downgrades the role of military power both as an instrument of foreign policy in peacetime and as the cornerstone of national security. In peacetime, claim the "new political thinkers," diplomacy is both cheaper and more effective than military power in furthering Soviet interests. They accuse Brezhnev and other previous leaders of overrating military means as a guarantee of Soviet security and paying too little attention to diplomacy as a tool of threat management:

> Security today should be ensured more and more by political means. In practical terms, this should be through arms limitations and reductions, a system of reliable control, and broader confidence-building measures, and also through easing and settling conflict situations and eliminating dangerous bones of contention in interstate relations.[120]

Since the armed forces' resource claims have traditionally rested on the overriding importance of their assigned roles, it is scarcely surprising that so searching a reassessment should have been seen by civilians and soldiers alike as raising serious questions about resources. It was clear by early 1988 that

---

[120] Eduard Shevardnadze, *International Affairs* (October 1988), 18.

the question of substantial cuts in military outlays had made its way onto the Soviet political agenda.

An early indication was General Tretiak's blunt warning, in an interview in the liberal publication *Moscow News* in February 1988, about the danger of diverting resources from defense to the consumer sector. Tretiak made his point by analogy with the troop cuts of the Khrushchev period:

> At the end of the fifties, the USSR reduced its army unilaterally by 1.2 million men. The economists estimated that this enabled us to double the size of old-age pensions and to set up ten house-building plants. On the surface it looked rather convincing. But only on the surface. As a professional military man, I'll tell you that the step was a rash one, it dealt a terrible blow at our defense capability, and at our officer personnel.[121]

By the summer of 1988, the advocates of budget cuts, to whom Tretiak had made only indirect reference months before, had begun to come out into the open. Several participants at a Ministry of Foreign Affairs conference favored unilateral troop cuts; others argued for cuts, but only on a bilateral basis.[122] Simultaneously, the media began to air a rising chorus of complaints about the high level of the military burden.

In July 1988 a political observer in *Izvestiia*, S. Kondrashev, maintained that it is possible to ensure security at cheaper cost by relying less on military means and more on political means:

> Don't get me wrong. Defense capability is a sacred matter, especially for a people with our historic memories. But it is not sacred in the sense of religious devotion, a fetish, or blind faith.[123]

In September *Sovetskaia kultura* published a letter from an economist complaining that the guns-versus-butter debate in the USSR had always been resolved in favor of guns:

> The old doctrine, which viewed the USSR as a fortress under siege, presupposes not simply national economic priority for hypertrophied defense needs, but also no hitches in satisfying them. And this impacts directly on the formation of the sum of funds that can be channeled into improving living standards. Is this doctrine's vitality not one weighty reason for the present neglect of the country's social sphere?[124]

Commentators also began to question in print the need for a massive standing army. The least intrusive of the solutions proposed involves a decrease in the service terms for draftees. One letter-writer to *Izvestiia*, who proposed a

---

[121] Tretiak, "Reliable Defense."

[122] Anatoliy Kovalev, "Soviet Foreign Policy Priorities," *International Affairs* (October 1988), 18.

[123] *Izvestiia*, 9 July 1988.

[124] *Sovetskaia kultura*, 17 September 1988, 5.

reduction of service terms to twelve to eighteen months, noted pointedly that several Western countries already have short terms of service.[125]

Other proposals go so far as to support a change in the very nature of the armed forces. In November 1988, *Moscow News* published an article by a Lieutenant Colonel Aleksandr Savinkin advocating a revival of the professional-militia system.[126] Savinkin's proposal involved replacing the large standing army with a system roughly analogous to that set up by the 1925 military reform, which combined a small professional core of volunteers with local militia units.

Savinkin's suggestion stirred up a storm of controversy. Some took his idea even further. One letter writer—an army captain from the Far Eastern Military District—proposed abandoning conscription completely in favor of an all-volunteer system.[127] There were many, however, who reasserted the familiar approach. A civilian economist, for example, questioned Savinkin's assumption that there is no longer a direct military threat to the Soviet Union.[128] The retired chief of the General Staff, Marshal Akhromeev, weighed into the argument with a ringing endorsement of the principle of universal military service:

> I cannot understand why some comrades are coming out against universal military service. I regard the volunteer principle of forming the army and navy and the emergence of "paid volunteers" as unacceptable for the Soviet Union. . . . The "volunteer" principle also contains a violation of social justice. All citizens should prepare for the defense of the motherland. Moreover, a mercenary army would cost our people far more than it costs at present. We must reckon with this too.[129]

At an election meeting in February 1989, MPA chief Lizichev strongly endorsed Akhromeev's position:

> At present there is a great deal of talk about our military building in the press and on radio and television. In the public consciousness, you could say, two different approaches to transformations in the armed forces are identified. The first envisages improving the existing system. The second is oriented toward changing the fundamental principles of the army's structure. It is claimed, in particular, that it is urgently necessary to go over to forming the army on the territorial militia principle. Others propose a mercenary army. People also say that each union republic is free to have its own army, its own national military formations. . . . The existing cadre system of military organization . . . withstood the test of both the Civil and the Great Patriotic War. That is the main argument in defense of the present system.[130]

[125] *Izvestiia*, 6 October 1988.

[126] Aleksandr Savinkin, *Moscow News*, November 1988.

[127] Ibid., no. 2, 8 January 1989, 8.

[128] Ivan Iudin, "I Disagree," ibid., no. 4, January 29–February 5, 1989, 4.

[129] S. F. Akhromeev, "The Army and Restructuring," *Sovetskaia Rossiia*, 14 January 1989, 1, 3.

[130] A. D. Lizichev, "Man Is at the Center of Restructuring," *Krasnaia zvezda*, 4 February 1989, 1–2.

On 7 December 1988, as the debate over conscription was gathering steam, Gorbachev made his announcement at the United Nations of a substantial, unilateral force reduction, which will trim the Soviet military by half a million men and ten thousand tanks. On 6 January 1989, speaking to a group of Soviet scientists and intellectuals, he noted that a "preliminary study" had shown that defense outlays could be reduced without degrading military capability— an unambiguous signal that substantial resource cuts were imminent. On 18 January, Gorbachev stated to visitors from the Trilateral Commission that the forthcoming manpower cuts would amount to 12 percent, while the military budget will be cut by 14.2 percent and weapons production by 19.5 percent.[131]

The manpower reductions affect both the officer corps (which will be trimmed through early retirements when possible) and draftees. The Soviets are adjusting their conscription system to the reduced conscript demand by expanding the educational deferment—a move the high command (as Iazov's earlier comments indicate) had firmly rejected. There is also some possibility that the leadership is toying with the idea of reducing the amount of time draftees serve. This latter possibility was indicated by Foreign Minister Eduard Shevardnadze in an October 1988 interview with a French newspaper. When asked why the conscript tour in the USSR was so long, he replied: "This question is also widely discussed in the press in our country and it is asking questions about the length and efficacy of military service. I am convinced that the new Supreme Soviet will examine this question."[132] Gorbachev himself raised the possibility of a decrease in the conscript term during an exchange with Komsomol members the same month. In response to the question, "Why do we need such a large army?" he answered: "I think we are moving in the direction of studying this important range of problems. . . . We must take a good look at the questions of army service and conscription. I think the question of length of service will also be raised. It could be changed."[133] Although neither Gorbachev nor Shevardnadze endorsed the most radical proposals for changing manpower policy, the continuation of the debate in the media indicates that proposals of various kinds are under consideration.

There is little doubt that the military elite finds these developments most disquieting. It was rumored that the removal of Akhromeev from the General Staff (a change announced shortly after Gorbachev's 7 December 1988 UN speech) was connected with military opposition to the announcement. Akhromeev's public denial of the reports—consistent with a long Soviet tradition of presenting a unified front in public on such occasions—was less than convincing.[134]

---

[131] Moscow Domestic Service in Russian 1800 GMT, 18 January 1989.

[132] *Le Nouvel Observateur*, 14–20 October 1988.

[133] Gorbachev's comments were reported in "Restructuring and Youth: Time for Action," *Pravda*, 1 November 1988, 1, 2.

[134] *Sovetskaia Rossiia*, 14 January 1989, 1, 3; and Sergei Akhromeev, "General Staff—

Media coverage of reaction to the reduction stressed strong military support, insisting that the officer corps' primary concern is how the cuts will be implemented and, in particular, how individual careers and the prestige of the military as a whole will be affected. Soviet officers, evoking "the mistakes made under Khrushchev," have expressed alarm that the reduction will mean "shattered lives" for many of their colleagues and greater difficulty in attracting high-quality young men to officer careers. Some have suggested procedures designed to ensure that decisions on which officers to force out will be made fairly, without the "protectionism" that allegedly flourished when Khrushchev's cuts were carried out. They have also urged that efforts be made to ease the inevitable problems that will accompany adjustment to civilian life.[135]

Despite these efforts to downplay resistance, it is clear that many in the military were dead set against the reduction. Shevardnadze, in a 10 January 1989 interview with *Le Figaro*, acknowledged military "concern" over the cuts, commenting that "obviously, it is not easy for them to change their way of life."[136] Defense Minister Iazov, while accepting the need for the policy change, admitted that "psychologically speaking, the reduction is not a simple factor for the army."[137]

The military leadership is also going on the defensive to repel what it apparently sees as even more serious potential assaults on the army's priority claim to resources. While civilian commentators are busily deflating the Western threat to justify the initial round of defense reductions and demand additional cuts, military leaders are issuing pointed reminders that the threat remains. "The disarmament process and the movement toward a nonnuclear and nonviolent world," Iazov has intoned, "have not yet become irreversible and are encountering powerful resistance."[138]

Akhromeev's successor in the General Staff, M. A. Moiseev, went considerably further. Although he conceded that the old principle that "savings can be effected everywhere except in defense" is no longer tenable, Moiseev echoed Iazov's warning that "imperialism's policy retains its aggressive orientation." Moreover, he vigorously rebutted what he portrayed as ill-informed charges that the military has been deliberately pumping up the threat to justify its mission and existence:

Changes," *Moscow News*, no. 5, 29 January 1989, 5. See also a denial from Valentin Falin, head of the Central Committee International Department, *Die Welt*, 24 January 1989, 6.

[135] *Krasnaia zvezda*, 15 December 1988, 2. See also the interview with Major General Lebedev, "Reduction of the Army and Defense Capability," ibid., 16 December 1988, 3; and the interview with Colonel General V. Lobov, "Proceeding from the Principles of Defensive Doctrine," *Pravda*, 17 December 1988, 4.

[136] *Le Figaro*, 10 January 1989, 5.

[137] Iazov's comments were reported in A. Vasilets and I. Kosenko, "Perestroika Requires Action," *Krasnaia zvezda*, 25 December 1988, 2.

[138] Ibid., 25 December 1988, 2.

The press has recently carried numerous noncompetent articles which essentially raise doubts about the existence of a real military threat and hence about the legitimacy of the defensive measures being taken. At times, it is bluntly said that an "alleged military threat" is invented by the military themselves in order to justify their existence.[139]

Coupled with the evidence of a lively internal debate over the wisdom of retaining a manpower-intensive conscription system, these developments indicate that a basic shift in the political leadership's priorities is now under way. After several decades as the unquestioned top national priority, the military has found itself in the unaccustomed position of having to justify its claim to resources. The high command is clearly uncomfortable in this new role, and signals of military-civil conflict (over the nature of the threat, the utility of military power, and the method of carrying out those reductions already announced) have multiplied.

Perhaps more threatening to the military's interests in the long term are the changes Gorbachev has initiated in the political system itself. These changes, which involve a partial dismantling of the coercive control system and a transfer of political authority from the party machine to the newly revamped legislature, are remolding the political landscape in ways that many in the military high command find alarming. Gorbachev's efforts to beef up the legislative system by incorporating some elements of real democracy in the electoral process and giving the Supreme Soviet a real role in the decision making process have set in motion a process that is bringing new players into the previously limited circle of military policy makers.

The implications of this development for the high command were dramatized by the harsh treatment accorded Iazov during his July 1989 confirmation hearings as defense minister.[140] Although the Supreme Soviet eventually approved his nomination, many legislators seized the opportunity to censure the military for its failure to reform and to bring forward proposals opposed by the Defense Ministry leadership. Deputies demanded that the reinstatment of student deferments be made retroactive (applying to those students already serving as conscripts). They also proposed changes in manning policy that would involve jettisoning conscription altogether. Others called for changes in stationing policy allowing minority draftees to be stationed in their home republic. Iazov predictably rejected these demands; but when Gorbachev eventually rose to defend his embattled defense minister, he criticized Iazov for dismissing proposals for the early release of students and objected to Iazov's uncompromising stand on republic proposals regarding stationing policies. Gorbachev's defense of Iazov, however half-hearted, was successful in securing

---

[139] Ibid., 10 February 1989, 1–2.

[140] The hearings took place on 3 July and were reported in *Pravda*, on 4 July. See also ibid., 5 July 1989, 1–2; and *Krasnaia zvezda*, 5 July 1989, 1–3.

Iazov's confirmation. While Iazov was spared the humiliation of Supreme Soviet rejection, the relatively large number of negative votes and abstentions reflects the mistrust with which both Iazov and the military are held by at least a minority of vocal deputies.

The hostile legislative reception to Iazov presages a series of stormy battles between the high command and the legislature on issues relating to military manpower and resource allocation. The military high command has already lost a minor skirmish; a week after Iazov's confirmation, the leadership, in a direct rebuke to Iazov, bowed to public pressure on the student deferment issue and endorsed a proposal allowing the early release of student conscripts.[141] Gorbachev's political reforms, then, have brought into the political process players who are in some cases highly dubious about the high command's claim on scarce resources and in others actively hostile to the military.

In addition, Gorbachev's reforms are igniting several explosive social issues with direct implications for the military. The loosening of coercive political controls, coupled with the greater toleration of political dissent, has resulted in a breakdown of social and political order and a series of challenges to Soviet rule on the USSR's periphery. This is threatening to the military in several ways. First, the Defense Ministry has in several cases been called upon to quell internal unrest, a role that only serves to diminish its prestige, as demonstrated by the public outrage after troops forcibly broke up an April 1989 rally in Georgia, leaving twenty dead.[142] Second, in several cases, nationalist demands have focused on both military presence and military service requirements. As noted above, during Iazov's confirmation hearings, legislators from the Baltic, Georgia, and Moldavia protested the Defense Ministry's distant stationing policy, demanding that conscripts from their republics be stationed closer to home. Popular-front activists in the Baltic have demanded the withdrawal of Soviet troops stationed on Baltic territory and the formation of republic armies. If implemented, these changes could mark the beginning of the end of the multinational Soviet Armed Forces. It is hardly surprising that Iazov and other members of the high command have been adamant in their opposition.

These developments—the shift in leadership priorities, the change in the nature of the decision-making system itself, and the increasing social and political unrest—have the potential of inducing revolutionary changes in the relationship between military and civilian institutions. Thus far, the military leadership has limited its public reaction to grumbling and reminders that the new congeniality in East-West relations may well prove temporary. There are no signs that the generals are actively planning more decisive action, such as

---

[141] *Izvestiia*, 13 July 1989.
[142] See D. T. Iazov, "New Quality for the Armed Forces," *Kommunist vooruzhennykh sil*, no. 15 (1989), 3–13.

a coup against the main architect of the offending policies, Mikhail Gorbachev. To be sure, publicly acknowledged rumors of a military coup surfaced in mid-1989, leading to a denial by Iazov, who noted that a military-led coup would be ''difficult.''[143] Military unease, however, may become important in the unlikely but not impossible event that Gorbachev's foes within the political leadership coalesce against him. In such a scenario, the high command may be forced to choose sides, and its chagrin at losing its status as the favorite son of the command economy and alarm at the adverse political and social trends may tempt it to join Gorbachev's opposition. In this sense, the increasing conflict between the military elite and the politicians has increased the likelihood of military intervention in politics, not perhaps as an initiator but as a participant in an attempt to oust Gorbachev or force him to reverse the offending policies.

However the political scenario is played out, it is apparent that civil-military relations have significantly deteriorated under Gorbachev. My findings suggest, however, that social changes and socially driven changes in the military environment do little to help explain the signficant shift in civil-military relations observed under Gorbachev. Rather, the increased conflict in civil-military relations is a consequence of developments set in motion by reform programs motivated primarily by the need to strengthen the economy. Although social trends have had some impact on the routine give-and-take between the two sides, the overall deterioration is not immediately the product of changes in the social environment, the starting point of this chapter. The key development has been a shift, quite possibly a fundamental one, in the nature of the political process itself and the priorities of the political leaders. As their perception of the world, of their country's problems, and of their own role has developed, they have begun to make choices that are moving the civil-military compact away from the mutual support characteristic of the Brezhnev era and toward a more troubled and conflictual relationship.

[143] *Moscow News*, June 1989.

Eight

The Military Abroad: Internal Consequences of External Expansion

BRUCE D. PORTER

THROUGHOUT the history of Imperial Russia, the return home of the Russian Army from fighting abroad was associated with revolution and upheaval. The Decembrist uprising was led by young officers who had fought in the Napoleonic Wars and become disillusioned by the contrast between Mother Russia and the prosperous lands to the West. The war in the Crimea encouraged the reforms of the 1860s and the abolition of serfdom. Russia's defeat in the Russo-Japanese War of 1905 precipitated the revolutionary upheavals of that same year. And as World War I dragged on, with disastrous Russian losses, a profound war-weariness helped make possible the October Revolution; soldiers returning home from the front played a prominent role in the dramatic events of 1917.

Mindful of this pattern, and not wanting to repeat it, Soviet leader Joseph Stalin at the end of World War II took the extraordinary step of sending almost all returning Soviet prisoners of war straight to Siberian labor camps. The same fate awaited other Soviet soldiers suspected of having had too much contact with the life and ways of Western Europe. Aleksandr Solzhenitsyn commented on this event in *The Gulag Archipelago*:

> They imprisoned all those POW's, of course, not for treason to the Motherland, because it was absolutely clear even to a fool that only the Vlasov men could be accused of treason. They imprisoned all of them to keep them from telling their fellow villagers about Europe. What the eye doesn't see, the heart doesn't grieve for.[1]

More than forty years have passed since World War II, but today's Soviet leadership may harbor similar concerns about the impact of service abroad on its officers and soldiers.

The 1970s and 1980s witnessed the extension of Soviet military power into many regions of the world where the USSR traditionally had not maintained a military presence. Particularly dramatic was the unprecedented level of involvement of the Soviet armed forces in Third World crises and conflicts, the

---

[1] Aleksandr Solzhenitsyn, *The Gulag Archipelago* (New York: Harper & Row, 1973), 1:243.

largest of which was the war in Afghanistan. As the Soviet military presence abroad expanded, Soviet officers and enlisted men came into contact with numerous unfamiliar cultures, political systems, and economies. The USSR's capacity for projecting military power abroad also grew substantially during this period, especially with respect to naval power. This in turn brought new problems and challenges. The impact of these various developments during the past two decades on the Soviet military itself and on civil-military relations in the USSR is the subject of this chapter.

The war of attrition along the Suez Canal, 1969–1970, marked the first massive extension of either Russian or Soviet military power outside the Eurasian continent, yet it was only the beginning of a decade of extraordinary Soviet involvement abroad. The war of attrition was followed by Soviet intervention in the October war of 1973, the Angolan civil war of 1975–1976, the Ogaden war of 1977–1978, and the war in Afghanistan, 1979–1989. The latter conflict marked the first large-scale invasion and occupation of a Third World country by the Soviet Union. Until their withdrawal in 1989, more than 100,000 Soviet troops occupied Afghanistan for a period of over nine years, locked in warfare with the tribally based Afghan resistance forces. In other troubled outposts of the Soviet "empire" abroad, much smaller numbers of Soviet advisers and troops engaged in counterinsurgency warfare against a variety of anti-Communist movements.

It seems improbable that the Soviet armed forces could have lived through such a period of flux—in which roles and mission evolved significantly, and tens of thousands of troops were stationed outside the borders of the Warsaw Pact for the first time—without experiencing significant internal changes. It is also difficult to believe that the events of the 1970s and 1980s could have passed without having some effect on civil-military relations and on society and politics in the USSR in general. But while the USSR's involvement in foreign conflicts during these decades has been studied extensively by various scholars,[2] I am aware of only one other study that has attempted to examine the impact of involvement in the Third World on the Soviet military itself or on civil-military relations inside the USSR.[3] This is clearly an area in which further research is needed.

The principal subject or "dependent variable" that this study seeks to analyze is the civil-military relationship in Soviet politics. This is no easy task, given the scarcity of hard data on the subject. Available information on Soviet

---

[2] See, for example, Stephen T. Hosmer and Thomas W. Wolfe, *Soviet Policy and Practice toward Third World Conflicts* (Lexington, Mass.: Lexington Books, 1983); Bruce D. Porter, *The USSR in Third World Conflicts: Soviet Arms and Diplomacy in Local Wars, 1945–1980* (Cambridge: Cambridge University Press, 1984); Francis Fukuyama, *Moscow's Post-Brezhnev Reassessment of the Third World*, R-3337-USDP (Santa Monica: Rand Corporation, February 1986).

[3] Francis Fukuyama, *Soviet Civil-Military Relations and the Power Projection Mission*, R-3504-AF (Santa Monica: Rand Corporation, April 1987).

military involvement in the Third World is fragmentary with respect to many of the "surrogate measures" of military or civilian influence identified by Timothy Colton in his introductory chapter. Data are particularly scarce with respect to conflicts occurring prior to the war in Afghanistan. One Western scholar has pointed out that the Soviets tend to praise publicly military officers who contribute to "motherland defense," while largely concealing efforts by the military to expand Soviet influence abroad—"foreign expeditions."[4] Beginning around 1983, the conflict in Afghanistan evidently moved at least partly into the category of "motherland defense," because the Soviet media began devoting considerable attention to the achievements of Soviet officers and men serving there. This wealth of data contrasts with the scarcity of detailed information about Soviet military activities in earlier Third World conflicts. This also means that the materials on which this chapter is based, as well as its conclusions, tend to be somewhat skewed by the Soviet experience in Afghanistan. This may be a minor handicap, given that the conflict in Afghanistan was by far the largest and most important the USSR was involved in since World War II—and certainly the one that has had the biggest impact on the military.

The Changing External Environment: Historical and Comparative Perspective

The Tradition of Limited Involvement

The Russian Empire, even in its imperial heyday, was almost entirely a continental power, with little overseas presence, military or otherwise. Russia's territorial ambitions were as vast as any of the great powers of Europe, but it fulfilled those ambitions by linear expansion, not by joining the race for empire overseas. This continental orientation and preoccupation with homeland defense remained a fundamental geopolitical trait of Russia long after the Bolsheviks assumed power. Prior to World War II, the Soviet Union did little of consequence in the developing world; most of that world was, in any event, under the dominion of other industrialized powers, and Moscow lacked the military wherewithal to engage them in the competition for territory or influence. The unsuccessful attempt of the Red Army to intervene in Poland in 1920 persuaded Lenin that Soviet armed forces should not be used directly for

---

[4] Henry S. Bradsher, *Afghanistan and the Soviet Union* (Durham: North Carolina Press, 1983), 216. One sign that this may be changing was the flurry of articles that appeared in *Krasnaia zvezda* in March 1989 on the subject of Soviet military advisers in the Third World. See *Krasnaia zvezda*, 25 March 1989 (two articles) and 27 March 1989. See also the discussion in a later section of this chapter.

advancing revolutionary causes abroad.[5] The Soviet Union did attempt to provide military assistance to Kemal Pasha in Turkey, and it became militarily involved in behalf of the Kuomintang, but by the late 1920s the Soviet regime had entered a period of internal consolidation, concentrating on the building of "socialism in one country."

The USSR's victory in World War II brought about the extension of Soviet military power and the Soviet political system into Eastern Europe. The immediate postwar period also witnessed a half-hearted Soviet effort to support the Chinese Communist struggle against the Nationalist government of Chiang Kai-shek, and massive Soviet military assistance to North Korea in its attack on the South in June 1950. These developments, however, reflected the traditional Soviet preoccupation with regions of the world contiguous to its own borders. It was not until after Stalin's death that the Kremlin began to extend its military reach into more distant regions of the globe.

Under Nikita Khrushchev, the Soviet Union became for the first time a large-scale supplier of arms to the non-Communist Third World. The USSR's debut as an extracontinental power took the form of a $250 million arms agreement signed in 1955 between Czechoslovakia and Egypt (but sanctioned and underwritten by Moscow). Within a decade, the Soviet Union had intervened by means of arms shipments in at least four Third World conflicts—in Yemen, Indonesia, Laos, and the Congo—and had undertaken additional arms deals with more than a dozen Third World countries. In none of these instances, however, were Soviet troops directly involved to any significant degree. Soviet military officers performed training and logistical assignments in various Third World countries but did not engage directly in combat. Outside the Warsaw Pact and Mongolia, probably no more than a few hundred Soviet military officers were stationed abroad at any given time. It is difficult to see how such a small presence overseas could have had much effect on the Soviet military as a whole.

Growing Involvement in the Third World

The external environment facing the Soviet military began to change significantly as a result of the USSR's growing involvement in the Middle East from 1967 to 1973. Following the June 1967 war, Moscow sent massive quantities of arms to Egypt, as well as thousands of Soviet military advisers. Prior to the war, approximately six hundred Soviet military advisers had been in Egypt; at the peak of involvement in the war of attrition, the Soviet presence in Egypt reached over twenty thousand troops. It represented the largest extension in

[5] Chiang Kai-shek, *Soviet Russia in China: A Summing-up at Seventy* (New York: Farrar, Strauss & Cuhady, 1957), 22.

history of either Russian or Soviet military power overseas. Nor was this a merely passive force of advisers and trainers. During the war of attrition, thousands of Soviet military advisers engaged in a wide variety of combat and combat support roles; among other things, Soviet soldiers flew air combat missions and manned SAM installations.

On 8 July 1972, President Anwar Sadat nationalized the military facilities constructed by the USSR in his country and ordered the withdrawal of all but about a thousand Soviet advisers from Egypt. Resentment had been building over the almost complete autonomy afforded the Soviet advisers and what many Egyptian officials felt were their overbearing and arrogant ways.[6] Within less than a year, however, a partial rapprochement had taken place, and thousands of tons of Soviet arms and numerous new military advisers poured into Egypt once again. This build-up culminated in the October 1973 Middle East war, in which Soviet troops and advisers were more extensively involved than in any Third World conflict up to that time.

An estimated three thousand to four thousand Soviet military advisers were in Egypt and Syria when the war broke out. Soviet military personnel participated in a broad range of combat support operations: air force technicians reassembled MiG-21s that had been shipped to Syria by air; Soviet troops drove tanks from Latakia and Tartous to Damascus; Soviet air traffic controllers operated radar equipment flown in from the USSR; Soviet military engineers repaired military equipment damaged in the fighting. Soviet officers accompanied Syrian air-defense and ground units everywhere except on the front line, and Soviet advisers reportedly were assigned to Syrian command posts from battalion level up. Soviet soldiers are reported to have participated in manning air-defense systems as well.

After the war, however, Soviet-Egyptian relations rapidly resumed their downward course. Sadat steadily reduced the Soviet presence in Egypt, diversified his country's sources of weaponry, and, in March 1976, terminated the Treaty of Cooperation and Friendship signed with the USSR in 1971. Moscow's loss of influence inside Egypt was almost total, a situation that did not change much during the following decade.

The Soviet fiasco in Egypt was no doubt a factor that led the Kremlin to rely more on radical, Marxist-Leninist parties and governments in its efforts to gain influence in the Third World during the remainder of the 1970s.[7] But despite

---

[6] See Mohamed Heikal, *Sphinx & Commissar: The Rise and Fall of Soviet Influence in the Middle East* (London: Collins, 1978), 238; Mohamed Heikal, *The Road to Ramadan* (New York: Quadrangle, 1975). Sadat also makes some interesting comments in *In Search of Identity: An Autobiography* (New York: Harper & Row, 1977).

[7] An excellent Western analysis of this shift in the USSR's policy is Donald Zagoria, "Into the Breach: New Soviet Alliances in the Third World," *Foreign Affairs* 57 (Spring 1979), 738. For Soviet sources, see the Ulianovskii article in *Pravda*, 3 January 1968; A. Iskenderov, "The National Liberation Movement in Our Time," *Third World, Problems and Prospects: Current*

the infelicitous outcome, the experience in Egypt did give thousands of Soviet military officers and enlisted men firsthand experience in dealing with nationals from a Third World country. Such large numbers of Soviet military men had never served outside the perimeters of the Warsaw Pact before, and their experience in Egypt must have shaped their outlook on the Third World for years to come. Soviet involvement in the war of attrition and the October war also gave the Soviet armed forces practical experience in combat and combat support (particularly logistics) that they could not have received except through involvement in an actual conflict.

The fall of Saigon in April 1975 marked a signal foreign policy success for the USSR that helped compensate for the continuing decline of Soviet influence in the Middle East. For over a decade the Soviet Union had provided massive military assistance to Hanoi, amounting to well over $3 billion in arms shipments and supplies. Soviet support was a critical factor in making possible North Vietnam's victory over the U.S.-supported regime in the South. The collapse of the South marked the first time in postwar history that a Soviet ally, supported by Soviet arms, had defeated a U.S. ally backed by American arms and support. By plunging the United States into a troubled period of neo-isolationism, the fall of Saigon also paved the way for a series of Soviet initiatives in the Third World during the latter half of the 1970s. From 1975 to 1980, no less than seven pro-Soviet Communist or radical leftist regimes came to power by armed force, all of them as the result of civil wars or coups in which Soviet-supplied weaponry and Soviet diplomatic support played a prominent role.

In terms of the magnitude of Soviet military involvement, the most significant of these conflicts were the Angolan civil war (1975–1976), the Ogaden war (1977–1978), and the war in Afghanistan (1979–1989). In the first two conflicts, massive Soviet military assistance helped consolidate the rule of pro-Soviet regimes over two strategically valuable African countries. Large numbers of Soviet forces were not directly involved in the conflicts, however. Instead, Soviet military advisers helped consummate a wedding between Soviet arms (shipped by air and sea in massive quantities) and Cuban troops (transported to Africa with Soviet assistance). Cuban troops enabled the USSR to claim dramatic military successes in both wars without committing its own forces on the ground.

Estimates of the number of Soviet military advisers in Angola range from 170 to 400.[8] The role of Soviet advisers in Angola was low-key and strictly limited in terms of involvement in actual combat. This was not the case in the

---

Stages of the National Liberation Struggle (Moscow: Progress Publishers, 1970), 11–43; and A. Kiva, "Strany sotsialisticheskoi orientatsii: nekotorye osobennosti politicheskogo razvitiia," *Mezhdunarodnaia zhizn* (September 1973), 38–47.

[8] *Strategic Survey* (1975), 32; *Newsweek*, 1 December 1975; 19 January 1976; *Washington Post*, 18 February 1976.

Horn of Africa, where as many as 1,500 Soviet military advisers participated in assisting Ethiopian forces against Somalia's incursion. In this instance, two high-level military officers, V. I. Petrov, first deputy commander-in-chief of Soviet ground forces, and G. G. Barisov, former commander of Soviet forces in Somalia, are reported to have played a prominent role in command and control of Cuban and Ethiopian forces on the ground.

At least some of the Soviet military advisers who served in Ethiopia had previously been stationed in Somalia, where the USSR for nearly fifteen years had been cultivating a client state and building an infrastructure that by 1977 was the closest thing to a Soviet military base anywhere in the Third World. Some 11,700 Soviet military advisers were stationed in Somalia by 1977, and the Soviet fleet enjoyed access to facilities at three Somalian ports. One of those ports, Berbera, was the site of extensive docking, communications, and missile support facilities constructed entirely by the USSR. As the conflict between Ethiopia and Somalia gradually heated up during the course of 1977, the USSR leaned increasingly toward Ethiopia, eventually precipitating a Somali decision on 13 November 1977 to expel all Soviet and Cuban military advisers. The loss of Somalia was more than compensated by the establishment of close ties with the radical, Marxist-Leninist regime of Haile Mariam Mengistu in Ethiopia. Ethiopia's size, resources, and influence in black Africa made it of far greater strategic importance to the USSR than Somalia had been.

Even as the Soviet Union was becoming embroiled militarily in Africa, it was also advancing its political influence and military presence in the Far East. This came about primarily by means of the special Soviet relationship with Vietnam, a relationship codified by a formal treaty of alliance signed in November 1978. The signing of that treaty was almost certainly a contributing factor in Vietnam's decision shortly thereafter to launch an invasion of Cambodia with the aim of overthrowing the pro-Chinese regime of Pol Pot. When China responded in February 1979 with a punitive military incursion into Vietnam, the USSR undertook a large-scale airlift of arms to Vietnam. China decided only a few months later to retreat from Vietnam, leaving the whole of Indochina under Vietnamese and hence (to some degree at least) Soviet influence.

As a natural outgrowth of these developments, the latter part of the 1970s and early 1980s witnessed a build-up of Soviet forces in Vietnam, particularly in Cam Ranh Bay, where the Soviet fleet began operating out of facilities at one time built by the United States. By 1986, between seven thousand and ten thousand Soviet forces were deployed in Vietnam. With the exception of East Germany, this was the largest single body of Soviet forces then deployed in any foreign country not contiguous to the USSR (i.e., beyond the reach of immediate ground reinforcements from the homeland). For this reason alone, the Soviet presence in Vietnam was an important experiment for the USSR. Relations with the host country, however, were anything but untroubled; there is much evidence to suggest that Vietnam was not happy with its near total dependence on Moscow.[9]

The invasion of Afghanistan in December 1979 was a watershed event in the military annals of the Soviet Union. It was the first time the USSR had invaded a Third World country; indeed, the first time since World War II that massive numbers of Soviet ground forces engaged in direct combat operations anywhere. The number of Soviet troops exceeded by a factor of four or five the number of Cuban troops involved in earlier conflicts in Africa. The war also resulted in numerous Soviet battlefield casualties for the first time since World War II. By comparison with Afghanistan, Soviet involvement in other postwar crises and conflicts amounted to little more than dabbling.

The war in Afghanistan also represents a striking example of an essentially new phenomenon of the postwar era: the USSR as a counterinsurgency power. Much like the United States in Vietnam, the Soviet Union in Afghanistan was supporting an urban-based regime with which it was allied against an insurgent force based largely in the countryside. The Soviets in the 1980s faced similar (albeit far smaller) situations in Cambodia, Ethiopia, Angola, Mozambique, and Nicaragua. (In the latter case, Cuba is the first-line ally of Managua, while the USSR plays a more distant role.) In Angola, Soviet advisers are reported to have played a direct role in combat operations conducted by the Angolan Army against UNITA forces in the southern part of the country, and in both Laos and Cambodia, Soviet advisers are reported to have lost their lives as a result of the fighting.[10]

As of 1989, the war in Afghanistan represented the pinnacle of Soviet military activities in the Third World. There has been no event or intervention even remotely approaching it in the 1980s, and Gorbachev's emphasis on international detente and internal reconstruction clearly lessens the likelihood of Soviet military activism in the Third World in the near term. In retrospect, the extraordinary Soviet activism abroad of the 1970s may have been but one manifestation of a "golden age" in Soviet foreign policy, parallel to the "golden age in Soviet civil-military relations" that Jeremy Azrael has suggested took place in the Brezhnev era.[11]

By contrast, the 1980s have been a period of consolidation, retrenchment, and even partial retreat for the Soviet Union. This trend began to emerge in the late Brezhnev years and developed under Andropov and Chernenko, but only under Gorbachev did its full significance become apparent. In his keynote address to the Twenty-seventh Party Congress, Gorbachev clearly down-

---

[9] An excellent study of the relationship is Douglas Pike, *Vietnam and the Soviet Union: Anatomy of an Alliance* (Boulder: Westview, 1987).

[10] AP and Reuters, 7 August 1986; *Bangkok World*, 17 May 1978; see also *New York Times*, 8 January 1978.

[11] Jeremy Azrael, *The Soviet Civilian Leadership and the Military High Command, 1976–1986*, R-3251-AF (Santa Monica: Rand Corporation, 1987), 2.

played the significance of the Third World, devoting less attention to it than any postwar Soviet leader ever had done in the equivalent forum. This shift in emphasis led to real changes in Soviet policy and behavior.

Shortly after coming to power, Gorbachev began to take steps to end the conflict in Afghanistan; by 1989, he had withdrawn all Soviet forces. The Soviet leadership also began to retreat from regional conflicts and counterinsurgency in general. Moscow took an active role in support of a U.S.-mediated settlement in Namibia, and it actively encouraged regional settlements of conflicts in Indochina and the Middle East. During the 1980s, the USSR significantly increased its military presence in only one country in the Third World (Syria) and, aside from Afghanistan, became involved militarily in only one new regional conflict, namely, the Lebanon crisis of 1982. This latter involvement arose out of the Soviet relationship with Syria, and Soviet behavior during the crisis suggests an effort to retain the confidence of its Syrian ally without doing anything that would escalate the hostilities. The involvement of Soviet advisers in Syria was strictly limited.[12]

A variety of factors—economic troubles, a profound social crisis, leadership instability, and perhaps concern over the U.S. military build-up of the Reagan years—impelled the Soviet leadership in the 1980s to concentrate on consolidating foreign advances and repairing the Russian heartland, rather than pressing for further gains in the Third World. In retreating from Third World activism, the leadership of the Kremlin was simply resuming a foreign policy approach more in line with traditional Russian and Soviet behavior than had been the case in the 1970s.

The Relative Magnitude of Soviet Military Involvement Overseas

The actual dimensions of the Soviet military presence in the Third World from 1945 to 1989 were relatively small by comparison with the U.S. presence overseas. In 1985, the year that Gorbachev became general secretary of the CPSU and the Soviet presence in Afghanistan was at its peak, the USSR had approximately 720,000 military personnel outside its borders. Of these, roughly half a million were stationed in the Warsaw Pact countries of Eastern Europe. Of the remaining 220,000, some 75,000 were in Mongolia and 115,000 in Afghanistan, both countries contiguous to the USSR. Even when troops stationed in the Warsaw Pact are included, less than 10 percent of total Soviet military personnel were based outside Soviet borders. Only 4.1 percent

---

[12] Sources vary on the number of Soviet military personnel stationed in Syria by the mid-1980s; estimates range from two thousand to six thousand, with several thousand more from other East Bloc countries. See *New York Times*, 16 December 1985; *New York Times Magazine*, 22 January 1984; *Foreign Report*, 9 July 1980; and Pedro Ramet, "The Soviet-Syrian Relationship," *Problems of Communism* (September–October 1980), 35–36.

were stationed outside Warsaw Pact territory (including the USSR), the vast majority in Mongolia and Afghanistan.

Measured as a percentage of total military forces, the Soviet commitment abroad is considerably smaller than that of the United States. The United States deploys over 16 percent of its total forces overseas, a much higher percentage than the USSR; moreover, approximately 7.8 percent of its total military forces are outside of NATO territory proper. In stark contrast to the USSR, most U.S. forces deployed outside NATO are at great distances from U.S. borders (with over 110,000 stationed in South Korea, Japan, the Philippines, or other Pacific bases, not counting forces afloat). This greater relative commitment of the United States overseas reflects the fact that it is predominantly a naval power, while the USSR has always been, and remains, a land power.

The Soviet intervention in Afghanistan is often compared with the U.S. experience in Vietnam. To put that analogy in perspective, however, the relative commitment of each superpower to the respective conflict must be analyzed. Over 21 percent of total U.S. forces were deployed in Vietnam in 1970, at the peak of that conflict; the corresponding figure for the Soviet Union in Afghanistan was only 2.1 percent in 1985. In other words, the relative commitment of the United States in Vietnam was ten times the Soviet commitment in Afghanistan. Total U.S. fatalities during the war in Vietnam were 47,321 (1964–1973); total Soviet fatalities in Afghanistan from the invasion to the signing of the Geneva accord (1979–1988) were 13,310.[13] As a percentage of total national population, the Soviet toll in Afghanistan was less than one-fifth that of the United States in Vietnam.

This is a finding of considerable importance, for it suggests that the impact of Afghanistan on the Soviet military or on civil-military relations is likely to prove far less dramatic than the impact of Vietnam on the U.S. military. This was all the more true given the closed nature of Soviet society, which enabled the public impact of the conflict to be contained and its full dimensions to be hidden from the Soviet population. By contrast, the war in Vietnam was graphically portrayed on television and openly criticized in the U.S. press.

If the relative impact of Afghanistan is likely to have been less than that of

---

[13] Soviet fatality figures were announced by General A. D. Lizichev at a press conference on 25 May 1988. *Krasnaia zvezda*, 26 May 1988. Some Western observers have questioned this Soviet estimate, but it accords fairly well with estimates by Western intelligence agencies (as reported in various Western media). Lizichev also announced that 35,478 had been wounded, and 311 were missing. There were undoubtedly numerous additional casualties from the time of this announcement until the final withdrawal over eight months later. Soviet television in February 1989 reported on one very late fatality; see *New York Times*, 10 February 1989. The Estonian Komsomol newspaper *Noorte Haal* claimed that the number of Soviet fatalities in the war reached 50,000 and that more than a million men served there in the course of the conflict. *Noorte Haal*, 24 January 1989, cited in Valerii Konovalov, ''Afghan Veterans in Siberia,'' *Report on the USSR*, 1, 21 (26 May 1989), 16.

Vietnam, the domestic consequences of the USSR's earlier foreign adventures must have been minute indeed. From 1945 until the invasion of Afghanistan, the Soviet Union lost no more than a few hundred military personnel as a result of its military involvement in the Third World; the vast majority of these were not engaged in front-line ground combat, but were involved in logistical support, training, or specialized support missions.[14]

No matter how the historical record is examined, the Soviet Union emerges as a continental power that has undertaken only minimum military activity outside Europe. It seems probable, therefore, that the impact of foreign involvement on the Soviet military has been relatively minor compared to its impact on the United States or on other ocean-going powers of the past. The one countervailing argument to this premise would be that the war in Afghanistan—precisely because it was the USSR's first major shooting war since World War II—may have affected the Soviet military to a degree disproportionate to the actual magnitude of the conflict. Afghanistan is also on the Soviet border and more directly related to historical Russian security concerns than was Vietnam to the United States. Additional data presented later in this chapter will shed light on this possibility.

The Evolving Soviet Force Structure: Internal Controls vs. Expansionist Imperatives

Growing Capabilities for Power Projection

At the end of World War II, the USSR possessed the largest land army in Europe, and by 1949, it had acquired the atomic bomb. These two factors made it a superpower, but they did not make it a global power—one capable of projecting military force into any part of the globe. The USSR's capabilities for power projection were quite limited in the immediate postwar period, but major investments in this area were already under way prior to Stalin's death. By the early 1960s significant advances had been made in naval power, and by 1970 real progress had been made in other mobility forces as well. The USSR had deployed several new classes of modern warships and had established a regular and substantial presence in the Atlantic, Mediterranean, and Indian oceans (from 1964 to 1970, annual ship-days in each ocean increased by a factor of ten or more). Soviet airlift capacity had increased through production of two new cargo aircraft, the An-12 and An-22, with the aggregate transport capability of Voennaia transportnaia aviatsiia (VTA, the air transport arm of the military) reaching an estimated 19.4 million ton-miles in 1970. Soviet sealift capacity had expanded dramatically, while the USSR had gained

---

[14] See Avigdor Haselkorn, "Soviet Military Casualties in Third World Conflicts," *Conflict* 2, 1 (1980), 73–86.

access to several port facilities in the Third World and had established anchorages in international waters at several critical geographical points.[15]

Soviet power projection capabilities continued to grow throughout most of the 1970s. The USSR added small attack carriers to its fleet (beginning with the 38,000-ton Kiev in 1975) and began construction of its first large-deck, nuclear-powered aircraft carrier. Large investments in the expansion and refurbishment of Soviet shipyards made possible the procurement of numerous new ocean-going vessels. By 1985, the number of Soviet principal surface combatants had reached about 285 major warships, 78 amphibious vessels, and over 500 small combatants and mine warfare units. The Soviet navy had undertaken construction of at least four new classes of nuclear-powered battle cruisers and a new class of logistics support vessels, the Berezina class. Soviet amphibious assault capabilities were modestly enhanced through enlargement of the size of its naval infantry forces and through acquisition of two Ivan Rogov class amphibious assault vessels, having three times the capacity of the earlier Alligator class vessels. The USSR also conducted a number of highly sophisticated, global naval exercises during the 1970s.[16] Soviet warships have not engaged in combat in any Third World conflict to date, but their presence offshore was evident in several regional conflicts in the 1970s, with deployments apparently aimed at deterring possible U.S. responses.[17]

The USSR's air and sea transport capabilities likewise increased substantially between 1970 and 1986. Its airlift capacity was greatly enhanced by the deployment, beginning in 1971, of the Il-76 jet transport plane, 310 of which were in service by 1986. The USSR was also developing a new transport plane, the An-400, with a capacity reportedly larger than the U.S. C-5. Total airlift capacity grew from 19.4 million ton-miles to over 30 million ton-miles between 1970 and 1986. The USSR still lagged behind U.S. capabilities in this respect, but its needs were proportionately less than those of the United States, given the closer proximity of Soviet air bases to most of Asia, the Middle East, and Africa.[18]

Soviet sealift capacity, primarily the responsibility of the Soviet merchant marine (which is entirely under military command), increased substantially during the period in question, reaching a total of 1,750 ships and a deadweight tonnage of 20.7 million. The addition of some seventeen roll-on/roll-off vessels to the merchant marine in the late 1970s was a particularly important

[15] See Porter, *The USSR in Third World Conflicts*, 49–52.

[16] *Understanding Soviet Naval Developments* (Washington, D.C.: Office of the Chief of Naval Operations, Department of the Navy, 1985), 25–33.

[17] On Soviet naval involvement in regional conflicts, see the relevant chapters in James M. McConnell and Bradford Dismukes, eds., *Soviet Naval Diplomacy* (London: Pergamon, 1978).

[18] *The Military Balance: 1986–1987* (London: International Institute for Strategic Studies, 1986), 39; Peter Borgart, "The Soviet Transport Air Force," *International Defense Review* (June 1979), 945–950.

addition to Soviet capabilities; it brought the total of Soviet Ro/Ro ships to over fifty-five, with at least thirty more on order.[19] This increase in Soviet military transport capabilities was an important factor enabling the USSR to intervene in the October war, the Angolan civil war, and the Ogaden war. However, as Soviet economic growth began to decline in the late 1970s, it became impractical for the USSR to sustain high levels of investment in power projection forces.

The New Thinking and the Decline in Mobility Investments

On 15 February 1989, the day the last Soviet troops departed Afghanistan, *Pravda* carried a lead editorial arguing that Afghanistan and Chernobyl had served as a school for "new political thinking" in the USSR. Since Gorbachev's accession to power in 1985, this phrase has become a convenient rubric for the adjustments in military doctrine, foreign policy, and international behavior that marked the Soviet Union's partial retreat from the Third World in the 1980s. These adjustments include reductions in the Soviet military presence abroad; a new emphasis on regional accommodations in the Third World; greater emphasis on arms control agreements as a component of Soviet security; changes in Soviet military doctrine, including focusing on defensive operations and advocating "reasonable sufficiency" rather than superiority; diplomatic support of international cooperation; and a repudiation of nuclear weapons as a practical military option.[20]

The "new political thinking" was obviously fraught with implications for Soviet policy toward the Third World and for civil-military relations in the USSR. Even during the later Brezhnev years, however, well prior to the advent of the "new thinking," the Soviet Union was reducing its investments in mobility forces. Because procurement schedules usually lag several years behind political trends, it is always problematic to draw firm conclusions about one from the other.[21] But the timing of these reductions suggests that the "new thinking" was as much a logical consequence of declining Soviet military capabilities in this area as a cause.

[19] *Understanding Soviet Naval Developments*, 73–74; see also Donald C. Daniel, "Merchant Marine," in *Soviet Armed Forced Review Annual 1977*, ed. David R. Jones (Gulf Breeze, Fla.: Academic International, 1977), 87.

[20] An excellent discussion of the new political thinking as it affects Soviet policy toward the Third World is Francis Fukuyama, *Gorbachev and the New Soviet Agenda in the Third World* (Santa Monica: Rand Corporation, 1989).

[21] On the relationship between procurement schedules and political decision making, see Dimitri N. Ivanoff and Frank M. Murphy, "A Methodology for Technological Threat Projections of Soviet Naval Antiship and Surface to Air Missile Systems," in *Naval Power in Soviet Policy*, ed. Paul J. Murphy (Washington, D.C.: U.S. Air Force, 1978), 135–154. In particular, see the subsection entitled "Analysis of Soviet Cyclical RDT&E Patterns," 136–137.

There was a noticeable decline, for example, in the rate of growth of Soviet naval forces in the 1980s. Michael MccGwire has made a persuasive case that this decline actually resulted from decisions made as early as 1976.[22] Programs such as the Berezina fast-replenishment ship and the Ivan Rogov landing ship were canceled or sharply curtailed as a result of these decisions; the large-deck, American-style aircraft carrier program may also have been canceled. The total per annum number of ship days in distant oceans logged by the various Soviet fleets also began to decline noticeably after 1984. By 1987, ship-days in the Mediterranean had declined by 30 percent from their peak in 1976, and in the Pacific by 44 percent from a 1979 peak.[23]

The tapering off of Soviet investments in mobility forces continued in the last half of the 1980s, which MccGwire argues was a direct consequence of the "new political thinking" and of decisions made by Gorbachev and his colleagues.[24] It is important to keep in mind, however, that the rate of growth of certain other, more important, Soviet weapons programs was also leveling off or declining during the 1980s, not only because of changes in doctrine and strategy, but also due to the stagnation of the entire Soviet economy. Moreover, most Soviet navy vessels suitable for power projection missions are also assigned anti–submarine warfare missions that are critical in Soviet planning for both conventional and nuclear war; cutbacks in naval forces are therefore not necessarily related solely to Soviet rethinking of Third World policy. Both the "new thinking" and the decline in Soviet mobility investments reflect a larger crisis of the entire Soviet system.

The Expanding Navy and the Challenge of Civilian Control

The Soviet leadership traditionally has been greatly concerned with maintaining tight political control over its military forces. The Soviet military leadership, in turn, has been fixated on maintaining operational control over its forces in the field, extending this even to small units and local tactical decisions that most Western armies leave to the discretion of lower-level commanders.

The rapid expansion of the Soviet fleet has posed special problems in this regard, which have not been obviated by the recent declines in naval spending. A warship, though nominally under the command of another ship or of land-

[22] Michael MccGwire, *Military Objectives in Soviet Foreign Policy* (Washington: Brookings, 1987), 107–112; MccGwire, "Gorshkov's Navy," unpublished manuscript, February 1989, 20–24.

[23] On the tapering off of Soviet naval programs in the 1980s, see Fukuyama, *Soviet Civil-Military Relations*, 44–48. Ship-day figures are from *Understanding Soviet Naval Developments*, 21, and from U.S. Naval Intelligence Command (Freedom of Information Act request).

[24] MccGwire, "Gorshkov's Navy," 26–34.

based headquarters, is highly autonomous; in practice it can and must make many decisions on its own. The far-flung distances over which modern naval warfare can take place, and the increasing importance of air power for naval warfare, make this all the more true today. Admiral V. N. Chernavin, commander-in-chief of the Soviet Navy, acknowledged the challenge in an article calling for perestroika in the fleet in connection with the Twenty-seventh Party Congress: "The magnitude and novelty of the tasks now facing the fleet present special demands on the political and professional quality of party workers."[25]

Maintaining political control over ships deployed worldwide is indeed a thorny problem. Political officers are aboard warships, of course, but they would have little opportunity to summon help in the event of mutiny or defection. Their own lack of direct contact with other political officers while afloat also increases the likelihood of their being co-opted by their shipmates. Soviet naval literature demonstrates an acute awareness of these problems. They have also been dramatized in a popular American novel, *The Hunt for Red October*, about the defection of a Soviet nuclear submarine to the United States.[26] In recent years, numerous articles in *Morskoi sbornik*, the navy's main journal, have discussed the challenges associated with maintaining political control on distant voyages.[27] One article minced no words in identifying the essential problem: "The departure of a ship to sea requires the immediate activation of ideological efforts. [This is] because long voyages presuppose stops at foreign ports, where bourgeois propaganda, particularly at the present time, is making attacks on the hearts and minds of Soviet seamen."[28] The possibility of defections, mutiny, or simply ideological contamination is obviously of growing concern for a fleet that is increasingly deployed thousands of miles from Soviet shores.

A particularly interesting article on this subject was written by the head of the political section of the Black Sea Fleet, Vice-Admiral S. Rybak, in the April 1986 issue of *Morskoi sbornik*.[29] Calling for new approaches in the work of political officers on long voyages, Rybak warned about the "provocative maneuvers of ideological diversionists" against young, inexperienced, and homesick Soviet seamen. In almost Orwellian terms, he spoke of the necessity of conducting "hate lessons" to inculcate hatred among Soviet seamen of

---

[25] V. Chernavin, "Voenno-morskoi flot—XXVII sezdu KPSS," *Morskoi sbornik* (January 1986), 6.

[26] Tom Clancy, *The Hunt for Red October* (Annapolis: U.S Naval Institute Press, 1984).

[27] "Distant Voyages—Schools for the Training of Seamen," *Morskoi sbornik* (September 1976); "Uroki dalnego pokhoda," ibid., (October 1986), 28–31; "Vospitanie politicheskoi bditelnosti v dalnem pokhode," ibid. (April 1986), 9–13; V. Chernavin, "Voenno-morskoi flot—XXVII sezdu KPSS," 3–11 (esp. pp. 5–6).

[28] Ibid. (September 1976), 7.

[29] Ibid. (April 1986), 9–13.

imperialist "pirates," and he suggested that any contact with American ships calls for political lessons on what various acts of aggression the specific ships encountered have been involved in. The article also contains the following interesting passage: "Experience shows that the ideological aktiv should devote steadfast attention to the communications specialists. . . . The absence of such attention led to seaman radio-telegraphist N. Grinchak violating radio discipline during a long voyage." Communications officers, of course, could establish direct contact with foreign warships at any time, placing them in a particularly sensitive position.

The difficulties faced by political officers on long voyages are one theme discussed repeatedly and frankly in Soviet naval literature. The dilemma of serving as "watchdogs" while still having to live in close proximity to the rest of the crew is very real. On the one hand, a series of articles in *Morskoi sbornik* admonished political officers to take "an individual approach," displaying concern about individual sailors' everyday life, and getting to know each sailor as a person.[30] On the other hand, General A. D. Lizichev, chief of the Main Political Administration, criticized the political organs of the Black Sea fleet for "cases of nonprescribed interrelations within certain ships' crews," evidently meaning excessive fraternization. In short: take an individual approach, but do not become so familiar with the crew that you are co-opted.[31]

The political risks and challenges associated with maintaining blue-water naval forces are obviously compounded by the increasing importance of naval power in the nuclear equation. Soviet warships are believed to conduct most exercises and voyages without nuclear weapons on board, but in times of crisis or war such weapons would have to be deployed. Clearly this presents the political leadership with the challenge of assuring a highly reliable command and control system over its nuclear forces afloat; technological methods of control, such as activation codes and security devices, may not be sufficient for this if there are serious failings in crew discipline and loyalty.

Another area of concern reflected in Soviet military literature during the 1980s is the reliability of naval aviators and the necessity of vigorous political work aimed at this group.[32] A large number of land-based aircraft are under

[30] See, for example, Captain A. Vorobev, "Dokhodit do sertsa kazhdogo," ibid. (November 1984), 29–32; Vice-Admiral N. D. Iakonskii, "Far from Home Shores," *Kommunist vooruzhennykh sil* (November 1984), 44–48.

[31] A. Lizichev, "Purposefulness and Professionalism in Restructuring Party-Political Work," *Kommunist vooruzhennykh sil* (July 1986), 9–18. Other examples of articles devoted to the work of political officers include G. Konovalov, "Partiinaia organizatsia—tsentr povsednevnoi ideino-vospitatelnoi deiatel'nosti," *Morskoi sbornik* (January 1986), 12–17; A. Nikolaev, "Zavershaia attestovanie kadrov politrabotnikov," ibid. (July 1986), 11–14; Major General A. Sereikov, "Usilivaia partiinoe vliianie," ibid. (August 1986), 27–29.

[32] See, for example, V. Strutovskii, "Distsiplina poletov," ibid. (July 1984), 34–35; "Distsiplina i bezaposnost poletov," and S. Gulyaev, "Moralno-politicheskaia i psikhologicheskaia podgotovka aviatorov," ibid. (August 1984), 24–26; "Politrabotnik eskadrili—dolzhnost osoben-

the control of the navy, and the Soviets have not forgotten the defection of Lieutenant Colonel Viktor Belenko to Hakodate, Japan, in a stolen MiG aircraft. An airplane or helicopter aboard a ship is potentially even more autonomous, once airborne, than a land-based aircraft—it is likely to be closer to foreign airstrips, giving the pilot ample opportunity for defection if he chooses. The Soviet fleet as of early 1987 still had only a handful of ships able to carry helicopters and VSTOL aircraft, but construction of a nuclear-powered, large-deck aircraft carrier was under way, so this problem may be a growing one for the Soviet leadership.

Individual Soviet sailors have attempted to defect in the past, and there is at least one case on record of an attempted defection by an entire Soviet vessel. Several articles in *Krasnaia zvezda* in 1986 acknowledged growing discontent among Soviet sailors with the rigors of sea duty.[33] This may be one sign of the challenges and difficulties the USSR will face as it becomes an increasingly prominent actor on the world stage.

The inordinate Soviet obsession with the problem of political control at sea may hamper the development of the navy into a modern and effective fighting force. It may mean that the Soviet leadership is having difficulty making the transition from the outlook of a continental power to that of a global, seafaring power. Historically, that has been an exceptionally difficult transition to make, and the only truly successful seagoing powers have evolved as such from their earliest history.

Participation and Promotion: Third World Conflict and the Civil-Military Balance

In any country possessing a large military establishment, there is a delicate and not necessarily stable balance between civilian and military authorities. Priorities and perceptions differ, often leading to political disagreements; in times of conflict, such differences are often exacerbated. At the heart of this civil-military balance is the relationship between the top civilian authorities and the most senior members of the officer corps.

The achievement of military victory during wartime and the maintenance of military might during peacetime are the foremost preoccupations of military leaders everywhere. But aside from these universal concerns, two more parochial concerns preoccupy senior military officers: their participation in decision making and their prospects for personal promotion. This section will examine the degree to which the top Soviet officer corps has been involved in

---

naya,'' ibid. (February 1986), 26–28; ''Krepit distsiplinu morskikh aviatorov,'' ibid. (August, 1986), 3.

[33] See *Krasnaia zvezda*, 28 December 1985; 11 January 1986; 12, 15, 25, and 26 February 1986; and 14 March 1986.

TABLE 8.1
Senior Soviet Military Officers Who Have Served in Third World Outside
Afghanistan

Rank and Name	Nature of Service
Gen. V. I. Petrov	Served in Ethiopia 1978–79, while deputy commander-in-chief of Soviet ground forces; then served as commander of Soviet forces in the Far East (would have included Vietnam); promoted to commander-in-chief of ground forces and deputy minister of defense; in late December 1984 or January 1985 promoted to first deputy minister of defense.
Gen. G. G. Barisov	Headed Soviet forces in Somalia until expulsion; then joined Petrov in Ethiopia. Later promoted to commander of forces in Czechoslovakia; dismissed after visit by Gen. Epishev. Present status unknown.
Col. Gen. V. V. Okunev	Head of Soviet military mission in Egypt at time of expulsion, 1972. A specialist on missiles and air defense.
Maj. Gen. V. Beliaev	First deputy to chief Soviet military adviser in Angola (*Krasnaia zvezda*, 25 March 1989). Promoted, evidently while in Angola, to Lt. General.
B. I. Zhaivoronok	Commander of anti-aircraft unit stationed in Egypt during the war of attrition.
K. I. Popov	Commander of anti-aircraft division stationed in Egypt during war of attrition. Awarded "Hero of the Soviet Union" for service rendered in Egypt.

decision making regarding Third World conflicts and the extent to which service in such conflicts has affected patterns of promotion or demotion among senior officers. It will begin with the early conflicts, then explore four different aspects of the war in Afghanistan: the decision to intervene; the career path of officers who served there; the decision to withdraw; and the impact on the military of the postwithdrawal domestic political backlash.

The Officer Corps and the Early Conflicts

Career paths are difficult to track in the case of regional conflicts prior to the war in Afghanistan. As table 8.1 indicates, the names of only a handful of high-ranking Soviet officers who served in these conflicts are known. It is important, therefore, to be cautious in making generalizations on the basis of the few cases where information exists.

The case of General V. I. Petrov may be enlightening, nevertheless. Prior to 1978, Petrov had served a distinguished career in the army, having risen to the rank of army general in 1972 at the age of fifty-five. Much of his career had been spent in the Far East, where from 1972 to 1976 he was commander of the Far Eastern Military District. In 1976 he became first deputy commander-in-chief of ground forces, and in 1978 he was sent to Ethiopia to head up Soviet military operations in the Ogaden war. He is believed to have had actual command of Cuban and Ethiopian forces while in Ethiopia. How many months he served there is not known, but it was the most visible and important command role any Soviet officer had ever played in a Third World conflict up to that time.

Exactly why Petrov was chosen to go to Ethiopia is not clear, but his service there, and the resounding battlefield successes that resulted, appear to have given his career a major boost. In 1979 he was responsible for setting up the Far Eastern Supreme Command (Theater), combining the Far Eastern, Trans-baikal, and Siberian military districts, their air forces, and the Pacific Fleet. Interestingly enough, this would have given him ultimate responsibility for Soviet forces stationed in Mongolia and in Vietnam, the latter being among Moscow's most important and sensitive overseas deployments. Petrov then became commander-in-chief of ground forces and deputy minister of defense in 1980, a rapid promotion by any standard. In 1982, he was named a Hero of the Soviet Union, and in February 1985, he was identified as first deputy minister of defense.[34] Petrov retired in 1986, probably for reasons of health (it was rumored he had cancer).

It is impossible, of course, to know the precise impact on Petrov's career of his service in Ethiopia and his responsibility for Soviet forces in Vietnam. Other factors may have contributed to his rapid advancement, as well. But it is clear, at least, that his experience in the Third World was no liability, and it may have been of considerable benefit in his rapid ascent.

Equally interesting is the career path of General G. G. Barisov, who served alongside Petrov in Ethiopia. Barisov was in charge of the Soviet operation in Somalia at the time of the Soviet expulsion in November 1977. While Barisov might have been held accountable for this debacle, this does not seem to have occurred. He was transferred to Ethiopia, where he assisted Petrov in the war against Somalia (having the advantage of first-hand knowledge of Somalia's forces), and then went on to become commander of the highly important Central Group of Forces in 1981. The Central Group of Forces constitutes the five Soviet divisions stationed in Czechoslovakia; the importance of this group was considerable when Barisov took over because the Solidarity movement in Po-

---

[34] *Pravda*, 2 February 1985.

land was then thriving, and there was a serious possibility of a Soviet invasion of Poland. Barisov served in this command post until 1984, when he was replaced by Colonel General V. F. Ermakov, who, interestingly enough, was coming from a major command post in Afghanistan.

The career paths of Petrov and Barisov suggest that service in the Third World can be a positive, career-enhancing step for senior military officers. Petrov and Barisov seem to have earned the respect and trust of the highest military and civilian authorities for their efforts in Ethiopia and elsewhere; their service in such posts seems to have been an advantage in their career advancement.

It is interesting to note that three of the names in table 8.1 first appeared in a series of articles published in *Krasnaia zvezda* in March 1989, just over a month after the Soviet withdrawal from Afghanistan. Two of the articles appeared under the heading of "Our Military Advisers," and another was in response to a letter from a reader entitled "We fought also. . . ."[35] The publication of these articles was probably as much in response to the return of Soviet forces from Afghanistan as it was a manifestation of glasnost. One of the articles reveals that several Soviet officers who served in Egypt in 1970–71 during the war of attrition received medals and honors, including at least two awards of the coveted "Hero of the Soviet Union."[36]

Non-Soviet sources also give some indication of what the early Soviet experience in the Third World was like. Unfortunately, many of these sources are Third World nationals whose view of the Soviets may have been marked by national or ethnic prejudice. Several accounts from the Middle East, for example, indicate that the Soviet advisers in both Egypt and Syria acquired a reputation for being rude, arrogant, and brusque. In Egypt, this was a factor in Sadat's decision to expel most Soviet advisers in 1972; in the case of Syria, there have been numerous reports of tension between the Soviets and the local population, and reliable accounts suggest that several Soviet advisers or diplomats have been murdered. From Angola have come reports that Soviet advisers were even less popular than Cuban troops, whose reputation also was not the highest.[37] One problem (which U.S. forces abroad have also faced) was that Soviet officers were accustomed to living in a style viewed as excessively luxurious by local nationals. A high-level Ethiopian official had this to say about the Soviet advisers serving in that country during the Ogaden war:

> Ethiopia was required to pay the living expenses of the foreign personnel. The Soviets are very condescending, unlike the Cubans. They expect to live very luxu-

[35] *Krasnaia zvezda*, 25 March 1989 (two articles), and 27 March 1989. These may have been the first open references in the Soviet media to senior officers who served as military advisers in the Third World prior to the war in Afghanistan. See also ibid., 5 September 1985, which mentions in passing that the cousin of a Soviet soldier served as a military adviser in North Vietnam.

[36] "Tot egipetskii god," ibid., 25 March 1989.

[37] *New York Times*, 31 May 1988; *Washington Post*, 9 July 1988.

riously. One of the Soviet generals who was coming to Addis Ababa wanted to bring a chauffeur for his personal use. The Defense Minister refused unless the chauffeur were also a technical adviser. The general took the request to Mengistu who acquiesced.[38]

Incidents like this doubtless contributed to the unpopularity of Soviet officers abroad; there is no evidence, however, that their reputation abroad negatively affected their careers at home.

The Decision to Invade Afghanistan

Was the decision to invade Afghanistan in 1979 a source of contention between military and civilian leaders? Leonid Brezhnev stated that the invasion "was no simple decision," and the authoritative commentator Aleksandr Bovin claimed that it was "a very difficult decision."[39] Even assuming this was true, it does not necessarily follow that the decision caused serious civil-military discord. Until the Soviet withdrawal in February 1989, the Soviet media gave almost no hint of any disagreement or difference between the military and the party over the issue. After the withdrawal, some articles appeared suggesting that various leaders, both military and civilian, were reponsible for the decision to intervene. But those so charged were either dead or long since out of power; moreover, those making these charges may well have had other political agendas in mind. It is difficult to know how much veracity can be given to such claims.

Jiri Valenta, a Western scholar who has studied closely the pattern of Soviet decision making in foreign interventions since World War II, wrote in 1980 that "analysts have little information about the decision-making process preceding the invasion."[40] Frances Fukuyama conceded this also in 1987: "Unfortunately, we have very little evidence—direct, Kremlinological, or otherwise—concerning Afghanistan's effect on Soviet civil-military relations. The dearth of information is particularly acute with regard to the military's role in the original decision to intervene."[41] The absence of smoke suggests that the civil-military fire, if it existed at all, was probably a small one.

Until new evidence appeared after February 1989, analysts could point only to the lengthy visit of General I. G. Pavlovskii, commander-in-chief of Soviet Ground Forces, to Afghanistan from August to October 1979, as well to visits by the head of the Main Political Administration, General Epishev, and the first deputy minister of internal affairs, General Paputin, that same year. These

---

[38] See interview quoted in Porter, *The USSR in Third World Conflicts*, 203.

[39] *New York Times*, 3 January 1980; *Corriere della Sera* (Milan), 2 April 1980.

[40] Jiri Valenta, "From Prague to Kabul: The Soviet Style of Invasion," *International Security*, 5, 2 (Fall 1980), 122.

[41] Fukuyama, *Soviet Civil-Military Relations*, 50.

visits indicate that the military at least participated in the Soviet leadership's assessment of the situation. Pavlovskii's earlier prominent role in the invasion of Czechoslovakia, and circumstantial evidence that he supported a later (never realized) invasion of Poland in 1980, have led several Western scholars to infer that he probably advocated intervention in Afghanistan.[42] The evidence is slim, however; and whether Pavlovskii did so or not, it says little about whether or not his recommendation was in line with other military advice and was consistent with or opposed to the thinking of the political leadership.

New evidence on this issue came to light at the time of the Soviet withdrawal from Afghanistan. In March 1989, the reformist Soviet politician Boris Eltsin told a preelection meeting of Soviet voters that four Politburo members had made the decision to invade Afghanistan: Brezhnev, Ustinov, Suslov, and Gromyko.[43] This list, though logical, reveals little about what internal debates may have occurred; moreover, every man on it is now dead. Marshal Kulikov, who was a deputy minister of defense (and commander-in-chief of the Warsaw Pact) at the time of the invasion, also blamed the whole decision on the past civilian leadership: "Around midnight, Ustinov arrived and declared that we would cross the border tonight. That was all. Who took the decision? The leadership—that is the one thing I do know. And you know who was leading then."[44] The notion that the decision to invade was made by a small group of top leaders has also received support from Soviet Foreign Minister Eduard Shevardnadze, who was a candidate member of the Politburo at the time of the invasion. Five weeks after the Soviet withdrawal, in an interview with *Izvestiia*, he denied playing any role in the decision to enter Afghanistan. He claimed that the decision was taken "behind closed doors" by "a few very high-ranking officials," and that junior members of the Politburo like himself (and Gorbachev, though he did not mention his name) were only informed of the decision afterward.[45]

While the actual decision to invade Afghanistan may have been taken by a small group of top Soviet leaders, there is considerable evidence that the General Staff was consulted on the issue. Following the Soviet withdrawal, two senior Soviet military officers claimed publicly that the military had been consulted and that the General Staff had opposed the decision. Colonel General Dmitrii Volkogonov, head of the Institute of Military History, claimed in *So-*

---

[42] Ibid., 50–55; Bradsher, *Afghanistan and the Soviet Union*, 150–153; Jiri Valenta, "The Soviet Invasion of Afghanistan: The Difficulty of Knowing Where to Stop," *Orbis* (Summer 1980); and Thomas Hammond, *Red Flag over Afghanistan: The Communist Coup, the Soviet Invasion, and the Consequences* (Boulder: Westview, 1984), 97–98.

[43] Sergei Belitski, "Authors of USSR's Afghan War Policy," *Report on the USSR*, 28 April 1989, 11.

[44] *Krasnaia zvezda*, 4 March 1989.

[45] *Izvestiia*, 23 March 1989.

vetskaia Rossiia in March 1989 that Marshal Ogarkov opposed the invasion, as did Epishev and Volkogonov himself (who was then a senior officer in the Main Political Administration). Army General V. I. Varennikov, a member of the General Staff at the time of the invasion, told the Soviet magazine *Ogonëk* in the spring of 1989 that the General Staff had opposed the decision, and he specifically named Ogarkov and Akhromeev as having opposed it. He refused, however, to blame the decision on then Defense Minister Ustinov.[46]

It is quite conceivable that the General Staff opposed the invasion, but its opposition must have been rather token, for all of the officers cited in these recent accounts as dissenting—Epishev, Volkogonov, Ogarkov, Akhromeev, and Varennikov—continued to serve in high positions, and even to prosper, well after the war was under way. The same was true of General (later Marshal) Sergei Sokolov, whom Akhromeev has identified as head of the Operational Group within the General Staff that organized combat operations in Afghanistan.[47] Until further evidence becomes available, the most plausible assumption may be that the General Staff recommended against the decision, but that the level of civil-military discord over the issue never reached serious proportions.[48]

Career Paths of Officers Serving in Afghanistan

The war in Afghanistan would appear to be one conflict in the Third World where the USSR's military involvement was large enough to have made civil-military disputes over policy likely. The nature of the war was tailor-made for such disputes: the involvement of the Soviet military was direct and massive; Soviet participation was deliberately limited, making it the type of conflict to which military officers are loathe to commit forces and prestige; and the war was brutal and long lasting, with debilitating effects on morale among the rank-and-file of the Soviet Army. If the USSR's top military leadership thinks at all like military officers elsewhere in the world, it probably would have preferred a less restricted campaign and a push for swift victory.

[46] Vokogonov's and Varennikov's statements appear respectively in *Sovetskaia Rossiia*, 14 March 1989, and *Ogonëk*, no. 12 (1989), quoted in Belitski, "Authors of USSR's Afghan Policy," 13. Just prior to the Soviet withdrawal, another senior Soviet officer, Colonel General Nikolai Chervov, also commented on the Soviet entry into the war. In an interview on Radio Moscow (in English to Great Britain), he criticized the original decision and stated pointedly that "it involved directly the defense minister and the chief of General Staff," i.e., Ustinov and Ogarkov. He gave no indication that either of them had opposed the decision. Radio Moscow, 10 February 1989, cited in *FBIS*, 13 February 1989.

[47] *Krasnaia zvezda*, 2 July 1989.

[48] Vladimir Kuzichkin, a Soviet defector and former major in the KGB, has claimed that the KGB opposed the decision to invade Afghanistan but was overruled. He claims the KGB predicted that the war could not be won. "Coups and Killings in Kabul," *Time*, 22 November 1982.

Unfortunately, the "black box" of Soviet politics makes it difficult to know what discussions on the issue took place between senior civil and military leaders. One indirect way of detecting possible disputes is to track the career paths of senior officers involved in the conflict, since at the highest levels of the armed forces, promotions and career paths are more likely to be influenced by civilian authorities than by military officers alone. If civil-military disputes over the conduct of the war were prevalent, one would expect that at least some of the military leaders involved would have suffered career setbacks as a result. This does not appear to be the case; in fact, the opposite is true.

Table 8.2 is a listing of senior Soviet military leaders known to have played a major role in the planning or execution of the overall operation in Afghanistan.[49] It is striking that almost every officer on the list has received one or more promotions since his involvement in Afghanistan; most of those not promoted were at a minimum assigned to posts of equal importance. This promotion pattern strongly suggests that service in Afghanistan has been a career-boosting step for the Soviet officer corps; much like Vietnam for the U.S. armed forces, it may have been a desirable career "ticket" for ambitious officers.

Perhaps the top party leadership deliberately elevated officers who served in (or in connection with) the war in Afghanistan to bolster the morale of the top officer corps. Such promotions also may have been a demonstration of party support for the war effort and a signal that the party welcomed the combat experience acquired in the conflict. Whatever the reasons, this promotion pattern continued right through the end of the Soviet occupation. On 15 February 1989, the day the last Soviet troops pulled out of Afghanistan, newspapers around the world carried a TASS photograph of Lieutenant General B. V. Gromov, the commander of the Soviet contingent in Afghanistan, crossing the Friendship Bridge from Afghanistan into the USSR. That same day Radio Moscow announced Gromov's appointment as commander of the Kiev Military District—an exceptionally prestigious command for an officer only forty-five years old.[50]

As if to leave no doubt about the leadership's intentions, Radio Moscow also announced on the same day the promotion of Varennikov, first deputy chief of the General Staff, to the post of commander-in-chief of Soviet Ground Forces and deputy minister of defense. Varennikov had played a key role on the General Staff in the planning of the original invasion and subsequent plan-

---

[49] This list is not inclusive. A number of other generals are believed to have served in Afghanistan, but little is known of their activities. Among others, the following names have been mentioned in various sources: Zakharov, Kasperovich, Aunapu, and Grekov. Several colonels who served in the war became generals after their return home. These are not listed in the table except as otherwise noted.

[50] Gromov continued to receive a hero's treatment in the military press after the withdrawal. See, for example, the interview with him in *Krasnaia zvezda*, 22 July 1989.

TABLE 8.2
Senior Soviet Military Leaders Involved with Afghanistan Conflict

Most Recent Rank and Name	*Nature of Involvement*
Marshal S. F. Akhromeev	In 1979, deputy chief of General Staff and chief of Main Operations Directorate within Ministry of Defense responsible for planning combat operations in Afghanistan early in war. Promoted to marshal in 1983 and to chief of General Staff in 1984, replacing Ogarkov. In 1988, removed from post and assigned as general inspector of the Group of General Inspectors. Later assumed role of military adviser to Gorbachev.
Army Gen. V. I. Varennikov	Assisted Sokolov in planning of invasion; promoted to first deputy chief and head of Main Operations Directorate of General Staff in November 1979. Beginning in late 1987, stationed in Kabul. Responsible for coordinating withdrawal from Afghanistan in 1988–89. On same day withdrawal was completed, promoted to post of commander-in-chief of Soviet ground forces and deputy minister of defense.
Maj. Gen. V. Vasen	Played role in withdrawal; responsible for control and protection of convoys along roads to and from Afghanistan.
Col. Gen. V. A. Vostrov	Deputy to Iazov in Central Asian Military District; promoted and appointed to command Siberian Military District in November 1984. Reportedly served as military adviser in Afghanistan toward end of conflict. By 1988 was serving as commander of Main Administration of Military Education of Ministry of Defense.
Lt. Gen. L. E. Generalov	Believed to have been commander of limited Soviet contingent early in conflict. After service in Afghanistan, appointed first deputy commander of Carpathian Military District.
Maj. Gen. P. S. Grachev	Played important role inside Afghanistan at time of withdrawal. Awarded "Hero of the Soviet Union."
Lt. Gen. B. V. Gromov	Commander in Afghanistan from sometime in 1986 until Soviet withdrawal; also had earlier tours in Afghanistan, beginning as early as 1980. Promoted from major general to lieutenant general while in Afghanistan, and awarded "Hero of the Soviet Union" for service in "Operation Magistral," which broke blockade of Khost. Last Soviet officer to leave Afghanistan (15 February 1989). Same day appointed commander of Kiev Military District.

TABLE 8.2 (*cont.*)

Most Recent Rank and Name	Nature of Involvement
Army Gen. M. M. Zaitsev	Appointed in July 1985 commander-in-chief of Southern TVD (Theater of Military Operations) from position as commander of group of forces in Germany. Remained in this position, with major responsibilities for Afghanistan, until summer of 1988.
Maj. Gen. V. S. Kot	A colonel and commander of a fighter-bomber unit; awarded "Hero of the Soviet Union" and promoted to major general as a result of service in Afghanistan. Subsequently promoted to deputy commander for aviation in the Far East Military District.
Army Gen. P. G. Lushev	Served as Central Asian Military District commander at time of invasion. Promoted to army general and appointed commander of Moscow Military District late in 1980; thereafter promoted (July 1985) to commander of group of forces in Germany. Subsequently promoted to first deputy minister of defense, then promoted again to commander-in-chief of Warsaw Pact (early 1989).
Army Gen. Iu. P. Maksimov	Commander of Turkestan Military District, 1979–1984; during that time possibly head of Southern TVD. Played major role in first five years of conflict. Awarded "Hero of the Soviet Union" in 1982 while holding rank of colonel general. Promoted to commander-in-chief of Strategic Rocket Forces and deputy minister of defense in July 1985, where he served until retirement in April 1989.
Lt. Gen. N. K. Martynuk	Commander of frontal aviation of Turkestan Military District during invasion.
Lt. Gen. V. G. Mikhailov	First deputy to Maksimov during latter's tour as commander of Turkestan Military District. Probably commanded ground forces during initial invasion. Present status or assignment unknown.
Lt. Gen. A. A. Mikoian	Aviation general; commander of frontal aviation of Southern TVD involved in initial invasion.
Marshal N. V. Ogarkov	Chief of General Staff of USSR at time of invasion. Removed from position in September 1984; transfered to important command, but transfer represented effective demotion. Retired early 1989.
Army Gen. N. I. Popov	Appointed commander-in-chief of Southern TVD in summer of 1988, replacing Zaitsev. As such, likely played an important coordinating role in final withdrawal.

TABLE 8.2 (*cont.*)

Most Recent Rank and Name	Nature of Involvement
Army Gen. I. G. Pavlovskii	As deputy minister of defense and commander of ground forces, visited Afghanistan in August 1979 with a contingent of some sixty officers. Later believed to have helped form headquarters and planning staff in Turkestan Military District. Had been commander of 1968 invasion of Czechoslovakia. Removed from command and made head of Group of General Inspectors in December 1980.
Lt. Gen. V. S. Paputin	First deputy minister of internal affairs in 1979, at time of invasion. Heavily involved in planning of operation; visited Kabul shortly prior to invasion. Died in Kabul on 28 December 1979, but the cause of his death is not known. Suicide has been widely rumored.
Lt. Gen. I. N. Rodionov	Believed to have held a major command in Afghanistan from sometime in the mid-1980s to April 1987, during which time he was promoted to rank of lt. general. Probably replaced Generalov as commander of limited contingent of Soviet forces. Appointed in April 1987 as first deputy commander of Moscow Military District. In June 1988 promoted to commander of Caucasian Military District.
Army Gen. G. I. Salmanov	Served in Afghanistan 1984–86. Then appointed head of General Staff Academy.
Maj. Gen. L. B. Serebrov	A political officer promoted to rank of major general while serving in Afghanistan. Served as spokesman of Supreme Army Command in Afghanistan.
Lt. Gen. V. I. Sivenok	First deputy to Gen. Lushev during latter's command of Central Asian Military District.
Maj. Gen. A. E. Sliusar	Believed to have served as commander of an airborne assault division in Afghanistan; awarded ''Hero of the Soviet Union.'' Later promoted to position as commander of Riazan Higher Paratroopers Command School.
Maj. Gen. V. S. Sokolov	Chief of staff of limited contingent of Soviet troops in Afghanistan at time of withdrawal.
Marshal S. L. Sokolov	First deputy minister of defense at time of invasion; headed the Operational Group within MoD that planned invasion and organized subsequent combat operations. Awarded ''Hero of the Soviet Union'' in 1980. Promoted to minister of defense in December 1984. Ousted as minister in May 1987 as a result of Rust affair. Unlike predecessors, made candidate, rather than full, member of Politburo.

TABLE 8.2 (*cont.*)

Most Recent Rank and Name	Nature of Involvement
Lt. Gen. M. M. Sotskov	Involved in 1986 partial withdrawal of Soviet forces. Held a press conference in Kabul to discuss the withdrawal.
Maj. Gen. K. M. Tsagolov	A military adviser to the Afghan Army from 1981 to 1984 and again in 1987. A military academician, later appointed chief of Department of Marxism-Leninism of Frunze Military Academy.
Gen. P. I. Shkidchenko	Served in Afghanistan; died in air crash in January 1982.
Lt. Gen. L. S. Shustko	First deputy commander of Turkestan Military District until some time in 1986, when he was promoted to commander of North Caucasus Military District.
Army Gen. D. T. Iazov	Replaced Lushev as commander of Central Asian Military District in 1980; appointed in July 1984 to command Far Eastern Military District. Subsequently promoted (1987) to deputy minister of defense, then in May 1987, promoted to minister of defense, replacing Sokolov.
Maj. Gen. M. Evanov	Commander of 105th Air Assault Division Group involved in initial invasion.
Col. Gen. F. Ermakov	Commander of Soviet forces in Afghanistan, 1982–84; replaced Barisov as commander of of Soviet forces in Czechoslovakia in July 1985.

ning of combat operations. Later in the war he went to Kabul, and eventually he played a major role in coordinating the withdrawal of Soviet forces. Varennikov's promotion to such a high position on the very day of the Soviet withdrawal and despite his prominent role in all phases of the conflict was a striking manifestation of civilian support for the military, an indication that civilian authorities would not seek to blame the military for the conflict.[51]

General Pavlovskii, removed as deputy minister of defense and commander-in-chief of ground forces in December 1980, was one notable exception to the general pattern of almost automatic promotion of the top military officers involved with the war in Afghanistan. Pavlovskii's assessment of the situation in Afghanistan during his 1979 visit almost certainly was a factor in the Politburo's assessment of the risks and costs of invasion. The fact that he was moved out of his position only a year after the invasion certainly suggests the possibility that he had fallen from favor partly due to the advice and coun-

---

[51] It is interesting to note that the promotion of at least five other Soviet generals was also announced on 15 February 1989. Radio Moscow Domestic Service, 15 February 1989, cited in *FBIS*, 16 February 1989.

sel he had offered or was offering on Afghanistan. Sources in the Soviet Union recently have claimed that Pavlovskii actually opposed the invasion of Afghanistan, and that he had informed the Soviet leaders of his own assessment that an invasion was not necessary. These same sources claim that Pavlovskii's removal was directly related to the advice he gave on Afghanistan; it is difficult to know, however, how true this information is, coming more than ten years after his visit to Afghanistan.[52] Pavlovskii was seventy-one years old when he was transferred from his command to the Group of General Inspectors, so it is more likely that this was an honorable way to ease out of service an older officer who could no longer meet the demands of the job under the stress of a real war on the ground.

It is extremely interesting to note that the three senior Soviet generals most closely associated with the General Staff's planning of the invasion—Sokolov, Ogarkov, and Akhromeev—were all removed from the highest circles of the officer corps during the course of the war in Afghanistan. This appears to be only an interesting coincidence, however, since each individual's fall from favor took place many years after the war was under way, and evidently not for reasons related to the war. While it is conceivable that each was removed at least partly due to his involvement and role in the conflict, the weight of evidence would suggest otherwise.

Ogarkov was removed as chief of the General Staff in September 1984. When his demotion and reassignment took place, some Western observers initially speculated about a possible link to the military's performance in Afghanistan. Both *Pravda* and *Krasnaia zvezda* were searched thoroughly for the period from July 1984, however, through October 1984, with not a hint found of any link. There is far more evidence pointing to differences between Ogarkov and the civilian leadership over spending priorities and the role of new military technologies. The marshal, known for his outspoken brashness, also may have been made an object lesson for other military officers. By removing Ogarkov, the civilian leadership clearly demonstrated who was in charge—but there is no evidence to suggest that this demonstration of civilian authority was specifically linked to Afghanistan or any other Third World issue.

As for Sokolov, in 1979 in his position as first deputy minister of defense, he was chief of staff of the operational group within the General Staff that was responsible for the organization of combat operations in Afghanistan.[53] The record suggests that he was heavily involved in the planning and execution of the original invasion, perhaps more so than any other military man save Defense Minister Ustinov himself. Sokolov's career prior to 1979 shows him to be a loyal party member and a military officer who had the highest confidence of the civilian leadership. For seven years prior to his elevation to first deputy

---

[52] *New York Times*, 20 September 1989.
[53] Marshal Akhromeev revealed this in an interview to *Krasnaia zvezda*, 2 July 1989.

minister in April 1967, he had been in senior command and staff posts in the Moscow and Leningrad military districts, positions that surely demanded the utmost political loyalty. The rest of his career was spent in the Ministry of Defense in Moscow, where he received two promotions in rank (to army general and then marshal).

Sokolov must have retained the confidence of the top party leadership following the invasion of Afghanistan, despite the military setbacks there, for in December 1984 he was elevated to the post of minister of defense. The only possible glimmer of discontent is that in that post he was not made a full member of the Politburo, unlike his two predecessors. But he was awarded the Order of Lenin on his seventy-fifth birthday, and there is no evidence that the failure to elevate him to full membership in the Politburo was in any way linked to Afghanistan. More likely, it was a civilian effort to demonstrate forcefully who was ultimately in charge on a whole range of issues affecting the military, Afghanistan being only one of many.

There is likewise no evidence that Marshal Akhromeev's removal as chief of the General Staff in December 1988 was in any way related to the Soviet military's role in Afghanistan (which was then rapidly winding down in any event). Most Western observers linked his resignation to his opposition to Gorbachev's proposals for unilateral reductions in Soviet force structure, made earlier the same year. Akhromeev himself, speaking in an interview with *Krasnaia zvezda* in July 1989, said only that the decision to replace him came after the U.S.-Soviet summit meeting in the summer of 1988, "when it became clear that military tensions were declining."[54] The fact that he remained as military adviser to Gorbachev certainly suggests he was not totally out of favor.

A decade is a long time, particularly in the rarefied upper echelons of the Soviet officer corps, and many other events and developments other than the war in Afghanistan appear to have affected the career paths of Sokolov, Ogarkov, and Akhromeev. The career paths of three other officers listed in table 8.2 are also of special interest from the point of view of civil-military relations: namely, Iazov, Lushev, and Maksimov.

When Sokolov was removed as minister of defense in May 1987 in connection with the Rust affair, his replacement was Army General D. T. Iazov, who, as commander of the Central Asian Military District from 1980 to 1984, played an important role in supporting Soviet forces in Afghanistan both logistically (via ground lines of supply) and from the air. The simple fact that Iazov, following his service in Central Asia, was appointed to command the prestigious Far Eastern Military District only a few months after the shooting down of KAL 007 in September 1983—when the political sensitivity of Far Eastern air defense was still very high—suggests that his work in Central Asia had brought him to the attention of the highest military and political leader-

54 Ibid.

ship. Had Gorbachev and the rest of the party leadership wanted to reflect their disagreement or dissatisfaction with the military's performance in Afghanistan, they perhaps would not have selected an officer closely linked to the war effort to replace Sokolov as minister.

Shortly after Gorbachev's accession, in July 1985, there took place a major reshuffle of Soviet military commanders, including some who were involved in the conflict in Afghanistan. It is possible that these shifts were connected in some way to Gorbachev's unusual meeting with a large group of top military leaders in Minsk on 10 July, the proceedings of which are not available in the West. One main result of the transfers was two highly noteworthy promotions for generals Lushev and Maksimov, both of whom had figured prominently in the Afghan conflict.

The promotion of Army General P. G. Lushev was reminiscent of Sokolov's early promotions, but in reverse. Whereas Sokolov's service in the Moscow and Leningrad military districts seems to have strengthened civilian confidence in his reliability and so to have paved the way for his later prominent role in Afghanistan, Lushev's service in connection with the war in Afghanistan was a stepping stone to command of the Moscow Military District, which he assumed late in 1980. This was, of course, an ideal post from which to establish close ties with the civilian leadership; but, more to the point, he would never have received the position if his service in Central Asia had not won him the trust and favor of the political leadership. From Moscow he assumed, in connection with the July 1985 transfers, the weighty position of commander of the Group of Soviet Forces in Germany, from where he was promoted to first deputy minister of defense in 1985.

As for Army General Iu. P. Maksimov, he was commander of the Turkestan Military District from 1979 to 1984 and commander of the Southern Theater of Forces from at least 1984 to 1985. This made him perhaps the most senior commander for Afghanistan during the first five years of the war. His promotion in July 1985 to commander-in-chief of strategic rocket forces (and deputy minister of defense) suggests not only a reward for a job well done, but a desire on the part of the civilian leadership to leaven a very important branch of the military not involved in Afghanistan with the combat-bred toughness of a senior ground commander. An alternative explanation would be that the civilian authorities wanted to replace Maksimov with a new commander in the hope that the war effort could be moved forward, but they wanted to do this in a way that would not fault him or suggest that the military was to blame for the Afghanistan quagmire. Yet it seems unlikely that the post of commander of missile forces would ever be used as a consolation prize, so the first explanation seems more plausible.

In short, there is considerable evidence that the war in Afghanistan was a career-boosting step for the majority of senior Soviet generals involved with the conflict. The civilian leadership appears to have gone out of its way to reward members of the officer corps who served in Afghanistan with some of the finest and most prestigious command posts available. If there had been major civil-military disagreements over the prosecution of the war in Afghanistan, or if the civilian leadership had wanted to make an example of certain generals for their failure to produce a victory, this pattern probably would not have held true. Nor is it plausible to argue that the civilian leadership promoted its *afgantsy* generals out of fear that demotions or discipline would cause unrest in the military; Sokolov's sacking demonstrated that the civilian leadership, under Gorbachev at least, had no problem exerting discipline or finding scapegoats when needed. The conclusion follows, therefore, that the civilian authorities accepted the military's performance in Afghanistan, and that there was a fair degree of agreement among civil and military authorities on the conduct of the war.

The Decision to Withdraw from Afghanistan

Samizdat literature and interviews with Soviet émigrés and travelers abroad indicate that public support for the Afghanistan campaign began to wane noticeably after 1984, and that some isolated public manifestations of discontent appeared.[55] This growing discontent at home with the war, combined with the deepening internal crisis of the Soviet system and the lack of military success in Afghanistan, undoubtedly contributed to top-level reassessments of the war and the ultimate decision to seek a political solution leading to withdrawal.

Not long after Gorbachev's accession to power, signs began to appear of possible Politburo-level rethinking of the war in Afghanistan. Shortly after Gorbachev replaced Chernenko in March 1985, he made a statement that suggested the USSR was eager to reach a settlement of the Afghanistan conflict. At the Twenty-seventh Party Congress in early 1986, Gorbachev pointedly referred to the war as "a bleeding wound," and articles began to appear in the Soviet media critical of various aspects of the conflict. Examined closely, however, Soviet statements in 1985 and 1986 still did not indicate a fundamental shift from the political line taken by Gorbachev's predecessors—that an end to the conflict would depend on a cessation of all Western aid to the Afghan resistance and on the security of the present regime in Kabul being assured.

When Gorbachev announced a modest withdrawal of Soviet troops from

---

[55] See, for example, *Sobesednik*, no. 50 (1986); no. 1 (1987); and *Molod Ukrainy*, 15 January 1987. See also the report on a Soviet documentary film, "Is It Easy to Be Young?" in *U.S. News and World Report*, 16 March 1987. On the general waning of public support, see "The Soviet Public and the War in Afghanistan: A Trend Toward Polarization," *Soviet Area and Audience Opinion Research*, AR 1-87, March 1987; and Sallie Wise, " 'A War Should Never Have Happened': Soviet Citizens Assess the War in Afghanistan," RL 226/88, *Radio Liberty Research Bulletin*, 1 June 1988.

Afghanistan on 28 July 1986, many Western observers suggested that he may have taken the move over the opposition of top Soviet military leaders.[56] This pull-out proved to be exceedingly modest, however. U.S. Secretary of Defense Weinberger claimed that U.S. intelligence had evidence that new Soviet troops moved into Afghanistan at the same time the withdrawal was announced; he stated that the net effect of the withdrawal had been neutral, or even positive, in terms of Soviet combat potential in Afghanistan. The timing of the withdrawal near to the convening of the U.S.-Soviet summit meeting in Rekjavik also suggests it was undertaken primarily for political and propaganda advantage, not as a prelude to larger Soviet withdrawals. There is no evidence of military opposition to the move.

During 1987 and the first four months of 1988, the Soviet position began to evolve noticeably. Domestic public opinion turned increasingly against Soviet involvement in the war, perhaps spurred on by the growing glasnost of the Soviet press.[57] Moscow began to press more actively for a political solution to the conflict, including the establishment of a coalition government in Afghanistan. Later, even this condition was dropped, and the Soviet government began to talk of unilateral troop withdrawals. The culmination of these shifts in the Soviet position, coupled with intensive international diplomacy, came on 14 April 1988, with the signing by the United States, Pakistan, Afghanistan, and the Soviet Union of accords in Geneva providing for a phased withdrawal of Soviet troops from Afghanistan. The Geneva accord called for 50 percent of Soviet troops to be withdrawn by 15 August 1988 and the remainder by 15 February 1989. The USSR met both deadlines.

The withdrawal from Afghanistan would seem to have provided ample cause for civil-military discord, either over the policy of withdrawal itself or over its execution. But again there is surprisingly little evidence of military dissatisfaction with the decision or its implementation. To the contrary, there is at least some evidence suggesting that the military was as disillusioned with the war as were the civilian leaders, and therefore may have supported the policy of withdrawal.

One telling indication of this was an article by Aleksandr Prokhanov that appeared in *Literaturnaia gazeta* on 17 February 1988. Writing with unprecedented frankness for the Soviet press, Prokhanov made a devastating indictment of the conflict in Afghanistan. He asserted that the Soviet-backed government was not socialist and was probably incapable of becoming so. He predicted that there would be a wrenching debate at home over the consequences of a war that had "sowed tragedy and pain in [Soviet] families."

---

[56] See, for example, Gary Lee, *Washington Post*, 29 July 1986.

[57] Wise, " 'A War Should Never Have Happened.' " This article, based on research conducted by the Soviet Area Audience and Opinion Research unit of Radio Free Europe/Radio Liberty, cites evidence that there was "a groundswell of discontent" about Soviet involvement in the war among virtually all segments of Soviet population, including party members.

Though the author claimed that "the departure of our troops is not a defeat," he acknowledged that the original aims of the war were not achieved. In seeking to place blame for the fiasco, he cast a wide net, faulting "experts" who "were wrong in their assessments of the situation in the country." Political and military leaders also shared the blame: "Mistakes were made by specialists in Islam, diplomats, politicians, the military."

What made Prokhanov's article particularly significant was the writer's reputation as an apologist for the war with close ties to the military. Although his views did not necessarily represent those of the armed forces, they were probably not dissimilar. The article seems to have been a clear signal that a high-level reassessment of the conflict was taking place on the part of both party and military leaders. Other, similar articles followed in various Soviet organs; none of them hinted at military dissent over the reassessment or the decision to withdraw from the country.[58]

A study of Soviet public opinion during the later years of the conflict in Afghanistan found that Soviet society was becoming increasingly polarized by the war, with larger percentages opposing it, but larger percentages also favoring it (while the number of undecided declined).[59] Such a development must have been of profound concern to the Soviet officer corps, the one group whose prestige and legitimacy had been recognized by virtually every sector of Soviet society in the past. This may partly account for why the military did not oppose the withdrawal from Afghanistan, despite the opportunities it afforded for combat experience and career promotion.

In summary, the bulk of available evidence suggests that no major manifestations of civil-military discord appeared over the withdrawal from Afghanistan. If they existed, they never surfaced publicly. This conclusion coincides also with the general picture presented in the previous two sections. It might even be said that the top civilian leadership and top military commanders of the Soviet Union stumbled into Afghanistan together, became mired down mutually, and decided jointly upon withdrawal.

The Postwithdrawal Backlash

The withdrawal from Afghanistan generated a debate within Soviet society about the origins of the conflict and the responsibility for what was widely

---

[58] See, in particular, the commentary by Oleg Bogomolov in *Literaturnaia gazeta*, 16 March 1988. See also Prokhanov's article, "Afganistan," in *Mezhdunarodnaia zhizn* (July 1988), 26–35, in which Prokhanov (p. 27) admits that his first highly prowar novel on Afghanistan was "written in a state of revolutionary euphoria." An excellent summary of Soviet press coverage of the war during its final years is Aaron Trehub, "Soviet Press Coverage of the War in Afghanistan: From Cheerleading to Disenchantment," *Report on the USSR* 1, 10 (10 March 1989), 1–4.

[59] "The Soviet Public and the War in Afghanistan: A Trend Toward Polarization," SAAOR AR 1-87, March 1987.

regarded as a blunder. Some of this backlash was directed against the military, which was forced to defend itself against accusations that it had encouraged entry into the conflict and committed serious errors in its prosecution.

On the day of the Soviet withdrawal, *Pravda* carried a front-page article attributing Soviet entry into the war to the "Brezhnev leadership," while nonetheless emphasizing the fundamental "good will" of the USSR. The article was critical of the way the original decision had been made: "It is possible to say that in the future such life and death questions as the use of troops should not be decided in chambers, secretly, without the sanction of the parliament of the country."[60] The same day, *Literaturnaia gazeta* carried a lengthy and shocking article (especially by Soviet standards) that described, among other things, the involvement of Soviet troops in the murder of Afghan civilians at a border checkpoint.[61] While the *Pravda* article seemed to reflect the determination of the top party leadership to put the war behind it, the piece in *Literaturnaia gazeta* perhaps reflected the equally strong determination of more liberal elements in Soviet society to debate the implications of the conflict and use it as an incentive for military reforms.

Leonid Mirov, *Pravda*'s first correspondent in Afghanistan, was reported to have told a meeting of the Soviet Peace Committee in February 1989 that the war was "a catastrophic stupidity," and that military overconfidence was to blame for the whole fiasco.[62] The prominent Soviet art historian and reformer Leonid Batkin published an article a few months later in *Moscow News* (a liberal Soviet publication aimed principally at foreign readers) in which he reported that the Soviet Army had committed "crimes against humanity" while in Afghanistan. He specifically accused Marshal Akhromeev of sharing responsibility for these crimes.[63]

Batkin wrote his article in defense of Andrei Sakharov, who had been shouted down at the Congress of People's Deputies by an angry group of delegates when he had criticized the role of the Soviet Army in Afghanistan. Sakharov's critique and the public airing of war-related issues at the congress were themselves indications of the depth of feeling over the war in Soviet society. The debate, however, has by no means been one-sided: as noted earlier, prominent Soviet military officers have defended the military's role and have claimed that the General Staff itself opposed entry into Afghanistan. Sakharov's charge that Soviet helicopters had sometimes fired on Soviet soldiers to prevent them from being taken prisoner by the Afghan resistance elicited vehement denials from the military.[64]

[60] *Pravda*, 15 February 1989.

[61] Gennadii Bocharov, "Afghan," *Literaturnaia gazeta*, 15 February 1989, 13–14.

[62] *Baltimore Sun*, 12 February 1989.

[63] *Moscow News*, no. 24 (1989).

[64] *Komsomolskaia pravda*, 2 March 1989; *Krasnaia zvezda*, 28 February 1989; and *Trud*, 12 March 1989, all cited in Dale R. Herspring, "The Soviet Military and Change," *Survival* 31, 4

A series of significant reforms was carried out in the Soviet military during
1988–89, during and following the withdrawal from Afghanistan. These included modest reductions in military force structure, deactivation of several
thousand members of the officer corps, making the armed forces more accountable to oversight from the Supreme Soviet, declassifying of some information about Soviet defense spending, redefining key points of military doctrine, and (perhaps most startling of all) the early deactivation of some
175,000 students from military service.[65] The latter step was taken over the
open opposition of Defense Minister Iazov and in the face of warnings from
the officer corps that it would reduce the combat readiness of the armed forces.

The timing of these initiatives certainly suggests that the pullout from Afghanistan gave impetus to the movement for military reform. On the other
hand, it must be kept in mind that Soviet society and government throughout
this period were undergoing far-reaching changes under the impetus of glasnost and perestroika. These changes predated the pullout from Afghanistan
and affected almost all sectors and institutions of Soviet society. Sorting out
cause and effect from the jumble of events occurring in 1988–89 is almost
impossible, but it seems likely that the Soviet withdrawal from Afghanistan
was not the immediate cause of the reforms initiated in the Soviet military
around the same time. Rather, both were consequences of the underlying crisis
of Soviet society as a whole; both represented Gorbachev's response to that
crisis.

The Soviet Military in Afghanistan: Four Concerns of the Officer Corps

The war in Afghanistan is the only serious shooting war that Soviet ground
forces have engaged in outside Eastern Europe since World War II, and the
only instance of large numbers of Soviet conscripts being sent outside the
Warsaw Pact for military service. It is also the only conflict during that time
for which a significant body of data exists on Soviet officers and enlisted men
who served there. This part of the chapter will examine four prominent concerns of the Soviet officers and (to a lesser degree) enlisted men who were
involved in the war in Afghanistan: recognition and honor; combat readiness;
the situation of veterans; and draft evasion.

(July/August 1989), 327. The fate of missing Soviet soldiers became a major political issue after
the withdrawal, with the formation of a special society, "Hope," to coordinate efforts aimed at
finding them or their remains. This society met with Gorbachev on 14 July 1989. *Pravda*, 15 July
1989.

[65] Some of these changes are discussed in greater detail in Herspring, "The Soviet Military and
Change." See also Stephen Foye, "The Soviet Military under Siege," *Report on the USSR*, 24
February 1989, 7–11.

Recognition and Honor

Even prior to the invasion of Afghanistan, Soviet advisers in Kabul and else-where in the country were enormously unpopular; many, possibly over one hundred, were murdered. American journalist Geoffrey Goodsell reported in September 1979, three months before the invasion:

> Already Soviet association with the Taraki regime has made the Russian the most hated of all foreigners in Afghanistan today. The 1,500 military personnel among the 4,000 Soviet advisers there do not wear Russian uniforms or even military insignia, because of the immediate identification these would offer. Non-Russian Westerners on the streets of Kabul hasten to assert that they are not Russians.[66]

After the invasion the life of Soviet officers and enlisted men serving in Afghanistan became vastly more hazardous, even in the central cities and other parts of the country. Once the casualties began to mount, it was probably inevitable that the military would press for public recognition to be given to the sacrifices being made by Soviet fighting men in Afghanistan.

Not until 1983, however, did the Soviet military and civilian press begin to devote significant attention to the war in Afghanistan, openly describing the sacrifices and heroics of Soviet servicemen. Quite likely the military brought pressure to bear on civilian authorities for a more open information policy regarding the war in order to help bolster the morale of the officer corps, whose achievements were not getting much public recognition.

This study has identified references in the Soviet press to more than 200 enlisted men and officers below the rank of general who served in Afghanistan.[67] While this number is minute compared to the more than 500,000 offi-

---

[66] *Christian Science Monitor*, 7 September 1979. See also *Los Angeles Times*, 10 January 1980.

[67] *Aviatsiia i Kosmonavtika*, no. 5 (1984), 31; no. 11 (1984), 32; no. 5 (1985); *Izvestiia*, 1 May 1986; 24 December 1985; *Jane's Defense Weekly*, 8 February 1986; *Kommunist vooruzhennykh sil*, no. 9 (1983); no. 23 (1984); *Komsomolskaia pravda*, 26 February 1984; 13 March 1984; 28 April 1984; 12 January 1986; *Krasnaia zvezda*, 7 August 1981; 10 October 1981; 25 November 1982; 5 December 1982; 15 January 1984; 24 March 1984; 7 and 15 April 1984; 23 June 1984; 17 April 1985; 7 and 8 May 1985; 4 and 8 June 1985; 20 and 30 July 1985; 5 September 1985; 1, 4, and 14 December 1985; 5, 11, and 21 January 1986; 11, 20, and 26 February 1986; 22 March 1986; 13 July 1986; 18, 29, and 31 October 1986; 11 November 1986; 2 May 1987; 3 and 30 January 1988; 13 and 28 February 1988; 2, 13, 22, and 27 March 1988; 2, 13, 15, 22, 23, 27, and 30 April 1988; 9, 15, 17, 19, and 22 May 1988; 5 June 1988; 17 and 19 August 1988; 10 September 1988; *Krylya rodiny*, no. 9 (1980); *Literaturnaia gazeta*, 9 January 1985; *Molod Ukrainy*, 10 July 1986; Moscow TV, 10 January 1986; *Ogonëk*, February 1985; *Pravda*, 2 August 1984; 24 July 1985; 10 September 1985; 19 November 1985; 22 January 1986; 27 May 1986; Radio Moscow, 23 March 1986; 6 and 11 July 1986; *Selskaia gazeta*, 1 April 1986; *Sovetskaia kultura*, 2 August 1986; Soviet TV, 8 July 1986; *Voennyi vestnik*, no. 9 (1984), photo supplement; no. 1 (1984); no. 8 (1985); no. 4 (1986); no. 11 (1986), supplement; *Voennie znaniya*, no. 2 (1985); *Vozdushnyi transport*, 17 August 1985; *Za rulem*, 2 February 1986; *Zvezdy podivga na zemle Afghanistana*, 97–107.

cers and men estimated to have served in Afghanistan between 1979 and 1989, it is far more data than was ever before available on Soviet involvement in a Third World conflict. It is important to keep in mind that these media reports may not accurately reflect the Soviet experience in Afghanistan, but they do indicate the kind of image that official Soviet organs sought to portray about the war.

It is noteworthy, for example, how many instances of combat described in the Soviet media involve either the defense of vehicle convoys or helicopter missions aimed at aiding convoys or units who had been attacked. Of the actual combat situations described in Soviet media reports, nearly half involved the defense of convoys, and approximately 25 percent were helicopter missions; many others involved attacks on garrisons and guard posts that were defending roads. The reports stressed the defensive nature of what Soviet forces in Afghanistan were doing. Soviet attacks on villages and Soviet ground offensives aimed at sweeping out centers of guerrilla resistance were ignored in the Soviet press. Also noteworthy was the heavy emphasis put on the standing officer corps. While some news reports mentioned the heroic accomplishments of enlisted men, the majority focused on officers. This may reflect the fact that information about the war tended to filter back to the Soviet Union through the officer corps; it may also indicate a conscious effort on the part of the official organs (particularly *Krasnaia zvezda*, the daily newspaper of the Ministry of Defense) to give maximum attention to the achievements of the professional military.

This emphasis on the valor and accomplishments of the officer corps showed up also in numerous press accounts of medals and combat awards won. The highest honor that can be granted to Soviet servicemen is that of Hero of the Soviet Union, an award similar to the coveted U.S. Medal of Honor. By February 1989, the time of the Soviet withdrawal, there were more than eighty instances of the honor being bestowed on Soviet military men serving in Afghanistan, sixty-five of whose names were known.[68] Fifty-three (nearly 82 percent) of these were officers, seven were sergeants, and only five were ordinary enlisted men. Five were generals, the most senior of whom was Varrenikov, chief of staff of the operational group of the General Staff that planned and executed the invasion, and a key figure in coordinating the final withdrawal when he was later stationed in Kabul.

The list of Heroes of the Soviet Union in Afghanistan also reveals that a disproportionately high percentage of the awards went to the airborne infantry or helicopter crews, suggesting that these groups may have borne the brunt of the combat. Of the twelve Soviet divisions in Afghanistan at peak strength,

---

[68] For more details and a complete listing of the sixty-five known awardees, see "Heroes of the Soviet Union—Afghanistan," *Jane's Soviet Intelligence Review* 1, 3 (March 1989), 111–15. See also Peter Kruzhin, "Geroi sovetskovo soiuza—'Afgantsy,' " *Radio Svoboda: Materialy issledovatelskogo otdela*, PC 195/86, 1 December 1986.

ten were motorized infantry and two airborne. Motorized rifle troops, however won only fifteen of the awards, airborne infantry and helicopter crews, twenty-six. Interestingly, six of the awardees were political officers, five of whom received the award after 1986.

Hero of the Soviet Union is, of course, not the only award available to Soviet servicemen. The Soviet media after 1983 carried several dozen reports of other awards being made to military personnel in Afghanistan: the Order of Lenin, Order of the Red Star, Order of the Red Banner, and others. A Radio Moscow interview with a Soviet lieutenant about his service in Afghanistan includes the following interesting passage: "When I first arrived in the platoon, exactly half of the men had received decorations. For me, of course, after military school, it was strange to see conscripted privates and sergeants with orders and medals."[69] If the ratio of 50 percent is anywhere near the norm, it certainly suggests that the military made a conscious effort to bolster the loyalty and morale of conscripts serving in Afghanistan.

It is also interesting to note that *Krasnaia zvezda* carried a veritable flood of lengthy articles on Afghanistan in the spring of 1988, around the time that the Geneva accords on the conflict were negotiated and signed. Most of these articles focused on individual soldiers and officers; many described their feats of valor at length and made note of the awards presented to them.[70] This series of articles (and the awards themselves, of course) appear very much as a deliberate effort to boost military morale and prestige at a time when withdrawal from the conflict was becoming a serious prospect.

In most cases, Soviet media reports did not indicate what happened to an identified officer or enlisted man following his service in Afghanistan. Where this information was provided, a large number of promotions or favorable assignments were mentioned, suggesting that service in Afghanistan often proved to be a career-boosting move. Only from Western correspondents and other non-Soviet sources do we learn of the numerous cases of Soviet officers who deserted, were punished or even executed for various actions, or suffered severe morale problems.[71]

Training and Combat Readiness

During the summer of 1985, the Soviet military press published a spate of articles describing how combat experience in Afghanistan was enabling officers to provide more effective training and leadership to troops back home

[69] Radio Moscow, 23 March 1986.

[70] *Krasnaia zvezda*, 2, 13, 22, and 27 March 1988; 2, 13, 15, 22, 23, 27, and 30 April 1988; 9, 15, 17, 19, and 22, May 1988; 5 June 1988.

[71] A Rand Corporation study concluded that poor morale was a major problem in the Soviet military throughout the war; see *New York Times*, 5 June 1988.

who had not personally experienced combat.[72] One article, for example, described a training exercise of a group of tank officers:

> The success of these tank officers was in large part due to the professional training of their officers, and in particular, of the commander of their company. By fulfilling his internationalist duty in the ranks of the limited contingent of Soviet forces in Afghanistan, Senior Lieutenant Stepanov received outstanding training.[73]

This and other articles around the same time made an obvious effort to glorify service in Afghanistan; several articles stated or implied that combat experience in Afghanistan was far superior to mere academic training. These articles all appeared in such short order, one after another, that they likely represented a high-level policy decision to emphasize the value of combat experience acquired in the war.

Another indication that service in Afghanistan was viewed as highly desirable for the education of Soviet officers was the appointment of senior veterans of the war to high positions in the military educational establishment. In mid-1986, for example, Army General G. I. Salmanov was appointed head of the General Staff Academy.[74] Salmanov had previously served for two years in Afghanistan; his appointment probably reflected a desire on the part of the top military (and perhaps civilian) leadership to insure that the practical experience of the war was made an integral part of the education of the senior officer corps. Other examples were the appointment of Major General A. E. Sliusar, a highly decorated commander of an airborne assault division in Afghanistan, as head of the Riazan Higher Airborne Troops Command School, and the appointment of Colonel General V. A. Vostrov as commander of the main administration of military education in the Ministry of Defense.[75]

The Soviet military learned many lessons from the war in Afghanistan. Early in the war, articles began to appear in the Soviet military press on mountain warfare and helicopter combat; many of these articles did not mention Afghanistan, but the lessons set forth in them were clearly applicable to that conflict.[76] The conflict saw a significant evolution of Soviet tactics and doctrine for fighting against guerrilla insurgencies. As the war progressed, the Soviets moved away from extensive reliance on heavy armored attacks, which often prove disastrous in rugged terrain, toward increased use of helicopters for transport and rapid insertion of small units of troops. Helicopter gunships,

[72] *Krasnaia zvezda*, 8 May 1985; 4 June 1985; 20 July 1985; 30 July 1985.

[73] Ibid., 8 May 1985.

[74] *Voenno-istoricheskii zhurnal*, no. 19 (1986), 85, cited in Richard Woff, "The Soviet High Command: Senior Personnel Changes: July–September 1986," The Center for Strategic Technology, Texas A&M, 8.

[75] *Voennyi vestnik*, no. 9 (1984), photo supplement; *Krasnaia zvezda*, 2 September 1988.

[76] An early, exceptionally well-researched study of Soviet military literature related to the war in Afghanistan is Douglas M. Hart, "Low-intensity Conflict in Afghanistan: The Soviet View," *Survival*, no. 2 (March/April 1982).

particularly the Mi-24 "Hind" D, came to play an important role in counter-guerrilla operations. Soviet tactics for helicopter warfare were substantially refined, and the helicopters themselves were fitted with new ventilator systems to reduce their heat signatures. The classic Soviet approach of relying on large formations of troops proved unworkable in Afghan terrain. Instead, there was a much greater reliance on *Spetsnaz* (special operations) forces. Moreover, once it became clear to the Soviets that the war would not be won quickly, emphasis on offensive operations diminished for a time, and Soviet forces concentrated on holding cities and highways.

Early in Gorbachev's tenure, however, the emphasis on offensive operations resumed as the military conducted large-scale border sweeps in eastern Afghanistan on the border with Pakistan. Innovative means of cutting off cross-border infiltration were used in these operations. There were also numerous cross-border incursions during this time, mostly by aircraft, which inflicted considerable damage in refugee settlements near the Pakistani side of the border. This tactic was reminiscent of U.S. practice in Vietnam, where the United States conducted bombing raids in Cambodia against Viet Cong forces who had sought safe haven.

But while the Soviet military in Afghanistan undertook a continual search for new and better means of prosecuting the war, this does not necessarily mean that the conflict heavily influenced Soviet tactics and operational doctrine in other theaters. The number of articles in Soviet military journals that were devoted to Afghanistan or related topics was relatively small, and Soviet strategy and force structure in Europe were not greatly affected by the war. Afghanistan was an important side arena for learning lessons; it did not precipitate an upheaval in Soviet doctrine or tactics.[77]

The Soviet novelist Aleksandr Prokhanov in an August 1985 *Literaturnaia gazeta* article emphasized the importance of the war in Afghanistan for giving Soviet officers combat experience:

> The commanders, graying at the temples, came under fire for the first time in the Afghan foothills. They saw wounded soldiers for the first time. For the first time they were sending their troops not on training attacks but to the weapons emplacements of the adversary, who had ignited a column of tankers. And they, the commanders, some with academic training, have only finally become soldiers here in the Hindu Kush.[78]

The reference to "graying temples" is a forceful reminder that many senior Soviet military officers are lacking in combat experience, having been too young to fight in World War II. Prokhanov is a prolific writer on contemporary

[77] George G. Weickhardt, "Democratization and *Glasnost* in the Soviet Armed Forces," *Report on the USSR* 1, 20 (19 May 1989), 10–15, discusses the impact of the conflict on Soviet thinking about command style. This may eventually lead to changes throughout the Soviet military, as the author suggests (see especially p. 12).

[78] "Zapiski na Brone," *Literaturnaia gazeta*, 28 August 1985.

military themes, whose prose throughout most of the war seemed to represent
a school of thinking that welcomed it as an opportunity for the Soviet Army
finally to get combat experience and as a necessary, almost ritualistic, rite of
passage for young Soviet soldiers. Prokhanov was reported to enjoy the patronage of the Main Political Administration and was the recipient of several
awards for his writing, including the Lenin Komsomol Prize and the Order of
the Red Banner of Labor. He wrote a tetralogy, *Goriashchie sady* (Burning
Gardens) set in Afghanistan, Cambodia, Mozambique, and Nicaragua, that
glorifies revolutionary violence as a means of self-revelation and self-re-
newal.[79] Western observers have commented on the almost Fascist sentiment
of his writing.[80]

Prokhanov's works, and the favorable attention given to them in the Soviet
press,[81] suggest that one consequence of the war in Afghanistan may have
been the increased militarism and hardening of the Soviet officer corps. A vast
number of corroborating sources—interviews with Soviet émigrés, samizdat
literature, and reports from Western correspondents—indicate that Soviet
commanders and officers in Afghanistan in numerous instances committed
atrocities, undertook brutal pacification campaigns, or performed assigned
missions with little regard for human life.[82] It is impossible to know what
fraction of Soviet officers or conscripts were involved in such atrocities, but
the experience is likely to have been one that permanently affected their outlook on war—either profoundly disillusioning them or inuring them to the
cruelty of combat. This is one effect of the war that is difficult to measure, but
that could be long lasting. The group most profoundly affected by the experience is, of course, veterans; the impact of the conflict on them has been substantial.

Soviet Veterans of Afghanistan

Not long after the Soviet withdrawal, there was a report in *Pravda* that the
graves of some soldiers who had perished in Afghanistan had been dese-
crated.[83] The report undoubtedly evoked powerful emotions among the officer
corps, where concerns over the honor of the dead and the treatment of veterans

---

[79] Aleksandr Prokhanov, *Goryashchie sady* (Moscow: Sovetskii Izdatel, 1984).

[80] See two excellent articles by Aaron Trehub, RL 81/85, "The Defense Genre: The Literature
of Tomorrow?" *Radio Liberty Research Bulletin*, 15 March 1985, and RL 307/85, "Afghanistan:
Portents of the Apocalypse?" *Radio Liberty Research Bulletin*, 11 September 1985.

[81] See, for example, *Literaturnaia gazeta*, 26 December 1984; *Krasnaia zvezda*, 6 March 1987.

[82] *Washington Post*, 26 November 1986; 3 January 1988; *New York Times*, 30 October 1986;
21 November 1986; 6 May 1987; *Christian Science Monitor*, 24 October 1988; *Los Angeles
Times*, 24 March 1988.

[83] *Pravda*, 10 March 1989.

are paramount. In the early years of the war, the situation of returned veterans—the so-called afgantsy—was largely ignored in the Soviet media, but in conjunction with the greater openness of the press after 1983, it became a major and widely aired issue.

One of the earliest news accounts appeared in *Komsomolskaia pravda* in February 1984. It was a story about a paralyzed veteran, Aleksandr Nemtsov, and his poor treatment by local officials. The story elicited widespread outrage and motivated local officials to pay sudden attention to Nemtsov's plight. The newspaper returned to Nemtsov's story at least two other times in the spring of 1984, in one case publishing a letter from the first secretary of the Dnepropetrovsk party committee assuring the public that "those at fault have been severely punished," and claiming that the committee was taking concrete measures to ensure that veterans of all conflicts were treated properly.[84] Possibly in partial response to the campaign being conducted in *Komsomolskaia pravda*, the newspaper *Sovetskaia Kirgiziia* carried an article in May 1984, discussing how the Naryn province was integrating returning veterans from the war into everyday life.[85] In July of the same year, *Pravda* took up the refrain with an article about Airborne Battalion Commander Leonid Khabarov, who had been seriously wounded in Afghanistan.[86] Over a year later, *Pravda* published a follow-up report to the effect that Khabarov had overcome his injury and succeeded in getting himself posted back to Afghanistan. There he had been wounded again, promoted to lieutenant colonel, and transferred to the Lenin Combined Operations Command School in Tashkent, where he was serving as a senior instructor.[87]

In January 1986, an article in *Komsomolskaia pravda* shed light for the first time on an interesting aspect of veteran life.[88] The author, a criminal investigator from Togliatti named Aleksandr Drobotov, describes meeting with a young Afghan veteran. The young veteran, Anatolii, informed Drobotov that he and other veterans of the war were displeased with the release of a local citizen on embezzlement charges and would take the law into their own hands and deal with the criminal if the state failed to punish him. Drobotov describes Anatolii's disillusionment with the materialism, corruption, and smugness of civilian life. Having lost a friend in Afghanistan, Anatolii asks, "What did my friend die for?" Drobotov portrays Anatolii as a troubled young man who has difficulty adjusting to civilian life, but admits that much of what he says is true, and that his fellow veterans from the war think much like he does.

Beginning in 1986, there was a flood of articles in the Soviet media on the situation of the afgantsy, some of which also mentioned the problem of vigi-

---

[84] *Komsomolskaia pravda*, 13 March 1984; see also 28 April 1984.
[85] *Sovetskaia Kirgiziia*, 5 May 1984.
[86] *Pravda*, 24 July 1984.
[87] Ibid., 10 September 1985.
[88] *Komsomolskaia pravda*, 8 January 1986.

lantism among veterans.[89] Soviet television turned to the subject in 1987 with a number of programs highlighting the frustrations and problems facing returning veterans from the war.[90] Soviet authorities, however, were not above using war veterans to further their own purposes: in many provinces, veterans of the war made officially sponsored speaking tours to encourage popular support for the conflict.[91]

Interviews with Soviet émigrés indicate that the plight of veterans of the war in Afghanistan has been real, but also that improvements were made in this area as the war dragged on: social services were increased, as were the pensions of war widows. In some parts of the country, local party organizations assisted veterans of the war to set up clubs where veterans could gather and renew their ties.[92] At a press conference held in Moscow in April 1987, two Soviet officials acknowledged that veterans of the war had experienced neglect and readjustment problems in some instances, but they claimed that the situation was improving and most veterans were well cared for.[93] Some six months later, however, the formation of a nationwide organization for Afghan veterans was announced following the conclusion of a Komsomol-sponsored conference in Askhabad of two thousand veterans of the war.[94]

During 1988, as the likelihood of a Soviet withdrawal from Afghanistan became more evident, the Soviet press continued to publish articles on the situation of veterans of the war.[95] The issue also became a point of discussion at the Nineteenth Party Conference, and in August 1988 the Council of Ministers of the USSR passed a resolution providing additional benefits to veterans of the war in Afghanistan.[96] Thus, while the issue was of particular concern to military officers, Soviet civilian authorities, too, showed concern about the difficulties of Afghanistan war veterans and the larger repercussions this might

[89] *Moskovskaia pravda*, 27 February 1987; *Radianska Ukraina*, 17 March 1987; *Pravda*, 4 April 1987; *Sobesednik*, no. 1 (1987); RLR 241/86, "Soviet Veterans of the War in Afghanistan: A New Social Force?" *Radio Liberty Research Bulletin*, 24 June 1986; on vigilantism and neo-Nazism among veterans see Valerii Konovalov, "Neo-Nazis in the USSR: From 'Mindless Childish Games' to a Program of Action," *Report on the USSR* 1, 24, (16 June 1989), 12.

[90] Soviet television, 31 January 1987 and 7 February 1987; see RLR 167/87, "More Selective Glasnost, about Afghanistan," *Radio Liberty Research Bulletin*, 28 April 1987.

[91] *Soviet Area Audience and Opinion Research (SAAOR)*, April 1986.

[92] *Sovsetskaia Rossiia*, 30 April 1986.

[93] Reuters, 27 April 1987. The Soviet press also reported several cases of young people passing themselves off as veterans of the war. See "Preemstvennost pokolenii: ot 'Izheveteranov' velikoi otechestvennoi k 'Izheveteranam' Afganistana," *Radio svoboda: materialy issledovatelskogo otdela*, RC 30/87, 12 March 1987.

[94] *New York Times*, 22 November 1987.

[95] *Krasnaia zvezda*, 14 January 1988; 19 January 1988; 13 February 1988; 14 May 1988; 9 October 1988. See also the interesting article by Valerii Konovalov, "Veterany afganistana, perestroika i 19-ia partkonferentsiia," *Radio svoboda: materialy issledovatelskogo otdela*, RC 59/88, 8 July 1989.

[96] *Krasnaia zvezda*, 21 August 1988.

have on society as a whole, including its effects on public perceptions of the military and military service. There is every indication that the problem will continue to trouble Soviet society for years to come.

Draft Evasion

A fourth issue that concerned the Soviet officer corps was draft evasion. Senior military officers were troubled, even outraged, by the attitude some civilian elites took toward the war in Afghanistan, and they made their feelings known in both the civilian and military press. As the quagmire deepened and the death toll mounted, a number of articles appeared in the Soviet press criticizing Soviet civilian elites for not caring enough about Soviet soldiers risking their lives in Afghanistan, and for seeking to have their own sons exempted from military service abroad. *Izvestiia* on 28 January 1982 criticized influential parents for trying to obtain special privileges for their children in a kind of Soviet draft evasion; this article did not explicitly link the problem to the war in Afghanistan, but later articles (particularly in the military press) did.

Krasnaia zvezda in December 1985 published a blunt, hard-hitting article on draft evasion. Written by a correspondent in Vladivostok, the article cited three particularly notorious cases of draft evasion, all of which fell under the jurisdiction of the military commissariat (recruitment office) of the city of Frunze. The following excerpt was particularly telling:

> Some officials and local bodies of power at times display a lack of principle or show indulgence toward various tricks used by certain insufficiently mature youth who are trying to have their military service deferred at any cost. For example, the Frunze Military Commissariat has repeatedly asked justice agencies to use the force of the law against those who are obviously evading service. But these requests are simply brushed aside.[97]

Six months later, the newspaper returned to the theme with an article charging that the sons of certain Soviet officials had avoided service in Afghanistan by questionable methods.[98] The officials involved, three of whom were cited by name, were all from Uzbekistan. The problem of draft evasion may have been particularly acute in that republic, as suggested by a speech to the Uzbek Komsomol congress in March 1987 by the first secretary of the Uzbek party, I. B. Usmankhodzhaev, in which he stated that "hundreds" of Komsomol members had been prosecuted for draft evasion, and that the numbers of such

---

[97] Ibid., 5 December 1985. The article also criticized the territorial Soviet executive committee for having failed to take action on building a local induction center.

[98] Ibid., 11 July 1986.

violators had been increasing; Usmankhodzhaev clearly implied a link between the draft dodging and the war in Afghanistan.[99]

It is perhaps significant that *Krasnaia zvezda* articles on draft evasion criticized the behavior only of local government officials in regions of the country
far removed from Moscow.[100] By doing so, the official organ of the armed
forces avoided any direct criticism of the central political authorities. The
newspaper also refrained from any direct criticism of the party—the individuals in question were government officials, not party functionaries (though
they were almost certainly party members). The broader intimation was un-
avoidable, however: the military expected the complete support of political
leaders for the campaign in Afghanistan but was not fully persuaded that such
support existed.

This should not be seen as necessarily reflecting a broader rift between military and civilian authorities. The top political leadership may, in fact, have
supported the military's campaign against local officials who were insuffi-
ciently supportive of the war. The appearance of most of the articles critical
of civilian elites after Gorbachev's accession to power suggests that this was
one more manifestation of glasnost—and that it was aimed precisely at middle-level bureaucrats, not at the top party leadership.

Further evidence that this campaign was not entirely of the military's making was a letter given prominent attention in a nonmilitary journal, *Molod
Ukrainy*. The letter was from a Ukrainian mother who criticized the war in
Afghanistan because "only the children of simple workers take part in the
battles; there are no children of officials there."[101] This mother's complaint
coincides closely with a main concern of the professional military: they want
to be sure that the party and government officials who run the country are with
them.

In Search of an Elusive Variable: Observations and Conclusions

The decade of the 1970s witnessed a dramatic expansion of Soviet military
power into the Third World; the 1980s, by contrast, saw the USSR retreat on
numerous fronts, after first becoming mired in ineffectual counterinsurgency
warfare in Afghanistan and other developing countries. This Soviet retreat
contributed to the loss of prestige and authority that the Soviet military suffered in the last few years of the 1980s, but it was not the only or even the
main factor behind the military's political difficulties. Those difficulties
stemmed from the profound social, economic, and ideological crisis that faced

---

[99] *Pravda vostoka*, 21 February 1987.

[100] The same pattern held true in a later article that touched on the issue in the civilian press.
See *Pravda*, 25 November 1987.

[101] *Molod Ukrainy*, 15 January 1987.

the Soviet system after the death of Brezhnev. As such, even the retreat from Afghanistan was more a consequence of Soviet troubles at home than a cause.

The domestic backlash against the war in Afghanistan was a small blip on the Soviet political screen by comparison with the profound impact on civil-military relations of glasnost, perestroika, and *demokratizatsiia*. The politics of reform instituted by Mikhail Gorbachev challenged encrusted institutions and traditional modes of behavior throughout the Soviet establishment, and the military was no exception. But Soviet military involvement in the Third World per se was not a major source of civil-military disagreement or political conflict at any time in the 1970s or 1980s.

This may seem a rather anticlimactic conclusion, much like Sherlock Holmes's "curious incident" of the dog that didn't bark. Yet it is eminently understandable, even logical, in view of the fact that the Soviet Union remains today, as ever, predominantly a continental power: the outlook, experience, organization, and force structure of its military establishment are primarily those of a country preoccupied with land warfare on or near its own territory. This focus has shifted somewhat as the USSR has expanded its naval forces and participated in foreign conflicts, but the fundamental orientation and thinking of the Soviet military remains "continental." Only a small percentage of total Soviet military personnel have ever served in foreign conflicts or overseas assignments, far less than their American counterparts.

The war in Afghanistan was the first regional conflict the USSR was involved in after World War II large enough to have had a significant impact on the Soviet military and on civil-military relations in the USSR. Soviet involvement in earlier conflicts in the Third World took place largely by proxy and had characteristics more like those of special operations than of outright warfare; there was little of interest with regard to civil-military relations in these smaller conflicts. But even in Afghanistan, despite the prolonged and difficult nature of the war, the traditional civil-military consensus endured. The conflict raised troublesome issues and caused minor tensions between the party and the military, but these were kept well within manageable bounds.

There is some evidence, hardly conclusive, that the Soviet General Staff disagreed with the decision to enter Afghanistan. This at least is what some Soviet generals claimed nearly a year after the invasion. But whatever disagreements may have taken place over the conflict in Afghanistan—and there undoubtedly were some—they transpired behind closed doors, and neither side felt compelled to take the debate "public" (even in the indirect manner of Soviet political debates). The officer corps was amply rewarded for its loyalty and service in the war in Afghanistan: service in the conflict was an almost certain path to quick promotion. This suggests that the senior civilian leadership and senior officer corps maintained a considerable degree of mutual trust and confidence throughout the war, perhaps even a consensual approach to decision making.

The officer corps did have certain sensitivities about prosecution of the war in Afghanistan: it wanted appropriate recognition for the sacrifice and efforts of the military; it worried over the plight of veterans; and it was outraged by instances of draft evasion by the sons of influential officials. The military was also acutely aware of the potential training value of the conflict in terms of combat experience, and the development of tactics, technology, and doctrine.

Though deeply felt by the officer corps, these concerns were not uniquely those of the military. The civilian leadership of the USSR did not want the loyalty, prestige, or combat readiness of the armed forces to decline as a consequence of the war. They, too, had good reason to be concerned about the welfare of veterans, the prestige of the military at home, and the problem of draft evasion. The simple truth is that the interests and goals of the civilian leadership and the senior officer corps coincided in Afghanistan far more than they diverged.

The civil and military leaderships of the USSR also have this in common: both would suffer a loss of prestige, authority, and legitimacy if the Soviet Union suffered a major military defeat abroad. For nearly a decade the Soviet Union experienced neither victory nor defeat in Afghanistan, but only a deepening quagmire. This must have been of growing concern to the military, since the longer the war was prolonged, the more unpopular it would be at home, and the more that unpopularity, by reference, would center on the military. An even worse prospect would have been an outright military defeat, since the military would likely be made a scapegoat for such a debacle. This may be one reason why, despite the opportunity for career advancement and combat training, the military did not oppose the withdrawal from Afghanistan.

One legacy of the war in Vietnam was the disillusionment of a generation of American youth, including both those who had opposed the war and those who had fought in it. The injection into U.S. society of hundreds of thousands of veterans, many of whom brought with them the psychological burdens of combat, physical addictions of various kinds, and resentment about the public's indifference toward them, has had an impact on American society that continues to be felt today. Likewise, it is at the level of the enlisted soldier that the analogy with Vietnam may be most applicable to the Soviet experience in Afghanistan and elsewhere.

Historically, armies have gone through their most profound changes in the wake of defeats. The Soviet military, like the U.S. military prior to Vietnam, has never experienced a major political or military defeat in any foreign conflict. Soviet clients have suffered such defeats, particularly in the Middle East, but Soviet forces themselves were not heavily involved in direct combat in those instances. The enormous impact of the war in Vietnam on the U.S. military was greatly compounded by the fact that the United States ultimately suffered defeat in the war. There was a sense that all the sacrifice and pain had been in vain; and the defeat led to a prolonged period of introspection among the U.S. professional officer corps.

Nothing similar has yet occurred in the case of the Soviet military. The withdrawal from Afghanistan did not, in and of itself, constitute a defeat so long as a Communist government remained entrenched in Kabul; as of this writing, the USSR is providing massive assistance to help insure the survival of that regime. Already it has survived longer than most Western observers predicted. But if Communist rule in Afghanistan should come to an end as the result of a military defeat, there may yet be serious repercussions at home for the Soviet military. The likelihood is that only such a defeat, or a similar defeat elsewhere in the world, would lead to a serious deterioration in the existing civil-military consensus in Moscow.

Nine

Conclusions: Toward a Crisis in Civil-Military Relations?

THANE GUSTAFSON

IT IS HARD to overstate the importance of the military factor in Soviet history. Since the beginning of the 1930s, when the Soviet Union began preparing for war with Germany, Soviet socialism has been so dominated by military spending and planning that it could fairly be called militarized socialism. For the last half-century, the uniformed military and the defense industry have been the most consistently and lavishly favored group in Soviet society. By the standard yardsticks of politics—such as "who gets what, when, and how" or the "authoritative allocation of values"—the Soviet military-industrial elite should be the dominant force in the Soviet political system.

But is it? No other question about the Soviet system has caused so much disagreement among Western observers or such wide swings in views. The aim of this book has been to put civil-military relations into perspective by taking the long and broad view, looking back over the last quarter-century and examining the subject in the context of the Soviet system as a whole.

Models of Soviet Civil-Military Relations

It may be helpful to restate our criticism of the earlier literature on Soviet civil-military relations. Most of it falls into two categories, which we have called Models I and II. Model I is a conflict model: it sees the party leadership and the military as alien to one another, and their ideal and material interests as competitive. Model II is a comity model: it portrays the two sides as having broadly similar views and parallel interests, and it holds that each acknowledges the legitimate place of the other. Despite their apparent differences, Models I and II share several basic faults. First, they both define their subject as a two-player relationship, consisting principally of the party leadership and the uniformed high command, whereas in fact the relationship of interest is not binary but triangular, since it includes the defense industry, a set of institutions with a history, values, and interests of its own. Indeed, other players are involved as well, such as the KGB.

Second, both models derive the motives of the players from supposed characteristics of communists and soldiers everywhere,[1] and from their supposed inherent interests; the only difference is that Model I finds them antagonistic, whereas Model II does not. The variety of views and the possibility of divergences and cleavages within each side are largely ignored, and consequently so is the possibility of coalitions across groups.

A third fault is that both models define the content of the relationship narrowly. The main issues they consider are political control and resource allocation; Model I treats these as zero-sum contests between the players, while Model II treats them as the basis for alliance against other players and institutions.[2] Both understate the variety of issues over which the players must deal with each other and with their surroundings.

Fourth, and most important, both models are essentially static: over the decades, the categories of players do not change, the basic issues do not change, the rules of the game hardly change; there is the unspoken assumption that the political system itself does not change. Finally, both models are based, in concept and method, on the sovietology of the 1960s: the implicit underlying concept of Soviet politics in both is that of elite relations within a quasi-totalitarian system,[3] and the essential method in both is Kremlinology, with its focus on shades of wording from leaders' speeches and bylined statements, and its broad inferences about political views and lineups from data about careers, ranks, and personnel movements.[4]

---

[1] Thus the features listed by Roman Kolkowicz to account for the military's "natural drive toward autonomy and their inherent professionalism" include institutional closure, detachment from the rest of society, an elitist value system, a hierarchical structure of authority, and limited possibilities for employing the soldier's professional skills in civilian life. See Roman Kolkowicz, *The Soviet Military and the Communist Party* (Princeton: Princeton University Press, 1967), 323.

[2] For William Odom the key point is that, while the military does not rule, the military and political elite have been at one in treating military power as an end social product rather than a social overhead cost, and they have worked together to achieve the militarization of the economy and society. See "The Soviet Military and Foreign Policy," *Survival* (November–December 1978), 276–281; "The Party Connection," *Problems of Communism* (September–October 1973), 12–26.

[3] The totalitarian model can lead to either Model I or Model II. Merle Fainsod's treatment of civil-military relations in *How Russia Is Ruled* (Cambridge: Harvard University Press, 1963), 463–500, is clearly Model I. Fainsod portrays a competitive, conflictual relationship, in which the party struggles (successfully) for control and primacy over a professional officer corps that, were it not largely atomized by all-pervasive political controls, would be only too glad to intrude in politics. Fainsod's lapidary formula sums it up: "The political insecurity of the military command is a guarantee of the military security of the political command" (p. 495).

[4] In fairness, the best Western work does take account of the complexity of the civil-military relationship and its evolution over time. Major external developments are not absent—such as the impact of technology on the composition of the officer corps, the evolution of doctrinal debates as a result of the advent of new weapons, or the constraining effects of economic stringency—but they are considered primarily from the standpoint of their immediate effect on the binary relationship. Thus Roman Kolkowicz, in an essay published in 1971, acknowledges the profound effects of technological change but lumps the different subgroups and tendencies within the Soviet mili-

For these reasons, Models I and II share common faults as explainers and predictors. Model I predicts conflict and has difficulty explaining harmony; with Model II, it is the reverse. Neither model is able to account for the fluctuations in the levels of conflict that have occurred over the decades,[5] and neither can explain the more subtle variations in the participation and influence of the players. As a result, scholarly and journalistic opinion based on these models has swung from extreme to extreme.[6]

Model III, described by Timothy Colton in chapter 1, improves on Models I and II by considering a broader range of civil-military dealings, distinguishing among three "domains" of issues (military proper, societal, and sovereign), and examining the variations of participation and influence within each. Model III also considers a broader array of players and gives more attention to cleavages within groups and alliances across them, and to individuals of mixed plumage who do not fit neatly into any group. It avoids the stark choice of Models I and II between conflict and comity by treating the relations among the players as bargained accommodations that proceed on several levels at once, and only occasionally break out into open conflict. Finally, Model III places Soviet civil-military relations in an evolutionary perspective, by showing the rise of a professional military, the gradual establishment of "objective control," and the eventual development, by Brezhnev's day, of something like a civil-military "contract," within which bargaining and competition nevertheless continued.[7]

But Model III, too, has difficulties as an explainer and predictor. The concept of a bargained contract between political and military-industrial leaders, as chapter 1 observes, leads to the prediction that the contract will come under strain if one side or the other perceives that its terms are no longer being prop-

---

tary into "radicals" vs. "conservatives," and "traditionalists" vs. "technocrats." See "The Military," in *Interest Groups in Soviet Politics*, ed. Gordon Skilling and Franklyn Griffiths (Princeton: Princeton University Press, 1971), 145–153.

[5] In particular, neither model is able to explain how the "power" gained by the military in the first half of the Brezhnev era could not be cashed in the second half, or how it waned during the subsequent interregnum, when the disarray in the civilian leadership was at its greatest. Even recent analysis sidesteps this problem. See, for example, F. Stephen Larrabee's otherwise illuminating essay, "Gorbachev and the Soviet Military," *Foreign Affairs* 66, 5 (Summer 1988), 1002–1006.

[6] In addition to the sources mentioned in chapter 1, one of the most eye-catching formulations of the early 1980s was Castoriadis's description of the Soviet system as a "stratocracy" (from *stratos*—army), in which the Communist Party has been replaced as the de facto ruler by the military, and Marxist-Leninist ideology by Russian imperial nationalism. Cornelius Castoriadis, *Devant la Guerre* (Paris: Fayard, 1981).

[7] Thus, Model III shares with Model I a common descent from Samuel Huntington's thinking in *The Solder and the State*. Though it qualifies several of Huntington's main concepts, it does not reject his framework. For a more radical critique of the Huntingtonian approach, see David E. Albright, "A Comparative Conceptualization of Civil-Military Relations," *World Politics* 32 (July 1980), 553–576.

erly met, that is, when (a) the political leadership or the military-industrial sector, whether by commission or by omission, is viewed as doing a poor job of safeguarding national security, or (b) the political leadership is seen to be failing to perform its civilian duties. If the contract is strained, one would predict that the level of civil-military conflict would rise, eventually spilling over into domains where there had been little previous interaction, as the players seek to widen the field or to enlist new allies. This in turn could lead (to borrow one of Gorbachev's phrases) to a "precrisis situation."

These predictions, at first sight, do not fare well when tested against the events of the last fifteen years. On the face of it, condition b was amply met during the last half of the Brezhnev era, and by the time Brezhnev died, some people in Moscow (notably Marshal Nikolai Ogarkov) worried that condition a threatened as well. Yet (to anticipate the argument to be developed below), the foregoing chapters of this book, even Bruce Parrott's chapter on politics, portray a much less turbulent civil-military relationship than one might have expected, considering that the Soviet domestic system was going through a period as bad as any since the end of World War II.

In contrast, one is tempted to say that under Gorbachev neither condition a nor condition b is met: the defects of the Brezhnev administration that most seriously threatened both national security and the viability of the state are both being vigorously addressed. Model III would therefore predict that the previous sources of strain on the civilian-military contract would ease, and that conflict should subside or disappear. Yet (to anticipate again the rest of the chapter) we now seem to be witnessing an increase in civil-military tensions, and the authors of this volume see more ahead.

In short, in the late Brezhnev period the civil-military relationship showed less strain than Model III would have predicted, whereas under Gorbachev it is now showing more. One of the main tasks of this book has been to explain this apparent paradox and to point the way toward a refined theory.

There appear to be two problems with Model III. The first is that if there is an unspoken contract among civilian politicians, defense industrialists, and uniformed commanders, we have not fully grasped its terms. This may be because Model III still has a conceptual flaw. Its emphasis on "contract" and "bargaining" suggests something like equality between the parties; this may reflect Model III's later origins in the 1970s, when Sovietologists were busy exploring the implications of the interest-group approach,[8] and spilling over

---

[8] An early example of the group approach to party-military relations, which emphasizes that "subgroups, as well as larger groups, make informal alliances with one another in opposition to similar formations on the opposite side," is the work of Vernon Aspaturian in the early 1970s. Aspaturian went so far as to write that the pressure from various "demand sectors" in Soviet politics (of which the "security demand sector" was only one) had "fractured the party apparatus." If, in the end, Aspaturian concluded that the phrase "military-industrial complex" did apply to the Soviet case, he emphasized that the complex included only the "conservative wing" of the

into the 1980s, when the concept of "contract" began to attract interest in the field.

But is the civil-military relationship one of contract or bargained accommodation alone? Or do these not take place within a relationship of *authority* in the sense in which Max Weber would have understood it, that is, one in which the military, on the basis of shared ideas and interests, consent to the rule of the party leadership and to certain basic rules laid down by the party leadership, but also to domination by the party and to the party's enforcement of the terms? Unlike a simple contractual relationship, an authority relationship is apt to endure after its terms have become strained, because it rests on a structure of habits and sanctions and an administrative apparatus, which themselves become invested with value and are slow to weaken. In this perspective, even if the zone of shared interests and values narrows, one should expect a lag between strain and response that would inhibit conflict for a time, thus explaining some of the apparent paradox above.

The second problem with Model III is that, although it moves beyond the simple two-player scheme of Models I and II, it still does not take full account of changes arising outside the party-military-industrial relationship and of the ways these are actually transmitted to the participants and acted upon by them. External changes may create or eliminate roles, add or subtract resources. They may bring organizational changes, new types of training, procurement, and force dispositions, and new careers. They may raise new civil-military issues and alter the pattern of civil-military participation. But none of these effects is automatic: external change does not have any single, simple, or immediate impact on civil-military relations, or even necessarily any impact at all. External changes will be variously perceived by the players, whose responses will therefore vary, and thus the effects of change may be dampened, deflected, or delayed.

In sum, in addition to the phenomenon of lag, the civil-military relationship may also be buffered against external change, thus further increasing its stability in the short term, but leaving open the possibility of sharp increases in conflict later on, if the sources of buffering should fail.

How can we test these ideas? Our approach has been somewhat like that of the physicist who studies an unknown structure by making controlled changes in its environment and observing its responses and changes. The last twenty-five years have provided something of a real-life equivalent. The Soviet military-industrial sector has been surrounded by changes in five basic areas: trends in politics and the political leadership, the declining performance of the economy, the challenge of new technologies, the sociocultural evolution of the country, and finally, the growing involvement of the Soviet military over-

---

party. See "The Soviet Military-Industrial Complex—Does it Exist?" *Journal of International Affairs* 26, 1 (1972), 1–28.

seas. Each of the chapters of this book has analyzed a different corner of the civil-military environment, and each has analyzed the responses of the principal players, and the consequences for their relationship.

This approach will be immediately familiar to historians as an attempt to stress the importance of the broad structure within which historical events are played out. In particular, we do not treat civil-military relations as a unique species, but as one illustration of Soviet politics. Thus the gradual development of military professionalization over the decades, culminating in an unspoken contract in the Brezhnev era, must be studied as just one aspect of a similar trend that has affected most Soviet professions and institutions, and indeed, to some extent, Soviet society as a whole.[9] And if there is strain developing in the civil-military contract under Gorbachev, it affects all groups in Soviet society, as the long-established premises of "militarized socialism" come under scrutiny along with the entire Stalinist strategy of development.

The reader may wonder why we have not included a chapter on the U.S.-Soviet relationship as a major environmental factor in Soviet civil-military relations. There is no question that the rivalry with the United States over the last forty-five years has ultimately been the most important driving force in Soviet foreign and domestic policy, the main cause of the unbalanced allocation of Soviet resources over the decades, and the main reason for the privileged position of its military sector.

But the key question is, just how does the U.S.-Soviet relationship influence civil-military relations in Moscow? There are two possible approaches to this question. One is to chronicle the key events and changes in U.S.-Soviet relations since 1965—the Vietnam years and the weakening of U.S. foreign policy, the rise and fall of detente, the evolution of the arms control process, the Carter-Reagan rearmament and the new U.S. assertiveness, and so forth. But structuring the subject in this way prejudges the conclusion, namely, that the shifting policies of successive American administrations are a major independent variable in civil-military relations.

Another approach, however, is to start from the realization that the American factor, as it actually impinges on the Soviet military sector, is almost independent of specific administrations and their policies, because it is much more long term. Thus, for example, the continuous pressure of the U.S.-Soviet rivalry on the economy and the technological system, as well as the Soviet responses to it, are best measured over decades. The practices and institutions developed to deal with that pressure have remained recognizably the same since they first arose in response to the rivalry with Germany in the 1930s. Finally, if the Soviet system has begun to change since the late Brezhnev period, it is not because of the briefly applied pressure of a particular American

[9] See Peter Hauslohner, "Gorbachev's Social Contract," *Soviet Economy* 3, 1 (1987), 54–85.

administration, but rather because of the cumulative strain of five decades of competition with the world's most powerful economy and technology.

In short, while there is no denying the importance of the American factor in Soviet civil-military relations, there is much to be said for breaking it up into its long-term political, technological, and economic aspects. That is what we have done in this book.

Summarizing the External Trends and Their Impact on the Military-Industrial Sector to 1985

The external environment of the Soviet military-industrial system, the fore-going chapters make clear, has changed a great deal over the last generation. But we must now deal with two fundamental questions about those changes: To what extent were they the culmination of long-standing trends, and to what extent were they the products of the passing circumstances of the Brezhnev era? If the changes observed are mainly long-range and not directly connected to the personality and circumstances of particular leaders, then they represent a continuous source of influence on civil-military relations, raising similar challenges and pressures regardless of the leadership in power. In other words, they are presumably still at work under Gorbachev as well. On the other hand, if the evidence points to short-range, contingent causes that change sharply from reign to reign, then their long-term significance for civil-military relations weakens, and the case for any model of long-term evolution weakens as well. A combination of Models I and II would then do as well as any other.

Assuming that we conclude that long-term trends are indeed dominant, then the second question is, are they likely to favor the continued growth of military professionalism, which is the core concept of Model III? A look at the intellectual ancestry of the idea of military professionalism reminds us that it is part of a family of theories of political modernization and development, which in turn are ultimately descended from Weberian thinking about the inevitable progress of rationalization of Western societies.[10] But it is hard to speak of rationalization in Brezhnev's *fin de regne* in the midst of the long-term slow-down of the Stalinist command economy, the spread of anomie in urbanized Soviet society, and signs of decay in an increasingly secularized ruling party. Ironically, each of these was the latter-day corruption of features—industrial growth, urbanization, secularization of policy making—that initially favored military professionalism. But if they culminated in a stagnant and corrupt system, how could military professionalism endure?

---

[10] On the concept of rationalization in Max Weber's thought, see Rogers Brubaker, *The Limits of Rationality: An Essay on the Social and Moral Thought of Max Weber* (London: George Allen and Unwin, 1984).

First, there is the question of long-term vs. short-term. For trends in the economy, technology, society, and foreign policy, the overall conclusion of this volume's authors is that the forces bearing on civil-military relations from the mid-1960s to the mid-1980s were not new in essence, they were more long-term than short, and they tended to originate more outside the triangle of politico-military-industrial leadership than within it. Each chapter of this book independently stresses the elements of long-term evolution.

This is most clearly apparent in the chapters dealing with economic, technological, and sociocultural sources of change. For Robert Campbell in chapter 4, as for most economists, the economic crisis of the late 1970s and early 1980s was the latest stage of a secular decline in growth rates that was ultimately due to systemic defects. The long-standing priority given to the military-industrial sector in resource allocation, particularly under Brezhnev, was an aggravating factor but not the root cause.[11] Ellen Jones's treatment of changes in Soviet society in chapter 7 similarly stresses the long-term forces— urbanization, education, social mobility, and stratification—shaping the cohorts from which conscripts and officers are drawn. These forces had little to do with the specific policies of the Brezhnev administration or with military policies on manpower. My own chapter 6 on technological change likewise emphasizes that the Soviet military-industrial sector, ever since the revolution, has faced the same essential problem of meeting continuous technological challenges from the West with an inferior industrial and technological base.

Trends in the presence and involvement of the Soviet military overseas, as described by Bruce Porter in chapter 8, are a somewhat more mixed case. It is true that of all the sources of change discussed in this book, this one is the most clearly connected to the policies of the Brezhnev leadership. But the dominant themes in Porter's chapter are long-term. In broad perspective, the setting for the expansion of the Soviet presence in the Third World was created by the weakening of the colonial empires and the gradual withdrawal of the Western powers, although the modern phase of Soviet interest in the Third World began with Khrushchev in the mid-1950s. Soviet naval expansion likewise has had a long-term component, since it was largely a response to evolving Soviet strategic missions and to long-term technological trends in Western naval deployments, although the Soviet response to them likewise accelerated under Khrushchev.[12] But most fundamental of all, the Soviet presence in the

[11] Most Western economists would subscribe to this systemic view; interestingly, this also seems to be the opinion of Soviet reformers, although lately there is a growing tendency to blame the long military priority for many of the ills of Soviet society. For an explicit statement of this case, see the speech by Minister of Health Evgenii I. Chazov at the Nineteenth Party Conference, reported in *Pravda*, 30 June 1988. For a summary statement of the systemic case, see Ed A. Hewett, *Reforming the Soviet Economy* (Washington, D.C.: Brookings, 1988).

[12] As Fukuyama observes, one of the forces leading to the expanded operating range of the Soviet Navy was the need to respond to similar expansion in the U.S. Navy. Thus the appearance

world remains what it has always been, that of a continental power, and this element of continuity dominates all other recent developments.

The question of long-term vs. short-term, systemic vs. contingent causation, is especially complicated when it comes to trends in politics and in the political leadership itself. Students of Soviet politics broadly agree on the character of the Brezhnev era; but they disagree over whether that character reflected mainly the man and his circumstances or a long-term evolution of the Soviet polity. The same disagreements continue today about Gorbachev: Do his accession and consolidation of power signal a reversal of the major political features of the Brezhnev era, or do they show, on the contrary, how deep-seated those are?

The case for the long-term, systemic view involves three issues. First, did the Brezhnev era mark a major change in the objectives of the elite, especially in the choice between "guns and butter"? George Breslauer describes the slow evolution of a "post-Stalinist consensus," consisting of a moving compromise between the traditional primacy of defense and heavy industry and a growing concern for living standards and worker incentives, with the latter slowly gaining ground.[13] On this reading, the "golden age" would stand out as an anomaly, and the period after 1975 as a return to the longer-term trend.

The second political issue concerns the nature of changes in the sources of power and authority in Soviet politics and their consequences for the personal power and authority of the party general secretary himself. The argument for the long-term trend is that the general secretary's classic levers of power—especially his control over the "personnel weapon" in the party and state apparatus—decayed, and with it his control over policy. It is not that the personnel weapon itself lost its importance, but it gradually slipped into other hands—republic, province, and city party bosses, and ministerial old-boy networks. At the same time, the range of resources that could be brought to bear in politics and policy making expanded to include such assets as publicity, technical expertise, local loyalties, and even private wealth; and the number of players who could wield them broadened. The general secretary was therefore obliged to proceed by persuasion and consensus building, building his authority through his success as policy maker and policy broker.[14]

The third part of the case concerns the style of policy formation. Whereas

of nuclear submarines on the American side and the growing range of U.S. sea-based nuclear strike forces led to longer-range ASW requirements on the Soviet side, and vice-versa. Thus Soviet navalism, at its origins, was not exclusively, or even primarily, aimed at power projection in the Third World. See Francis Fukuyama, *Soviet Civil-Military Relations and the Power Projection Mission*, R-3504-AF (Santa Monica: Rand Corporation, April 1987), 25–26.

[13] George W. Breslauer, *Khrushchev and Brezhnev as Leaders: Building Authority in Soviet Politics* (London: Allen and Unwin, 1982), esp. 269ff.

[14] This is a composite of arguments by various Western scholars in the 1970s. For a review of major sources, see Thane Gustafson and Dawn Mann, "Gorbachev's First Year: Building Power and Authority," *Problems of Communism* 35, 3 (May–June 1986), 1–19.

in classic views of Soviet politics the policy process was described as "trickle down" rather than "bubble up," more recent studies of policy initiation, agenda formation, specialist participation, and leadership learning stress the growing importance of the latter. The politicians have gradually lifted their hand, first from the life sciences, then from the social sciences, and most recently from international relations and security studies. The expert is increasingly respected and consulted, and the range and quality of his participation have increased. Policy debate is more open, the zone of "closed" issues has shrunk, and institutions and interest groups are freer to argue their case. These trends began under Khrushchev and continued under Brezhnev; the era of glasnost is thus the latest stage of a long evolution.

Bruce Parrott's analysis in chapter 2 does not address these issues directly. He portrays a general secretary whose power grew so slowly that he had to bargain for the support of Marshal Grechko and the military for his arms-control policy until the early 1970s, and did not have his hands completely free until Grechko died and Ustinov was appointed defense minister in his place. Both in this chapter and elsewhere, however, Parrott argues that Brezhnev was then strong enough politically to the end of his life to defend his essential priorities against challenge, through conventional power politics and aggressive policy initiatives.[15] On balance, Parrott's portrait of Brezhnev is not that of a weak general secretary, and he would not agree with the idea that the post of general secretary has weakened over time. Parrott is in good company; Mikhail Gorbachev evidently does not agree either. In this connection one can only observe that even the weakest of all general secretaries to date, Chernenko, got rid of Ogarkov with no sign of hesitation or difficulty once Ogarkov had overstepped himself. The question of the powers of the general secretary is at once the most important and the least settled issue about Soviet politics.

Nevertheless, in the background of Parrott's portrayal one glimpses the longer-term trends at work. Brezhnev's change of course in 1973–1974, as Parrott describes it, cannot be explained solely by Brezhnev's consolidation of power, especially in light of Parrott's earlier description of Brezhnev as a man of strong military sympathies. His shift makes sense only if one assumes

[15] A slightly different but not incompatible view, held by George Breslauer and Peter Hauslohner, portrays Brezhnev as a man whose policy reverses toward the middle of the 1970s forced him to go on the offensive to forestall a massive authority collapse. In this view, Brezhnev's appointment of Ustinov in 1976, the Tula Line in 1977, and his efforts to slow down the growth of military spending from the mid-1970s on, would be seen as part of a larger pattern of increasingly desperate policy initiatives coming from a general secretary who won every battle yet knew he was losing ground, in energy, agriculture, manpower, foreign affairs, arms control, and more. The pattern, then, is one of political *fuite vers l'avant* by a leader whose powers are weakened by policy failure. (In addition to Breslauer's *Khrushchev and Brezhnev as Leaders*, see Peter A. Hauslohner, "Managing the Soviet Labor Market: Politics and Policy-Making under Brezhnev," Ph.D. dissertation, University of Michigan, 1984, esp. chap. 5.)

that inside Brezhnev two objectives contended—military might and social welfare. On this reading, by the mid-1970s Brezhnev was satisfied that the former objective was being well served, so he shifted his focus to the second. The actual allocation of resources showed no such "moving compromise": it consistently favored heavy industry and the military, except for the brief period 1955–1959. In terms of budget shares, the first half of the Brezhnev era was no more "golden," and the second half no less, than the period 1960– 1985 as a whole; and in terms of actual resource allocations, the golden age continued through Brezhnev's death.[16] But Campbell's chapter suggests that this was not Brezhnev's intention, and agrees that Brezhnev's mix of objectives may well have shifted by the end of his life.

The "respect for specialists" and the greater freedom of technical debate behind the scenes benefited military experts in the Ministry of Defense in the first instance. It was only in the second half of the Brezhnev era that a further stage in the process began to affect civil-military debate, namely, the rise of civilian experts on security affairs and their increasing ability to make themselves heard.

On the whole, then, the authors of this volume all stress the long-term, systemic trends in the shaping of the civil-military environment. If these are long-term trends, then they must also be at work under Gorbachev. Indeed, Gorbachev's political strategy must be interpreted in part as an effort to restore the general secretary's power and authority, as well as that of the political system as a whole.[17]

Buffering and the Impact of Change

However long-term and systemic the external forces bearing on the party-military-industrial triangle may have been, after the mid-1970s they moved toward a crux. The early 1980s were the lowest point in Soviet fortunes, and the

---

[16] For summary data on the defense burden as a share of GNP, see Abraham S. Becker, *Sitting on Bayonets: the Soviet Defense Burden and the Slowdown of Soviet Defense Spending*, JRS-01 (Santa Monica: Rand/UCLA Center for the Study of Soviet International Behavior, December 1985), 13.

Similarly, the share of heavy industry (defined as "Group A") in total Soviet investment reached its post-Stalin peak under Khrushchev, then declined sharply in 1966–1970 before resuming steady growth from 1970 to 1985. See State Statistical Committee, *Narodnoe khoziaistvo za 70 let* (Moscow: Finansy i Statistika, 1987), 328–329.

[17] This argument is developed in more detail in Thane Gustafson, "The Crisis of the Soviet Political System and Gorbachev's Political Strategy," in *Gorbachev's Russia and American Foreign Policy*, ed. Seweryn Bialer and Michael Mandelbaum (Boulder: Westview Press, 1988), 187–230.

most potentially threatening time for the authority of the regime and the stability of the country, since the aftermath of World War II. Surely, one might have thought, such a decline in regime performance would have brought a crisis in civil-military relations. But the second broad conclusion of this book is that, on the whole, the "crisis of effectiveness" from 1975 to 1985 produced surprisingly few signs of deep-seated civil-military conflict. It may have strained the terms of the civil-military contract, but it did not rupture it.

This conclusion is rather different from that of other recent analyses of civil-military relations, and it may even seem to conflict with the evidence presented in Bruce Parrott's chapter. Did not the "golden age" come under strain as early as 1974? Was there not growing civil-military tension throughout the second half of the decade, and open conflict by the beginning of the 1980s? Parrott's evidence is consistent and persuasive, and we do not disagree with it. But our conclusion is based on the larger framework of the civil-military "contract," and particularly on the following three points.

First, what was the actual impact of the changes in the economic and political environment on the flow of resources to the military-industrial sector? We have already noted that the military maintained its share of GNP. But since overall GNP growth dropped steadily with every five-year plan under Brezhnev, does this not mean that the growth rate of military spending slowed as well? Not necessarily: Robert Campbell's evidence suggests that when one looks below the level of official money allocations to the actual flow of material resources and manpower, the military-industrial sector continued to receive a growing share of the total growth in investment resources for machine building, including particularly R&D personnel. The civilian leadership may have intended to slow the growth rate of resources for the military-industrial, and they may even have thought they were succeeding, but the "informal priority system" continued to operate as before, insuring continued preferential treatment for military-industrial needs.

Ellen Jones's essay reaches much the same conclusion: universal service and premilitary training, on the one hand, and a well-nourished network of officers' academies, on the other, ensured a preferential flow of manpower to the military. The manpower pool may have been less healthy, less docile and martial, and less fluent in Russian (not to mention less computer-literate) than senior officers would have liked, but the combination of internal "streaming" arrangements and the shortage of real battlefield challenges meant there were few military consequences, even allowing for Afghanistan, where, as Bruce Porter argues, only about 2 percent of the Soviet military ever served. One might add to all this one more important resource: the preferential personal benefits enjoyed by the officer corps, and especially by the senior officers, which continued unaffected by the general economic downturn. As Jones observes, an officer's career was not quite so attractive as it once was, compared to a civilian life that had grown much more prosperous than a generation ago, but it still provided a comfortable living. In short, the long-established system of preferential allocation of resources acted to buffer the military-industrial sector against the consequences of economic and sociodemographic deterioration, although no doubt that very buffering worsened the consequences of decline for the rest of the economy.

The second question is, what was the impact of environmental changes on the military's main missions? Here the conclusions from Bruce Porter's chapter and my own are instructive. Porter observes that the actual number of Soviet troops and officers involved in duty overseas has been very small compared to that of the United States. The Soviet Union remains overwhelmingly a continental power, and its main military forces and missions are configured accordingly. Moreover, in a variety of ways the Soviets have limited the impact of their overseas investments on their own organization, whether by employing Cuban surrogates, limiting ship-days on cruise, or keeping large parts of their overseas forces in a low state of readiness.[18]

In my chapter on Soviet adaptations to changing military technologies, I argue that two things cushioned the impact of external change on the military-industrial sector. First, until the mid- to late 1970s, the Soviets did not perceive the technological challenge from the West as different in essence from the ones they had been meeting successfully since World War II. Then, after the mid-1970s, though alarm mounted in some military circles (notably in Marshal Ogarkov's entourage), the "emerging" military technologies were still at a sufficiently early stage of development, and their impact on actual warfare sufficiently ambiguous, that they did not cause immediate and acute anxiety throughout the services. (The military became much more openly worried after about 1983–84, but that is a later part of the story.)

In short, buffered once against the impact of change on its flow of resources, the military-industrial sector was buffered again by the large size of its traditional missions compared to its newer overseas ones, and by the relative adaptability and effectiveness of its traditional methods of weapons design and procurement, combined with the ambiguity of the implications of the latest technological challenges for warfare.

A third source of buffering, this time on the political level, was the fact that, as decrepit and corrupt as certain parts of the machinery of state had grown, for the most part it continued to turn, and even to turn more or less normally, especially in the Central Committee apparatus and the military-industrial ministries. The technocratic apparatus, particularly in the military-industrial sector, remained reasonably well-staffed and continued to follow long-established and time-tested procedures; it is enough to recall that most of

---

[18] See also Francis Fukuyama, *Soviet Civil-Military Relations.*

the current members of Gorbachev's Politburo and Council of Ministers already occupied relatively senior positions under Brezhnev.

Moreover, long-established political practices probably prevented most of the officer corps, even at relatively senior levels, from becoming fully aware of the rot in the party leadership or the disarray at the top, or from communicating their views among themselves. Limits on news, the compartmentalization of participation, the isolation of most of the officer corps from most of the civilian population, including the political class, the successes of Soviet foreign policy and of military modernization until the late 1970s—these features must have slowed the loss of the leadership's prestige and authority in the eyes of all but the most senior and well-informed military officers. And this latter group was presumably still sufficiently inhibited by long-inculcated norms of nonpolitical service and severe sanctions for disloyalty not to voice unfavorable political views to junior officers and thus contribute to a "community of opinion" within the officer corps.[19]

Ironically, this triple buffering may not have prevented a double misunderstanding: as Campbell observes, the Soviet leaders, looking at the statistics on military spending, may have firmly believed that, even allowing for their own efforts to slow down the rate of growth of military spending, they were giving the military steadily increasing budgetary support. Yet the military, for their part, looking at the flat procurement rates that prevailed from the mid-1970s on, may have perceived that their actual buying power was being cut back.[20] As both sides waved conflicting figures at one another, civil-military tensions rose while the allocation system below continued to operate more or less as usual, steadily building up the military's actual share of resources.

Another pair of misperceptions may have played a role in building up civil-military tensions over the gravity of the "American threat." The Soviet General Staff, perceiving the American rearmament and the tough rhetoric of the Reagan administration, may have overreacted to it, to the point of convincing

[19] This is distinct from grumbling or even snickering. Jeremy Azrael, for example, makes much of the military's resentment over Ustinov's appointment as minister of defense in 1976, and of stories that the military greeted Brezhnev's promotion to the rank of marshal, in May of the same year, with derision, and probably that of Ustinov as well. See Jeremy R. Azrael, *The Soviet Civilian Leadership and the Military High Command, 1976–1986*, R-3521-AF (Santa Monica: Rand Corporation, June, 1987), 5–6. To begin with, the two cases were probably perceived as quite different from one another. It is not difficult to believe that the military would have preferred a uniformed officer in the Politburo, but did they really resent the appointment of a man who during his entire career had overseen the modernization of the Soviet arsenal? Their resentment probably grew later, as Ustinov clearly associated himself with policies of Brezhnev that the military increasingly disliked. As for phony military rank, surely the tradition of political generals was so well established in the Soviet Union that officers merely shrugged at the sight of another one.

[20] Abraham S. Becker, *Ogarkov's Complaint and Gorbachev's Dilemma: The Soviet Defense Budget and Party-Military Conflict*, R-3541-AF (Santa Monica: Rand Corporation, December 1987).

itself by 1982–83 that there was a serious danger of war. The political leadership, perhaps understanding better its changeable American opponent but underestimating the impact of its own actions on American opinion, clung to its military modernization and to arms control and detente, Brezhnev-style, and insisted that all was well.

In short, to say that the essentials of the contract were maintained is not to say that civilian and military leaders saw eye to eye. Nevertheless, the overall conclusion that emerges from our study is that during the Brezhnev years the military-industrial sector was relatively insulated from the many-sided crisis that gripped the Soviet Union in the decade 1975–1985, and consequently was relatively unaffected by the changes taking place in the "external variables" surrounding it. If that is the case, then as we move on to the next section we should observe, first, relatively limited adaptive responses by the military-industrial sector, and correspondingly few changes in internal organization, structures, roles, and procedures; and second, internal disagreements and tensions within the military-industrial sector as those more affected argued with others who saw less need for change. This would imply that the military-industrial sector was further buffered against change by a fourth factor: the inertia of its own internal structures and procedures, and internal disagreements that inhibited change.

Military-Industrial Responses to Change, 1965–1985

The structures, procedures, and official views of large organizations represent complex compromises and alliances, and much trial and error goes into adapting to their surroundings; it is little wonder, therefore, that organizations resist change. When a response becomes necessary nevertheless, organizations typically proceed step-wise, trying the familiar solutions first, adapting existing structures and procedures wherever possible, and reaching for new ones only in cases of dire necessity.[21]

Adaptive Responses

The responses of the Soviet military-industrial sector to the changes of the mid-1960s to the mid-1980s illustrate this general pattern. We have argued that the sector was triply buffered against the changes in its environment during this period, even during the dire decade of 1975–1985. Its responses were correspondingly muted: While they varied with the type and perceived sever-

---

[21] For two samples of the large literature on these subjects, see John D. Steinbruner, *The Cybernetic Theory of Decision: New Dimensions of Political Analysis* (Princeton: Princeton University Press, 1974), and Richard M. Cyert and James G. March, *Behavioral Theory of the Firm* (Englewood Cliffs, N.J.: Prentice-Hall, 1963).

ity of challenge, overall the military-industrial sector's answers to change consisted of limited adaptations along familiar lines.

The impact of change was least great in the sociocultural realm, and consequently this is also the area in which the military's own responses were the smallest. As Ellen Jones shows, where the military perceived that the available manpower was physically unfit, unfamiliar with Russian, inclined toward pacifism, or inadequately educated, they reacted by criticizing the schools, the family, and the media, in other words, by heightening their demands on civilian institutions. But their own adaptations were minimal, consisting of marginal improvements in living conditions for soldiers, symbolic efforts to curtail physical discipline, a modest affirmative action program for non-Russian officer candidates, and the like.

Economic stringency and technological change presented a more complex challenge. We have argued that the economic pressure on the military-industrial sector was not the result of a slowdown in the growth rate of real resources. Nevertheless, because simultaneously the costs of new weapons were rising rapidly and several development programs were encountering problems and delays, officers and defense industrialists increasingly perceived stringency. The uneasiness produced by these changes was severe enough to cause lively debate and some conflict.

Only part of this, however, was directed at the leadership; more often, different military-industrial players argued with one another.[22] How they actually responded depended on the breadth and severity of the perceived stress and on the availability of "off-the-shelf" options for adaptation.

Three types of responses will illustrate the point. First, in the area of weapons design and procurement, the Soviet defense industries responded to technological challenge with options that had long been part of the standard arsenal, and which therefore involved no fundamental internal changes of structure, personnel, or procedure: closer ties with basic science, more use of Western design concepts and know-how, greater centralization of decision making, and still more systematic use of traditional design conventions and management techniques. In some cases, this produced a partial "Westernization" of design; in other cases, the result was parallel lines of new weapons, some more "Soviet-style" and others more "Western-style" in design. But overall, the Soviets did not abandon the basic design and procurement strategies that had served them well for decades.[23]

---

[22] See in particular Rose E. Gottemoeller, "Conflict and Consensus in the Soviet Armed Forces," in *The Dynamics of Soviet Defense Policy*, ed. Bruce Parrott (Washington, D.C.: Wilson Center Press, 1990).

[23] An interesting current example is sea-launched cruise missiles. The SS-N-21 shows considerable Western influence in design concept but represents at the same time an impressive display of microminiaturization and other industrial advances. The SS-NX-24, which has not yet reached operational deployment, is an older, "incremental" design. I am indebted to Rose Gottemoeller

Second, in response to the growing technological challenge to conventional forces, particularly in Europe, the Soviets made substantial changes in the organization of their forces: the adoption of the "theater" as the central unit of organization, the formation of operational maneuver groups, special air-assault brigades, and the like.[24] Similarly, the increasing vulnerability of their silo-based ICBMs led the Soviets to move to a more elaborate triad of strategic weapons, including in particular an expanded and modernized strategic bomber force. These were not trivial changes: they were associated with new kinds of equipment (such as the "MAINSTAY" AWACS airplane or the extensively reconfigured BEAR-H bomber), new command systems and training programs, and new priorities among the services.

Nevertheless, these were still incremental responses. In conventional weaponry, their effect was to retain and strengthen the traditional combined-arms concept, based on mechanized armor. The Soviet military conducted at least two rounds of debate on the future of the tank, and on both occasions rejected the view that the tank was doomed.[25] In this case as in others, Marshal Ogarkov's more radical prescriptions were rejected, and a new consensus formed around a more incremental approach to modernization.

This reassertion of traditional concepts was part of a larger response to perceived economic stringency, namely, the reassertion of central missions. The principal victim was the navy and especially its power-projection mission in the Third World. The military high command, traditionally dominated by officers of land-based services, had never been unanimously enthusiastic about the rise of Soviet navalism or power projection in the Third World. Following the death of the navy's most important advocate, Marshal Grechko, its priority was cut back to size and its doctrinal pretensions rejected.[26]

The third example concerns the Soviet responses to more acute but more narrowly military challenges. Where Soviet equipment and tactics were found wanting on the battlefield—notably in the 1973 war, in the 1982 Beka'a Valley incident, and in Afghanistan—the military and defense industries responded with major changes. Perhaps the most striking, as Bruce Porter tells us, was the development of effective attack helicopters and new tactics to match. Other examples included improvements in artillery training[27] and tactical air

---

of the Rand Corporation for these observations. For background, see her "Land-Attack Cruise Missiles," *Adelphi Papers*, no. 226 (London: International Institute for Strategic Studies, Winter 1987–88).

[24] See, for example, Phillip A. Peterson and John G. Hines, "The Conventional Offensive in Soviet Theater Strategy," *Orbis* (Fall 1983); and John G. Hines and Phillip A. Peterson, "Changing the Soviet System of Control: Focus on Theater Warfare," *International Defense Review* (March 1986).

[25] Gottemoeller, "Conflict and Consensus."

[26] See Fukuyama, *Soviet Civil-Military Relations*, 39–42.

[27] The repercussions of the 1973 war for Soviet artillery training are discussed in Richard Woff, "Soviet Missile Troops and Artillery," pamphlet published jointly by Defence Studies, Univer-

operations.[28] But the main point about these responses is that they were "point changes"—specific, largely technical, and local in scale, and therefore comparatively easy for large organizations to make. Moreover, even in these cases the changes were limited to the least sweeping; the Soviet preference for close ground control of tactical air operations, for example, did not change substantially.

In sum, the military-industrial sector reached for traditional solutions, reasserted central concepts and missions, and made point changes in weaponry and tactics. This pattern of responses suggests the "step-wise" style typical of large organizations when not confronted with critical challenges. The relatively leisurely reactions of the military-industrial sector from the mid-1960s to the mid-1980s appear consistent with the image of a buffered system.

Evolution of Participation and the Creation of New Roles

Ten years ago, Timothy Colton challenged students of Soviet civil-military relations to move beyond their traditional preoccupation with political control to a more flexible framework for understanding the relations of soldiers and politicians and for assessing the power and influence in the hands of each. The balance of influence between them depends above all on the nature and extent of the participation of military officers—and, by extension, of defense industrialists—in the business of decision making. The nature of that participation, and its significance for power, depend on the scope of participation and the means employed in it.[29]

In line with that challenge, the next step is to ask how the changes surveyed have affected the military's participation in decision making. We turn first to the issue of scope. The scope of military participation depends, first of all, on whether there have been major changes in the military's roles. Some scholars have predicted vastly changed roles for the Soviet military; twenty years ago, for example, Roman Kolkowicz wrote that with the passing of terror and the dilution of the party's vanguard role, the military would become (indeed, had already become) "the main instrument of coercion."[30] There is very little sign of that. Throughout the Brezhnev era the KGB remained the leadership's main instrument of domestic coercion, and more recently, despite the spread of civil

---

sity of Edinburgh, and the Center for Strategic Technology, Texas A & M University, College Station, Texas, December 1983.

[28] Benjamin Lambeth, *Moscow's Lessons from the 1982 Lebanon Air War*, R-3000-AF (Santa Monica: Rand Corporation, September 1984).

[29] Timothy J. Colton, *Commissars, Commanders, and Civilian Authority: The Structure of Soviet Military Politics* (Cambridge: Harvard University Press, 1979), 231–249.

[30] Roman Kolkowicz, *The Soviet Military and the Communist Party* (Princeton: Princeton University Press, 1967; reprint, Boulder: Westview Press, 1985), 337.

disturbances under Gorbachev, it is primarily the police and the KGB, and not the military, that have dealt with them, although if disturbances were to spread that would surely change. But in principle, new civilian responsibilities could indeed create new military-industrial roles and alter the scope of participation.

Another set of predictions concerns the effects of technological progress. Stephen Meyer, for example, has argued that trends in technology alter the respective roles of politicians and military commanders, by giving the latter more and more of a monopoly of understanding of the increasingly complex skills and data of high-tech warfare. Jerry Hough has suggested, on the contrary, that a new generation of civilian experts is coming along to dilute that monopoly.[31] In both cases, the logic is that technological change creates new roles and alters old ones.

How should one go about thinking about the possible impact of such changes on participation, and thus on the civil-military balance of influence? It will be useful to begin by distinguishing among three sorts of roles, analogous to the three main domains of decision making used by Colton and others who have used a similar approach since then, notably Condoleezza Rice.[32] There are internal roles, corresponding to the military's own professional functions; institutional roles, that is, those in which soldiers and defense industrialists represent their institutions in dealings with the political leaders, notably as advisors on military-political issues; and finally, societal roles, or roles that bring officers and defense industrialists into working contact with the society and the economy, as trainers, educators, gatherers of information, and so forth.

INTERNAL ROLES

In the Western literature on civil-military relations of a generation ago, the key issue was the military's striving for "professional autonomy" and the efforts of the party leadership to keep it under control. For a scholar such as Merle Fainsod, therefore, the two principal roles of interest were those of military commander and political officer.[33] But within a few years, Kolkowicz was describing a growing diversification of internal roles among the commanders,[34] and somewhat later Colton's work, based partly on the biographies of hundreds of officers from the 1930s through the 1960s, drew attention to a similar diversity of roles among the political officers.[35] This picture of greater diversity of roles came partly from a closer look at the past, but it also reflected

---

[31] These ideas are discussed in detail in the first chapter by Gustafson.

[32] Condoleezza Rice, "The Party, the Military, and Decision Authority in the Soviet Union," *World Politics* 40, 1 (October 1987), 55–81.

[33] Fainsod, *How Russia Is Ruled.*

[34] Kolkowicz, *The Soviet Military and the Communist Party*, 309–321.

[35] Colton, *Commissars, Commanders and Civilian Authority.*

new developments, as the military adapted to their expanding missions and more demanding technologies. As a result, Western analysts became more aware of the complexity of civil-military relations in the management of the military's internal affairs. The simple dichotomy of "commander" versus "commissar," struggling over the issue of "professional autonomy," no longer fit reality, if it ever had.

From the mid-1960s to the mid-1980s, as the foregoing chapters suggest, professional roles within the Soviet military and defense industries continued to diversify. It is no longer simply that the officer-technocrat has displaced the old-style tank commander, or that political officers' careers have become more distinct from those of commanders. Within the General Staff alone, there are now specialists on arms control and diplomacy, systems analysis, foreign intelligence, counterinsurgency warfare, power projection and airlift logistics, space-based command and control, not to mention more conventional specialties.[36] The same has occurred within the VPK, the apparatus of the Ministry of Defense, and the major design bureaus.

These new roles and missions have broadened the variety of interests and viewpoints within the military-industrial sector; and if American experience is any guide, this makes internal cohesion and unity more difficult to achieve. (In this respect, the military-industrial sector differs only in degree from other Soviet institutions, notably the party apparatus itself.)[37] In particular, there may be a greater division of roles at the top of the military leadership, notably between the minister of defense and the chief of the General Staff, creating greater potential for differences between them.[38]

At the same time, the military-industrial leadership has attempted to impose order on this more complex scene by expanding the roles of centralizers and coordinators. Since the 1960s the General Staff has sought to develop unified training and planning, to preserve the combined-arms doctrine against the tendency of the services to advocate specialized missions, and to centralize communications and troop control.[39] Whether this effort has been successful is not the point here; rather, the new centralizers themselves add to the diversity of roles, thereby adding to the potential variety and complexity of civil-military interaction.

[36] Kenneth Currie, "The Soviet General Staff's New Role," *Problems of Communism* 33, 2 (March–April 1984).

[37] Jerry Hough, in an essay published nearly twenty years ago, called attention to the potential cleavage lines within the party apparatus as a result of the party's increasingly diverse roles. See "The Party Apparatchiki and Interest Group Theory," in Jerry F. Hough, *The Soviet Union and Social Science Theory* (Cambridge: Harvard University Press, 1977), 71–108.

[38] This theme is developed in particular in Dale Herspring, *The Soviet High Command, 1964–1989: Politics and Personalities* (Princeton: Princeton University Press, 1990).

[39] Rice, "The Party, the Military, and Decision Authority."

INSTITUTIONAL AND SOCIETAL ROLES

One might have thought that the economic and social trends of the last twenty years would have led military-industrial institutions to play larger societal roles. Yet our study suggests that very little of the sort took place between the mid-1960s and the mid-1980s, at least on the level of whole institutions. The military, unlike their grandfathers in the 1920s, resisted taking additional responsibility for shaping Soviet youth or teaching them Russian, insisting instead that that was the job of the civilian authorities. Similarly, the military's commitment to power projection roles in the Third World was never single-minded, and it appears to have receded after the death of Defense Minister Grechko in 1976.[40] Lastly, neither the military nor the defense industries developed major new roles in the mobilization or assimilation of new science and technology; instead, they strengthened their ties with the traditional sources of such expertise, especially the USSR Academy of Sciences and its major divisions and republican affiliates, and expanded traditional information-gathering activities overseas.[41]

One interesting new development is the military's increased expertise in economic analysis and industrial management, in response to economic stringency and the increased political salience of economic issues in civil-military bargaining. The evidence, unfortunately, is slim and ambiguous.

It has long been the case, for example, that military officers are detached to Gosplan and other major state committees, but it is likely that they are, in effect, high-level *voenpredy*, charged with monitoring the flow of physical resources. Abraham Becker suggests that the military may have used studies of military spending to bolster their case for increased budgets, but he does not claim to know whether such studies (if they really existed) were developed internally or commissioned elsewhere.[42] Meyer, Rice, and David Holloway document the growth of systems analysis in the General Staff and in military institutes, but they are unable to say how much such analysis may have affected actual decision making.[43] Perhaps the most eloquent indirect evidence concerning military roles in economic decision making are the somewhat embarrassed admissions heard recently from Soviet spokesmen to the effect that

[40] See Fukuyama, *Soviet-Civil Military Relations*. One would like to know, in particular, what role Soviet military leaders played in the decision to use Cuban surrogates in place of Soviet troops in Ethiopia and Angola.

[41] Thus, sources cited in my technology chapter argue that the GRU has greatly expanded its activities in the illegal acquisition of Western technology. That is plausible, but the point here is that this does not represent a new role.

[42] Becker, *Ogarkov's Complaint*.

[43] Rice, "The Party, the Military, and Decision Authority." See also Meyer and Holloway sources cited in chapter 6.

they do not really know how much their defense costs. One suspects that the military role in economic decision making remains underdeveloped, other than in the final bargaining over who gets what at the top.

If the military and the defense industries did not assume major new roles in social and economic policy, they certainly did—or, at least, individuals did—in foreign affairs. Admiral Gorshkov himself traveled the world as diplomat and arms salesman, as did other high-ranking officers and defense officials. The growing Soviet military presence overseas was accompanied by new reporting functions; thus, the intervention in Afghanistan was prepared by high-level visits by then–ground forces commander General Pavlovskii, and there were naturally many others after that.

A handful of officers with backgrounds in arms control have been attached to offices in the party Central Committee, the Ministry of Foreign Affairs, and elsewhere, and military officers have played leading roles in all arms-control negotiations since the 1960s. Military intelligence operatives have played a growing part in the VPK's technology transfer program. Each of these activities is backed up by larger, if less visible, staff support and specialized institutions. They add up to growing military roles, or at least capabilities, in foreign-policy advice and decision making.

The most eye-catching case of role expansion from the mid-1960s to the mid-1980s was the military's growing visibility in the formation of military doctrine. This clearly began as a military reaction against Khrushchev's lopsided stress on nuclear weapons and his efforts to cut back conventional armaments. But in the first half of the Brezhnev era the military developed more elaborate institutions for work on doctrine (notably the General Staff Academy) and more numerous and assertive specialists. By the second half of Brezhnev's rule, as Parrott's chapter argues, civilian leaders reasserted their jurisdiction over doctrine, but the military were not denied their new voice and continued to participate actively in doctrinal debates.

In sum, during the two decades from the mid-1960s to the mid-1980s, the military-industrial sector expanded its roles, but in a definite pattern: not at all in social roles, more in foreign and doctrinal than in economic, and most of all in internal roles. Outside its internal arena, the military's role expansion was more of scope than of means: small numbers of individuals were involved, or at most individual offices, academies, and the like. In contrast, the expansion of the defense industries' participation in the civilian economy was one of means rather than scope: though they produced more civilian goods, they took no greater part in economic policy or increased responsibility for the performance of the civilian economy.

The next question is, how did these limited expansions of roles affect military participation in policy making? Did they create new assets, and thereby new influence?

Roles, Assets, and Influence

A number of Western observers, noting the expanded roles of the military and the defense industry, argued that these created new assets for them, while those of the civilian side diminished. This, indeed, is the reasoning behind most of the claims that the military-industrial sector gained influence, even power, as the Brezhnev era wore on. We have already noted, for example, Meyer's argument that the military's monopoly of technical expertise represented a growing asset in decision making for national security from the mid-1960s to the mid-1980s. Similarly, one might infer that the added information and expertise gained from the military's growing roles overseas would represent assets in decision making, as would the growing presence of military officers in key civilian offices.

But the essays in this book suggest a different interpretation. The military-industrial expansion of roles was limited and uneven. Instead of creating lasting assets for the military-industrial sector, such role expansion as did occur may have created only fragile assets and even liabilities. This would help to explain the seeming collapse of the sector's influence after Gorbachev's accession.

The reasoning is this: the bulk of the military's role expansion occurred in areas of foreign policy and doctrine. These were precisely the areas that were coming to be seen by the political elite as sources of expense, danger, and failure. The military's monopoly of expertise and its autonomy in technical operations, in particular, were increasingly perceived as a threat (nowhere more clearly, perhaps, than in the deployment of the SS-20 in the mid-1970s and the resulting fiasco of the fall of 1983). Meanwhile, in the area of mounting social and economic problems, the military and the defense industries had developed no roles or expertise at all, and in fact had resisted doing so. Ogarkov's demands for increased civil defense, industrial preparedness, and patriotic education thus came from a man who had essentially no seat at the social or economic policy-making table, and who did not have behind him an apparatus of officers involved in planning, education, public health, and so on, or a history of useful proposals. Indeed, the military must have been perceived as one of the aggravating causes of problems in these areas, precisely because of the tenacity with which they clung to a growing share of resources and manpower, while insisting that the civilian sector bear responsibility for all problems.

Thus the military's expanded roles and seeming assets, rather than increasing the authority and influence of the military, may ironically have lessened them instead, because the areas in which they were concentrated were themselves coming under scrutiny and criticism by the political class and the rising leadership. Assets and roles are not directly cashable into influence and authority; they must be seen to be associated with success.

Summing Up the Evolution of Civil-Military Relations in the Brezhnev Era

This analysis of the Brezhnev era begins with the first of two paradoxes arising out of Model III: Given the multiple "crisis of effectiveness" in the Soviet Union in the second half of Brezhnev's rule, together with the growing perceived threats to Soviet national security, one would have expected the terms of the unspoken contract among the parties of the civil-military triangle to come under severe strain. Why, then, was there no crisis in civil-military relations?

The foregoing chapters suggest the outlines of an answer: The military-industrial sector was heavily buffered against change by a long-standing network of arrangements that protected it (even against the wishes of the civilian leaders) from changes in its preferential share of resources, sheltered the bulk of the military from the effects of marginal changes in its missions, and partially insulated it from direct contact with the political corruption and disarray that affected the civilian leadership and the growing anomie in civilian life. Consequently, the military-industrial sector did not suffer the full effects of the crisis.

To the lesser changes they did feel, military-industrial leaders were able to respond with limited adjustments along largely established lines, or with no changes at all. (Marshal Ogarkov's jeremiads, lest we forget, were directed at least as much against the inertia of his colleagues as against the party leadership.) But as a result, there was no fundamental alteration in the organization of the services, the procedures for recruiting and training manpower, the style of weapons design and procurement, the participation in the civilian economy, or the mix of missions and their relative priority. Indeed, of all the major institutions in Soviet society, the military and the defense industries appeared to have responded least, and perhaps learned least, from the changes taking place around them.

As a further consequence, the roles and assets of the military-industrial side within the civil-military triangle changed little, as did the range of their participation. In particular, the military-industrial players did not venture into the "societal" domain of policy making, let alone that of "sovereignty," any more than they had in the past. In foreign policy and in doctrine, such role expansion as occurred may well have created liabilities rather than assets, detracting from the military influence and authority in the eyes of the political generation coming to power.

Much has been made of the fact that under Brezhnev the military broadened their roles in at least one area of "high politics," namely, the formation of doctrine. But this issue is best seen in long-term perspective: issues of doctrine, strategy, and force structure have long been debated and bargained between civilian and political leaders, even under Stalin. It is probably the case that over the decades the military's participation in this area has become more institutionalized, more public, and more accepted, but those are trends characteristic of all participation by technical specialists in Soviet policy debates. In any case, the extent of the military's sole jurisdiction over doctrine during the so-called golden age should not be exaggerated; if in reaction to Khrushchev's blunders the civilian leadership left the field of doctrine to the military in the first half of the Brezhnev era, by the second half they were back in force. Once again, the golden age looks like a passing anomaly.

In sum, the military-industrial sector remained privileged, protected, and subordinated, as it had ever since the early 1940s. The first apparent paradox disappears: There was no crisis in civil-military relations from 1975 to 1985 because the terms of the contract were not unduly strained. If the rest of the Soviet system remained surprisingly stable during this decade, it is less surprising that the civil-military relationship remained so, because the crisis affected it less.[44] The golden age, or at least the essential foundations of it, did not end until after Gorbachev took office.

The Outlook for Civil-Military Relations under Gorbachev

Brief as Gorbachev's tenure as leader has been, one can already distinguish two broad phases in it, and perhaps now the beginning of a third. During his first year, Gorbachev stuck essentially to Andropovian lines: while scattering symbolic gestures suggesting change, he remained cautious in his rhetoric, leaned to an industry-first, technocratic approach to policy, emphasized discipline over reform, and avoided challenging the major institutions. During his second year, both his speech and his policies grew bolder, more innovative, and more confrontational, and by the winter and spring of 1987 they turned distinctly radical. Since the fall of 1987, Gorbachev has tried to hold the political center, to quell the radical fringes, and to placate alarmed conservatives, but he has stuck to his reform agenda, which if anything has grown still bolder.

Gorbachev's treatment of the uniformed military and the defense industries, as seen in the earlier chapters, followed much the same course. Yet, from the beginning, Gorbachev was noticeably less solicitous in public of the uni-

---

[44] It is striking that this description of the civil-military relationship fits many of the conditions of stability described by Seweryn Bialer in *Stalin's Successors: Leadership, Stability, and Change in the Soviet Union* (Cambridge: Cambridge University Press, 1980), 127–226.

formed military than his predecessors had been. With the beginning of the radical phase of perestroika and the embarrassment of the Rust affair in the spring of 1987, Gorbachev became both more openly critical of the military-industrial sector personally and more willing to allow public criticism by others.[45] In the summer of 1988, at the Nineteenth Party Conference, Gorbachev brought the radical implications of his economic program home to the military-industrial sector by calling (and allowing others to call) for transfers of resources and priority from the military to the civilian side.[46] Since December 1988 he has stated explicitly that both military spending and the size of the armed forces will be reduced, and the 1990 plan contains the first explicit implementation of the new priorities.

Western observers, noting these trends and watching the disturbed responses of leading officers, have begun to speculate that the Soviet Union is headed for a new era of civil-military tension and confrontation. This book has discussed the main issues: Gorbachev's symbolic slights of the military and changes of military-industrial personnel, signs of a slowdown in military spending and efforts to challenge the informal allocation system, public criticism of the military by journalists and intellectuals, the new doctrine of "defensive sufficiency" and radical innovations in arms control, the newly prominent role of civilian advisers, and lastly, the withdrawal from Afghanistan.

In the perspective of this book, however, it is important to distinguish carefully between what one might call "manageable friction" at the edges of established civil-military boundaries, and threats to the very basis of the civil-military contract. Each of the issues just mentioned is ambiguous in its possible political effects. Personnel turnover may threaten senior officers, but it opens up glittering promotions for junior ones. Glasnost may ruffle military pride, but it also gives military-industrial people new latitude to criticize the leaders' policies and the ills of civilian society. A slowdown in military spending is disturbing, but it need not cause a crisis if the military retain priority in de facto resource allocations at lower levels, if enough officers are convinced that the long-term goal of technological modernization is being served, and if in the process the military are not threatened in their status and livelihood. The

---

[45] See Dale R. Herspring, "Gorbachev, Yazov, and the Military," *Problems of Communism* 36, 4 (July–August 1987), 99–107; and F. Stephen Larrabee, "Gorbachev and the Soviet Military."

[46] Gorbachev's own speech at the party conference criticized his predecessors for allowing the country to be drawn into an all-out arms race and for basing Soviet foreign policy too much on military strength. He omitted any ritual phrases to reassure the military that they would get "everything necessary" to maintain a strong defense, stating instead that "the effectiveness of our defense must be measured henceforth in terms of qualitative parameters, both in technology and in manpower." Gorbachev also called for "deep transformations" in defense industry and repeated his previous exhortations to the defense industries to give greater emphasis to consumer goods. ("O khode realizatsii reshenii XXVII s"ezda KPSS i zadachakh po uglubleniiu perestroiki," *Pravda*, 29 June 1988.)

withdrawal from Afghanistan might lead the military to blame the civilian leadership for their defeat, but as Bruce Porter observes, the size of the Soviet contingent in Afghanistan was only one-tenth that of the United States in Vietnam, and consequently operations in Afghanistan never affected the Soviet military as deeply, especially since the military have not been blamed for defeat. Finally, Gorbachev's arms-control policies, and the prominent role of civilian advisers in shaping them, may be unsettling to some officers, but one should also observe that military officers have been given unprecedented latitude and public visibility in negotiations, and there are military officers attached to all of the major civilian offices dealing with security policy.

In sum, the most visible surface signs of tension within the civil-military triangle over the last two years—the signs that Model I would make the most of—turn out on reflection to be ambiguous. Taken by themselves, they need not cause a crisis in civil-military relations, particularly if Gorbachev takes care to stand above the fray.

But they are symbols and portents of something much more fundamental: perestroika itself, if actually carried out, threatens the threefold buffering of the military-industrial sector and thus the very basis of the civil-military contract.

First, the most important single guarantor of the position of the military-industrial sector is the informal allocation system. If ministries are weakened, if the branch industrial departments of the party apparatus (most of which were dissolved in the autumn of 1988) remain shut down, if the local soviets gain a more powerful voice in resource allocation and are encouraged to use it to raise local living standards, if producer goods are allocated through a wholesale market system, it will be more difficult for the military-industrial system to assert its priority. To be sure, the defense industry department of the party Central Committee remains in business (as do its counterparts at lower levels of the apparatus), and the device of "state orders" (*goszakazy*) will protect the commodities of direct strategic significance; but as the coverage of *goszakazy* is restricted, military customers will be forced to compete by rules that are not so much in their favor as formerly.

Gorbachev's efforts to enlist the defense industry into the campaign to modernize civilian industry, described in chapter 5 by Julian Cooper, could threaten the military's informal priority by diluting it and by distracting the VPK ministries from their core mission of serving the military. To be sure, the defense industry has been producing civilian goods and equipment for decades. But the threat could be much greater this time, if civilian ministries are transferred to the jurisdiction of the VPK, or if VPK ministries are given major and visible roles in the service sector, and actually held to account for them.[47]

---

[47] Consumer electronics is the most prominent example so far. For example, three VPK ministries (Minpromsviazi, Minradioprom, and Minelektronprom) produce 94 percent of all Soviet

Then a natural process would begin to occur: a "civilian" wing of the VPK network would come into being, providing new careers, offices, and resources, and the hitherto unchallenged military customer might find that a powerful competitor had been introduced inside its own boundaries. So far, that has not happened, and the VPK ministries have fought a grumbling rearguard action against the role expansion being proposed for them.[48] But the battle is only beginning.

Second, the fundamental threat of glasnost is not so much that it ruffles the military's sense of honor, but that it could contribute to breaking down the isolation of the Soviet officer corps from the rest of society, making officers more aware of ferment in society, of the government's difficulties, of nationalist views, of revisionist history—in short, creating the basis for *opinion* among a much larger group of military people than heretofore. The threat is that glasnost, as in the rest of society, can be a catalyst for the formation of true interest groups, that is, groups not simply derived from the state, but increasingly aware of their own views and interests, able to communicate them internally, and increasingly resolved to defend them.

The other deep threat of glasnost to the underpinnings of the military-industrial sector is the prospect that in the early 1990s, in the wake of price reform, detailed information about military spending will become widely available to the Soviet public. One of the most essential features of the informal allocation system was precisely that it operated out of sight. No detailed figures were publicly available; those that circulated within even the highest elite were probably unreliable; and the flow of physical goods and services to the military-industrial sector was largely uncharted and unchartable. But if the Soviet political class ever became more fully aware of the full burden of defense, this information could heighten competition for resources from the Politburo on down.

It is not only perestroika that will affect the position of the military, but also

television sets. These have been fiercely criticized in the Soviet media under Gorbachev, and their manufacturers held up to ridicule. Some of them have now been instructed to set up a network of repair shops. See Tatiana Boldyreva, "Tele—ele-ele," *Ekonomika i organizatsiia promyshlennogo proizvodstva*, no. 5 (1987), 115ff; and M. Maksimovskaia, "Televizor otdai vragu," *Izvestiia*, 8 May 1988. The latter article, devoted to the problem of exploding television sets, criticizes the manufacturers for hiding behind state secrecy to keep outside inspectors away.

[48] Two examples among many: the Ministry of the Aviation Industry played a key role in supplying jet engines to power the Soviet gas transmission network in the wake of the Reagan compressor embargo of 1982–83. Recently there have been reports that, now that the emergency has passed, the ministry is lagging in supplying more engines and in servicing those it supplied. See V. T. Fadeev, "Effektivnost gazotransportnoi sistemy: sovremennaia taktika tekhnicheskogo obnovleniia," *Gazovaia promyshlennost*, no. 11 (1987), 26–29; also *Ekonomicheskaia gazeta*, no. 50 (1987), 3. The second example concerns the failure of Minpromsviazi to support Gorbachev's program to modernize the domestic telephone network. *Elektrosviaz*, no. 9 (1987), 2. I am grateful to Robert Campbell for calling my attention to these sources.

the unanticipated side-effects of perestroika. Nothing was so great an irritant in civil-military relations under the tsars as the task of maintaining civil order and repressing dissent, which was entrusted to the army. As nationalist tensions continue to grow, the military may well be drawn into a new and unwelcome role.

Finally, if the agenda of the Gorbachev reformers is to reduce the size of the military factor in the Soviet system, this is ultimately the greatest threat to the basis of the traditional civil-military contract and therefore the single most explosive issue in the reform program, because it would affect the military's core missions and the very standing of the officer corps as a social group. The size of the officer corps could drop, but, more serious, the perquisites, social prestige, and professional pride of the officer corps could all be diminished simultaneously. It is symptomatic that the strongest military grumbling registered under Gorbachev to date concerns not budgets or doctrine per se but the recollection of Khrushchev's mass cashiering of officers and men.[49] Simultaneously, massive cuts in Soviet conventional forces and the adoption of an operational defensive doctrine would drastically affect the traditional dominance of the land forces and their traditional offensive strategy.

Such drastic changes seemed unthinkable under the Gorbachev of 1985, implausible in 1986, unlikely in 1987. But events since the Nineteenth Party Conference in 1988 must suggest to the military-industrial sector that unless Gorbachev is stopped, he will remove much of their traditional buffering. The military's resources, internal structures, roles, and assets will all be changed. If the civil-military relationship is essentially one of contract, as Model III argues, then a crisis surely lies ahead. The second paradox disappears: the golden age is truly coming to an end, not under Brezhnev, but under Gorbachev.

But if, as was suggested at the beginning of this essay, the civil-military relationship is more than one of contract, but of authority based on shared interests and ideas, it is possible that Gorbachev and the reformers can avoid a crisis after all. Soviet officers and defense industrialists are not simply soldiers and munitions makers; they are also Soviet citizens. It would be surprising if they were entirely insensitive to the appeal of a man who (to use Weberian language), in addition to his own undoubted personal charisma, is determined to restore the charisma of the Leninist system, to break the creep toward neotraditionalism of the Brezhnev period, and to introduce elements of modern authority based on legal-rational principles. If Soviet soldiers are

---

[49] The commander of the VVS, General Ivan M. Tretiak (himself a former ground forces officer), wrote in 1988, "Any changes in the army have to be weighed a thousand times. For instance, at the end of the 1950s the Soviet Union unilaterally reduced the army by 1.2 million men. Economists have calculated that this enabled us to increase old-age pensions two-fold, to create housing-building combines. But that step was hasty, it dealt a colossal blow to our defense potential, the officer corps included" (*Moscow News*, 21 February 1988).

modern men, then they may acknowledge not only the rationality but the legitimacy of what Gorbachev is trying to do, however uncomfortable it may be for them. In that case, it is conceivable that a new "contract" can be negotiated. It hardly requires saying that these are heroic assumptions; it is far more likely that there is open battle ahead.

Final Points and Speculations

This study has developed five broad themes. The first is that the "external" forces bearing on civil-military relations in the last generation are of long standing and have shaped the entire Soviet system, not just the civil-military triangle. The crisis that struck the Soviet Union after the mid-1970s and launched the present leaders on their extraordinary careers was connected to long secular movements: the extended slowing of economic growth; the steady pressure of technological change; the side-effects of evolution of Soviet society (urbanization, ethnic mix, birthrates); gradual changes in the effective, if unwritten, rules of politics; and the steady expansion of Soviet interest and presence overseas.

The second broad theme is that the military-industrial sector was less affected by these trends than the rest of the Soviet polity, economy, and society. The military-industrial sector has been buffered against change, first, by the system (formal and especially informal) of resource allocation; second, by the inertia of its established missions and the availability of "off-the-shelf" options for change; and third, by the traditional rules and procedures governing participation and communication, which isolated the military from most political life and facilitated the development of an inward- and backward-looking professionalism.

As a result, this study argues, military roles and views, the range and types of military participation, and, finally, the balance of influence among civilian and military players have been slow to change. The "golden age" of civil-military relations of the first half of the Brezhnev era seems to the authors of this study less golden, and the second half less brazen, than commonly portrayed. And while the end of the Brezhnev era brought crisis to every part of the civilian system, the military system was relatively unscathed, and there was no crisis in civil-military relations, although there was certainly growing friction.

But the multiple buffering that sheltered the military-industrial sector had delayed side-effects that are only now becoming apparent. First, the special priority given to the military-industrial sector aggravated the crisis of the rest of the economy, by continuing to draw off an expanding share of scarce resources even after growth had virtually ceased. Second, a sheltered military-industrial elite learned less from the experiences of the last decade than many parts of the civilian elite, and consequently it represents more of a conservative force today. It is no accident that the "technocratic wing" of the new leadership consists largely of former officials of the VPK ministries.

Finally, the last broad theme of this study is that the Gorbachev program, which is itself a response to the long-term trends in the Soviet system, has the potential to disrupt the stability of civil-military relations, not so much because of arms-control agreements with the West, symbolic slights to the military, criticism by intellectuals, or even budgetary cutbacks, but above all because perestroika and the *novoe myshlenie*, "new thinking," threaten the very basis of the civil-military relationship, and especially the traditional multiple buffering. If the military's missions are radically transformed, if the informal resource-allocation system is weakened, if glasnost is allowed to penetrate deeply into the military and defense industry, then more change will be visited upon the military-industrial sector in the next few years than over the last forty. Perestroika threatens the system of objective control and thus the basis of the military's professionalism, by exposing it to politics and possibly drawing it into political, or at any rate extramilitary, roles, while weakening and downgrading its traditional ones. If "objective control" now becomes tinged with "subjective," civil-military relations will become more politicized, less sheltered, and far less stable.

As one reflects on the broad sweep of civil-military relations over the postwar period, the most striking thing is the essential stability of the relationship, which must be seen as part of the remarkable stability of the Soviet regime as a whole. The same broad features of the Soviet regime that have served as hedges against disruption and discord, when added to the extra protections with which the military-industrial sector is surrounded, account for much of that stability. But the greatest source of stability of all is the fact that the Soviet leadership maintained for over thirty years after Stalin's death the essential priorities, growth strategies, and institutional structures it had inherited.

Gorbachev is now being driven by the logic of his own reform program to question these features, although it would be too much to say that he has yet attempted to dismantle them altogether. But if he does so, he will be striking simultaneously at the heart of the militarized socialism that the traditional priorities, strategies, and structures were there to sustain, and at the very basis of the traditional civil-military relationship.

Index

Academy of Sciences, USSR, 49, 80, 146, 150; ties to military, 157, 224–226, 354
Adamovich, A. M., 85
Afanasev, S. A., 167, 172, 178
Afgantsy. See Afghanistan, veterans of
Afghanistan, 43, 247–248, 259; compared to Vietnam war, 294–295; decision to invade, 305–307; domestic opinion on, 318–320; media treatment of war in, 271–272; veterans of, 272, 316, 321, 327, 328; war in, 286–287, 292; withdrawal from, 243, 247, 300, 304, 316–318, 360
Akhromeev, S. F., 79, 82, 83, 279, 309, 319; chief of General Staff, 33, 72, 74; removal of, 33n.77, 88, 280, 313, 314; opposed to invasion of Afghanistan, 307
Alcohol, abuse of, 246–247; campaign against, 248–249; and KGB, 116
Aleksandrov, A. P., 146, 225
Andropov, Iu. V., 29, 56, 70, 90, 98, 103, 105; detente, 119–120; Polish crisis, 118; Third World policy, 119
Arbatov, G. A., 68
Army, Red, 17, 21; Tsarist, 15–17. *See also* Professionalization
Artemev, P. A., 95
Azrael, Jeremy, 25, 26, 31

Badamiants, V. G., 116
Bakhirev, V. V., 167
Baklanov, O. D., 174, 182, 183
Balmont, B. V., 172, 178
Balzer, Harley, 154
Barisov, G. G., 291, 302, 303–304
Barmin, V. P., 205
Batkin, Leonid, 319
Becker, Abraham, 354
Belenko, Viktor, 301
Beliaev, V., 302
Beliakov, O. S., 174, 183
Belianin, P. N., 184
Belousov, B. M., 176
Belousov, I. S., 149, 151, 175, 180, 182, 183
Beriia, L. P., 19, 23, 99, 201

Berkhin affair, 108
Bessmertnykh, A. A., 81
Bialer, Seweryn, 28
Bondarenko, V. M., 57
Bovin, A., 87
Breslauer, George, 342
Brezhnev, L. I., 6, 25–29, 42, 44–45, 63–64, 83, 90, 98, 343, 344; consolidation of power, 52–53, 58–62; defense industry under, 220–222; influence of military under, 29–33, 46ff.; invasion of Afghanistan, 306; and KGB, 101–103
Brzezinksi, Zbigniew, 28, 29
Budennyi, S. E., 19, 20
Buffering, military, against social change, 267, 269; against external forces, 344ff., 357, 363. *See also* Military
Burlatskii, Fedor, 23

Campbell, Robert, 40, 341, 345, 347
Central Committee, 48, 52, 72, 74, 134, 149, 165, 271, 272, 346, 355, 360; and defense industry, 167, 168; January 1987 Plenum of, 4–5, 82–83, 84; KGB and, 100, 103, 107, 110; under Khrushchev, 202; military representation on, 22; under Stalin, 19, 22; State-Legal Department of, 95
Chebrikov, V. M., 76, 95, 101, 105, 106, 117; and foreign policy, 120
Chelomei, V. N., 167
Chernavin, V. N., 299
Chernenko, K. U., 62, 63, 70, 106, 133; policies of, 65, 73–75
China, 10–11
Civilian politicians, 9, 19, 343. *See also* Civil-military relations
Civil-military relations: approaches to, 7ff., 12–14; accommodation under Brezhnev, 26–29, 46ff., 53, 357–358; civil society, 158; defense industry, 189–191, 234–236; economic competition and, 143, 146, 152, 156ff., 194; future of, 92, 358ff.; influence of Afghanistan on, 189–191, 234–236; Model I, 12–14, 20, 28–29, 31, 32, 89,